Digital Cinematography

Today's successful cinematographer must be equal parts artist, technician, and business-person. The cinematographer needs to master the arts of lighting, composition, framing, and other aesthetic considerations, as well as the technology of digital cameras, recorders, and workflows, and must know how to choose the right tools (within their budget) to get the job done. David Stump's *Digital Cinematography* focuses on the tools and technology of the trade, looking at how digital cameras work, the ramifications of choosing one camera versus another, and how those choices help creative cinematographers to tell a story.

This book empowers the reader to correctly choose the appropriate camera and workflow for their project from today's incredibly varied options, as well as understand the ins and outs of implementing those options. Veteran ASC cinematographer David Stump has updated this edition with the latest technology for cameras, lenses, and recorders, as well as included a new section on future cinematographic trends.

Ideal for advanced cinematography students as well as working professionals looking for a resource to stay on top of the latest trends, this book is a must read.

David Stump, ASC, has worked on numerous motion pictures and television productions as Director of Photography, as Visual Effects Director of Photography, and as a Visual Effects Supervisor, garnering Emmy nominations and an Academy Award for Scientific and Technical Achievement. A member of the Producer's Guild of America (PGA), the Visual Effects Society (VES), the Society of Motion Picture & Television Engineers (SMPTE), the Academy of Television Arts & Sciences (ATAS), and the Academy of Motion Picture Arts and Sciences (AMPAS), Stump has worked in Digital Visual Effects for over 25 years, since the advent of Computer Generated Images for film. In 2001 he was accepted for full membership into the American Society of Cinematographers, where he is currently chairman of the Camera and Metadata Subcommittees of the ASC Technical Committee.

Digital Cinematography

Fundamentals, Tools, Techniques, and Workflows

Second Edition

David Stump ASC

NEW YORK AND LONDON

Second edition published 2022
by Routledge
52 Vanderbilt Avenue, New York, NY 10017

and by Routledge
2 Park Square, Milton Park, Abingdon, Oxon, OX14 4RN

Routledge is an imprint of the Taylor & Francis Group, an informa business

First edition published by Focal Press 2014

Library of Congress Cataloging-in-Publication Data
Names: Stump, David, author.
Title: Digital cinematography : fundamentals, tools, techniques, and workflows /
    David Stump, ASC.
Description: Second edition. | New York, NY : Routledge, 2021. | Includes
    bibliographical references and index.
Identifiers: LCCN 2021001894 (print) | LCCN 2021001895 (ebook) | ISBN
    9781138603851 (hbk) | ISBN 9781138603868 (pbk) | ISBN 9780429468858 (ebk)
Subjects: LCSH: Digital cinematography.
Classification: LCC TR860 .S78 2021 (print) | LCC TR860 (ebook) | DDC 777—dc23
LC record available at https://lccn.loc.gov/2021001894
LC ebook record available at https://lccn.loc.gov/2021001895

ISBN: 978-1-138-60385-1 (hbk)
ISBN: 978-1-138-60386-8 (pbk)
ISBN: 978-0-429-46885-8 (ebk)

Typeset in Times
by Apex CoVantage, LLC

Contents

Goldsmith, Brian Legrady, Alexander Schwarz, Peter Martin, Wolfgang Baumler, Sylvia Gossner and Heidi Lippert of Hawk Vantage, Bill Turner of Schneider Optics and Susan Lewis of Lewis Communications, Pete Anderson of Leader, Belinda Merritt and David McClure of MTI Film, Yuri Neyman of 3CP, Rick Harding of FotoKem, Syrous Nabatian, Sarah Priestnall, Kelly McCall, Christopher "CB" Brown, and Johnathan "JB" Banta.

This work is dedicated to the memory of my parents,
David Stump Sr. and Laura Stump,
who always encouraged my scientific curiosity
and artistic expression.

The most thanks of all go to my wife, Jennifer,
the greatest contributor of all!

Foreword

I love shooting film. I love shooting digital. I love analog technology. I love digital technology. I have no agenda for either, and I make my living by knowing and using both effectively. A new era of cinematography has emerged – the era of digital cinematography.

What This Book Is About

This is a book about the tools and technology of digital cinematography. It explains how digital cinematography cameras work, and it will teach the theory and practice of using them.

What This Book Is *Not* About

This book is not about film, television broadcasting, composition, storytelling, screenwriting, lighting or lighting equipment, grip equipment, or how to become a cinematographer. There are plenty of very good books on all of those subjects that are already in publication.

Why Should a Cinematographer Read This Book?

If you want to be a cinematographer in this new age of digital cinematography, you almost can't afford *not* to read it. Today, a director of photography must be three things: first, an artist; second, a technician; and third, a businessman. There are plenty of books written to teach and coach you in the artistry of cinematography, lighting, composition, framing, camera movement … but very few that give you the information you will need to master the techniques of digital cinema cameras and even fewer to give you an appreciation of the ramifications of the decision you make to use one camera and its resulting workflow over another. Increasingly, cinematographers are being judged by their employers: the studios, the producers, the directors, the editors, and the post producers, on the basis of *all three* of these criteria.

Don't Bluff with Buzzwords, *Do Your Homework*

When one considers that there are literally dozens of cameras to choose from to make a movie, television show, commercial, documentary, or video clip, the choice of a camera for any given project can sometimes seem bewildering, The freedom to choose imposes a responsibility on the cinematographer, the responsibility of education. The cinematographer is responsible to his director and his producers to may not be available for or invited to attend final color correction, so attention to look management during production is a very good step toward assuring the look of the final image.

Where We Are Now

The "dark days" of the invention and development of digital cameras for cinematography are mostly behind us. We have crossed a tipping point into the era of digital motion picture imaging. We have emerged from the era of the evolution of digital cinematography that suffered from "early adopter syndrome" and we are at the point where single chip Bayer pattern CMOS digital cinema cameras own the greater percentage of the market.

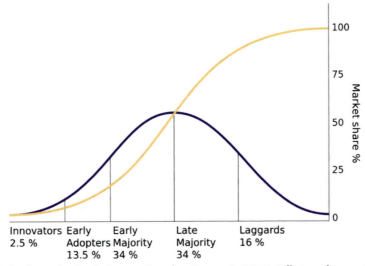

Figure 0.1 Technology adoption bell curve. Based on Rogers, E. (1962) *Diffusion of Innovations*. Free Press, London, NY, USA, Public Domain, https://commons.wikimedia.org/w/index.php?curid=8043923.

With successive groups of consumers adopting a new technology (shown in blue), its market share (yellow) will eventually reach the saturation level. The tools of digital cinematography have spent enough time in the hands of working professionals to mature and evolve. The great news is that it only gets better from here, and the tools seem now not only to meet the capabilities that film gave us, but in some ways to exceed the imaging capabilities of film. That further dictates that we educate ourselves thoroughly on the use of those tools on a daily basis from here on out.

Chapter 1

Understanding Digital Theory

How Digital Cinema Cameras Work

Cinematography is the art of capturing, recording, and manipulating motion pictures on a medium such as film or a digital image sensor.

Figure 1.1 Making movies.

The discipline that underlies cinematography is the mastery of matching the tonal range of creative scenes in front of the lens to the measured capability of the sensor medium behind the lens in order to artistically capture and record that tonal range.

Figure 1.2 The scene has a tonal range.

Human Visual Response to Light

Human visual response to the intensity of light is not linear. Human eyes are capable of responding to an enormous range of light intensity, exceeding a minimum-to-maximum intensity variation of over 10-billion-fold, but our vision recognizes light intensity in a way similar to the way film negative records light. Both human vision and film negative respond to a doubling (or halving) in intensity as approximately one stop of change in perceived brightness.

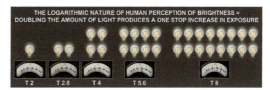

Figure 1.3 A doubling in luminance is perceived as a one stop increase.

Both human vision and exposure of silver halide crystals in film emulsion exposure are similarly nonlinear, and can be approximately modeled either by a logarithm or by a power law function.

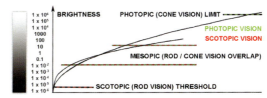

Figure 1.4 Human vision perception of brightness is nonlinear.

Psychophysicist Stanley Smith Steven's power function laws of psychophysical response to luminous intensity observe that human visual response to brightness is very close to a logarithmic or power function.

Sensing Light

For more than a hundred years, photographic film used light sensitive silver halide crystals to record images.

Figure 1.5 Silver halide crystals under an electron microscope.

When the exposed silver halide grains were developed and fixed, the crystals were converted to metallic silver, creating the darker areas of film negative. The more light received, the darker the silver halide crystals.

Digital sensors use silicon-based semiconductor devices called photodiodes – essentially microscopic light-controlled valves – which when struck by light allow electrons to pass through. Microscopic photodiodes allow electrons to pass and build up electrical charge when light hits them, and once per frame the camera will count how many electrons were accumulated, drain the charge, and reset the counter to zero.

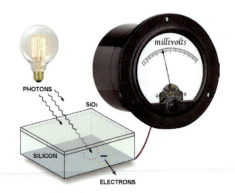

Figure 1.6 Photodiodes turn light into voltage.

A digital camera sensor is composed of a grid of photodiodes arranged in rows and columns. Each photodiode allows electrons to build up a charge as light rays from the lens form an image on the sensor grid, which can be measured by the camera. This accumulation of charge is very similar to building up a static charge by walking on carpet with sneakers on a dry day. The more you walk, the more charge you build up. With more light, more charge is built up on each photodiode, and conversely with less light, less charge is built up.

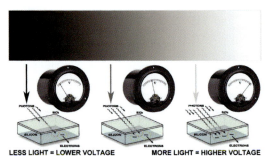

LESS LIGHT = LOWER VOLTAGE   MORE LIGHT = HIGHER VOLTAGE

Figure 1.7 Less light produces lower charge, more light produces higher charge.

In digital imaging these individual photodiodes are referred to as photosites and their signal product is referred to as sensels). Camera sensors have thousands of rows and columns of photosites that work like independent microscopic light collectors, converting light into voltage on a photosite for photosite, frame for frame basis. This arrangement of photosites is called a raster, a closely spaced rectangular grid of photosites that capture an image.

These rows and columns of photosites are not capable of discriminating color on their own, they are only capable of individually sensing the intensity or power of light hitting them and converting that into voltage. They must be given a means by which color information can be derived. The topic of deriving color from photosites will be addressed later in this chapter.

The number of photosites (usually in the horizontal dimension) is what manufacturers use to give the number of "K" (or thousands of photosites) of a camera. When a camera is said to be "4K," that means it has *at least* 4096 photosites in the horizontal dimension. As we will see in the next chapter, the number of photosites does not necessarily translate into the effective resolution of the images from a camera, as photosites are not pixels.

Figure 1.8 Rows and columns of photosites turn light into electron counts.

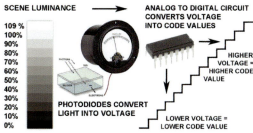

LIGHT IS CONVERTED INTO VOLTAGE AND VOLTAGE IS CONVERTED INTO CODE VALUES

Figure 1.10 Photosites turn light into static electric charge, and A to D conversion turns accumulated charge into digital code numbers.

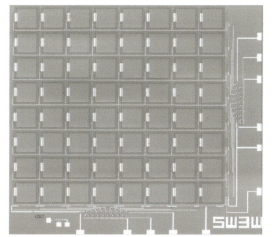

Figure 1.9 Electron microscope view of rows and columns of (monochrome) photosites on a sensor.

Analog to Digital (A to D) Conversion

Through the process of analog-to-digital (A to D) conversion, the amount of each photosite's electric charge is converted by a sampling circuit into binary digits. In digital images, each photosite value is represented by a discrete numerical code value on a frame to frame basis. The process of converting the individual charges from photosites into numerical code values (or samples) is called quantization. The charge built up on each photosite is dumped into the analog-to-digital converter electronics at the end of every frame. A "sample" is a numerical code value that represents this photosite's accumulated charge that was built up over the exposure time of the frame. Because digital samples are numbers, they can be stored in a computer's memory and saved to a computer hard drive as data.

Encoding Luminance to Numerical Code Values

Sensor response to light is linear. For twice the amount of light, a photodiode delivers twice the amount of charge. For half the amount of light a photodiode delivers half the amount of charge. If we begin to assign linear numerical code values to linear charges from sensors, we can quickly intuit the issues created by encoding luminance in a linear fashion. This method is inefficient and does not provide enough code values at the dark end of the tone scale.

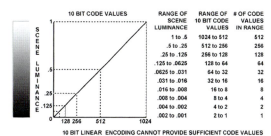

10 BIT LINEAR ENCODING CANNOT PROVIDE SUFFICIENT CODE VALUES

Figure 1.11 Linear light encoded in linear code values.

Figure 1.11 shows us a one-to-one linear encoding scheme, where scene luminance is plotted in an arbitrary range from 0 to 1, and encoded into digital code values that are plotted directly as a linear function.

The Problem with Linear Encoding

The range in relative scene luminance from 1 down to 0.5 covers a one-stop (factor-of-2) difference. In a 10-bit linear encoding scheme, this range is represented by the code values 1024 to

512, so there would be 512 discrete code values assigned to the brightest single stop of light. From 0.5 luminance down to 0.25 luminance is also one stop, but here there are 256 code values available (from code value 512 down to code value 256). From 0.25 luminance down to 0.125 luminance is again only one stop, but here there are 128 code values available (from code value 256 down to 128). From 0.125 luminance down to 0.0625 is also one stop, but here there are only 64 code values assigned (from code value 128 down to 64). The fifth stop down from 1 receives 32 code values, the sixth stop down receives 16 code values, the seventh stop down receives 8 code values, the eighth stop down receives 4 code values, the ninth stop down receives 2 code values and the tenth stop is left to be encoded with one single code value.

If we encoded in a one-to-one linear scheme, we would have more than enough numerical code values to represent the first and brightest stop of luminance, and almost none to represent the bottom toe of the exposure. In a linear encoding, the lower the luminance, the fewer the number of code values available to represent it.

This is why we *do not* encode 10-bit images in a linear scheme. The problem with encoding images this way is that while there are more than sufficient code values to display the brightest stop of light, the lowest six stops are allocated far too few code values to be displayed with any precision at all. The significance of this is that we must very carefully and suitably allocate the number of code values per stop of light in our encoding to make the most efficient and economical use of our available bits.

Because human visual response to brightness is very close to a logarithmic or power function, it makes sense to encode digital images from sensors either logarithmically or through a power function for human viewing.

The Just Noticeable Difference (JND) and Square Root Integral (SQRI)

How many code values (discrete digital luminance steps) must be used in encoding images to ensure that quantizing is never visible in an image over the dynamic range of the camera? The sensitivity of the human visual system to contrast is limited. If two gray levels are close enough in luminance, the difference is indistinguishable to human vision. The ability to discriminate tonal differences varies over the range from dark to bright.

There has been extensive scientific research into how many shades of color humans can distinguish in images. The acknowledged threshold of that ability to distinguish differences in tonal value is described by the concept of the "Just Noticeable Difference," or "JND." In imaging, a just-noticeable difference is the amount a color or shade must be changed in order for a difference between two adjacent colors or shades to be noticeable or detectable by human observers at least half the time.

This concept is important to us now because if we employ an encoding scheme that has fewer code values than "Just Noticeable Differences" per stop of light, we can perceive the different shades that make up subtle gradations of color as distinct bands of color. This banding is often referred to as "color aliasing," which significantly detracts from faithful reproduction of original images, and which detracts from viewing of those images. The number of "Just Noticeable Differences" per stop of light varies dependent on color and luminance, and the eye is more tolerant of greater differences in tone or color at lower luminance levels than at higher luminance levels.

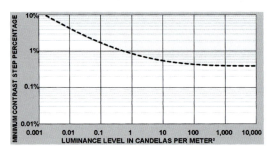

Figure 1.12 Barten ramp expressing noticeable contrast step percentages as a function of brightness.

A general rule of thumb is that an encoding scheme should allow roughly 60 to 70 code values per stop of light in medium tonal ranges. The optimum distribution of code values per stop of light varies from dark (permitting larger percentage increments of variance in contrast) to bright (demanding smaller percentage increments of variance in contrast), and this distribution varies according to what is referred to as a Barten ramp.[1]

Each photosite is assigned a specific digital red, green, or blue tonal intensity code value. The number of tonal values available is called the color bit depth. The higher the bit depth, the more tonal values available, the fewer the just noticeable color differences. In digital cinema bit depth refers to the number of digital bits used to encode each color component of a single pixel. A "bit" is a binary digit that can have one of two states. These state values are most commonly represented as either 0 or 1, *true/false, yes/no, +/−*, or *on/off*. 1-bit color means *on/off*, a binary pair of tones; *black/white*. 10-bit color means 2 to the 10th power bits; $2^{10} =$ 1024 tones per color, $2 \times 2 \times 2 \times 2 \times 2 \times 2 \times 2 \times 2 \times 2 \times 2 = 1024$ tones each for red, green, and blue (RGB). Of the 1024 code values available for encoding color in 10-bit encoding, we reserve the top and bottom 4 bits for other data, so roughly speaking, RGB 30-bit color means we have 1015 values of red, 1015 values of green, and 1015 values of blue available, $1015 \times 1015 \times 1015 =$ for a total of 1,045,678,375 possible shades of color.

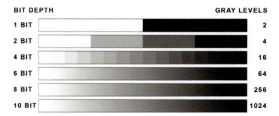

Figure 1.13 Luminance discrimination in bits.

Practical testing of human sensitivity to "just noticeable differences" in display contrast has determined that the minimum quantizing level needed to exceed the threshold of banding visibility in digital cinema is at the very least 10 bits per color (red, green, and blue), encoded logarithmically. A logarithmic scale is a nonlinear scale that quantifies values in orders of magnitude rather than in constant increments.

Linear vs. Gamma/Logarithmic Encodings

Gamma γ A Video Power Function

Early television engineers had to solve the problems of the difference between human visual perception of brightness and display output brightness long before digital cinema was invented. Cathode ray tube (CRT) television monitors converted a video signal to light in a nonlinear way, because the CRT electron gun's intensity (brightness) as a function of applied video voltage is also nonlinear. When a middle gray video signal of 0.5 is fed to a CRT display, the resulting brightness results in a mid-gray of about 22% the intensity of white.

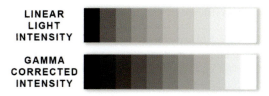

Figure 1.14 Linear light intensity visually compared to gamma corrected intensity.

Their solution was to apply a power multiplier function called gamma to the input signal that approximates the relationship between the encoded luminance in a television system and the actual desired image display luminance. Gamma and other similar multiplier functions such as log encodings are referred to as Opto-Electronic Transfer Functions (or OETFs). The Greek letter Gamma – γ – is used to denote a multiplier that enables efficient coding of linear light for broadcast video recording, transport, and distribution. Gamma is perceived as a change in contrast. Gamma bends the middle tonal values between black and white, while pure black (0.0) and pure white (1.0) are unaffected. Gamma of 1 (unity gamma) means no change, values greater than 1 increase contrast, values less than 1 (fractions) decrease contrast.

Power-law gamma coding is a nonlinear way of encoding used primarily in the RGB video world at 8 bits, and at 10 bits for HDTV as stipulated in Rec 709. The code values for RGB are proportional to the corresponding light coming out of a CRT raised to a power of about 0.45.

For image processing and post production operations such as compositing and CGI, an inverse Opto Electrical Transfer Function (denoted as OETF⁻¹) is often used to linearize the data back to radiometric code values.

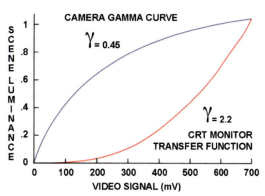

Figure 1.15 Gamma = .45454545 for cameras (blue) and gamma = 2.2 for monitors (red).

To compensate for the application of an encoding gamma function, an Electro Optical Transfer Function such as gamma 2.2, gamma 2.4, gamma 2.6, Perceptual Quantizer (PQ) or Hybrid Log Gamma (HLG) is applied to the signal going to the monitor or projector so that the end-to-end response of the image system is visually linear. In other words, the recorded signal is deliberately gamma distorted so that after it has been equally inversely distorted again by the display device, the viewer sees the correct perceptual tonal scale of brightness.

ITU-R Recommendation BT.709

ITU-R recommendation BT.709 specifies a transfer function for HDTV gamma encoding of camera signals. The Rec 709 mathematical gamma transfer function of γ 0.45 is a sloped straight-line near zero that blends to a power function so that the overall curve exhibits a continuous slope.

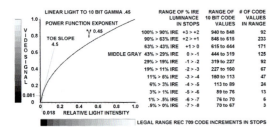

Figure 1.16 ITU Rec 709 gamma curve for encoding camera signals.

In HD video signals the video signal output voltage of a photosite exposed to 100% diffuse white yields 714 mV or in video engineering terminology, 100 IRE. Overbright white values up to 109% yield up to 785 mV, or 109 IRE. Black level in video signals is set at 53.57 mV or 7.5 IRE. (IRE is a unit used in the measurement of composite video signals. The acronym name is derived from the initials of the Institute of Radio Engineers.)

Most camera manufacturers' implementations of Rec 709 yield close to the same results when viewed on a monitor or waveform scope. Tonal scales in Rec 709 can be encoded into two different code ranges. Legal range encodes the tonal scale from code values 64 at the low end to 940 at the high end, leaving a –4% margin for underexposure at the toe and a +9% margin for overexposure at the high end. Full (or extended) range encodes the signal from code value 4 at the toe to code value 1019 at the high end, reserving

bits 0 through 3 and bits 1020 through 1023 for video timing reference.

This difference in Rec 709 encodings frequently leads to confusion when transforming from one encoding to the other, and when monitor or projector settings do not match the signal input. Most often legal range is the correct choice for video levels. Choosing incorrectly shows up most visibly in black levels. Excessive black or black clipping usually means that you are looking at full range video on a monitor set up for legal range, and when monitoring legal range on a monitor set up for full range the blacks will look lifted or slightly gray. The choice between Data Level or Video Level is almost always dictated either by the codec you are recording or the codec you're rendering to, and 90% of codecs are designed for Legal (Video) Levels. Some processing systems make use of all 1024 color code values for processing, but this encoding is not a documented broadcast standard.

Logarithmic Encoding for Film: a History Lesson

The Cineon System was created by Eastman Kodak in the early 1990s to solve these same issues of encoding linear light efficiently. The Cineon System was one of the first computer-based end-to-end 4K resolution 10-bit log digital film systems. It was an integrated suite of components – a film scanner, a digital film workstation (with Cineon software for compositing, visual effects work, restoration, and color management) and a film recorder for output back to film. In the late 1980s the Cineon digital film system developed a logarithmic encoding for film scanning. The Cineon log encoding curve became the basis for development of the wide variety of log encodings in digital cameras today.

The Cineon project was responsible for the creation of the Cineon (.cin) 10-bit log file format, designed to handle digital film frames. The Cineon file format became the basis for the later SMPTE standardized Digital Picture Exchange (.dpx) format. The Cineon image file format is very similar to the ANSI/SMPTE DPX file format, and they are for all intents and purposes used interchangeably. Both file formats have variable metadata header (headers contain the data about what the file is and how to use it) lengths and DPX file headers are more flexible, allowing variable image headers to accommodate the needs of different industries, while the Cineon file format is more specific to digital film.

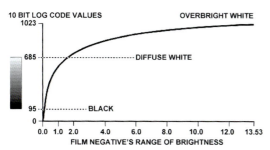

Figure 1.17 Cineon 10-bit log encoding curve.

10-Bit Log Cineon/DPX File Format

In a Cineon (.cin) or (.dpx) file, each channel (R, G, B) is encoded with 10 bits, typically in a range from a "black point" at code value 95 to "diffuse white" at code value 685 on the 0–1023 scale of code values. Code value 685 diffuse white is mapped to record a diffuse white reflection, such that rays incident on a white surface are scattered at many angles in a Lambertian reflection, equal in luminance in all directions, rather than at just one angle as in the case of specular reflections.

A "soft clip" was introduced to make the rolloff of whites appear more natural. Values above 685 are reserved for "brighter than white" tones like specular highlights or the sun, and values below 95 are reserved for blacker-than-black information. When negative is "printed up" at the lab to be brighter for artistic reasons or for scene-to-scene color matching, the blacker-than-black information can reveal itself. Similarly, negative can be "printed down" darker, revealing picture information from the over bright detail.

Cineon log film scans capture the entire exposure range of each frame of film and store that range as individual frame 10-bit log Cineon files. Because film negative (like human vision) has a logarithmic response to light, the negative determines the log response curve and the file only needs to faithfully and accurately store the negative's density at each tone level. More encoding values are perceptually useful as exposure to light increases.

Film is measured in logarithmic density units proportional to the negative's optical density. When encoding the exposure latitude of film, we must very carefully and suitably allocate the number of code values per stop of light in our encoding to make the most efficient and economical use of

our bits. If we try to squeeze the range of brightness of film into the full 0 to 1023 code range that would only leave 75 code values for the 0 to 1.0 stop range, the same number of code values as we have allocated to the range from +12 to +13 stop range. Over bright highlights on film do not require the same number of code values, and the human eye cannot discriminate between two over bright film highlights that are close in value at very high brightness levels. Because black is mapped to code value 95, that would leave only a range of 928 code values for the entire remaining exposure range. A scene with very bright highlights can result in values above the Cineon range. Those highlights can be lost in a standard DPX encoding, and that effect is called *clipping*.

The enormous dynamic range of film could not be preserved through the post process without characterizing the response of film with its unique exposure shoulder and toe, and log encoding it, so the Cineon Log encoding curve was devised by Eastman Kodak to preserve the maximum latitude from film scans for digital manipulation into a 10-bit log file. Notice that black is mapped to Cineon code value 95 (out of 1024) instead of 0. The Cineon white code value is 685, which represents 90% of a 100% reflector. In this way, Cineon files store both film Dmin values and Dmax values in order to emulate film's latitude and response characteristics.

Cineon/DPX Encoding Ranges

Table 1.1 Various Cineon/DPX Encoding Ranges

Cineon / DPX Encoding Ranges				
Encoding Type	Description	Black Point (out of 1024)	White Point (out of 1024)	Gamma
ITU Rec 709	Legal (Video) Range	64	940	2.2
DCI Gamma	Full DCI Range	4	1019	2.6
Print Density	For Use in Film Scans and Film Print Work	95	685	1.66
sRGB	Full Range	0	1023	2.2

Logarithmic Encoding for Digital Cinema

In the late 1990s into the early 2000s digital cameras began an evolution that would eventually lead them to compete with and displace film. In 1998 SONY's 1920 × 1080 F900 CCD camera with their HDCAM video tape recorders posed a threat to the supremacy of film, but one of the many impediments to its success in the cinema world was Rec 709 color. In June 2000, *Star Wars Episode II – Attack of the Clones* began principal photography shot entirely on a SONY HDW-F900 camera in a Rec 709 workflow with an HDCAM tape deck record solution. Subsequently, the F900 quickly proved insufficient to the giant screen world of cinema, and as the race to develop new and better digital cinema cameras and workflows began, it quickly became apparent that a 4:4:4, 10-bit full bandwidth signal would be essential to the success of any digital camera that wanted to compete in the world of film.

In 2005, the American Society of Cinematographers and the Producer's Guild of America conducted the ASC/PGA Camera Assessment Series, a landmark test of seven digital cameras: ARRI's D-21, Panasonic's AJ-HPX3700, Panavision's Genesis, Red's One, SONY's F23 and F35, and Thomson's Grass Valley Viper shooting alongside an ARRI 435 using four Kodak stocks, two tungsten (Vision2 250T 5217 and Vision3 500T 5219) and two daylight (Vision2 250D 5205 and Vision3 250D 5207). The decision to post the material in a film style digital intermediate dictated that where possible, cameras would record a log encoded signal to emulate the characteristics of film negative, reproducing a wider dynamic range of scene tones within a wider color gamut that is closer to film than a Rec 709 encoding. One direct result of these tests was that the manufacturing community seriously took up the challenge of creating film style log encodings and wider color gamuts that propelled the success of digital cameras into motion picture production.[2]

The proliferation of log encodings in digital cinema cameras is now ubiquitous. Every camera that aspires to be taken seriously in the cinema world now supports its own log workflow. I will briefly cover a few log encodings here, but there will be more on the subject in later chapters.

ARRI Log C

The Log C curve is a logarithmic encoding of scene tonal values where the relationship between exposure measured in stops and the number of

code values used to encode the signal is constant over a wide range. The overall shape of the Log C curve is similar to the Cineon exposure curve of film negative. Because of fundamental differences between a digital sensor and film negative, the color characteristics are different.

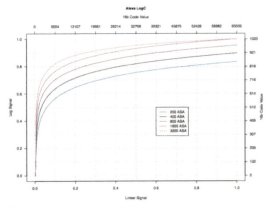

Figure 1.18 ARRI Log C curves for several ASA settings.

Log C actually is a set of curves for different EI values/ASA ratings. Each curve maps the sensor signal, corresponding to 18% gray scene luminance, to a code value of 400 in a 10-bit signal. A 10-bit signal offers a total code value range of 0 to 1023. The maximum value of the Log C curve depends on the set EI value. The reason is quite simple: when the lens is stopped down, by one stop for example and the EI setting is increased from, say, 800 to 1600, the sensor will capture one stop more highlight information. Since the Log C output represents scene exposure values, the maximum value increases.

SONY S-Log

S-Log, S-Log2 and S-Log3 are a set of log encoding curves that have been specifically optimized for SONY digital motion picture cameras to maximize the performance of the image sensor. S-Log curves are designed to record and transmit as much of the information recorded by your camera's sensor as possible, to preserve the wide color gamut and dynamic range recorded by the sensor. Using SONY S-Log1 the cinematographer can preserve up to 1000% dynamic range of Rec 709. Using S-Log2, dynamic range increases to 1500%. S-Log3 provides a similar result to S-Log2, but with more detail in the shadows, while extending the dynamic range between midtones and highlights.

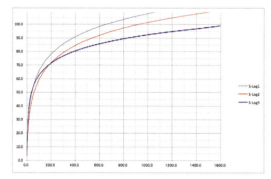

Figure 1.19 SONY S-Log1, 2, and 3 log curves.

S-Log3 is based on Cineon Digital Negative as revised in 2007. The S-Log3 tone curve has no shoulder and reduced toe (with a non-linear curve in shadow area). It is more like a pure log encoding than S-Log2, to provide greater dynamic range in log-based grading.

Display Referred vs. Scene Referred

What we can learn from the evolution from Rec 709 encoding to log encoding is that the creative intent of cinematography has driven us from a *Display Referred* perceptual coding approach where images are transformed directly into the nonlinear light power of the display being used toward a *Scene Referred* approach where the image data is maintained in a format that as closely as possible represents the original radiometric linear light values, preserving all the color and high dynamic range of the scene.

Log encoding captures the integrity of original images from digital cameras more faithfully than Gamma encoding, storing images in much smaller files for storage and use than radiometrically linear encoding; so for now, log encoding gives us our most effective workflow.

Every manufacturer now understands that characterizing the performance of a new sensor

Table 1.2 Table of log encodings with code values and % IRE levels for waveform monitor reference

Log / Gamma Encoding Function	0.0088% Black -13 stops IRE %	0% Black 10-bit Code Value	18% Gray IRE %	18% Gray 10-bit Code Value	90% White IRE %	90% White 10-bit Code Value
ARRI Log C	3.60%	95	38.4%	400	58.00%	572
Blackmagic 4.6K Film	1.00%	75	41.0%	420	68.00%	664
Blackmagic 4K Film	4.00%	95	38.0%	400	78.00%	743
Blackmagic Film	4.00%	95	38.0%	400	66.00%	642
Canon Log	7.30%	128	32.8%	351	62.80%	614
Canon Log 2	3.60%	95	39.2%	408	58.40%	575
Canon Log 3	7.00%	128	31.3%	351	59.00%	577
Cineon Film Log	3.54%	95	46.0%	481	70.90%	685
DJI D Log	0.00%	64	39.3%	498	86.00%	814
Gamma 2.2	0.00%	64	40.9%	444	100.00%	940
Gamma 2.6	0.00%	64	54.0%	536	100.00%	940
Linear	0.00%	64	18.0%	239	100.00%	940
Panasonic V Log	7.30%	128	42.1%	433	61.00%	602
Rec BT 709	0.00%	64	40.9%	444	101.10%	940
Rec 2100 HLG	0.00%	64	22.0%	260	50.00%	502
RED Log 3 G10	3.40%	94	31.6%	341	49.20%	495
RED Gamma 3	4.00%	95	45.0%	455	77.00%	736
RED Gamma 4	1.00%	72	45.0%	457	81.00%	778
RED Log Film	3.54%	95	46.1%	481	70.90%	685
Sony S Log	3.00%	90	37.6%	394	65.40%	637
Sony S Log 2	3.00%	90	32.3%	347	59.20%	582
Sony S Log 3	3.60%	95	40.6%	420	60.90%	598
sRGB	0.00%	64	48.0%	488	100.00%	940

and writing a log encoding curve to accommodate that unique sensor is one of the keys to a camera's success.

Notice the variations in IRE % and code values from black to middle gray to 90% white from one encoding to another. The decisions that camera manufacturers make in encoding their cameras varies widely. One downstream effect is that post production must have access to accurate de-log profiles for every camera used in order to accurately post produce and color correct their images. It is not unusual for an editorial timeline to include material from half a dozen cameras in one scene, so access to and use of the correct encoding and decoding profiles is imperative.

Sampling Rate

Now that we have an understanding of how digital encodes gradations of the scene luminance and tonal scale to code values, let's move on to a discussion of how a digital camera samples those tonal scales over time.

Sampling rate refers to the frequency in megahertz (MHz) at which the analog to digital process in a camera samples analog values from the sensor.

A good way to visualize the process of sampling video is to imagine the analog signal voltage coming from each photosite as a continuous waveform that varies over time. For the sake of this example, I will represent the video signal coming from a photosite with a sine wave varying in luminance from 0 to 100%.

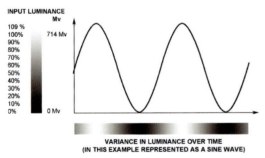

Figure 1.20 Video signal luminance varies over time.

In this example, the variation of luminance ranges from 1 to 100%, the full dynamic range of the sensor, over time. Now let's study how to slice this analog signal for the purpose of reproducing the original wave shape from our numerical samples. The regular frequency at which we take these samples is referred to as the sampling rate.

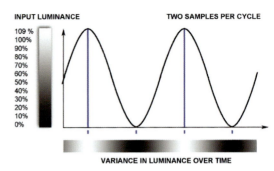

Figure 1.21 Two samples per cycle of the sine wave.

In order to visualize the sampling of this analog voltage signal, it is useful to imagine the digital samples as slices along those waveforms. In order to create digital video, the samples must be useable to accurately and faithfully reconstruct the original wave form. If there are not enough samples of the analog wave, the reconstructed waveform cannot recreate the original waveform. The more frequently the original wave form is sampled, the more accurate the digital reproduction will be. The code value of each sample endures until it is replaced by a new sample, so digital code values are illustrated as flat top square waves.

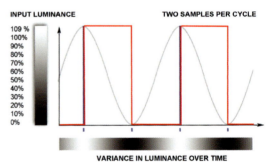

Figure 1.22 Reconstruction from two samples per cycle.

When we try to recreate the original sine wave from just two samples per cycle we can see that the digital representation does not resemble the original waveform. Digital sampling records a code value for each sample, and that value persists until it is replaced by another value. In this example, the only samples available are alternating values for 0 luminance and 100 luminance. This reconstruction is not sufficient to accurately reproduce the original analog video signal. Too few samples cannot serve to reconstruct original analog waveforms.

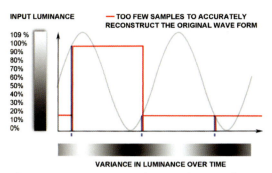

Figure 1.23 Reconstruction from too few samples fails to reconstruct.

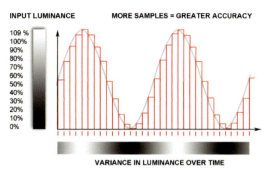

Figure 1.25 More samples results in greater accuracy of reconstruction.

When even fewer samples are taken from the original waveform, the digital reconstruction does not resemble the original wave form in any way. This reconstruction is said to be an "alias" of the original waveform.

Nyquist Shannon Sampling Theory

To accurately reconstruct the analog wave forms that form the original picture signal the sampling rate must be more than twice the highest frequency contained in those analog signals.[3]

If the frequency of analog wave forms is sampled at less than two times the highest frequency of the original analog wave form, the digital samples cannot be used to accurately recreate that waveform. Under sampling results in inaccuracies of reconstruction, the original analog waveform cannot be recreated from the under sampled data.

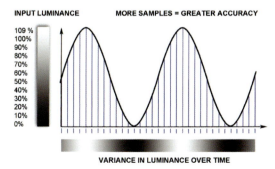

Figure 1.24 More samples per second (than Figure 1.23) results in greater sampling accuracy.

By sampling at a higher frequency, we can more faithfully reconstruct the original analog wave shape from the digital samples. When represented as digital samples it is much easier to recognize the fidelity of the samples to the original waveform.

Samples must be taken at a high enough frequency to enable accurate reproduction of the original analog wave forms in order to recreate the picture that the camera originally photographed from digitally recorded and stored data. The more samples per cycle, the greater the accuracy in reproduction of the original wave form.

When a waveform is grossly under sampled reconstruction becomes impossible because the resulting reconstructed wave form bears no resemblance to the original. In this case we call the inaccurate reconstruction an "alias" of the original. If, theoretically, we increased the sampling frequency to approach infinitely high frequency, the width of each sample would approach zero, and we could theoretically increase the accuracy of our reconstruction of the analog phenomenon being sampled to approaching 100% precision. This solution is not practical, as it would result in enormous files sizes for each image, so the number of samples per picture becomes an economic compromise.

There were two factors that determined the sampling rate for digital video. The first factor was this concept that sampling had to happen at a high enough frequency to reproduce the original analog signal. The second factor was that any new digital broadcast system design had to fit within the framework of the existing legacy analog broadcast system.

All of this data from sensors must be conveyed per pixel, per frame, per second in real time from the sensor to the record media or broadcast/display system. Data rate is the amount of digital information (bits) that is conveyed or recorded per unit of time, expressed as bits per second (bit/s) or megabits per second (Mb/s) that makes up the digital video signal or recording stream. The photosite count of the sensor, times the bit depth, times the frame rate (plus some bits for metadata and timing signals) equals the bits per second output. The higher the bit rate, the more data being transmitted, and the higher the quality of the video signal.

In 1920 × 1080 4:2:2 HD broadcast video, the sample rate was set at 74.25 MHz for luminance (Y) and 37.125 MHz for the blue (Cb) chrominance, and red (Cr) chrominance components. The bit rate of a standard 1920 × 1080 RGB video signal is approximately calculated as the number of samples per second times the number of bits per sample. The number of samples per second is the number of samples per picture times the number of pictures per second. A 1920 × 1080 10-bit RGB signal frequency is 74.25 MHz. As the number of pixels increases, so does the bit rate. Ultra High Definition TV cameras have twice as many samples (3840 × 2160) in both the horizontal and vertical dimensions, so the sampling rate for UHD TV is four times the sampling rate of High Definition television. In non-broadcast digital cinema cameras, sampling rates run much higher and are no longer related to the original analog broadcast system sampling rates.

Color

Rows and columns of photosites are not capable of discriminating color on their own, they are only capable of individually sensing the intensity or power of light hitting them. They must be given a means by which color information can be derived.

Figure 1.26 The human visible spectrum.

The perception of color in human beings begins with specialized retinal cells in our eyes – called cone cells – that contain pigments with different spectral sensitivities. In human eyes, there are three types of cones sensitive to three different spectra, resulting in what is called trichromatic vision. These cones are called short (S), medium (M), and long (L) cones, and although the three types do not correspond precisely to red, green, and blue, they give us the RGB color model, which is (for human beings) a convenient means for visually representing color in images.

In order to understand how color photography works, it is important to understand how

visible light gets separated by color filters into the three primary colors (red, green, and blue) that we use to reproduce images.

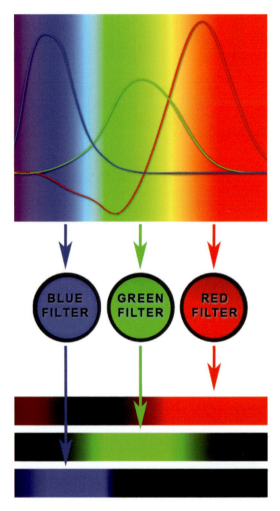

Figure 1.27 Visible light divided into its RGB components.

Similar to the way the pigments in the three types of cones on our retinas filter light into red, green, and blue, photographic filters can be used to separate light into its primary colors.

Bayer Pattern CMOS Sensors

Almost all cameras currently in use for digital cinematography employ a single chip monoplanar **C**omplimentary **M**etal **O**xide **S**emiconductor (**CMOS**) image sensor. The rows and columns of photosites on a CMOS sensor are covered by a painted on transparent **C**olor **F**ilter **A**rray (**CFA**) composed of a regular repeating pattern of microscopic red, green, and blue filters. Each photosite can only capture light of one of the primary colors, while rejecting light of the other two primary colors.

Just like on the human retina, the individual red, green, and blue color separation filters are microscopic in size. This color filter array is arranged in a pattern commonly called a Bayer pattern, named after its inventor, Dr. Bryce Bayer of Eastman Kodak.[4]

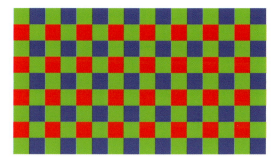

Figure 1.28 Enlarged section of a Bayer pattern color filter array.

The light falling on such an array of photosites is largely wasted. A green photosite can only collect the green light that falls on it; red and blue light are blocked. A red photosite can only collect the red light that falls on it; green and blue are rejected, and a blue photosite can only collect the blue light that falls on it, rejecting red and green light.

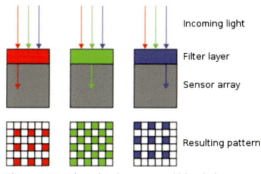

Figure 1.29 Filtered red, green, and blue light landing on non cosited photosites.

In summary, a Bayer pattern sensor is composed of thousands of rows and columns of adjacent, non cosited photosites covered by a color filter array arranged in a repeating pattern of red, green, and blue filters. By this method, a Bayer pattern sensor discretely samples each of the three primary colors from adjacent photosites for use in interpolating one RGB color for each photosite with the assistance of its neighboring photosites. These *photosites* are not yet tricolor *RGB pixels*.

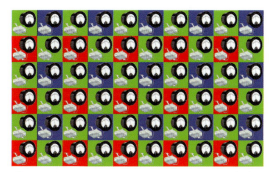

Figure 1.30 A Bayer pattern sensor is comprised of rows of red, green, and blue filtered photosites.

Color in the Digital Realm: What Are Pixels?

The word **pixel** is a contraction of pix (for "pictures") and el (for "element").

A pixel is the smallest, addressable three color (RGB) element in a digital imaging device. The address of a pixel corresponds to its physical coordinates on a sensor or screen.

The word **sensel** is a contraction of sens (for "sensor") and el (for "element").

A sensel is the signal value from one single monochrome photon collecting element on a sensor. In other words, a sensel value is the electrical signal value product of a photosite. On a Bayer pattern sensor, individual photosites can only sense one color: either red only, or green only, or blue only, and as such, sensels and/or photosites) are NOT pixels.

Pixels are full color RGB samples of an original image. More pixels provide a more accurate representation of the original image. The color and tonal intensity of a pixel is variable. In digital motion picture cinematography systems, any unique color is typically represented by 10-bit log digital code values for each of the three component intensities of red, green, and blue.

Color Bit Depth

Color bit depth refers to the number of gradations of tricolor RGB brightness value or tonal range, and describes the amount of color information stored in each pixel. As we increase bit depth, we increase the number of colors that can be represented. In a 10-bit RGB image, each color channel (red, green, and blue) carries $2^{10} = 1024$ variations of color. Excluding reserved bits from code values 0–4 and

1019–1023, that enables up to 1,045,678,375 colors per RGB pixel.

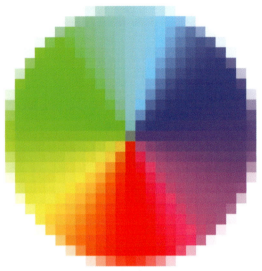

Figure 1.31 Only pixels contain RGB (red, green, and blue) information.

Photosites Are NOT Pixels!

One of the most important distinctions we can make when talking about digital cinema cameras is that photosites are *not* pixels. It is important to note here that if a camera manufacturer advertises that a sensor is 4K, the cinematographer must dig deeper to learn whether that means 4K photosites or 4K pixels. In this book, the author may also use these terms ambiguously where citing a manufacturer's usage. 4K of photosites does not necessarily produce 4K pictures with 4K of real world resolution.

Figure 1.32 Red, green, and blue photosites combine to create RGB pixels.

RGB pixels must be created from RAW Bayer images by mathematically interpolating samples from adjacent, non co-sited, red only, green only, and blue only photosites. This mathematical combining of values is called deBayering. The mathematical processes of deBayering average adjacent photosites in a wide variety of ways, and the process also averages effective real world resolution as well. This subject will be covered in more depth in Chapter 2.

Color Bit Depth: How Many Crayons in the Box?

Higher color bit depth gives you more shades of color – it's like having more crayons in your coloring box.*

Figure 1.33 Fewer colors to choose from reduces the accuracy with which subtle graduations in colors can be reproduced.

Figure 1.34 More colors to choose from means that subtler graduations of color can be reproduced.

As we learned earlier, bit depth refers to the number of digital bits used to store the tonal scale or color information of each pixel as a digital representation of the analog world. The higher the bit depth the more shades or range of colors in an image, and accordingly, the bigger the file size for that image.

The Math of Color Sampling

If we take enough samples often enough, and divide each of those samples into enough discrete

---

* Quote attributed to Scott Billups

colors, we can reproduce our pictures more accurately.

Figure 1.35 Low color bit depth results in color aliasing – notice the banding in the RED cards!

Insufficient color bit depth (too few discrete colors) results in color aliasing, which looks like distinct separate bands of red shades across this image instead of a subtle graduation of color. Higher color bit depth means the more discrete colors the encoding of each color channel (red, green, or blue) divides the tonal scale into, the less banding in subtle gradations of color can be seen. More crayons in the box means less difference between the colors of the crayons from one to the next.

Figure 1.36 With more colors to choose from we can make more beautiful pictures.

Source: detail from True Color Series – "Girl 1" crayon art courtesy of artist Christian Faur – www.christianfaur.com/.

The More Crayons, the Prettier the Pictures

If we take enough samples often enough, and divide each of those samples into enough discrete colors, we can reproduce our pictures more accurately.

Sampling color bit depth is the maximum number of color tonal bits each sample's RGB components can use to reconstruct pictures from digital samples. DPX file systems used in digital cinema operate in 30-bit color, which means 10 bits (logarithmic encoded) per channel of red, green, and blue. Of those 1024 code values available for encoding each color we reserve the top and bottom 4 bits for other data, so roughly speaking, RGB 30-bit color means we have 1015 values of red, 1015 values of green, and 1015 values of blue available, $1015 \times 1015 \times 1015 =$ for a total of 1,045,678,375 possible shades of color.

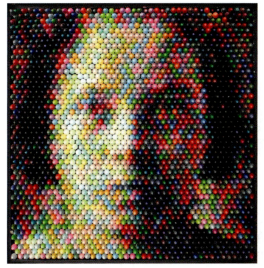

Figure 1.37 More colors to choose from means prettier pictures.

Source: "Girl 1" crayon art courtesy of artist Christian Faur – www.christianfaur.com/.

The more we oversample analog signals, the more accurately we can recreate those original signals from our digital samples. The tradeoff comes in storage space. If we excessively over sample, then the size of media storage of our images is increased, so the tradeoff is economic. Some degree of oversampling is beneficial to the quality of the images, but excessive oversampling wastes resources and slows processing.

ACES

There is much effort being given to refining a new file format as the eventual future of digital cinema, and there are research and development efforts under way to implement a 16-bit half float file coding for image manipulation purposes. Floating point math carries code values as exponents rather than as integers, which makes the process reversible without the decimation (rounding errors) inherent in integer mathematics. The Academy of Motion Picture Arts and Sciences (ACES – Academy Color Encoding System) project is an attempt to create a ubiquitous 16-bit half float motion picture file format that will serve our industry all the way from color correction through archive. 16-bit sampling quantizes to 2 to the 16th power or 65,536, code values (65,536 shades of red, 65,536 shades of green, and 65,536 shades of blue) which provides much more accuracy and subtlety of color shading.

This is especially important when working with wide-gamut color spaces where most of the more common colors are located relatively close together, or in digital intermediate, and where a large number of digital transform algorithms are used consecutively. At this time, ACES version 2.0 is under construction, and the Academy of Motion Picture Arts and Sciences have put in motion an initiative to put ACES into the public domain through an open source project called the Academy Software Foundation. These efforts will be covered more deeply in later chapters of this book.

Notes

1. Researcher Peter G. J. Barten has developed and refined a number of equations for understanding human visual capabilities in this realm. He defines a metric for describing perceived image quality that is based on the square root of the normalized modulation of the picture. He calls this metric the SQRI or square root integral. He observes experiments where comparable image contrast was varied in steps of one "Just Noticeable Difference" (or JND); the minimum amount of contrast change that is detectable more than 50% of the time in test subjects, and his tests show a very close correlation to the results of real world testing. Detection of "Just Noticeable Differences" depends on many factors, resolution, luminance, refresh rate, and others, and the number of "JNDs" per stop of light varies dependent on color and luminance, but humans are quite sensitive to these differences in contrast. For a scholarly look at human vision and our ability to distinguish subtle differences in contrast please read *Contrast Sensitivity of the Human Eye and Its Effects on Image Quality* by Peter G. J. Barten.
2. https://theasc.com/ac_magazine/June2009/CASPart1/page1.html; https://theasc.com/ac_magazine/September2009/CASPart2/page1.html.
3. The Nyquist–Shannon sampling theorem provides a condition for the sampling and reconstruction of a band-limited signal. When reconstruction is done using the Whittaker–Shannon interpolation formula, the Nyquist criterion is a necessary condition to avoid aliasing. Basically, the theorem states that if samples are taken at a slower rate than twice the highest frequency limit, then there will be some signals that cannot be correctly reconstructed. The minimum required bandwidth sampling frequency theorem was implied by the work of Harry Nyquist in 1928, in which he showed that up to $2 \times B$ independent pulse samples could be sent through a system of bandwidth B. Nyquist did not consider the problem of actual sampling and reconstruction of continuous signals. The Shannon sampling theorem was an extension of Nyquist's work that proved that analog frequencies could be reconstructed from samples.
4. Bryce E. Bayer was the American scientist who invented the Bayer Color Filter Array, which is used in most modern digital cameras. In 1975, while working for Eastman Kodak, Bayer filed a patent application and received U.S. patent number 3,971,065. The filter employs what is called the "Bayer Pattern," a checkerboard-like arrangement of red, green, and blue photosites on a square grid of photosites that allows digital cameras to capture color images. Half of the photosites collect green light, and the others are evenly divided between red and blue light. The patent application described the filter as "a sensing array for color imaging" that "includes individual luminance- and chrominance-sensitive elements that are intermixed so that each type of element occurs in a repeated pattern with luminance elements dominating the array."

Chapter 2

Camera Sensors, DeBayering, Sensitivity, and Noise

The Practical Differences between Film and Digital Sensors

Figure 2.1 Cinematography is now film *and* digital.

The single best piece of advice that I can offer with regard to the difference between exposing film and exposing digital is this: it's okay and sometimes desirable to slightly overexpose film, but it's not okay or advisable to overexpose digital unless that overexposure is EXACTLY what you want!

Cinematographers have widely varying methodologies for determining an exposure, some simple, some convoluted. Film negative has enormous exposure latitude and is very forgiving of a wide variety of exposure techniques.

Modern digital cinema cameras are now achieving wide latitude too. The difference between digital video cameras with a Rec 709 heritage and limited ability to capture dynamic range and digital cinema cameras with a filmic heritage is quickly widening.

Digital is like reversal (or auto positive) film stocks. There can sometimes be very little margin for error in exposure, especially at the high end of the tonal scale, and once a photosite reaches full light well capacity (or clip) it cannot continue to record any more detail. When using film negative one could always "print down" a bit to save some detail in excessively bright areas, and this can frequently save an overexposed area in the frame. The same overexposure in digital traditionally could not be corrected. The attempt to "print down" overexposed highlights usually did not result in any detail regained, but rather, a similar amount of highlight detail, just rendered at a lower gray level.

The real distinction to be understood here is the difference between HD broadcast type cameras that render internally and produce a display-ready output, which is like shooting on slide film, and digital cinema cameras producing an output in log or raw format that needs an additional step to be display-ready, which is more like shooting on negative film.

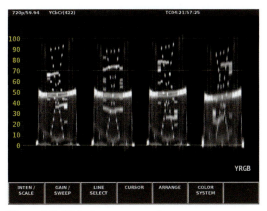

Figure 2.2 Spectra light meter.

Figure 2.3 Digital exposure tools.

Figure 2.4 Overexposed sky with clipped exposure in clouds.

Figure 2.5 The same image color corrected to lower levels (note that the clipped areas do not gain any detail by "printing down" the image).

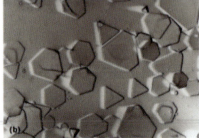

Figure 2.6 Film grains as photographed by an electron microscope

Source: reproduced with permission of AccessScience (www.AccessScience.com), ©McGraw-Hill Education.

A good rule of thumb in digital work has traditionally been that at the bright end of the exposure range, digital cameras are not WYSI-WYG (what you see is what you get) but rather WYSIAYG (what you see is *all* you get). When a photosite reaches 100% saturation it is said to be at "full well capacity" or "clip," and any picture detail that arrives above that "clip" level is lost (overexposed) forever! This happens when photosites reach their maximum electrical charge level and cannot produce any additional voltage from more photon arrivals.

Film has a random pattern of different sized grains that (depending on the sensitivity of the particular film stock) can achieve very high resolution.

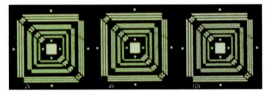

Figure 2.7 Film scanned at various resolutions.

Scanning film at resolutions higher than 4K (such as up to 10K) yields very well resolved grain.

Figure 2.8 Silver halide film grains compared to a sensor grid pattern.

Source: Silver Halide Photo Copyright (c) 2013 Kodak. Used with permission; Sensor Photo Micrograph Elsevier Science Direct Used with permission www.sciencedirect.com/science/article/pii/S0924424702003928.

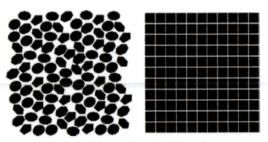

Figure 2.9 How film emulsion and digital sensors see differently.

Digital sensors have an exact grid of discrete photosites. Their resolution is very predictable and can be calculated as the result of several mathematical factors; sensor type; CCD vs. CMOS, Bayer pattern sensor vs. 3-chip sensor, deBayer algorithm, photosite count, optical low pass filter and recording workflow all figure into the resolution equation (as we will soon learn).

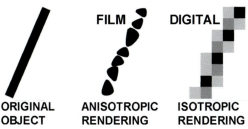

FILM   **DIGITAL**

ORIGINAL OBJECT   **ANISOTROPIC RENDERING**   **ISOTROPIC RENDERING**

Figure 2.10 Isotropic and anisotropic renderings of a real-world object.

As a result, digital reproduces real world images in a more isotropic way. A photosite array has isotropic spacing because the shape and space between any two adjacent photosites is the same along each axis, x and y.

Film renders images in a more anisotropic way, systemically different for every orientation or size of the original object. Anisotropy is the property of being directionally dependent, which implies different properties in different directions.

Sensor Size Has an Effect on the Image We See

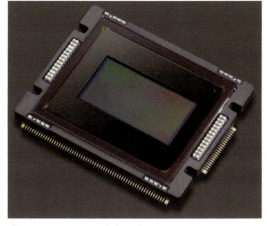

Figure 2.11 A typical digital sensor.

The desire to work with a sensor the size of a 35mm film frame is a strong force driving

development in this area, and many of the issues of digital cinema revolve around the very basic differences between sensor technologies.

Figure 2.12 There is a *huge* supply of good 35mm film lenses in the world.

A great deal of effort has been expended on the development of single chip 35mm and Super 35mm sensors for digital cinema because there is a great demand to use existing cinema lenses to acquire images on digital cameras and because film makers prefer the depth of field characteristics of the 35mm format for aesthetic reasons. Gathering the image using a single chip camera with a sensor the size of a 35mm film frame means that we can use existing cinema lenses, without many of the problems digital camera builders encountered designing 3-chip CCD television cameras around the inherent chromatic aberration of prismatic color separation.

Generally speaking, single sensor cameras render images with the same depth of field and image characteristics that we have become accustomed to in a hundred years of filmic experience.

Bayer Pattern Sensors

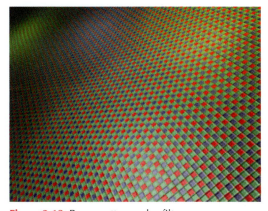

Figure 2.13 Bayer pattern color filter array.

Digital motion picture camera sensor design has moved away from CCD (Charge Coupled Device) technology to CMOS (Complimentary Metal Oxide Semiconductor) technology, partly because of improvements in CMOS capabilities, and partly because of the cost to manufacture. The Bayer pattern mosaic sensor employs a color filter array pattern for arranging *non co-sited* (side by side) RGB color filters over a square grid of adjacent photo sensors on a monoplanar chip. CMOS' particular arrangement of color filters is used in most single-chip sensors in digital motion picture cameras, camcorders, and scanners to create a color image. This filter pattern is composed of 50% green, 25% red, and 25% blue photosites, and is also frequently called GRBG, RGBG, or BGGR based on a repeating 2×2 pattern which begins at the upper left-hand side. There are two green photosites for each red and blue photosite. Because green is the source channel for luminance in digital pictures, this color ratio makes sense in the design of a single plane sensor. This pattern constitutes an orthogonal sampling lattice, with photosite order numbering from left to right, top to bottom. There are many other color filter array patterns and sensor types in use for other purposes in other devices, but for now we will limit the discussion to the patterns and sensor types most commonly used in digital cinema cameras.

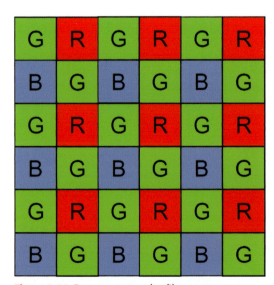

Figure 2.14 Bayer pattern color filter array.

Because of the human visual system, a minimum of three color planes are required to represent a full color digital image. The spectral response of these planes usually corresponds to the sensitivities of cones in the human eye.

A typical camera sensor detects light intensity but no color information. Most digital cinema cameras use a single light sensor together with a Color Filter Array (CFA). The CFA allows only one color of light to reach the sensor at each photosite. The result is a mosaic image, where a pixel location captures either red, green or blue light. The Bayer pattern is the most commonly used CFA design. (B. E. Bayer, "Color imaging array," U.S. Patent 3,971,065, 1976.)[1]

Figure 2.15 Closeup view of a Bayer pattern sensor.

The convenience of this single chip sensor method of gathering images comes with a price. A Bayer pattern array lays out a red, a blue, and (usually) two green photosites side by side in offset rows to achieve an average color and luminance sample of the image. Because all three colors are recorded by separate and non-co-sited photosites, the resulting images initially contain color sampling errors that result from the difference between the light sampled or not sampled by each photosite.

To reiterate, the light falling on a Bayer pattern array is largely wasted. A green photosite can only collect the green light that falls on it, red and blue light are blocked. A red photosite can only collect the red light that falls on it, green and blue are rejected; and a blue photosite can only collect the blue light that falls on it, rejecting red and green light.

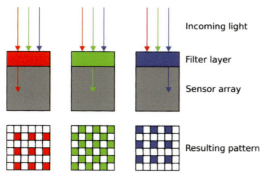

Figure 2.16 Filtered red, green, and blue light landing on non co-sited photosites.

The white squares in each color record represent sites where there is no color information. Values will be synthesized and assigned to those areas by a process of interpolation. A Bayer pattern sensor discretely samples and records each of the three primary colors from adjacent photosites for use in later interpolating one RGB color for each photosite on the sensor with the assistance of its neighboring photosites. These *photosites* are not yet tricolor *RGB pixels*.

RAW File Formats

A camera RAW image file contains minimally processed image data from a Bayer pattern image sensor in a digital motion picture camera. RAW files are not yet ready to be viewed or edited until the image is processed by a RAW converter into a usable image file format. There are dozens of raw formats in use by different manufacturers of digital image capture equipment.

A RAW digital image usually holds a wider dynamic range and color gamut than the resulting deBayered frame it will parent; the purpose of RAW image formats is to save, with minimum loss, the data obtained from the sensor. Raw image formats are intended to capture the scene-referred radiometric characteristics of the scene, the physical information about the light intensity and color of the scene, at the highest level of the camera sensor's performance.

RAW files contain a file header which conveys the byte ordering of the file, a file identifier, and an offset into the main file data, camera sensor size, and color profile map of the Bayer pattern Color Filter Array (CFA) required to assign discreet colors to the sensor image data. They also contain image metadata required including exposure settings, camera and lens model, date, time, and place, authoring information, and an image thumbnail (a JPEG or

other temp conversion of the image), which is used to view the file on the camera's viewfinder.

DeBayering (De Mosaicing) RAW Bayer Pattern Images

Figure 2.17 A typical RAW Bayer pattern image before color assignment.

Photosites in this Bayer pattern arrangement cannot be said to be pixels, as they only carry RAW monochrome tonal values until they are assigned colors in either red only, green only, or blue only, corresponding to the dye color covering each individual photosite. Once each photosite has been told whether it is a red, green, or blue photosite, the image then consists of discrete red only, blue only and green only values, which look like this:

Figure 2.18 RGB Bayer image before deBayering.

Figure 2.19 The same image after deBayering.

The process of "deBayering" interprets from adjacent discreet red or green or blue photosites to create RGB pixels that attempt to accurately reconstruct the scene. We will learn more about this process.

If we take a closer look at the image we can gain some insight into the imaging process before and after deBayering.

Figure 2.20 Bayer image (not yet deBayered).

Figure 2.21 Bayer image magnified.

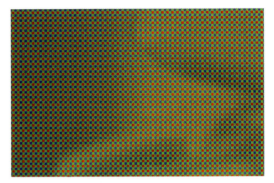

Figure 2.22 Very close on a Bayer pattern image before deBayering

Close examination of the image reveals that it is still constructed of individual photosites values that all fall on either a red tonal scale, a green tonal scale or a blue tonal scale.

None of the camera original photosites yet contains full RGB information; as a result, their digital code values can be stored as a value one third the size of an RGB pixel. Raw images are generally about one third the size of RGB images.

The process of de mosaicking these images is called de Bayering, a mathematical operation that interpolates the missing color data for each photosite in the array from surrounding known data in order to synthesize a full color RGB pixel at every photosite location on the imager.

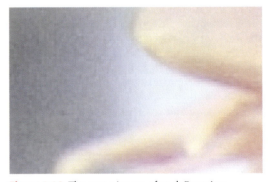

Figure 2.23 The same image after deBayering.

De Bayering Algorithms

A variety of deBayer reconstruction processes are used to mathematically generate and assign full color RGB values to all of these single color value photosites based on color information shared and interpreted from neighboring photosites. There are numerous mathematical algorithms for interpolating missing color information for red only, blue only, and green only photosites, and each algorithm can deliver different aesthetic results. I will summarize a few (of the many) here.

Nearest Neighbor

The simplest of all interpolation algorithms is a nearest neighbor interpolation. Using a 2×2 neighborhood from the Bayer pattern, missing color values are interpolated by simply adopting the nearest sampled value.

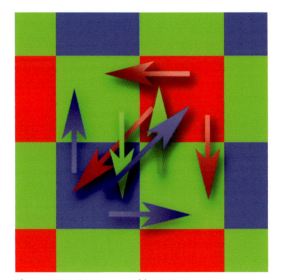

Figure 2.24 "Nearest neighbor" DeBayering.

The sampled blue and red values in a 2×2 neighborhood are used at the three remaining locations. The sampled green values can be shared in either a vertical or horizontal direction to fill in color values for the photosites without green information.

Bilinear Interpolation

Another simple interpolation algorithm is bilinear interpolation. A 3×3 neighborhood is taken from the CFA and missing color values are calculated by averaging nearby values.

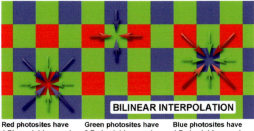

BILINEAR INTERPOLATION

Red photosites have 4 Blue neighbors and 4 Green neighbors	Green photosites have 2 Red neighbors and 2 Blue neighbors	Blue photosites have 4 Red neighbors and 4 Green neighbors
Red photosite assumes Blue Value as average of 4 Blue neighbors and Green value as average of 4 Green neighbors	Green photosite assumes Red Value as an average of 2 Red neighbors and Blue value as average of 2 Blue neighbors	Blue photosite assumes Red Value as an average of 4 Red neighbors and Green value as average of 4 Green neighbors

Figure 2.25 How bilinear "deBayering" works.

This interpolation method performs well in smooth areas where the colors change slowly from one to the next. When utilized along edges where color changes occur abruptly, false color and zipper artifacts are introduced, sometimes resulting in a poor image quality.

The simplest demosaicking methods interpolate each color channel separately. One such technique is bilinear interpolation, which uses the average of the surrounding photosites. In bilinear interpolation, each missing green value is calculated as the average of the four surrounding green values, and each missing red or blue value is calculated as the average of the two nearest neighbors or four nearest neighbors, depending on the position relative to the edge. Other standard interpolation methods, such as cubic spline interpolation, can be used to slightly improve the performance when processing each color channel separately.

The problem with methods that interpolate the color channels independently is that they usually fail at sharp edges in images, resulting in objectionable color artifacts.

To minimize the problems caused by simple channel independent methods that interpolate the color planes separately, adaptive demosaicking algorithms have been developed which utilize the correlation between the color channels.

Advanced demosaicking algorithms put a lot of computational effort into reconstructing high frequency detail in the red and blue color channels. If the image is compressed afterwards, it will often be converted to YCbCr 4:2:0 format. In this format, the chroma channels (Cb, Cr) are downsampled by a factor of two in both the horizontal and vertical directions, resulting in a loss of the high frequency color information.[2]

Cubic Interpolation

Cubic interpolation is similar in nature to linear interpolation. Cubic interpolation suffers from the same artifacts as linear interpolation, but to a lesser degree. The expanded 7×7 neighborhood reduces the appearance of these artifacts, but they are still present in the final image.

High Quality Linear Interpolation

High quality linear interpolation improves linear interpolation by exploiting interchannel correlations between the different color channels. A 5×5 neighborhood is used, wherein the nearby photosites of the corresponding color channel are averaged and then added to a correction term calculated from information in a different color channel. Despite a modest increase in the number of computations performed compared to the linear and cubic interpolations, this method outperforms many more complicated, nonlinear methods, with greatly reduced edge artifacts.

Smooth Hue Transition Interpolation

The key assumption of high quality linear interpolation is that hue is smoothly changing across an object's surface. The false color artifacts of linear and other methods of interpolation result when hue changes abruptly, such as near an edge. In this case, hue is defined as the ratio between color channels, in particular the ratio between red/blue and green.

Pattern Recognition Interpolation

Thus far, all of the interpolation algorithms cited have flaws estimating colors on or around edges. In an attempt to counteract this defect, pattern recognition interpolation describes a way to classify and interpolate three different edge types in the green color plane. Once the green plane is interpolated, the red and blue color planes are interpolated using the smooth hue transition interpolation described previously. The first step in this procedure is to find the average of the four neighboring green photosites, and classify the neighbors as either high or low in comparison to this average. This photosite is then defined as an edge if three neighbor photosites share the same classification. If not, then the photosite can either be a part of a corner or a stripe. If two adjacent neighbor photosites have the same classification, then the photosite is a corner. If two opposite pixels have the same classification, then the photosite is a stripe.

Adaptive Color Plane Interpolation

Up to this point, the interpolation of the green color plane has occurred using only information from the green samples from the CFA data. However, certain assumptions can be made regarding the correlation between the color planes. One well-known assumption is that the color planes are perfectly correlated in a small enough neighborhood. It works well to interpolate missing photosite values along edges, rather than across them. In order to utilize the edge detection capability of adaptive color plane deBayering, it is useful to consider many directions. In some methods, as many as 12 directions are considered in which all the G information in a 5×5 neighborhood is used.

Resolution in Bayer Pattern Cameras

It is a bit disingenuous to cite a camera's resolution as the resolution of the final image created demosaicking. The deBayering process is a process of *averaging* or *interpolating* color values across the sensor, and decimation of resolution is inherent in that averaging. It is *not* accurate to cite the resolution of a sensor as the number of photosites. Photosites are *not* RGB pixels. The real world resulting effective resolution of deBayered images depends on the deBayer algorithm used. For this reason, it makes no sense to assess a Bayer pattern camera's resolution in terms of photosite count. Any given deBayer algorithm can produce the same number of RGB pixels from the same original raw image, so the real question is what is the efficiency of the deBayer algorithm employed in terms of resolution delivered?

Depending on the deBayer math used, the resulting color information can vary in real world measurable spatial resolution, most often less than the photosite count of the sensor. Depending on the math used, the effective output spatial resolution can be expressed as a percentage of the Bayer sensor photosite count. The most widely used methods of deBayering usually result in from 66% to 80% of the photosite count of the sensor, and higher with some algorithms. It is possible to deBayer to higher pixel counts, but the methods that result in higher measurable real world spatial resolution are mathematically intensive, usually not real-time.

Converting Raw Images to RGB Images

Converting a raw image to an RGB image takes a fair amount of image processing. It includes much more than just deBayering. This processing also bakes in a look in the image.

In a video or JPEG workflow, this processing is done entirely in the camera.

In a raw image workflow, most of the image processing is done in post. As post gets the original sensor data, post can apply and reapply different looks without the loss of quality that would occur should you drastically edit a video image in post.

The image processing often includes the following steps in the order shown below:

Dead Pixel Removal

The values of dead or stuck photosites are restored through interpolation with the nearest good same-color photosites.

Noise Reduction

Noise reduction is an early stage in the image pipeline. This assures that later non-linear stages produce results that are more predictable without sporadically amplifying the noise. Beware that too much noise reduction can destroy image detail.

Linearization

The sensor's response to light is rarely truly linear. Many sensors have a soft knee, a slightly reduced sensitivity above 70%. The linearization step restores this to a linear signal.

Black Level Subtraction

The signal recorded by unexposed photosites is rarely zero. Non-light sources such as thermal noise and electrical interference within the sensor can generate a small signal.

The average level of this black signal can be calculated and then subtracted from the image. After the subtraction, on average the unexposed photosites will have a value of zero. Due to sensor noise, some photosites may now get negative values. These values must be retained, as clipping to zero can result in visible artifacts such as blotchy shadows.

Demosaic to RGB

The demosaicking stage restores the RGB image pixels from the color-filtered photosites. Bayer (RG/GB) is the most common layout for the color filter mosaic, but since other color filter layouts are in use, the general name for this process is demosaicking, (often loosely referred to as deBayering).

The demosaicking algorithm varies from vendor to vendor, and the most advanced methods are protected by patents or trade secrets.

Here we can only give a sampling of the available algorithms:

Nearest Neighbor of Same Color

The very crude nearest neighbor method fills in the missing color values from a nearest photosite of the desired color. While the method is fast, the results are inferior. Sharp edges will show severe color bleed. For Bayer patterns, the effective image resolution is half the photosite resolution, as that's the spacing of the red and blue samples. This method can be acceptable when the image is downsampled to the effective (meaning eventual output) resolution.

Averaging Same Colors

A missing color value can be calculated by averaging the colors of the surrounding photosites of the desired color. This method is slower than the nearest neighbor method, and the results usually are slightly better, although edges get jaggies instead of color bleeds. For Bayer patterns, the effective image resolution is yet again half of the photosite resolution. Unfortunately, this method is very common, as it is very easy to implement.

Using All Photosites

The better methods use all available colors and photosites for restoring each color. Just like in the eye, the spectral curves of the different color filters are designed to overlap. It is rare to find a color on set that registers in only one set of color filters. And almost all natural objects have wide spectral reflectance curves. The extreme exceptions would be laser lights. Thus, all objects provide details in all photosites, and the advanced methods utilize this using all photosites to calculate each color plane. The effective image resolution is now *the same as* the photosite resolution. As these methods often detect gradients, they may be more sensitive to image noise.

We now have an RGB image in the color space of camera RGB, and we can now apply the processing steps that require RGB pixels.

Lens corrections

When the lens characteristics, including the focal length for a zoom, are well known, lens artifacts such as barrel distortion and chromatic aberration can be reduced by applying the appropriate geometric counter-distortions.

Cropping

Next, the image is cropped. The demosaicking methods can produce artifacts in the edge pixels, so these are cropped off. The cropping can also set the desired aspect ratio, such as 2.39:1, 16:9, or 4:3.

Scaling

The RGB image can be scaled up or down to the desired image-sampling rate, such as 1920 × 1080. This must be done with methods that don't introduce moirés or discard image details. Upsampling will not provide more image detail, but may be needed to fit a specific workflow, such as HD.

White Balance

In the white-balance step, the RGB values read off a gray card are used to scale the RGB channels to equal values for gray. This can be as simple as just dividing with the gray card RGB values, or more advanced, taking into account chromatic adaptation, and applying a matrix.

This step is easily combined with the color conversion step for better overall performance.

This step may also include clipping overexposed pixels to the max neutral value. If not all three channels are clipped, then advanced methods may also try to restore the actual exposure values.

Partial Exposure

Partial exposure happens if a strobe or flash or lightning goes off during the shot. If the flash occurs at either of the two vulnerable moments of the shutter cycle when some percentage of the photosites are turned on and some are turned off, a partial exposure of the frame can occur.

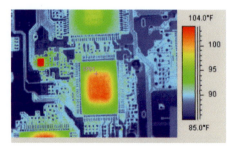

Figure 2.39 Partial exposure.

Dark Frame Subtraction

CMOS devices do their analog to digital conversion right on the image sensor, adjacent to the light wells. This on-board processing generates heat, which digital sensors see as randomly scattered light that contributes to the noise level of the sensors. This commonly demands that most CMOS (and some CCD sensors) sensors perform a dark cycle subtraction of that noise from pictures on a frame-by-frame basis.

Figure 2.40 Infrared photograph of a hot circuit board.

Thermal noise can be mathematically cancelled by taking sample *dark frame* images at the same operating temperature as the adjacent image file. The resulting thermal noise template will consist largely of thermal noise and fixed-pattern read noise, and when subtracted from the image, thermal noise effects can be very significantly reduced. Excessive noise reduction can reduce

shadow detail in pictures, so the amount of noise reduction applied must be carefully controlled.

This noisy image:

Figure 2.41 Before noise subtraction.

Minus this dark frame sample:

Figure 2.42 Noise state of the sensor.

Equals this quiet relatively noise-free frame:

Figure 2.43 After noise subtraction.

Frequent camera black balancing with a closed shutter or with a lens cap on the lens generates dark frame exposures that are used to subtract the accumulation of dark current caused by thermal, electronic, and random noise.

Dynamic Range and Exposure Latitude

The dynamic range (or tonal range) of a scene is the ratio of the maximum and minimum light levels in the scene.

The dynamic range of a camera is the ratio of number of stops of latitude a sensor is capable of recording.

The exposure latitude of a camera is the range of tones that the camera can accurately capture from dark to light that will produce an image that is acceptable in color and tone without clipping highlights and with an acceptable noise level in dark areas of the frame.

The discipline that underlies cinematography is the mastery of matching the tonal range of scenes in front of the lens to the capability of the sensor medium behind the lens in order to artistically capture and record that tonal range.

Exposure choices that deliberately introduce clipping in highlights or noise in black levels can be made as subjective artistic decisions by educated knowledgeable cinematographers who understand the limitations of the technology, the tonal range of the scene being photographed, and the consequences of their decisions.

Human vision is capable of sensing up to 30 stops of light. Dynamic range of such magnitude cannot be recorded by any current photographic device except by integrating numerous successive bracketed exposures. The resulting high dynamic range (HDR) Image can be contained in a 32-bit floating point file that preserves the values of the original scene ranging from the darkest darks to the brightest highlights, all with full detail. This will be explained in further detail later in this book.

Modern color negative films are capable of recording between 12 and 14 stops of latitude. Digital sensors have come a long way in the last ten years in this respect. Some digital cameras now legitimately claim to have dynamic range equaling or exceeding that of film. This improvement in dynamic range can largely be attributed to advancements in log encodings in digital cinema cameras.

Dynamic range in digital sensors is traditionally defined as the range of signal from the brightest signal (full well capacity of the photosites or signal clip) to the dimmest signal (background noise). The difference between the photonic and/or electronic noise in the system with no signal present and the maximum signal the system can record without clipping or distorting the signal is considered to be the dynamic range of the sensor. This ratio is usually measured in units of decibels or in f stops of latitude.

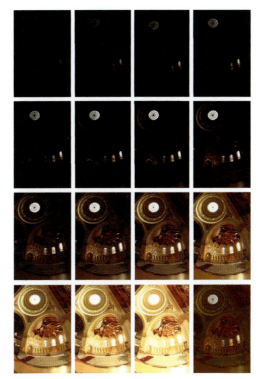

Figure 2.44 A high dynamic range photograph, which integrates 15 exposures to create one 32-bit image (bottom right), which cannot be satisfactorily reproduced by print media.

Image courtesy Dr. Paul Debevic

One of the biggest sources of dispute in digital cinema today resides in the argument of how to determine the zero decibel baseline for measuring a digital sensor, and which of the two log equations to use in assessing the signal to noise ratio of that sensor. Hearing two manufacturers defend their differing viewpoints on the subject is a bit like listening to a comedy routine about the incongruity of the term "jumbo shrimp."

As general guideline, the *signal-to-noise ratio* can be determined from the sampling resolution n by SNR (dB) = $20 \cdot \log_{10} 2n \approx n * 6$, so 8-bit signal-to-noise ratio for 8-bit sampling is 8*6=48 dB and for 16-bit sampling resolution is 96 dB.

As an example, one typical professional digital cinema camera in common use advertises a 63 dB signal to noise range. To understand what this means we divide that 63 dB number by 20, then raise 10 to that power:

$$63 \text{ dB} / 20 = 3.15 \quad 10^{3.15} = 1412.5$$

The dynamic range of this camera expressed as a ratio is about 1412:1

Similarly, the dynamic range of our example camera can be expressed in bits or stops. Measured in bits our camera is said to be just under 10.5 bits – $\log_2 1412$. Bits can be roughly equated to stops, and this sensor can capture a scene that is 10.462 stops from low to high, or a 1:1412 lighting ratio from darkest to brightest.

To convert bits to a ratio: where n is the number of bits, 2^n is the ratio.

$$10.462 \text{ bits} = 2^{10.462} = 1412$$

Once again, the dynamic range of this camera can be expressed as a ratio of about 1412:1.

What does that mean in practical terms? Nearly nothing! It's a sales pitch! Either the pictures look distractingly noisy or they don't. Most manufacturers of digital cameras expend great effort to determine a relationship between ISO rating and noise level that keeps this discussion out of screening rooms.

How Much Picture Noise Is Acceptable in Digital Cinema?

Dynamic range and exposure latitude are intimately intertwined. The latitude of a sensor changes in distribution of the number of stops above and below middle gray as one alters the ISO rating. The cinematographer can rate a sensor's ISO higher and reduce the number of stops above middle gray, or rate the sensor ISO lower to prevent excessive noise in dark areas of the frame. In one type of project, the creative team might take great precautions to suppress and minimize noise in images while another type of project might use noise as a creative tool. In color correction of dailies or vfx plates, some camera workflows allow the colorist to change the embedded ISO rating to brighten or darken an image globally before performing primary corrections, greatly reducing noise. In one circumstance the cinematographer might expose to avoid highlight clipping while in another scene some level of clipping might be acceptable. These are among the many creative choices cinematographers have in telling stories. Just remember to let everyone involved in the project know when these choices are being made and how they will be used. It is urgent to have the producers, the director, and the studio all involved in such a choice so that such decisions don't come back to haunt during post production or quality control. Digital noise reduction is an expensive and time consuming post production process. Noise can be a subjective creative tool, but one that must be used with caution – your mileage may

vary. The best advice is to do tests. Test to confirm that the manufacturer's ISO rating of the camera is realistic, test to determine what noise floor is acceptable for the production, and test to learn at what level the sensor clips or loses the ability to reproduce color correctly. These tests will enable the cinematographer to expose with confidence on the set.

Figure 2.45 Universal Studios City Walk at night from the air.

When viewed on a big screen in the context of the story, this noise level doesn't seem to stand out.

Figure 2.46 Let's examine part of the picture more closely.

Close examination of code values shows that there is over 10% variance in code values in many of the smooth gradations of this scene.

Figure 2.47 Even closer.

Many digital camera signal to noise ratio (S/N) performance levels are quoted in dB (decibels) to compare baseline noise to top signal power. In order to meaningfully understand the dynamic range of a photographic sensor it is therefore essential to define what is an acceptable level of noise at the lowest end of the scale.

The top end of the signal to noise equation is much easier to define and even the novice can quickly learn to identify "signal clip" on a waveform monitor, that point when photosites have reached their maximum saturation "full well" capacity.

Figure 2.48 A sky with clipped highlights.

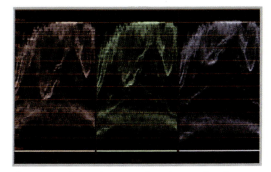

Figure 2.49 Wave form monitor picture showing clipping in areas of overexposure, which show up as flat line areas at the top of the scale.

Noise and Lower Dynamic Range Issues

Noise is inherent in all digital cameras, and shows up as an indecisive and frequently annoying dither in an otherwise stabile and unchanging image. Film, on the other hand, has an inherent grain structure that results in overall random grain pattern that usually (when properly exposed and processed) does not call attention to itself, and therefore doesn't result in a fixed pattern noise like that of digital cameras.

Figure 2.50 Noise in a clear blue sky.

In excess, digital noise can attract attention and detract from storytelling by taking the audience out of the moment, interrupting the willing suspense of disbelief.

Figure 2.51 Image from ICAS 2012.

Figure 2.52 The same image with noise.

Noise usually shows up most noticeably at the dark end of the tonal scale, and can sometimes be very difficult if not impossible to remedy in post production.

There are several basic phenomena that contribute to noise in digital cameras.

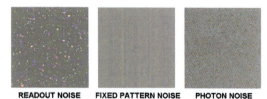

READOUT NOISE   FIXED PATTERN NOISE   PHOTON NOISE

Figure 2.53 Readout noise, fixed pattern noise, photon noise.

Fixed Pattern Noise, Dark Noise, Readout Noise, Circuit Noise, and Photon Noise

Fixed pattern noise refers to a constant non-uniformity in an image sensor's output. For a variety of reasons, photosites have variances in sensitivity and performance, resulting in inconsistencies in their output signal. Photosites may vary widely in their output when given no external illumination, the deviation of a photosite's output from the average output of the sensor's photosites can be attributed to dark signal non uniformity which is the amount any given pixel varies from the average dark signal across the sensor, and can result from individual photosites' reaction to temperature and integration time. Photosites see heat and infrared energy as light, and the circuitry surrounding the sensor contributes to a base level of dark exposure just by virtue of the operational heat it generates. A camera working in a hot desert environment will generate a different dark noise level than a camera working in a cold Arctic environment, so it is important to perform a black balance operation frequently in cameras that allow for that operation. Some cameras actually perform black balance in an automated fashion, performing flat field correction on a frame to frame basis.

Figure 2.54 Template of fixed pattern noise.

Because fixed pattern noise is usually consistent on a frame-to-frame basis, dark frame subtraction can help to control noise by taking a black picture when the shutter is closed, and subtracting the resultant black image from the subsequent exposure. This technique can also frequently help to correct stuck pixels or hot pixels as well.

In situations where thermal noise is a factor, it helps to subtract off the contribution of that thermal noise from the image, by taking dark frame images at the same exposure time and operating temperature as the image file and averaging them together. The resulting thermal noise template will consist largely of thermal noise and fixed-pattern read noise, and when subtracted from the image, thermal noise effects can be reduced.

Photosites may also vary in output when given an equal quantity of light due to photo response non uniformity, which results from differing sensitivity levels from photosite to photosite, and from inconsistent performance from the amplifiers attached to each individual photosite. This phenomenon is usually referred to as readout noise or bias noise. Readout noise can be exacerbated by variances in voltage or current in the camera circuits, and by electromagnetic inductance, such as a walkie-talkie badly placed near the camera.

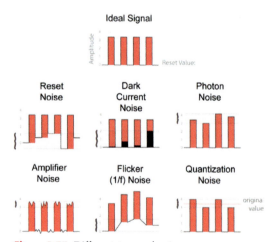

Figure 2.55 Different types of noise.

Analog electronic circuits are vulnerable to noise. This random noise does the most harm where the signal being amplified is at its smallest, the CCD or CMOS analog to digital conversion stage. This noise originates from the random movement of electrons in the transistors that amplify the analog signal for sampling, and this noise level depends on how the electronics are designed, but not on the level of the signal being amplified.

Digital cameras record images in a very strict and methodical way. When presented with an exact quantity of light, they attempt to report a precise resulting voltage, but in certain lighting situations, when the amount of light striking the image sensor varies randomly and minutely from frame to frame, the resultant change in individual pixel values can result in another kind of noise called photon noise, also known in imaging science as Poisson noise. Very subtle random variations in the number of photons arriving from objects being photographed causes a variation in the voltage generated from the photosites sampling them, and this variation is a fairly constant factor.

Imagine that you have two different size hourglasses, one that is 4 inches tall and one that is two feet tall.

Figure 2.56 Small hourglass.

Figure 2.57 Large hourglass.

Now you flip each one to begin timing an hour, and observe the sand that falls through the opening into the bottom. The smaller hourglass drops fewer grains of sand than the larger one while measuring the hour, so it is intuitive that the difference in the number of grains of sand dropping could be greater or lesser on a second to second basis. The small hourglass might drop 20 grains in one second, 18 grains in the next second, and 23 grains in the next second. The larger glass might drop 220 grains of sand in one second, 218 grains of sand in the next second, and 223 grains of sand in the next second.

The difference in the number of grains of sand dropped on a second to second basis is consistent between the two glasses, but the percentage of difference between the number of grains of sand dropped per second is vastly different. Similarly, photons arriving at a sensor can be randomly different, producing random photon noise, and that noise is prone to being greater in percentage at lower quantum levels.

When an object being photographed is very dark in the scene, this variation in photon arrivals is more significant in comparison to the overall signal being sampled, but when the object being photographed is brighter, the same statistically random variation in photon arrivals becomes vastly less significant in comparison to the overall signal being sampled. The result is that dark areas of the frame are more susceptible to photon noise than bright areas.

Highlight Handling and Headroom

Figure 2.58 Clipped highlights.

Highlight headroom is a difficult concept to understand. Put very simply, most movies were historically originated on negative film, which handles overexposure extraordinarily well. The highlight capture characteristics of digital capture can sometimes more closely resemble an auto positive Ektachrome stock, which has a tendency to lose overexposed highlight detail much sooner in its exposure cycle. The result is that these two media achieve color and exposure saturation in differing ways.

Figure 2.59 Deanna Durbin, beautiful in backlight.

Consider that many cinematographers have made great reputations for beautiful cinematography, earning many an Oscar, by knowing the fine art of hot backlight, and you can begin to understand the sensitivity that cinematographers have to the capabilities of film vs. the capabilities of digital. Digital cameras reach their saturation point very decisively. When the light well of a photosite reaches saturation (or "full well capacity") it reaches that point with absolute certainty, and is said to be at "clip" level. Any more light arriving at that photosite during that accumulation cycle is likely to spill out of that photosite and into adjacent photosites, resulting in bloomed areas of overexposure, that cannot be reduced in size or color corrected in post production. Understanding the inherent differences in highlight and upper dynamic range issues between digital cameras and film is essential to the art and craft of the cinematographer.

For these reasons, cinematographers have great cause for concern in evaluating the new digital toolset being presented by a wide variety of manufacturers. The cinematographer must educate him or herself in the fine art of exposing for digital cameras, and this means mastering the tools of exposure metrics. The topic of exposure tools is covered thoroughly in Chapter 10 in this book.

Fill Factor

Fill factor refers to the ratio of usable photon gathering area to processing or non-photon collecting area on a digital sensor. Fill factor is defined as the ratio of the actual maximum obtainable power, to the theoretical (not actually obtainable) power from a photosite. As an example, let's compare two theoretical camera sensors, identical in size and photosite count.

Figure 2.60 A high fill factor sensor.

The first diagram depicts a CCD sensor with a fill factor of above 80%. That means that 20% or less of the sensor area is devoted to wiring, circuitry, and the electronics of removing the charge from the sensor.

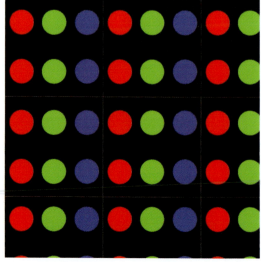

Figure 2.61 A lower fill factor sensor.

The second diagram depicts another CCD sensor in common usage today, this sensor only yields about 25% fill factor.

Comparing the two sensors we can see that one is clearly more efficient than the other sensor, making better use of the light available arriving from the scene.

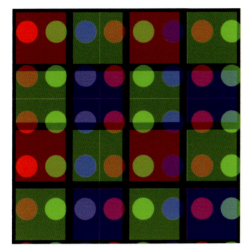

Figure 2.62 An overlay of the high and low fill factor sensors.

The calculation of maximum obtainable power and resultant noise is directly related to the number of photons collected in each light well and to the mathematics of how that ratio is converted into color information.

Fill factor is also intimately tied to the Nyquist resolution limit in digital sensors. (We will cover this in more depth later!).

Figure 2.63 Aliasing above the Nyquist frequency.

The lower the fill factor of a sensor, the more prone the sensor is to aliasing problems beyond the Nyquist frequency of that sensor.

Spatial aliasing and Moire occur above the Nyquist limit of the sensor in this case, and must be optically filtered out to prevent ugly image artifacts.

In current generation CCD and CMOS sensors, the full well capacities run from about 100,000 to 200,000 electrons. Fill factor for CCDs is typically 80–90% and is much lower for CMOS, around 30% for many designs, but that number is improving as transistor size is reduced through new and more efficient manufacturing techniques.

Figure 2.64 Filtered image.

Figure 2.65 Moire alias artifact.

Microlenses on Photosites

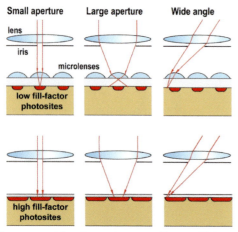

Figure 2.66 Microlenses increase effective fill factor.

Full well capacity in modern digital camera sensors varies according to photosite size. A photosite of 5.5 μm structure size can accumulate approximately 20,000 electrons, a 7.4 μm photosite can accumulate up to 40,000 electrons. This quantity figures in sensor and camera design, and is intimately tied to the mapping of camera data to digital code values. It also affects noise in sensors – higher photosite charge capacities yield less noise in the resulting pictures. Micro lenses help to capture light that would have otherwise fallen onto sensor circuitry and direct it into the light wells, effectively increasing fill factor, but as ray angles increase toward the edges of the frame light may scatter and reflect. This results in uneven illumination of the sensor, called falloff or shading. Newer, more image space telecentric lens designs are helping to direct light toward photosites at angles closer to perpendicular.

Sensitivity and ISO/ASA rating

Figure 2.67 Technicolor shot with ASA 5 film stock.

Image courtesy of Laurent Mannoni Directeur scientifique du Patrimoine et du Conservatoire des techniques - Cinémathèque française

Sensitivity and ISO/ASA rating are very important factors in any digital cinema camera. Long gone are the days of the Technicolor three-strip system, with its ASA 5 rating, dictating that an entire soundstage would be ringed with as many Brute and Titan arc lamps as could be fitted bale to bale on the stage lighting rails, and dictating enormous power requirements for lighting films.

Figure 2.68 Ray Rennahan's Technicolor light meter (which reads in hundreds of foot candles).

Modern cinematographers now rightfully expect to be able to shoot scenes lit by candles, or practical household light bulbs. We fully expect to photograph night exterior cityscapes using mostly existing light. Manufacturers of motion picture film stocks have invested millions upon millions of research dollars into designing high quality film stocks with very high ASA ratings, fine grain characteristics, vivid color reproduction, and deep rich blacks. Film has raised the bar very high in terms of image quality, and digital cameras have now reached a level where the technology has exceeded the capabilities of film.

Figure 2.69 Eastman Kodak 5219 ASA 500 film stock.

Sensitivity

ASA, ISO, sensitivity, and film speed are measures of a film stock or digital sensor's sensitivity to light. Film stocks or sensors with lower sensitivity (lower ISO/ASA speed) require more light, and/or a longer exposure time to achieve good color reproduction. Stocks or sensors with higher sensitivity (higher ISO/ASA speed) can shoot the same scene with a shorter exposure time or less light.

Sensitivity refers to the ability to capture the desired detail at a given scene illumination. Matching imager sensitivity with scene luminance is one of the most basic aspects of camera design.

Silicon imagers capture image information by virtue of their ability to convert light into electrical energy through the photoelectric effect. Incident photons boost energy levels in the silicon lattice and knock loose electrons to create an electric signal charge in the form of electron-hole pairs.

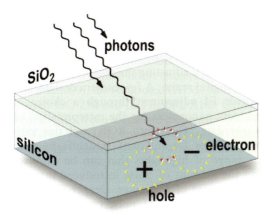

Figure 2.70 How photosites turn photons into electrical charges.

Image sensor sensitivity depends on the size of the photosensitive area. The bigger the photosite, the more photons it can collect. Sensitivity also depends on the quantum efficiency of the photoelectric conversion. Quantum efficiency is affected by the design of the photosite, but also by the wavelength of light. Optically insensitive structures on the photosite can absorb light (absorption loss); also, silicon naturally reflects certain wavelengths (reflection loss), while very long and very short wavelengths may pass completely through the photosite's photosensitive layer without generating an electron (transmission loss). Sensitivity requires more than merely generating charge from photo-generated electrons. The imager must be able to manage and measure the generated signal without losing it or obscuring it with noise.

ISO/ASA Rating/Exposure Index

The ISO arithmetic scale corresponds to the ASA (American Standards Association, which is now renamed American National Standards Institute – ANSI) scale, wherein a doubling the sensitivity of a film (halving the amount of light that is necessary to expose the film) implies doubling the numeric value that designates the film speed.

Figure 2.71 ISO logo.

In the ISO (International Organization for Standards) logarithmic exposure index (EI) scale, which corresponds to the older European DIN (Deutsches Institut für Normung or translated; German Institute for Standardization) scale, doubling the speed of a film implies adding 3° to the numeric value that designates the film speed. For example, a film rated ISO 200/24° is twice as sensitive as a film rated ISO 100/21°.

Usually, the logarithmic exposure index speed is omitted, and the arithmetic exposure index speed is given, the quoted "ISO" speed is essentially the same as the older "ASA" speed.

Figure 2.72 ASA wheel on a light meter.

Signal gain refers to the ratio of amplification of the electronic signal coming from the sensor and going into the analog to digital convertor. In digital camera systems, the arbitrary relationship

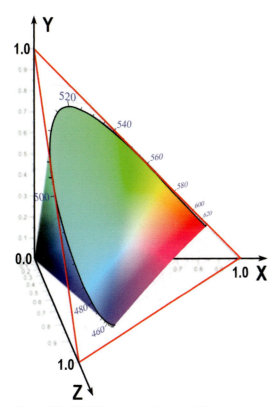

Figure 3.6 CIEXYZ spectrum locus in 3D.

If one imagines depth behind the diagram, colors transition along a centerline from light to dark, and the resulting shape slightly resembles the Hollywood Bowl Band Shell. The colors along any gamut border line can be made by mixing the primaries at the ends of the lines.

Color Temperature and White Balance

Film and digital are projected or viewed on illuminated monitors or screens, so we use an additive RGB (red, green, and blue) model when defining film and digital color spaces. In an RGB color model, the addition of all three colors produces white. The definition of white in an RGB color model is much stricter than the perception of white by human vision. The human eye has three types of color receptors which reduce colors to three sensory quantities, called tristimulus. Human vision has a tendency to interpret white from a wide variety of different color illuminants. This ambiguity in visual perception is called metamerism, a perceived matching of colors under illumination from lighting with different spectral power distributions. Metamerism occurs because each of the three types of cones on the human

retina responds to light from a broad range of wavelengths, so that different combinations of light can produce an equivalent color sensation. Digital sensors do not suffer from this ambiguity in the interpretation of colors, so careful attention must be paid to defining white in the digital world. Scenes that seemed to match in color to the eye on set or on location can look very different in dailies or in the color correction suite.

The color temperature of a near white light source is defined by the temperature of a black body thermal radiator that radiates light of a color comparable to that of the light source. For example, a tungsten filament incandescent light bulb emits thermal radiation, and because the tungsten filament approximates an ideal blackbody radiator, it's color can be expressed as the temperature of the filament. This range of color is indicated by a curved line across the middle of the CIE chromaticity diagram called the blackbody curve. Color temperature is conventionally expressed in degrees Kelvin, using the symbol K, a unit of measure of absolute temperature. A tungsten filament incandescent light bulb emits thermal radiation, and because the tungsten filament approximates an ideal blackbody radiator, its color temperature is essentially the temperature of the filament.

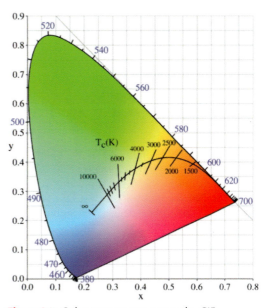

Figure 3.7 Color temperature across the CIE spectrum locus.

Color temperature is a characteristic of near white light at the center of the CIE 1931 chromaticity diagram in a range going from red to orange to yellow to white to blueish white.

Illuminants with higher color temperatures of 5000K and over appear bluer and cooler, lower color temperatures of 1700–3200K appear redder and warmer. The spectrum of white in illuminants transitions from 1700 to 4500K roughly along the blackbody locus of Planckian radiation (incandescent light), then it is averaged from about 4500K to 5500K to meet the CIE D series daylight locus. While color temperature is a scalar measure of near white color, many colors with different appearances can have matching color temperatures, and some illuminants with identical color temperatures vary in how much green they contain. The tonal scale for any given color temperature white point extends from along the blackbody curve in a straight line all the way to the narrow back of the spectrum locus in a gray scale range from white to black.

Table 3.1 Color temperature of light sources

Color Temperature	Source
1700K	Match flame, low pressure sodium lamps
1850K	Candle flame, sunset/sunrise
3000K	Warm white tubular fluorescent lamps
3150K	Studio tungsten lamps
5000K	Horizon daylight
5000K	Daylight/cool white tubular fluorescent lamps
5600K	Studio HMI lamp
6200K	Xenon short arc lamp
6500K	Daylight, overcast
6500–9500K	LCD or CRT screen

Colors on the daylight end of the color temperature scale are often preferred in display calibrations due to their "neutral white" appearance. Rec 709 specifies the use of a D65 (6500K) illuminant, and other defined daylight illuminants including D50, D55, and D60.

Because cinematographers use a wide variety of light sources interchangeably, it becomes important to set white balance in cameras to match the artistic intent of the scene being photographed. Digital cinema cameras can white-balance both in hardware settings and metadata to bring more or less warmth into a picture. White balancing is a global adjustment of the relative intensities of red, green, and blue in order to render neutral colors correctly under a variety of light sources and color temperatures. White balance is covered more deeply in Chapter 10 of this book under camera setup and operation.

Light sources and illuminants that do not emit light by thermal radiation are now necessarily being more accurately characterized by their spectral power distribution. The cinema industry now demands that relative spectral power distribution curves be provided by manufacturers of LED and other illuminants in increments of 5nm or less on a spectroradiometer in order to evaluate their usability for photographic use. The subject of LED spectra will be covered in more depth in Chapter 11 of this book.

Color Space as It Relates to Cinematography

With an understanding of the vast spectrum of colors that human beings can perceive, it is important to understand the compromises we make in reproducing those colors in the pictures that we create.

A color model is a mathematical system used to specify and describe particular colors. A color that can be specified in a color model corresponds to a single point within a color space. There are numerous color models including RGB (red, green, blue), CMYK (cyan, magenta, yellow, key), YIQ (luminance, in phase, quadurature), HSI (hue, saturation, intensity), among others. Digital cinema uses an RGB color model.

For the cinematographer's purposes, a color space is a specific three-dimensional organization of colors defined by a set of primaries inside a color model. In combination with camera and viewing device profiles, a color space allows for reproducible digital representations of color and tonal scale.

When defining a color space, the usual reference standards are the CIELAB or CIEXYZ color spaces, which were specifically designed to encompass all colors the average human can see. Cinematographic systems function in an RGB color space, which is a subset of the full human visible color palette defined by the CIE study.

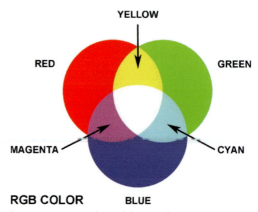

Figure 3.8 RGB color (additive color mixing).

In digital cinematography, the RGB color model is the mathematical method used to describe colors as numerical triples of chromaticity coordinate numbers denoting red, green, and blue values.

Chromaticity is defined as an objective specification of the quality of a color regardless of its luminance. Chromaticity consists of two independent parameters, hue and saturation. RGB color is defined by specific chromaticities of red, green, and blue additive primaries, and can produce any color that lies within the volume defined by those primary colors.

When these chromaticities are extended through the range of their tonal scale from fully saturated (called mass tone), and as they mix toward white (called a white letdown), they extend along individually curving lines of colors bowing toward black (at near coordinates 0,0), they define a color space or color volume.

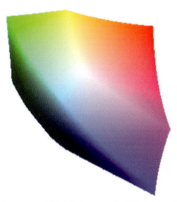

Figure 3.9 1976 CIELAB isometric 3D plot of sRGB color space.

Source: courtesy of Ron Penrod.

We use an additive RGB (red, green, and blue) model when defining film and digital color space. The addition of all three colors produces white, and the darkening of all three colors yields black. RGBA is RGB color space with an additional channel, alpha (or matte channel) to control transparency.

Figure 3.10 An RGB image from ASC/PGA ICAS 2012 "Serious News."

In these illustrations, we can see an example scene (above) and it's RGB waveform scope representation (below). The waveform picture graphically tells us how much of each primary color is present to make up the picture.

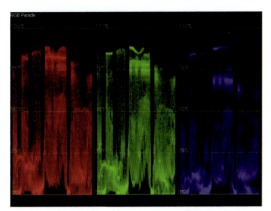

Figure 3.11 RGB wave form monitor screen grab.

RGB color is an additive way of making our palette of colors, in which red, green, or blue light is added together to create color from darkness, and it is defined by what quantities of red, green, or blue light needs to be emitted to produce a given color.

This

Figure 3.12 The red record.

plus this

Figure 3.13 The green record.

plus this

Figure 3.14 The blue record.

equals this:

Figure 3.15 The RGB image.

The digital camera senses individual color channels from the scene, and the images are recorded as RGB information. Those individual red, green, and blue components are then recombined to recreate the colors of the original scene. How a camera samples and derives individual color records is a complex process, especially in Bayer pattern cameras that record raw images. Bayer pattern cameras employ complicated math to derive their individual color records, and that case is discussed in Chapter 2 of this work.

Color Gamut

A set of RGB primary chromaticities functions within the larger CIE XYZ reference color space to define a three dimensional "footprint," a subset of colors known as a gamut.

A gamut is a subset of values in a color space. Gamut is the term we use to refer to all the colors in a defined color space. Frequently a gamut will be pictorially represented in only two dimensions on a plot of the CIE XYZ spectrum locus, where saturation and tonal scale are implied. Color gamuts are device dependent, each defined for specific output devices, such as projectors, monitors, and printers. The various RGB color gamuts

used in digital cinematography employ mapping functions to and from other color spaces to create a system of color interpretation.

In cinematography, a gamut is a subset of colors from the visible spectrum. The most common usage refers to the subset of colors which can be accurately represented in a given circumstance, such as within a color space or by a display device. In digital imaging, a gamut is approximately defined by XYZ red, green, and blue primary colors and bounded by straight lines between each of the three primary colors (in a 2D representation diagram).

Gamut also refers to the complete set of colors found within an image at a given time. Converting a digitized image to a different color space alters its gamut, and when the target color space is smaller or more confined than the original, some of the colors in the original image are lost in the process.

Pointer's Gamut

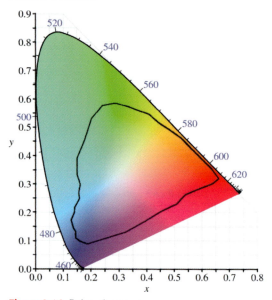

Figure 3.16 Pointer's gamut.

Pointer's gamut is a measured approximation of the gamut of every color that can be reflected by the non-specular surface of any object of any material. Pointer's gamut is not defined by RGB primaries but rather, by observation. In 1980, Michael R. Pointer published an empirical maximum gamut for real surface colors, based on 4089 samples, establishing a widely respected target for color reproduction. Pointer's gamut also forms the basis of the subset of human visible colors that can be reproduced using subtractive color mixing.

Because we as artists and image authors study endless paintings, prints, and books as reference for our work, and because we frequently employ printed media for communicating our artistic intent, we should understand color space as it relates to reflective or print media. In printed media, a reflective palette of colors can be created by using the subtractive primary colors of pigment: cyan, magenta, yellow, rather than by the additive primary colors of red, green, and blue. This color process is referred to as CMYK, an acronym for cyan, magenta, yellow and key (or black).

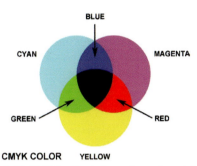

Figure 3.17 CMYK color (subtractive color mixing).

A CMYK color model uses ink values for cyan, magenta, yellow, and black, and employs subtractive color mixing, starting with a white canvas or page and using inks, dyes, or paints to subtract color from the white base to create an image. The addition of all three colors at full saturation results in black, and CMYK adds an additional dye, K (Key) to create deeper blacks.

SWOP CMYK Color Space

CMYK subtractive colors define their own specific color space. To create a 3d representation of this color space, we measure the amount of magenta color along the X axis of the cube, the amount of cyan corresponds to the Y axis, and the amount of yellow to its Z axis.

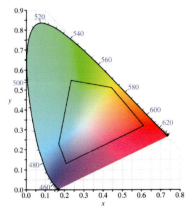

Figure 3.18 SWOP CMYK color space.

Specifications for Web Offset Publications (SWOP), is an organization and the set of specifications that they produce that specifies the consistency and quality of professionally printed material. The resulting CMYK color space provides a unique position for every color that can be created by combining these four pigments. Because the printed color palette depends on the reflectance of the medium on which it is printed, the intensity and range of colors in print is generally limited by the combination of paper, ink, and illumination. The addition of all three colors results in black, and CMYK adds an additional dye, K (Key) to create deeper blacks. White is created in the absence of color by the paper or media on which the image is printed.

Figure 3.19 RGB vs. CMYK color.

Film and digital are projected or viewed on illuminated monitors or screens, so we use an additive RGB (red, green, and blue) model when defining film and digital color space. In an RGB color model, the addition of all three colors produces white, and careful attention must be paid to defining white in the digital world.

Rec 709 HDTV Color Space

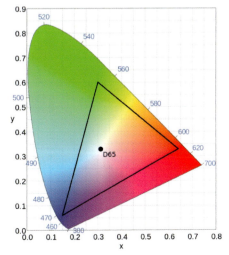

Figure 3.20 Rec 709 high definition television color space.

ITU BT709 defines a modest color palette which was originally designed and engineered to accommodate the limited capabilities of cathode ray tube (CRT) television screens.

The high definition television Rec 709 specification defined both an $R'G'B'$ encoding and a $Y'C_BC_R$ encoding, each with either 8 bits or 10 bits per sample in each color channel. In the 8-bit encoding, the R', B', G', and Y' channels have a nominal range of [16..235], and the C_B and C_R channels have a nominal range of [16..240] with 128 as the neutral value. So in $R'G'B'$, reference black is (16, 16, 16) and reference white is (235, 235, 235), and in $Y'C_BC_R$, reference black is (16, 128, 128), and reference white is (235, 128, 128). Values outside the nominal ranges are allowed, but typically they would be clamped for broadcast or for display. Values 0 and 255 are reserved as timing references, and may not contain color data. Rec 709's 10-bit encoding uses nominal values four times those of the 8-bit encoding. Rec 709's nominal ranges are the same as those defined years before in ITU Rec 601 (standard-definition television), and were originally based on the subset of visible colors that could be reproduced by CRT monitors. Rec 709 color space covers 35.9% of the CIE human visible spectrum.

DCI P3 Color Space

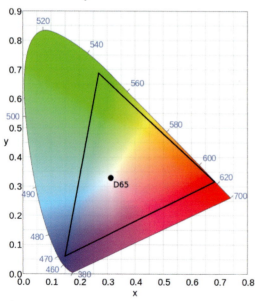

Figure 3.21 Digital cinema initiatives (DCI) P3 color space.

DCI-P3, or DCI/P3, is the SMPTE standard RGB color space designed by the Digital Cinema Initiative (DCI) for digital motion picture exhibition by the (then) seven major studios of American film industry. DCI-P3 color space covers 45.5% of all CIE human visible spectrum. The Digital Cinema Initiative (which set the standards for Digital Exhibition of Motion Pictures) chose a gamut larger than Rec 709, but smaller than motion picture release print film. Now, many new generation digital cinema cameras are capable of capturing colors outside the range of either film or television, and the development of wide gamut high dynamic range workflows, displays, and projectors is under way.

BT Rec 2020 UHDTV Color Space

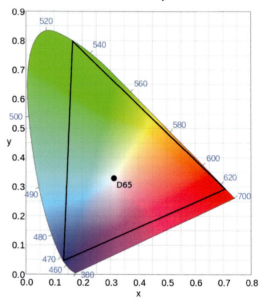

Figure 3.22 BT Rec 2020 UHDTV color space.

ITU-R Recommendation BT.2020 specifies a new ultra high definition television (UHDTV) system that includes both standard dynamic range and wide color gamut display capability, ultra high (3840 x 2160) definition, a wide variety of picture resolutions, frame rates, bit depths, color primaries, chroma samplings, and an opto-electrical transfer function. It is expanded in several ways by Rec BT.2100. Rec. 2020 (UHDTV/UHD-1/UHD-2) color space can reproduce colors that cannot be shown with Rec 709 (HDTV) color space. Rec 2020 color space covers 75.8% of the CIE human visible spectrum.

AMPAS ACES AP0 Color Space

The Academy Color Encoding System (ACES) is a color image encoding system created by hundreds of industry professionals under the auspices of the Academy of Motion Picture Arts

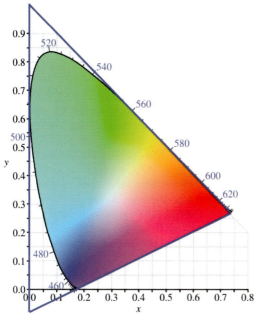

Figure 3.23 ACES AP0 color space.

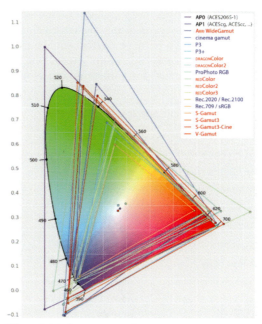

Figure 3.24 Camera encoding gamuts.

and Sciences. The system defines color primaries that completely encompass the visible spectral locus. The white point is approximate to the CIE D60 standard illuminant, and ACES files are encoded in 16-bit half float values allowing ACES Open EXR files to encode 30 stops of scene information.

Camera Color Gamut

In images captured from digital camera sensors, the values of the primaries relate to the amount of light seen through red, green, and blue color filter pigments on the Bayer color filter array. Cameras do not have a gamut per se, so it does not make sense to talk about the gamut of a camera, but it is very important to specify a color space or color into which colors from cameras are to be encoded. Camera encoding gamuts are selectable in many cameras, but exercise caution when selecting a gamut, consult your lab, and test, test, test!

- ALEXA wide gamut is the color encoding space used in combination with ARRI Log C.
- Canon cinema gamut is used to encode log images from Canon cinema cameras.
- RED color, RED DRAGON color, RED DRAGON color2, RED DRAGON color3, are all RED digital cinema camera color encoding spaces.

- REDWideGamutRGB is designed to encompass the colors a RED camera can generate without clipping any colors.
- Panasonic V-Gamut encodes wide color from Panasonic Varicam cameras by optimizing the on-chip filter characteristics for splitting light into RGB.
- SONY S-Gamut3 color space is wider than S-Gamut3.Cine. SONY S-Gamut3 color space covers the same range as S-Gamut, but has improved color reproduction
- SONY S-Gamut.Cine color space is slightly wider than DCI-P3. Combining S-Gamut3. Cine with S-Log3, which has gradation characteristics similar to those of scanned negative film, makes SONY camera images easier to grade.
- SONY S-Gamut color space is wider than S-Gamut3.Cine.

Gamuts Compared

Color gamuts are device dependent, each defined for specific output devices, such as projectors, monitors, and printers. Cameras do not have defined RGB primaries per se. They have spectral sensitivities based on the pigments used in their Bayer pattern color filter arrays, and some sensors may register many more colors than the defined color spaces we use in digital cinematography. A camera's unique look is based on how a color scientist maps those colors into a gamut.

The colors available from a sensor are normally scaled to fit into a gamut that includes as many usable colors as a particular gamut can contain. It is from this process that we are given a long list of "camera gamuts" from which we can re-map

Table 3.2 Gamuts and transfer functions

Color Spaces	Transfer Functions
ACES Primaries 0	ACEScc
ACES Primaries 1	ACEScct
ACEScc	ACESproxy10i
ACEScct	ACESproxy12i
ACEScg	ARRI LogC EI 200
ACESproxy	ARRI LogC EI 400
Adobe RGB	ARRI LogC EI 800
ADX10 Film Scan	ARRI LogC EI 1600
ADX16 Film Scan	ARRI LogC EI 3200
ARRI Wide Gamut	BMDFilm
BMD Wide Gamut	BMDFilm 4.6K
BMDFilm (Legacy)	BMDFilm 4K
BMDFilm 4.6K (Legacy)	BMDFilm Pocket 4K EI 3200
BMDFilm 4.6K V3 (Legacy)	BMDFilm Pocket 4K EI 400
BMDFilm 4K (Legacy)	Bolex Log
BMDFilm 4K V3 (Legacy)	BT.1886
Bolex Wide Gamut RGB	CanonLog
Canon Cinema Gamut	CanonLog2
Canon DCI-P3+	CanonLog3
CIE-XYZ	Cineon
DJI D-Gamut	DJI D-Log
Fuji F-Log Gamut	Fuji F-Log
GoPro ProTune Native	Gamma Function
P3	GoPro ProTune Flat
Panasonic V-Gamut	Hybrid Log Gamma
ProPhoto RGB	JPLog
Rec. 2020	Nikon N-Log
Rec. 709	Panasonic V-Log
RED DRAGONcolor	Phantom Log 1 Normalized
RED DRAGONcolor2	Phantom Log 2 Normalized
REDcolor	PQ ST 2084
REDcolor2	RED Log3G10
REDcolor3	RED Log3G12
REDcolor4	REDLogFilm
REDWideGamutRGB	SONY S-Log
SONY S-Gamut/S-Gamut3	SONY S-Log2
SONY S-Gamut3.Cine	SONY S-Log3
	sRGB

colors to display dependent gamuts. It is sometimes useful to deBayer camera RAW files to a "camera native" color space that does not limit color to a specific display dependent gamut in order to take advantage of the wider spectral sensitivities of such sensors.

After that, color science can transform those colors into other color spaces such as Rec 709, Rec 2020/2100, and DCI-P3 that displays and projectors can reproduce by the use of an optical transfer function (OTF). The optical transfer function of an optical system such as a camera, monitor, or projector specifies how the system presents light from the image file onto screen, or to the next device in the optical transmission chain. Images are transformed from one transfer function to another with regularity in finishing and display.

Color Space Conversion or Transformation

$$\begin{cases} Y &= 0.2989 \times R + 0.5866 \times G + 0.1145 \times B \\ Cb &= -0.1688 \times R - 0.3312 \times G + 0.5000 \times B \\ Cr &= 0.5000 \times R - 0.4184 \times G - 0.0816 \times B \end{cases}$$

Figure 3.25 Example *RGB* to *YCbCr* color space conversion math.

Color space conversion is the mathematical transformation of the numerical representation of a color from one color space definition to another. This normally happens in the course of converting an image that is represented in one color space to another color space, and the obvious goal is most often to make the colors of the transformed image look as close as possible to the colors of the original image. Transformations use explicit mathematical functions to convert from one set of color values to another, so the resulting transitions in color and tone are generally continuous and smooth, with no interpolation errors. Needless to say, transformations from one color space to another can lose or decimate color information in the process, and that information frequently cannot be regained by reversing the transformation.

Color Sampling and Subsampling

What is 4:4:4? It has become HD slang to refer to images and systems in which all three color records have been sampled at equal maximum system frequencies. In the era of digital HD acquisition, 4:4:4 is a bit of a misnomer. Denoting an image as 4:4:4 traditionally refers to a standard definition RGB digital video image in which all three color components have been sampled at full bandwidth 13.5 mhz. HDTV sampling was based on the original

electronic timing parameters of standard definition digital TV. For the purposes of doing efficient
standards conversions between PAL and NTSC,
it made sense to design the timing, or sampling of
both standards, from a common point of reference. A 2.25 MHz frequency is the lowest common
multiple between NTSC and PAL systems for digital sampling. Six times 2.25 equals 13.5 MHz, so
that number was internationally decided upon as
the (over) sampling rate used for both PAL and
NTSC formats in standard component digital
video. HDTV maintains an integer relationship for
the same reasons. A 1920 × 1080 active pixels high
definition system utilizes a 74.25 MHz sample rate.
Multiply 2.25 by 33 and get 74.25. There is a total
sampling capability of 2200 samples per line and
1125 lines in such a schema, and this was thought
(at the time) to be a sufficient number for all broadcast cases. Because HD images are sampled at
74.25 mhz they should actually be said to be sampled at a 22:22:22 ratio. This history lesson should
be read, understood, and then forgotten. It essentially means that none of the three color records has
been undersampled or subsampled at a lower rate.

Most digital cameras can also output 4:2:2,
(or properly 22:11:11), which is usually either
downsampled internally in 3 CCD cameras, or
deBayered directly from Bayer pattern cameras.

What is 4:2:2? What is 4:2:1? What is 4:1:1?
What is 4:2:0? What is 3:1:1? They are all subsampling schemes wherein one or more of the three
color components are sampled at lower frequencies than the green (or luma) picture component;
4:2:2 is a practical way of sending RGB images
as approximations of the original colors at much
lower bandwidth for transmission or storage. All
subsampling schemes depend on deriving the
resolution from the luminance (green channel)
component of the scene and using it to create a
sense of resolution in the red and blue channels
of the image. Color subsampling is widely used
in prosumer cameras, HDV cameras, and many
inexpensive cameras. Broadcast HDTV is almost
always sampled at a 4:2:2 sampling ratio. Raw
Bayer pattern cameras sample at 4:2:0 (line by
line) by their very nature, and then derive other
sampling ratios from the deBayer process.

While *any* camera *could* produce the next
Oscar winner for best cinematography, it is probably wiser for professional cinematographers to
insure success with quality than to hope for it
while saving too much money. Capture the biggest
color space, highest resolution, and lowest compression you can afford with the budget you have,
especially if you intend to do any visual effects
work at all. If you think this is of no importance
to the movie you are preparing to shoot, think

about that again for a moment, and then try to
name a movie that you saw this year that had no
visual effects. Some of the most effective visual
effects are the ones that the audience has no idea
are visual effects. Set extensions, beauty cleanups
on performer's faces, wire removals, sky replace-
ments, adding reflections, etc. – are all visual
effects that really refine the image without drawing
attention to themselves. Do a little homework and
you will probably learn that there were numerous
visual effects shots in almost every movie made
today. One of the most important factors in doing
invisible visual effects work is starting the process
with the best images you can get, and shooting at
full bandwidth color is a great start!

YCbCr and Y'CbCr Color

Even though HD video displays are driven by red,
green, and blue voltage signals, full bandwidth
RGB signals were not an economically efficient
means for storage and broadcast transmission,
as they have a lot of inherent color redundancy.

YCbCr and Y'CbCr (where Y' denotes luminance) are practical ways of encoding RGB images
as approximations of color and perceptual uniformity, where primary colors corresponding roughly to
red, green, and blue are processed into images that
closely resemble the original RGB image, but at
much lower bandwidth for transmission.

Figure 3.26 The early days of color television.
Source: NBC Universal – used with permission.

A digital image can be represented using three
color values per pixel. However, the colorimetric
storing of images in RGB space is inefficient, as
there is considerable correlation between the channels. Alternatively, when images or video are to be
compressed, they are usually converted into YCbCr
color space. In YCbCr space, an image is represented by one luma (Y) and two chroma (Cb, Cr)

components. The luma channel contains "brightness" information; it is essentially a gray-scale version of the image. The chroma values are color offsets, which show how much a pixel deviates from grey scale in the blue (Cb) and red (Cr) directions.

For most natural images, the RGB to YCbCr conversion strongly de-correlates the color channels, so the Y, Cb, and Cr components can be coded independently.

In YCbCr space, the bandwidth of an image tends to be concentrated in the Y channel. This leaves the Cb and Cr channels with less information, so they can be represented with fewer bits.

Another advantage of the YCbCr space comes from the characteristics of the human visual system. Humans are more sensitive to brightness information than color information. Consequently, the chroma signals (Cb, Cr) can be down-sampled relative to the luma (Y) without significant loss of perceived image quality. Chroma down-sampling is almost always done when compressing image or video data.

In YCbCr 4:4:4 format, the chroma values (Cb, Cr) are sampled at the same rate as luma (Y). This format is rarely used, except in professional applications.

Conversion from Bayer cell to YCbCr 4:4:4

Figure 3.27 Conversion from Bayer cell to YCbCr 4:4:4 (Cb is represented as plus blue and minus blue values, Cr as plus red and minus red values).

Source: Mitch Bogdonowicz.

In YCbCr 4:2:2 format, the chroma values (Cb, Cr) are down-sampled by a factor of two relative to the luma (Y) in the horizontal direction. Most higher end digital video formats use YCbCr 4:2:2 sampling.

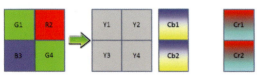

Conversion from Bayer cell to YCbCr 4:2:2

Figure 3.28 Conversion from Bayer cell to YCbCr 4:2:2 (Cb is represented as plus blue and minus blue values, Cr as plus red and minus red values).

Source: Mitch Bogdonowicz.

However, the most common color format used in compressed images and video is YCbCr 4:2:0.

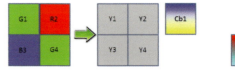

Conversion from Bayer cell to YCbCr 4:2:0

Figure 3.29 Conversion from Bayer cell to YCbCr 4:2:0 (Cb is represented as plus blue and minus blue values, Cr as plus red and minus red values).

Source: Mitch Bogdonowicz.

In YCbCr 4:2:0 format, the chroma signals are down-sampled by a factor of two in both the horizontal and vertical directions. It should be noted that there are different chroma positions used in YCbCr 4:2:0 format. Sometimes the chroma samples are considered to be half-way between the luma samples vertically, or in the center of a group of four luma samples. In the down sampling process the chroma channels should be low-pass filtered to limit aliasing.[2]

Figure 3.30 ICAS "Serious News."

In this illustration, we can see our original RGB example scene and it's YCbCr wave form scope representation. The Luminance Y (on the left) is used to multiply the chrominance components (chroma blue, center, and chroma red, on the right) to reproduce the scene from a smaller subset of the original color data.

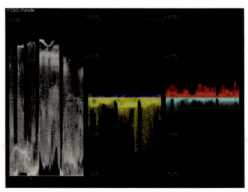

Figure 3.31 YCbCr wave from monitor screen grab of the scene.

Y'CbCr color encoding is used to separate out a luma signal (Y') that can be stored with high resolution or transmitted at high bandwidth, and two chroma components (Cb and Cr) that can be bandwidth-reduced, subsampled, and compressed for improved system efficiency.

Figure 3.32 The full color scene.

Figure 3.33 The luminance or Y component.

Figure 3.34 The blue chroma or Cb component expressed as plus and minus blue values.

Figure 3.35 The red chroma or Cr component expressed as plus and minus red values.

The blue and red chroma components are effectively half the bandwidth of the green luma component, not a problem in many ordinary viewing circumstances, but a huge potential source of headaches for visual effects work.

Figure 3.36 Green screen compositing.

Blue screen or green screen mattes are more difficult to extract from chroma subsampled images, as the difference in sampling resolution between color records in composites can cause fringing and matte edge lines that are clearly visible and nearly impossible to mitigate. If you are doing big screen VFX, shoot 4:4:4 (or should I say, 22:22:22).

Color Has Traditionally Been Device Dependent

Traditionally, most image color data has been what we call *output referred or display referred* imagery, because it is dependent on the limited dynamic range and color gamut of a particular output device or display. Display referred color achieves the appearance of the correct creatively intended color by mathematically mapping the original photometric signal with a transform or transfer function specific to a particular display device such as a monitor or projector.

Figure 3.37 The early days of color television.

Preparation for Using ACES

Using ACES in practice, as with any production pipeline, requires advance preparation to achieve satisfying results. Key issues to consider when using ACES include:

- If shooting with digital cameras, acquisition or creation of appropriate IDTs to produce well-formed ACES-encoded images.
- If shooting film, proper calibration of film scanners to produce well-formed ADX-encoded images.
- If creating CGI images, keeping to an ACES EXR pipeline for all interchange of images throughout the VFX process to avoid traditional color pipeline ambiguities and issues.
- Use of appropriate RRT/ODT combinations for on-set viewing, editorial viewing, VFX department viewing, and mastering, as well as support for any LMTs that might be used on-set, through post and vfx, and into the mastering suite.
- Confirmation of ACES support either natively or through input and output LUT support in color correctors and other image-processing hardware and software.

With a correctly implemented ACES-based workflow, visual effects artists, cinematographers, animators, matte painters, compositors and I/O departments can rely on properly exposed source images as the best starting point for visual effect integration and mastering. ACES will enable clear and well-defined solutions to the many problems currently associated with correct usage of color space and dynamic range in the realm of visual effects work.[3]

Digital Cinema Color Spaces: P3, XYZ, X′Y′Z′, and ACES

Digital Cinema Initiatives, LLC (DCI) was founded in 2002 as a joint venture between Walt Disney Studios, 20th Century Fox, MGM, Paramount, SONY, Universal, and Warner Brothers Studios. DCI's purpose was to create uniform specifications for digital cinema projection, and to establish voluntary open standards for digital motion picture exhibition to insure a uniform and high level of interoperability, reliability, security, and quality control.

One of the most important of the many goals of Digital Cinema Initiatives was to make digital cinema as extensible, or as immune to obsolescence, as possible. Color space is one of several areas where the benefit of this approach is evident.

The DCI specification published in 2005 built in the capability to encode color information in the DCDM (Digital Cinema Distribution Master) in a notation for color space that would be universal and future-proof. They decided to base it on CIE 1931, an internationally recognized standardization of the human visual system color matching functions. The tristimulus values expressed here describe the gamut of color humans can see. The CIE notation is called XYZ or "cap XYZ" and DCI specified use of the system's x, y coordinates to describe the color primaries X, Y, and Z as a gamut container.

This XYZ space far exceeds the visual perception capability of humans. The joke was if aliens ever landed on earth, the DCI spec would provide for whatever color gamut they might be able to see. In reality, it provides an important enabling foundation that technology improvements in digital cinema are being built upon.

This "extensible and interoperable" mindset of DCI has been carried forward and dramatically expanded by the Academy's ACES methodologies described elsewhere in this book. ACES is a wide gamut representation as is XYZ. Both are mathematically transformable to the other. While ACES "RGB like" primaries in x–y space are optimized for use in motion picture production, post/DI/grading, distribution, archive, and television, when selected by DCI, CIE's XYZ was far better known internationally and across all industries.

From a practical standpoint, most real-world color spaces are a subset of the human ability to perceive color as described by the tristimulous values expressed in CIE. For example, the Rec 709 gamut in wide use in HDTV is considerably smaller than film's, and much more limited than CIE, and now, ACES.

A new color encoding, X′Y′Z′ (called "x-prime, y-prime, z-prime"), was specified for DCI image encoding. X′Y′Z′ is an output-referred, gamma 2.6 encoding of CIE-XYZ, with a reference white point at 48cd/m2. Because the X′Y′Z′ color space is larger than the human visual gamut, a smaller display gamut, P3, was also defined.

The DCI spec allows that productions are free to master to any white point they prefer, provided all mastered colors fall within the allowed DCI gamut. The DCI (0.314, 0.351) white point is often eschewed because it exhibits a greenish cast when compared to the daylight curve. X′Y′Z′ coding space is display-referred, so that the full color appearance of the theatrical imagery (such as any film emulation 3D-LUTs) is fully baked into the X′Y′Z′ image. Images in X′Y′Z′ are intended to be unambiguous so that there should be no color variation between calibrated DCI digital cinema projectors.

In the current Texas Instruments DLP implementation of DCI color space (DCI X'Y'Z' P3) the gamut, described by the designation "P3," approximates that of film. This gamut covers the vast majority of real-world colors, although highly saturated colors (as you might find on a butterfly's wing or a tropical fish) are outside the P3 gamut.

The reason the P3 color gamut in digital cinema is not as large as the human visual response gamut (CIE) is due to the combination of limitations in the xenon light sources used in projectors coupled with the capabilities of the color-splitting components of the DLP projector light engine. While excellent compared with most previous methodologies, its capability is now being exceeded by the progression of technology with methods such as laser projection.

Since lasers are truly monochromatic or "pure," the three laser primaries can be selected to be more saturated, which naturally creates a larger gamut. Deeper green primaries are available in laser light that wouldn't be practical with Xenon. From a cinematic standpoint, this is most significant in how the broader primaries permit expanded reproduction of the cyan and yellow secondaries. The benefits of this expanded color gamut can be fully realized in ACES, and utilized with new RRTs and ODTs as new laser projection systems find their way into the market.

As lasers come into wider use for mastering, DI will be able to be done in these significantly greater color gamuts, especially in the context of ACES. While not immediately directly applicable in the tens of thousands of converted Xenon P3 digital cinema projection systems in use worldwide (which will require either a gamut conversion from the expanded laser color space to P3, or the continued use of the ACES P3 ODT), it will be beneficial in the most premium venues that have laser projection as well as providing superior picture DI's for ancillary and archive use.

As lasers expand into exhibition, and manufacturers cease producing xenon projectors, the foundational DCI spec will not need to be redone to include this progressive improvement, or others like it in the future. Inside ACES, in addition to the P3 ODT in current use, new expanded-gamut laser ODT's can be utilized for improved theatrical presentation.[4]

Notes

1. Studies suggest that many women (and a few men) have a fourth type of cone whose sensitivity peak is between the standard red and green cones, giving them an increase in color differentiation called tetrachromacy.
2. Courtesy of Mitch and Jim Bogdonowicz.
3. Courtesy of AMPAS, Andy Maltz, Curtis Clark, Jim Houston, and David Reisner. For more information on ACES, please visit oscars.org/aces.
4. Courtesy of Jay Spencer.

reflection and absorption by the pigments and dyes themselves. The colored dye of a solid object will absorb (or subtract) unwanted frequencies from white light and reflect the desired frequency – say, blue. As another example, a piece of glass dyed yellow subtracts the unwanted frequencies from white light and allows the yellow frequency to pass through.

Plato believed that our eyes contained fire placed there by the gods. The fire produces rays that extend from our eyes and interact with the particles that emanate from all the objects in the sight line to create visual perception. Obviously, Plato's theory has since been proven false. Even Aristotle, Plato's pupil, refuted this theory by arguing that if it were true, vision at night would not be any different than vision during the day. But, he noted, it *is* different.

Human Color Perception

Back to the more logical explanation. Three kinds of light-sensitive pigments in our eyes are contained in three types of cones: blue (short wavelengths), green (medium), and red (long). These color vision cells (or photoreceptors) truly are shaped like cones. Because there are three cones, color spaces are mapped in three dimensions. In reality, each is sensitive to a range of colors, but they peak at the correlating primary-color wavelengths. How the brain sees and interprets color signals sent from the cones is still not fully understood, but it is known that processing in the brain plays a big role in determining the perceived color. Though the blue cone's peak sensitivity is to blue light, when only those cones fire, our brains for some reason perceive violet rather than what we would assume to be a typical blue. Call it one of nature's quirks. Other quirks are color vision abnormalities, where some of a person's cones may be absent or deficient in a particular pigment, which causes the interpretation of some colors to be affected. This is known as color-blindness, and it predominantly affects about 8 to 12% of males. Only about half of 1% of females has a form of color-blindness. Red–green color blindness is the most common form.

Rods, too, are not immune to abnormalities. Rods are retinal cells that are indeed shaped like rods and function more at low light levels. They do not distinguish color, only picture detail and intensity, or white and black. Rods are saturated above about one foot-lambert and are not considered to play a significant role in normal

color vision. However, the shadows in a typical motion-picture presentation fall into a light level where both cones and rods are active, known as mesopic vision, which falls between photopic (under normal light conditions) and scotopic (human vision in the dark). Few people have total color-blindness with no cone activity, in which they see only in black-and-white or shades of gray. (For the Internet-savvy, the Website http://colorfilter.wickline.org allows you to type in a Web address and view that page as though you are color-blind.)

Humans can see an estimated 10 million different colors, and each of us perceives every color differently. I could point to a light-skinned tomato and say it is red in color, but someone else might say it is more orange due to a color deficiency or through a difference in color nomenclature as a result of culture. (Tomato, to-mah-to.) Culture and gender are other possible factors that affect color perception. Women perceive a greater range of colors than men do, particularly shades of red. To explain the reason for this difference, researchers in this area point to our ancestors. The men hunted for animals while the women, when not tending to offspring or the cave, sought out fruits, vegetables, and insects, and these were identified and rated poisonous or safe based on color. Women also are the only ones who could have the rare and theoretical tetrachromacy condition: a fourth type of cone. The result of a mutation in the two female X chromosomes, tetrachromats can have either red, red-shifted, green, and blue cones or red, green, green-shifted, and blue cones. In theory, this should result in a "heightened" sense of color and a broader color space, but the exact effects are not known and difficult to pinpoint because most of us are trichromats and we cannot see what they see. It would be as though we were trying to see ultraviolet radiation. A tetrachromat describing what they see would be like describing the color of UV; we trichromats have no reference for that perception. Another unknown is whether the brain and nervous system, wired for three-color input, can adapt to four colors to put those cones to use.

Genetically, men are relegated to trichromacy forever. But there is some hope for trichromats: it is thought but not yet proven that when rods kick in at low light intensities, they may contribute to color vision, providing a small region of tetrachromacy in trichromatic color space.

be no color variation between calibrated DCI digital cinema projectors.

In the current Texas Instruments DLP implementation of DCI color space (DCI X'Y'Z' P3) the gamut, described by the designation "P3," approximates that of film. This gamut covers the vast majority of real-world colors, although highly saturated colors (as you might find on a butterfly's wing or a tropical fish) are outside the P3 gamut.

The reason the P3 color gamut in digital cinema is not as large as the human visual response gamut (CIE) is due to the combination of limitations in the xenon light sources used in projectors coupled with the capabilities of the color-splitting components of the DLP projector light engine. While excellent compared with most previous methodologies, its capability is now being exceeded by the progression of technology with methods such as laser projection.

Since lasers are truly monochromatic or "pure," the three laser primaries can be selected to be more saturated, which naturally creates a larger gamut. Deeper green primaries are available in laser light that wouldn't be practical with Xenon. From a cinematic standpoint, this is most significant in how the broader primaries permit expanded reproduction of the cyan and yellow secondaries. The benefits of this expanded color gamut can be fully realized in ACES, and utilized with new RRTs and ODTs as new laser projection systems find their way into the market.

As lasers come into wider use for mastering, DI will be able to be done in these significantly greater color gamuts, especially in the context of ACES. While not immediately directly applicable in the tens of thousands of converted Xenon P3 digital cinema projection systems in use worldwide (which will require either a gamut conversion from the expanded laser color space to P3, or the continued use of the ACES P3 ODT), it will be beneficial in the most premium venues that have laser projection as well as providing superior picture DI's for ancillary and archive use.

As lasers expand into exhibition, and manufacturers cease producing xenon projectors, the foundational DCI spec will not need to be redone to include this progressive improvement, or others like it in the future. Inside ACES, in addition to the P3 ODT in current use, new expanded-gamut laser ODT's can be utilized for improved theatrical presentation.[4]

Notes

1. Studies suggest that many women (and a few men) have a fourth type of cone whose sensitivity peak is between the standard red and green cones, giving them an increase in color differentiation called tetrachromacy.
2. Courtesy of Mitch and Jim Bogdonowicz.
3. Courtesy of AMPAS, Andy Maltz, Curtis Clark, Jim Houston, and David Reisner. For more information on ACES, please visit oscars.org/aces.
4. Courtesy of Jay Spencer.

The Color–Space Conundrum

American Cinematographer Magazine explores the historical relevance of color space and its impact on the cinematographer's work.

The Beginnings of the Digital Intermediate
BY DOUGLAS BANKSTON

When John Schwartzman, ASC wanted to avoid the resolution-degrading optical blowup of the 2003 film *Seabiscuit*, he took the Super 35mm footage into a digital-intermediate suite at Technicolor's DI facility, Technique (now known as Technicolor Digital Intermediates, or TDI), where the process was accomplished on a computer. Though the digital era was in its infancy, its tools offered cinematographers unprecedented control over their imagery. And new digital tools – file formats, projectors, Look-Up Tables, cameras, algorithms for color sampling, compression and conversion, etc. – were being developed at a breakneck pace. As manufacturers pursued their own directions and goals, a digital realm without order was created, beyond the controlled borders of a small, select group of post facilities that engineered their own proprietary DI workflow solutions.

During his color-timing sessions in the DI suite, Schwartzman encountered some of the variances that can plague the hybrid imaging environment. The suite had been calibrated for a regular Vision print stock filmout. Sometime during the process, the production switched to Vision Premier stock, resulting in a color shift on the new stock because of the now mismatched Look-Up Table (LUT), which maps an input value to a location in a table, such as a pixel, and replaces that value with the table entry. Rather than start over and calibrate the suite and LUTs for Premier, through testing and familiarization, Schwartzman discovered that a certain magenta push in the digitally projected image

would correspond to his intended perfect result on Premier film. In essence, he had experienced a collision of the digital and film color spaces.

Figure 4.1 In this simulated visual from *Seabiscuit* (2003), John Schwartzman, ASC had to have a magenta push in the digitally projected image (right splitscreen), which would correspond to his intended image that had no color shift on the Premier print stock filmout (left splitscreen).

What Is Color Space?

Color space, quite simply, is the geometric representation of colors in a three-dimensional space, such as with a cube, sphere, or cone. They are tools to analyze and digitally encode color. There are many color spaces, including HSV, CIE XYZ, HSL, sRGB, CMY, CIE L*u*v*, CIE L*a*b*, and CMYK. Volumes have been written about color, color space, and color science and their applications to imaging. While I do not have an infinite number of pages in which to discuss this topic, I will broadly discuss color, how we perceive color, and how color has been handled in the motion-picture and television industries.

For a good starting point, just look at the sun – and I don't mean that literally. This G2-class, main-sequence star at the center of our solar system heaves electromagnetic energy into space in the form of waves of varying lengths, or frequencies. These waves bombard Earth. The atmosphere reflects or absorbs most of this energy, but some waves make it through to strike the planet surface and its countless sunbathers. This is known as light, and it is good, for we need it to see. However, humans are able to visually perceive a very narrow frequency band of this radiant energy.

The ancient Greeks postulated that the four elements of earth, wind, water, and fire correlated with a four-color theory, though their philosophical writings never directly tied an element to a specific color. Other theories were that a color was based on the smoothness of the atoms that constituted it, or that color consisted of quantities of energy where white was pure energy and black had none. While investigating color mixtures, Aristotle offered philosophical waxings that were also well off the track, but his approach at least began to steer the concepts in a better direction. As the story goes, one afternoon Aristotle spied some daylight hitting a white marble wall, and he held up a yellow glass fragment. The daylight that passed through the glass and struck the wall turned yellow. He then held a blue glass fragment between the yellow glass and the wall. The resulting light on the wall surface was blue, yellow, and *green*. He therefore surmised that blue and yellow create green when mixed together, which isn't quite true when it comes to light. Rather than mix to form green, the dyes in the glass subtracted portions of the light until all that was left to pass through in a certain spot was green.

Well over 1,500 years passed before Sir Isaac Newton ate the apple he saw fall from the tree – the one that led him to formulate the Universal Law of Gravitation – and turned his attention to the light that allowed him to see said fruit. He placed a prism in front of a pencil-thin beam of sunlight, which, because of a prism's variable refractance properties, caused that white light to disperse into its component frequencies: red, orange, yellow, green, blue, indigo, and violet, in ascending order from lower to higher in wavelength.

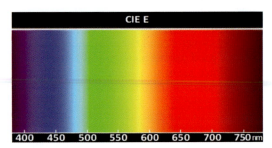

Figure 4.2 The visible spectrum of light.

Wavelengths of visible light range from 380 nanometers to 760 nanometers, and the length of a wave affects its color. A shorter wavelength, such as that of violet, has a higher frequency – that is, it cycles faster with less distance between peaks in the wave. Newton didn't get this far in his thinking, however – he passed the component light through an upside-down prism, which reconstituted the frequencies into white light.

Rainbows aside, all radiant energy is "colored." The colors that we can see fall within the visual spectrum, and this spectrum makes up what we commonly refer to as light. An example of a higher frequency that radiates just outside the bounds of the visual spectrum is ultraviolet. Although often referred to as ultraviolet light, that phrase is a misnomer – it is actually what we call ultraviolet *radiation*. If you can't see it, it can't be light. Bees can, so UV is light to them. Can you describe the color of ultraviolet, a color you cannot see? (And don't say purplish, based on the groovy black light you once had in your dorm room. That novelty's high-UV-output fluorescent tube allows some visible violet light to pass through so you would know that it is on.) UV-A energy also is emitted but can't be seen. Only the *effect* this frequency of energy has on certain substances can be seen, causing them to fluoresce. (Rest assured, the tube doesn't allow the shorter wavelength UV-B and UV-C frequencies to pass through and cause skin cancer.)

An example of a lower frequency is infrared radiation. When shooting with black-and-white infrared film, a stock that has a higher sensitivity to the infrared spectrum, the lens focus must be set differently than you would for visible light because the glass does not bend the longer wavelengths as much. Doing so enables the film to record a sharp image that takes advantage of what infrared reveals about the subjects by how the subjects and their variations in reflectance modulate the IR waves.

When light strikes an object, certain wavelengths are absorbed and others are reflected. Those that are reflected make up the color of the object – orange, for example. Orange has many variations that can be described as light, deep, rusty, bright, etc., and each is its own individual color. To explain this in more scientific terms than "deep" or "rusty," orange is distinguished by several characteristics: hue, lightness, and colorfulness. Hue is the property that identifies a color with a part of the spectrum – for example, orange is between red and yellow. The lightness description simply locates the color somewhere between light and dark colors. The colorfulness label indicates whether a color is either pale or pure (vivid).

Turn on a fluorescent Kino Flo and a tungsten 10K and then look at the output. What do you see besides spots before your eyes? You will perceive white light emanating from each, yet the two fixtures have vastly different spectrums. Though the two throws of light may be of different spectrums, an object illuminated by each will look the same – a phenomenon known as metamerism. The reason we see white light from two different sources is due to the fact that the eye reduces the full spectral distribution of light into three bands, and there are an infinite number of different spectral distributions that can result in the same three signals to the eye. The spectral distributions that appear visually identical are called metamers.

Of the colors that make up the visible spectrum, red, green, and blue are called primaries. Newton argued that each color of the visible spectrum was a primary, but he considered the definition of primary to mean "simple," as in simply a lump-sum color called red or yellow, etc., without getting into characteristics such as lightness or colorfulness or a specific wavelength of red within the red range. The other four colors,

known as secondary colors, are made by combinations of the three pure colors.

Orange light is created by roughly two parts red to one part green. In addition to creating the secondary hues, adding these three primary colors together in various combinations builds every other color up from black, and this is known as the *additive* color process. The three bands in our color vision cells correspond directly to the three primary spectral colors, and because of this, it is possible to match a wide range of colors via a mixture of just three primary colors.

Yes, we learned in art class that red, blue, and yellow are primary colors (and that we aren't supposed to eat paint). But those primaries apply to dyes and pigments, and they actually are called subtractive primaries.

In light, the subtractive primaries are cyan, magenta, and yellow. Visible light, whose primaries consist of red, green, and blue (RGB), is what allows those primary red, blue, and yellow pigments (or cyan, magenta, and yellow) to have color through varying degrees of wavelength

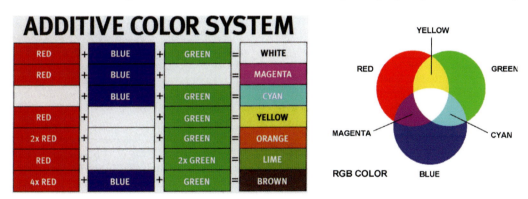

Figure 4.3 The additive color system, where equal parts of red, green, and blue yield white.

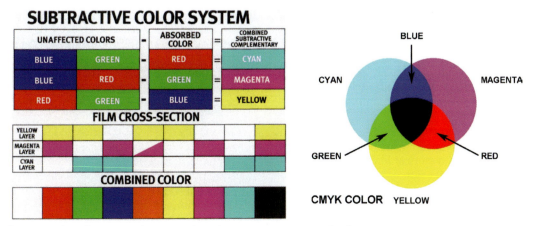

Figure 4.4 The subtractive color system based on cyan, magenta, and yellow primaries.

reflection and absorption by the pigments and dyes themselves. The colored dye of a solid object will absorb (or subtract) unwanted frequencies from white light and reflect the desired frequency – say, blue. As another example, a piece of glass dyed yellow subtracts the unwanted frequencies from white light and allows the yellow frequency to pass through.

Plato believed that our eyes contained fire placed there by the gods. The fire produces rays that extend from our eyes and interact with the particles that emanate from all the objects in the sight line to create visual perception. Obviously, Plato's theory has since been proven false. Even Aristotle, Plato's pupil, refuted this theory by arguing that if it were true, vision at night would not be any different than vision during the day. But, he noted, it *is* different.

Human Color Perception

Back to the more logical explanation. Three kinds of light-sensitive pigments in our eyes are contained in three types of cones: blue (short wavelengths), green (medium), and red (long). These color vision cells (or photoreceptors) truly are shaped like cones. Because there are three cones, color spaces are mapped in three dimensions. In reality, each is sensitive to a range of colors, but they peak at the correlating primary-color wavelengths. How the brain sees and interprets color signals sent from the cones is still not fully understood, but it is known that processing in the brain plays a big role in determining the perceived color. Though the blue cone's peak sensitivity is to blue light, when only those cones fire, our brains for some reason perceive violet rather than what we would assume to be a typical blue. Call it one of nature's quirks. Other quirks are color vision abnormalities, where some of a person's cones may be absent or deficient in a particular pigment, which causes the interpretation of some colors to be affected. This is known as color-blindness, and it predominantly affects about 8 to 12% of males. Only about half of 1% of females has a form of color-blindness. Red–green color blindness is the most common form.

Rods, too, are not immune to abnormalities. Rods are retinal cells that are indeed shaped like rods and function more at low light levels. They do not distinguish color, only picture detail and intensity, or white and black. Rods are saturated above about one foot-lambert and are not considered to play a significant role in normal color vision. However, the shadows in a typical motion-picture presentation fall into a light level where both cones and rods are active, known as mesopic vision, which falls between photopic (under normal light conditions) and scotopic (human vision in the dark). Few people have total color-blindness with no cone activity, in which they see only in black-and-white or shades of gray. (For the Internet-savvy, the Website http://colorfilter.wickline.org allows you to type in a Web address and view that page as though you are color-blind.)

Humans can see an estimated 10 million different colors, and each of us perceives every color differently. I could point to a light-skinned tomato and say it is red in color, but someone else might say it is more orange due to a color deficiency or through a difference in color nomenclature as a result of culture. (Tomato, to-mah-to.) Culture and gender are other possible factors that affect color perception. Women perceive a greater range of colors than men do, particularly shades of red. To explain the reason for this difference, researchers in this area point to our ancestors. The men hunted for animals while the women, when not tending to offspring or the cave, sought out fruits, vegetables, and insects, and these were identified and rated poisonous or safe based on color. Women also are the only ones who could have the rare and theoretical tetrachromacy condition: a fourth type of cone. The result of a mutation in the two female X chromosomes, tetrachromats can have either red, red-shifted, green, and blue cones or red, green, green-shifted, and blue cones. In theory, this should result in a "heightened" sense of color and a broader color space, but the exact effects are not known and difficult to pinpoint because most of us are trichromats and we cannot see what they see. It would be as though we were trying to see ultraviolet radiation. A tetrachromat describing what they see would be like describing the color of UV; we trichromats have no reference for that perception. Another unknown is whether the brain and nervous system, wired for three-color input, can adapt to four colors to put those cones to use.

Genetically, men are relegated to trichromacy forever. But there is some hope for trichromats: it is thought but not yet proven that when rods kick in at low light intensities, they may contribute to color vision, providing a small region of tetrachromacy in trichromatic color space.

In the late 1700s and early 1800s, Johan Wolfgang von Goethe penned poetry and dramatic plays, and his masterpiece was *Faust* (which spawned his less-successful sequel, *Faust II*). The German master poet and playwright also dabbled in painting and color theory, writing the philosophical treatise *Theory of Color*. Goethe's theory was interesting, in that it brought an emotional element to color, along with a keen sense of observation. Different colors make us feel various emotions, and humans knew this well before Goethe was born. He just happened to put forth these concepts on paper.

Goethe sketched a color circle of paint pigments but did not place the primary blue and yellow opposite the other – as primaries normally would be, with complementary colors in between. (A complementary, or secondary, color in paint, such as orange, is a mixture of red and yellow primaries and therefore falls between them. A tertiary color is created by mixing a primary and a secondary and would reside between those.) Goethe extended the blue and yellow into a large triangle within the circle. Next to the color circle he drew various triangles that represented alternative possibilities for the internal triangle, with emphases on considerations such as brightness and intensity, the complementary colors or the sensual–moral point of view he explained as force, sanguineness, or melancholy. His intent with the early color wheel was to show how the colors were "sensual qualities within the content of consciousness," and to relate their effects on the eye and mind. On the yellow and red side of the circle, what he called the plus side, colors were considered warm and comfortable, but on the blue side, or minus side, colors had an unsettled, weak, and cold feeling.

Colors have meaning to us and stir emotions within us. Culture and our individual upbringing, as mentioned before, may play a role in how we perceive color. A number of studies into this possible psychological connection have been done and continue to be done. By studying groups in isolated locations, it has been hypothesized that humans are most likely born with a basic set of responses to color, but as we age, certain preferences and perceptions come to be held, based on experiences and cultural practices. Culture and/or location could have an impact. For example, Marc H. Bornstein, Ph.D., of the National Institute of Child Health and Human Development, found evidence in 1973 that populations with a closer proximity to the equator have less ability to discriminate shades of blue, but culture played no role. He did find that some cultures'

languages did not lexically discriminate blue from green. Studies indicate that these languages make semantic confusions that mimic tritanopic vision (the inability to distinguish the colors blue and yellow).

Studies of memory indicate that memory can also influence our perceptions of color. In remembering a significant moment that occurred on an otherwise bland, low-contrast day, we may recall the sky as a richer blue, the sand whiter, the water a lighter crystalline blue, the wetsuit a more saturated royal blue, the shark a darker gray, and the blood a brighter red. (If I may use a grim example.) These "memory colors" tend to have narrow gamuts (color ranges) toward the primaries and more saturation, and they develop from the combined memories of many observations. They also must have context, because that's what defines them. A memory color is not "green"; a memory color is "grass." It's as though we have formulated a perception and laid it on top of the original image that is stored away in our brains, and that formulated image is the one recalled. Memory colors do not affect what we see in the present. They could, however, affect our preferences. Cinematographers more often than not adjust at least some color in a scene – making the sky richer, the grass more vibrant or the tennis ball more vivid – by selecting certain filters such as color grads or by making adjustments using Power Windows in the DI suite, hoping to jog the audience's memories and tap into the emotions that are attached to them, but also to present what we generally consider "pleasing" images.

However, changing color in a scene by way of the lighting doesn't work as well when it comes to the tricky human vision system. Say, for example, a scene calls for a smug mogul to slide a letter of termination across the board table toward the company embezzler, and it is lit with some 2Ks shining through blue theatrical or party gels. In our perception of the scene, neither the actors, the table nor the white piece of paper change colors to blue. There is built-in context in that scene: we know what a boardroom typically looks like, what color human skin should be and that the paper is white. Our vision system has the ability to adjust the "white point" (or the point in the CIE chromaticity diagram where all primary and secondary colors of the spectrum come together to form white) to better match the light conditions – in this case, toward blue. Our eyes and brains make the adjustment based on reference – for example, the piece of paper that we assume to be white from experience. Take that same piece of paper and look at it when it's lit by warm, orange candlelight, then by a tungsten 10K, then by a hard HMI, and finally by daylight. To a first approximation, we see the paper as white no matter what color temperature the light source may be.

Quantifying Human Color Perception: CIE 1931

As you can see, there are *many* variables for cinematographers to consider if they are not seeing eye to eye with a production designer or director (who, unknowingly, may have a touch of color blindness). More importantly, there are just as many factors to consider when one is trying to record, emulate, and display the tristimulus color space of the human vision system in other media, such as film, television, and digital projection. Trying to describe a color to someone can be difficult when you function within your tristimulus color space model and the other person functions within his or hers. Color spaces naturally do not translate very well to each other. In 1931, the confusion and ambiguity in color led the Commission Internationale de l'Eclairage (also known as the CIE, or the International Commission on Illumination), to derive a *three-dimensional* color space from color-matching experiments using a small group of volunteer observers. This by no means was the first attempt at modeling color space, just the first standard that allowed us to calculate whether two spectral distributions have matching color.

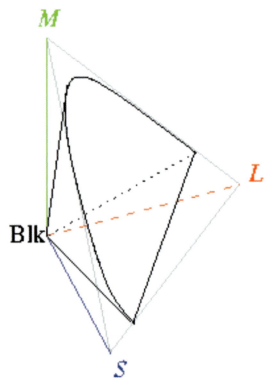

Figure 4.6 The human tristimulus color space model resembles a cone or the shape of the Hollywood Bowl's band shell.

A little more than 100 years earlier, in 1810, the German painter–theorist Philipp Otto Runge, a Romantic artist and admirer of Newton's handiwork, made one of the earliest attempts to coordinate hues and values (light and dark content) into a coherent whole by using red, blue, and yellow as primaries in a three-dimensional color space rendering, which he titled simply *Colour Sphere*. Some 50-odd years later, the brilliant British mathematician and physicist James Maxwell, after correctly theorizing that Saturn's rings consisted of particles, conducted Rumford Medal–winning investigations into the classification of colors and color-blindness. His color-classification system denoted colors in terms of hue, intensity, brightness, and tint. (Early color television sets ended up with similar controls.)

The CIE based their additive CIE XYZ color–space model, also known as CIE 1931, on Maxwell's work, which used the additive color mixture of red, green, and blue primaries. X, Y, and Z define the primary colors in virtual 3-D space (like XYZ axes), with the

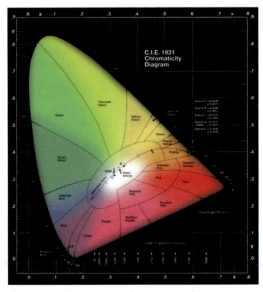

Figure 4.5 The CIE's 2-D chromaticity diagram.

locus of spectral colors forming a conical horseshoe shape that diminishes toward the rear to the point of black (at X=Y=Z=0) – a shape resembling the shell of the Hollywood Bowl if viewed from a 45-degree angle. The model represents all colors in the visible spectrum, and colorimetric spaces are always three-dimensional.

Color Photography

Really, the fault lies with Maxwell for setting the stage for eventual color–space clashes in motion pictures and television. In 1861, Maxwell, who actually is recognized more for his work in electromagnetism, stood before his learned colleagues at the Royal Society of London and demonstrated that any shade of colored light could be produced by combining various amounts of red, green, and blue-violet: the additive color process. He used three lanterns and placed colored solutions before the lens of each. For his grand finale, he only happened to show the first color photograph. He had chosen a tartan ribbon as his subject, probably because he was a Scotsman, and had photographer Thomas Sutton photograph it three times – once with a red filter on the lens, once with a green and once with a blue – using wet collodion plates. At the Royal Society, Maxwell placed those primary filters on the three lanterns and projected the plates onto a screen. He then lined the three images up so they overlapped properly, producing one image with somewhat unnatural colors because, unbeknownst to Maxwell, photographic emulsions at that time were not sensitive to red and green light – meaning the red- and green-filtered photographs were not true records, unlike the blue-filtered photograph. But there on the screen a *color* image was projected. (And Maxwell didn't even charge admission.)

Color in Cinematography

In 1889, George Eastman introduced a transparent celluloid roll to replace the fragile paper rolls in the Kodak camera he had designed a year earlier. Those interested in motion photography latched onto the new base for its thinness and flexibility. Naturally, one would assume that black-and-white dominated the early motion pictures. (It had to, because that was the only film stock available.) However,

attempts to colorize the black-and-white imagery in both still and motion-picture photography were being attempted from the get-go. In fact, the first film made for screen projection was in color. In 1894, *Annabelle's Butterfly Dance* wasn't like one of Thomas Edison's 5-cent Kinetoscope peep shows; it was to be seen by a mass audience (well, at least by more than one person at a time). A product of American inventor C. Francis Jenkins, the short movie simply depicted dancer Annabelle Moore fluttering about in a long, flowing white dress. Frame by frame, the film was hand-tinted to make Annabelle appear to be dancing under colored lights. Apparently, *Annabelle's Butterfly Dance* was a hit, because seven sequels were spawned.

Jenkins was a busy innovator. In 1895, he and his partner, Thomas Armat, invented the phantoscope, a superior projector in its day, but lost their shirts at the Cotton States and International Exposition in Atlanta, Georgia. Fairgoers turned their noses up at a technology they had never heard of at a steep cost of 25 cents per admission. The phantoscope ended up in the hands of Edison for pocket change. He turned around and manufactured it under the name Vitascope, making a tidy fortune. Jenkins also was a founder and the first president of the Society of Motion Picture Engineers (SMPE); created "radiovision," which first transmitted images over radio waves for public viewing in 1925; and constructed and managed a radiovision transmitter – the first television station, W3XK – near Washington, D.C. In 1947, he was presented with a Special Academy Award for his significant contributions to the industry.

Hand-tinting long films was a difficult task, and audiences were becoming annoyed with the fact that tinters could not color within the lines. The French company Pathé streamlined the process in an assembly-line fashion they called the Pathécolor stencil process, and it was performed entirely by women because they had smaller hands. The film was rear-projected onto a ground-glass screen with a stencil overlay, and certain areas were cut out. The stencil and the film were registered and run through a staining machine. A velvet loop saturated with dye applied the color, which reached the film through the holes. As many as six colors were applied, requiring multiple passes.

Figure 4.7 Hand-painting of film, such as this example from *The Great Train Robbery* (1903), was replaced by tinting and stencil processes such as Pathécolor as films grew longer in length.

Modeling a color space for the tinting method would produce a very narrow gamut that probably shifted on a per dye-per-film basis, and perhaps per frame. Still, it was color and a wider space than black-and-white, which had the narrowest of color spaces: a straight line of grays stretching from the white point to the black point. Tinting was around for a while. Cecil B. DeMille painted a heart red in his 1922 film *Fool's Paradise*, and Sergei Eisenstein painted a flag red and the sky blue for a sequence in his 1925 epic *The Battleship Potemkin*.

Toning was a method of giving an overall colorcast to a scene or full-length film. A kind of forefather of the traditional photochemical timing method, toning required the film to sit in a chemical bath. The types of chemicals determined the color, and the amount of time determined intensity. Toning met with a hasty demise when sound on film became *de rigueur* – the chemicals destroyed the variable-density soundtracks.

Developers, cinematographers, and other experts knew that *natural* color films would be the way of the future for motion pictures (natural color meaning that the colors would either exist in the film stock or be added by optical or mechanical

means). The result would be a more realistically colored image. Still photographers were already enjoying the advantages of three-color RGB film. In 1877, Louis Ducos du Haron, considered the father of photo colors, made the earliest natural color photograph on record, also by using the collodion process. However, the glass plate had an RGB additive-color network engraved onto it.

A number of RGB additive color processes were developed for motion pictures during its early years. Though the processes were natural color, they were beset with problems inherent to film. Sequential RGB processes photographed red-, green-, and blue-filtered images successively via a rotating color wheel on the camera.

Figure 4.8 Walt Disney selected Technicolor for his "Silly Symphony" animated shorts, using a color wheel to record blue, green, and red records sequentially on black-and-white film.

When projected, the red, green, and blue frames took advantage of the latent-image aspect of a human's persistence of vision, whereby the mind combined the images into a single color image. However, if a subject moved even the slightest bit, those three frames were not exact and color fringing occurred, causing red, green, or blue halos around the subject. Furthermore, the inherently unsteady movement of film virtually guaranteed color fringing, whether the subject moved or not. The additive processes that depended on separate projectors combining to form a color image on screen, à la James Maxwell, also were prone to fringing because of the films' shifting movements within the gate.

In 1912, Arturo Hernandez-Mejia invented what possibly was the first *subtractive* method of natural color motion pictures, using simultaneous red-sensitive and green-sensitive negative stocks that alternated exposure. Whereas red, green, and blue light are added to form colors in the additive process, the subtractive color process uses the primaries' complementary colors – yellow (equal parts red and green), cyan (green and blue), and magenta (red and blue) – to subtract wavelengths of white light, passing the red, green, and blue wavelengths. RGB is captured and stored as various amounts of cyan, magenta, and yellow colorant. Because it wasn't prone to additive-process problems, the subtractive YCM process eventually became the de facto standard for motion picture film, and so did the inversely arranged CMY color space.

Technicolor was *the* leading color company for about 20½ years. MIT alumni Herbert Kalmus and Daniel Comstock, who put the "Tech" in Technicolor, worked with W. Burton Wescott and William Coolidge to develop Technicolor Process Number One (1915–16), Two (1921), and Three (1926). All three processes exposed two strips of panchromatic film in a special camera using a prism to create red and green "records." The first process was additive, but the second and third were subtractive. The third used the dye-transfer or "imbibition" process to create positive gelatin relief images that yielded rich colors when printed.

However, because only two records were recorded, the two-strip process didn't reproduce certain colors and some colors were inaccurate, which audiences didn't buy. In 1930, when Hernandez-Mejia's patents became available, Technicolor scooped them up in order to secure the company's unique process. In 1932, they turned their two-strip Process Number Three into three-strip Process Number Four .

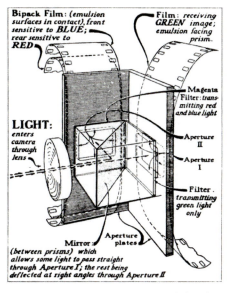

Figure 4.11 How the images are recorded in the three-strip Technicolor camera.

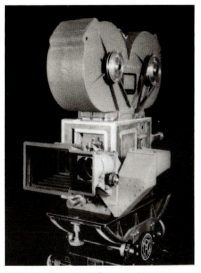

Figure 4.12 Technicolor's famous three-strip subtractive camera.

Figure 4.9 Technicolor's two-color additive camera.

Figure 4.10 Technicolor's two-color subtractive camera.

This process had three true RGB records, accomplished in-camera by joining two prisms of

discrepancies became easy to trace, and they were either ameliorated or subjected to compensation.

The adjustment of printer lights was sometimes a confusing practice for cinematographers. On the lab's traditional RGB 50-point, incremental scale, if a point of blue was added, more yellow was introduced into the scene. Huh? Remember, you were working in a subtractive CMY color space. Technicolor was the one lab that broke from the pack to use the YCM scale, rather than RGB. In the end, however, it was the cinematographer, with the help of the colorist, who controlled the image at all times, and if one point of blue was added at FotoKem and one point of blue was added at Deluxe, though their scales may differ, the results were basically the same: one point equaled one point. When the results were recorded to a film wedge test, a computer punch card or metadata, the look theoretically could be matched at any lab and print house.

The only intangible *was* human perception. Film recorded what it literally saw. Humans could adjust their white point; film cannot. To film, a white piece of paper under candlelight was orange. But for all its minor faults, the film system worked because it remained consistent, and the results were repeatable with no color–space transforms taking place. Motion-picture production had one less headache to worry about.

Color in Television

Television, on the other hand, can cause imaging experts to reach for the Advil. There is more than one color space. No two cameras match exactly. A host of intermediate equipment and personnel, broadcast nuances, network politics, and different phosphors on televisions (and different colorimetries on LCD, LED, OLED, and plasma monitors) all come into play. Television has a complicated and tangled history, and this chapter doesn't have the bandwidth to explain it all. Nevertheless, I will attempt a brief overview: in 1884, the brilliant inventor Nikola Tesla came to the U.S. and went to work getting the bugs out of Edison's DC (direct current) system of electricity. (A major drawback of the DC system is that the longer electricity has to travel, the more the voltage drops.) After Edison gave Tesla the shaft, the Croatian immigrant devised the *AC* (alternating current) system, which allowed electricity to travel great distances by wire. Tesla chose a 60 Hz cycle because anything lower than that introduced flicker into streetlamps. In 1888, inventor George Westinghouse signed Tesla to a contract,

and despite the Edison group's best attempts to discredit Tesla and the system – which caused Edison to lose a potential monetary windfall in the millions – Westinghouse managed to install the *AC* system in the U.S. (Edison's smear campaign did keep Tesla from taking credit for many innovations for decades.)

In the ensuing years, a number of other battles emerged in the field of television: Philo Farnsworth vs. Vladmir Zworykin and RCA Victor; DuMont Laboratories vs General Electric vs. RCA-NBC – the list goes on. In the early 1930s, the British Broadcasting Company kick-started the U.S. drive toward TV with a short-range broadcast to about 1,000 test subjects. Those in the U.S., with their wait-and-see attitude, realized how behind they were.

Because flicker needed to be reduced, both Farnsworth and Zworykin agreed that a minimum of 40 pictures per second were necessary (a standard that they adapted from the motion-picture industry, in which each frame was projected twice for 48 fps). The required bandwidth for such a signal was greater than the technology allowed. In came interlace, which split a picture into two alternating fields, and a rate of 30 frames/60 fields per second was selected to match the screen refresh rate to the 60Hz power source. This figure also fit within the restriction of the bandwidth available at the time and didn't reduce spatial resolution. The original 343-line process was upped to 441 lines in the mid-1930s, then to 525 lines in 1941 for black-and-white by the year-old National Television System Committee (NTSC), but picture size was locked from the get-go at 4 × 3 to mimic the cinematic 1.33:1 aspect ratio at the time.

Color was inevitable. After a few years of manufacturer skirmishes, the NTSC adopted the CBS field-sequential system in December of 1953, but manufacturers and broadcasters clamored for compatibility with their current black-and-white TV sets – which meant that a color signal had to be shoehorned into the bandwidth space of the black-and-white transmission signal. Bandwidth was tight because TV's "wise men" thought that 13 channels would be plenty. Color information for television was based on red, green, and blue; therefore, three signals were needed. Engineers added two to the black-and-white composite signal, using the existing black-and-white signal (the luminance) as the third. This was modeled in the YIQ color space, where Y= +30% red, +59% green, +11% blue, I= 60% red, –28% green, –32% blue. In the conversion from YIQ to RGB at the television set, I and Q were compared to Y and the differences that result were converted into three channels (red, green, blue) while Y still served its original luminance function. So, television required a color–space transform from RGB camera pickup tubes to YIQ for transmission and vice versa at the television set.

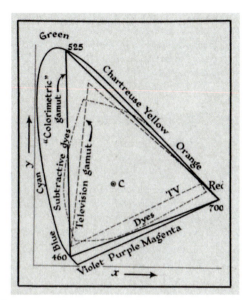

Figure 4.19 The electronic tube camera's image take-up schematic used in early color television.

WHEN prints of good quality are being televised, there should be no need for monitors to alter density controls. Uniformity of density and shading is inherent in the film itself.

Figure 4.20 The color gamuts resulting from certain arbitrary sets of primary colors plotted on the chromaticity diagram. The 700–525–460 millimicron set encloses the widest range of colors, but most of the vivid spectrum colors lie outside even this satisfactory gamut.

At the 30 Hz rate, I and Q encoded color information into a color subcarrier positioned in previously unused areas, or side bands, of the black-and-white composite signal. Harmonics from encoded audio subcarrier that resided in close proximity caused interference in the color signals degrading image quality. As a fix, the frame rate was lowered to 29.97 Hz to put the color out of phase with audio, eliminating interference. The color signals' amplitudes determined color saturation, and their phases in relation to the phase of the colorburst (a sinusoidal reference signal for each scanline) determined hue. The first coast-to-coast color broadcast featured the Tournament of Roses Parade on January 1, 1954. However, Michigan State's 28–20 Rose Bowl victory over UCLA was not shown in color.

NTSC color does have its faults. The encoding process causes some overlapping, or mixing of information, among the three signals, and no filter can separate and reconstruct the three signals perfectly, impairing quality.

Also, high-frequency phase-dependent color signals require timing tolerances that are difficult to maintain. That's why the color and image integrity of an NTSC signal degrades significantly with each generation removed from the original. Despite these faults, NTSC actually has decent color rendition, but there are compromises when it comes to the television sets.

A major problem lies in cabling: over distance, the nature of the NTSC color signal does not allow it to maintain phase integrity very well, so by the time it reaches the viewer, color balance is lost (which is why technological wags often deride NTSC with the phrases "Never the Same Color" or "Never Twice the Same Color"). Because of this problem, NTSC necessitates a tint control on television sets.

The European systems PAL and SECAM have no need for a tint control. PAL, or "phase alternating line," reverses the phase of the color information with each line, which automatically corrects phase errors in the transmission by canceling them out. PAL exists in a YUV color space, where Y is luminance and U and V are the chrominance components. SECAM ("sequential couleurs a memoir," or "sequential, with memory") was developed in France because the French like to do things differently. Functioning in a YDbDr color space, where Db and Dr are the blue and red color differences, SECAM uses frequency modulation to encode the two chrominance components and sends out one at a time, using the information about the other color stored from the preceding line.

PAL and SECAM are 625-line, 50-field systems, so there can be a bit of flicker. In the 19th century, the German company AEG selected the less-efficient 50 Hz frequency for their first electrical generating facility because 60 did not fit the metric scale. Because AEG had a virtual monopoly on electricity, the standard spread throughout the continent.

The ultimate destinations for broadcast images were television sets, which used cathode ray tubes (CRTs) to fire red, green, and blue electron beams at the back of a screen coated with red, green, and blue phosphors. Therefore, no matter what the system's color space, it must once again be transformed into RGB at the television. TVs have limited brightness and can reproduce saturated colors only at a high brightness level. Green is saturated naturally at a low brightness – this is where one of those NTSC compromises comes in. The contrast range of typical motion-picture projection has a sequential (best-case) contrast ratio of about 2,000:1, but it could be more than 50,000:1 with Vision Premier print stock in a good theater. A professional high-definition CRT broadcast monitor was typically set up with a sequential contrast ratio of about 5,000:1. An early standard-definition CRT television set's contrast ratio was very low. Newer television sets had much higher contrast ratios due to phosphor and CRT improvements. Higher brightness and saturated colors gave the appearance of good contrast. (The same holds true for LCD, LED, OLED, and plasma monitors. The TV also must compete with ambient lighting, however dim, in the TV room. So, when you get your new TV home and turn it on, the manufacturer has (incorrectly) set the brightness to "nuclear."

Video engineers, who are not cinematographers, "assist" the images in getting from point A to point B. However, a video engineer is a middleman who is human and therefore subjective. This fact led Arthur Miller, ASC to pen the following diatribe for the May 1952 issue of *American Cinematographer*: "Much of the poor quality of video films as observed on home receivers is due to faulty electronic systems of the telecaster, to poor judgment of the engineer handling the monitor controls in the station, or both …. In short, much of the trouble still exists because of the lack of standardization in the television industry.

Figure 4.21 Arthur Miller, ASC noted in 1952 that "poor judgment of the engineer handling the monitor controls" has led to poor quality in television.

Perhaps the strongest point here is the fact that a new factor enters into the telecasting of

motion pictures: the privilege vested in the network's engineering staff to control contrast and shading as TV films are being broadcast." This passage may have been written in 1952, but Miller's complaint is *still* valid today.

In 1956, Ampex Corporation launched the VRX-1000 (later called Mark IV), its 2" black-and-white magnetic tape recorder for the motion picture and TV industries.

Figure 4.22 In 1956, Charles Ginsburg (left), Ampex Corporation's senior project engineer in charge of video development, and Philip Gundy, audio division manager, inspect the magnetic assembly of the new VRX-1000.

The higher resolution put the kinescope out to pasture, and when videotape was able to record in color, telecine took advantage. Color on videotape involved compression of some sort. For example, Betacam and Bosch Quartercam recorded the chroma signals in 2:1 compression, mostly to expand the wavelength of the luminance and thereby increase the signal-to-noise ratio, but the generational degradation still applied.

Figure 4.23 Thirty years later, tape-to-tape color correction was the norm, but a major drawback was a loss of image integrity in each generation removed from the original.

CIE 1976: CIE L*a*b*

During this time, CIE saw where color was headed and, in 1976, standardized a more perceptually uniform color space. Known as CIE L*a*b*, it made up for some of the deficiencies of the CIE 1931 or XYZ model. L* was a nonlinear function of luminance, a* was a value for which –a* is green and +a* is red, and b* is a value for which –b* is blue and +b* is yellow. The advantage of L*a*b* over XYZ is that equal numerical differences between color values correspond roughly to equal perceptual differences. In other words, with XYZ you could tell whether two colors would match, but L*a*b* goes a step beyond to allow you to calculate how different they look.

Around 1983, component video was introduced to the professional market, providing significant advantages over composite video. Component separated the chroma signals from the luminance and transmitted them individually. By keeping the color and black-and-white information separate, there was no overlapping of information, nor was there any resultant degradation caused by separation-filter circuits. Color fidelity was much better, as was resolution. Component video functions in the YPbPr color space, a derivative of the YUV color space.

The Birth of High Definition Video

NHK, Japan's broadcasting corporation, took advantage of component video in the development of high-definition video. They developed the HD monitor and then worked *backwards* to create the equipment and camera to support it. This was an opportunity to start TV anew, and though the goal was 1,500 or more lines of resolution, the developers, SMPTE (now with a "T" for television) and, to an even greater degree, the manufacturers, aimed low: 1,125 lines or lower. Most scientists agree that 1,125 lines or less (and broadcasters and manufacturers have selected the lower resolutions) is below the optimum that the human eye can effectively process. Also, the selection of 16 × 9 as the aspect ratio was a head-scratcher. HD's inroads into the homes of viewers progressed at a snail's pace for more than 20 years, until receiving a boost in 2008 when SONY ceased CRT production. But with a higher resolution than NTSC standard video, HD did improve post production quality and film-to-tape and tape-to-film transfer. (But incidentally, picture resolution does not affect color rendition.) *Julia and Julia*, shot by Guiseppe Rotunno, ASC, AIC in 1987 on high definition and posted in HD, was the first HD feature transferred to 35mm film for theatrical presentation.

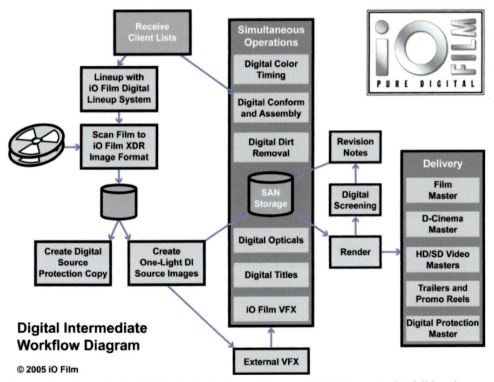

Figure 4.24 *Julia and Julia* (1987), shot by Guiseppe Rotunno, ASC, AIC, was the first full-length feature to originate in high definition and be transferred to film for theatrical exhibition.

During this time of rapid technology influx and change in video and television, film was a constant. Sure, print stocks and lab development/printing improved dramatically, but film's color process endured and remained unchanged because of its simplicity (compared to electronic algorithms, compressions, etc.) and reliability (again, compared to electronic algorithms, compressions, etc.).

In the late 1970s and early 1980s, CCDs (charge coupled devices) began to proliferate, given their ability to read out RGB charges as signals to corresponding pixels. As a result, digital bits slowly began to pervade the entertainment industry without constraints, essentially opening a Pandora's box. Digital required standards, but was it too soon? As history has shown, the powers-that-be have not made ideal choices. However, during those years, no ASC Technology Committee existed to present unified "best-practice recommendations." Now one does, and its members have something to say.

In January 1848, while overseeing the construction of a sawmill on a bank of the American River just outside Sacramento, foreman James Marshall happened upon a pea-sized gold nugget in a ditch. That moment set the California Gold Rush in motion; hundreds of thousands of people headed west to stake their claims to the precious metal. Soon enough, encampments sprouted and grew into mining towns. At the time, however, California had not yet attained statehood and functioned in a political vacuum. Squatters pervaded the land, and the prospectors, many of whom were squatters themselves, defended their territories with vigor. Frontier justice reigned, and trees were frequently decorated with nooses. In 1850, California officially became the 31st state, and the new government established at the end of 1849 took shape with laws that began to bring a sense of order to the land.

History is cyclical, and digital imaging for motion pictures experienced a "gold rush" of its own. In the quest for bits rather than nuggets, the fortune seekers (and squatters) included a variety of competing entities: the philosophically conflicted studios, beholden to the bottom line yet striving for the best imaging elements; the manufacturers, who naturally are beholden not only to the bottom line, but also to market share; and the post production facilities and theater owners, who would prefer not to invest heavily in new formats and equipment that become outmoded upon installation. When smelted together, these camps' ideologies did not form a utopian imaging environment. As a result, cinematographers, the artists responsible for turning ideas and words into big-screen visuals, endured a piecemeal workflow that frequently was compromised, inefficient, and expensive. In short, the process sometimes produced bad images, despite the wealth of image-control tools and techniques that were available.

Philosopher George Santayana (1863–1952) wrote, "Those who cannot remember the past are doomed to repeat it." Digital/high-definition television was already a mess of seemingly irreversible missteps. Digital cinema was not as much of a muddle – yet. The frontier of digital motion imaging was like pre-1850 California: wide open and lawless.

Managing the Digital Revolution

Enter the ASC Technology Committee. The goal of this august body is to formulate a series of "best-practice recommendations" for working in a hybrid film/digital environment – recommendations that will allow room for innovations to come. So far, the committee has worked closely with the Digital Cinema Initiatives (DCI) studio consortium in creating the Standard Evaluation Material, or StEM, for testing digital-projection technologies. The ASC is not proclaiming standards; that function is the province of the Society of Motion Picture and Television Engineers (SMPTE) and the Academy of Motion Picture Arts and Sciences (AMPAS). Just because a technology becomes an official standard doesn't mean it is the best choice (see television for countless examples). Likewise, just because a manufacturer introduces a new product does not automatically make it the de facto best choice for serving filmmakers' needs. The Technology Committee was formed by ASC cinematographers, its associate members, and industry professionals in an effort to marshal this burgeoning field of digital motion imaging; the group's true function is to serve as an advisory council and provide leadership within the current vacuum of ad hoc technology implementation.

The graphics industry was in a similar state in the early 1990s. The Internet and computer networks were taking hold, and traditional film proofs were giving way to file sharing. However, with the variety of software, monitors, and printers available – none of which communicated with each other – that gorgeous spokesmodel in your print ad might look great on the ad agency's computer, but not so pretty in the actual pages of a magazine; if the printer shifted the blacks, you could end up with a hazy image. In 1993, to promote its ColorSync color-management system, Apple Computer formed the ColorSync

Consortium with six other manufacturers. A year later, Apple, though remaining an active participant, handed the responsibility of cross-platform color profiling to the rest of the group, which then changed its name to the International Color Consortium, or ICC. Today, all hardware and software support ICC color profiles, and while not perfect, the system ensures that displays and printers are calibrated, and that shared files remain as true to the creators' intentions as possible.

Maintaining image integrity in a hybrid workflow – in other words, preserving the intended look – is the digital nirvana that cinematographers seek. As discussed earlier, the human visual system is subject to a number of variables, all of which ensure that none of us perceives the same image in exactly the same way. Film and its photochemical processes have their own tendencies. Over time and through technical development, the closed-loop system of film became manageable and consistent, with repeatable results. However, the introduction of digital bits has thrown the traditional methods of image control into flux: no two facilities are alike, no two processes are alike, and no two workflows are alike.

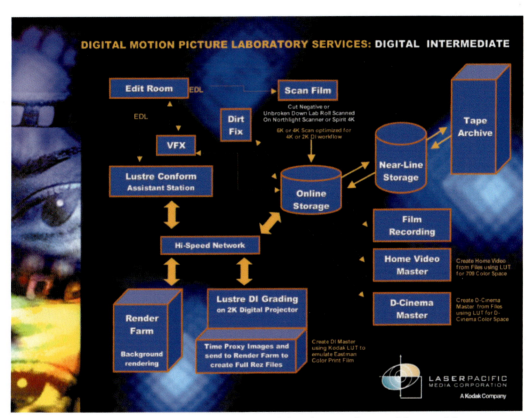

Figure 4.25 Though the diagram shows iO Film's general digital intermediate workflow, workflows are tailored to a particular project. No two workflows are exactly the same.

As a result of this situation, managing a hybrid film/digital workflow is similar to creating a computer workstation from the motherboard up – choosing various brands of graphics, capture, output, and ethernet cards, installing memory and hard drives, upgrading the BIOS, picking out software, and selecting multiple monitors for display. Murphy's Law of electronics guarantees that all things will not function as a perfect, cohesive whole upon initial startup; hence, tech-support operators in India await your call. Of course, despite the numerous faults inherent to today's hybrid cinema workflows, the digital environment offers far greater potential for image control than the photochemical realm. It's no small fact that of the five feature films nominated for 2004 ASC Awards (*The Aviator, A Very Long Engagement, The Passion of the Christ, Collateral*, and *Ray*), all went through a digital–intermediate (DI) process. (Now, one would be hard-pressed to find a movie that has *not* undergone a DI.)

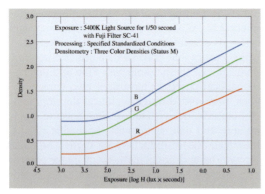

Figure 4.26 Though the basic workflow steps may appear the same when comparing DI facilities, within those steps the processes and equipment vary. Each facility designs a system to accomplish its goals, much like how one would build up a computer workstation.

The DI process was born out of the marriage between visual effects and motion-picture film scanner- and telecine-based color grading. Of course, digital imaging began impacting the motion-picture industry a long time ago. While at Information International, Inc. (Triple-I), John Whitney Jr. and Gary Demos (who now chairs the ASC Technology Committee's Advanced Imaging subcommittee) created special computer imaging effects for the science-fiction thriller *Westworld* (1973) and its sequel, *Futureworld* (1976). The duo subsequently left to form Digital Productions, the backbone of which was a couch-sized Cray XM-P supercomputer that cost $6.5 million. With that enormous hunk of electronics (and an additional, newer supercomputer that the company later acquired), Whitney and Demos also produced high-resolution, computer-generated outer-space sequences for the 1984 feature *The Last Starfighter*. The substantial computer-generated imagery (CGI) in that film was impressive and owed a debt of gratitude to a groundbreaking predecessor: *Tron*. That 1982 film, to which Triple-I contributed the solar sailer and the villainous Sark's ship, featured the first significant CGI in a motion picture – 15 minutes' worth – and showed studios that digitally created images were a viable option for motion pictures.

During that era, computers and their encompassing "digital" aspects became the basis of experiments within the usually time-consuming realm of optical printing. Over 17 years, Barry Nolan and Frank Van Der Veer (of Van Der Veer Photo) built a hybrid electronic printer that, in 1979, composited six two-element scenes in the campy sci-fi classic *Flash Gordon*. Using both analog video and digital signals, the printer

output a color frame in 9 seconds at 3,300 lines of resolution. If optical printing seemed time-consuming, the new methods weren't exactly lightning-fast, either, and the look couldn't yet compete with the traditional methods.

The Birth of Digital Imaging

In 1989, Eastman Kodak began research and development on the Electronic Intermediate System. The project involved several stages: assessing the closed-loop film chain; developing CCD-based scanning technology with Industrial Light & Magic; and, finally, constructing a laser-based recording technology and investigating the software file formats that were available at the time. The following year, Kodak focused on the color space into which film would be scanned. The project's leaders determined that if footage were encoded in linear bits, upwards of 12–16 bits would be necessary to cover film's dynamic range. Few file formats of the day could function at that high a bit rate. Logarithmic bit encoding was a better match for film's print density, and Kodak found that 10-bit log could do a decent job (more on this later). The TIFF file format could handle 10-bit log, but was a bit too "flexible" for imaging purposes (meaning there was more room for confusion and error).

Taking all of this into account, Kodak proposed a new format: the 10-bit log Cineon file format. The resulting Cineon system – comprising a fast 2K scanner capable of 4K (which was too slow and expensive to work in at the time), the Kodak Lightning laser recorder and the manageable Cineon file format – caused a radical shift in the visual-effects industry. In just a few short years, the traditional, labor-intensive optical died out. Though Kodak exited the scanner/recorder market in 1997, the Cineon file format is still in use. Kodak received an Academy Sci-Tech Award for another component of the system, the Cineon Digital Film Workstation.

In the early 1990s, the arrival of digital tape formats was a boon to telecine. Multiple passes for color-correction and chroma-keying could be done with little or no degradation from generation to generation. The first format, D-1, worked in ITU-R BT.601(Rec 601) 4:2:2 component video with 8-bit color sampling. Rec 601 is standard definition as defined by the ITU, or International Telecommunication Union. (This body's predecessor was the International Radio Consultative Committee, or CCIR.) 4:2:2 chroma describes the ratio of sampling frequencies used to digitize the luminance and color-difference components in component video's color space of YCbCr, the digital derivative of YUV. (YPbPr is component's analog derivative.) Thus, for every four samples of Y, there are two sub-samples each of Cb and Cr.

Composite 8-bit D-2 was a replacement for 1" analog tape. It functioned under SMPTE 244M, the recommended practice for bit-parallel digital interface, and was susceptible to contouring artifacts. D-3 was a composite 8-bit videotape recording format using 1/2" tape. Because these digital formats were being developed in Japan, D-4 was skipped. (Japanese culture has its superstitions, and the characters for "four" and "death" are both pronounced in Japanese as shi – an ominous association.)

D-5 was a common post facility format because it could record uncompressed Rec 601 component digital video at up to 10-bit depth. With compression of 4:1, it can record 60p signals at 1280 × 720p and 24p at 1920 × 1080p resolutions in 4:2:2. D-6 was a high-definition format better suited to storage because of cost and size but not widely used; it recorded uncompressed in the ITU-R BT.709 (Rec 709) high-definition standard at full-bandwidth 4:4:4 chroma. D-7 served Panasonic's DVCPro standards: 480i 4:1:1 DVCPro with 5:1 compression, 480i 4:2:2 DVCPro50 with 3.3:1 compression, and 1080i 4:2:2 DVCPro HD at 6.7:1 compression. (Almost all tape formats are now obsolete. SONY HDCam SR became the tape format of choice, but the 2011 earthquake and subsequent tsunami in Japan destroyed SONY's manufacturing facility caused significant HDCam SR tape shortages. As a result, many facilities accelerated a switch to file-based workflows with LTO – Linear Tape Open Data – backups. The HDCam SR market never fully recovered.)

These varying numbers beg the question: What qualifies as high definition? Really, high definition is any format that is even the slightest bit better than the component standard-definition resolution. This has allowed the "hi-def" label to be tossed around rather haphazardly.

The year 1998 marked a turning point, when two teenagers were sucked through their television into the black-and-white world of a 1950s-style TV show, and their presence added a little "color" to the environs. *Pleasantville* was pure fantasy, but the isolation of colors against black-and-white backgrounds was not. The color footage shot by John Lindley, ASC underwent a Philips Spirit DataCine 2K scan at 1920x1440 resolution (which actually was not full 2K resolution). The data files then were handed over to visual-effects artists who selectively desaturated areas of a given shot. Kodak's digital laboratory, Cinesite, output the files to a color intermediate stock via a Kodak Lightning recorder. Nearly

1,700 shots were handled in this manner, a very time-consuming visual-effects process.

In telecine, isolating an object or color and desaturating the background was a relatively simple task. Looking at what was done in *Pleasantville* and what could be done in telecine, filmmakers and industry engineers began putting two and two together; they realized that film images could be converted into digital files, manipulated via telecine-type tools, and then output back to film. This concept, pioneered by Kodak, became known as the digital–intermediate process, which replaces the traditional photochemical intermediate and color-timing steps. Of great benefit was the ability to skip the image-degrading optical blowup for Super 35mm footage, which could then be unsqueezed in a computer with no loss of resolution.

Many in the industry point to the Coen brothers' 2000 feature *O Brother, Where Art Thou?*, shot by Roger Deakins, ASC, BSC, as the first commercial film to undergo a true DI. Deakins was well aware of *Pleasantville*, and therefore knew that a DI was the only way he could achieve a highly selective, hand-painted postcard look for the Depression-era film without every shot being a visual effect. With the DI still in its less-than-ideal infancy, *O Brother* was a learning process for all involved, including Cinesite, where a workflow was created somewhat on the fly. Footage was scanned on the DataCine, and the loss of definition from the pseudo-2K scan worked in the film's favor, further helping to mimic the era's look. After spending ten weeks helping to color-grade the film, Deakins said he was impressed with the new technology's potential, but remarked in the October 2000 issue of *American Cinematographer* that "the process is not a quick fix for bad lighting or poor photography."

While Deakins was sowing DI seeds at Cinesite, Australian director Peter Jackson decided to tackle the *Lord of the Rings* trilogy – all at once. Maintaining consistency in the look of three films, each well over three hours long with extensive visual effects, was a Mount Doom-sized task. Colorist Peter Doyle and cinematographer Andrew Lesnie, ASC, ACS sought the help of a little company in Budapest called Colorfront. In a nutshell, the duo asked Colorfront to build, to their specifications, a hardware/software digital-grading system that had typical telecine tools, but could be calibrated for any lab and could emulate the printer-light system of traditional photochemical color timing. In integrating the beta system into the workflow, Doyle discovered that the color management of electronic displays quickly became an issue. "At the time, digital projectors just simply were not good enough," he recalls. "We stayed with using CRTs, but just in getting the monitor to match the print, there was the discussion of defining what we wanted the monitor to really be. Obviously, we had to deviate away from a perfect technical representation of a film print."

In piecing together a workflow, the filmmakers struck upon a clever idea. To ease the amount of work later in the DI chain, the voluminous number of plates shot for the digital effects were pregraded before they went to the visual-effects artists. This practice gained in popularity and became standard operating procedure in all workflows. Lesnie picked up an Academy Award statuette for *The Fellowship of the Ring*, and Colorfront teamed up with U.K.-based 5D to release the beta system commercially as 5D Colossus.

Colossus, which was later purchased and improved upon by Discreet, then re-released as Lustre, unleashed a flood of color-grading and color-management tools upon the film industry. This flow of products shows no sign of abating, and, as in the computer industry, updates are unremitting and obsolescence is an ever-present factor. With the lack of viable standards, the technologies introduced were often proprietary or did not play well with others in the digital-imaging arena. Could you put 10 basketball players from around the world on a court, each wearing a different uniform and speaking a different language, and expect an organized game? Not without coaches and decent translators. Who better to coach digital imaging than those who have the most experience with creating high-quality visuals: i.e., the members of the ASC Technology Committee?

Many factors are involved in navigating the hybrid film/digital-imaging environment, and to discuss each of them comprehensively would turn this chapter into a sizable textbook of hieroglyphic equations found in higher collegiate math courses. This article isn't even an overview, something that also would be textbook-sized. Rather, I will analyze some key elements that affect workflow choices, because no two workflows are currently the same; each is tailored specifically to a particular project.

Hybrid Workflows: Film and Digital Coexist

Despite decades of Paul Revere-like cries of "Film is dead!," celluloid was still the dominant recording and presentation medium. (However, there may be more truth than ever to the "film is dead" cry, with Kodak entering receivership in 2012 and Fujifilm shutting down its motion picture film division in 2013.) Digital, for reasons mentioned earlier, quickly became the dominant intermediate medium. Thus, the typical analog–digital–analog hybrid workflow comprised

shooting on film, manipulating the images in the digital realm, and then recording back to film for display and archiving purposes.

Let's begin with analog camera negative as the recording medium. As of now, there is no proven digital equal to the dynamic range of camera negative. The negative records as close to an actual representation of the scene we place before it as the emulsion allows, but it is not necessarily how we see things. Film does not take into account differences in human perception, nor our eyes' ability to adjust white point, as discussed earlier in this article.

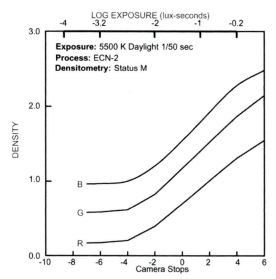

Figure 4.27 The sensitometric curve of camera negative film with a more gradual gradient, or wider latitude. Pictured here: Fujicolor Reala 500D 8596/8692.

A film's sensitometric curve is plotted on a graph where the Y axis is density and the X axis is log exposure. The curve determines the change in density on the film for a given change in exposure. The uppermost portion of the curve that trails off horizontally is known as the shoulder, and this is where the negative is reaching maximum density. In other words, the more light reacts with the emulsion, the denser it gets, and, of course, a lot of light will yield highlights. What?! Remember, this is a negative working material that is making an inverse recording of a scene, so on your negative, bright white clouds will be almost black, and when positively printed, the clouds become a light highlight area. The bottom portion of the curve that also trails off horizontally is known as the toe. Density is lighter here from less light exposure, giving you shadows and blacks. The endpoints of the toe and shoulder where the curve flattens to constant densities are known as D-min and D-max, respectively. Measuring the slope of the curve between two points of the straight-line portion on negative film typically will yield the number .6 or close to it, depending on the stock, and this is called gamma. (There is no unit of measurement for this number per se, much like exposure stops aren't accompanied by one. They are actually ratios, density change to log-exposure change.) Now, measure the density difference between D-min and D-max, and you end up with that negative's maximum contrast range.

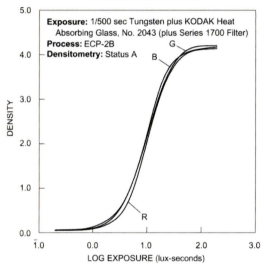

Figure 4.28 The sensitometric curve of Kodak Vision2 250D 5205/7205.

Negative film is not tasked with having to display the recorded image. To do so, the negative must be directly printed onto positive print film or, for releasing large numbers of prints, go through the intermediate photochemical processes of creating an interpositive (IP) and then mulitple internegatives (INs). A check print is made from the IN, and then the images found on the original camera negative finally can be displayed. Print film does not reproduce everything that was recorded on the negative. "The purpose of the negative is to capture a virtual scene," says Kodak image scientist Douglas Walker, "but there is no practical way to reproduce those same luminance ratios. A scene can have a dynamic range of 100,000:1 or 1,000,000:1, and it would be cost-prohibitive to try to reproduce that in every theater. So you need a way of creating a rendition of the scene that is convincing, yet more practical to re-create. The purpose of print film is to do just that."

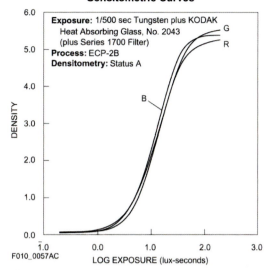

Figure 4.29 As reflected in the steep S-curve, print film has less latitude and higher contrast than negative film and a gamma of 2.6 as opposed to .6 for negative. Kodak Vision Color Print Film 2383 (left) has a contrast ratio of 13 stops.

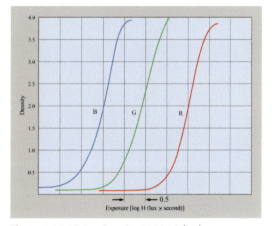

Figure 4.30 Vision Premier 2393 (right) has a contrast ratio of about 18 stops.

The sensitometric curve of print film is much steeper than that of negative film. Just compare gammas: .6 for negative vs. 2.6 or more for print. As a result, highlights and shadows compress in the toe and shoulder of the print stock, respectively. "This is kind of the 'film look,'" says Technology Committee chair Curtis Clark, ASC, "which still has gradation in the shoulder and toe, whereas with video it just clips. That's something I think we have grown accustomed to culturally and aesthetically as well – having that ability to see particularly in the highlights and shadows because there are vital nuances and details there."

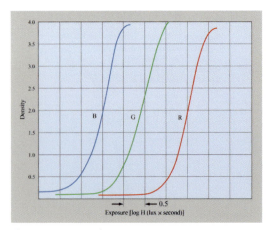

Indeed, the cinematographer can control how much the audience sees into the highlights and shadows by increasing or decreasing print density via printer lights. In one of the eccentricities of the photochemical chain, print film's sensitometric curve is the inverse of the negative curve, where the shoulder contains shadows instead of highlights. To visualize the relationship of the two curves, you place the print curve on top of the negative curve and rotate the print curve 90 degrees. (This is known as a Jones diagram, named after its inventor, Lloyd Jones.)

Figure 4.30 Fujicolor Positive Print 3513/3516. As reflected in the steep S-curve, print film has less latitude and higher contrast than negative film and a gamma of 2.6 as opposed to .6 for negative.

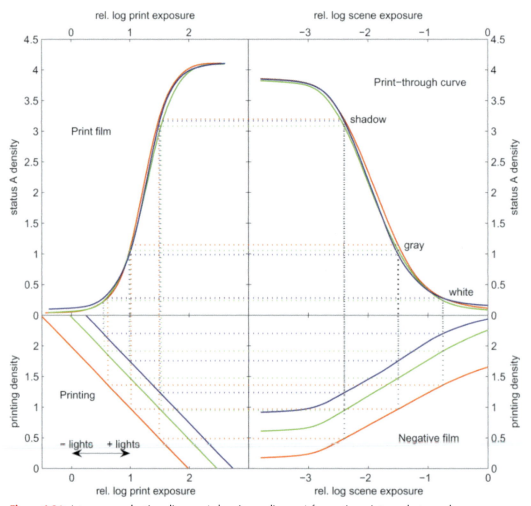

Figure 4.31 A tone reproduction diagram (a.k.a. Jones diagram) for motion-picture photography.

Sensitometry for a camera negative film is shown in the southeast quadrant. Increasing the camera exposure one stop, for example, slides the white, gray, and shadow points 0.3 units to the right. The northwest quadrant shows the sensitometry of the print film. The southwest quadrant shows the negative densities being mapped to exposures onto the print film (e.g., via a printer at the lab). Adjusting the timing lights effectively slides the 45-degree curves left or right. The northeast quadrant shows the overall tone reproduction of the system (i.e., the density on print that results from a given scene exposure).

By adjusting a printer light during print film exposure, say green by +3 points, the negative's curve slides by a fixed amount of $+3 \times 0.025$ log exposure along the print curve, modulating the amount of light that hits the print film. The print film's curve remains fixed. The vertical-density axis of the negative maps onto the horizontal log-exposure axis of the print. It is because of this that printer light changes are quantifiable and repeatable.

The June 1931 issue of *American Cinematographer* contains a one-paragraph blurb about a new natural-color motion-picture process shown to England's premier scientific body, the Royal Society of London, the same society that witnessed James Maxwell's exhibition of the first color photograph. This motion-picture process used a film base imprinted with a matrix consisting of a half-million minute red, green, and blue squares per inch of film. That sounds like a "pixelated" concept – about 40 years ahead of its time.

An image can be scanned and mathematically encoded into any number of lines both horizontally and vertically, and this is known as spatial resolution. Typically, there are more lines of resolution horizontally than vertically because a frame is wider than it is tall, meaning more information is found in a scan line from side to side than one from top to bottom. Each line is made up of individual pixels, and each pixel contains one red, one green, and one blue component. Based on the encoded values for that pixel, the components will dictate what color the pixel will be along with the characteristics of the specific display device.

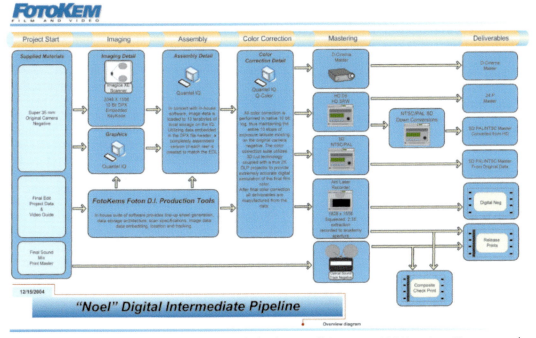

Figure 4.32 The diagram for the 2004 release *Noel*, shot by Russell Carpenter, ASC (American Cinematographer "Post Process," Jan. '05), reveals the specifics that went into that project's DI, accomplished in native 10-bit log space at FotoKem.

Scanning at 2K resolution has been the most popular and feasible. A true 2K frame is 2048 × 1556 × 4 or 12,746,752 bytes in file size. (It is ×4 because the three Cineon 10-bit RGB components that equal 30 bits are packed into 32 bits, which is 4 bytes. Two bits are wasted.) 4K 4096 × 3112 fast became viable as storage costs dropped and processing and transport speeds escalated. *Spider-Man 2* was the first feature to undergo a 4K scan and 4K finish. Bill Pope, ASC screened for director Sam Raimi, the editors and the producers a series of 2K and 4K resolution tests, and all preferred the 4K input/output. The perceived improvement in resolution was that obvious. Beginning with 6K, that perception starts to wane for some people. There are scanners on the market that can scan a frame of film at 10K resolution. But scanning an entire movie at 10K is as rapid as using the Pony Express to send your mail. The ideal scanning resolution is still a topic for debate, though 8K is favored by many. "In order to achieve a limiting resolution digitally of what film is capable at aspect ratio, you really need to scan the full frame 8000 by 6000 to get a satisfactory aliasing ratio of about 10 percent," says Research Fellow Roger Morton, who retired from Kodak. Limiting resolution is the finest detail that can be observed when a display system is given a full-modulation input. (This deals with the concept of modulation transfer function – I'll get to that shortly.) Aliasing is the bane of digital. In the May/June 2003 issue of *SMPTE Motion Imaging Journal*, Morton identified 11 types of visible aliasing that he labeled A through K. They include artifacts such as: variations in line width and position; fluctuations in luminance along dark and light lines that create basket-weave patterns; coloration due to differences in response of color channels (as in chroma sub-sampling); and high-frequency image noise (also known as mosquito noise). "They're more serious in motion pictures than in still pictures" he points out, "because many of the aliasing artifacts show up as patterns that move at a different speed than the rest of the image. The eye is sensitive to motion and will pick that motion up."

Scanning (digitization) turns an undulating analog frequency wave into staircases. Converting the digital wave back to an analog wave does not necessarily take the smoother diagonal route between two sample points along the wave; it often moves in a very calculating manner horizontally and then up to the next point on the wave. It's like terracing the rolling hillsides, but the earth that once occupied the now-level terraces has been tossed aside, and so has the image information contained between the two samples. Missing information can lead to artifacts, but the higher the sample rate, the closer together the sample points will be, thereby throwing out less information. The result is a smoother wave that can be reconstructed from its digital file. Deficiencies in the encoding/digitization process, including low resolution and undersampling, are the root of these distracting digital problems. Sampling at a higher rate alleviates this.

Nyquist Sampling Theory

A 2K image is a 2K image is a 2K image, right? Depends. One 2K image may appear better in quality than another 2K image. For instance, you have a 1.85 frame scanned on a Spirit DataCine at its supposed 2K resolution. What the DataCine really does is scan 1714 pixels across the Academy frame (1920 from perf to perf), then digitally up-res it to 1828 pixels, which is the Cineon Academy camera aperture width (or 2048 if scanning from perf to perf, including soundtrack area). The bad news is, you started out with somewhat less image information, only 1714 pixels, and ignored 114 useful image pixels, instead re-creating them to flesh the resolution out to 1828. You know how re-creations, though similar, are not the real thing? That applies here. Scan that same frame on another scanner with the capability of scanning at 1828, 1920 or even 2048 pixels across the Academy aperture, and you would have a digital image with more initial information to work with. Now take that same frame and scan it on a new 4K Spirit at 4K resolution, 3656 × 2664 over Academy aperture, then downsize to an 1828 × 1332 2K file. Sure, the end resolution of the 4K-originated file is the same as the 2K-originated file, but the image from 4K origination looks better to the discerning eye. The 4096 × 3112 resolution file contains a tremendous amount of extra image information from which to downsample to 1828 × 1332. That has the same effect as oversampling does in audio.

In 1927, Harry Nyquist, Ph.D., a Swedish immigrant working for AT&T, determined that an analog signal should be sampled at twice the frequency of its highest frequency component at regular intervals over time to create an adequate representation of that signal in a digital form. The minimum sample frequency needed to reconstruct the original signal is called the Nyquist frequency. The problem with Nyquist sampling is that it requires perfect reconstruction of the digital information back to analog to avoid artifacts. Because real display devices are not capable of this, the wave must be sampled at well above the Nyquist limit – oversampling – in order to minimize artifacts.

In the same way that analog audio is digitized, the analog film's RGB frequency waves are sampled, which measures the intensity at each location and forms a two-dimensional array that contains small blocks of intensity information for those locations. Through the process of quantization (analog-to-digital conversion), that data is converted by an imaging device to integers (natural numbers, their negative counterparts, or 0) made up of bits (binary digits). Each pixel is assigned specific digital red, green, and blue intensity values for each sampled data point. This is color bit depth. Usually for imaging, integers are between 8 and 14 bits long but can be lower or higher. For example, if the stored integer is 10 bits, then a value between 0 and 1023 may be represented. The higher the bit rate, the more precise the color and the smoother the transition from one shade to another. If an image is quantized at 8-bit color bit depth, each component's integer will have a value that is 8 bits long. The higher the bit depth, the more sample points, the fewer the artifacts. Scanners and telecines today operate at bit depths ranging from 8 to 16 bits per color component.

A further consideration is how to stack the representations of intensity to represent the color values of the scene. This stacking is known as the "transfer function," or characteristic curve of the medium. In the physical world of film, the transfer function is fixed when the film is manufactured and is determined by the sensitivity of the film to light in the original scene.

Human vision is more sensitive to spatial frequency in luminance than in color, and can differentiate one luminance intensity value from another as long as one is about 1% higher or lower than the other. The encoding of these luminances is done in either a linear or nonlinear fashion. The term "linear" has been used somewhat erroneously in the industry to describe encoding methods that are quite different from each other. In the most common of these usages, linear (as in a "log to lin conversion") actually refers to a form of power-law coding.

Power-law coding is not pure linear, but not quite logarithmic either. It is a nonlinear way of encoding done primarily in the RGB video world at 8 bits, 10 bits for HDTV as stipulated in Rec 709. The code values for RGB are proportional to the corresponding light coming out of a CRT raised to a power of about 0.4. If your eyes are now starting to glaze over, that's understandable. This is the type of equation taught in the higher math class that might have been skipped.

The other method of encoding commonly described as linear is the representation of scene intensity values in a way that is proportional to photons. (To put it simply, a photon is a unit of intensity of light.) In other words, a one-stop increase in exposure doubles the photons, and hence would double the corresponding digital value. Visual-effects artists prefer to work in this scene-linear space because it seamlessly integrates with their like-valued CGI models.

Although the way human vision recognizes light intensity and the way film records light can be modeled either by logarithm or by power-law, "neither description is completely accurate," points out Walker.

Matt Cowan, co-founder of Entertainment Technology Consultants (ETC, and now RealD's chief scientific officer) notes: "For luminance levels we see in the theater, we recognize light intensity by power-law. Film actually records light by power-law, too; the transmission of film is proportional to the exposure raised to the power gamma. Film-density measurement is logarithmic, but we do that mathematically by measuring the transmission, which is linear, of the film and converting to density, or $D = \log(1/T)$, where the log transformation is not inherent to the film."

Logarithmic, power-law, and linear. To avoid any possible confusion – if it's not too late – I will speak mostly in logarithmic terms, because they are used more often to describe photography.

Film is measured in logarithmic units of optical density, something that Kodak used in its Cineon system. (Just look at a sensitometric graph – the X–Y axes are respectively log-exposure and density, a form of log.) The values are proportional to the negative's optical density, and this ensures that more of the encoded values will be perceptually useful as exposure to light increases. Although different density standards have been used to measure density on a negative, such as the ISO standard status M, the Cineon system introduced the use of printing density, which is based on the spectral sensitivity of the print material and the light source used for exposure. For a particular film, printing density is analogous to the way the print film sees the negative film. This allows for a more accurate simulation of the photographic system in the digital world. Using the same concept of printing density to calibrate the scanner and film recorder to an intermediate film stock allows accurate reproduction of the original camera negative, regardless of which film stock was used.

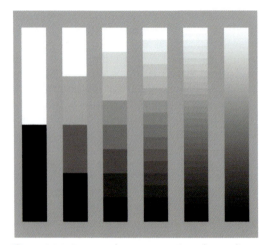

Figure 4.33 A grayscale representation of encoding images at various bit depths – from the top: 1 bit, 2 bits, 3 bits, 4 bits, 5 bits, and 8 bits.

computer calculations performed as straight integer quantities or as floating point. Current computers process at 32 or 64 bits, with 32 being more widely supported. Now this is a computer microprocessing bit rate; these bits are different than color bits. Calculating as integers is often a faster process, but it can lead to errors when the calculation rounds up or down to an incorrect integer, thereby throwing the value of the RGB components off. Floating point is a somewhat slower but more precise method of rounding because it allows for decimal fractions (the floating "point"), leading to fewer errors. The color shift that results from an error is generally too small to perceive. Instead, what is seen are artificial structures or edges that have been introduced into the image known as banding, which disrupts the smooth color gradient. The same banding also can be caused by low color bit depth.

Notice the banding at lower bit depths. The color transitions at the higher bit depths are much smoother. The printing process is not capable of reproducing gradients with more than 8 bits. However, in a dark room using professional equipment, it is easy to demonstrate the difference between 8-bit and 10-bit gradients.

In the DI, 10-bit log has been the de facto historical standard, though some felt 12-bit log was a sufficient level of encoding that should have been supported internally within DI pipelines. The SMPTE DC28 digital cinema committee found that 12 bits used with a 2.6 power-law coding in RGB adequately covers the range of theater projection expected in the near future. Again, this could have been another one of those myopic instances. (However, ACES, or Academy Color Encoding System, 16-bit floating point has since been developed and is now in use.) Lou Levinson, (former) senior colorist at Post Logic and chair of the ASC Technology Committee's Digital Intermediate Subcommittee, has greater aspirations: "What I am going to propose as the optimum pipeline is that you have a very high bit depth backbone – XYZ bits, 16 bits per channel minimum – and that it's bipolar. Rather than counting from 0 and going all the way up to 1, I'm going to make the middle 0 and then plus or minus how many bits you have. So if you have 16 bits and 0 is middle grade, then you can go all the way to +15 bits and –15 bits. There are lots of reasons why I like having 0 in the middle because certain things fail to 0. When they stop working, they won't add or subtract anything bad to the picture."

When the bits are calculated to create and display an image file, one can choose to have those

Modulation Transfer Function and Contrast Sensitivity Function

We humans value detail and sharpness more than resolution in an image. High resolution is synonymous with preservation of detail and sharpness, but high pixel count does not always translate into high resolution. "As you try to increase the amount of information on the screen," explains Cowan, "the contrast that you get from a small resolution element to the next smallest resolution element is diminished. The point where we can no longer see [contrast difference] is called the limit of visual acuity." It's the law of diminishing returns, and a system's ability to preserve contrast at various resolutions is described by the modulation transfer function (MTF). The eye is attuned to mid-resolution information, where it looks for sharpness and contrast. A higher MTF provides more information in the mid-resolution range. You just want to make sure that the resolution doesn't drop so low that you pixelate the display, which is like viewing the image through a screen door.

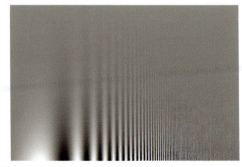

Figure 4.34 The contrast sensitivity function.

The contrast sensitivity function (CSF) shows that visual sensitivity to contrast is highest at lower resolutions than the threshold of acuity (the point where we can no longer see contrast difference). This is noted by the envelope of modulation that looks like a Gaussian curve, a symmetrical bell-shaped curve of normal distribution that encompasses the more-defined blacks. If the pattern is observed up close, the Gaussian shape moves right; as you view the pattern from greater distances, it will continue to move left. The peak on this curve represents the spatial frequency where contrast discrimination is most sensitive.

Effect of Different MTF

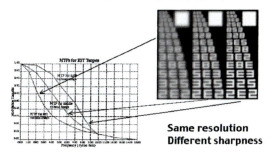

Same resolution
Different sharpness

Figure 4.35 Modulation transfer function.

The modulation transfer function (MTF) is a 2-D plot that shows the degradation in contrast ratio, or modulation, against increasing spatial frequencies, or higher resolution. This diagram shows an image that is much sharper at a higher modulation (higher contrast ratio) than a lower modulation, even though all three are the same resolution.

Preserving Image Quality across File Formats

All of the encoded values must be contained within a storage structure or file. A number of file formats exist that can be used for motion imaging, but the most common ones being transported through the DI workflow are Cineon and its 16-bit capable offshoot DPX (Digital Motion-Picture eXchange in linear or logarithmic), OpenEXR (linear) and ACES (linear and log), which originated from OpenEXR, and TIFF (Tagged Image File Format in linear or logarithmic). All of

these formats contain what is known as a file header. In the header, you and whatever piece of electronic gear that is using the file will find grossly underutilized metadata that describe the image's dimensions, number of channels, pixels, and the corresponding number of bits needed for them, byte order, key code, time code … and so on. Fixed-header formats such as Cineon and DPX, which are the most widely used as of right now, allow direct access to the metadata without the need for interpretation. However, all information in the fixed headers is just that – fixed. It can be changed, though, but with great effort. These two formats do have a "user-defined area" located between the header and the image data proper, allowing for custom expansion of the metadata.

TIFF has a variable header, or image file directory (IFD), that can be positioned anywhere in the file. A mini-header at the front of the TIFF file identifies the location of the IFD. "Tags" define the metadata in the header, which has room for expandability. Open EXR, a popular visual-effects format which originally was developed by Industrial Light & Magic for internal use, also is a variable-header format.

"You can convert from one format to another," says Texas Instruments' director of DLP Cinema Technology Development Glenn Kennel (now president of ARRI USA). Kennel worked on the original Cineon system while at Kodak. "The important thing, though, is that you have to know enough information about the image source and its intended display to be able to make that conversion. What's tricky is whether the color balance is floating or the creative decisions apply to the original image source. If the grading has been done already then you have to know the calibration of the processing and display device that was used."

Pacific Title & Art Studio eventually opted for the TIFF format when formulating a DI workflow for the StEM digital projection test film. StEM was conceived by the ASC and the DCI studio coalition as high-quality evaluation imagery that was offered to digital cinema product developers of servers, digital projectors, etc. Pacific Title scanned the footage at 6K resolution in 16-bit DPX resolution on a Northlight scanner – 164 MB per frame. When the data was stuffed into a 16-bit DPX container, the facility ran into problems because few software implementations correctly supported the format's full specifications.

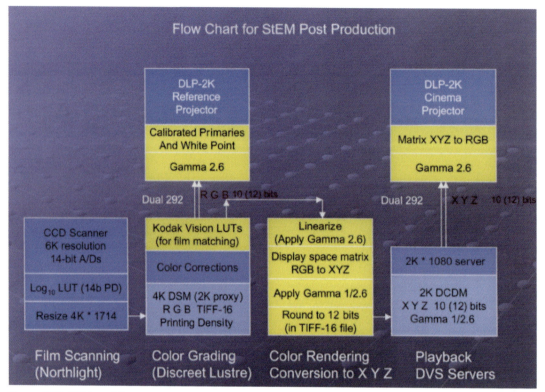

Figure 4.36 StEM workflow.

The Standard Evaluation Material DCI and the ASC created for digital projection testing was scanned at 6K resolution into 16-bit DPX files by Pacific Title & Art Studio. Sixteen-bit DPX was not yet well supported in the industry so PacificTitle had to convert to the 16-bit TIFF for storage. File transport was accomplished at 10 and 12 bits at various points during the workflow, with all 12 bits used upon final display

"After casting about for a solution," recalls Denis Leconte, (former) head of software development at Pacific Title, "we settled on 16-bit TIFF as a reasonably well-supported data exchange standard. This was first intended to be converted prior to Lustre-ready delivery. But as we found more software having trouble with 16-bit DPXs, we moved the TIFF conversion higher into the pipeline, to the point where it ended up being done during the first resize from 6K to 4K straight off the scanner.

"One important note regarding the use of TIFF," he continues, "is that the file format was used as a container for printing density values that were stored as 16-bit printing density values over a 2.048 density range [the range of values that the format can store]. The TIFF spec does not allow for this type of data format per se, so

the photometric interpretation tag was left as RGB color and further processing was done with the assumption that pixel data represented printing density." Thus, one of the problems of file formats arises: you can use any format to store the bits, but unless you know exactly what the original data represents, your image may not look the way it was intended.

Adds (former) Pacific Title producer Jim Houston, "The Academy's Science and Technology Council is taking on pilot projects to work on some industry-wide problems. One of them is working on this file-format issue to come up with a simplified format for a digital source master that will satisfy the user requirements for higher bit depth, higher resolution files. We're just at the beginning stages. If we can have a digital file format that is as widespread and compatible as 35mm negative, digital workflow will be greatly improved." (Houston is a principal architect of ACES.)

If the StEM footage were taken to a different post facility, the general workflow steps – scanning and converting to a file format, dust-busting and sharpening, color grading, and digital cinema master creation, and possibly a DI filmout – would be the same, as would many of the tools, but the processing and transport would be different. Each facility designs (or cobbles together) a system to accomplish its goals. However, just because a "Lustre" logo is on the box doesn't mean that two high-end DI facilities' Discreet Lustres will function the same, just like a 1979 Camaro Z28 with a blower, ported and polished heads and straight pipes won't perform the same as a showroom-stock '79 Z28. DI facilities hot-rod their gear, optimizing the performance to fit within their custom workflows. EFilm senior colorist Steve Scott (now with TDI) and Roger Deakins ASC, BSC graded *The Village* on a proprietary system that had its foundation in Colorfront technology. It is updated continually with EFilm's own modifications. (More likely than not, all facilities have juiced every piece of gear, from scanners to color correctors to recorders, at least a little to get their respective pipelines flowing the way they prefer.)

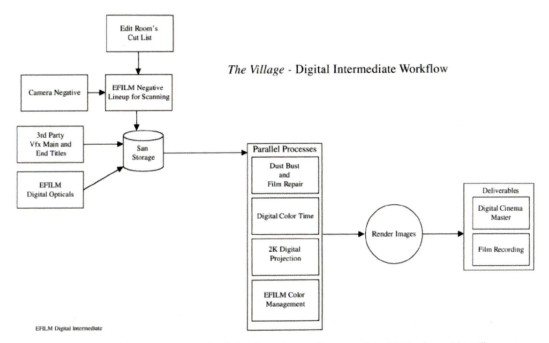

Figure 4.37 Roger Deakins, ASC, BSC and colorist Steve Scott color graded the 2004 release *The Village* using a proprietary color-grading system from Colorfront that had been completely customized by EFilm. Every DI facility "hot rods" its equipment to better integrate with its chosen workflow.

Look-Up Tables (LUTs)

The Colonel has his recipe, Coca-Cola has its formula, and DI facilities have their "secret sauce," which undoubtedly includes proprietary Look-Up Tables (LUTs). Most projects that are shepherded through a DI strive to maintain the CMY filmic look and quality, but you don't see that naturally on an RGB color space display. That doesn't work when the cinematographer and colorist are grading a motion picture on a monitor and digital projector and the motion picture will be shown on film print stock in theaters across the globe. This is where LUTs come in. A LUT is a facility's tool to shift from one color space to another – to get a scan to display correctly on the monitor requires a certain LUT, and to display on a digital projector requires a different LUT. LUTs shift an input value to a particular output value; for example, they shift a specific color of yellow to a deeper shade to emulate how the yellow would be created on Kodak Vision print stock. There are limits to this shifting, however. For a more numerical example, a 10-bit log file has assigned values from 0 to 1023 ($2^{10}-1=1023$) that correspond to densities on the negative. If a LUT is written to emulate the look of a +1 stop increase (which would equal approximately +90 code values), 0 becomes 90, 1 becomes 91, and so on. However, 934 + 90 = 1023, not 1024. 935 + 90 = 1023, not 1025, etc. 1023 is the limit, and all numbers beyond that are clipped back to 1023 because they fall out of the gamut of reproducible colors. That means it is an artifact, but one that may not be perceivable. "If you look at RGB space as a cube," says Joshua Pines, vice president of imaging research and development at Technicolor Digital Intermediates (TDI), "you actually can warp it, which is what happens to the densities as they go from a negative to a print. Some of it may fall out of gamut. It depends on what the gamut is that you are producing.

"What we're doing at TDI is taking spectral radiometer readings in XYZ [color space] of the film projection of each of the lattice points, and then figuring out what digital values we must send out to the digital projector to produce those same XYZs." A lattice, or table, is a more manageable grid of points from which to measure. "You don't construct a table that has every single value – it will be such an enormous table!" Pines exclaims. "But you can do a bunch of points and interpolate between them. Let's say that instead of doing 1,000 reds, 1,000 green, and 1,000 blues, we do 20 reds by 20 greens by 20 blues, or perhaps $16 \times 16 \times 16$, $25 \times 25 \times 25$, $65 \times 65 \times 65$, etc. The points are equally spaced from white to black, and it's a more reasonable table to measure. We have our input coming in, and if we are lucky enough to hit on one of those points, we already will know what the output will be for digital emulation of that film print. More often than not, we will not hit one of those points. We will be in between in RGB space, the middle of the cube. That means we will have to take an average of the known values depending on where we will have to interpolate between the known values at the corners of the cube, and that is how a 3-D LUT works. I prefer to call them 'interpolated lattice deformations' because the lattice is deformed when we interpolate between actual lattice points."

So, LUTs can emulate the characteristics of actual negative and print film stocks. Kodak and Fuji have their own LUTs for their stocks. Kodak LUTs are available with the Kodak Display Manager and Look Management System products. Fuji's LUTs for its negative and print stocks are available by request. A DI lab like TDI may also craft its own custom LUT by analyzing and measuring the film stock, writing the LUT code and then perfecting it through trial and error. LUTs also can shift colors and create unique looks, as well as transform color spaces. The LUTs' key role in the DI workflow has led several companies, such as Filmlight (Truelight), Kodak (TCS), Thomson (Luther), Imagica (Galette), and others to introduce color–space converter boxes that come with LUTs designed by the manufacturers. Many facilities also download their custom

LUTs into these boxes. Scanner manufacturers, such as ARRI with its Arrilaser and Celco with its Fury, have gotten into the color mix as well with onboard color-management systems that don't require LUTs to be plugged in – they operate with preset color profiles.

There is a simple LUT, a 1-D LUT, that you may not realize is at work during basic color correction. If you tell your colorist to make a scene cooler and he then adds a little blue, a 1-D LUT for the blue channel has just been applied to the digital file for display. Notes Pines, "An LUT is a table of numbers – a single number goes in, another comes out. Blue goes in, blue comes out, and so on. Something you can never do with a 1D LUT is saturation, taking color and turning it into grayscale values, because the final red output, for example, doesn't just depend on the red, but also the green and the blue input values."

For the DLP digital projector used in color grading, Pines wrote the Technicolor two-strip- and three-strip-emulating LUTs for *The Aviator*, shot by Robert Richardson, ASC, based on emulated looks visual-effects supervisor Rob Legato had produced in Adobe After Effects and Photoshop. "Marty Scorsese has a collection of old two-strip films," says Pines. "We took a whole reel of a print, scanned it, put it through our calibrated digital projector and tweaked it side by side with the film projector so that they looked identical. Therefore, we had a digital footprint of what the two-strip film-print color gamut was. We did the same thing with three-strip with frames from *Robin Hood*. We got that information not only for visual reference, but also to map the color canvas [with tables]. We characterized those, turning them into 3-D LUTs."

Figure 4.38 For Robert Richardson, ASC to achieve two-strip and three-strip Technicolor looks for *The Aviator*, Josh Pines of TDI wrote Look-Up Tables (LUTs) that were applied to the images. At the top is the image before color grading and beneath it is the image after the two- strip LUT was applied. TDI's efforts aided Richardson in achieving the nostalgic looks, and Richardson took home the Academy Award for Best Cinematography.

Figure 4.39 The resulting image after the LUT is applied.

A 3-D LUT has three input channels and three output channels. The red, for example, could be dependent on all three channels of input. The same goes for blue and green. "In practice, a full-blown 3-D LUT would be way too big for current computers and electronics," Pines indicates. "Instead, we use a 'sparse 3-D LUT' and interpolate between the lattice points."

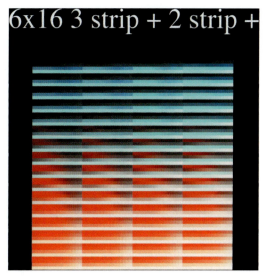

Figure 4.41 Center: with the two-strip emulation LUT applied.

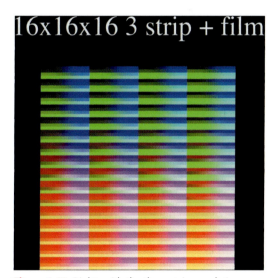

Figure 4.42 Right: with the three-strip emulation LUT applied.

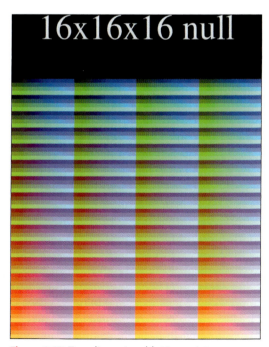

Figure 4.40 Two-dimensional lattice-point representations of the 16 × 16 × 16 3-D LUTs used in *The Aviator*. At left, null: which represents the input that contains all colors with no color processing yet applied

Figure 4.43 This scene featuring Pan Am head Juan Trippe (Alec Baldwin) marks a switch to the three-strip Technicolor look. Top: before the LUT is applied.

Figure 4.44 The result after the three-strip LUT was applied.

The digital image files with these LUTs applied were recorded to print film via an Arrilaser. Had *The Aviator* undergone a digital cinema release, those LUTs could not have been placed in every digital projector throughout the world, so Pines would have had to do some digital "cooking." "They will not let me control the [digital] projectors in the theaters," he reveals, "so I would've had to 'bake in' that film look through the mastering process." Having a look "baked in" means that the file has been changed and saved to permanently reflect that look. It is a way to protect the integrity of the image, because the digital environment opens the process up to meddling by other hands.

The Aviator

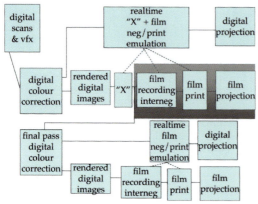

Figure 4.45 *The Aviator* workflow.

Though the LUT is doing the processing, the human element certainly isn't removed from the process. "We run it through this LUT and get HD video, and we run it through that LUT and get standard definition – it doesn't work that way," contends Levinson. "You still need a fair amount of human invention, and that is why we have people trained in color correction doing the scanning. We have the people who will be responsible

for the DI color correction overseeing the trimming of the color for some of the other target deliveries."

"Le Gant" Hybrid DI

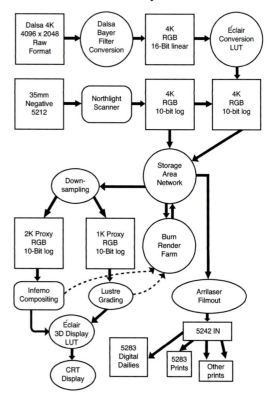

Figure 4.46 Éclair tested a 4K DI process – the facility normally works at 2K – on *Le Gant*, a film shot simultaneously on 35mm and digitally with the Dalsa Origin digital data camera. The Origin's Bayer filter pattern was deBayered to RGB. Color grading was done using 1K proxies on a CRT display because the facility's Barco DLP projectors were in use on other projects.

Compression

The hybrid digital workflow does not have to start with film origination. High-end digital video cameras, such as SONY's HDW-F900 CineAlta and HDW-F950 (which has data-only output capability) and Panasonic's VariCam, have been around for several years and record in the Rec 709 high-definition RGB color space. However, they record compressed signals to tape: SONY in 8-bit to heavily compressed (upwards of 7–10:1) HDCam or, in the case of the F950, lesser 2–4:1 compression for 10-bit to HDCam SR, depending on the chroma sampling and the specific recording deck; and Panasonic to heavily compressed DVCPro HD.

"Pandora's Box is open," says David Stump, ASC, chair of the Digital Camera subcommittee. "The future is going to be digital somehow, some way, and will at least include a hybrid of film and digital cameras. However, there is no reason to give up a perfectly good toolset for one that does less. As a cinematographer, you can always raise an eyebrow by suggesting compression. The bad kinds of compression create sampling errors and the okay compressions use a little less disk or tape space."

There are two distinctions in compression, lossy or lossless, and they both involve higher math algorithms to shrink a file's size to make it more manageable and transportable. No sense in boring you with these algorithm details. Lossy can be of any factor of compression – 10:1, 50:1, 100:1, etc.; the algorithm used causes the loss by throwing out what it calculates to be unnoticeable by the viewer chroma subsampling is a form of lossy compression. To achieve losslessness, generally only a small amount of compression is applied, but this doesn't shrink the file size much. The earlier compression is applied within the workflow, the more its errors compound. Errors show up as squares of color rather than picture detail.

If compression is necessary, it is best to apply it as close to the last stage of the workflow as possible. Remarks Kennel, "From an image-quality standpoint, it's risky to apply compression up front in the process, whether it's in the camera footage or in the image being used in the visual effects compositing process. It's better to stay with the whole content of the image while you are twisting, stretching, color correcting, and manipulating the image. If you apply compression up front and you decide to stretch the contrast or bring detail out of the black during a color-correction session, you may start seeing artifacts that weren't visible in the original image. I think compression is a good enabler and cost reducer on the distribution side, just not a good thing up front."

An algorithm does not necessarily have to be applied to achieve a compressed image file. Compression can occur by the very nature of the workflow itself. The StEM image files were 6K 16-bit TIFF files but were unsqueezed from the original anamorphic camera negative and down-converted to 4K for sharpening. They were then downsampled to 1K 10-bit files for color correcting as proxies on a Lustre. After grading, the files were converted again to 12-bit files in XYZ color space. During the first pass of the material through the workflow, those 12-bit files were being pushed through 10-bit-capable pipelines to

a digital projector, meaning 2 bits were lost as the pipeline truncated the files for display purposes. However, the end display and film-out used all 12 bits.

Manufacturers such as ARRI, Panavision, Dalsa, and Thomson (and eventually SONY, RED, Vision Research, Panasonic, Canon, and Blackmagic) developed so-called "data cameras" that could avoid video color space. They recorded uncompressed to hard-disk storage and had better image quality than HD – 4:4:4 chroma sampling, so no short-shrifting sub-samples, wider latitude, 10-bit or higher color bit depth and resolution close to 2K and higher. Dalsa claimed 4K × 2K and at least 12 linear stops for the Origin and went so far as to offer workflow support through post. And Thomson's Viper, for example, captured in raw mode, meaning the picture wasn't pretty but had the most picture information at your disposal in post for possibly endless manipulation. Michael Mann's film *Collateral*, shot by Paul Cameron and Dion Beebe, ASC, ACS, made excellent use of digital-video and digital-data camera technology, in addition to shooting traditional Super 35 film elements that were down-converted to Rec 709 color space to match the predominant high-definition footage. Basically, Rec 709 served as the lowest common denominator among the formats.

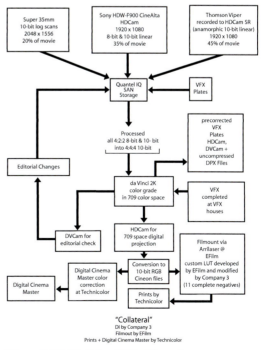

"Collateral"
DI by Company 3
Filmout by EFilm
Prints + Digital Cinema Master by Technicolor

Figure 4.47 *"Collateral"* Workflow diagram.

Collateral, shot by Paul Cameron and Dion Beebe, ASC, ACS, was shot on digital video and digital-data cameras, as well as 35mm. The multiple formats were converted into 1920 × 1080 4:4:4 10-bit DPX files in Rec 709 color space. "We did test after test after test to make sure that what we were seeing at Company 3 was exactly what we wanted on film," says senior colorist Stefan Sonnenfeld of Company 3, where the DI was performed. "It was tricky, especially with the types of transfers we were doing, but I'm used to doing multiple formats, coming from commercials and music videos. Part of my job as a colorist is to utilize what's there and make it into what people want it to be." Sonnenfeld also graded the digital cinema master at TDI.

Director of photography Sean Fairburn believes that waiting until post to decide on an image's look – for example, when shooting in the raw format – will lead to a loss of image control for the cinematographer. "If we train a new generation of directors of photography who can't decide whether to put a filter on the lens or on in post," he asserts, "then maybe the colorist or the director might choose a different filter. I am the one on the set that looks at an actress's dress and says, 'This is what it is supposed to look like.' The colorist doesn't know that the teal dress was actually teal. If the film or the electronic medium slightly shifts, he is not going to know that it needs to be pulled back to teal. I am the guardian over this image. If I can capture an image that looks closer to where I want to be, then my colorist, my visual-effects producer and whoever else is down range already sees where I am going. Let's defer very expensive decisions until later on? This isn't that kind of job."

Fairburn has touched on an unavoidable problem in post production: the differences in human perception that were discussed earlier in this article. The more people involved in making judgment calls, the more your image could drift away from its intended look. The raw format, and digital in general, does offer more manipulation possibilities in post, but creating a look from the ground up takes time, something that the post production schedule is usually lacking. And more hands are involved in the post process. (Tuning the matrix, knee, and slope and permanently "baking" that tuned look into the original recorded image, became unnecessary with the dawn of log and hyper gamma curve outputs for 2/3"-sensor cameras. During this period in time, cinematographers' philosophy on look creation changed, and with the development of full-frame/Super 35 sensors that record raw log data, "baking in" is avoided now specifically to allow for image manipulation in post.)

Looking into the Digital Future

No matter what manipulation an image goes through, the file inevitably must undergo a color space conversion, sometimes several, during the workflow. Upon scanning, the colors on the negative typically are encoded in some form of RGB density. The look may be adjusted either in a look management system or a color corrector, sometimes in density (log) space or sometimes in video space. The colors may be converted to scene space for visual-effects work. Another color conversion may happen when preparing the final version for output to film or digital cinema. SMPTE DC28 settled on conversion to CIE XYZ color space for the digital cinema distribution master (DCDM) because it can encode a much wider color gamut than those of monitors, projectors, and print film, allowing room for better display technologies in the future.

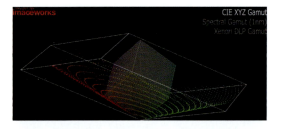

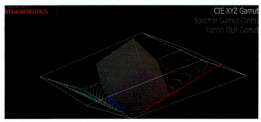

Figure 4.48 and 4.49 Two views of a graphic comparison of three color gamuts. The innermost cube represents the colors that can be reproduced by a particular RGB display device. The curved surface illustrated by colored contour lines represents the boundary of colors visible to human beings; that it lies outside the RGB cube shows that many colors cannot be reproduced by an RGB device. The outermost figure, the white wireframe rhombohedron, represents the colors that can be specified by the CIE XYZ primaries; since this gamut encompasses all the visible colors, XYZ can be used to specify any color.

"Before the advent of ACES, where anything can be mapped without losing any data, every transfer from one color space to another color space, even if it's the same color space, ran risks of sampling errors," says Stump. "By re-sampling to any other color space, especially a smaller space, you can concatenate (link together) errors into your data that then cannot be reversed. They cannot be corrected by expanding that data back into a bigger color space.

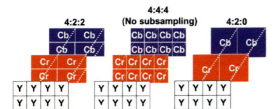

Figure 4.50 Chroma sampling models for YCbCr color space. 4:4:4 is uncompressed chroma sampling.

Some people will argue that you can correct the errors using large mathematical formulas, but I don't think that is error correction. I think that is error masking. That's a lot of work to correct an error that didn't have to be created in the first place. On the Cinematographers Mailing List, I read something that was well said: 'You should aspire to the highest-quality acquisition that you can afford.' There are numerous hidden pitfalls in post."

Displays, whether monitors or digital projectors, are the driving force behind color–space transformation and LUT creation. They function in device-dependent RGB color space. In digital projection, Texas Instruments' DLP (Digital Light Processing) and JVC's D-ILA (Digital Direct Drive Image Light Amplifier) are the two technologies currently in use (in 2005). DLP, used in Barco and Christie projectors, for example, has an optical semiconductor known as the Digital Micromirror Device (DMD) that contains an array of up to 2.2 million hinge-mounted microscopic mirrors. These mirrors either tilt toward the light source (on) or away from it (off). For the 3-DMD chip system, the cinema projector splits the white light into RGB and has three separate channels – red, green, and blue. Each chip is driven with 16 bits of linear luminance precision resulting in $2^{48} = 281$ trillion unique color possibilities. Resolution is 2048 × 1080. D-ILA, a variant of LCOS (Liquid Crystal on Silicon), utilizes a 1.3" CMOS chip that has a light-modulating liquid crystal layer. The chip can resolve up to 2048 × 1536 pixels – 2K resolution. DLP has the most installations in theaters and post facilities. JVC was the first to introduce a 4K (3860 × 2048) D-ILA projector. SONY began showing its 4K 4096 × 2160 digital projector that uses Silicon X-tal Reflective Display (SXRD) technology. Contrast was stated as "high."

The consensus on the 2K DLP projectors of today (in 2005) is that sequential contrast, roughly

1,800:1 (D-ILA has less) in a typical viewing environment, is approaching the appearance of a Kodak Vision release print. Vision print stock actually has a density contrast ratio of 8,000:1, or 13 stops, but the projection booth's port glass, ambient light, and light scatter caused by reflection reduce it to a little over 2,000:1. The more expensive Vision Premier print stock has a contrast ratio of about 250,000:1, or 18 stops to the power of 2. (Humans can distinguish 30 stops.)

The chosen light source for digital projection is xenon, which has a slightly green-biased white point. Shown as the "tolerance box" in the lower-left diagram. "Xenon produces a pretty broad spectrum white," explains Cowan, "but included in that white is infrared and ultraviolet. One of the things you have to do to avoid damage to optical elements within the system is filter out the IR and UV. Along with the IR and UV, you end up filtering a little of the red and the blue but leaving all the green. The green component accounts for about 70% of the brightness."

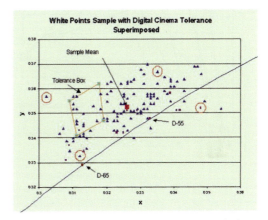

Figure 4.51 This diagram shows a sampling of where the white points of various digital cinema projectors fall along the daylight curve. D-65 and D-55 refer to daylight curve positions with the correlating color temperatures of 6500°K and 5500°K.

Analog film projectors are set up to output 16 foot-lamberts of luminance with an open gate. Put film in the gate and only 11 to 14 foot-lamberts hit the screen. Fourteen is the target for digital cinema projectors as well. (And now for the rhetorical question: are these luminance levels maintained in theaters?) You can go much brighter with analog projectors, and the perceived colorfulness would increase, but flicker would be introduced, especially in the peripheral vision. Flicker is not so much a problem with digital projection because there is no shutter. However, lamp size and heat management are the roadblocks to increased brightness.

"With the xenon light source," adds Kennel, "you can actually push color gamut out beyond TV, beyond Rec 709, and out beyond most of the colors in film, except for the really deep, dark cyans." An interesting example of this constraint can be seen in *The Ring*. Projected on film, cinematographer Bojan Bazelli's overall cyan cast to the imagery comes through, but when viewed on a Rec 709 or Rec 601 RGB display that lacks most cyan capability, that cyan tint shifts to a bluish-gray because shades of cyan aren't reproduced well, if at all, in those RGB color gamuts.

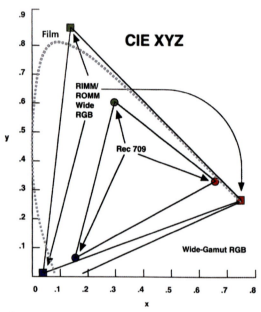

Figure 4.52 A color gamut comparison of various color space formats within CIE XYZ. As a note, the film gamut is at one particular density. Film's chromaticity varies, depending on the density.

DLP projection also offers onboard color correction, but loading a LUT for a particular film into every theater's projector isn't feasible. Instead, DLP projectors function within preloaded color profiles. Typical RGB has three primary colors, and its corresponding color profile for the DLP digital projector is known as P3. Pixar's animated *Toy Story 2* (1999) used a P3 color profile for its digital cinema master. But other colors can be designated as primaries to expand the mix and match palette, as Texas Instruments has done with the P7 system – red, green, blue, magenta, cyan, yellow, and white. "We were trying to color correct a scene that had red geraniums, green grass, and warm skin tones," remembers Cowan. "When we balanced out the green grass and red geraniums so they looked natural, the skin tone

went dead. When we balanced the skin tones, the green grass and red geraniums looked fluorescent, so we had a fundamental color-balance problem. Skin tones end up in the yellow area a lot. Yellow should be a combination of red plus green, but in order to get bright enough yellows, we had to crank the red and green brightness too high. What we did in the P7 world was reduce the target luminance of the red and the green but left the target luminance of yellow high. In fact in P7, we can get very bright yellows without getting very bright greens or reds associated with it."

Throw in some inverse gamma 2.6 to get good quantization to go with the P7 profile (it's P7v2 now [in 2005]), and you're ready for digital projection. Well, not quite. The goal of DCI was to establish digital cinema distribution parameters and out of that came the DCDM, the Digital Cinema Distribution Master, which stipulates a conversion of the materials to wide-gamut CIE XYZ color space and the use of the MXF (Material eXchange Format) file system and JPEG 2000 codec. JPEG 2000 uses wavelet transform compression and offers the capability of compressing a 4K file and extracting only the 2K image file out of that.

The future of projection could be in lasers. Lasers can produce true black (because when they're off, they're off without slow light decay) and will widen the color gamut beyond all current display technologies. For now, questions about the technology remain: Is it feasible for commercialization? What happens to your hair when you stand up into the laser beam? (Christie demonstrated a laser projector in 2013, projecting *Hugo* and *G.I. Joe: Retaliation* in 3-D and achieving 14 foot-lamberts of brightness on screen.)

The ASC Technology Committee is well aware of the possibility that any standards to come out of the current workflows actually may undermine rather than assist image quality and marginalize those best equipped to manage the image – cinematographers. For this reason, they are serving as a sort of forest ranger in the digital frontier. In doing so, Clark has created an ideal workflow guide that includes all the tools needed to maintain image integrity throughout the hybrid film/digital process. Rather than being equipment-centered and rigid, the workflow specifies best-practice recommendations, allowing for inevitable technological innovations. "We're stepping in with a proposal of what needs to happen," he indicates. "We're not only assessing currently available workflow management tools and applications, but also identifying a set of functions that need to be integral to these workflow solutions in order to maximize both creative potential and cost efficiency."

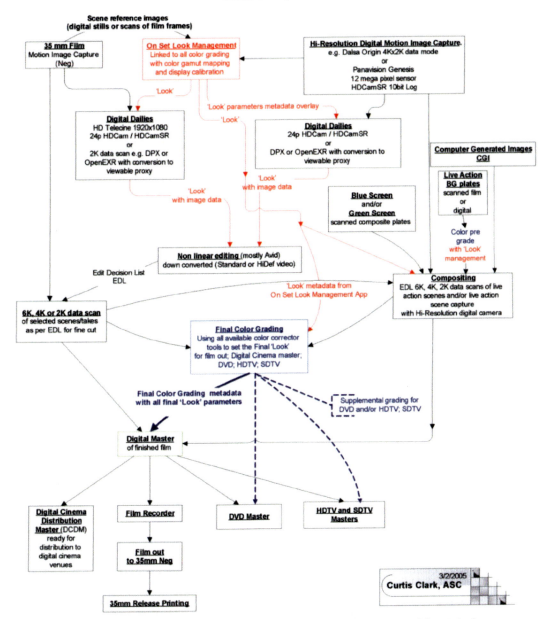

Figure 4.53 Key to the ASC Technology Committee's best-practice hybrid imaging workflow is look management, a burgeoning field in the motion picture industry. This also includes the Color Decision List (CDL) proposal. The committee's workflow allows for inevitable technological improvement and innovation.

Key to this workflow is the integration of "look management" that begins on the set. "This optimized workflow incorporates the provision for a look management function that can be utilized at every stage of the filmmaking process, from previsualization through to final color correction, with tool sets that are designed for the cinematographer," he says. "This reinforces the importance of the cinematographer's traditional role in the creative process, which not only includes setting the look in terms of the image capture but also managing that look all the way through final color correction and digital mastering to the distribution of a theatrical release on film, DCDM, DVD, HDTV, SDTV, etc.

A Technological History of Motion Pictures and Television (Fielding)
The History of Movie Photography (Coe)
Color and Culture (Gage)
A History of Motion Picture Color (Ryan)
Mr. Technicolor (Kalmus)
Color Television and Theory: Equipment Operation (RCA)
The Natural Philosophy of James Clerk Maxwell (Harman)

Publications:

American Cinematographer
SMPTE Motion Imaging Journal
Understanding Digital Cinema: A Professional Handbook (C. Swartz, editor)

Web Sites:

fcc.gov tvhandbook.com discoverychannel.com colormatters.com wordiq.com colorsystem.com
DCImovies.com (Digital Cinema Initiative)
Molecularexpressions.com
SMPTE.org (Society of Motion Picture and Television Engineers)

Chapter 5

MTF, Resolution, Contrast, and Nyquist Theory

Resolution (for our purposes) is defined as the lity of an imaging system to resolve detail in the object that is being imaged. Resolution is a measure for the smallest spatial detail an imaging system can resolve. The resolution of the human eye is indicated as "*visual acuity*." The primary metric of resolution in imaging is modulation transfer function (MTF). The perception of sharpness depends, to a lesser degree, on the resolution and more on the micro contrast in the image, which is called *acutance*.

It is important to distinguish between sharpness and resolution. *Sharpness* is a perceived quality which is a combination of the measurable properties of resolution and contrast. The relationship of resolution to contrast is expressed as MTF, which is a curve that plots resolution vs. contrast. However, sharpness can be deceiving, which is why engineers prefer the metric of MTF. A high-resolution image with low contrast may look *less sharp* than a low resolution image with high contrast. This is because our human perception pays more attention to contrast at certain line pairs per mm than others.

Raster and Resolution

Resolution is NOT the number of photosites or pixels in a file. The term *definition* refers to the raster of an image. HDTV, high definition television has a definition of 1920 pixels by 1080 pixels. The number of pixels in an image defines the ability of the container, but resolution defines the content, i.e. what MTF can actually get through a camera system. If a camera records a 4K file, that only means that the file has a raster of 4K pixels horizontally. It does not refer to the resolution of the content. The real world resolution of that image, as measured in line pairs per millimeter (or image width) could easily be well below 4K, 2K, or 1K.

Modulation Transfer Function (MTF)

In 1927, Harry Nyquist, Ph.D., a Swedish immigrant working for AT&T, determined that an analog signal should be sampled at (at least) twice the frequency of its highest frequency component at regular intervals over time to create an adequate representation of that signal in a digital form. The minimum sample frequency needed to reconstruct the original signal is called the Nyquist frequency. This chapter will show us the importance of his research.

To determine resolution, a raster is normally used, employing increasingly fine bars and gaps. A common example in real images would be a picket fence displayed in perspective. In the image of the fence, shown in Figure 5.1, it is evident that the gaps between the boards become increasingly difficult to discriminate as the distance becomes greater. This effect is the basic problem of every optical image. In the foreground of the image, where the boards and gaps haven't yet been squeezed together by the perspective, a large difference in brightness is recognized. The more the boards and gaps are squeezed together in the distance, the less difference is seen in the brightness.

Figure 5.1 A real world example of MTF.

To better understand this effect, the brightness values are shown along the yellow arrow into an *x/y* diagram (Figure 5.2). The brightness difference seen in the *y*-axis is called *contrast*. The curve itself functions like a harmonic oscillation; because the brightness does not change over time but spatially from left to right, the *x*-axis is called *spatial frequency*.

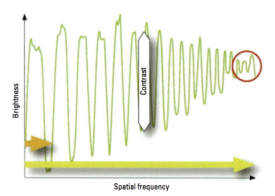

Figure 5.2 Mathematical analysis of the picket fence example.

The distance can be measured from board to board (orange arrow) on an image. It describes exactly one period in the brightness diagram (Figure 5.2). If such a period in the film image continues, for example, over 0.1mm, then there is a spatial frequency of 10 line pairs/mm (10 lp/mm, 10 cycles/mm, or 10 periods/mm). Visually expressed, a line pair always consists of a bar and a "gap." It can be clearly seen in Figure 6.4 that the finer the reproduced structure, the more the contrast will be smeared on that point in the image. The limit of the resolution has been reached when one can no longer clearly differentiate between the structures. This means the resolution limit (red circle indicated in Figure 5.2) lies at the spatial frequency where there is just enough contrast left to clearly differentiate between board and gap.[1]

MTF(v) = Mi (image)/Mo (object)

The object being photographed modulates in frequency and contrast.	The lens attempts to accurately transfer that information to the sensor. But is made out of glass by human beings!	The ratio of the resulting reduction in contrast to the image of the original object contrast is a mathematical function that referred to as MTF.

Figure 5.3 Essentials of MTF.

Using test patterns called square wave gratings (and or sine gratings) with dark and light bars as subject matter, we can measure the amount of light reflected in front of the lens.

Figure 5.4 Square wave test grates of varying frequency.

The maximum amount of light will come from the white bars and the minimum from the dark bars. When we take the ratio of the illumination from the light bars to the illumination from the dark bars we can measure and express the contrast ratio of the test scene we are using to evaluate the system.

If this reflected light is measured in terms of luminance (L) we can define scene modulation according to the following equation: Modulation = (Lmax – Lmin)/(Lmax + Lmin) where Lmax is the maximum luminance of the grating and Lmin is the minimum.

For simplicity, modulation transfer function is generally abbreviated to MTF. MTF is a tool for assessing the resolution behavior of individual components of a total imaging system (such as a lens, a camera, a display, a printer etc.) It also allows an assessment of the overall resolution of that total system – which, is after all, what ultimately impacts our human visual system. And yes, the human visual system itself is endowed with an MTF of some considerable complexity.

What is being modulated, what is being transferred, and how does all of this bear upon resolution? These terms help us provide a linkage between the resolution capability of an imaging component and the contribution that component makes to the perceived sharpness seen when we look at the final reproduced image.

The role of the lens is to intercept the optical wavefronts emanating from an illuminated three-dimensional object within a given scene and to transfer that information into an output two-dimensional object image. The lens creates an optical representation of that scene.

Consider a lens imaging a very low frequency set of adjacent black and white bars (two or three pairs of lines) as depicted in Figure 5.5. As the lens transmits the light from that scene object there will be a modest loss of the white and there will be an elevation of the black (due to internal flare phenomenon). Thus, the output optical reproduction of the black and white scene will incur a small loss of contrast – and the formal contrast ratio of that lens will then be as defined in Figure 5.5.[2]

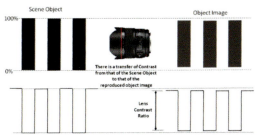

Figure 5.5 Transfer of contrast from scene to image.

All lenses have less than 100% transmittance and also have some degree of black contamination due to flare and internal reflections – that combination defines the lens contrast ratio.

As the spatial frequency of the black and white bars being imaged by the lens is increased, the contrast of their optical reproduction at the lens output lowers. This is simulated in Figure 5.6. The higher that spatial detail becomes, the lower its contrast at the lens output port. Thus, there is a modulation of the transfer of contrast through the lens as a function of spatial frequency, hence the term modulation transfer function.[3]

Contrast Is Decreased as a Function of Frequency

Lenses (including the human lens) are not perfect optical systems. As a result, when light is transmitted through them it undergoes some unavoidable degradation.

Figure 5.7 Cutaway view: inside of a typical lens (Duncan Meeder, LeicaShop Henny Hoogeveen the Netherlands).

Optical design and modern glass coatings help to hold down internal reflections inside a complex lens, but some light scatters as it passes through multiple glass elements and optical cements, and as it bounces off of internal mechanical surfaces.

MTF has spatial frequency (v) as a parameter. Lens systems behave differently dependent on the frequency of the optical information that passes through them. Lens system contrast varies as a function of the spatial frequency of the stimuli that they attempt to transmit.

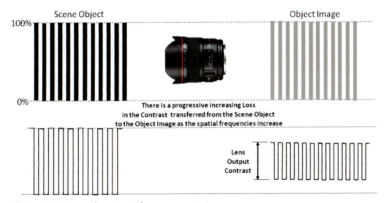

Figure 5.6 Loss of contrast from scene to image.

Let's assume that we have as our subject a square wave grating of a specific frequency (v) and modulation (contrast), and this image is passed through a variety of lenses.

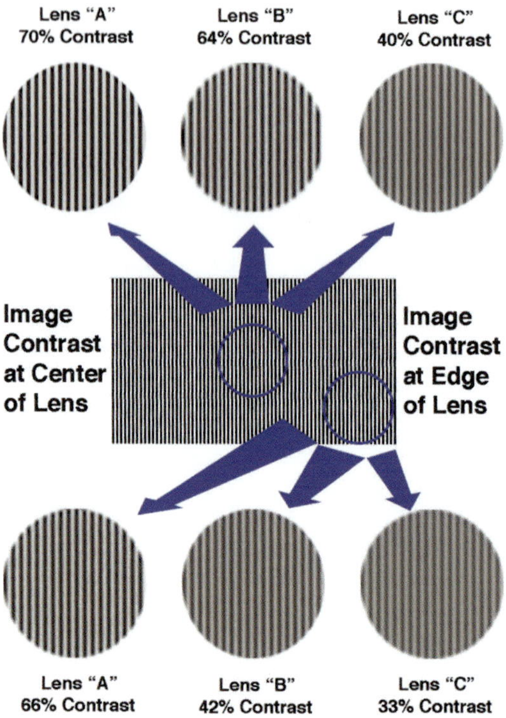

The contrast modulation of the resulting photographed images can now be measured and expressed as percentages.

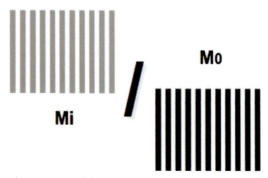

Figure 5.9 Modulation of the image of the object divided by the modulation of the object.

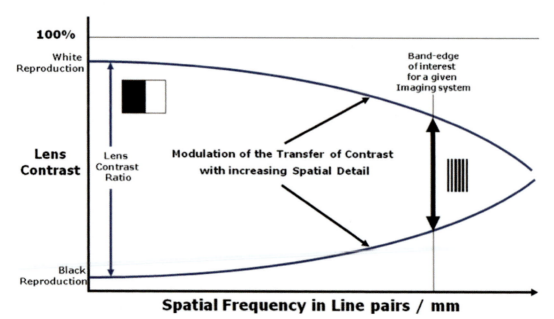

Figure 5.8 The decrease of contrast in the resulting images.

The modulation transfer function is defined as the modulation of the resulting image, M_i, divided by the modulation of the stimulus, the object being imaged, M_0, as described in the equation: $\mathbf{MTF(v) = M_i/M_0}$.

Modulation transfer function is the ratio of the contrast in the scene object to the contrast in the object image as a function of spatial frequency.

If the lens output optical level relative to the level of the input scene object (100% black and white bars) is plotted as a function of spatial frequency it would plot this progressive loss of contrast within the lens in the manner shown in Figure 5.10.

Figure 5.10 Showing a representative falloff in lens contrast – spanning very low spatial detail to the highest spatial detail that defines the pass band of interest for a given imaging system.

If this contrast characteristic of a given lens is plotted as a graph with spatial frequency as the horizontal axis we have the portrayal of the MTF of that specific lens. In the optical world, the unit of spatial frequency is typically in lines per mm – that is, the number of black and white line pairs passed through each millimeter width of a lens. The spatial frequency at which the MTF has dropped to a level below 10% is referred to as the limiting resolution or the resolving power of the lens.

MTF is very important because in its association of lens contrast with spatial detail it is conveying a great deal of information about the image sharpness that that lens can deliver. The human visual system is very sensitive to contrast.

Clearly, the task of the optical designer is to maintain the contrast level as high as possible out to the extremity (the "band edge") of the imaging system in question. Achieving a high contrast ratio requires elevation of the light transmission efficiency through the lens and a lowering of the black contamination. Sophisticated multilayer optical coatings are required to achieve both.

Lenses having a high contrast ratio will likely offer the higher MTF across the system pass band of interest.

As shown in Figure 5.12, a lens having a high contrast ratio offers the better opportunity to hold up that contrast with increasing spatial frequency.[4]

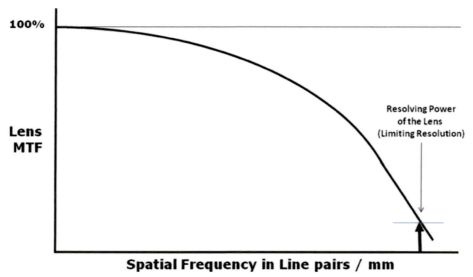

Figure 5.11 MTF characteristic.

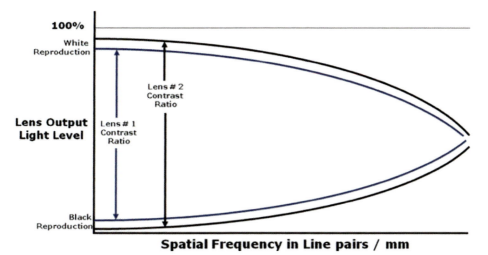

Figure 5.12 Contrast as a function of frequency.

It now becomes very important to evaluate lens MTF in the context of the overall system, and we will see how the lens is just one factor in a cascading series of percentages that yields an overall MTF number for the entire imaging system.

Modulation Transfer Function of a Solid State Camera

The role of the camera is to accept the object image projected by the lens onto the image sensor(s), and, in turn, transform that optical representation into a digital representation at the camera output. The task of the image sensor is to effectively transfer as much as possible the contrast of the optical image – over the spatial frequency range of interest – to the analog voltage representation that it creates (which is subsequently digitized). Unlike the lens, however, which is a spatially continuous surface, the image sensor (CCD or CMOS) is a sampled system in both the horizontal and vertical domain. Like the lens, the image sensor manifests a progressive loss of output contrast with increasing spatial detail. This is generally referred to as the "aperture" of the CCD or CMOS image sensor, and its shape is a function of both the number of sampling photosites and the spacing between each photosite. There is an aperture for the horizontal domain and a separate aperture for the vertical domain of the image sensor.

Sampling theory mathematics applies here, and while this does facilitate an assessment of an effective MTF for the image sensor, it must also, of necessity, take into account the inevitable aliasing that is created by the sampling mechanism. Sampling theory predicts that a sideband frequency is created that is centered at the spatial sampling frequency of the image sensor. This horizontal sampling frequency for an image sensor having N photosites per vertical line is calculated as N photosite samples divided by the aspect ratio (AR) = N/AR line pairs (or cycles) per picture height.

Because the Nyquist frequency is half the spatial sampling frequency, any scene detail having a spatial frequency above Nyquist will create an unwanted "beat" frequency within the useful passband below that Nyquist frequency. All professional cameras utilize an optical low pass filter in front of the image sensor which is usually Cosine shaped with a null at the sampling frequency. The multiplication of this filter shape with that of the image sensor aperture will produce the final effective MTF for the image sensor as shown in Figure 5.13.

As we have seen, modulation transfer function describes the ability of adjacent pixels to change from black to white in response to patterns of varying spatial frequency, the actual capability to show fine detail. Neither the lens MTF nor the camera MTF tells the whole story. An image reproduced with an overall system optical transfer function that "rolls

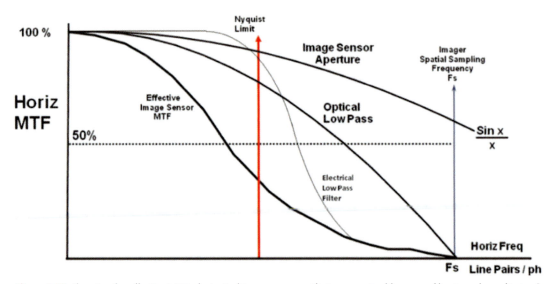

Figure 5.13 Showing the effective MTF of a typical image sensor utilizing an optical low pass filter to reduce aliasing.[5]

off" at high spatial frequencies will appear blurred.

The optical transfer function of an imaging system is the measure of resolution that the entire system is capable of. It is the overall optical transfer function (OTF) of the complete system, including lens and anti-aliasing filter as well as other factors, that defines true performance in delivering sharp high contrast images.

Most HD cameras output a picture that is 1920 × 1080 pixels in dimension. In real world terms, that means that a 1920 × 1080 pixel image projected onto a 40′ × 22′ movie screen would be composed of pixels 1/4″ square.

It takes two horizontal pixels (one white and one black) to create one visible *cycle*. A 1920 pixel horizontal by 1080 vertical HD projection can accurately display a maximum of 960 *cycles* of horizontal resolution and 540 *cycles* of vertical resolution on a 40′ wide screen.

If an unfiltered 1920 × 1080 HD system is presented with a subject matter with a higher frequency than 960 horizontal cycles or 540 vertical cycles (the Nyquist limit), it is unable to accurately reproduce that frequency, and it will exhibit spatial aliasing.

Figure 5.16 Frequency sweep exhibiting aliasing

Aliasing is the effect that causes high frequency signals above the Nyquist frequency (fewer than two samples per cycle) to become indistinguishable or distorted when sampled. It also refers to the distortion or artifacting that results when the picture that is reconstructed from samples is different from the original picture.

Figure 5.14 Horizontal square wave grate.

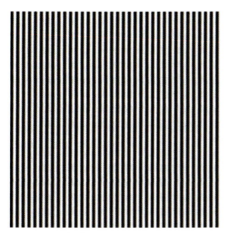

Figure 5.15 Vertical square wave grate.

Figure 5.17 OLPF filtered image.

Higher Contrast Images Will Be Perceived as Sharper than Lower Contrast Images

Are resolution and sharpness the same thing? By looking at the images shown in Figure 5.23, one can quickly determine which image seems sharper.

Although the image on the left comprises twice as many pixels, the image on the right, whose contrast at coarse details is increased with a filter, looks at first glance to be distinctly sharper.

The resolution limit describes how much information makes up each image, but not how a person evaluates this information. Fine details such as the picket fence in the distance are irrelevant to a person's perception of sharpness – a statement that can be easily misunderstood. The human eye, in fact, is able to resolve extremely fine details. This ability is also valid for objects at a greater distance. The decisive physiological point, however, is that fine details do not contribute to the subjective perception of sharpness. Therefore, it's important to clearly separate the two terms, resolution and sharpness.

The coarse, contour-defining details of an image are most important in determining the perception of sharpness. The sharpness of an image is evaluated when the coarse details are shown in high contrast.[6]

The perception of sharpness doesn't depend solely on spatial resolution. High resolution would seem synonymous with preservation of detail and sharpness, but high pixel count does not always translate into high resolution. The contrast sensitivity function (CSF) tells us that our visual sensitivity to contrast is higher at lower spatial resolutions than at the threshold of visual acuity (the point where we can no longer see contrast difference). Our eyes are attuned to middle resolution information for sharpness and contrast. A more effective MTF provides more information in that middle resolution range. Modulation of contrast at lower to middle spatial frequencies in coarse detail is considerably more significant in giving the impression of sharpness than contrast at the highest resolution limit.

Figure 5.23 Which of these images appears to be sharper?

1000 Pixels

higher resolution at lower contrast

500 Pixels

higher contrast at lower resolution

Figure 5.24 The left image has higher resolution, but the right image seems sharper.

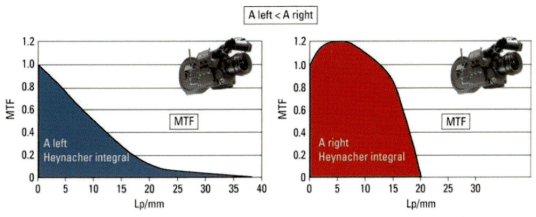

Figure 5.25 Heynacher integral graphs illustrating the effect of contrast over resolution in perceived sharpness.

In the 1970s, Erich Heynacher from ZEISS provided the decisive proof that humans attach more value to coarse, contour-defining details than to fine details when evaluating an image. He found that the area below the MTF curve corresponds to the impression of sharpness perceived by the human eye (called the Heynacher integral) (Heynacher, 1963).

Expressed simply, the larger the area under the integral curve, the higher the perception of sharpness. It is easy to see that the coarse spatial frequencies make up the largest area of the MTF. The farther right into the image's finer details, the smaller the area of the MTF. Looking at the camera example in Figure 5.25, it is obvious that the red MTF curve frames a larger area than the blue MTF curve, even if it shows twice the resolution.[7]

Fine picture detail near the Nyquist frequency limit of a sensor can help contribute to greater *perceived* image texture and (to some degree) image sharpness. Cloth and medium high frequency subject areas give images more apparent sharpness, but they stress every component of the imaging system and present MTF challenges at every step of the way.

Fill factor in sensors also affects lens performance and aliasing. Lower fill factor sensors can yield more apparent picture sharpness than high fill factor sensors with the same lens, but at the cost of increased noise.

Figure 5.27 Very fine picture details.

Image courtesy of Bob Primes

Extremely fine detail above the Nyquist frequency (testing the resolving power of the lens) has not traditionally been valued as contributing to perceived image sharpness in HD systems, and is routinely filtered out of images by both optical low pass filters and software filters in accordance with SMPTE recommended broadcast practice.

This is not true for digital cinema cameras that are capable of acquiring in 4K, 5K,

Figure 5.26 Contrasty vertical and horizontal lines and low frequency high contrast picture edge detail, contribute to *perceived* sharpness in images.

6K, and up to 8K. Higher resolution cameras offer detail and sharpness that approaches the diffraction limits of photographic systems. There is much discussion about whether this resolution is of value in film making, but the eventual planned increase in DCP bit rates and larger screens will make the differences more obvious and apparent to viewers. In addition, higher resolution acquisition has great value in visual effects work. Finer detail in blue screen and green screen shots enables finer detail in compositing. Whether delivering to 4K, 2K, or HD, the additional detail of higher definition acquisition adds greater resulting detail at higher Nyquist frequencies that show up in the final delivery of composited VFX work.

Important Trends to Consider Regarding Picture Sharpness

To summarize, 1920 × 1080 HD systems are limited in frequency response at Nyquist limits of 960 cycles in the horizontal domain and 540 cycles in the vertical, but the Digital Cinema Initiative (DCI) specs for digital cinema exhibition provides for much higher definition exhibition systems.

In order to continue to attract audiences to see our movies in theaters, we are continuing to develop ways to deliver motion picture images at a new quality level; higher resolution, higher dynamic range, higher frame rate, brighter projection systems and new standards to accommodate these advances continue to be developed and implemented.

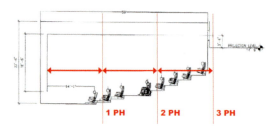

Figure 5.28 Viewing distance in picture heights.

If we view our 1920 × 1080 pixel HD image projected onto our 40′ × 22′ movie screen from a distance of one and a half screen heights (or about 33′) trigonometry tells us our horizontal viewing angle is approximately 62 degrees, yielding an average of just over 30 pixels per degree, and therefore

just over 15 cycles per degree of perceptible detail. It is important to note here that the original design spec for the 1920 × 1080 HD standard called for a viewing distance of 3.5 screen heights away, yielding 30 cycles per degree of resolution for the same pictures.

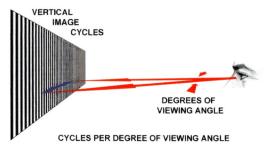

Figure 5.29 Cycles per degree of viewing angle.

The human eye is generally capable of detecting 44 to 60 (and in some cases 80 and over) cycles per degree of detail. Images of 10 to 12 cycles per degree are almost universally perceived as blurry, images of 22 cycles per degree are generally perceived to be sharp, images of 30 cycles per degree are generally acknowledged as satisfactory to human visual acuity, so it is readily apparent that an imaging system that operates at 15 to 16 cycles per degree is barely satisfactory for use in large screen theatrical applications.

For a more in-depth discussion on the resolving powers and capabilities of the human vision system I would highly urge that you should read Michael F. Deering's scholarly paper "A Photon Accurate Model of the Human Eye," or better still attend one of his lectures on the subject. It is a very detailed work, and once understood, it yields many critical and valuable insights into the physiology and mechanics of human vision.

The accepted science of modulation transfer function tells us that many other factors enter into the effectiveness of any acquisition system at delivering resolution to a screen, but we can surmise that an image generated at 1920 pixels across (which at 1.5 screen heights yields 15.36 cycles per degree) is slightly inferior to the de facto digital cinema standard of 2048 × 1556 (16.45 cycles per degree) which is accordingly inferior to 4K shown at 4096 × 3112, which yields an effective screen resolution of about 33 cycles per degree, a number more in accord with human visual acuity.

This is not to say that *every* movie made needs to be made to higher criteria of resolution! Every story dictates a different look and resolution. Some movies demand a softer gentler look, some performers need a gentler photographic treatment, but if we provide for the capability of working at higher resolution, film makers will find stories to tell that require *those* tools as well.

Figure 5.30 Blowup of an image from a typical HD camera.

Figure 5.31 The same image blowup from a 4K digital camera.

The Case for 4K

1920 × 1080 HD and 2K are not sufficient to position the cinema as *clearly superior* to HDTV. Visible pixels, jagged outlines, and screen door effects won't work when your audiences can enjoy superb pictures of nearly identical resolution at home. The value of 2K

cinema has value in much of the content being produced for the big screen, but as the studios roll out 4K high dynamic range releases at the next generation of DCI specs implementing much higher DCP bit rates, it is hoped that higher image quality can prolong the life of theatrical exhibition.

Like color, widescreen, stereo, and surround sound before it, 4K HDR is another advance in technology in the ongoing competition between the theater experience and electronic entertainment in the home. 4K makes a visible difference on screens big and small. For 3D movies, 4K can project left-eye and right-eye information simultaneously, eliminating the limitations of triple-flash presentation. 4K projection is scalable, accommodating 4K, 2K, HD and other digital content. In fact, the smaller pixels of 4K projection and contemporary signal processing actually improve the presentation of 2K material.

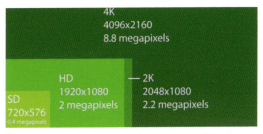

Figure 5.32 Relative resolutions compared

Because we are moving into a world of digital projection which will eventually afford us the ability to project images at 4K (and above), perhaps we should consider that the constraints imposed on us by release print film stocks will soon be ancient history, and empowered by our new ability to project at higher levels of resolution and brightness, we can attract audiences into theaters for a more powerful experience, an experience unavailable in the best home theater, well worth the prices that cinema tickets now cost.

There Is 4K and Then There Is 4K

As we have learned, photosites are *not* pixels. When a sales brochure proclaims that a camera boasts any number of "K," whether it is 3K, 4K, or 5K, it is important to understand whether they are citing monochrome photosites or RGB pixels. As Nyquist theory and deBayer in practice show us, Bayer pattern sensors yield less real world resolution than their photosite count. The mathematical ratios of photosites to actual resolution usually range between 50% and 66% of the sensor photosite count, though some deBayer algorithms claim to produce as much as 80% efficiency. It is always important to understand the factors that yield resolution in motion picture cameras, and it is equally important to distinguish between 4K files and 4K resolution. It is possible to carry standard definition resolution in files resized to 4K, but those pictures do not resolve any more picture detail by virtue of having been resized to fit in a 4K file.

Let's assume that:

- the scene has no color, is entirely black and white
- the optical low pass pre-filter and lens MTF are at the photosite size
- the red, green, and blue photosites all make the same value from every gray in the scene under that scene's black-and-white color temperature and illumination spectrum.

We would then have full resolution at the full photosite count of the sensor. In other words, a 4K Bayer pattern sensor would yield a full 4k resolution.

If, on the other hand, there are numerous very small color details in the scene, then either:

- The colors and/or luminance and/or green will alias, or
- The optical low pass filter and lens MTF frequencies must be at least the same as the number of red and blue photosites each, not red plus blue.

This optical low pass prefilter and MTF corresponds to half resolution, yielding 2K resolution, and should yield alias-free at 2K.

Somewhere in between these two worlds (black and white everywhere in the scene, vs. small color details), some middle-ground optical prefilter, and the lens MTF, a 4K Bayer pattern sensor should usually be able to yield somewhere around 3K – that is, between 2k and 4k on practical scenes.[8]

Resizing and Resampling

Resampling is the mathematical method whereby new and different sized versions of a digital image with a different width and height

in pixels is created. It can also refer to the process whereby an image is reduced in color bit depth or transferred into a larger color space. Enlarging an image is called upsampling; reducing its size or bit depth is called downsampling. When images are upsampled, the number of pixels in the picture increases, but extra image detail and resolution cannot be created in the image that was not already present in the original picture. Images normally become softer the more they are enlarged, as the amount of information per pixel is reduced. When images are downsampled, the data in the original image has to be combined and discarded to make the image smaller. This results in *decimation*, which is defined as the reduction of the number of samples in a discrete-time signal. Decimation occurs when images are downsampled in either resolution or color bit depth. It occurs because as we reduce sampling precision as a byproduct of re sampling, individual samples cannot modify fractionally, there are no fractional code values.

If we downsample and then upsample an image, we cannot ever get all of the original image detail back – detail decimated by re sampling is lost forever. When images are downsampled into a smaller color space they lose color information, that information is not recoverable if they are then re sampled into a larger color space. An image originated at 1920 × 1080 will never exist at greater definition than 1920 × 1080.

There are some very expensive sharpening tricks that can increase the apparent resolution of these pictures, and an image that originated at higher resolution will seem apparently sharper when downsampled, but in any image pipeline there is a lowest common denominator. Once an image has been rendered at 1920 × 1080 that is the greatest resolution it can have. Camera original recorded at 1920 × 1080 is still effectively 1920 × 1080 even when resized to or projected at 4K. It will still have a best effective resolution of approximately 15.36 cycles per degree even on the best projection system in the world. Similarly, images cannot gain any new color information by upsampling to a larger color space. Once an image has been sampled into 10 bit color space, that is all the color information it can have.

Re sampling errors are irreversible bottlenecks in the digital pipeline. Data decimated is data lost forever. Color information lost in re sampling cannot be recovered. Resolution lost in re sampling cannot be truly recovered.

Figure 5.33 Close on an original HD image.

Figure 5.36 The re-upsampled image is sharpened in (an unsuccessful) attempt to recreate the original resolution.

Figure 5.34 The same image re sampled to one half resolution.

Spatial upsampling involves interpolating between the existing pixels to obtain an estimate of their values at the new pixel locations. *Interpolation* is defined as a method of constructing new data points within the range of a discrete set of known data points. Downsampling involves interpolating a weighted average of the original pixels that overlap each new pixel. Numerous re sampling algorithms are available, most work by computing new pixels as a weighted average of the surrounding pixels.

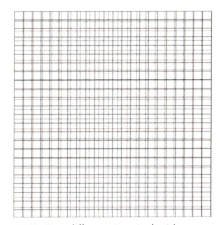

Figure 5.37 Two different size pixel grids superimposed.

Figure 5.35 The one half resolution image re sampled back to its original size.

The weights of surrounding pixels depend on the distance between the new pixel location and the neighboring pixels. The simplest methods consider only the immediate neighbors, more advanced methods examine more of the surround pixels to attempt to produce more accurate and better looking results.

Why is re sampling of concern to cinematographers? Frequently cinematographers, directors and editors may blow up an image for dramatic purposes, or to frame out a microphone dipping into the top of the frame, or to frame out a flag or even a small part of an actor at the edge of frame.

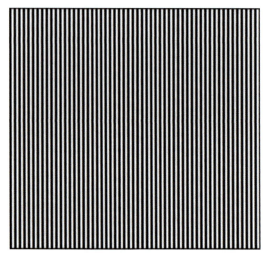

Figure 5.38 Vertical sine wave grate.

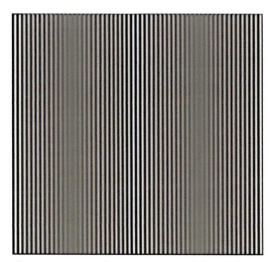

Figure 5.39 Vertical sine grate resampled (note the uneven decimation in the resized grid)

When designing a workflow for digitally captured motion picture images, it is important to give careful attention to choosing the best the working image size when a choice is available from the camera. The goal is to avoid resizing the image multiple times which can cause a reduction in image quality. It is important to consider the deliverable requirements and determine which

output size is the hero resolution and use this size as the native working resolution for the project. For example, if a DCP is the hero deliverable and the project's format is anamorphic then a working resolution of 2048 or 4096 would avoid additional resizing. Of course in this case, the HD deliverables would have to be resized from the 2048 or 4096 working resolution to 1920, but the hero DCP would remain un resized. Another consideration might be safe area protection. In this case, the designated safe action area inside of the full image area should be the hero deliverable size. It is also very important that the camera's "ground glass" properly represents the working area if it is to be a cutout of the full sensor area.

It is important to consult all parties working with the images before beginning production to determine the best working size for the project.[9]

The ideal workflow would resize the image of the "hero format" only one time in order to obtain the highest image quality for our target format. Let's imagine the hero distribution format is a 1:2.40 DCI and the camera has a 1:1.78 sensor using a flat lens, which gives us a 2880 ×1620 image. The SMPTE 240 delivery spec specifies a 2K DCI pixel count of 2048 × 858 for a film out done with a 1:2.35 extraction area. This framing will reflect the creative intent of the director and cinematographer if the frame lines in the camera's viewfinder showed 1:2.35 and 1:2.40 framing lines.

In this workflow, a good ultimate resolution for output to a 2K 1:2.35 image would be 2144 × 1206. The deBayer from the camera raw original image would be done from 2880 × 1620 to 2144 × 1206. Visual effects and DI would be done at 2144 × 1206. For output to digital cinema, the 2144 × 1206 working image resolution would be cropped to 2048 × 858 distribution resolution. For a filmout, the 2144 × 1206 image would be resized, cropped, and anamorphically stretched to 4096 × 3432. The Rec 709 HD TV output would be cropped from 2144 × 1206 to 2048 × 1152 and resized to 1920 × 1080. Depending on how the DP framed the image, letter box bars might be added to the HD TV image.[10]

Resizes can ultimately have an effect on the sharpness and resolution of an image, so much so that it sometimes becomes noticeable to the audience, taking them out of the moment and interrupting the willing suspense of disbelief.

There are numerous resizes already built into the process of finishing a film; a 1920 × 1080 HD picture has to be resized to 2048 × 1144 for the digital cinema package (DCP) process, and likewise, it has to be resized to

1998 × 1116 for output to film. A film originated, 2K scanned movie has to be resized from 2048 × 1107 to 1998 × 1080 for a film out to negative stock. There is a non-integer (and therefore decimative) resize waiting around every corner!

MTF and the Final Step in the Imaging Chain: Projection

We now expend tremendous effort in designing and building lenses to exacting specifications and extremely high MTF to put onto cameras designed to equally demanding specifications. We exercise great care in designing workflows to preserve that precious signal all the way through to output to a digital cinema package in order to preserve every bit of contrast, resolution, and fidelity from the original creative intent as we possibly can. Then we hand our work off for projection in uncontrolled environments that can sometimes carelessly discard much of the effort and cost expended in the name of showing our work at the highest level of quality possible. What am I talking about? Projection.

When the cinematographer goes to a theater, or a screening room, or a post production facility, or even a digital intermediate facility, the very first thing one should check is *how clean or dirty is the projection booth's port glass window*? Projection booths have traditionally used a glass window between the projection lens and the theater in order to keep the noise of a film projector from distracting from the movie. Because port glass windows are usually specially coated with anti reflective coatings, they have dielectric properties that give them the

ability to store static electric charges on their surfaces, much like a capacitor. This static charge attracts pollen, dust, cigarette smoke, and smog, sometimes quickly accumulating a hazy layer that can contaminate the images projected through them.

Figure 5.40 A typical projection booth port glass window.

Would you put a filter on the camera taking lens that looks like this? The net effect is the same, whether this glass is in front of the taking lens or in front of the projector! Images projected through dirty, dusty, smog covered port glass can exhibit the same decrease in contrast as images shot through bad or dirty lenses or filters. You wouldn't expect to get great looking 4K images shooting through a Harrison Double Fog #3 filter, so it stands to reason that you cannot expect to get great looking 4K images by projecting through a port glass that is as dirty as a bus station window!

Notes

1. Courtesy of Dr. Hans Kiening, ARRI.
2. Courtesy of Laurence Thorpe, Canon USA.
3. Courtesy of Laurence Thorpe Canon USA.
4. Courtesy of Laurence Thorpe, Canon USA.
5. Courtesy of Laurence Thorpe Canon USA.
6. Courtesy of Dr. Hans Kiening, ARRI.
7. Courtesy of Dr. Hans Kiening, ARRI; E. Heynacher (1963). Objective image quality criteria based on transformation theory with a subjective scale, Oberkochen, Germany. *Zeiss-Mitteilungen*, 3 (1); G. Simpson, http://de.wikipedia.org/wiki/George_Gaylord_Simpson. Accessed January 2008; T. Tani (2007). AgX photography: present and future. *Journal of Imaging Science and Technology*, 51 (2), 110–116.
8. From Gary Demos.
9. Attributed to Bill Feightner – Colorfront.
10. Joachim Zell, Imaging Scientist.

insufficient image brightness, 3D artifacting, and general visual discomfort. Recently it has widely been proposed that increasing cinema frame rates could improve the cinema experience in 3D.

Interest in higher frame rates in 3D increased when Peter Jackson announced he would be shooting *The Hobbit: An Unexpected Journey* at 48 fps per eye, and soon after that James Cameron showed tests shot at both 48 fps per eye and 60 fps per eye and declared he wanted to use one of those camera speeds for his next series of *Avatar* films.

Figure 6.9 *Avatar* Director James Cameron.

Figure 6.10 *Hobbit* Director Peter Jackson.

Ang Lee's 2016 film *Billy Lynn's Long Halftime Walk* was the first ever feature film shot at the extra high frame rate of 120 frames per second. The movie was released in a limited number of theaters in 4K 3D, and was an early experiment in pushing the limits of digital acquisition and exhibition.

The combination of higher frame rates, increased resolution (4K and up) and higher brightness display can all exacerbate camera judder if not correctly managed. *Billy Lynn* employed an early version of RealD's TrueMotion "synthetic shutter" processing system to creatively manage and manipulate judder and strobing. Judder is a camera problem that arises from the gap in picture data during shutter closed intervals, and strobing is a projection problem caused by the way a projector reproduces motion from frame sequences. The TrueMotion process can be used to eliminate judder and strobing, and further, judder effects can be controlled, localized, and even added or enhanced as a creative choice using this tool.

Shooting at 120 frames per second with a 360-degree shutter angle captures everything that happens in front of the camera with no shutter closed image gap between frames. Then the software allows adjustments to sharpness, motion blur, and judder after capture. In *Billy Lynn*, TrueMotion software used five integrated exposures of the original 120 fps footage to create each single frame of 24 fps output. With True-Motion, the user can derive any shutter angle after capture, as a post production process, even shutter angles greater than 360 degrees, with the ability to also adjust the attack and decay of the shutter waveform. The result can either be a more traditional, cinema-like look at 24 fps, or if preferred, more staccato looks can be created without the addition of judder. Cranking and ramping options can also be applied selectively to areas in a frame, so foreground, including localized elements or actors, can be masked.

As these developments in the creative community have thrust the subject of higher frame rates into the forefront in the filmmaking community, it is clear that the exhibition world will need guidance and standards if they are to reap benefits of showing movies at higher frame rates. In addition, providers of mastering software will also need guidance with regard to which frame rates and compression ratios they should develop and include in their applications.

Cinematography has entered the digital age, and film makers are free of most of the constraints imposed on the traditional processes of film making. Higher frame rates, higher bit depths, increased resolution, and increased projection brightness are all coming into our collective awareness, promising new freedoms in image creation. Those freedoms will first be discovered, then explored, and then employed to creative purpose by cinematographers everywhere.

Frame rate capability depends on hardware and software bandwidth. Bit-rate is impacted by that frame rate, and also by the size of each frame/image in bits. Higher resolution means more bits, as do many other aspects of higher image quality. Each system combination – server, connections, and projector – has a resulting cascaded bandwidth limit.

Historical Perspectives

Todd AO: 65mm at 30 fps

Figure 6.11 A frame from Todd AO's *Oklahoma*.
Image courtesy of Rodgers and Hammerstien

Figure 6.12 The Showscan 65mm camera.

The 65mm Todd-AO process of the mid 1950s shot and projected at 30 frames per second, 25% faster than the 24 frames per second that was then standard. The slightly higher than normal frame rate combined with the extra resolution of 65mm gave Todd AO movies noticeably less flicker, and made them play steadier and smoother than standard 35mm prints. Unfortunately, Todd-AO required its own cameras, projectors, and sound systems, and like several other enhanced formats of the same period such as Cinerama, VistaVision, Technirama, it was ultimately surpassed in popularity by the success of Panavision.

Showscan at 60 Frames per Second in 65mm

The Showscan film process was developed in the early 1980s by Douglas Trumbull, a VFX pioneer famed for his work on *2001: a Space Odyssey*, *Close Encounters of the Third Kind*, *Blade Runner*, and numerous other VFX epics. Using his own design 65mm cameras, he shot and projected films at 60 frames per second, giving audiences an experience in both extremely high temporal and spatial resolution.

Trumbull did research on the physiology of cinema frame rates, running tests filmed at assorted higher speeds and then shown to audiences who were wired to test their responses. He learned that as the frame rate increased toward 72 frames per second, the audience's emotional reaction increased.

Figure 6.13 Douglas Trumbull.

Trumbull is now deeply engrossed in a new digital acquisition process that captures images at 120 frames per second at a 359.99 degree shutter angle and then allows for integration of those images to a wide variety of lower frame rates and effective shutter angles. Designed to work in both 2D and 3D, it will enable cinematographers and directors to tell stories in an incredibly realistic new way.

Coming Soon to a Theater Near You: Even Higher Frame Rates!

There is now even a camera that can capture at one trillion frames per second, freezing light itself!

Figure 6.14 Light photographed at one trillion frames per second!

Image courtesy of Dr. Ramesh Raskar

The camera chapters of this book will go into greater detail on the high speed and variable frame rate capabilities of the cameras available today.

Formats and Aspect Ratios

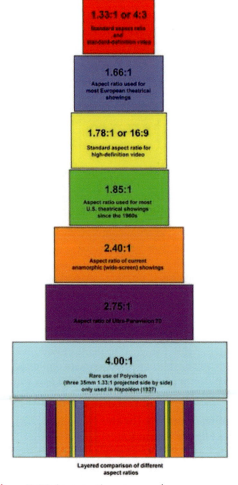

Figure 6.15 Aspect ratios compared.

Aspect Ratios

The aspect ratio of an image is its width divided by its height. Aspect ratios are mathematically expressed as a ratio of "x-to-y" or "x-by-y". Historically, there have been innumerable aspect ratios in film and television. The most common aspect ratios used today in the exhibition in movie theaters are 1.85:1 and 2.39:1. The two most common video aspect ratios are 4:3 (1.33:1), for standard-definition video formats, and 16:9 (1.78:1), for high-definition television. Aspect ratio was traditionally used as a storytelling tool, taller ratios such as 1.33:1 could be used effectively to give a claustrophobic feel to a story told in close quarters, conversely, 2.39:1 worked very well in exterior settings such as westerns.

Cinema Terminology

The movie industry historically assigns a value of 1 to the image's height – a Cinemascope anamorphic frame is usually described as 2.40 to 1 or 2.40:1. In American cinema, the most common acquisition and projection ratios are 1.85:1 and 2.39:1. Europe historically used 1.66:1 as their widescreen standard. The "Academy ratio" of 1.37:1 was historically used for cinema until about 1953, when television, with a screen ratio of 1.33:1, became a threat to movie box office. The minor difference between 1.33:1 and 1.37:1 results from a small area of the frame that was used to carry a vertical interval signal essential in analog broadcast television. In reaction to the TV threat, Hollywood gave birth to a large number of widescreen formats – Cinemascope, Todd-AO, and Technirama to name just a few. During and after that period, the 1.85:1 aspect ratio became the most common cinema projection standard in the United States and generally worldwide.

1.33:1 or 4 × 3 Academy

Figure 6.16 1.33:1 or 4 × 3 Academy.

The 1.33:1 (technically 1.37:1) ratio or "Academy Aspect Ratio" is the aspect ratio that was defined by the Academy of Motion Picture Arts and Sciences as a framing standard at the introduction of optical composite sound on film. It has been used for NTSC television since its inception. Because broadcast television also used this aspect ratio, films made in this format could be easily viewed on NTSC TV sets. With the advent of the widescreen 16 × 9 aspect ratio, the 4 × 3 aspect ratio is quickly becoming a legacy format.

1.5:1, Full Frame, Large Format (LF), VistaVision

The 1.5:1 aspect ratio was facilitated by Kodak's development of 135 format cartridge film for still photography in 1934. The format quickly grew in popularity thanks to cameras like the Leica, eventually surpassing 120 film by the late 1960s to become the most popular photographic film size. The 36mm × 24mm usable negative size of the 135 film frame has long been commonly referred to as "Full Frame," and has subsequently been adopted and evolved by digital SLR cameras.

In 1953 Paramount Studios extended the format to motion picture imaging when they modified two Stein "Fox Color" cameras built for a 1930s two color process which used a two-frame over under a pair of frames. Instead of an image four perforations high, the camera simultaneously exposed two frames, eight perforations consisting of one 4-perf image through a red filter and one 4-perf image through a green filter in an over/under orientation. Paramount engineers removed a septum in the film gate that divided the over under frames, and turned the camera on its side. The film was run horizontally through the camera rather than vertically, and the entire eight perforations were used for one image. The cameras were used to photograph *White Christmas*, and VistaVision was born.

In the digital cinema era, the demand for 4K and higher resolution, coupled with the physical limitations of photosite size has driven a revival of the format as "Full Frame" (FF) or Large Format (LF), and occasionally even still referred to as "VistaVision." Numerous larger high resolution

digital sensors now approximate the size of a 135 negative, and cinematographers find the depth of field and lens bokeh characteristics of the format to be familiar and inviting. Just remember this format usually requires lenses with a much great coverage circle to fill the frame.

1.66:1 or 3 × 2

Figure 6.18 1.66:1.

1.66:1 was the native aspect ration of super 16mm film, and served as the standard TV and theatrical aspect ratio in many European countries. Up until the introduction of 16 × 9 HD in the United States, the 1.66:1 ratio served as a compromise aspect ratio between the 1.85:1 theatrical exhibition ratio and the 1.33:1 ratio used for standard definition television. When cinema attendance dropped, Hollywood began to create widescreen aspect ratios such as 1.85:1 and 2.39:1 in order to differentiate the cinema experience from television.

1.85:1

Figure 6.19 1.85:1.

Introduced by Universal Pictures in 1953, 1.85:1 became the most popular 35mm widescreen standard for theatrical film. Wider than 1.33 or 1.66, but not quite as wide as anamorphic 2.39, it could be captured on any 4-perf camera to give a more widescreen experience. The format projects 3 film perforations ("perfs") high by the full width of 35mm Academy aperture, out of a 4-perf frame.

In order to save money, many cameras were modified to shoot 1:85 in a 3-perf mode to save 25%

phones when the phone is reoriented. As content plays and the user rotates the device, the composition switches between portrait and landscape modes, as if cutting between wide shots and closeups. The image is automatically reframed to fill the screen, (discarding picture at the sides of the frame in portrait mode) and users can choose between two framings of the content. Designed for a generation that watches content on mobile devices, this also allows creators to use the different orientations for interactive content.

Figure 6.28 16 × 9 to 9 x 16 switchable framings.

Film Camera Aperture Sizes and Digital Cinema Sensor Sizes

Film aperture and sensor sizes have historically varied widely, affecting many of the factors of cinematography. As we have already seen, sensor size affects the resulting image in many ways. Smaller sensors are more prone to noise and Nyquist issues, while larger sensors become more expensive. Super 35mm sensors have become the norm for many reasons, partly because we have been working in that format for such a long time that there is a huge supply of great lenses, and partly because over the history of cinema we have come to agree that the format is generally very pleasing to look at. It is important for the cinematographer to acquaint him or herself with the wide variety of sensor sizes available today:

Digital sensors range in size closely relative to film formats, so familiarity with both formats creates a vocabulary of visual communication

Table 6.1 Digital cinema sensor sizes

Cinema Sensor Sizes		
Camera	Sensor Size in mm	Lens Type
2/3" B4 mount broadcast	8.8 × 6.6 mm	B4 mount
Super 16mm	12.52 × 7.41	Super 16mm
Academy 35 mm	22 × 16 mm	Academy 35mm
Sony FS5, FS7, F35	23.6 × 13.3	Super 35mm
Panasonic Varicam PURE / 35 / LT	23.6 × 13.3 mm	Super 35mm
ARRI Alexa 4 x 3	23.8 × 17.8 mm	Super 35mm
Canon C200, C300MkII, C500MkII, C700	26.2 × 13.8 mm	Super 35mm
ARRI Alexa 16x9, Amira	24.8 × 13.4 mm	Super 35mm
Sony F55, F5, FS700	24 × 12.7 mm	Super 35mm
Sony F65	24.7 × 13.1 mm	Super 35mm
Super 35 mm	24.89 × 18.66mm	Super 35mm
Blackmagic URSA Mini Pro 4.6 / G2	25.34 × 14.25mm	Super 35mm
RED Mysterium X 5K	27.7 × 14.6mm	Super 35mm
Phantom Flex 4K	27.7 × 15.5mm	Super 35mm
ARRI Alexa Open Gate	28.17 × 18.13 mm	Super 35mm
RED Dragon 6K	30.7 × 15.8mm	Super 35mm
Sony Venice	36 × 24mm	Full Frame (FF)
ARRI Alexa LF Open Gate	36.7 × 25.54 mm	Full Frame (FF)
VistaVision	37.72 × 24.92mm	Full Frame (FF)
Canon C700	38.1 × 20.1mm	Full Frame (FF)
Panavision Millenium DXL2	40.96 × 21.60 mm	Full Frame (FF)
RED Dragon / Monstro 8K / Ranger 8K	40.96 × 21.60 mm	Full Frame (FF)
Sony A7, Canon 5D	36 × 24mm	Full Frame (FF)
Phantom 65	51.2 × 28.8 mm	65mm LF
65mm 5 perf	52.51 × 23.07mm	65mm LF
ARRI Alexa 65	54.12 × 25.59 mm	65mm LF
70mm Imax 15 perf	70.41 × 52.62 mm	IMAX

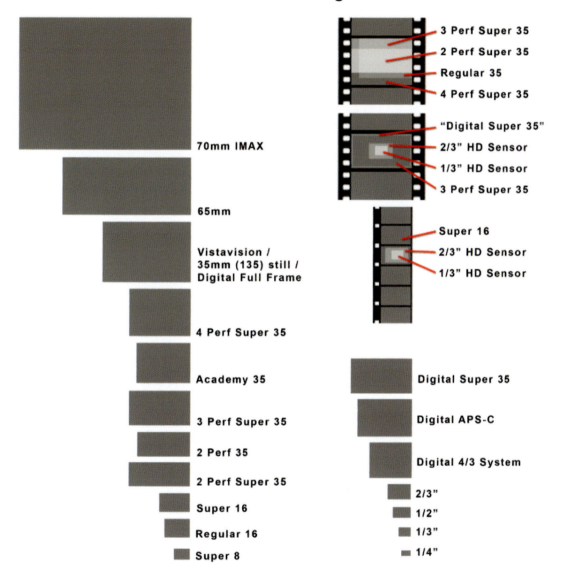

© Bennett Cain 2009

Figure 6.29 Film camera aperture sizes compared to digital sensor sizes.

between cinematographers, directors, producers, and their audiences.

The aspect ratio of an image describes the proportional relationship between its width and its height. It is commonly expressed as two numbers separated by a colon, as in 16:9 or 2.39:1. For an "x-to-y" or "x-by-y" aspect ratio, no matter how big or small the image is, if the width is divided into x units of equal length and the height is measured using this same length unit, the height will be measured to be y units. Professional acquisition and display is always measured in square pixels. Some older HD cameras and prosumer devices acquire and store images in non-square pixel formats but we can ignore those cases for our purpose.

Below is a table of pixel values for most of the common aspect ratios in use for cinema and television, with pixel dimensions. The first set of values ignores display constraints and simply defines an aspect ratio in pixel numbers. The second table is display referred and defines aspect ratios as constrained by display devices. The table is color coded to indicate where letter boxing or pillar boxing and image is required to display it at the highest possible resolution for the display device aspect ratio while still viewing the entire composition.

Table 6.2 Digital aspect ratio resolutions

Aspect Ratio	Pixel Resolution Independent of Container Aspect Ratio					
	HD	2K	UHD	4K	8K UHD	8K
1.33 (4:3)	1920×1440	2048 × 1536	3840 × 2880	4096 × 3072	7680 × 5760	8192 × 6144
1.66 (5:3)	1920 × 1152	2048 × 1229	3840 × 2304	4096 × 2458	7680 × 4608	8192 × 4915
1.78 (16:9)	1920 × 1080	2048 × 1152	3840 × 2160	4096 × 2304	7680 × 4320	8192 × 4608
1.85	1920 × 1038	2048 × 1107	3840 × 2076	4096 × 2214	7680 × 4151	8192 × 4428
1.90	1920 × 1011	2048 × 1078	3840 × 2021	4096 × 2160	7680 × 4042	8192 × 4320
2.00	1920 × 960	2048 × 1024	3840 × 1920	4096 × 2048	7680 × 3840	8192 × 4096
2.35	1920 × 817	2048 × 871	3840 × 1634	4096 × 1743	7680 × 3268	8192 × 3486
2.37 (64:27)	1920 × 810	2048 × 864	3840 × 1620	4096 × 1728	7680 × 3240	8192 × 3456
2.39	1920 × 803	2048 × 858	3840 × 1607	4096 × 1714	7680 × 3213	8192 × 3428
2.40 (Blu-Ray Scope)	1920 × 800	2048 × 853	3840 × 1600	4096 × 1707	7680 × 3200	8192 × 3413
2.44	1920 × 787	2048 × 839	3840 × 1574	4096 × 1679	7680 × 3148	8192 × 3357
	Pixel Resolution Constrained by Defined Aspect Ratio Container					
Aspect Ratio	HD	2K Cinema	UHD	4K Cinema	8K UHD	8K Cinema
1.33 (4:3) Pillar Boxed	1440 × 1080	1440 × 1080	2880 × 2160	2880 × 2160	5760 × 4320	5760 × 4320
1.66 (5:3) Pillar Boxed	1800 × 1080	1800 × 1080	3600 × 2160	3600 × 2160	7200 × 4320	7200 × 4320
1.78 (16:9)	1920 × 1080	1920 × 1080	3840 × 2160	3840 × 2160	7680 × 4320	7680 × 4320
1.85 Letter Boxed	1920 × 1038	1998 × 1107	3840 × 2076	3996 × 2160	7680 × 4151	7992 × 4320
1.90 Letter Boxed	1920 × 1011	2048 × 1078	3840 × 2021	4096 × 2156	7680 × 4042	8192 × 4312
2.00 Letter Boxed	1920 × 960	2048 × 1024	3840 × 1920	4096 × 2048	7680 × 3840	8192 × 4096
2.35 Letter Boxed	1920 × 817	2048 × 871	3840 × 1634	4096 × 1743	7680 × 3268	8192 × 3486
2.37 (64:27) Letter Boxed	1920 × 810	2048 × 864	3840 × 1620	4096 × 1728	7680 × 3240	8192 × 3456
2.39	1920 × 803	2048 × 858	3840 × 1607	4096 × 1714	7680 × 3213	8192 × 3428
2.40 (Blu-Ray Scope) Letter Boxed	1920 × 800	2048 × 853	3840 × 1600	4096 × 1707	7680 × 3200	8192 × 3413
2.44 Letter Boxed	1920 × 787	2048 × 839	3840 × 1574	4096 × 1679	7680 × 3148	8192 × 3357

Aspect Ratio	Pixel Resolution Constrained by DCI Spec Aspect Ratio Container	
	2K DCP	4K DCP
1.78 (16:9)	1920 × 1080	3840 × 2160
1.85	1998 × 1080	3996 × 2160
2.39	2048 × 858	4096 × 1716
Full Container	2048 × 1080	4096 × 2160
Pillar Boxed for Container		
Letter Boxed for Container		

High Dynamic Range (HDR) and Wide Color Gamut (WCG) Video

High dynamic range (HDR) refers to the newly extended luminance and contrast range of television displays, to the maximum and minimum amount of light the television display is capable of producing. High dynamic range video displays brighter whites, darker blacks, and more vivid colors that more closely resemble human visual perception. The enhancement of viewing experience that HDR brings is appreciable under any viewing condition. High dynamic range systems can display large luminance variations from very dark values of 0.00005 cd/m² (candelas per meter squared, otherwise referred to as "nits") to very bright values greater than 1000 cd/m². Standard dynamic range (SDR) television systems can display luminance values in a range from approximately 0.0005 to 100 cd/m².

Wide color gamut (WCG) refers to the level of saturation and number of colors that a TV or monitor can reproduce. Wide color gamut describes a capability of displaying images with a wider range of colors than have been supported by conventional systems. Video systems up to now have been based on Rec 709 color, which can only reproduce about a third of all CIE visible chromaticity values.

SMPTE ST2084 standardizes an electro-optical transfer function (EOTF) for HDR that was developed by Dolby Laboratories to define the process of Dolby Vision perceptual quantization (PQ) high dynamic range encoding. ST 2084 perceptual quantization is the EOTF or signal encoding function that Dolby Vision is based on. The perceptual quantizer function is license-free

for users under a RANZ (reasonable and non-discriminatory) declared for both SMPTE and ITU.

SMPTE standard ST2086 defines a static metadata specification that does not change local screen brightness during playback of video content, and SMPTE standard ST2094 defines content-dependent dynamic local screen brightness metadata. SMPTE ST2086 static metadata is supported by HDMI 2.0a, and is included in HDR content to convey the color volume and luminance of the content. These are described by the chromaticity of the red, green, and blue display primaries and by the white point of the mastering display, its black level, and its peak luminance level. ST 2086 specifies the mastering (reference/grading) display color volume using (*only*) the maximum and minimum luminance, primaries (xy-chromaticities), and white point (xy-chromaticity).

ST2086 carries the MaxCLL (maximum content light level) from player to display. MaxCLL level expressed in cd/m² describes the luminance of the brightest pixel in the content. ST2086 also conveys the MaxFALL (maximum frame-average light level), which describes the average luminance of all pixels in each frame. The MaxFALL (also expressed in cd/m²) level is the maximum value of frame-average max RGB for all frames in the content. CTA 861-G defines the calculation of the content light level metadata items: MaxCLL and MaxFALL. The Blu-ray Disc Association (BDA) originally defined this in the 2012–2013 time frame. The BDA disappeared when most of its membership moved to the UHD Alliance (UHDA). The definition was standardized by the CTA (formerly CEA, the CES organizer).

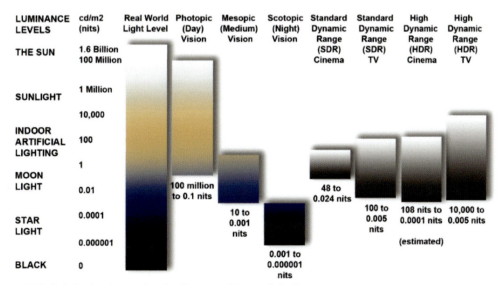

Figure 6.30 Relative luminance levels of human vision and displays.

The CTA and ITU-R plus H.265 documents are available freely online, searchable on Google.

ITU-R Rec BT.2020 defines a new television specification wide gamut color space, with a resolution of 3840 × 2160, an EOTF of SMPTE ST2084 and peak luminance levels of (either) more than 1,000 nits, black level less than 0.05 nits, (or) a peak luminance more than 540 nits and black level of less than 0.0005 nits for a new UHDTV system. ITU-R BT.2020 specifies the color primaries, white point, for UHD, the EOTF is ITU-R BT.1886 same as 709 (approximately gamma = 2.4). ITU-R BT.2100 is the overall HDR specification for TV broadcast. The specification includes both EOTF of PQ and HLG. The conversion between PQ and HLG is given in ITU-R BT.2390.

Hybrid Log Gamma (HLG)

Hybrid Log Gamma ITU.BT2100 was jointly developed as a high dynamic range broadcast standard by the BBC and NHK. HLG is an open source royalty-free standard which specifies system parameters essential for extended image dynamic range in television broadcast including system colorimetry, signal format, and digital representation. Hybrid Log Gamma specifies a nominal peak luminance of 1,000 nits and a system gamma value that can be adjusted depending on background luminance.

HDR10 and HDR10+

HDR10 is an open source standard for high dynamic range video broadcast and display. Every TV that is HDR-capable is compatible with HDR10 – it is the minimum HDR specification. HDR10 is a de facto standard, i.e. there is not a specification document that defines the system. Back in the 2012–2013 time frame, BDA specified that the next gen UHD Blu-ray "shall be in BT.2020 primaries/white-point system, signal encoded in PQ while compressed in the H.265/HEVC Main 10 profile (thus 10-bit), w/ SMPTE ST 2086 mastering display color volume and content light level (MaxCLL, MaxFALL) metadata." HDR10 is supported by a wide variety of companies, which include monitor and TV manufacturers such as Dell, LG, Samsung, Sharp, VU, SONY, SONY Interactive Entertainment, Vizio, Microsoft, and Apple. HDR10 employs wide-gamut Rec 2020 color space, a bit depth of 10 bits, and the SMPTE ST 2084 (PQ) transfer function. It also uses SMPTE ST 2086 mastering display color volume static metadata to send color calibration data of the mastering display,

such as MaxFALL and MaxCLL as static values, encoded as SEI messages within the video stream. HDR10+ is Samsung's extension of the HDR10 system to include dynamic (content dependent) color mapping metadata based on SMPTE ST 2094-40 (dynamic metadata for Color Volume Transform Application #4).

The practical difference between HDR10 and HDR10+ is in the additional picture brightness data that gets transmitted along with an HDR movie or TV show that controls brightness and contrast on a scene to scene basis. This dynamic metadata tells a TV or monitor how to modulate high dynamic range content. HDR10 has static metadata, one setting for the entire program. HDR10+ and Dolby Vision incorporate dynamic scene to scene, shot to shot metadata.

Dolby Vision Perceptual Quantization (PQ)

Dolby Vision PQ perceptual quantization (SMPTE ST 2084) is a standard that uses the SMPTE 2084 electro-optical transfer function (EOTF). PQ ranges of 1,000, 2,000, and 4,000 nits are specified for mastering and reference viewing, and a 10,000 nit numerical code range is defined to allow system overhead range to achieve color saturation at 1,000 to 2,000 to 4,000 nit levels. Dolby Vision employs dynamic metadata which controls how HDR looks from scene to scene, or even on a frame to frame basis. This extra level of control lets film makers decide how a movie should look on your TV. Dolby Vision is a brand name for an overarching ecosystem for content production to distribution vertically, and for mobile to games to cable to OTA/OTT horizontally. The Dolby internal system is not bit-depth dependent. For example, the calculations in SDR do not need to be 8-bit, or HDR 10-bit.

Table 6.3 HDR code values vs. brightness levels

Brightness	Video	SMPTE 2084-PQ			HLG
cd/m² (nits)	WFM %	10-bit Legal Range Code Value	10-bit Full Range Code Value	12-bit Code Value	10-bit Legal Range Code Value
0	0	64	0	0	64
0.078	5.6	113	55	220	76
0.625	12.7	176	129	516	99
5	24.8	281	254	1016	162
20	35.7	377	366	1464	260
40	41.9	431	429	1716	341
80	48.6	490	497	1988	456
100	50.8	509	520	2080	502

Brightness	Video	SMPTE 2084-PQ			HLG
cd/m² (nits)	WFM %	10-bit Legal Range Code Value	10-bit Full Range Code Value	12-bit Code Value	10-bit Legal Range Code Value
640	70.3	680	720	2880	838
1000	75.2	723	769	3076	911
1200	77.2	740	790	3160	940
2000	87.6	788	847	3388	
4000	90.3	855	924	3696	
10000	100	940	1023	4092	

Wide Color Gamut: ITU-R Rec 2020

ITU-R recommendation BT.2020 specifies a new ultra high definition television (UHDTV) system that includes both standard dynamic range and wide color gamut display capability, ultra high (3840 × 2160) definition, a wide variety of picture resolutions, frame rates, bit depths, color primaries, chroma samplings, and an opto-electrical transfer function. It is expanded in several ways by Rec BT.2100. The Rec 2020 (UHDTV/UHD-1/UHD-2) color space can reproduce colors that cannot be shown in Rec 709 color space, and Rec 2020 color space covers about 75% of the CIE human visible spectrum.

Wide color gamut enables more vivid hues and color saturation levels. To produce a wider color gamut, a display needs to employ RGB primary colors further out toward the CIE chromaticity spectrum locus. Rec 2020 color primaries are pure, monochromatic, 100% saturated colors, created by light energy that is concentrated at a single wavelength.

The current color gamut standard for HDTV is specified by ITU-R Rec. BT.709. The DCI P3 color gamut that is currently specified for digital cinema presentation is significantly larger than the Rec 709 HDTV gamut. Digital cinema packages (DCPs) are encoded in gamma 2.6, so the playback projection decodes a DCP at a gamma of 2.6.

ITU-R Rec BT.2020, the new color space specification for the latest UHDTV system for HDR, has more pure and saturated RGB primary colors and is larger still. BT.2020 also covers almost all of Pointer's gamut leaving very few real-world colors that cannot be displayed in the BT.2020 color space. BT.2020 is also a sufficiently large color space to allow television broadcast to display saturated colors like neon lights, emissive source lights, and highly saturated CGI images.

History and High Dynamic Range Imaging

Log encoding has made high dynamic range acquisition possible, both on film and from digital capture. Film has had the ability to capture high dynamic range for decades. Film negative can capture scene tones of 13 to 14 stops. To help understand high dynamic range capture, let's spot meter a real day scene.

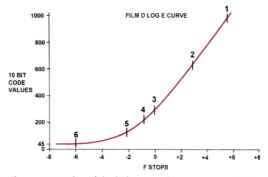

Figure 6.32 Exposure value measurements of daylight scene luminance.

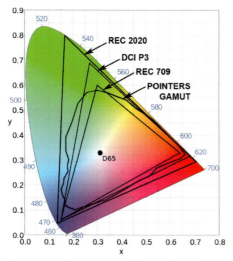

Figure 6.31 Rec 709, DCI P3, and Rec 2020 UHDTV color spaces compared.

Figure 6.33 Plot of daylight scene luminance vs. 10-bit code values.

Let's spot meter a real night scene.

Figure 6.34 Exposure value measurements of night scene luminance.

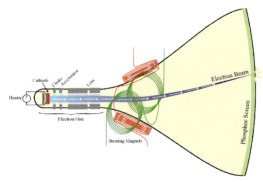

Figure 6.36 CRT display structure.

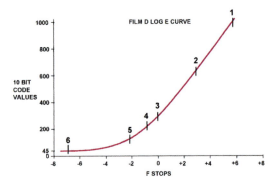

Figure 6.35 Plot of night scene luminance vs. 10-bit code values.

Standard dynamic range display device imaging parameters for TVs, monitors, and cinema projection have historically constrained the display of images captured. Film negative has long been capable of capturing far more dynamic range than theatrical projection could show. Standard dynamic range technology could only display a limited range of scene tones using screen brightness of up to 14 foot lamberts (48 nits) for projection (both film print and digital cinema) at contrast ratios between 2000:1 and 4000:1.

Standard dynamic range monitors and televisions could display up to 100 nits, and up to 250 nits when overdriven, but excessive SDR display brightness significantly lifts black and reduces overall contrast, both to the detriment of the viewing experience.

Standard dynamic range display performance was originally born of cathode ray tube (CRT) display technology. A CRT is a vacuum tube that fires electrons at a phosphorus-covered screen area in order to display images. By modulating and magnetically deflecting the electron beam onto the screen in a fixed pattern called a raster,

the entire front area of the tube is scanned repetitively and systematically. Controlling the intensity of each of the three additive primary colors (red, green, and blue) beams, produces color images on the screen. Needless to say, the limitations of this technology were many and varied.

New display technology is not limited by the traditional limitations of color and brightness that were characteristic of CRT displays. The development of light emitting diode (LED) and subsequently organic light emitting diode (OLED) technologies has revolutionized the capabilities of modern displays. An OLED is a solid-state device consisting of a thin, carbon-based semiconductor layer that emits light when electricity is applied by adjacent electrodes. In order for light to escape from the device, at least one of the electrodes must be transparent. The intensity of the light emitted is controlled by the amount of electric current applied by the electrodes, and the light's color is determined by the type of emissive material used. To create white light, most OLED devices use red, green, and blue emitters that can be arranged in several configurations.

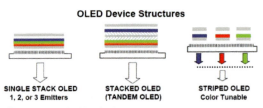

Figure 6.37 OLED device structures.

New generation monitors (and very soon, digital projectors) are engineered to display high dynamic range images at much brighter screen luminance, color saturation, and contrast levels than SDR displays. Quantum dot red and green nanocrystals, which emit light at very narrow bandwidths when excited by blue LED photon energy, are now beyond DCI-P3 color space and are getting narrower and more saturated as the technology matures. HDR display levels reach up to 1,000 nits on SONY and Canon HDR monitors and on some consumer television sets. HDR can be viewed at up to 2,000 and even 4,000 nits on specialized Dolby monitors.

Laser light sources in Dolby Cinema and IMAX Laser Cinema projection systems produce narrow bandwidth, highly saturated colors and are getting very close to accurately reproducing the BT.2020 color gamut currently at up to 108 nits (32 ft./lamberts) in Dolby vision digital cinemas.

Higher dynamic range display requires the use of a new electro-optical transfer function (EOTF) encoding that more closely resembles the log and power functions that are used in digital cinema than a gamma function from the days of video encoding.

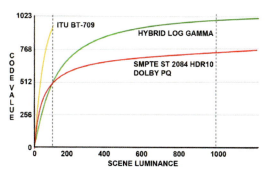

Figure 6.38 HDR electro optical transfer functions.

Tips for Shooting for HDR

Important factors to understand in capturing high dynamic range images:

- White balance every scene for best high dynamic range.
- Use an on set HDR display and a wave form monitor that is HDR capable.
- Expose carefully to preserve and protect your highlights and shadows, protecting from +6 stops to -6 stops.
- Record using a SONY S-log 2, S-log 3, RED Log3G10, or ARRI log C or the best quality log encoding for the camera you are using.
- Record uncompressed or the least possible compressed signal possible.
- If you must record a compressed signal, record 4:4:4:4, ProRes XQ, or ProRes HQ, RGB.

Day Exterior Shooting

Figure 6.39 Bright puffy clouds can be creatively controlled (courtesy of Bill Tondreau).

Day exterior skies with bright puffy clouds can be creatively controlled, but only if exposed below clipping for the sensor. Log encoding enables preservation of highlight details when day exteriors are correctly exposed.

Interiors with Windows

Figure 6.40 Interiors with windows must be carefully controlled.

In scenes that see views outside windows and doors, we now have a new ability to control brightness, but exercise caution. HDR finish may reveal detail outside over bright windows and window treatments that was never visible before. This situation can present an enormous range of light levels from T22 outside to T2 inside.

Low Light Scenes

Figure 6.41 Beauty in the dark areas of the frame.

Low light can also be great, and scenes without highlights are OK. In many HDR scenes the beauty happens well below 400 nits!

Shooting Backings

Figure 6.42 Shooting with backings.

Backings outside doors and windows must be controlled in contrast and highlights. In standard dynamic range and on film the rule of thumb was if you lit a backing so that it is *almost* about to *burst into flames* it might be bright enough! While that might no longer be true, badly lit or under lit backings (especially old hand-painted backings) shot in high dynamic range reveal themselves very quickly. Audiences today are too sophisticated to be fooled with badly lit or badly painted backings outside doors and windows. A calibrated HDR monitor on set will quickly reveal any issues, and modern backings like Rosco Softdrop backings are much more convincing than old hand-painted backings.[1]

Makeup in HDR

Figure 6.43 Makeup must be blended more carefully (credit: Eamon Shannon, Tim Lott, Ron Vidor, Tia Goossen, and Kohanna Kay).

Other HDR Shooting Concerns

Figure 6.44 Hide cables, tape marks, stands, and gear.

Things we counted on hiding in the dark – cables, sandbags, C-stand feet, can show up more visibly in HDR. Reflections in windows, glass, car doors, and other reflective materials also become more visible, and therefore more difficult to remove from footage in post.

Important Lens Criteria for Shooting HDR: Modulation Transfer Function (MTF)

If you are trying to achieve a look with the highest dynamic range possible, remember that dynamic range begins at the lens. A low contrast lens will prove ill-suited to rendering wider dynamic range. Lens flares, aberrations, and light transmission characteristics are also different in HDR. Newer, sharper, and more contrasty lenses with modern coatings are needed if the story you are telling requires a more HDR look. To make the most of HDR, an understanding of MTF in optics is important.

Figure 6.45 Modulation transfer function.

MTF refers to the measurement of how a lens transfers scene contrast to an imager. The scene being photographed modulates in frequency and contrast, the lens attempts to accurately transfer that information to the sensor, but the lens is a real physical object made out of glass, which has a refractive index. The degree to which the lens succeeds in transferring scene contrast to the sensor is expressed as a percentage of the original scene contrast. The ratio of the resulting reduction in contrast from the original scene contrast

Higher Brightness Display Increases the Effect of 24/25p Judder

HDR high contrast scene elements shot at 24 fps are vastly more prone to strobing on screen at higher light levels. 24 fps judder and flicker are MORE PRONOUNCED in HDR, shutter speed, and angle and strobing/judder are exacerbated with higher dynamic range display. Higher frame rate capture and display lessens the effects of 24/25p judder, and new higher acquisition frame rates will likely be necessary in the near future.

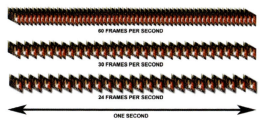

60 FRAMES PER SECOND

30 FRAMES PER SECOND

24 FRAMES PER SECOND

ONE SECOND

Figure 6.46 HDR will eventually drive higher frame rates.

Finishing in Dolby Vision and HDR

Dolby Vision is Dolby's branded implementation of their perceptual quantization electro-optical transfer curve (EOTF) content encoding in combination with dynamic metadata delivery. Dolby Vision supports either Rec 2020 or DCI-P3 primaries, color spaces, and white points, and 12 bits per color channel for both home and theatrical exhibition. Television and monitor manufacturers incorporating Dolby's technology pay a licensing fee. Dolby's content mapping process is now incorporated in most high-end finishing software to allow creation of multiple nit level target versions ranging from 100, to 600, 1,000, 2,000, 4,000, and 10,000 nits. The 10,000 nits range provides overhead for mastering saturated colors at very high brightness, 1,000 nits output is becoming fairly common, but most consumer HDR TVs are only capable of between 400 and 750 nits, with only a couple of models exceeding 1,000 nits at time of publishing.

Color grading can be viewed on a Dolby PRM-4220 monitor, a SONY BVM X-300 monitor, or a Canon DP-V3120 monitor. Scene to scene and shot to shot dynamic metadata is generated by the colorist during a trim pass on Dolby Vision HDR grade; when complete, the metadata is output as a sidecar XML file. This metadata allows scene to scene and shot to shot HDR to be properly decoded and displayed as film makers intended them on consumer televisions. Additionally, the metadata instructs displays how to interpolate 10-bit SDR video and 12-bit HDR video at between 100 nit SDR baseline and other luminance values up to the peak luminance of the master source file. A Dolby Vision TV with 400, 600, or 1,000 nits will display the video content correctly using the metadata to "map" to the performance characteristics of the viewer's television.

There is much discussion about whether to grade the SDR deliverables first, or the HDR deliverables. I prefer to do the HDR and SDR grades in parallel when possible, but others prefer to do the HDR grade first and then do an SDR trim, re-grading for the areas of the picture that exceed 100 nits and matching it as closely as possible to the HDR grade. Unfortunately, the SDR version can sometimes seem a disappointment after doing the HDR grade.

Working at higher bit depth means using new tools and techniques. Your high dynamic range project will benefit from higher bit depth workflows, so plan your workflow carefully. Don't let transcoding or resampling decimate your precious data.

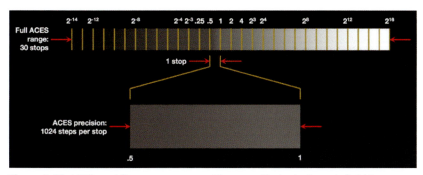

Figure 6.47 ACES workflows can preserve 30 stops of latitude through finishing.

High dynamic range imaging demands a sufficient Rec 2020 color space and 16-bit floating point workflow. BT Rec 709 is the default broadcast color space. Take care not to resample Rec 2020 images to Rec 709. Down samples rendered to smaller color spaces or to lower bit depth file sizes are not reversible. An ACES workflow will preserve maximum dynamic range and color in your images through finishing. An ACES Open EXR 16-bit half-float encoding workflow provides for 30 stops of range at a precision of 1,024 steps per stop of light.

Note

1. For more on using Rosco Softdrop backings follow these links: www.rosco.com/spectrum/index. php/2015/07/softdrop-the-easiest-backdrop-ever/; www.youtube.com/watch?v=muH_k-IV4Xk; www.youtube.com/watch?v=0NnOU0lYr4Y; www.youtube.com/watch?v=vGkBMC8niHA; www. youtube.com/watch?v=CM3ZmuGWIJ0; www.youtube.com/watch?v=uHnAbiitx1w.

Chapter 7

Lenses

Figure 7.1 Mike Todd reflected in his Todd AO 12.7mm "Bug-Eye" lens (1955).

I am going to begin on the subject of lenses before I talk about cameras, because *lenses are just as important as cameras*! A camera is a box to hold a sensor in the dark. Yes, the quality of the sensor makes a *big* difference, but when all we had to make movies with was film, the only *real* difference between one camera system and another was the lens that captured the image. Good lenses don't happen accidentally, they are the result of well-intentioned and skilled design, attention to detail in the formulation and manufacture of glass, enormous research and development of coatings, and high precision in mounting and alignment. There is no free lunch. An old still lens bought on eBay will *never* deliver the crisp, sharp results that a Panavision Primo 70, or a ZEISS Signature Prime, or a Cooke, or a Leica Summicron or Fujinon or Schneider or Canon or any well designed modern lens will deliver, but if you want an interesting creative period or artistic "look" then a very old set of Baltar lenses might be just the sort of thing you are looking for!

Creative intent might compel a cinematographer to use lenses that have character or flares or any number of inherent flaws to help tell a story, and that's okay, as long as you have agreement with your director and your producers. Many projects are made with vintage or specialty lenses to achieve a look, but many projects require a less experimental, more commercial approach. An informed cinematographer can make lens choices from among many types and brands, so do the homework. A solid understanding of lens parameters such as chromatic aberration, contrast, distortion, the relationship between center and edge behavior, differences between high and normal speed lenses, coatings, design, anamorphic squeeze factors all give cinematographers a basis for choosing the right lenses for achieving a "look." Understanding the importance of holding certain lens parameters as constant values from lens to lens in a set and over the course of a production is very important for achieving a consistent image style and look.

When you are prepping to shoot your project, no matter what the creative intent, begin by selecting the *best lenses you can afford*! No matter what your creative intent is, putting a bad lens on the best camera is going to make the camera look bad. Putting a high-quality lens on a lesser camera will make the lesser quality camera look as good as it can look. There are vast numbers of high quality lenses for all sizes of sensors available at rental houses that can be used for digital filmmaking. With the advent of computer aided design, modern glass recipes, aspheric elements, and modern coatings, lens design has made enormous strides in the last 30 years.

Anamorphic vs. Spherical

Two types of lenses are typically used in production: spherical and anamorphic. Spherical lenses are more commonly used. Spherical lenses project images onto the sensor without affecting their aspect ratio. Anamorphic lenses, on the other hand, capture an image that is compressed along the horizontal dimension, and the images they produce require subsequent stretching in post-production in order to be properly displayed.

Figure 7.2 75mm Bausch and Lomb Cinemascope Prime Lens (1955).

The decision to use anamorphic lenses is usually creatively motivated, but it is a decision that can only be taken with consultation and consent of the director, producers, and studio. It is a decision that implies that the finished product will be exhibited in a widescreen aspect ratio, which will dictate that viewers will see the finished product as a letterboxed image.

Anamorphic lenses were originally designed so that widescreen imagery could utilize the entire frame area of an Academy 4 perf 35mm film, but today, anamorphic squeeze ratio is no longer tied to a specific display aspect ratio. One of the important innovations of ARRI's ALEXA camera was a 4 × 3 sensor mode specifically designed to accommodate 2x squeeze anamorphic lenses, with a sensor area similar to 35mm film. Some anamorphic lenses employ other squeeze ratios to produce widescreen images from 1.78:1 sensors, with a narrower relative angle of view than traditional anamorphic.

Film makers are attracted to anamorphic lenses for a number of reasons. Lens flares can appear as blue horizontal or vertical streaks which span the entire frame, and out of focus objects and highlights are vertically elongated as opposed to circular. Anamorphic focus shift changes objects in frame to and from an oval to a circle; some film makers find this artifact is very cinematic. Anamorphic and spherical lenses technically exhibit the same depth of field, but in practice cinematographers must use longer focal lengths with anamorphic in order to capture the same horizontal angle of view. For the same subject magnification, anamorphic lenses produce a

shallower, more cinematic depth of field. Zoom lenses with rear anamorphs do not exhibit the same bokehs as lenses with front anamorphs, and their depth of field characteristics are closer to those of spherical lenses.

Distinctions that Go into Evaluating Lenses

Resolution

Resolution (for our purposes) is defined as the ability of an imaging system to resolve detail in the object that is being imaged. Resolution is a measure for the smallest spatial detail an imaging system can resolve. The resolution of the human eye is referred to as "visual acuity." The primary metric of resolution in imaging is MTF. It is important to distinguish between sharpness and resolution. Sharpness is a perceived quality which is a combination of the measurable properties of resolution and contrast. The perception of sharpness depends, to a lesser degree, on the resolution and more on the micro contrast in the image, which is called acutance. A high-resolution image with low contrast may look less *sharp* than a low-resolution image with high contrast. This is because our human perception pays more attention to contrast at certain line pairs per mm than others.

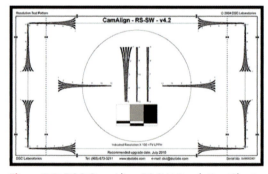

Figure 7.3 DSC Cam Align RS SW Resolution Chart.

The resolving power of a lens is measured by its ability to differentiate two lines or points in an object. The greater the resolving power, the smaller the minimum distance between two lines or points that can still be distinguished. Optics design, mechanical design, coatings, and glass quality all contribute to the overall resolution of a lens, and digital cinema has among the most demanding design of criteria anywhere. While film projection long ago settled into an accepted quality and resolution level, digital cinematography now continues to increase in resolution on an almost daily basis!

Lenses for cinematography are designed to give their best results at an optimized stop, usually somewhere between T2.8 and T5.6 depending on the brand and manufacture philosophy. Lens resolution performance can decrease slightly at stops above or below the optimized stop, and at very deeps tops such as T16 or T22 diffraction can occur, greatly decreasing the resolution and performance quality of a lens.

f-Stop/T-Stop

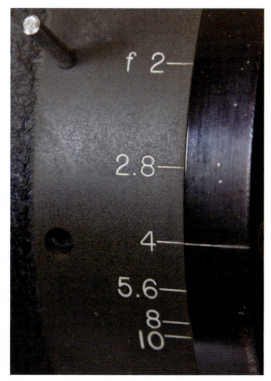

Figure 7.4 *f*-stops.

The mathematical *f*-number (*N*) of a lens is the ratio of its focal length (*f*) divided by the diameter of the aperture (*D*). For example, if a lens focal length *f* is 100mm and its entrance pupil diameter *D* is 50mm, the *f*-number of that lens is 2.

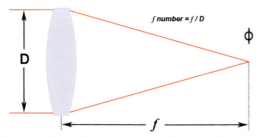

Figure 7.5 Formula for determining *f*-number of a lens.

From the calculation of the wide open *f*-number of a lens, we can begin to mark the scale of *f*-stops to stop down on a lens. For the sake of calculation, the aperture of a lens is considered a circle. The area (*A*) enclosed by a circle of radius (*r*) is πr^2. The Greek letter π represents a constant, approximately 3.14159, which is the ratio of the circumference of a circle to its diameter.

$$A = \pi r^2$$

When a lens' aperture diameter increases by the square root of two, the surface area of the aperture circle is doubled, and the amount of light that hits the sensor is therefore doubled.

Figure 7.6 Single *f*-stop increments.

As the diameter of the aperture decreases in increments of the square root of 2, the amount of light reaching the sensor is halved. Therefore, the scale of *f*-stops or T-stops is expressed as a function of the square root of 2, in one stop increments.

Table 7.1 Actual *f*-stops expressed as a numerical function of the square root of 2

Aperture Value	Mathematical Formula	f Number (N)	Mathematical Value
0	$\sqrt{(2^0)}$	1	1
1	$\sqrt{(2^1)}$	1.4	1.414...
2	$\sqrt{(2^2)}$	2	2
3	$\sqrt{(2^3)}$	2.8	2.828...
4	$\sqrt{(2^4)}$	4	4.525...
5	$\sqrt{(2^5)}$	5.6	5.657...
6	$\sqrt{(2^6)}$	8	8
7	$\sqrt{(2^7)}$	11	11.31...
8	$\sqrt{(2^8)}$	16	16
9	$\sqrt{(2^9)}$	22	22.62...
10	$\sqrt{(2^{10})}$	32	32

(Continued)

Table 7.1 (Continued)

Aperture Value	Mathematical Formula	f Number (N)	Mathematical Value
11	$\sqrt{(2^{11})}$	45	45.25...
12	$\sqrt{(2^{12})}$	64	64
13	$\sqrt{(2^{13})}$	90	90.51...
14	$\sqrt{(2^{14})}$	128	128
15	$\sqrt{(2^{15})}$	180	181.02...
16	$\sqrt{(2^{16})}$	256	256

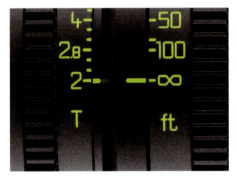

Figure 7.7 Cinema lenses are calibrated in T-stops.

Cinema lenses are rated in T-stops ("T" for "transmission"), instead of mathematical *f*-stops. T-stops are measured and calibrated on a photometer and are very accurate and reliable. Cinema lens sets are usually designed to have closely matching maximum wide open T-stop apertures so that the cinematographer doesn't have to be concerned about lighting to accommodate the slowest lens in the set or re-lighting when changing lenses. Depending on where the stop is set, the cinematographer can manipulate the optical performance characteristics of the lens; depth of field, aberration, bokeh, center to edge performance, contrast, vignetting, etc.

Contrast/MTF

Figure 7.8 The lens transfers scene contrast to the Imager.

Contrast is one of the factors that gives us a sense of sharpness in pictures. The metric of contrast in lenses is modulation transfer function, or MTF. Modulation transfer function in a lens depends on how much of the scene contrast the

lens can deliver to the sensor. The scene being photographed modulates in frequency and contrast. The lens attempts to accurately transfer that information to the sensor, the ratio of the resulting reduction in contrast to the original scene contrast is a mathematical function expressed as a percentage; that percentage is the metric of MTF.

Figure 7.9 Lenses are solid objects (Duncan Meeder, LeicaShop Henny Hoogeveen the Netherlands).

Lenses are solid objects made out of glass, which has a refractive index. That glass is held in place on metal surfaces and suspended inside a metal cylinder. There are many glass elements with many optical coatings, numerous mechanical surfaces, and many optical cements in any lens. Most of the glass lens blanks used in modern lens construction come from one of two glass manufacturers; either Ohara or Schott. The glass used in lens manufacture today is far more restricted in formulation than it was in the past. From the 1940s through the 1970s it was common to infuse some glass elements with radioactive Thorium 232 (advertised as "rare earth"), and lead (flint glass) to modify refractive index. EPA regulations have restricted the use of lead in glass, so glass manufacturers now use other additives such as cadmium, boric oxide, zinc oxide, phosphorus pentoxide, fluorite, and barium oxide.

The edges of the lens elements are painted and the interiors of the barrels are baffled and coated to reduce internal light dispersion. No lens will ever be able to achieve 100% transmittance, and there will never be a perfect lens.

The performance of any lens varies across the frame from center to corner. Most lenses perform well at the center and not as well towards the corners. Measuring only the center portion of a lens to assess its performance would be misleading, MTF graphs include multiple data points along the diagonal from the center of the frame to the corners of the frame. When optical technicians test MTF, they generally rotate the lens through 360 degrees, and the measured MTF at the edge of frame is taken as an average.

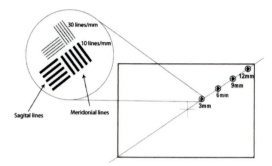

Figure 7.10 Measuring lens MTF.

Lens MTF is evaluated using square wave grid patterns, evenly spaced black and white lines at two sizes, 10 lines/mm, and 30 lines/mm. There are two groups of data plotted on an MTF chart, Sagital and Meridonial lines. The Sagital lines are the pairs of lines that run along a central diagonal line that passes through the middle of the lens from the bottom left-hand corner to the top right-hand corner. Meridonial lines are line pairs perpendicular to that central diagonal line. These square wave grid patterns are placed at regular increments to measure contrast and resolution, respectively. For MTF measurements, comparison of Sagittal and Meridonial data is useful in quantifying lenses that exhibit astigmatism.

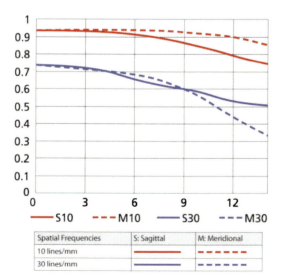

Spatial Frequencies	S: Sagittal	M: Meridonial
10 lines/mm		
30 lines/mm		

Figure 7.11 Sample MTF chart for an AF-S DX NIKKOR 35mm f/1.8G lens.

The vertical axis of an MTF chart plots the transmission of scene light that the lens transmits on a scale from 0 (or 0%) to a maximum value of 1 (or 100%). The horizontal axis measures the distance from the center of the lens to its furthest corner along the diagonal. So, the "0" in the lower left corner represents the center of the lens and the numbers along the lower axis represent the distance out towards the edge of the lens along the diagonal in millimeters.

The contrast of the Sagital and Meridonial line pairs at various points from the lens' center are read and plotted on a chart. This particular MTF chart includes measurements for the Sagital and Meridonial lines at both 10 lines per millimeter and 30 lines per millimeter. This produces a chart with 4 separate lines.

In general, the higher and flatter the lines the better. Higher lines indicate better contrast (10 lines/mm) or resolution (30 lines/mm) while a flatter (left to right) line shows that the optical performance is close to the same at the edge of the image compared to the center.

The red 10 line/mm (10 lines per millimeter) indicates the lens' ability to reproduce low spatial frequency or low resolution. This line indicates the lens' contrast values and the higher and straighter this line is the better. The higher the line appears the greater the amount of contrast the lens can reproduce. The blue 30 line/mm (30 lines per millimeter) indicates the lens' ability to reproduce higher spatial frequency or higher resolution; this line relates to the resolving power of the lens and again the higher the line the better. The line starts on the left of the chart which represents the center of the lens. As the line moves to the right it indicates the edge of the lens, so you can see how the contrast and sharpness of the lens decreases from the center to the edge of the image.[1]

Focal Length and Field of View

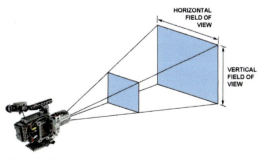

Figure 7.12 The lens sees a frustum view.

Lenses see a frustum view of the world. A frustum is like a pyramid lying on its side with the tip clipped off. Everything between the lens and the furthest plane in the field of view is the viewing area. The exact shape of the frustrum varies depending on what focal length of lens (wide-angle, normal or telephoto) is being used, and on the aspect ratio of the sensor.

Lens Types

Prime lenses are lenses of a fixed focal length. Zoom lenses cover a range of focal lengths using movable elements within the barrel of the lens assembly. In cinema usage, a zoom lens must be parfocal, that is, it must stay in focus as the focal length is changed. A normal lens is a lens with a focal length close to the diagonal size of the film or sensor format. A normal lens generally magnifies the image the same amount as the human eye, and produces field of view that looks "normal" to a human observer. A wide-angle lens is a lens that reproduces perspective wider than a normal lens. A wide-angle lens with a field of view greater than 90 degrees is considered an ultra-wide-angle lens. A Fisheye Lens is an extremely wide-angle lens with a strongly convex front element, and which exhibits strong barrel distortion. Long lenses and telephoto lenses have a focal length greater than the diagonal of the film frame or sensor.

Anamorphic Lenses employ optical elements that squeeze the image in the horizontal dimension (by a variety of different ratios) to produce widescreen images with a different ratio of height to width than that of the sensor or film plane.

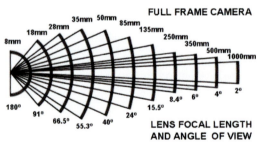

Figure 7.13 Full frame camera lens angles and fields of view.

For the purposes of this book, it is no longer practical to include field of view tables for cameras and lenses. If extended to include every lens available on every current modern camera sensor, the tables alone would encompass hundreds of pages. Detailed format coverage and field of view information ranging from 2/3", 16mm, 35mm, Super 35mm, Full Frame, VistaVision, and 65mm can be researched from one of many apps available for this purpose. Field of view and

sensor coverage information can be calculated from the coverage data provided by lens manufacturers and the sensor dimensions of any given camera by using an app such as pCAM.

Figure 7.14

Source: www.davideubank.com/Good_Focus/pCAM_Film+Digital_Calculator.html

Focal Length, Field of View, Distance, and Perspective

Each focal length of lens has an inherent perspective, dictated by the way it magnifies the image. Similar framings of a scene can be made from different distances by using different focal length lenses and adjusting the distance from which the picture is made. As we compare similar framings of the same subject, the perspective differences inherent in each lens are obvious.

Figure 7.15 The same framing on different lenses at different distances.

The camera can make similar framings from different distances by compensating with focal length of the lens. The space between the cans seems expanded or contracted, exaggerated by the wider lenses and compressed by the more telephoto lenses. Compositions made on telephoto lenses render distant objects as compressed in size while compositions made from close in with wide-angle lenses exaggerate the scale of objects as they move closer or further away. The common misconception is that the focal length of the lens entirely determines the perspective of an image, but the other factor that determines the perspective of a scene is where you put the camera. Telephoto lenses are often said to compress the scene and make everything look flat, but it's not just the focal length that's doing this. Generally, when using a telephoto lens, the camera is placed further from the scene being photographed in order to create a similar framing to what the camera would get from closer in on a normal or wide-angle lens.

A COMPOSITION AT CLOSE DISTANCE WITH A WIDE ANGLE LENS

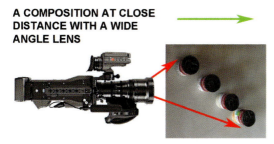

AT THIS DISTANCE THE OBJECTS OCCUPY A LARGE PERCENTAGE OF THE SCENE DEPTH

Figure 7.16 Wide-angle shot – objects occupy a greater percentage of scene depth.

IF WE PULL THE CAMERA AWAY, THE DISTANCE BETWEEN OBJECTS BECOMES A SMALLER PERCENTAGE OF THE OVERALL SCENE DEPTH

A SIMILAR COMPOSITION TAKEN FROM GREATER DISTANCE WITH A LONGER FOCAL LENGTH LENS EXHIBITS LENS COMPRESSION

Figure 7.17 Telephoto shot – the same objects occupy a smaller percentage of scene depth.

If the camera is moved further away from the subject while compensating the framing with a longer focal length lens, the subject's depth becomes a relatively smaller percentage of the overall scene depth. If the camera is moved closer to the subject while compensating the composition with a shorter focal length lens, the subject's dimensions become a much larger percentage of the overall scene depth. It is this phenomenon which gives perspective along with focal length. Similar framings can be made with many combinations of camera-to-subject distance and lens viewing angle, so matching a setup is not simply a matter of adjusting a zoom lens until the subject appears the right size.

Figure 7.18 Volume and perspective as a function of lens and distance.

This has consequences in making close-up shots of actors. If we photograph an actor's face from a foot away, we sense the shape and volume of their face pretty clearly, but as we move the camera further away from them, compensating the composition with a longer focal length lens, the perspective of the face will begin to flatten.

The perspective depth cues of the subject vary as a percentage of the overall scene depth. If the subject is a small percentage of the overall scene depth place further away, its depth cues flatten out. If the subject is placed closer, depth and perspective cues increase as the subject occupies a greater overall percentage of the scene depth. This factor becomes a great tool in story telling when artfully employed.

Lens Illumination and Coverage

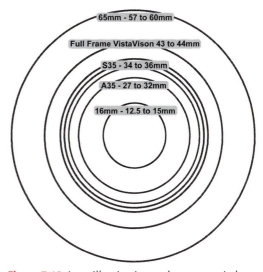

Figure 7.19 Lens illumination and coverage circles in mm.

The useable sensor coverage range of a lens is called the "image coverage circle." To define the coverage circle of a lens simply by the size of the illuminated area is overly simplistic. There are several distinctions that go into determining the "usable coverage area" of a lens. A lens may supply a very large illumination circle, but how much exposure falloff is acceptable at the corners of the frame? Does the lens go too dark at the edge of coverage? How much MTF falloff is acceptable across the frame? How does the performance of the lens vary from center to edge for what size sensor?

One philosophy of the definition of coverage area promotes the concept that performance falloff in MTF at the edges of frame is acceptable,

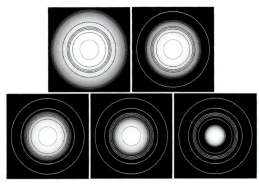

Figure 7.25 Coverage dots of lenses are designed for specific sensor areas.

The illustrations in Figures 7.21–7.25 demonstrate that lens coverage dot areas are tailored to fit specific sensors. A 50mm lens designed for a 65mm sensor produces a much larger coverage area than a 50mm lens designed for a 16mm film coverage area, but both lenses are 50mm lenses! A 50mm lens on a 65mm camera is actually a very wide-angle lens, while on a VistaVision or Full Frame sensor it is a modestly wide-angle lens. A 50mm lens on a 35mm or Super 35mm camera is a normal lens, but on a 16mm camera it is a modestly telephoto lens. Focal length, coverage, and sensor size are all closely interrelated, and the cinematographer must pay close attention to matching lenses to sensors!

Table 7.3 Comparison of horizontal field of view of ZEISS CP3 lenses on various sensors

Zeiss Compact Primes CP.3 & CP.3 XD Horizontal Angles of View for Various Sensors						
Sensor Dimensions	36mm × 24mm 1.42" × 0.94"	30.2mm × 16.7mm 1.19" × 0.66"	24.9mm × 18.7mm 0.98"× 0.74")	22 mm × 16mm 0.87" × 0.63"	22.3mm × 14.9mm 0.88" × 0.59"	17.3mm × 13mm 0.68" × 0.51"
Focal length	**Full Frame**	**APS-H**	**Super 35mm**	**Academy 35mm**	**APS-C**	**Micro FT**
15mm CP.3 & CP.3 XD	100°	90°	79°	73°	73°	60°
18mm CP.3 & CP.3 XD	89°	80°	69°	63°	64°	51°
21mm CP.3 & CP.3 XD	81°	71°	61°	55°	56°	45°
25mm CP.3 & CP.3 XD	72°	62°	53°	47°	48°	38°
28mm CP.3 & CP.3 XD	65°	57°	48°	43°	43°	34°
35mm CP.3 & CP.3 XD	54°	47°	39°	35°	35°	28°
50mm CP.3 & CP.3 XD	40°	34°	28°	25°	25°	20°
85mm CP.3 & CP.3 XD	24°	20°	17°	15°	15°	12°
100mm CP.3 & CP.3 XD	20°	17°	14°	14°	13°	10°
135mm CP.3 & CP.3 XD	15°	13°	11°	9°	9°	7°

ZEISS have published a table comparing the relative field of view obtained by placing their CP3 Compact Primes on a variety of sensors, and the result is very informative. The CP3s cover all the way up to full-frame sensors, but the table details the differences in horizontal field of view from sensor to sensor, and from lens to lens. This chart reinforces the cinematographers need to understand coverage, illumination, and focal length in lenses. It's notable that the field of view of an 85mm lens on a full-frame sensor is almost the same as the field of view of a 50mm lens on an Academy sensor.

Large format cinematography is quickly becoming very popular, but it challenges the cinematographer to carefully manage matching lenses to cameras. Cinematographers can no longer make assumptions about lens illumination circles and angle of view. We can't assume every lens in a set will cover the sensor as well as any other lens in the set. Test test test!

ARRI Lens Illumination Guide

ARRI Frame Line & Lens Illumination Tool: https://tools.arri.com/flt/index.html?_ga= 2.177182182.2134117720.1563735561- 2080774220.1518721526

Looking for the old frame line composer? You'll still find it here: https://tools.arri.com/ fileadmin/adapps/frameline_v4/index.html

Looking for the old lens illumination tool? You'll still find it here: https://tools.arri.com/fileadmin/ adapps/lensilluminationguide/index.html

Figure 7.26

ARRI have created an online tool for creating custom frame lines for ARRI cameras and for checking how different lenses illuminate different ARRI sensor sizes, recording formats, target aspect ratios, and frame lines.

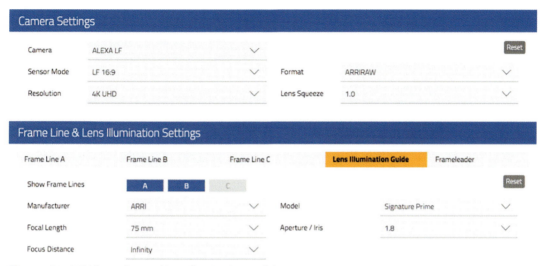

Figure 7.27 ARRI frame line and lens illumination tool data entry page.

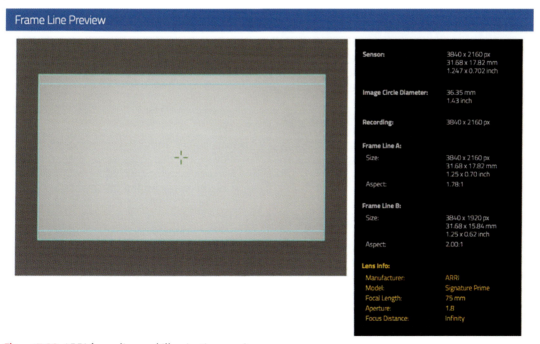

Figure 7.28 ARRI frame line and illumination preview screen.

This tool includes options for numerous framing reticles, and if you click on the Download – All Lens Settings at the bottom right a .zip archive for each lens set will appear in your downloads folder.

Below are a number of examples of the kind of data that is available from this resource. The ARRI frame line and lens illumination tool can provide the cinematographer with a wealth of lens coverage and illumination data.

Figure 7.29 Cooke ᴹᴵᴺᴵS4/i lenses (18, 25, 32, 50, 65mm) coverage on ALEXA mini sensor.

Figure 7.30 Cooke S4/8 lenses (18, 25, 32, 50, 65mm) coverage on ALEXA Large Format Sensor.

Figure 7.31 ZEISS Ultra Primes (16, 24, 32, 50, 85mm) coverage on ALEXA Mini Sensor.

Figure 7.32 ZEISS Ultra Primes (16, 24, 32, 50, 85mm) coverage on ALEXA Large Format Sensor.

Figure 7.33 ZEISS Master Primes (18, 25, 35, 50, 75mm) coverage on ALEXA Mini Sensor.

Figure 7.34 ZEISS Master Primes (18, 25, 35, 50, 75mm) coverage on ALEXA Large Format Sensor.

Figure 7.35 ZEISS Signature Primes (18, 25, 35, 47, 75mm) coverage on ALEXA Mini Sensor.

Figure 7.36 ZEISS Signature Primes (16, 24, 32, 47, 75mm) coverage on ALEXA Large Format Sensor.

From the illustrations above, it becomes apparent that not all lenses are created equal. A 50mm lens designed for a 35mm or Super 35mm sensor delivers a smaller coverage circle, and will not cover a large format or 65mm sensor. Similarly, a 50mm lens designed for a 65mm or large format camera will deliver an image circle that is much larger than a 35mm sensor, resulting in excess light scatter inside the lens cavity and reduced MTF performance. Both lenses are 50mm lenses, both lenses magnify the image by the same amount, but the individual coverage and illumination designs are tailored for specific camera sensors.

The cinematographer must match lens coverage requirements to sensor size carefully.

Figure 7.37 Coverage area of lenses can differ from wide-angle to normal lenses.

It is not sufficient just to test coverage only on the wide-angle lenses of any given lens set (as intuition would suggest). The cinematographer must test every lens in the set, as lens coverage in any given set changes as their design transitions from retrofocal wide-angle lens designs to normal lens designs, and then again as normal lens designs transition to telephoto lens designs. These transitions in coverage happen fairly predictably around multiples of the focal distance of the lenses, usually somewhere between 32mm and 50mm, and then again around 65mm to 100mm.

Abel Cine FOV Tool 2.0

www.abelcine.com/articles/blog-and-knowledge/tools-charts-and-downloads/abelcine-fov-tool-20

Figure 7.38

AbelCine's FOV Tool 2.0 (field of view) comparator allows a cinematographer to compare camera and lens combinations, including a variety of sensor sizes, recording resolutions, and aspect ratios.

Figure 7.39 Abel Cine FOV Tool Camera and Lens Data Entry Page.

Select a specific recording mode on one camera to compare with another. For example, compare the 8K Full Frame mode on the RED Helium 8K to the 4.4K Open Gate mode on the ALEXA LF. The tool includes most available cameras including the latest full-frame cameras, such as the SONY Venice, ARRI ALEXA LF, and RED Monstro.

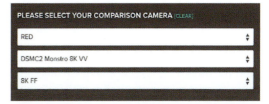

PLEASE SELECT YOUR CAMERA

ARRI	↕
Alexa LF	↕
Open Gate	↕

PLEASE SELECT YOUR COMPARISON CAMERA [CLEAR]

RED	↕
DSMC2 Monstro 8K VV	↕
8K FF	↕

PLEASE SELECT YOUR LENS

ARRI	↕
Signature Prime	↕
75	↕
Infinity T1.8	↕

Figure 7.40 Abel Cine Field of View Tool.

Figure 7.42 CVP Lens Tool Camera and Lens Data Entry Panel.

In addition, the cinematographer can specify an image circle to overlay over the sample image to determine lens coverage. Abel have included many lenses to choose from, so you can select a lens and see if it will cover the new full format modes.

It is important to note that these values are not 100% accurate. You should always test a lens to know for sure if it will give you the coverage you need. The AbelCine FOV Tool 2.0 is a work in progress.

From the cinematographer's data entry, the Lens Coverage and Camera Comparison Tool provides practical information in a visual format for checking whether a lens covers a sensor format, comparing field of view for a lens on a given sensor format, comparing sensor data, accessing lens data, and for seeing which focal lengths to use to match a B camera to an A camera.

CVP Lens Coverage and Comparison Tool

https://cvp.com/tools/cameralens

Figure 7.41

Figure 7.43 CVP Lens Coverage and Camera Sensor Comparison Screen.

Creative Video Productions in the United Kingdom have created a database to quickly show how different lenses will cover a camera or to compare sensor coverage on different cameras using the same lens.

The database can show coverage of each lens, but it is recommended that cinematographers shoot their own tests, as the database will not show other characteristics such as resolution falloff and aberrations towards the edges.

Figure 7.44 CVP Lens Tool Camera and Lens Data Panel.

In addition, the tool provides a thorough data panel with information about the camera and lens choices entered, and it also gives you the option to print the results. Please note that CVP urges that while all images have been taken with a medium format camera and with each lens, results may vary depending on the camera choice and differences in manufacturing tolerances of the lens chosen.

On Line Lens Test Resources

www.oldfastglass.com/lens-tests/
https://blog.sharegrid.com/ultimate-vintage-cinema-lens-test

Figure 7.45

Old Fast Glass have compiled a very large collection of lens evaluation tests that are available free, on line. Their goal is to have a library of test videos of every lens in their inventory. The approach was to be scientific, but also shoot a "real world" subject and scene.

Figure 7.46 Old Fast Glass lens tests.

For all of their lens tests they made sure to keep the camera, lighting, model, her wardrobe, and even her make-up consistent from lens to lens. The only variable is the lens itself. Because they tested different speed lenses at multiple apertures, exposure was compensated using the camera's shutter. Each lens was shot wide open and stopped down. No post processes were applied to the footage. Videos shot on RED were exported with DRAGONcolor2 and REDgamma4 applied. Videos shot on ARRI ALEXA Mini were recorded Log-C and ARRI's Rec 709 was applied. Images were captured in incandescent lighting only, and no lights were dimmed at all. They set ISO to 500 to get cleaner shadow detail.

Many lenses were shot RED Dragon 6K HD, and since most of the lenses in this test were designed to cover the Super-35mm format or smaller, so you will see heavy vignetting. They wanted to show that shooting on sensors larger than Super-35 can be done. The Cineovision and Lomo Round Front anamorphics were shot with an ALEXA Mini at 2.8K.

Telecentricity

Until recently almost all cine lenses have been entocentric in design. An entocentric lens is a lens which has its entrance or exit pupil inside the lens. The entrance pupil is defined as the image of the aperture stop as seen from an axial point on the object through those elements of the lens which precede the stop. The exit pupil is the image of the aperture stop as seen from an axial point in the image plane.

In entocentric lenses objects further away have lower magnification, and the apparent size of objects changes with distance from the camera. The word telecentric derives from the words tele ("far" in ancient Greek) and center, referring to the entrance pupil, the actual center of the optical system. An object–space telecentric lens is a lens that has its entrance pupil at infinity. This means that the chief (oblique rays that pass through the center of the aperture stop) are parallel to the optical axis in front of or behind the system, or both.

Placing the entrance pupil at infinity makes the lens object–space telecentric. In true telecentric lenses the image size is unchanged with object displacement, provided the object stays within the depth of field or telecentric range of the lens. Object–space telecentric lenses are used in machine vision systems because image magnification is independent of the object's distance or position in the field of view.

Placing the exit pupil at infinity makes a lens image–space telecentric. Image–space telecentric lenses are used with image sensors that do not tolerate steep angles of incidence. If both pupils are placed at infinity, the lens is double telecentric (or bi-telecentric).

For the purpose of this discussion we are interested in cine lenses designed for increased *image–space* telecentricity. I ask the reader to assume that I do not mean fully telecentric lenses, but rather what I will call or "more telecentric" lenses.

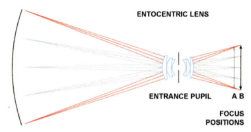

Figure 7.47 Traditional entocentric lenses.

Entocentric lenses have a fixed angle of the light toward the object as well as toward the sensor and yield different magnification at different distances. When the subject moves toward or away from the lens, the size of its image changes in proportion to the object-to-lens distance. In Figure 7.47 we can see that as the lens is focused by moving the group toward or away from the image plane, the result is a change in image size that is called "breathing."

This change in image size occurs because light exits an entocentric lens at an angle determined by the exit pupil of that particular lens design. Optics quantifies this angle as étendue, the property of light in an optical system that characterizes how "spread out" the light is in area and angle. Étendue is a geometric quantity that measures the light gathering capability of the optical system. Simply defined, it is Power = étendue {solid angle} × {times} radiance area {intensity of the source (Watts/meter²/sr)}. Because of this angle of spread, when the lens is moved closer to or further from the imager to focus (from focus position A to B), the image changes in size and the lens changes in effective focal length.

The angle at which rays exit a lens did not matter very much when the sensor of choice was film.

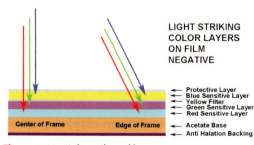

Figure 7.48 Light striking film.

Lenses for film cameras have traditionally been designed with the assumption that the image is formed on a set of photosensitive layers that are relatively insensitive to the variances in the angle of light from the lens. Film lenses can direct light to the film plane at fairly steep ray angles without a substantial exposure penalty. The image formed in the center of the film frame and the image formed at the edges of the film frame are relatively evenly exposed because film's capture layers are composed of randomly oriented photo-sensitive grains.

In a digital camera, microlenses on top of photosites may not correctly accept light that is incident at too steep a ray angle at the edges of the image sensor, those rays can actually be detected by a neighboring photosite or reflected off the sensor and scattered randomly.

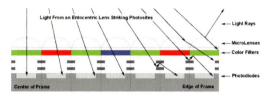

Figure 7.49 Issues of light striking microlenses at steep angles.

The result can be that red-filtered light can mix with a green photosite and green filtered light is mixed in with a red photosite. Misdirected light can scatter between photosites causing cross-talk, reduction in color saturation, and color fringes on sharp edges.

One approach to solving the issues of scattered and wasted light is to design lenses which are more near-telecentric. Increased image–space telecentricity can be designed into fixed focal length lenses for cinema, but their design requires additional elements to achieve telecentricity, they necessarily become larger in diameter depending on the sensor size that is being used, and they require shorter flange focal distance.

The main benefit of more image–space telecentric lenses for use on digital cinema cameras is that they do not suffer as much from radiometric $\cos^4\theta$ roll-off in sensor illumination and vignetting, since the rays land more perpendicular to the sensor across its entire area. An interesting by-product is that an increase in image–space telecentricity in a lens reduces both breathing and edge falloff in that lens.

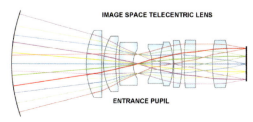

Figure 7.50 A more near image–space telecentric lens.

the lens. The radius of curvature in an aspheric changes with distance from the optical axis, unlike a spherical lens, which has a constant radius.

Wide-angle rectilinear lenses can cause objects moving across the frame to appear to stretch or enlarge as they near the edge of the frame. Rectilinear correction is accomplished by using aspheric elements to effectively change the focal length of a lens across the field of view of the lens. A rectilinear lens' variable power of magnification pushes the middle of the frame away by making the focal length more wide angle there, while pulling the corners of the image closer by making the outer diameter of the image area slightly more telephoto. The resulting overall focal length of such a lens is then calculated diagonally from corner to corner. Optics designers use aspheric elements to accomplish this variation in focal length and magnifying power across the image, and the mathematical curve that quantifies this effect is called the "mustache curve," because when plotted, it can resemble the shape of a gentleman's handlebar mustache.

Chromatic Aberration, Coma, Astigmatism, and Diffraction

Chromatic aberration or color fringing or purple fringing occurs when a lens cannot focus red, green, and blue wavelengths at the same focal plane. Lenses capture incoming light and bend it to record on the film/digital sensor plane.

Chromatic Aberration

Chromatic aberration is caused by lens dispersion, when different colors of light traveling at different speeds pass through a lens. When a lens bends the light, it can act as a prism and separate the various color wavelengths, sometimes resulting in color fringing, varied in colors depending on the subject in front of the lens. Wide-angle lenses must bend light at some very steep angles of incidence toward the imager plane without allowing any wavelengths to be prismatically offset in order to avoid chromatic aberration. As a result, images can look blurred or have colored fringed edges (red, green, blue, yellow, purple, magenta) around objects, especially in high-contrast situations. The refractive index for each wavelength of light is different in lenses, resulting in two types of chromatic aberration – longitudinal chromatic aberration and lateral chromatic aberration.

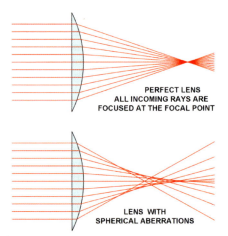

Figure 7.66 A "perfect lens" (above) and a lens with spherical aberration (below).

A perfect lens would focus all wavelengths into a single focal point, where the best focus with the "circle of least confusion" is located.

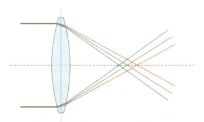

LONGITUDINAL CHROMATIC ABERRATION

Figure 7.67 Longitudinal chromatic aberration.

Longitudinal chromatic aberration occurs when different wavelengths of light do not converge at the same plane after passing through a lens. Longitudinal chromatic aberration shows fringing around objects across the entire image, even in the center. Red, green, blue or a combination of these colors can appear around objects. Longitudinal chromatic aberration can be dramatically reduced by stopping down the lens, or by using post production software.

Figure 7.68 Longitudinal chromatic aberration as a function of distance.

Notice the green color fringing at the (farther) top of the image, shifting to neutral in the middle (in focus) area, becoming magenta at the (nearer) bottom part of the image.

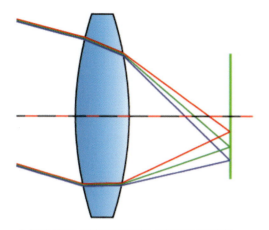

LATERAL CHROMATIC ABERRATION

Figure 7.69 Lateral chromatic aberration.

Lateral chromatic aberration (or transverse chromatic aberration) occurs when different wavelengths of color arrive at an angle and focus at different positions along the focal plane. Lateral chromatic aberration shows up towards the corners of the image in high-contrast areas. Blue and purple fringing is often common on some fisheye, wide-angle, and low-quality lenses. Lateral chromatic aberration cannot be mitigated by stopping down the lens, but it can be reduced using post processing software.

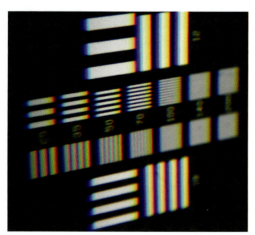

Figure 7.70 Corner crop showing severe lateral chromatic aberration.

Some lenses exhibit both longitudinal and lateral chromatic aberration at the same time. The only way to reduce such aberrations is to stop

down the lens to reduce longitudinal chromatic aberration and then remove the lateral chromatic aberration in post production by resizing two out of the three color records.

Coma

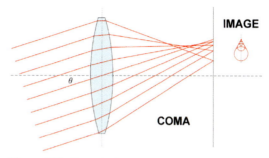

Figure 7.71 Coma in lenses.

Coma, or comatic aberration, refers to aberration that results in off-axis point sources appearing distorted, appearing to have a tail like a comet. Coma is a variation in magnification over the entrance pupil of a lens. Aspheric elements, achromatic/apochromatic optical designs and special extra-low dispersion elements in lenses are designed to correct spherical aberration, coma, and chromatic aberration.

Astigmatism

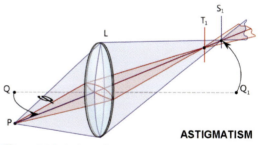

Figure 7.72 Astigmatism.

Astigmatism can occur even when the optical system is perfectly symmetrical. This is often referred to as a "monochromatic aberration," because it occurs even for light of a single wavelength. The amount of aberration can vary strongly with wavelength in an optical system.

Diffraction

The performance of a lens will usually increase as one stops down from wide open, reaching a maximum of performance at intermediate apertures, and then declining again at very narrow apertures due to diffraction.

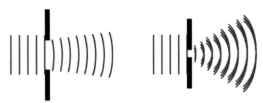

DIFFRACTION OF LIGHT THROUGH WIDE AND NARROW APERTURES

Figure 7.73 Diffraction through wide and narrow apertures.

Diffraction occurs when waves encounter an obstacle or a very small aperture. It is the bending of light waves around the corners of an obstacle or aperture into the region of shadow of the obstacle. Similar effects occur when a light wave travels through a medium with a varying refractive index such as glass or an aperture. Diffraction in lenses shows up as arbitrarily softer pictures at deeper stops, diminishing the benefits of added depth of field that stopping down should intuitively yield. Diffraction sometimes creates odd artifacts that look like dirt on the lens.

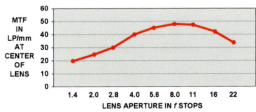

Figure 7.74 Diffraction – lens performance can decline at deeper stops.

Bokeh

Figure 7.75 Out of focus point source lights show lens bokeh.

Bokeh is a Japanese word that describes the out of focus character of a lens. Bokeh is a subjective quality, and is individual to the taste of cinema-

tographers. Can you detect the shape of the lens iris in high contrast highlights? Do objects go out of focus gracefully? Are the depth of field characteristics of the lens pleasing throughout the stop range of the lens? Lenses with matching iris assemblies will usually provide matching out of focus bokeh characteristics. A set of lenses where one lens has a triangular iris assembly, another a hexagonal iris, another octagonal, and another with 12 blades, can result in very different bokeh shapes from shot to shot. Bokeh is usually approximately circular in spherical lens images and oval in anamorphic lenses with a front anamorphic element. In anamorphic lenses the more things go out of focus, the more their bokehs are elongated vertically.

Bokeh is one of the more misunderstood concepts in optics. It is a term that was coined for photographic use only in 1997, a relatively short time ago. It is from the Japanese word "boke," meaning blur or haze. In recent years, many people have simplified bokeh to refer to how the shape of a lens' iris is rendered in out of focus points of light in an image, such as streetlamps at night. Much talk is made of how many iris blades are used and how round the iris aperture is as it is stopped down, but this is a minor aspect of bokeh.

The bokeh of a lens defines how that lens renders the out of focus portions of the image. In representing a three-dimensional space on the two-dimensional field of a photographic plate, the geometry of the path light takes through the lens elements can become apparent. As elements with the frame move out of focus (further from the third dimensional "Z-axis" center of the image) and further from the middle of the frame (the two dimensional "X-axis" and "Y-axis" center of the image), the Z-axis distance can begin to interact with the X- and Y-axis distances, causing a curving of the image. The visual effect is to create a spherical or tunnel-like rendering of the image as it progresses from the plane of focus. The more pronounced this effect the more "coarse" the bokeh. A highly corrected bokeh minimizes the rounding effect, rendering a more flat field as the image shifts focus.

A "coarse or fine" bokeh does not necessarily translate to a "bad or good" bokeh as it is more of a personal preference. One man's artifact is another man's art.[2]

Optics Design and Lens Groups

The earliest known lenses were made from polished quartz crystal; the Nimrud lens has been dated as early as 700BC. The Romans and

Greeks filled glass spheres with water to make lenses. Heiroglyphs from the 5th century BC describe simple glass meniscal lenses. Alhazeni wrote about lenses in his "Book of Optics" in the 11th century. Between the 11th and 13th century "reading stones" were used to assist in illuminating religious manuscripts, Roger Bacon used parts of glass spheres as magnifying glasses.

The telescope and the microscope were both invented around 1600, although for about 150 years, the achievable image magnification could not be increased beyond a factor of 10x. Using the simple glass of that time, it was not possible to eliminate the limiting color blur. In the 1750s, a new lead-containing flint glass made optical systems with better color imaging possible, producing another factor of 10x in magnification. When Otto Schott introduced boron oxide, barium oxide, and phosphorus oxide into glassmaking in the 1880s, yet another factor of 10x magnification opened to optics.

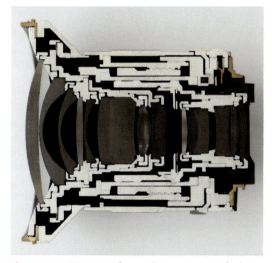

Figure 7.76 Diagram of optical construction of a lens.

Lenses have historically evolved in their construction from specific groups of elements. The Petzval Portrait lens of 1840, the 1890 ZEISS Protar anastigmat, the 1893 Taylor, Taylor & Hobson Cooke Triplet, the 1902 Tessar, the 1918 Plasmat, the 1926 Sonnar, and many other lens groupings led formula developments in advancing the design of optics. These design parameters determine many of the optical qualities and performance of lenses. Sturdy durable construction will give the owner a long use life over which the cost can be amortized. Focus barrels and *f*-stop mechanisms should be durable, front and rear elements should be quick to service, and the lens design should not allow dirt to work its way into the barrel easily. Manufacturers expend great effort to construct sets of prime lenses that ideally weigh the same amount across the range of focal lengths, and that place focus and iris gears at the same position on the barrel so that rebalancing a Steadicam or a gimbal is less time consuming on set. Front diameter should be the same throughout the set so that a clip-on matte box can be quickly remounted after lens changes.

As lens design expanded to include a wide variety of convex, concave, and meniscus lenses, lens makers began to understand the issues of spherical aberration, coma, chromatic aberration, and diffraction. The Petzval Portrait lens of 1840, the 1890 ZEISS Protar anastigmat, the 1893 Taylor, Taylor & Hobson Cooke Triplet, the 1902 Tessar, the 1918 Plasmat, the 1926 Sonnar, and many other lens groupings led formula developments in advancing the design of optics.

Anamorphics

The process of anamorphosing optics was developed by Henri Chretien during World War I to provide a wide-angle viewer for military tanks. The optical process was called Hypergonar by Chrétien and was capable of showing a field of view of 180 degrees. The technology was subsequently adapted to film, and anamorphic capture and projection arose from the desire to display wider aspect ratio images while still using standard 4 perf cameras and projectors.

Anamorphic widescreen developed as a response to the image detail shortcomings of non-anamorphic, spherical widescreen projection. When photographing wide screen with a spherical lens, the picture was recorded onto the film negative so that its full width fit within the film frame, but not its full height. The result was that a substantial part of the frame area was wasted, masked out, either on the print or in the projector in order to project a widescreen image.

It might seem that it would have been easier to simply use a wider film gauge for shooting movies, but because 35mm film was already in widespread use, it was more economically appealing for film producers and exhibitors to simply attach a special lens to the camera or projector, rather than invest in an entirely new film format, new cameras, new projectors, new editing equipment etc.

Twentieth Century Fox original Cinemascope lens system photographed a 2:1 horizontally squeezed image onto the film negative. The horizontal squeeze introduced in the taking lens had to be corrected when the film was projected, so another anamorphic lens was used on the projector to un-squeeze the picture to its correct proportions, resulting in an aspect ratio that was twice as wide in on-screen aspect ratio as the negative's frame.

A simple anamorphic lens consists of a regular spherical lens, plus an anamorphic attachment (or an integrated lens element) that does the anamorphosing. The anamorphic element operates at infinite focal length, so that it has little or no effect on the focus of the primary lens it is mounted on but still squeezes the optical field. A cylindrical 2:1 anamorphic has no effect in the vertical axis of the picture, but effectively halves the focal length in the horizontal. A 50mm spherical lens fitted with a 2:1 horizontal anamorphic becomes a 25mm lens in the horizontal axis. Numerous other squeeze ratios are employed in anamorphic taking lenses, and some lenses place the anamorphoser at the rear element instead of the front of the lens.

There are artifacts that occur in anamorphic lenses that do not occur in spherical lenses. Long blue horizontal flares result from bright lights in the frame in an otherwise dark scene. This artifact has become associated with a cinematic look, and is sometimes emulated by using a filter with non-anamorphic lenses. Anamorphic bokehs are elliptical rather than round, and when the camera racks focus objects can appear to stretch vertically. Additionally, wide-angle anamorphic lenses of less than 40mm focal length produce a barrel distortion which many directors and cinematographers like. Another characteristic, "anamorphic mumps" occur when an actor's face is positioned in the center of the screen, and actors standing in full-length view at the edges of the screen can become skinny-looking. Also, in medium shots, when an actor walks from one side of the screen to the other, he or she can appear to increase and decrease in apparent girth.

Panavision was the first company to produce an anti-mumps system in the late 1950s. They used a second lens which was mechanically linked to the focus position of the primary lens. This changed the anamorphic ratio as the focus changed, resulting in the area of interest on the screen having a normal-looking geometry. Later cylindrical lens systems used two sets of anamorphic optics; one was a stronger "squeeze" system, which was coupled with a slight expansion sub-system. The expansion sub-system was counter-rotated in relation to the main squeeze system, by mechanical linkage with the focus mechanism of the primary lens. This combination changed the anamorphic ratio and minimized the effect of anamorphic mumps in the area of interest in the frame.

There has been a years long revival of interest in wide screen and anamorphic cinematography, and many designs are available for cinematographers to choose from. Many of those choices are covered in depth later in this chapter.

Construction, Dimension, Durability, and Design

Many factors influence lens performance and character; the type and chemistry of the glass, lens group formulas, coatings, edge blackening, and manufacturing workflow.

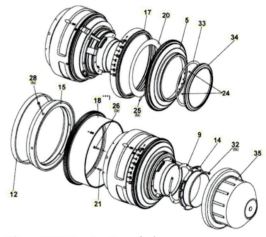

Figure 7.77 Construction of a lens.

The cinematographer and camera assistants must learn the craft of evaluating the physical attributes and condition of lenses. Focus scaling should be easily readable (even in the dark), and properly spread out with adequate distance between marks for ease in focus pulling. Gears should be uniformly spaced from one lens to another in the entire lens kit to accommodate fast lens changes and minimize rearranging lens motors and focusers.

Lenses use a variety of linear and helical cams for moving elements while focusing. Do the focus barrels turn easily? Does the barrel deflect the image when focused in opposing directions? Is there backlash or looseness in the focus barrel? Does the zoom mechanism deflect when changing direction? Does the zoom gearing have backlash? Do the crosshairs weave throughout the zoom or focus travel ranges?

Don't be shy when evaluating a lens package for a project. If the lenses seem inferior, or not well maintained, point it out to the rental agent. Your reputation is on the line!

Ideally, focus and iris ring spacing and front lens diameters should be uniform throughout the set so that matte box, follow focus, and lens motors can remain in the same position for lens changes. Torque required to turn focus should be consistent and set for the best combination of easy movement and smooth feel. Well-designed cine lenses typically feature about 300 degrees of barrel rotation for the full range of focus, while exhibiting little or no barrel extension. The focus ring should have interchangeable scales for both feet and meters. Consistent size and length, and lightweight are essential when working hand held or especially when working on a steadicam.

Zoom lenses can continuously change focal length without losing focus. Zoom lenses used for movie making must be parfocal maintaining focus as the focal length and magnification change as functions of zooming. This capability also allows the cinematographer to set accurate critical focusing at maximum focal length and then to zoom back to a shorter focal length to compose the image.

The optical path of an ordinary zoom lens has a four-lens group structure. The first group is called the focusing group, because it is used to focus the image. The second group is the variator which changes the image size. The third group is a compensator which maintains focus. The fourth group is a stationary lens group called the relay lens.

At the wide-angle end of the zoom, the variator group is moved forward, creating a retrofocus lens structure. At the telephoto end, the variator is moved back, so the lens structure resembles the telephoto type. To keep the image in the same position as the two lens groups move, the lens groups must move along parameters determined by the laws of optics. The movements of the variator and compensator groups are usually controlled by barrel cam mechanisms. A normal zoom lens has a divergent variator and a divergent compensator. The track followed by the compensator takes it forward, then back. The inner barrel has a linear guide cam groove, and the outer barrel has a curved cam groove matching the track of the lens motion. When the outer, curved cam barrel is turned, the variator and compensator move in unison following the curved cam grooves.

Zoom lenses must correct optical aberrations so that the image will stay sharp as the focal length is changed. To correct for aberrations at all focal lengths, the aberrations caused by each of the lens groups must be minimized. Aberrations that individual lens groups cannot correct on their own must be corrected by another lens group. If the correct cam curve, designed for a particular lens, is not followed very precisely, focus will be lost during zooming. Because of the need for precision, the cams are machined to micron tolerances by computer controlled machining tools.

Focus and Zoom Scaling

Figure 7.78 Focus marks at macro focus.

The amount of rotation required to focus or zoom the lens efficient for cinema focus pullers is a critical practical factor. When evaluating lenses, look for an extended focus scale with more space between focus marks for distant shots, but not so much travel that the entire range cannot be used in a single focus pull. Precise, accurate, easily visible focus marks that do not require the first assistant to dislocate his arm getting from a near mark to a far mark are essential on a fast moving set. Focus scales should be precisely calibrated and engraved with large bright markings for better visibility in low light conditions.

Ramping

Figure 7.79 Stop difference from *f*4.5 to *f*5.6 over focal length range due to lens *f* drop ramping.

Ramping (or *f* drop) refers to a drop in exposure at the telephoto end of a zoom lens focal length range. The entrance pupil of a zoom lens changes in diameter as the focal length is changed, as one zooms toward the telephoto end, the entrance pupil gradually enlarges. When the entrance pupil diameter reaches a diameter equal to or greater than the diameter of the focusing lens group the amount of light transmitted drops. In many zoom lenses the focusing group is large enough that no *f* drop occurs. *F* drop is a major factor in zoom lenses used in live sports broadcasts, which require long focal lengths and must frequently work in twilight or low light levels. To eliminate ramping completely, the focusing lens group has to be at least equal to the focal length at the telephoto end divided by the *f*-number.

A certain amount of ramping at the telephoto end is one of the tradeoffs in designing zoom lenses to reduce their size and weight for hand held use.

Depth of Field

The depth of field is that area behind and in front of the primary focal point that remains acceptably in focus at any given T-stop or range of the lens. Smaller apertures with higher T-stop numbers yield greater depth of field and wider apertures with lower T-stop numbers yield less depth of field. Depth of field is generally greater in wide-angle lenses and shallower in telephoto lenses.

The depth of field of a lens is the range of acceptable sharpness before and behind the plane of focus obtained in the final screened image. It should be understood that the determination of depth of field involves a subjective sensation that requires taking into account the condition under which the final projected image is viewed. The following two formulas are used for calculating the depth of field with the help of the hyperfocal distance and the circle of confusion.

$$\text{DN: Camera to Near Limit} = \frac{H \times S}{H + (S - F)}$$

$$\text{DN: Camera to Far Limit} = \frac{H \times S}{H - (S - F)}$$

H = Hyperfocal distance

S = Distance from camera to object

F = Focal length of lens

Depth Total = DF-DN

The following example shows how simple hyperfocal distance and depth of field calculations can be made by use of the above formulas:

Given a 35mm camera lens of 50mm focal length focused at 20 feet and utilizing a stop of f/2.8

$$H = \frac{F^2}{f \times Cc}$$

Convert focal length from 50mm to 2 inches (approximately),

$$H = \frac{2^2}{2.8 \times .002} = \frac{4}{.0056} = 714 \text{ inches or } 59.5'$$

Therefore when the lens is focused at 59.5 feet everything from half that distance, or 29.7 feet, to infinity will be acceptably sharp.

Using H in the depth of field formula we proceed:

$$\text{DN: camera to near limit} = \frac{H \times S}{H + (S - F)}$$

Convert all values into inches: H is 714 inches; S (distance of subject from camera) is 20 feet, or 240 inches; F is 50mm or 2 inches.

$$DN = \frac{714 \times 240}{714 + (240 - 2)} = 172.6 \text{ inches or } 14.3 \text{ ft.}$$

$$\text{Camera near to far limits} = \frac{H \times S}{H - (S - F)}$$

$$DF = \frac{714 \times 240}{714 - (240 - 2)} = 360 \text{ inches or } 30 \text{ ft.}$$

Therefore when the 50mm lens at f/2.8 Is focused at 20 feet it has a depth of field ranging from 14.3 ft. to 30 ft., or a total depth of:

$$D\,(\text{Total}) = DF - DN = 30 - 14.3 \text{ ft.} = 15.7 \text{ ft.}$$

Note: Since in the above depth of field formula

$$\frac{H \times S}{H \pm (S - F)}$$

the focal length F will always be small compared to S, it is allowable to simplify it to:

$$\frac{H \times S}{H \pm S}$$

in which case the above example looks like this:

$$DF = \frac{59.5 \times 20}{59.5 + 20} = \text{approximately } 15 \text{ ft.}$$

$$DN = \frac{59.5 \times 20}{59.5 - 20} = \text{approximately } 30 \text{ ft.}$$

$$D\,(\text{Total}) = 30 - 15 = 15 \text{ ft.}$$

After calculating the hyperfocal distances for all *f*-stops desired, the above formula permits a quick and easy way to calculate depth of field tables.

Where,
F=focal length of lens
f=f/stop number
Cc=circle of confusion

The circle of confusion for the hyperfocal distance can be briefly described as the image of a point situated outside the focused distance plane that will therefore not form the image of a point in the film plane but a blurred circle of a specified diameter Cc.

Circle of Confusion

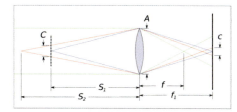

Figure 7.82 Circle of confusion formula.

Figure 7.82 shows lens and ray diagram for calculating the circle of confusion diameter *c* for an out-of-focus subject at distance S_2 when the camera is focused at S_1. The auxiliary blur circle *C* in the object plane (dashed line) makes the calculation easier.

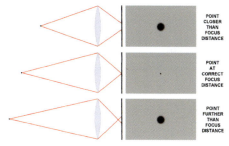

Figure 7.83 Circles of confusion, too close, in focus, and too far.

In photography, the term "circle of confusion" is used to define acceptable sharpness of points in an image. A standard value circle of confusion is usually defined for each sensor size or image format-based perceived visual acuity in a viewing environment, and on the amount of enlargement of the image. Real world lenses cannot focus all rays to a perfect point. Even at best focus, a point is imaged as a spot rather than a point. The smallest such spot that a lens can produce is referred to as the "circle of least confusion."

A lens can precisely focus objects at only one distance; objects at other distances are defocused.

Figure 7.80 Deep focus scene from *Citizen Kane*.

Figure 7.81 Shallow focus scene from *The Trident*.

Hyperfocal Distance

Hyperfocal is a specific distance/aperture combination for a focal length in which the far end of depth of field hits the photographic infinity point. It is the combination with the greatest depth of field because one cannot get sharpness beyond infinity. Once one focuses beyond the hyperfocal point, depth of field shortens because the close distance gets farther away but the far distance is always infinity.

The formula for hyperfocal distance (using inches or fractions) is:

H = Hyperfocal distance

$$H - \frac{F^2}{f \times Cc}$$

Any lens has two focal points, one on the object side, called the primary focal point, and one on the image side, called the secondary focal point. Defocused object points are imaged as blur spots rather than points. The greater the distance an object is from the primary focal point, the greater the size of the blur spot. Objects at greater distances from the plane of lens focus can still appear sharp, and the range of object distances over which objects still appear acceptably sharp is referred to as the depth of field. The common criterion for acceptable sharpness in the final image is that the blur spot be indistinguishable from a point. The zones in front of and in back of the primary focal point in which defocus is less than the acceptable circle of confusion is called the depth of focus.

Depth of Focus

In some cases, it may be desirable to have the entire image sharp, and deep depth of field is appropriate for the artistic intent of a shot.

Figure 7.84 Depth of focus in a shot.

For other cases, a shallower depth of field may be better suited to tell the story, focusing the viewer on a specific subject or area of the frame and de-emphasizing the foreground and background either side of the subject.

Depth of focus should be distinguished from depth of field. Depth of focus is an infinitely small range behind the lens at the focal plane within which the film is positioned during exposure. This is most critical, particularly with short focus lenses. If the film moves out of this precise position, either forward or backward, it will cause unsharp images produced by an increase of their diameter of the circle of confusion. The circle of confusion is no longer an acceptably sharp point but a larger circle which is blurred. Precise placement of the film in the film aperture is a most important consideration for motion picture camera designers to avoid film buckling or breathing, or other mechanical problems such as variable pressure plates or poor registration

causing displacement of the film behind the lens during actual exposure. Each frame must be held securely in position and in perfect register in the exact focal plane and remain absolutely motionless during exposure. For close approximation, the formula for depth of focus for a lens at a given f-stop is plus or minus:

$$\frac{50mm \times 2.8}{1000} = 0.14mm = 0.0055"$$

$$\text{or about} \pm 0.00275"$$

Therefore a 50mm lens at $f/2.8$ has a depth of focus of:

$$50mm \times 2.8$$
$$1000 = 0.14mm = 0.0055" \text{ or about } \pm0.00275"$$

This represents nearly 0.003" or slightly over the diameter of the circle of confusion for the 35mm camera and shows the degree of precision required in motion picture camera design.

Focal Reducers, Expanders, Doublers, and Diopters

A focal reducer or speed booster is an optical element used to reduce focal length, increase lens speed, and in some cases improve modulation transfer function (MTF) performance. Speed boosters/focal reducers allow for larger format glass to cover smaller format sensors with the benefit of added light gathering ability.

The effects and uses of the focal reducer are largely opposite to those of the teleconvertor. The combined system of a lens and a focal reducer has smaller back focus than the lens alone. About one stop in light collection ability can be achieved due to the concentration of light on a smaller sensor. A focal reducer can also improve your MTF by virtue of magnification, but remember, you are adding additional elements to the optics.

Figure 7.85 Metabones E-EF Speed Booster.

A Metabones E-EF Speed Booster turns a 70mm T2.8 into a 50mm T2 lens. The resulting image coverage circle is smaller than the original 70mm lens, but that doesn't matter if the combination covers the format size of your camera.

Drawbacks of focal reducers can include added distortion, chromatic aberrations, subtle bokeh character differences, a different look to the flare, and increased vignetting in comparison to the lens on a larger format sensor at maximum aperture. Stopping down 1 or 2 stops can help mitigate some of the issues.

Figure 7.86 Duclos 1.7x Expander.

Expanders are optical devices that take a collimated beam of light and expand its size.

The Duclos 1.7x Expander effectively increases the image coverage circle of a taking lens, providing a narrower effective field of view while maintaining a high level of image quality. The Expander converts S35mm lenses to cover Full Frame and VistaVision sensors, introducing a 1½ stop of light loss. By using an expander, older lenses can be used with PL-mounted digital cameras with sensors larger than the Academy aperture, up to a 34mm image circle. The Duclos 1.7x Expander features an integrated back focus adjustment for quick, easy field tuning with no need for shimming. Designed and manufactured with high grade, anodized aluminum body and stainless steel PL to PL mounts. The 1.7x Expander will work with any S35 lens with a maximum aperture of T2.0 or greater.

Figure 7.87 Schneider 2.0x PL Mount Doubler.

A doubler (sometimes called teleconverter or tele extender) is a secondary lens mounted between the camera and a lens. A doubler enlarges the central part of an image obtained by the lens. For example, a 2x teleconverter for a 35mm camera enlarges the central 12 × 18mm part of an image to the size of 24 × 36mm. Teleconverters are typically made in 1.4x, 1.7x, 2x, and 3x models. The use of a 2x teleconverter effectively makes a lens double the focal length. It also decreases the intensity of the light reaching the film by a factor of 4.

Diopters/Closeup Lenses

Diopters can be used when no lens in the lens package can focus close enough to get really tight on the subject even at minimum object distance. The most common type of diopter is a plano convex lens, flat on one side and convex on the other side. Like all filters, plano convex diopters reduce resolution and can sometimes introduce strong chromatic aberrations.

Figure 7.88

The strength of diopters is measured in millimeters, and the diopter value is the reciprocal of the focal length in meters. Diopters come in a variety of strengths such as: +1/4 diopter, +1/2 diopter, +1 diopter, +2 diopter, and +3 diopter.

When using a diopter in combination with a camera lens, if one sets the camera lens at infinity, a +1 Diopter close-up lens will be in focus 1 meter away from the object. A +2 diopter will be in focus at .5 meter away from the object and a +3 diopter will be in focus at .333 meter away from the object. Split diopters can allow subjects to be in focus in two different planes, but the split area must be carefully concealed to keep the viewer from detecting the diopter edge in the image.

Always mount diopters with the convex side facing away from the lens, and exercise caution in handling diopters, the convex side is very easily scratched and damaged.

Filters

Figure 7.89 Glass filters affect resolution.

Keep in mind that placing filters in front of the lens alters the effective resolution, the more filters, the less resolution. Using glass filters is frequently a necessity, sometimes the only way to insure that a creative look or a cinematographer's care for the beauty of an actress endures all the way through post. Exercise caution when using filters, use a donut around the lens to keep any stray reflections from behind camera from bouncing off the back of the lens. Stacking multiple filters can also create reflections from bright picture highlights, sometimes tilting filters can fix the problem. Weigh the differences between filtering with glass filters on set as opposed to using digital filters in post. Glass filters affect the whole image, they permanently alter the image, they vary in effect from wide lenses to telephoto lenses, and they are easily destroyed on set. In addition, a beauty filter like a glimmer filter or a diffusion filter or a Pro Mist filter can make a blue screen or green screen shot into a compositing nightmare! Digital filters offer an infinite range of permutations, they allow for an "undo" button, and they can be applied in post to match very closely any look that can be achieved on set.

Polarizing Filters

Polarizing filters can be used to reduce haze, to darken blue skies, to reduce reflections and sheen, and to reduce specular highlights. When used with locally polarized lighting, a polarizer can eliminate specular highlights on faces for face replacement plates. Polarizing filters come in two types: liner polarizers and circular polarizers. A linear polarizer is manually oriented to polarize light in one direction, and must be adjusted when the camera is moved or when shooting circumstances change. A circular polarizer is a linear polarizer backed with a quarter wave retarder that depolarizes the light after the unwanted reflections have been attenuated. This is frequently necessary when using polarizers on digital cameras as the polarizer may interact badly with optical low pass filter packs, 3D beam splitters, and prism optics. When using a circular polarizer remember to mount the filter with the polarizing side facing out and the wave retarder side facing the lens front element. A circular polarizer should always be labeled for correct orientation by the manufacturer. As with any glass filter, there will be a slight loss of resolution, and between one and two stops of light loss.

Nodal Point or (More Correctly) the No-Parallax Point

The nodal point is a misnomer in cinematography. For practical purposes in cinema, the term "nodal point" is used to mean the no-parallax point. Because the image arriving at the sensor is rolled 180 degrees, it makes sense that somewhere before the light strikes the image plane the ray traces of incoming light cross. With most lenses, there is usually one optical center point around which one can rotate the camera and observe no-parallax change in the image as you are panning or tilting the camera. This special "no-parallax point" is a virtual aperture, usually (but not always) contained within the lens. This point is defined by the location of the entrance pupil. In most prime lenses the no-parallax point is usually fixed, in a zoom lens the no-parallax point can move forward and back as the focal length changes, sometimes even moving outside the lens.

Some wide-angle and fisheye lenses do not have a single no-parallax point. Instead, they have a range of "least-parallax points" that depend on the angle off of the lens axis. Such lenses can be recognized easily – just look into the front of the lens and observe that the location of the entrance pupil moves forward or backward as you rotate the lens off-axis.

Anamorphic lenses have two no-parallax points, one in the vertical axis and one in the horizontal axis. By design, the two no-parallax points cannot exist in the same place. A 50mm 2:1 squeeze anamorphic lens is only a 50mm lens in the vertical axis; it is actually a 25mm in the horizontal axis because the 2:1 squeeze element only affects the image in the horizontal axis. As one might imagine, the task of reverse engineering the optics in an anamorphic lens for the purpose of adding 3D objects into a panning, tilting, rolling, dollying shot in a CGI environment can be very *very* difficult!

Finding the No-Parallax Point

We can empirically find the no-parallax point by shooting two C-stands, lined up in a row so that one blocks the other. We will need two printed cards with black and white squares, two C-stands, a gearhead on a tripod or dolly, a camera, and a lens. On a fluid head like an O'Connor 2575 the center of the tilt axis rotation is at the middle of the head, making it impossible to use in this case. On an "L" type head like a Cartoni Lambda, Weaver-Steadman, or Ronford F7 head the lens can be centered at the rotation points of the pan and tilt axes. Placing the lens no-parallax point at the centers of rotation on an "L" head ends up very back heavy. An Arrihead or a Panahead or other geared head will allow you to place the lens at the center of the pan and tilt rotation axes and still manage balancing the camera.

Figure 7.90 Stage setup for finding no-parallax point.

Mount the two cards at the top of the C-stands at lens height, straight and level, and set one stand about 6 feet from the camera and the other at about 12 feet from the camera.

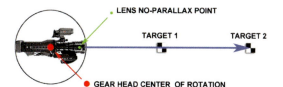

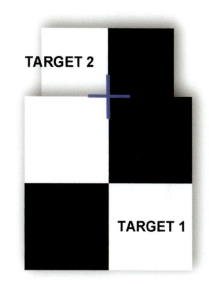

Figure 7.91 Setting up targets in order to find the lens' "no-parallax point."

Line the two targets up on the crosshairs of the viewfinder so that one set of squares is visible above the other, aligned at the center.

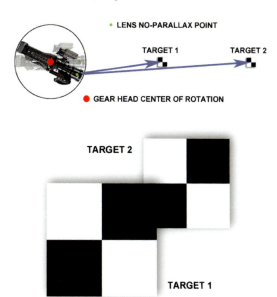

Figure 7.92 The relationship of the charts changes as the camera is panned.

In this case, when we pan to the right, the two targets will probably move out of alignment slightly (unless you have accidentally placed the lens no-parallax point precisely on the gearhead center of rotation!), and when we pan left, they will move out of alignment by the same amount in the opposite direction. This parallax shift indicates that the lens' no-parallax point is forward of the center of rotation of the pan tilt head.

Figure 7.93 Relationship of lens no-parallax point and P/T head center of rotation.

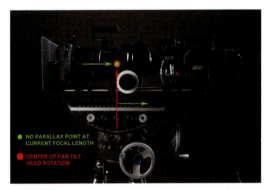

Figure 7.94 Aligning the no-parallax point to the P/T head center of rotation.

With the camera panned until the two charts are at the edge of frame to one side or the other, loosen the detent on the gear head's balance plate and slide the camera back (or forward as needed) until the two charts are aligned again. When the lens is over the rotation point of the head, the camera may become back heavy, so exercise caution when releasing the tilt lock detent.

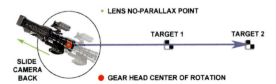

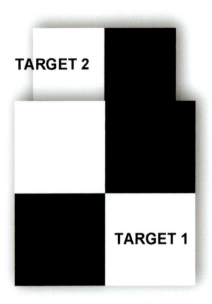

Figure 7.95 Aligning the "no-parallax point" at the center of rotation.

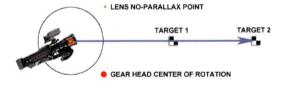

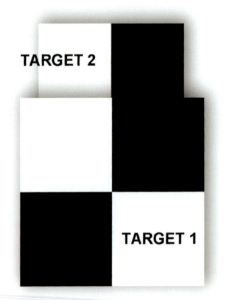

Figure 7.96 Once aligned, panning or tilting the camera does not affect parallax.

Pan back and forth to move the charts from one side of frame to the other and observe that their alignment doesn't change. We no longer observe any parallax shift between objects at different distances from the camera as we pan and tilt. When the relationship between the two charts remains constant as we pan, we have successfully placed the no-parallax point directly over the center of rotation of the gear head. If you set the lens at the no-parallax point before shooting panoramic plates or tiles the images can be stitched easily, as fixed objects in the scene do not move from one tile to the next.

Lens Metadata

Cooke /ℹ̃ Technology

Cooke's /ℹ̃ Technology enables film and digital cameras to automatically record key lens data for every frame shot and provide it to post-production teams digitally. Focal length, focus distance, and *f*-stop are digitally recorded for every frame, at any frame rate up to 285 fps, film or digital, and stored as metadata. This improves efficiency in Visual Effects workflows by reducing the amount of time spent reverse engineering VFX plates. It digitally records vital lens data frame-by-frame, all synced to timecode, including focus setting, T-stop, and depth-of-field. Cooke's /ℹ̃ "Intelligent" technology is standard on all new Cooke 35mm lenses: Anamorphic/ℹ̃ , S7/ℹ̃ , 5/ℹ̃ , S4/ℹ̃ , PANCHRO/ℹ̃ Classic , and ᴹᴵᴺᴵS4/ℹ̃ lenses. Using a Cinematography Electronics /ℹ̃ Lens Display Unit assistants can see a continuous remote readout of the precise focus setting, T-stop, and depth-of-field using Cinematography Electronics' /ℹ̃ Lens Display Unit in conjunction with their Cinetape. Digital cinema cameras that are /ℹ̃ equipped include ARRI ALEXA, RED, SI 2K, and current SONY models.

The Cooke /ℹ̃ Technology User's Guide and Technical Manual can be found at this URL: www.cookeoptics.com/techdoc/F1279020D F268AF185257F95006FDC11/i2-user-guide+ technical-manual-v4.0-2016--.pdf.

ZEISS' application of /ℹ̃ technology adds information about the lens' distortion and shading characteristics in real time to speed-up the workflow on set and in post production. Lens settings and shading characteristics are now captured on every frame, integrated into the image stream, and output to post.

Panavision DXL Lens Data

Panavision DXL is the latest entry into the camera data field. DXL2's internal gyro and accelerometer measures XYZ in orientation and movement through Z space, and that data is captured per-frame and saved into the R3D RAW file for use in any VFX workflow or database. Lens data including Focus, Iris, and Zoom are also incorporated into the data stream, which greatly improves reliability and efficiency in Visual Effects workflows.

Speeding up VFX Work with ZEISS eXtended Data

by Christophe Casenave, Edited by Jon Fauer

I Technology is an open lens data protocol designed and developed by Cooke Optics, the open standard can be extended by partners. ZEISS added lens data parameters that had been requested by Visual Effects artists: distortion and shading (also called vignetting).

Having this data and being able to record it together with video clips would simplify, accelerate, and make image compositing much more accurate than it is currently.

As this was an extension to what Cooke's I Technology originally offered, ZEISS named it "eXtended Data (XD)" and has opened the specifications to all Cooke /ℹ̃ technology partners both on the camera side as well as on the lens side. Cooke was kind enough to make this officially part of the Cooke /ℹ̃³ protocol so everybody has access to this technology.

Early on, companies such as Transvideo, Ambient, RED, and Pomfort decided to support this initiative and implemented the use of this data in their products. Most recently, FUJINON also decided to implement XD in their new Premista zooms and SONY is adding XD recording into the VENICE camera.

In order to make this data easy to use, ZEISS also provides different tools to prepare the data and use it in VFX – among these are plug-ins for Foundry's NUKE and Adobe After Effects.

Let's look at some examples of how to use eXtended Data technology to speed up your VFX work. There is also a lot more information available on the ZEISS eXtended Data web page: zeiss.com/cine/xd.

VFX, Compositing and CGI Integration Today

The process is well established: whenever there is a plan for Visual Effects work in a feature, the VFX supervisor should ask the film crew to provide grids, "checkerboards," and grey cards. These help calculate the lens characteristics that will then be applied onto the CGI elements so they match the geometry and the look of the footage. However, this way of working has some drawbacks:

- The crew (usually the camera assistant) needs to shoot grids in pre-production or prep at the rental house. This is tedious, eats up time, and is redundant from job to job.

- Grids and cards are usually only shot at a couple of focus distances. But distortion and shading characteristics of a lens vary continuously when the focus and T-stop change.
- There is a lack of precision inherent in shooting grids and charts. Let's assume you are doing VFX work on footage where the AC did a focus change. You will need to choose one distance as the best compromise and use the grid associated with this distance to calculate the lens characteristics.

Easier, Faster, More Precise Compositing with Lens Data

The idea of ZEISS eXtended Data technology is to replace the hassle and complexity of shooting charts with a simple method:

- ZEISS CP.3 XD and Supreme Prime lenses integrate distortion and shading characteristics. These can be recorded on set. Each frame will get a set of accurate distortion and shading data. (Cooke measures each lens at the factory so that their /i^3 distortion mapping is unique to each individual lens.)
- The DIT prepares and hands over this data, together with the footage, to the VFX team. The easiest way to do this is to ingest the data directly into the EXR files. This can be done with the command line tool ZEISS-XDCP which is available for download on the ZEISS eXtended Data website. eXtended Data /i Technology contacts in lens mount for direct connection to camera. eXtended Data /i Technology 4-pin external connector.
- VFX teams can use this data to either correct or exaggerate geometric distortion and shading or apply these parameters to the VFX elements. ZEISS plug-ins for Foundry NUKE and Adobe After Effects are for this purpose.

Benefits of eXtended Data

- With XD, there is no need to shoot grids during prep.
- The recorded characteristics are much more accurate than any grid and are available for any distance and for any T-stop. This means that if you pull focus during a shot, each frame will receive the correct lens characteristics.
- The way to correct or apply the characteristics in VFX is easier, faster, and more accurate. ZEISS provides plugins for Foundry NUKE and Adobe After Effects that let the VFX artist use the recorded lens characteristics in a very simple way with one click.

VFX compositing with eXtended Data: use grid to evaluate lens distortion and apply to images. Above: NUKE Analyzer Checkerboard. Below: NUKE with EXR Clip. Using eXtended Data, this step is much easier: ZEISS plug-in uses the lens data to undistort / distort. This is a one-step process and there is no guesswork.

What Are the Choices to Record and Use ZEISS eXtended Data?

This is the most common question: how do I record the lens data on set and how do I prepare it?

In fact, there are different ways to record eXtended Data depending on the camera setup.

- The easiest: RED DSMC2 cameras (V. 7.1 and later) or SONY VENICE (V. 4.0) can already communicate with eXtended Data lenses and record the distortion and shading data into R3D and X-OCN files respectively.
- ARRI cameras can record Cooke /i data but not the distortion and shading included in eXtended Data. The best way to record XD with ARRI cameras is to use the new Transvideo Starlite HDm Metadator monitor. This will record the data in a way that is directly usable by the ZEISS plug-ins.
- Ambient MasterLockitPlus is camera agnostic. It works with any camera that has the ability to receive timecode externally. It records the lens metadata and Pomfort Silverstack DIT software is used to prepare it for post production.

There are many different ways to work with eXtended Data. Production teams should pick the one that works best for them. We will go through 3 examples.

ZEISS eXtended Data Using a RED DSMC2 for VFX

RED DSMC2 Cameras can already record distortion and shading data provided by ZEISS CP.3 XD and Supreme Prime Lenses. The lens data travels through the connectors in the lens mount and the recorded data is then embedded into the R3D files. The workflow is quite simple:

- Lens data is automatically recorded into the video files.
- The DIT generates EXR files out of the R3D files as usual.
- The DIT extracts the lens data out of the R3D files and ingests them into the EXR files using zeiss-xdcp command line software.
- The VFX artist can then use Foundry Nuke or Adobe After Effects plug-in to apply the lens data to the footage or to computer graphics.

stop tester made by Steffelbauer (or other) stop tester. This measures the average illuminance in the picture gate and is supplied with a calibrated lens.

Physical/Mechanical QC Issues in Lenses

Whether renting or buying lenses, a thorough checklist of QC questions in prep can save a lot time and money during production.

- Are there any chips or scratches on elements?
- Are there any blemishes or imperfections on the coatings?
- Are the engraved markings for the scales clean and legible?
- Are there any dings or defects in the zoom/focus gear that would interfere with a follow focus?
- Is there any sign of impact damage that could cause internal jamming or limitations?
- Are the elements secured in their proper position? Does the lens flare more in one direction than another?
- Is the viscosity of the zoom, focus, and iris acceptable?
- Does the zoom/focus scale move without any visible result?
- Does the zoom/focus barrel shift back and forth, changing focus?
- Are there certain areas of the zoom/focus that are harder to turn than others?
- Are there any rings or parts that seem to be loose or shifted?
- Is the mount secured and in good, clean condition, free of dings or dents?
- Does the zoom/focus scale stop firmly at the end of travel both ways?
- Are the helix threads loose causing image shift or focus loss?
- Is the cam free of dents and is the follower secure and in proper form?
- Are the zoom/focus mechanisms free of grit from sand or other dirt?

Additional more rigorous lens testing methodology is described in a 1995 EBU white paper; *Measurement and Analysis of the Performance of Film and Television Camera Lenses* (Tech. 3249–E), European Broadcasting Union, Case Postale 67, CH–1218 Grand–Saconnex (Geneva) Switzerland.

Lens Resources for Repair and Service

www.ducloslenses.com/pages/ice-box

Duclos Lenses provides quality service to professionals and companies who own and rent top-of-the-line cinema optics. They have the test equipment and experience required to optimize and maintain all makes and models of lenses. They are a family owned and operated business who not only appreciate and respect customers in a way only a small business could, but also survive on customer satisfaction and repeat business.

Lens Section

There is a very wide variety of both old and new lenses available today in the world of digital cinema. This chapter could easily end up being a book unto itself if the author detailed every lens that could potentially be fitted to a digital cinema camera, so I will keep to modern lenses and brands, and I will attempt to outline as many of those choices as I reasonably can. Here they are in alphabetical order:

Angénieux Optimo Lenses

Figure 7.106
www.angenieux.com/

Angénieux Optimo Prime Lenses

Figure 7.107 Angénieux 40mm Optimo Prime Lenses.

Angénieux's Optimo Primes provide full frame 46.5mm image circle coverage with a consistently fast 1.8 T-stop except for the extreme wide and telephoto lenses. All focal lengths provide maximum flexibility with fully interchangeable mounts in PL and LPL. Engineered as smart lenses, Optimo Primes will support both Cooke /ı̄ and ARRI LDS and feature common gear size and position across the entire set. Focal lengths for the Optimo Primes include 18mm, 21mm, 24mm, 28mm, 32mm, 40mm, 50mm, 60mm, 75mm, 100mm, 135mm, and 200mm.

Table 7.4 Angénieux Optimo prime lenses

Focal Length	T-Stop	Close Focus inches/m	Image Circle
18mm	T2.0	14"/0.36m	FF 46.5mm
21mm	T1.8	14"/0.36m	FF 46.5mm
24mm	T1.8	14"/0.36m	FF 46.5mm
28mm	T1.8	14"/0.36m	FF 46.5mm
32mm	T1.8	14"/0.36m	FF 46.5mm
40mm	T1.8	14"/0.36m	FF 46.5mm
50mm	T1.8	16"/0.4m	FF 46.5mm
60mm	T1.8	20"/0.5m	FF 46.5mm
75mm	T1.8	24"/0.6m	FF 46.5mm
100mm	T1.8	28"/0.7m	FF 46.5mm
135mm	T1.8	39"/1.0m	FF 46.5mm
200mm	T2.4	48"/1.2m	FF 46.5mm

Angénieux Optimo Zoom Lenses

Angénieux's Optimo line of zoom lenses are very sharp, exhibiting good MTF and pleasing image characteristics. Optimo lenses feature optical design that minimizes breathing and ramping, and offers high levels of performance across the entire zoom range. Optimos generally rotate through about 320 to 330 degrees of barrel rotation for the full extent of focus, and their focus and zoom mechanisms are very solidly engineered.

Figure 7.108 The Angénieux 15–40mm Optimo Zoom.

The 15–40mm Optimo has a very fast wide open aperture of T2.6 with good contrast and color reproduction, and it is light enough for hand held and steadicam operation, available in ARRI PL, Panavision, Nikon, or Canon mount.

Figure 7.109 The Angénieux 28–76mm Optimo Zoom.

The Angénieux 28–76mm T2.6 Optimo Zoom began its life as a film lens, but is becoming very popular for digital cameras because of its size and the images it creates. The 28–76mm yields very good contrast and color reproduction. It is ideal for Steadicam, Technocrane, or hand held work, and is available in PL, Panavision, Nikon, or Canon mount.

Figure 7.110 The Angénieux 45–120mm Optimo Zoom.

The 45–120mm zoom lens, PL mount, was designed to be used with 35mm cameras as well as the latest generation of digital cameras. It features a fast aperture of T2.8. Available for handheld cameras, steadicam, or crane, the focus ring has a 320° focus rotation with over 50 precise focus witness marks. It offers superior optical performance rivaling prime lenses at equivalent focal lengths.

The 45–120 is a great complement to the 28–76mm and the 15–40mm. All three lenses are small and light enough for handheld cameras, steadicam, or crane work, and long enough for close-ups.

Figure 7-111 The Angénieux 17–80mm Optimo Zoom.

The Optimo 17–80mm features a very fast aperture speed of T2.2, available in PL mount.

Figure 7.112 The Optimo 19.5 to 94mm Zoom.

The Optimo 19.5 to 94mm has been specially designed for an image coverage up to 31.4 mm diagonal for a compatibility with S35 Film and Digital cameras including the full frame 5K format of RED Epic. The 17–80 and 19.5–94 share the same 4.7x zooming architecture, while the 19.5–94 offers a larger imaging circle.

Figure 7.113 The Angénieux 24–290mm Optimo Zoom (non Ultra).

The 24–290mm (frequently lovingly nicknamed "the Hubble" after it's amazing reach!) has a very fast aperture speed of T2.8. It displays outstanding performance across the entire range of focal lengths while exhibiting very good contrast and color reproduction, available in PL mount.

Figure 7.114 The Optimo 28–340mm Zoom (non Ultra).

The Optimo 28–340mm was also designed for an image coverage up to 31.4 mm diagonal for a compatibility with all S35 film and digital cameras, including the 5K format of RED Epic (among others). The Optimo 24–290 (non Ultra) and the 28–340 (non Ultra) share the same 12x zoom architecture, and the 28–340 has a larger image circle.

Figure 7.115 The Angénieux Ultra 12x S35 24–290mm Zoom.

The workhorse 24–290mm has a fast aperture speed of T2.8. It displays outstanding performance across the entire range of focal lengths while exhibiting very good contrast and color reproduction. Now the 24 to 290 has been optically and mechanically redesigned to enable Full Frame and VistaVision coverage. New features include no ramping, minimal breathing, and efficient use of aspheric elements to minimize color fringing. The lens comes in original PL mount lens, but is now compatible with ARRI LPL mount. The new mechanical design features very short minimum focusing distances of 1.22m/4'1" in S35 – 1.24m/4'1" in Ultra S35 and 1.5m/5' in Full Frame/VistaVision.

Other features include weight reduction of moving components, reduced dust intake by improved air flow and dust traps, precise and ergonomic focus ring with scale rotation of 321 degrees and over 70 focus marks. User changeable focus marking rings with focusing scales available in feet or metric.

Configurations include:

ZoomS35 + U35 kit (Standard Optimo Ultra 12X U35 package)

ZoomS35 + U35 kit + FF/VV kit (Full Optimo Ultra 12X FF/VV package)

Figure 7.116 The Optimo Ultra 12x U35 26–320mm Zoom.

The Optimo 12x U35 26–320 is the successor model to the 28–340mm. Like the 24 to 290mm, the lens features a new optical and mechanical design, offering better mechanical stability and serviceability. New features include no ramping, minimal breathing, and efficient use of aspheric elements to minimize color fringing. The lens comes in original PL mount lens, but is now compatible with ARRI

The new ARRI LPL (Large Positive Lock) lens mount sits at a 44mm flange depth and has a 62mm diameter that is optimized for the ALEXA LF larger sensor. Numerous camera companies are losing the spinning mirror reflex shutter and heading to shorter flange depths to accommodate more telecentric lens design options. This allows ARRI's Signature Primes and future large-format lenses to be smaller and more lightweight, with a fast T-stop and pleasing bokeh on a larger format sensor. A PL-to-LPL adapter offers backward compatibility with PL mount lenses that cover Super 35 or full frame. The adapter attaches securely to the LPL lens mount without tools, allowing assistants to switch between PL and LPL lenses on set, and offering cinematographers greater lens choice. The mount is compatible with the new LDS-2 lens data protocol, and will also be able to read data from LDS-1 and i lenses.

ARRI Large Format Lenses

ARRI Rental's ALEXA 65 system is available exclusively through its global network of rental facilities. The ALEXA 65 system offers a complete large-format solution for high-end motion pictures, television productions, and commercials, and now, a new and wide variety of custom-designed prime and zoom lenses. Capturing uncompressed 65 mm ARRIRAW images of ultra high resolution, ALEXA 65 is the flagship of the ALEXA camera platform. An integral part of the ARRI ALEXA 65 camera system is the wide range of 65 mm prime and zoom lenses specifically designed to cover the full image area of the ALEXA 65 sensor.

ARRI Vintage 765 Lenses

The Vintage 765 lens range, originally developed for the ARRIFLEX 765 film camera has been adapted for use with the ALEXA 65. These are the original eleven ARRIFLEX 765 vintage lenses from the late 1980s. They give the cinematographer a classic look with good contrast and a gradual fall-off across the image. Vintage 65 lenses provide full ALEXA 65 sensor coverage.

Table 7.11 ARRI Vintage 765 Lenses

Focal Length	T-Stop	Close Focus	Image Circle
30mm	3.6	0.32m/13.5"	65mm
40mm	4.2	0.50m/20"	65mm
50mm	3	0.50m/20"	65mm
60mm	3.6	0.30m/12"	65mm
80mm	2.8	0.64m/25"	65mm
100mm	3.6	0.70m/28"	65mm
110mm	2.1	0.80m/37"	65mm
120mm	4.2	0.75m/29"	65mm
150mm	3	1.40m/56"	65mm
250mm	4.2	2.06m/102"	65mm
350mm	4.2	1.90m/75"	65mm

ARRI Prime 65 Lenses

ARRI Rental have commissioned a range of 65 mm prime and zoom optics utilizing Hasselblad lens elements from the HC series of large-format lenses. These lens elements have been re-housed in sturdy and uniform cine style lens barrels, co-developed with IB/E Optics including a new iris system for the prime lenses, and a new focus/iris/zoom control mechanism for the zoom lens. These lenses use a new XPL mount system that enables LDS functionality and ARRI's LPL mount system as well.

Figure 7.135 Vintage 100mm 765 Lens.

Figure 7.136 ARRI Prime 65 Lenses.

ARRI's classic ALEXA 65 lenses (originally developed to meet the immediate needs of the

ALEXA 65 Camera) provide full ALEXA 65 sensor coverage, utilizing crisp, contrasty glass. The set consists of eight original prime 65 lenses, housed in robust cine lens barrels with uniform front diameters and featuring smooth focus and iris operation. This set also provides full ARRI Lens Data System capability (LDS) for lens metadata. The Prime 65 lens series delivers very high MTF, excellent contrast and geometry, with very low chromatic aberration or focus breathing. The usability and ruggedness of these lenses is comparable to ARRI/ZEISS Master Prime lenses.

Table 7.12 ARRI Prime and Zoom 65 Lenses

ARRI Prime 65 Lenses			
Focal Length	**T-Stop**	**Close Focus**	**Image Circle**
24mm	4.8	0.38m/15"	65mm
28mm	4	0.25m/10"	65mm
35mm	3.5	0.50m/20"	65mm
50mm	3.5	0.60/24"	65mm
80mm	2.8	0.70m/28"	65mm
100mm	2.2	0.90m/35"	65mm
150mm	3.2	1.30m/51"	65mm
300mm	4.5	2.45m/96"	65mm
ARRI Zoom 65 Lenses			
Focal Length	**T-Stop**	**Close Focus**	**Image Circle**
38–210mm	6.3		65mm
50–110mm	3.5–4.5		65mm
80–200mm	2.8		65mm
150–600mm	6.3		65mm

ARRI Rentals Prime 65 S Lenses

Figure 7.137 Prime 65 S Lenses.

ARRI's Prime 65 S lenses are an extension of the Prime 65 range, with seven higher-speed lenses, all T2.8 or faster. Prime 65 S lenses provide full ALEXA 65 sensor coverage with beautiful bokeh and slightly lower contrast, and include ARRI Lens Data System (LDS) for lens metadata.

Table 7.13 ARRI Prime 65 S Lenses

Arri Prime 65 S Lenses			
Focal length	**T-Stop**	**Close Focus**	**Image Circle**
35mm	2.5	0.55m / 21.5"	65mm
45mm	2.8	0.45m / 18"	65mm
55mm	2.8	0.50m / 20"	65mm
75mm	2.8	0.60m / 24"	65mm
90mm	2.8	0.40m / 16"	65mm
120mm	2.5	0.57m / 22"	65mm
150mm	2.8	1.20m / 47"	65mm

ARRI Prime DNA Lenses

Figure 7.138 ARRI Prime DNA Lenses.

ARRI Rental's Prime DNA lenses utilize new custom designed 65 mm format optics in 14 lenses (actually more than 14 with close focus variants) that provide full ALEXA 65 sensor coverage, refit with ARRI's LPL mount. DNA lenses use a combination of proprietary vintage and modern optics to meet cinematographers needs. This evolving collection is customizable and has interesting characteristics that can be mixed and matched specific to the project.

Table 7.14 ARRI DNA Lenses

Focal Length	T-Stop	Close Focus	Image Circle
28mm	2.8	0.45m/18"	65mm
35mm	2.3	0.45m/18"	65mm
35mm	2.8	0.45m/18"	65mm
45mm	2.3	0.45m/18"	65mm
45mm	2.8	0.45m/18"	65mm
50mm	2	0.81/32"	65mm
55mm	2.8	0.45m/18"	65mm

(Continued)

Table 7.14 (Continued)

Focal Length	T-Stop	Close Focus	Image Circle
60mm	2	0.60m/24"	65mm
65mm	1.6	0.70m/28"	65mm
70mm	2.8	0.60m/24"	65mm
80mm	1.9	0.70m/28"	65mm
110mm	2.8	0.94m/36"	65mm
150mm	2.8	1.50m/59"	65mm
200mm	2.8	2.50m/98"	65mm

ARRI Rental DNA LF Primes

Originally developed for the 65mm format of ARRI Rental's exclusive ALEXA 65 camera, the new DNA LF series is purpose-designed for the ALEXA LF format.

Figure 7.139 ARRI DNA LF Lens.

Comprising re-housed vintage optics with a new iris for circular bokeh, DNA LF lenses incorporate coating options and tuneable internal elements. Prime DNA lenses for the larger ALEXA 65 format can be used on the ALEXA LF, but that frames out some of the interesting elements at the edges and corners of the image. DNA LF lenses are purpose-made for the ALEXA LF, featuring a 49mm image circle that is matched to the LF sensor.

DNA LF lenses have been designed from the ground up to be customizable in ways that can be accurately recorded. Internal markings and mechanisms allow each lens to be personalized to a measurable, repeatable extent, and afterwards set back to its base settings. Adjustments can be made to focus fall-off, halation, contrast, spherical aberration, and field curvature, to meet the needs of a cinematographer or production.

Focus fall-off is natural and pleasing, highlights are rendered in a mellow way, and the flare characteristics respond organically to direct light sources. New multi-blade irises have been built into every lens, providing consistent out-of-focus highlights and attractive bokeh. Robust housings, uniform lens rings, and full LDS-2 metadata make DNA LF lenses practical, characterful companions for ALEXA LF and Mini LF, as well as other full-frame cameras.

DNA LF lenses are available in nine focal lengths ranging from 21mm to 135mm.

Table 7.15 ARRI DNA LF Lenses

Focal Length	T-Stop	Close Focus	Image Circle
21mm	T1.5	7"/.177m	49mm
25mm	T1.5	8.6"/.218m	49mm
29mm	T2.0	11"/.279m	49mm
35mm	T2.0	11"/.279m	49mm
50mm	T1.5	18"/.452m	49mm
75mm	T1.5	2'/.6m	49mm
85mm	T1.5	2'3"/.685m	49mm
100mm	T2.0	2'6"/.762	49mm
135mm	T2.0	4'2"/1.27m	49mm

ARRI 65 LDS XPL Lens Mount

Figure 7.140 LDS XPL Mount.

The Prime 65, Zoom 65, and new Prime 65 S lenses feature an XPL mount (now also adapted with ARRI's new LPL mount to provide cross camera compatibility with the same lens sets) equipped with the ARRI Lens Data System (LDS) that allows frame-accurate metadata about focus, iris, and zoom settings to be recorded with the image stream. This data can be used on set for wireless remote lens control, but it can also be used to help match a virtual lens with the recorded image in post production, reducing the time and cost involved in generating complex visual effects shots.

ARRI Ultra Wide Zoom Lenses

Figure 7.141 ARRI 19–36mm Anamorphic Ultra Wide Zoom.

ARRI's Anamorphic Ultra Wide Zoom AUWZ 19–36/T4.2 complements ARRI ZEISS Master Anamorphics to cover extreme wide-angle focal lengths between 19 mm and 36 mm. Telecentric optical design in the AUWZ gives it a more uniform field illumination from the center to the corners of the image. Focus breathing and distortion are minimized even at close focus. The AUWZ renders an inverted image compared to other lenses (actually right side up) at the sensor plane that is easily inverted on most digital cinema cameras.

ARRI's intent was to create a very wide range of anamorphic lenses, with a 19mm wide angle zoom at one extreme and a 360mm prime (180mm Master Anamorphic with 2 x Alura extender) at the long end. The entrance pupil doesn't change when zooming on either the Ultra Wide Zoom or the Anamorphic Ultra Wide Zoom, making them ideal for VFX work.

Minimum object distance is 2', just beyond the front lens element, so the AUWZ allows anamorphic close-ups that haven't been possible before. Flares, which are very well controlled by the multilayer, anti-reflective lens coating, generate a creaminess around highlights that gives night shots an ethereal and magic quality. ARRI Lens Data System (LDS) provides lens metadata for zoom, focus, and aperture settings, simplifying visual effects workflows in post.

Table 7.16 ARRI Ultra Wide Anamorphic Zoom Lens

Arri Ultra Wide Anamorphic Cine Zoom Lens			
Focal length	Aperture	Close Focus mm/ft	Image Circle
19-36mm Anamorphic Zoom	T4.2	0.6 m / 2'	Super 35mm
Arri Ultra Wide Cine Zoom Lens			
Focal length	Aperture	Close Focus mm/ft	Image Circle
9.5-18mm	T2.9	0.55m / 21.654"	34.4mm

The ARRI Ultra Wide Zoom UWZ 9.5–18/T2.9 is a super wide-angle zoom lens with an image circle of 34.5 mm, the UWZ is designed for both existing and future generations of large-sensor digital cameras. The optical performance of this telecentric design is comparable to that of high-end wide-angle prime lenses, and the UWZ can replace a range of wide-angle primes.

Figure 7.142 ARRI 9.5–18mm Ultra Wide Cine Zoom Lens.

Optimized for VFX applications, the UWZ is ideal for plate shots, distortion is less than 1% at 9.5mm and less than 0.1% at 18mm, straight lines stay straight, even at close focus. New coatings reduce flare and veiling glare to a minimum. Near telecentric optical design gives the UWZ very good field illumination from the center to the corners of the image. Built-in ARRI Lens Data System (LDS) provides lens metadata for zoom, focus and aperture settings.

Table 7.17 ARRI Ultra Wide Cine Zoom lens

Arri Ultra Wide Cine Zoom Lens			
Focal length	Aperture	Close Focus mm/ft	Image Circle
9.5-18mm	T2.9	0.55m / 21.654"	34.4mm

ARRI/Fujinon Alura Zoom Lenses

Figure 7.143

Source: www.arrirental.com/lenses/35mm_alura.html.

Caldwell Chameleon 1.79x squeeze anamorphic primes feature classic blue flare and anamorphic bokeh reminiscent of vintage widescreen cinema. The 1.79x anamorphic squeeze ratio is the perfect balance of anamorphic look and maximal use of sensor area.

Chameleon Primes are compact in size and capable of high resolution, with bright easy to read markings and consistent 95mm front element size.

An interchangeable rear lens group provides either an image circle capable of covering Super35mm sensors or large format, full frame, and Vista Vision cinema cameras. Available in PL mount, the Chameleons have the distinctive aberrations one would expect from anamorphic lenses, but with restraint and control. Having two series with different image circles allows the cinematographer to embrace character and edge aberrations, or opt for a cleaner, more restrained image, depending on the shot or project. The conversion kit converts Standard Coverage (SC) Series to Extended Coverage (XC) Series and includes optics, aperture rings, and focal length plaque. The SC series covers most Full Frame sensors with moderate levels of edge aberration, the XC series covers Full Frame sensors with lower levels of edge aberration.

Table 7.20 Caldwell Chameleon 1.79x Squeeze Prime Lenses

Caldwell Chameleon 1.79x anamorphic prime lenses			
Focal Length	**T-Stop**	**Close Focus**	**Image Circle**
SC – Standard Coverage			
25mm SC	T2.0	0.76m/2'6"	33mm
32mm SC	T2.0	0.76m/2'6"	33mm
40mm SC	T2.0	0.76m/2'6"	33mm
50mm SC	T2.0	0.76m/2'6"	33mm
60mm SC	T2.0	0.76m/2'6"	33mm
75mm SC	T2.0	0.76m/2'6"	33mm
100mm SC	T2.6	0.76m/2'6"	33mm
XC – Extended Coverage			
48mm XC	T3	0.79m/2'7"	50mm
60mm XC	T3	0.79m/2'7"	50mm
75mm XC	T3	0.79m/2'7"	50mm
90mm XC	T3	0.79m/2'7"	50mm
112mm XC	T3	0.79m/2'7"	50mm
150mm XC	T4	0.79m/2'7"	50mm
225mm XC	T6	0.79m/2'7"	50mm

Canon Cine Lenses

Figure 7.154

Source: www.usa.canon.com/internet/portal/us/home/products/professional-video-solutions/cinema-lenses.

Figure 7.155 Canon Sumire Prime Lenses.

Canon Sumire Prime Lenses

Until recently, Canon had been focused on producing Super 35mm zoom lenses in PL and EF mounts, while manufacturing their cine prime lenses in EF mount only. Canon has a long legacy in cinema optics, most cine lens enthusiasts know something of the legend of Canon's legendary K35 cine prime lenses. The recent interest in full frame lenses and cameras for cinema motivated Canon to create a contemporary set of prime lenses with PL mounts. Canon designed a sharp 4K full frame lens over most of the aperture range, but as wide aperture (from about F/2.8 to full open) is approached they also designed in some modifications to that sharpness, "a unique optical design introduces a nuanced look as the lens aperture approaches its maximum setting that subtly modifies the textural rendering of close-ups. It smooths the transition from areas that are in focus to out of focus regions of the image, with gentle fall-off and pleasing bokehs."

Canon's Sumire Prime lenses have markings on angled surfaces on both sides of the barrel, making it easy to read focus and aperture settings from behind or from either side of the camera. Focus markings can be switched from standard labeling to metric. The control rings are engineered to maintain the proper amount of resistance with consistent operating torque. Sumire lenses meet 4K production standards, featuring a full-frame imaging circle in a lightweight, compact design. They feature an 11-blade aperture diaphragm for pleasing bokeh and all share the same gear position, front diameter, and rotation angle, the lenses' compatibility with third-party accessories allows crews to easily change lenses without making adjustments to the camera setup.

Table 7.21 Canon Sumire PL Mount Prime Lenses

Canon Sumire PL Mount Prime Lenses			
Focal length	T-Stop	Close Focus Inches / mm	Image Circle
14mm	T3.1	8" / 200mm	Full Frame
20mm	T1.5	12" / 300 mm	Full Frame
24mm	T1.5	12" / 300 mm	Full Frame
35mm	T1.5	12" / 300 mm	Full Frame
50mm	T1.3	18" / 0.450mm	Full Frame
85mm	T1.3	38" / 0.950mm	Full Frame
135mm	T2.2	39" / 1m	Full Frame

Canon EF and PL Mount Cinema Zoom Lenses

Canon's EF Cinema Zoom lenses offer fluorite coated aspheric lens elements, and advanced optical design, covering ranges of focal lengths most commonly used. These lenses are light and small, with consistent form factor. They share the same gear position, diameter and rotation angle, and front diameter; good compatibility with third-party accessories allows assistants to quickly and easily change lenses.

The EF Cinema Zoom lens CN-E14.5–60mm T2.6 L SP (PL mount) provides wide angle coverage in a 4.1x zoom lens for the Super 35mm format, and delivers 4K+ optical performance. It features markings on angled surfaces on both sides of the barrel, making it easy to read settings from behind, or from either side of the camera. Focus markings can be switched from standard labeling to metric.

Figure 7.156 The Canon 14.5–60mm 4K+ Cinema Zoom.

Designed for 4K+ production, it's optical performance exceeds the requirements of HD imaging systems. This lens has consistent operating focus and zoom barrel torque, and a covered flange-back focus adjustment mechanism. It features advanced optical design with fluorite coatings

and large aspheric lens elements to achieve sharp images at T2.6 over the entire focal range. Canon incorporated geared inner focusing that minimizes focus breathing. The 11-blade iris ensures pleasing bokeh, and opto mechanical design avoids temperature-induced marking discrepancies and optical performance impairments. Available as CN14.5–60mm T2.6 L SP (PL mount) and CN14.5–60mm T22.6 L S (EF mount).

Figure 7.157 The Canon 15.5–47mm Cinema Zoom.

The CN-E15.5–47mm T2.8 L SP (PL mount) or CN-E15.5–47mm T2.8 L S (EF mount) features a good range of zoom magnification and wide-angle focal length range for the Super 35mm format, and is engineered to combine 4K optical performance with lighter weight and a lower price point.

Figure 7.158 The Canon 30–105mm Cinema Zoom.

Canon's CN-E30–105mm T2.8 L SP (PL mount) or CN-E30–105mm T2.8 L S (EF mount) offers a good range of zoom magnification and mid-range focal lengths for the Super 35mm format, and is engineered to combine a lower price point and lighter weight with 4K optical performance.

mance. All four zooms are similar in size and weight, with uniform gear placement and front barrel diameters, enabling quick and efficient lens changes.

Table 7.33 Fujinon HK Premiere zoom lenses

Fujinon HK Premier PL Mount Cine Zoom Lenses			
Focal length	Aperture	Close Focus m/ft	Image Circle
14.5 - 45mm (HK3.1x14.5)	T2.0	0.71m/2.3ft	S35
18-85mm (HK4.7x18)	T2.0	0.82m/2.7ft	S35
24 - 180 mm (HK7.5x24)	T2.6	1.24m/4.1ft	S35
75-400mm (HK5.3x75)	T2.8 (75-270mm) T3.8 (270-400mm)	2.0m/6.6ft	S35

Fujinon Cabrio Zoom Lenses

Figure 7.186 Fujinon Cabrio 19–90mm Zoom Lens.

The 19–90mm Cabrio (ZK4.7×19) Zoom features a detachable servo drive unit, making it suitable for use as a standard cinema lens or as an ENG-Style lens. With a 19–90mm focal range, a wide open T-stop of 2.9, and a weight of 2.7kg including servo motors, it features a very long focal range for such a lightweight zoom. The ZK4.7×19 also features flange focal distance adjustment, macro function, and is LDS (Lens Data System) and /ȿ technology metadata compatible when employing the servo drive.

Figure 7.187 Fujinon Cabrio 14–35mm Zoom Lens.

Fujinon's Cabrio PL 14–35mm wide angle lens offers exceptional optical performance in the center of the image and in the corners of the frame in a wide angle lens. It supports the ARRI Lens Data System (LDS) and /ȿ metadata formats when employing the servo drive and can be controlled using FUJINON wired broadcast lens controls. The drive can also interface with existing cinema industry standard wireless controllers.

Figure 7.188 Fujinon Cabrio 25–300mm Zoom Lens.

A 12x PL mount cine lens, starting at 25mm and reaching to 300mm, gives the versatility to cover a wide variety of shooting situations, great for shooting documentaries, nature and wildlife, and car commercials. The PL 25–300 covers 31.5mm sensor size on a digital cinema camera for full-frame resolution. A nine-blade iris part of the design as well, creating the most natural-looking imagery possible. Features include flange focal adjust, LDS and /ȿ technology metadata compliant when employing the servo drive, smooth focus action, and an optional detachable digital servo.

Figure 7.189 Fujinon Cabrio 85–300mm Zoom Lens.

The Cabrio PL 85–300mm offers focal lengths of 85–218mm at T2.9 and 300mm at T4.0 at just over 3 kilograms (3.1kg), making it ideal for shooting documentaries, nature and wildlife, car commercials, and many other demanding production scenarios. Like the PL 19–90 Cabrio, the PL 85–300 is equipped with the same features including flange focal distance adjustment, Lens Data System (LDS) and /ẞ metadata formats when employing the servo drive, a MOD of 1.2m, a macro function for objects as close as 97cm (38 inches), and covering a 31.5mm diagonal sensor size. The PL 85–300 can be controlled using cinema industry standard wireless controllers as well as existing detachable FUJINON wired units.

Figure 7.191 Gecko-Cam Genesis G-35 Full Frame Prime Lenses.

Table 7.34 Fujinon ZK Cabrio zoom lenses

Fujinon ZK Cabrio PL Mount Cine Lenses			
Focal length	**Aperture**	**Close Focus m/ft**	**Image Circle**
14.5 - 35mm (ZK2.5x14)	T2.9	0.6m / 2ft	S35 31.5mm
19 - 90mm Cabrio (ZK4.7x19)	T2.9	0.85 m	S35 31.5mm
25-300mm (ZK 12x25)	T3.5 (25-273mm)	1.2m / 3' 11"	S35 31.5mm
	T3.85 (273-300mm)		
85-300 mm (zK3.5x85)	T2.9 (85-218mm)	1.2m / 3' 11"	S35 31.5mm
	T4 (218-300mm)		

Figure 7.192 Gecko-Cam Genesis Vintage 66 Full Frame Prime Lenses.

The Special Edition Gecko-Cam Vintage 66 Lenses are the same lenses with uncoated and re-coated glass elements for a softer look with more flares. Features include changeable focus rings for metric and imperial markings, an optional motor for focus and iris, four lenses in the set open to T 1.4. Gear rings are all in the same position, lens front diameters are 114mm, 6K ready.

Gecko-Cam G-35 Lenses

Figure 7.190

*Source:*www.gecko-cam.com/products/lenses/genesis-g35/.

GECKO-CAM Genesis G-35 lenses combine modern mechanics made in Germany with a Canon K35 vintage look, the Genesis G35 lens series is available in focal lengths of 14.5mm, 16mm, 20mm, 25mm, 35mm, 50mm, 85mm, and 135mm. G-35 full frame image circle covers 46.3mm for use with RED 8K Monstro, ALEXA LF, and SONY VENICE. Available lens mounts are PL and LPL. Changeable focus rings are available in either metric or imperial markings, and there is an optional motor for focus and iris. All lenses in the set share the same gear position, and have 114mm fronts.

Figure 7.193 Gecko-Cam Macro 100mm Lens.

Gecko-Cam have added a 100mm macro lens which reaches maximum magnification of 1:1 at a T-Stop of 2.9. It features internal focusing for constant lens length, floating element design for breathing control, cam-follower driven focus mechanics, 95 mm front diameter, and is available in PL and LPL mounts.

The 100mm Macro is available either as a Genesis G-35 with multi-layer coating for high flare reduction, or as a Genesis Vintage '66 for more flares and softer bokeh.

Table 7.35 Gecko-Cam Genesis G35 full frame prime lenses and Gecko-Cam Vintage '66 full frame prime lenses

Focal Length	T-Stop	Close Focus m/inches	Image Circle
14.5mm	T3	0.28m/11.5"	46.3mm
16mm	T2.4	0.30m/12"	46.3mm
20mm	T1.8	0.20m/8"	46.3mm
25mm	T1.4	0.25m/9.84"	46.3mm
35mm	T1.4	0.33 m/13"	46.3mm
50mm	T1.4	0.45m/17.71"	46.3mm
85mm	T1.4	1.1m/43.3"	46.3mm
100mm Macro	T2.9–22	0.30m/12" 1:1	46.3mm
135mm	T2	0.8 m/31.5"	46.3mm

Hawk Anamorphic Prime Lenses and Zoom Lenses

Figure 7.194

*Source:*www.hawkanamorphic.com/en/index.php.

HAWK 65 Large Format Anamorphics

Figure 7.195 HAWK 65 Anamorphic Lenses.

HAWK65 anamorphic lenses are specifically designed for the new generation of large format sensors that have renewed interest in the 65mm format. The 1.3x anamorphic squeeze allows large format sensors to utilize the entire sensor to create anamorphic images. New coating technology with soft contrast gives HAWK 65 lenses a gentle look on digital sensors. These lenses give cinematographers the opportunity to shoot anamorphic 65mm with modern glass made for ARRI ALEXA 65 or RED Weapon 8K sensors.

Table 7.36 HAWK 65 large format anamorphic lenses

HAWK65 – Large Format Anamorphics			
Focal length	T-Stop	Close Focus m / ft	Image Circle
Hawk65 40 mm	T2.2	1 / 3' 3"	50 mm
Hawk65 45 mm	T2.2	1 / 3' 3"	50 mm
Hawk65 50 mm	T2.2	0.8 / 2'7"	50 mm
Hawk65 60 mm	T2.2	1 / 3'3"	50 mm
Hawk65 70 mm	T2.2	1 / 3'3"	50 mm
Hawk65 80 mm	T2.8	0.8 / 2'7"	50 mm
Hawk65 95 mm	T2.8	1 / 3'3"	50 mm
Hawk65 120 mm	T2.8	1 / 3'3"	50 mm
Hawk65 150 mm	T2.8	1 / 3'3"	50 mm
Hawk65 200 mm	T4	1 / 3'3"	50 mm
Hawk65 280 mm	T4	1 / 3'3"	50 mm

Hawk Class-X Anamorphic Lenses

Figure 7.196 Hawk class-X Anamorphic Lenses.

Hawk class-X anamorphic lenses deliver a classic 2x anamorphic look in newly designed and built lenses. Hawk class-X lenses deliver improved definition, close focus and improved edge distortion characteristics.

Table 7.37 Hawk class-X anamorphic lenses

Hawk class-X Anamorphic Lenses			
Focal length	T-Stop	Close Focus	Image Circle
28 mm	T2.2	0.6 / 2'	28 mm
35 mm	T2.2	0.75 / 2'6"	30 mm
45 mm	T2.2	0.75 / 2'6"	32 mm
55 mm	T2.2	0.75 / 2'6"	34 mm
55 mm macro	T2.2	0.35 1'3"	30 mm
65 mm	T2.2	0.5 1'8"	33 mm
80 mm	T2.2	0.75 2'6"	36 mm
110 mm	T3	0.75 2'6"	40 mm
140 mm	T3.5	0.75 2'6"	42 mm
38-80 mm zoom	T2.8	0.62 2'	30 mm
80-180 mm zoom	T2.8	1 3'3"	32 mm

MINIHAWK – Hybrid Anamorphics

Figure 7.197 MINIHAWK – Hybrid Anamorphics.

MiniHawk anamorphics solve many of the problems associated with anamorphic lenses while preserving classic anamorphic characteristics. These hybrid lenses are compact, lightweight, and fast, a good fit for hand-held work, drone shooting, and stabilizing systems. They have super-close focus, almost like macro lenses, no breathing while focusing, and are geometrically well corrected, while still preserving classic anamorphic characteristics, such as elliptical bokeh and shallow depth of field that create a cinematic feel.

Table 7.38 MINIHAWK hybrid anamorphics

Minihawk Hybrid Anamorphics			
Focal length	T-Stop	Close Focus	Image Circle
35 mm	T1.7	0.25 m 10"	30 mm
40 mm	T1.7	0.25 m 10"	32 mm
50 mm	T1.7	0.25 m 10"	34 mm
65 mm	T1.7	0.25 m 10"	36 mm
80 mm	T1.7	0.35 m 1'2"	35 mm
100 mm	T1.7	0.35 m 1'2"	40 mm
135 mm	T1.7	0.35 m 1'2"	40 mm
180 mm	T1.7	0.5 m 1'8"	42 mm

Hawk V-Lite 2x Squeeze Anamorphic Prime Lenses

Figure 7.198 Hawk V-Lite 2x Squeeze Anamorphic Lenses.

Hawk V-Lite 2x Anamorphics are designed to minimize distortion and increase resolution and contrast. V-Lites are fully color matched to all other Hawk Anamorphics. Vantage employs telecentric optical design, T-Stops on the Hawk V-Lite lenses are constant from infinity to close focus and there is no light loss while focusing. Maximum even field light transmission is maintained throughout the whole focus range, and Hawk V-Plus and V-Lite 2x squeeze lenses also perform very well at close focus. New design features include lighter weight, improved PL mount and redesigned focus scale ergonomically optimized for parallax free reading from both sides of the lens. V-Plus and V-Lite 2x Squeezed Anamorphics locate the anamorphic element at the front of the taking lens.

Figure 7.199 Hawk V-Lite 2x Squeeze 45m Anamorphic Prime Lens.

Table 7.39 Hawk V-Lite 2x Squeeze series primes

Focal Length	Aperture	Close Focus ft/m	Image Circle
V-Lite 28 28mm	T 2.2–T16	0.8m/2'7"	28mm
V-Lite 35 35mm	T 2.2–T16	1m/3'3"	30mm
V-Lite 45 45mm	T 2.2–T16	1m/3'3"	32mm
V-Lite 55 55mm	T 2.2–T16	1m/3'3"	34mm
V-Lite 65 65mm	T 2.2–T16	1m/3'3"	34mm
V-Lite 80 80mm	T 2.2–T16	1m/3'3"	36mm
V-Lite 110 110mm	T 3–T16	1m/3'3"	40mm
V-Lite 140 140mm	T 3.5–T22	1m/3'3"	42mm

The range of Hawk V-Lite Anamorphics are designed from scratch and are unique in their construction. V-Lite focus scales are optimized for adjustment during camera prep. The focus gear ring has been designed to be responsive, reliable, and durable, and the follow focus gear has also been moved closer to the camera body in order to optimize ease in focusing. A new labeling design makes it easier to distinguish the different focal lengths, and every lens is marked clearly with the corresponding focal distance on both sides.

Hawk V-Lite Vintage '74 Prime Lenses

Figure 7.200 Hawk V-Lite 45mm Vintage '74 Anamorphic Prime Lens.

Hawk's Vintage '74 anamorphics employ coatings from the 1970s that create more internal barrel flare, hazing, lower contrast, bluer streaks, and all the artifacts that anamorphic lens manufacturers have been working so hard to eliminate for years.

Figure 7.201 Hawk V-Lite Vintage '74 2x Squeeze 35mm prime lenses.

Table 7.40 Hawk V-Lite Vintage '74 Primes

Focal Length	Aperture	Close Focus ft/m	Image Circle
V-Lite 28 28mm	T 2.2–T 16	2'7"/0.8m	28mm
V-Lite 35 35mm	T 2.2–T 16	3'3"/1m	30mm
V-Lite 45 45mm	T 2.2–T 16	3'3"/1m	32mm
V-Lite 55 55mm	T 2.2–T 16	3'3"/1m	34mm
V-Lite 55 Macro 55mm	T 2.2–T 16	1' 2"/.35m	30mm
V-Lite 65 65mm	T 2.2–T 16	3'3"/1m	34mm
V-Lite 80 80mm	T 2.2–T 16	3'3"/1m	36mm
V-Lite 110 110mm	T 3–T 16	3'3"/1m	40mm
V-Lite 140 140mm	T 3.5–T 22	3'3"/1m	42mm

The Hawk Vintage '74 series feature distinctive white barrels, and are targeted at a nostalgic cinematographer that loves the look of old

Cinemascope and Panavision anamorphics. Digital cameras now are almost all capable of delivering quality images, so it falls to optics to deliver an image that differentiates a look. These newly designed "old school" lenses give the cinematographer oval bokehs, blue streaks, secondary images and flares, and unpredictable aberrations. Hawk also added a V-Lite 55mm macro lens which is available in multiple configurations, as a 2x squeeze anamorphic lens, a 2x anamorphic Vintage '74 lens, a 1.3x anamorphic lens, and as a 1.3x Vintage '74 lens. All versions of the 55mm are T2.2 with close focus distance of 0.35m/1'2" and an image circle of 30mm.

Hawk V-Plus Vintage '74 Front Anamorphic Zoom Lenses

Figure 7.202 Hawk V-Plus Vintage '74 Front anamorphic Zoom Lenses.

Hawk V-Plus Vintage '74 front anamorphic zoom lenses 45–90mm/T 2.9 and 80–180mm/T2.9 give cinematographers the versatility and advantages of zoom lenses while delivering the same look as the '74 anamorphic primes. They are also available as standard, non-vintage versions, and their technical data is identical.

Table 7.41 Hawk V-Plus Vintage '74 front anamorphic zoom lenses.

Hawk V-Plus Vintage '74	Front Anamorphic Zoom Lenses		
Focal Length	**Aperture**	**Close Focus Ft / m**	**Image Circle**
V Plus 45-90mm	T2.8–T16	2'6"/0,75m	31 mm
V Plus 80-180mm	T2.8–T16	3'3"/1m	32 mm

Hawk V-Plus Anamorphic Prime Lenses

Figure 7.203 Hawk V-Plus Series Prime Lenses.

Hawk V-Plus lenses feature close focus optics and have been built with a "masking" of the image area. The system consists of three strategically positioned masks within the lens: one mask at the front element, a second mask positioned before the cylindrical elements and a third mask at the rear element. The cut outs of those masks are individually designed for every lens according to its optical path, and the result is a vast improvement in flare and veiling performance. V-Plus lenses feature newly designed focus scales, ergonomically optimized for clear parallax free reading from both sides of the lens employing new engraving techniques.

Table 7.42 Hawk V-Plus anamorphic prime lenses

Hawk V Plus Anamorphic Prime Lenses

Focal Length	Aperture	Close Focus Ft / m	Image Circle
V Plus 35mm	T2.2–T16	2'6"/0,75m	29 mm
V Plus 40mm	T2.2–T16	2'6"/0,75m	30 mm
V Plus 50mm	T2.2–T16	2'/0,6m	32 mm
V Plus 65mm	T3–T22	1'2"/0,35m	30 mm
V Plus 75mm	T2.2–T16	2'/0,6m	34 mm
V Plus 85mm	T2.2–T16	2'/0,6m	34 mm
V Plus 100mm	T2.2–T16	3'3"/1m	34 mm
V Plus 120mm	T3.5–T32	1'5"/0,42m	31 mm
V Plus 135mm	T3–T22	3'3"/1m	36 mm
V Plus 150mm	T3–T22	3'3"/1m	36 mm

Hawk V-Series Anamorphic Primes and Zooms

Figure 7.204 Hawk V-Series Anamorphics.

These lenses are some of the first lenses produced by Hawk, featuring robust construction and excellent glass. Hawk V-Series features good close focus ability and recent improvements to the overall performance of the lenses.

Table 7.43 Hawk V-Series 2x Squeeze lenses

Hawk V Series 2x Squeeze Primes and Zooms

Focal Length	Aperture	Close Focus Ft / m	Image Circle
V 25mm	T2.2-16	3'6"/1m	28 mm
V 30mm	T2.2-16	2'8"/0.8m	28 mm
V 35mm	T2.2-16	2'6"/0.75m	29 mm
V 40mm	T2.2-16	2'6"/0.75m	30 mm
V 50mm	T2.2-16	2'/0.6m	32 mm
V 60mm	T2.2-16	2'/0.6m	32 mm
V 75mm	T2.2-16	2'/0.6m	34 mm
V 100mm	T2.2-16	3'6"/1m	34 mm
V 135mm	T3-32	3'6"/1m	36 mm
V 180mm	T3-32	6'6"/2m	36 mm
V 250mm	T3-32	6'6"/2m	37 mm
V 350mm	T4-32	6'6"/3m	37 mm

Hawk V Series 2x Squeeze Zooms

Focal Length	Aperture	Close Focus Ft / m	Image Circle
V 46-230mm	T4-32	9'9"/3m	30 mm
V 300-900mm	T4-32	9'9"/3m	41 mm

Hawk C-Series Anamorphic Primes and Zooms

Figure 7.205 Hawk C-Series Anamorphics.

The C-Series first generation of Hawk anamorphic lenses were designed and produced over 20 years ago and are still in superb working condition. Many cinematographers love the beautifully classic look of these lenses.

Table 7.44 Hawk C-Series 2x Squeeze lenses

Hawk C Series 2x Squeeze Primes			
Focal Length	Aperture	Close Focus Ft / m	Image Circle
C 40mm	T2.2-16	3'3"/1m	28 mm
C 50mm	T2.2-16	3'3"/1m	32 mm
C 60mm	T2.2-16	3'3"/1m	36 mm
C 75mm	T2.2-16	3'3"/1m	36 mm
C 100mm	T3-22	3'3"/1m	39 mm
Hawk C Series 2x Squeeze Zoom Lens			
Focal Length	Aperture	Close Focus Ft / m	Image Circle
C 55-165mm	T4-22	3'3"/1m	30 mm

Table 7.45 Hawk V-Lite Series 1.3x Squeeze lenses

Hawk V-Lite 1.3x Squeeze Primes			
Focal Length	Aperture	Close Focus Ft / m	Image Circle
V-Lite 20 20 mm	T 2.2 - T 16	2" / 0.6m	32 mm
V-Lite 24 24 mm	T 2.2 - T 16	2" / 0.6m	32 mm
V-Lite 28 28 mm	T 2.2 - T 16	2" 7" / 0.8m	28 mm
V-Lite 35 35 mm	T 2.2 - T 16	3'3"/1m	30 mm
V-Lite 45 45 mm	T 2.2 - T 16	3'3"/1m	32 mm
V-Lite 55 55 mm	T 2.2 - T 16	3'3"/1m	34 mm
V-Lite 65 65 mm	T 2.2 - T 16	3'3"/1m	34 mm
V-Lite 80 80 mm	T 2.2 - T 16	3'3"/1m	36 mm
V-Lite 110 110 mm	T 3 - T 16	3'3"/1m	40 mm
V-Lite 140 140 mm	T 3.5 - T 16	3'3"/1m	42 mm
Hawk V-Plus1.3x Squeeze Zooms			
Focal Length	Aperture	Close Focus Ft / m	Image Circle
30-60mm	T 2.8 - T 16	2" / 0.6m	30 mm
45-90mm	T 2.8 - T 16	2' 6" / 0.75m	31 mm
80-180mm	T 2.8 - T 16	3' 3" / 1m	32 mm

Hawk V-Lite 1.3x Squeeze Anamorphic Primes and Zooms

Figure 7.206 Hawk V-Lite 1.3x Squeeze Prime Lens.

IB/E RAPTOR

Figure 7.207

*Source:*www.ibe-optics.com/en/products/cine/lenses/raptor-primes

Both 1.3x and 2.0x squeeze ratio anamorphics are popular in use on digital cameras, but Hawk 1.3 squeeze anamorphic lenses are used frequently with the ARRI ALEXA, EV/EV+, and many other 16 × 9 single sensor cameras. Simple math shows that a 1.85 aspect ratio × 1.30 (the Hawk squeeze factor) = 2.40 scope aspect ratio. A fairly simple post production un squeeze resizing of the image can yield a beautiful 2.40 scope picture that utilizes almost every pixel on a 16 × 9 sensor. Using a 4 × 3 sensor area, the image can be unsqueezed to 1:78 for a 16 × 9 HDTV release. 1.3x Hawks give oval bokehs, shallow depth of field and interesting anamorphic flares. Despite a small amount of barrel distortion (normal in anamorphic lenses), they handle contrast very well and yield clean sharp images. Because the squeeze factor is smaller, the anamorphic effects are not as pronounced as they are with conventional 2x anamorphics, but they are still evident. The V-Lite 1.3 Squeeze series are also available as Vintage '74 lenses, with identical technical specifications.

IB/E OPTICS Raptor large format macro lens set comes in four focal lengths; 60mm, 100mm, 150mm, and 180mm. The Raptors are designed to cover up to RED Weapon 6K and 8K, SONY A7, and ARRI's ALEXA 65. Raptor lenses featuring full frame (24×36) coverage, 1:1 magnification, T-Stop 2.9 at all focal lengths, as well as robust and durable mechanics. They exhibit no breathing or change in focal length when focusing, and internal focusing enables no change in lens length through the entire range of focus. Features include extended color correction, consistent distance from flange to iris to focus ring, common front diameters of 95 mm, M 0.8 gears for focus and iris. Focus barrel travel is 320 degrees and nine leaf iris travel is 60 degrees for all lenses. Lenses feature a Universal Mounting

System available for PL, Nikon F, Canon EF, SONY NEX E, etc. Maximum magnification is 1:1 on all four lenses, with a maximum aperture at infinity of T 2.9 and at near focus of T 5.3.

The movement toward larger format sensors is in progress and the number of large format cameras available keeps growing and includes the ALEXA LF, ALEXA 65, SONY VENICE, RED MONSTRO 8K VV, Panavision Millennium DXL2, and others. Larger sensors deliver a film-style look with interesting bokeh due to their very shallow depth of field and require lenses that can cover the complete area. The IBE Raptor large format prime lens set is building to fit the needs of the larger format cameras.

Table 7.46 IB/E Raptor lenses

IB/E Raptor macro lenses			
Focal Length	T-Stop	Close Focus	Image Circle
60mm	T 2.9–T 22	19cm/7.5"	50mm/1.97"
100mm	T 2.9–T 22	31.2cm/12.2"	50mm/1.97"
150mm	T 2.9–T 22	38.0cm/15.0"	50mm/1.97"
180mm	T 2.9–T 22	47.0cm/18.5"	50mm/1.97"
IB/E Raptor prime lenses			
40mm	T2.4–T22	28.6cm/18"	50mm/1.97"
80mm	T2.4–T22	66cm/26"	50mm/1.97"

Illumina S35 MKII and MKIII Lenses by LOMO/LUMATECH

Figure 7.208

Source: www.lomo.ru;www.lumatechinc.com/S35.html.

Figure 7.209 LOMO ILLUMINA Super 35 MKII and MKIII Lenses.

Illumina Super 35 lenses are built by the LOMO optical design Bureau, St. Petersburg, Russian Federation. Glass is supplied to LOMO by Schott of Germany. Illumina primes are available in focal lengths of 14mm, 18mm, 25mm, 35mm, 50mm, 85mm, and 135mm.

PL lens mount front diameters are 95mm from 18mm to 135mm and 120mm for the 14mm. PL back focus is 52mm with clearance for spinning mirror shutters, gearing is 0.8 metric for both iris and focus. Minimum image circle for the Illumina S35 T1.3 primes covers the 5.5K 15×30mm format, most units cover a RED Dragon sensor.

Illuminas employ a double-helical thread focus mechanism with a bearing system. The focus gear does not move forward or back when focusing, but the front of the lens and the iris gear track in and out up to 5mm. Focus movement rotates through 270 degrees and front elements do not rotate when focusing. All lenses in the set weigh under 3.5 lbs.

Table 7.47 LOMO ILLUMINA Super35 MKII and MKIII prime lenses

LOMO ILLUMINA	MKII S35 lenses		
Focal Length	T-Stop	Close Focus inches/m	Image Circle
14mm	T1.8	9.8"/0.25m	30.8mm
18mm	T1.2	9.8"/0.25m	30.8mm
25mm	T1.2	11.8"/0.3m	30.8mm
35mm	T1.2	14"/0.35m	30.8mm
50mm	T1.2	28"/0.7m	30.8mm
85mm	T1.2	37"/0.91m	30.8mm
135mm	T1.8	5'/1.5m	30.8mm

LOMO ILLUMINA	MKIII S35 lenses		
Focal Length	T-Stop	Close Focus inches/m	Image Circle
14mm	T1.8	9.8"/0.25m	30.8mm
18mm	T1.2	9.8"/0.25m	30.8mm
25mm	T1.2	11.8"/0.3m	30.8mm
35mm	T1.2	14"/0.36m	30.8mm
50mm	T1.2	24"/0.6m	30.8mm
85mm	T1.2	37"/0.91m	30.8mm
135mm	T1.8	5'/1.5m	30.8mm

Kinefinity Lenses

Figure 7.210

*Source:*www.kinefinity.com/shop/mavo_prime_lens/?lang=en.

Figure 7.211 Kinefinity MAVO Lenses.

Kinefinity MAVO Prime lenses are designed specifically for large format cinema cameras up to 8K Full Frame with a coverage area of 46.5mm and wide open stop of T2.0. Apochromatic optical design minimizes purple or green fringing at wide open aperture for natural, color-matched rendition. MAVO Primes minimize breathing effects, even at 75mm and 100mm. High MTF performance supports up to 8K resolution on Full Frame cameras, with good sharpness and contrast, beautiful bokeh, natural focus transitions, and natural highlight fall-off.

Front diameters are 3.7" (95mm) and weighing 2.5 to 2.9 lbs. (1.1 to 1.3kg), uniform length of 4.5"(117mm), make these lightweight and compact lenses ideal for Large Format cameras working handheld, with Steadicam, or even on drones. Large cine-style focus and iris rings on MAVO primes allow for smooth focus and iris adjustments. Focus/iris ring locations are in exactly the same location on all lenses for convenience in lens changes. Focus rotation is 270 degrees, and iris rotation is 70 degrees. The large iris ring provides continuous adjustment from T2.0 to T22 with 1/3 and 1 stop marks and every lens has large legible focus marks from infinity to minimum object distance. MAVO primes are available in PL mount, Canon EF, and SONY E mounts. The MAVO Prime 100mm lens features close focusing ability with minimum object distance of 56cm.

LEITZ Cine Lenses

Figure 7.212

Source: www.LEITZ-cine.com.

LEITZ PRIMES

Figure 7.213 LEITZ PRIME Lenses.

Designed to cover the frame, the **LEITZ PRIME** Lenses feature stainless steel **ARRI LPL** mount and project a usable VistaVision image circle of 46.5mm diameter, compatible with the ARRI ALEXA LF and LF Mini. The T1.8 maximum aperture is consistent among the range except for the 180mm at T2. Geared focus and iris control rings share the same position among every lens in the set and with consistent front diameter, lens changes can be made without having to move follow focus or lens control systems.

Table 7.48 Kinefinity MAVO lenses

Kinefinity Mavo Lenses			
Focal length	T-Stop	Close Focus	Image Circle
25mm	2.1	0.21m / 8"	46.5mm
35mm	2	0.3 m / 12"	46.5mm
50mm	2	0.44m / 17"	46.5mm
75mm	2	0.69m / 27"	46.5mm
100mm	2	0.56 m / 22"	46.5mm

Figure 7.214 LEITZ PRIME Lens 35mm.

An internal focus cam-follower mechanism provides the lens with a non-rotating front, perfect for clip-on matte boxes. A generous number of focus marks are distributed along the focus scales, and 270° of focus rotation makes for accurate focus pulls. The 114mm diameter front is standard across the set of lenses, which also speeds up lens changes when working with a matte box.

Modern lens design and tight tolerances ensure low distortion, high resolution, and excellent color rendition. A 15-blade circular iris provides a natural-looking bokeh and 270° of focus rotation allows for extremely accurate focus marks and focus pulls.

Table 7.49 LEITZ PRIME lenses

Focal Length	T-Stop	Close Focus ft/m	Image Circle
18mm	T1.8	1'2"/.36m	46.5mm
21mm	T1.8	1'10"/.55m	46.5mm
25mm	T1.8	1'10"/.55m	46.5mm
29mm	T1.8	1'2"/.35m	46.5mm
35mm	T1.8	1'6"/.45m	46.5mm
40mm	T1.8	1'2"/.36m	46.5mm
50mm	T1.8	1'7"/.47m	46.5mm
65mm	T1.8	2'2"/.65m	46.5mm
75mm	T1.8	2'6"/.75m	46.5mm
100mm	T1.8	3'11"/1.2m	46.5mm
135mm	T1.8	3'11"/1.2m	46.5mm
180mm	T2	4'11"/1.5m	46.5mm

LEITZ ZOOMS

Figure 7.215 LEITZ 25–75mm Zoom Lens.

The LEITZ ZOOM 25–75mm PL Lens features an LPL mount and has an image circle that covers the VistaVision format, that covers full-frame sensors. Parfocal design and a T2.8 aperture throughout its zoom range, the lens holds focus throughout the zoom and does not ramp exposure. The lens design also reduces the

breathing and image shift sometimes encountered while zooming and focusing. It is color-matched to LEITZ PRIMES for seamless intercutting between the lenses. A 15-blade iris produces a natural looking round bokeh in out-of-focus areas. The focus, iris, and zoom control rings have cine-style 0.8 MOD gears, and the focus ring features approximately 270 degrees of rotation. The 25 to 75mm zoom features a 114mm front diameter common to many cinema-style matte boxes. Clickless 15-bladed iris gives an attractive bokeh, 114mm front diameter is compatible with most matte boxes.

Figure 7.216 LEITZ 55–125mm Zoom Lens.

The LEITZ ZOOM 55–125mm Lens has an image circle that covers the VistaVision format and LPL lens mount. Featuring a parfocal design and a T2.8 aperture throughout its zoom range, the lens holds focus throughout the zoom and does not ramp exposure as you get to the extremes of the range. The lens design also reduces the breathing and image shift sometimes encountered while zooming and focusing. It is color-matched to LEITZ PRIMES for seamless intercutting between the lenses. A 21-blade iris produces pleasing round bokeh in out-of-focus areas. The focus, iris, and zoom control rings have cine-style 0.8 MOD gears, and the focus ring features approximately 270 degrees of rotation. The 25 to 75mm zoom features a 114mm front diameter common to many cinema-style matte boxes. The lens has a built-in support foot with a 3/8"–16 threaded mounting hole that helps support the lens with the aid of an optional 3/8"–16 rod-mounted lens support.

Table 7.50 LEITZ ZOOM lenses

Focal Length	T-Stop	Close Focus ft/m	Image Circle
25–75mm	T2.8	36"/.91m	46.5mm
55–125mm	T2.8	41"/1.04m	46.5mm

LEITZ SUMMILUX-C Cine Lenses

Figure 7.217 LEITZ SUMMILUX-**C** Cine Lenses.

LEITZ's SUMMILUX-**C** high speed T1.4 close focus primes employ a multi-aspheric design and precision lens mechanics to provide very good flat field coverage across the entire 35mm frame. LEITZ SUMMILUX-**C** lenses feature uniform distance focus scales, and similar location of focus and iris rings allows for quick lens changes. Lightweight and rugged, the lens mounts are made of glass impregnated titanium for smoothness and strength, and focusing exhibits no appreciable breathing. LEITZ SUMMILUX-**C** lenses weigh between 3.5 and 4.0 pounds each. Available in focal lengths of 16mm, 18mm, 21mm, 25mm, 35mm, 40mm, 50mm, 75mm, 100mm, and 135mm.

SUMMILUX-**C** PRIMES feature very high resolution, the entire set is capable of 4k and beyond. They exhibit extremely high contrast image transfer, exceptionally low chromatic aberration across the full image, high relative illumination with flat field and minimal shading, and consistent image quality throughout the range of focus.

LEITZ's SUMMILUX-**C** lenses employ a linear iris that stops to closure, and both front and rear filter fit capability. They also feature a small diameter focus scale, with expanded focus mark spacing in critical focus range, constant focus mark spacing on all lenses in critical focus ranges. The focus rings of all the LEITZ SUMMILUX-**C** PRIMES have 270 degrees of rotation. A feature unique to the LEITZ SUMMILUX-**C** PRIMES is that the focus ring is divided in half. Minimum object distance to 6' is 135 degrees of rotation, and 6' to infinity is 135 degrees of rotation on the barrel, providing a uniform focus scale for all the lenses from 6' to infinity.

Table 7.51 LEITZ SUMMILUX-C lenses

Focal Length	Aperture	Close Focus inches/m	Image Circle
16mm	T1.4–22-closed	1'6"/0.45m	33mm
18mm	T1.4–22-closed	1'6"/0.45m	33mm
21mm	T1.4–22-closed	1'3"/0.38m	33mm
25mm	T1.4–22-closed	1'3"/0.38m	33mm
29mm	T1.4–22-closed	1'6"/0.45m	33mm
35mm	T1.4–22-closed	1'6"/0.45m	33mm
40mm	T1.4–22-closed	1'6"/0.45m	33mm
50mm	T1.4–22-closed	2'/0.60m	33mm
65mm	T1.4–22-closed	1'6"/0.45m	33mm
75mm	T1.4–22-closed	2'6"/0.76m	33mm
100mm	T1.4–22-closed	3'3"/0.90m	33mm
135mm	T1.4–22-closed	4'1"/1.25m	33mm

LEITZ SUMMICRON-C Lenses

Figure 7.218 LEITZ SUMMICRON-**C** Cine Lenses.

The LEITZ SUMMICRON-**C** lenses bring much of the look and feel of the SUMMILUX-**C** lenses but with one less stop and at a much lower cost. They retain the natural focus transitions, good color rendition, and creamy sharpness that is distinctive of the LEITZ look and feel but in a smaller, more accessible package. The SUMMICRON-**C** lenses are as well suited for big budget feature films and TV shows as they are production companies and growing businesses looking for a beautiful set of lenses to invest in that will provide a timeless and workable image for all kinds of productions. They are designed to color match and intercut with the LEITZ SUMMILUX-**C** lenses.

Like the SUMMILUX-**C** lenses, the LEITZ SUMMICRON-**C** lenses focus falls off gently to give a dimensionality to faces. Their ability to cleanly resolve edges and other fine details makes them one of the sharpest sets of cine lenses available. SUMMICRON-**C** lenses were designed for larger digital sensors and have a larger image circle to maximize resolution while maintaining even illumination and holding focus all the way into the corners of the frame.

Table 7.52 LEITZ SUMMICRON-**C** lenses

Focal Length	T-Stop	Close Focus ft/m	Image Circle
15mm	T2–22 close	1'/.3m	36mm
18mm	T2–22 close	1'/.3m	36mm
21mm	T2–22 close	1'/.3m	36mm

Focal Length	T-Stop	Close Focus ft/m	Image Circle
25mm	T2–22 close	1'/.3m	36mm
29mm	T2–22 close	1'/.3m	36mm
35mm	T2–22 close	1'2"/.36m	36mm
40mm	T2–22 close	1'6"/.45m	36mm
50mm	T2–22 close	2'/.6m	36mm
75mm	T2–22 close	2'7"/.8m	36mm
100mm	T2–22 close	3'3"/1m	36mm
135mm	T2–22 close	4'6"/1.35m	36mm

Table 7.53 LEITZ THALIA prime lenses

Focal Length	T-Stop	Close Focus	Image Circle
24mm Makro	3.6	0.2m/7.8"	60mm
30mm	2.9	0.5m/20"	60mm
35mm	2.6	0.55m/22"	60mm
45mm	2.9	0.6 m/24"	60mm
55mm Makro	2.8	0.3m/11.7"	60mm
70mm	2.6	0.5m/20"	60mm
90mm THALIA-T	2.2	0.9m/36"	60mm
100mm	2.2	0.7m/28"	60mm
120mm Makro	2.6	0.57m/22.5"	60mm
180mm	3.6	1.5m/60"	60mm

LEITZ THALIA Lenses

Figure 7.219 LEITZ THALIA Cine Lenses.

LEITZ THALIA PRIME lenses offer a consistently cinematic look and feel throughout the range of ten lenses from 24mm to 180mm covering an image circle of 60mm that covers sensors from the ARRI ALEXA 65, to VistaVision and Super 35 sensors. They are lightweight and compact with matched front diameters of 95mm and are available in PL mount with /i Technology metadata contacts. The iris design of THALIA lenses maintains a circular iris through all aperture stops, creating a cinematic bokeh. THALIA lenses offer many of the image characteristics that have driven cinematographers to pair older lenses with digital sensors. They are clear without being overly sharp, focus is smooth and forgiving without looking soft.

Figure 7.220 LEITZ THALIA MAKRO Lenses with THALIA **T**-90.

LEITZ M 0.8 Lenses

Figure 7.221 LEITZ M 0.8 Cine Lenses.

For over 60 years LEITZ M full frame lenses have still images around the world. Now LEITZ Cine Wetzlar, sister company to LEITZ Camera, are bringing the characteristics of these legendary still lenses to cinema with their M 0.8 series. The M 0.8 lenses interpret light and skin tones with a unique sense of clarity, color and charisma.

LEITZ offers five lenses in this series, choosing the fastest in each focal length. They include: 21mm f/1.4, 24mm f/1.4, 28mm f/1.4, 35mm f/1.4, 50mm f1.4 (and the 50mm f/0.95 Noctilux), 75mm f2.0, and 90mm f2.0. Lenses will be available individually or as a set. LEITZ M 0.8 lenses are among the smallest lenses that can be used with cine accessories on professional cameras. They are well suited for compact cameras, drones, gimbals, and underwater camera configurations.

LEITZ M 0.8 lenses are only available in LEITZ M mount, mounts are available for SONY VENICE, ARRI ALEXA mini, and ARRI AMIRA cameras.

Table 7.54 LEITZ **M** 0.8 prime lenses

Focal Length	T-Stop	Close Focus	Image Circle
21mm LEITZ M mount	1.4	2'3"/0.7m	FF 24mm × 36mm
24mm LEITZ M mount	1.4	2'3"/0.7m	FF 24mm × 36mm
28mm LEITZ M mount	1.4	2'3"/0.7m	FF 24mm × 36mm
35mm LEITZ M mount	1.4	2'3"/0.7m	FF 24mm × 36mm
50mm LEITZ M mount	1.4	2'3"/0.7m	FF 24mm × 36mm
50-N LEITZ M mount	0.95	3'3"/1m	FF 24mm × 36mm
75mm LEITZ M mount	2.1	2'3"/0.7m	FF 24mm × 36mm
90mm LEITZ M mount	2	3'3"/1m	FF 24mm × 36mm

Panavision Lenses

Figure 7.222

Source: www.panavision.com/home.

Panavison have spent 66 years building a dizzying assortment of optics to be available to cinematographers. They are currently engaged in adapting much of their lens catalog for use on Full Frame sensor cameras, and they can adapt almost any lens the customer asks for to fill Full Frame. For this reason, the lens tables in the Panavision section do not specify lens coverage circle. In any event, even if you don't see it in their catalog, ask them, they probably have it. If they don't have it, they would probably build it for you, and enjoy doing it!

Primo L-Series Prime Lenses

Figure 7.223 Panavision Primo L-Series Family of Lenses.

Panavision's Primo lenses combine high contrast and good resolution with even field illumination, minimal veiling glare, minimal geometric distortion, and

no ghosting. Primos are designed to intercut with all other lenses in the Primo line. Although they were originally designed and optimized for film, they can and are being re-optimized for digital sensors.

The L-series of Primo prime lenses are available in focal lengths ranging from 10mm to 150mm. All lenses are a T1.9 with close focusing distances ranging from 2 feet to 5 feet 9 inches depending on focal length.

Table 7.55 Panavision Primo L Series prime lenses

Focal Length	Aperture	Close Focus inches/cm
SL10 10mm	1.9	24"/61cm
SL 14.5 14.5mm	1.9	24"/61cm
SL17.5 17.5mm	1.9	24"/61cm
SL21 21mm	1.9	24"/61cm
SL27 27mm	1.9	24"/61cm
SL35 35mm	1.9	24"/61cm
SL40 40mm	1.9	24"/61cm
SL50 50mm	1.9	24"/61cm
SL65 65mm	1.8	24"/61cm
SL75 75mm	1.9	36"/91.4 cm
SL85 85mm	1.8	24"/61cm
SL100 100mm	1.9	36"/91.4 cm
SL125 125mm	1.8	26"/66cm
SL150 150mm	1.9	60.8"/154.3cm

Primo Close Focus Lenses

Panavision also offers the option of close focus prime lenses ranging from 14.5mm to 35mm. All lenses are T1.9 with close focusing distances ranging from 7½ inches to 11 inches from the film plane, depending on the focal length of the lens you are using. This translates to close focus of 2 inches or less from the front of the lens. A wide-angle adapter is available for use on the Primo Close Focus 14.5mm creating an 11.5mm wide-angle lens.

Table 7.56 Panavision Primo close focus prime lenses

Panavision Primo Close Focus Series		
Focal length	Aperture	Close Focus Cm / Inches
SL14.5-CF 14.5mm	1.9	21cm / 8.25"
SL17.5-CF 17.5mm	1.9	19.1cm / 7.5"
SL21-CF 21mm	1.9	24.1cm / 9.5"
SL24-CF 24mm	1.8	27.9cm / 11"
SL27-CF 27mm	1.9	24.1cm / 9.5"
SL30-CF 30mm	1.8	25.4cm / 10"
SL35-CF 35mm	1.9	27.9cm / 11"

Primo "Classic Series" Prime Lenses

Figure 7.224 Panavision Primo Classic 75mm Lens.

Panavision Primo Classic Series lenses deliver the same color and performance as the original Primo line of lenses while incorporating some unique upgrades and options.

These classic lenses are available in focal lengths ranging from 21mm to 125mm. Five (21mm, 27mm, 35mm, 50mm, and 100mm) utilize existing glass designs with new mechanics all with a speed of T1.9 and close focusing distances ranging from 9½ inches to 16 inches. An additional five focal lengths (24mm, 30mm, 65mm, 85mm, and 125mm) utilize new glass and mechanics with speeds of either T1.7 or T1.8 and close focusing distances ranging from 10 inches to 25½ inches.

All the lenses have cam drive mechanisms with linearly spaced focus scales from close focus to infinity. The lens focusing mechanisms transition into a continuous close focus to macro focusing capability. Three of the longer lenses (65mm, 100mm, and 125mm) employ linear bearing technology. All of the lenses accept a screw-on rear gel filter holder. All of the Primo classic lenses are color matched to the original Primo L-series Primes.

The Primo Classic 24mm, 30mm, 65mm, 85mm, and 125mm are available in versions which offer a special feature called soft effect. This effect can be variably selected (using an internal optical system) manually or with a motor. The soft effect system is calibrated with indexed markings that go from 0 to 3. At the "0" setting you can expect the same performance as the rest of the Primo line of lenses. At levels 1, 2, and 3 the lenses will progressively build up to provide a more classic soft focus, deep field effect reminiscent of cine lenses from the past. It is important to note that the soft effect is only present at or near full aperture and will be difficult to see through the viewfinder. The lenses can be used both normally, without the soft effect, or with the soft effect, which can be varied in shot.

The same focal lengths that comprise the Classic Soft Effect lenses are also available in smaller, lighter versions without the Soft Effect option. The focal lengths of this version are 24mm, 30mm, 65mm, 85mm, and 125mm.

The soft effect calibrated scale correlates to the lenses set to a constant object magnification and results in the same effect for different focal length lenses. Unlike normal filters, which depend on scattering of light, the soft effect is achieved by disturbing the wave-front so there is no apparent milky diffusion look. Objects at or near the best focus are affected, leaving shadow detail and blacks unaffected as well as highlights with little or no blooming.

Table 7.57 Panavision Primo Classic Series prime lenses

Panavision Primo Classic Series		
Focal length	**Aperture**	**Close Focus Inches**
SL21-M 21mm	1.9	9.5" / 24.1cm
SL24-MS 24mm	1.7	10" / 25.4cm
SL27-M 27mm	1.9	9.5" / 24.1cm
SL30-MS 30mm	1.7	10" / 25.4cm
SL35-M 35mm	1.9	11" / 27.9cm
SL50-M 50mm	1.9	11" / 27.9cm
SL65-MS 65mm	1.7	13.5" / 34.3cm
SL85-MS 85mm	1.7	16.5" / 41.9cm
SL100-M 100mm	1.9	16.5" / 41.9cm
SL125-MS 125mm	1.8	25.5" / 64.8cm

Primo Zoom Lenses

Primo Zooms are built to match the color and performance of the Primo Prime lenses. Primo Zoom lenses combine high contrast and resolution with even field illumination, minimal veiling glare, minimal geometric distortion, and no ghosting. The overall performance of the Primo Zoom allows seamless intercutting of shots from primes to zoom.

4:1 Primo Zoom – SLZ

Figure 7.225 Panavision 17.5–75mm 4:1 Primo Zoom Lens.

The 4:1 Primo Zoom is T2.3 with a focal length range of 17.5–75mm, maintaining a constant aperture through all zoom and focus positions. It has continuous close focusing to macro 1:6 with a minimum distance of 2½ feet. There is minimal breathing when focusing at short focal lengths. When using the optional Primo 1.4x extender it becomes a 24.5–105mm, T3.2 lens with a 1:4 macro magnification and a close focusing distance of 2 feet 10 inches.

11:1 Primo Zoom – SLZ11

Figure 7.226 Panavision 24–275mm 11:1 Primo Zoom lens.

The 11:1 Primo Zoom is a high contrast ratio, high-performance zoom. With an aperture of T2.8 and a focal length range of 24–275mm, it has become the measure by which all cine zoom lenses are judged. It maintains a constant aperture throughout zoom and focus. It has continuous close focusing to macro 1:3.5 with a minimum distance of 4 feet. There is minimal breathing when focusing at short focal lengths (24mm–60mm).

It is matched in color balance to the full range of Primo prime lenses, and can be used for both zooming and as a variable prime lens. Using the Primo 1.4x extender, it becomes a 34–395mm, T4 lens with a 1:2.5 macro magnification and a close focus distance of 4 feet 1 inch.

3:1 Primo Zoom – SLZ3

Figure 7.227 Panavision 135–420mm 3:1 Primo Zoom Lens.

The 3:1 Primo Zoom is a high speed, high performance telephoto zoom, with an aperture of T2.8 and a focal length range of 135–420mm

that maintains constant aperture at all zoom and focus positions. It has continuous close focusing to macro 1:6 with a minimum distance of 8 feet. There is minimal breathing when focusing at short focal lengths (135mm–200mm). Using the optional Primo 1.4x extender the lens becomes a 190–595mm, T4 lens with a 1:4 macro magnification and a close focusing distance of 8 feet 7 inches.

Primo Macro Zoom – PMZ

Figure 7.228 Panavision Primo 14.5–50mm Macro Zoom Lens.

The Primo Macro Zoom is T2.2 with a focal length range of 14.5–50mm, and is a versatile zoom lens that can replace a set of close-focus primes. It combines wide angle zooming and continuous close focusing in a compact, lightweight design weighing only 9.5 lbs. The Macro zoom covers Super 35 format over its entire zoom range and down to 15 inches close focus. It can yield a 2.2:1 reproduction ratio and due to its unique design, the macro zoom creates a unique bokeh that is unlike any other zoom.

Table 7.58 Panavision Primo Zoom lenses

Panavision Primo Zooms		
	Aperture	Close Focus Inches / cm
SLZ 17.5-75mm	2.3	33" / 83.8cm
SLZ11 24-275mm	2.8	48" / 121.9cm
SLZ3 135-420mm	2.8	102" / 259.1cm
PMZ 14.5-50mm	2.2	15" / 38.1cm

Panavision Compact Zoom Lens – PCZ

Figure 7.229 Panavision Compact Zoom 19–90mm.

The PCZ is a proprietary zoom lens that covers a focal length range of 19–90mm and has a T-stop of T/2.8. The PCZ represents the latest generation of Panavision S-35 compatible spherical zoom design options. The PCZ utilizes a unique design that contain concepts not encountered in other zoom types in the motion picture industry. The compact zoom maximizes contrast, resolution, and field illumination while minimizing breathing, veiling glare, ghosting, distortion, and other aberrations. The PCZ utilizes multiple aspheric surfaces and carefully selected components to produce a lens that is more compact than any other comparable zoom lens in the motion picture industry.

The compact zoom features zero-backlash mechanics, which is especially critical when following focus. Ergonomic considerations include expanded dual-side scales and standard gear locations for focus, zoom, and T-stop.

Panavision PZW

The PZW is a Panavision exclusive lightweight zoom that covers a focal length range of 15–40mm and has a T-stop of T/2.6. The PZW utilizes a patented design that incorporates aspheric lens technology and proprietary design concepts to produce a zoom lens with excellent contrast and resolution performance, very little focus breathing, consistent performance throughout zoom and focus, and very little geometric distortion. The PZW is suited to Steadicam and handheld rigs and the PZW imaging performance rivals prime lenses. The PZW has excellent image illumination across the entire S-35 imaging diagonal and the PZW maintains a constant aperture at all zoom and focus positions. The PZW has a close focus of 2 feet.

Panavision PZM

Figure 7.230 Panavision PZM 70–185 Zoom Lens.

The PZM 70–185 T3.5 zoom lens incorporates the latest optical and mechanical design and fabrication techniques such as aspheric surfaces

and internal bearing group guides. The PZM has image performance equal to or surpassing most prime lenses. The low zoom ratio, modest aperture, and advanced aspherics provide superior imaging with well controlled breathing in a compact form factor that is ideal for handheld and Steadicam situations. Multiple moving groups ensure consistent performance throughout the zoom and focus ranges. The aperture remains constant at all the zoom and focus positions and the field illumination is very consistent from the center to the edge of the designed S-35 imaging diagonal. The PZM has a close focus of 2 feet and a wide open aperture of T/2.6.

Panavision PNZT

The PNZT rounds out the longer end of the light-weight Panavision zoom lenses. The PNZT has a focal length range that spans 60–125mm and has a maximum aperture of T/2.6. The PNZT has a close focus of 3½ feet and is capable of a macro magnification ratio of 1:7. The PNZT utilizes moving groups to ensure consistent performance throughout the zoom and focus range. The PNZT maintains constant aperture at all zoom and focus positions and the field illumination is very consistent from the center to the edge of frame. The PNZT's compact design is well suited to hand-held and Steadicam use and its unique design qualities yield optical performance that rivals any modern prime lens in all aspects of imaging quality.

Panavision Primo 70 Lenses

Figure 7.231 Panavision Primo 70 Lenses.

Panavision's Primo 70 lenses are designed for high-resolution large format sensors and are a great complement to the Panavision DXL and DXL2 cameras. They won't fit on film cameras because their short flange focal depth and shallow rear element proximity to the image plane and would interfere with the spinning mirror reflex shutter. Because the Primo 70s are designed for digital cameras, they take advantage of a shorter flange focal depth, shallower rear vertex working distances, and near telecentric prescriptions. The resulting lenses are "closer" to the imaging sensor than traditional motion picture lenses. The Primo 70 flange distance is a nominal 40mm to the sensor. By comparison, the 35mm Panavision flange depth is 57.15mm and the PL flange distance is 52mm. Primo 70 Series lenses are designed to have very high technical performance. Some of the attributes that are associated with the Primo 70 lenses are very high resolution with very high contrast, matched colorimetry characteristics, and even field illumination across the entire 52mm imaging diagonal.

Unlike film cameras, digital cameras have an infrared (IR) cut-off filter, an optical low-pass filter (OLPF), and a cover glass in front of the sensor. The total thickness of these behind-the-lens elements varies from camera to camera, and the combined thickness and make-up of the optical components have an effect on the optical path that the lens encounters. The Primo 70s are optimized for a 4mm thickness of the glass components in a digital camera.

Primo 70 floating focus elements allow for very good performance at all distances, especially at close focus. In addition, the lenses act like very "weak zooms" that change the focal length just enough to eliminate breathing due to focus change. Primo 70s are designed to cover a 52mm diagonal sensor, so the widest lens in the Primo 70 series, the 24mm on a 70mm sensor would have roughly the same field of view as a 12mm on Super 35mm sensor.

Primo 70s designs include multiple aspheric elements. A single aspheric element can correct optical errors that would take several spherical elements to correct. The use of aspheric elements allows for a 70mm lens to be the same size as a Primo 35mm, but lighter. The Primo 70 design includes elements with anomalous dispersion, which have non-linear refraction of color wavelength characteristics and have the ability to achieve color correction that is normally not possible with standard line glass types. In short, this allows for finer correction of chromatic aberrations. Some of the hallmarking characteristics of the Primo 70 optics are there is very little color fringing (lateral color), coma and astigmatism have been corrected to a very high degree throughout the entire range of focus, and geometric distortion has been controlled to be rectilinear at all field positions. The Primo 70s were designed to produce near diffracted limited performance MTF numbers for the high spatial frequencies encountered in today's modern UHD cameras. The MTF performance of the Primo 70 lenses is consistent from on-axis to the edge of the designed 52mm diagonal.

A unique feature of the Primo 70 lenses is they are equipped with internal t-stop and focus drive motors (24mm excluded). The internal motor drive system is designed to recognize the protocol of various remote focus handsets and can be driven and powered up without any cables via electronic contacts within the camera mounts of the DXL and DXL2 cameras. The Primo 70 lenses are also equipped with metadata capability that can be accessed from the electronic pogo contacts on the lens mounts.

Table 7. 59 Panavision Primo 70 Series lenses

Panavision Primo 70 Series prime lenses			
Focal Length	T-Stop	Close Focus m/inches	Image Circle
24mm	2	0.3m/12"	52mm
27mm	2	0.36m/14"	52mm
35mm	2	0.36m/14"	52mm
40mm	2	0.36m/14"	52mm
50mm	2	0.41m/16"	52mm
65mm	2	0.51m/20"	52mm
80mm	2	0.61m/24"	52mm
100mm	2	0.76 m/30"	52mm
125mm	2	0.91m/36"	52mm
150mm	2	1.2m/48"	52mm
200mm	2.8	1.2m/48"	52mm
250mm	2.8	1.2m/48"	52mm

Panavision Primo 70 Series zoom lenses			
Focal length	T-Stop	Close Focus	Image Circle
15–30mm	2.8	.5588m/22"	52mm
28–80mm	3	0.84m/33"	52mm
70–185mm	3.5	1.5m/60"	52mm
70–200mm	2.8	1.52m/5'	52mm
200–400mm	4.5	1.9m/78"	52mm

Primo Artiste Lenses

Figure 7.232 Panavision Primo Artiste Lenses.

The Primo Artiste lenses are a full series of T/1.8 lenses making them one of the fastest optics available for large-format cinematography. The Artiste lenses have been designed to cover a 52mm image diagonal. The Artiste series is an evolutionary step in design, becoming the second series from Panavision to include a fully internalized motor and complete metadata compatibility. The essence of the Artiste concept is an innovative configuration that takes advantage of the aesthetic flexibility available within large format digital sensors, with the resulting look evoking a quality reminiscent of vintage optics. In addition, the Artiste lenses incorporate multi-layer anti-reflective coatings that keep veiling glare down to a minimum. The series incorporates modern features such as focus breathing control, even field illumination, and optimized close focus performance.

The Primo Artiste come equipped with a Primo 70 lens mount and are capable of working with all S-35 and full-frame digital camera options. Due to the position of the rear optics, the Artiste lenses cannot be used on film cameras. All of the Artiste lenses come with a 4.440" or 113mm front diameter and come in focal lengths ranging from 27mm to 250mm.

Table 7.60 Panavision Primo Artiste lenses

Focal Length	T-Stop	Close Focus inches/m
27mm	1.8	14"/35.6cm
35mm	1.8	14"/35.6cm
40mm	1.8	14"/35.6cm
50mm	1.8	16"/40.6cm
65mm	1.8	20"/50.8cm
80mm	1.8	24"/60cm
100mm	1.8	30"/76.2cm
125mm	1.8	36"/91.44cm
150mm	1.8	48"/121.9cm
200mm	2.6	48"/121.9cm
250mm	2.6	48"/121.9cm

Panaspeed Lenses

Figure 7.233 Panaspeed 50mm T1.4 Lens.

The Panaspeed is the latest lens prime offering from Panavision. The Panaspeed line is designed to cover a 46.5mm image diagonal and range in focal length from 17mm to 180mm. All but the 180mm and 150mm have a T-stop of T/1.4 and the 180mm and 150mm are a T/1.9. The Panaspeed lenses incorporate multi-aspheric lens elements and floating element groups that produce consistent performance from infinity to close focus as well as minimizing focus breathing. The resolution and contrast qualities associated with the Panaspeed optics are similar to the Primo lenses designed for the 35mm format. Some of the hallmarking characteristics of the Panaspeeds are there is very little color fringing (lateral color), coma and astigmatism have been corrected to a very high degree throughout the entire range of focus, and geometric distortion has been controlled to be nearly perfectly rectilinear at all field positions.

Multi-layer coating used throughout the design maintains excellent control of veiling glare and unwanted ghosting artifacts. The flaring characteristics of the Panaspeeds are controlled by the careful selection of both mechanical and optical design traits used consistently within the focal lengths of the series. The Panaspeed lenses have been optimized to work on all of the modern digital cameras and they are also compatible to work with film cameras.

The Panaspeeds come equipped with module .8 metric gears on both the focus and T-stop rings and are standardized with a 4.440" or 113mm front diameter. The Panaspeeds come equipped with a Primo 70 mount and can be fitted with PL mount. Though the Panaspeeds have been designed to cover the 46.5mm diagonal, the Panaspeeds provide excellent performance at the S-35 image diagonals and serve as an excellent addition to the existing Primo series.

Table 7.61 Panavision Panaspeed lenses

Focal Length	T-Stop	Close Focus inches/m
17mm	1.4	17"/43.2cm
24mm	1.4	14"/35.6cm
29mm	1.4	15"/38.1cm
35mm	1.4	16"/40.6cm
40mm	1.4	16"/40.6cm
50mm	1.4	19"/48.3cm
65mm	1.4	24"/60.9cm
80mm	1.4	37"/94cm
100mm	1.4	42"/107cm
135mm	1.4	48"/122cm
150mm	1.9	36"/91.44cm
180mm	1.9	59"/149.9cm

Panavision Sphero 65 Lenses

Figure 7.234 Panavision Sphero 65 Lens.

Sphero 65 lenses feature moderate focus roll-off with subtle aberration accompanied by rounded out-of-focus properties. The attributes of the Sphero 65 optics produce images with blended layers of contrast, natural background separation, pleasing flesh tones, and a glamorous, soft classic look. Updated with modern mechanics and designed around modern multi-layer coatings, the Sphero 65 optics are less susceptible to flare and glare than the System 65 series. Sphero 65 lenses are compatible with both film and digital cameras fitted with a PV 65 mount.

Table 7.62 Panavision Sphero 65 lenses

Focal Length	T-Stop	Close Focus m/inches	Image Circle
24mm	2.8	0.48m/19"	65mm
29mm	2.8	0.5m/20"	65mm
35mm	2.8	0.5m/20"	65mm
40mm	2.8	0.4m/16"	65mm
50mm	2	0.56m/22"	65mm
75mm	2	0.69m/27"	65mm
100mm	2	1.07m/42"	65mm
135mm	2.8	1.53m/60"	65mm
180mm	2.8	1.53m/60"	65mm
300mm	2.8	3.05m/120"	65mm

Super Panavision 70 Lenses

Figure 7.235 Super Panavision 70 Lens.

Super Panavision 70 lenses are true vintage optics. Their optical layouts are epitomized by classic designs from an earlier era. The coatings on the lenses tend to be single layer and produce unique flares and glare that are not represented by modern optics. They produce an image with a lower contrast look with more radiant flaring characteristics. Many of the lenses in this series originate from the early MGM lens inventory Panavision acquired in its early years. The Super Panavision 70 lenses offer a glamorous, softer "vintage" look with a gentle focus roll off, a uniquely contoured bokeh and a smooth texture. SUPER PANAVISION 70 lenses are compatible with both film and digital cameras fitted with a Panavision 65 mount.

Table 7.63 Super Panavision lenses

Super Panavision Prime Lenses			
Focal length	T-Stop	Close Focus	Image Circle
28mm	2.8	0.61 m / 24"	65mm
35mm	2.8	0.38 m / 15"	65mm
50mm	2	0.91 m / 36"	65mm
50mm	2	0.61 m / 24"	65mm
75mm	2.8	0.84 m / 33"	65mm
100mm	2.5	0.99 m / 39"	65mm
150mm	3	0.84 m / 33"	65mm
300mm	2.8	2.59m / 102"	65mm

Panavision System 65 Lenses

Figure 7.236 Panavision System 65 Lens.

System 65 lenses modern coatings and new mechanics make the lenses less susceptible to flare and glare. They give the image the established "classic" 65mm look with organic focus roll off, rounded bokeh, pleasing flesh tones, and a warm, contouring look. The System 65 lens series was originally developed for Far and Away in 1990 and was designed to create a look that complemented the imaging capabilities of motion picture emulsion of that time. The classic design specifications that were applied to the System65 optics lend well to modern digital photography. Panavision System 65 lenses are compatible with both film and digital cameras fitted with a PV 65 mount.

Table 7.64 Panavision System 65 lenses

Panavision System 65 prime lenses			
Focal length	T-Stop	Close Focus m/Inches	Image Circle
24mm	3.5	0.46m/18"	65mm
28mm	3	0.46m/18"	65mm
35mm	2.8	0.61m/24"	65mm
40mm	2.8	0.69m/27"	65mm
50mm	2	0.44m/17"	65mm
75mm	2	0.69m/27"	65mm
100mm	2	0.61 m/24"	65mm
150mm	1.9	1.22m/48"	65mm
180mm	2	1.6m/63"	65mm
300mm	2.8	2.59m/102"	65mm

Panavision System 65 zoom lenses			
Focal length	T-Stop	Close Focus	Image Circle
150–600mm	6.3	3.05/120"	65mm
210–840mm	9	3.05/120"	65mm

Ultra Panavision 70 Lenses

Figure 7.237 Panavision Original Ultra Panatar Lens.

Ultra Panavision 70 anamorphic lenses are built to cover an ultra wide 2.76:1 aspect ratio by means of a 1.25x squeeze and utilizing the full aspect ratio of the film. They give the image multiple anamorphic artifacts including flares, vertical defocus,

and elliptical bokeh. Their organic focus roll-off and intrinsic edge-layering depth cues give the cinematographer soft, glamorous, classic-looking images and a vintage large format anamorphic look. There is still one set of Ultra Panatar optics that is designed around a prism anamorphic squeeze system. This system comes in a 57mm, 75mm, 104mm, and 150mm. The characteristics of this set is unique and produces a softening around edges that is in a class of its own.

Figure 7.238 Panavision Updated Ultra Panatar Lens.

Ultra Panavision 70 lenses have been given updated modern mechanics and are compatible with both film and digital cameras fitted with a PV 65 mount. In addition, a newer version of the Ultra Panatar lenses were developed to have a more modern look. The newer version introduced some new focal lengths, utilized modern multi-layer coatings, and better contrast capabilities.

Table 7.65 Ultra Panavision 70 lenses

Ultra Panavision 70 Lenses			
Focal length	T-Stop	Close Focus m / Inches	Image Circle
AP35 35mm	2.8	0.61 m / 24"	65mm
AP40 40mm	2.8	0.76 m / 30"	65mm
AP50 50mm	2.8	0.61 m / 24"	65mm
AP65-01 65mm	2	0.56m / 22"	65mm
AP65-02 65mm	2	0.48 m / 19"	65mm
AP75-01 75mm	2	0.91 / 36"	65mm
AP75-02 75mm	2.8	0.61 m / 24"	65mm
AP100 100mm	2.8	1.07m / 42"	65mm
AP135 135mm	2.8	1.6m / 63"	65mm
AP180 180mm	2.8	1.53m / 60"	65mm
AP290 290mm	4	2.75m / 108"	65mm
AP400 400mm	6	2.44m / 96"	65mm

65 Vintage Lenses

Figure 7.239 Panavision 65 Vintage Lens.

The 65 Vintage series utilizes classic designs to produce a line of optics that closely assimilate the qualities associated with vintage medium format optics from the pre 1980s era. The 65 Vintage line covers the 65mm imaging diagonal and range in focal length from 18mm to 200mm. The T-stops vary from T/2.5 to T/1.4. The series utilizes single layer coating technology that brings out veiling glare artifacts and unique pupil flares that are reminiscent of optics from that era. The 65 Vintage optics are driven by modern mechanical transports that are based on the Primo mechanical housings. The Vintage 65 lenses are built around the System 65 mount that has a flange focal depth of 2.080" and the series is compatible with both film and digital cameras. The imaging characteristics of the 65 Vintage optics complement digital sensors nicely and offer a softer look that rolls off pleasantly and has a good layered transition between the foreground and the background. The MTF quality of the 65 Vintage optics is such that there is plenty of volume and as result, the depth of field appears to be very forgiving while imparting an image that is glamorous.

Table 7.66 Panavision 65 Vintage lenses

Focal Length	T-Stop	Close Focus inches/m
24mm	1.4	24"/61cm
29mm	1.4	21"/53.3cm
35mm	1.4	24"/61cm
40mm	2	24"/61cm
50mm	1.4	24"/61cm
65mm	1.4	27"/68.6cm
80mm	1.4	30"/76.2cm
100mm	1.4	36"/91.44cm
135mm	1.8	48"/122cm
180mm	2	60"/152cm
300mm	2.8	60"/152cm

Panavision PVintage Lenses

Over 60 years ago Panavision began creating precision lenses for the motion picture industry. Today many cinematographers seeking an economical solution have asked Panavision to reach into their vaults and offer these classic Panavision lenses for modern digital camera systems.

Figure 7.240 Panavision PVintage Prime Lenses.

The PVintage series of lenses were originally designed in the 1970s. Re-engineered by Panavision to include modern external housings and a new, smooth action internal opto-mechanical design, the PVintage series was developed. The original optical imaging characteristics of the Panavision Super and Ultra Speed optics that are used to create the PVintage lenses were not changed and as a result, the PVintage lenses have a classic look enveloped in a modern mechanical assembly. The standard 4.440" Primo diameter eliminates the need for adapter rings, and the bold, easy to read dual-side focus and aperture scales allow you to easily work on both sides of the camera.

Table 7.67 Panavision PVintage primes

Panavision PVintage Primes		
Focal length	Aperture	Close Focus Inches
PVS14 14mm	1.9	24" / 61cm
PVS17 17mm	1.9	24" / 61cm
PVS24 24mm	1.2	24" / 61cm
PVS29 29mm	1.2	24" / 61cm
PVS35 35mm	1.6	24" / 61cm
PVS40 40mm	1.3	24" / 61cm
PVS50 50mm	1.4	24" / 61cm
PVS75 75mm	1.6	24" / 61cm
PVS100 100mm	1.6	48" / 121.9cm

The PVintage Ultra-Speed lenses have never been out of circulation, consistently maintained and cared for, these lenses are the original Panavision Ultra-Speed lenses, called back to duty for another era of cinematography.

Standard Primes – SP

Panavision's Legacy Standard Primes are the oldest spherical lenses in the Panavision line, made in the late 1960s. The SP lenses exhibit imaging characteristics that are a blend of good contrast and residual pupil imaging aberrations. This combination of imaging traits has given way to a rebirth of theses lenses when combined with modern day digital imagers. Surprisingly, despite their small size, many of the SP lenses cover a 46mm diagonal and can be used with the larger format cameras. Typical to lenses of that era, the older coatings can produce more flaring and veiling glare artifacts. These lenses are available in focal lengths ranging from 8mm to 150mm, and the lens speeds vary from T1.9 to T4, and close focusing distances vary from 9 inches to 5 feet. There are two 8mm wide angle lenses available in this series, one is a Nikon Fisheye and the other is a Distortion lens. Due to the extended exposed rear group of the SP9.8mm T2.8, the lens must be carefully test fitted on a camera by camera basis!

Super Speed "Z" Series SZ Ultra Speed "Z" Series USZ

Figure 7.241 Panavision Super Speed Lens.

Legacy Super Speeds and Ultra Speeds from the mid-1970s are available in focal lengths ranging from 14mm to 200mm, speeds vary from T1.1 to T2.1 and close focusing distances vary from 2 feet to 5 feet, depending focal length lens. Ultra Speeds are available in focal lengths ranging

from 14mm to 150mm. Those lens speeds vary from T1 to T1.9 and close focusing distances vary from 2 feet to 5 feet. The Legacy Ultra and Super Speed lenses are generally treated with multi-layer coatings and have better flare and glare control over the SP series of optics. The Ultra and Super Speed lenses are compatible with both film and digital cameras and some of the focal lengths cover the larger 46mm diagonal sensors. The Ultra and Super Speed lenses have a classic look that complements digital photography well. It was the advent of full size digital sensors and the ability of the lenses to blend lines between the foreground and background that helped bring this series of lenses out of retirement.

Figure 7.242 Panavision Ultraspeed Z Series Prime Lenses.

The Z series lenses were developed in the 1980s and incorporate ZEISS optics combined with Panavision mechanics. Available in focal lengths ranging from 14mm to 180mm, lens speeds vary from T1.9 to T2 and close focusing distances vary from 2 feet to 5 feet depending on focal length. Ultra Speed Z lenses are available in focal lengths ranging from 14mm to 180mm. Those lens speeds vary from T1.3 to T2.8 and close focusing distances vary from 2 feet to 5 feet.

The version of ZEISS Optics within the "Z" series are unique to Panavision and are not the same as those used by competitors. All of the "Z" series lenses come with round iris assemblies which yield round specular bokeh highlights. The "Z" series lenses come with multi-layer coating and utilize better corrected lens prescriptions. The resulting images of the "Z" lenses will have better flare and glare control accompanied by a higher degree of contrast and resolution reproduction.

Table 7.68 Panavision Legacy primes

Series MKII		
Focal length	**Aperture**	**Close Focus Inches / cm**
USZ14 14mm	1.9	24" / 61cm
USZ24 24mm	1.3	24" / 61cm
USZ29 29mm	1.3	24" / 61cm
USZ35 35mm	1.4	24" / 61cm
USZ50 50mm	1.4	24" / 61cm
USZ85 85mm	1.4	24" / 61cm
USZ100 100mm	2	36" / 91.4cm
USZ135 135mm	2	60" / 152.4cm
USZ180 180mm	2.8	60" / 152.4cm

Series MKII		
Focal length	**Aperture**	**Close Focus Inches / cm**
SZ14 14mm	1.9	24" / 61cm
SZ24 24mm	1.9	24" / 61cm
SZ29 29mm	1.9	24" / 61cm
SZ35 35mm	1.9	24" / 61cm
SZ50 50mm	1.9	24" / 61cm
SZ85 85mm	1.9	30" / 76.2cm
SZ100 100mm	2	36" / 91.4cm
SZ135 135mm	2	60" / 152.4cm
SZ180 180mm	2	60" / 152.4cm

Ultra Speed MKII		
Focal length	**Aperture**	**Close Focus Inches / cm**
SS14 14mm	1.9	24" / 61cm
SS17 17mm	1.9	24" / 61cm
SS20 20mm	1.9	30" / 76.2cm
SS24 24mm	1.3	24" / 61cm
SS29 29mm	1.3	28" / 71.1cm
US35 35mm	1.3	24" / 61cm
SS40 40mm	1.3	24" / 61cm
US50 50mm	1	24" / 61cm
SS75 75mm	1.6	24" / 61cm
SS100 100mm	1.6	48" / 121.9cm
SS125 125mm	1.6	42" / 106.7cm
SS150 150mm	1.5	60" / 152.4cm

Table 7.69 Panavision Legacy primes

Super Speed MKII		
Focal length	**Aperture**	**Close Focus Inches / cm**
SP24 24mm	2	24" / 61cm
SS28 28mm	2	24" / 61cm
SS35 35mm	1.6	24" / 61cm
SS50 50mm	1.4	27" / 68.5cm
SS55 55mm	1.1	30" / 76.2cm

Normal Speed MKII		
Focal length	**Aperture**	**Close Focus Inches / cm**
SPN8 8mm	2.8	12" / 30.5cm
SP8D 8mm	2.8	14" / 35.5cm
SP9.8 9.8mm	2.8	24" / 61cm
SP16 16mm	2.8	20" / 50.8cm
SP20 20mm	3 or 4	30" / 76.2cm
SP24 24mm	2.8	27" / 68.5cm

H-SERIES

Figure 7.243 Panavision H Series Lens.

The H-series consist of focal lengths ranging from 12mm to 150mm and have apertures ranging from T/3.0 to T/1.0. The H-series lenses cover a 47mm diagonal and share imaging characteristics similar to the SP and Super speed lenses. The H-series are a compact lens that utilizes a constant 95mm front diameter and are suited to work with the vista format cameras and are well suited to compact handheld situations. The H-series produce images that have an organic fall-off and utilize the lifted contrast to create a layered separation between the foreground and background. The lenses produce a unique flare and glare quality

Table 7.75 Panavision B Series anamorphic lenses

Focal Length	T-Stop	Close Focus inches/m
35mm	2.3	42"/106.7cm
40mm	2.5	42"/106.7cm
50mm	2	42"/106.7cm
75mm	2.5	45"/114.3cm
100mm	2.8	54"/137.2cm

Panavision AL Primo Anamorphic Lenses

Figure 7.251 Panavision AL Primo Anamorphic Lens.

As a way to showcase the optical qualities of the Primo lenses, Panavision created the AL Primo anamorphic series of lenses. The Primo anamorphic use the actual Primo primes and wed them to a modified cylindrical layout that matches the pupil of the primes. The Primo anamorphic lenses produce the same contrast as the spherical Primos while producing the familiar aesthetic of Panavision anamorphic lenses. The Primos deliver consistent performance from the center to the edge of frame. There is a variation of the original Primo anamorphic lenses that is a close focus version. The close focus version utilizes a cam drive instead of a helical drive and the close focus lenses allow the user to focus down to 2½ feet for all of the lenses (2¾ feet for the 100mm). Though the Primo anamorphic lenses are large, they are frequently used and favored by many contemporary cinematographers because of their beautiful photographic qualities. The Primo anamorphic cylinders use multi-layer coating and produce an iconic blue horizontal flare that is well defined.

Table 7.76 Panavision Primo anamorphic lenses

Focal Length	T-Stop	Close Focus inches/m
35mm	2	42"/106.7cm
40mm	2	42"/106.7cm
50mm	2	42"/106.7cm
75mm	2	54"/137.2cm
100mm	2	54"/137.2cm

Panavision T Series Anamorphic Lenses

Figure 7.252 Panavision T Series Anamorphic Lenses.

Panavision T Series lenses combine new optical layouts with mechanical advances from the G series, but have a larger sweet spot and focus closer than some of their predecessors. They are compatible with digital sensors without losing any of the imaging characteristics that have become part of Panavision's anamorphic grammar. Optical features of the T Series lenses include high contrast, balanced aberration control, glare resistance, tightly controlled anamorphic squeeze ratio, and minimal breathing. Like all of the other Panavision anamorphic lens series, the T-series have flaring characteristic that help identify the uniqueness of that particular series.

T Series lenses engraved focus and T-stop scales appear on both sides of the lens, with metric focus and T-stop gears arranged in the standard Panavision locations. The T Series focal lengths include 28mm, 35mm, 40mm, 50mm, 60mm, 75mm, 100mm, 135mm, 150mm, and 180mm primes which are augmented by the AWZ2.3 37–85mm and ALZ10 42–425mm zooms. The primes have a typical speed of T2.3 and close focus of 2 feet. The T60 and T40 focus down to 1½ ft. All the lenses in the T Series primes have a common front diameter of 4.44 inches to make changing lenses simpler.

Table 7.77 Panavision T Series anamorphic lenses

Panavision T Series Anamorphics		
Focal length	T-Stop	Close Focus
28mm	2.3	0.61 m / 24"
35mm	2.3	0.61 m / 24"
40mm	2.3	0.46m / 18"
50mm	2.3	0.61 m / 24"
60mm	2.3	0.46m / 18"
75mm	2.3	0.61 m / 24"
100mm	2.3	0.61 m / 24"
135mm	2.3	0.84m / 33"
150mm	2.8	1.07m / 42"
180mm	2.8	1.07m / 42"

Panavision T Series Anamorphic Zooms

*T Series Anamorphic Wide-Angle Zoom
AWZ2.3 37–85MM T2.8*

Figure 7.253 Panavision T Series 37–85mm T2.8 Anamorphic Wide-Angle Zoom.

The AWZ2.3 complements the T Series primes. The front anamorphic construction follows Panavision tradition. The AWZ2.3 is optimized for electronic sensors (not compatible with spinning mirror cameras) while retaining desirable anamorphic flaring and breathing characteristics. It weighs 14 lbs. and measures 12.8 inches long. Speed is T2.8 and close focus is 2¾ ft. Focus, zoom, and iris scales are engraved on both sides. The gears are metric module 0.8 and zoom motor and follow focus mounting points are integrated. The AWZ2.3 incorporates a higher degree of horizontal breathing control which closely follows the focusing characteristics of the anamorphic prime lenses.

The optical layout adopts mechanical advances from the G series, and provides a large sweet spot of focus. Optical features include high contrast, well balanced aberration control, excellent glare resistance, tightly controlled anamorphic squeeze ratio, and minimal breathing.

*T Series Anamorphic Zoom ALZ10
42–425MM T4.5*

The AZL10 is the latest addition to the T Series anamorphics. The rear anamorphic construction follows Panavision tradition and the associated imaging performance. The ALZ10 is optimized for larger sensor coverage and can cover the Millennium DXL 7K anamorphic at all zoom, focus, and iris settings. The ALZ10 covers DXL 8K anamorphic to 44mm.

The optical layout provides a large sweet spot of focus. Optical features include high contrast, better field illumination, well balanced aberration control, excellent glare resistance, tightly controlled anamorphic squeeze ratio, and minimal breathing. The ALZ10 measures 16.4 inches long and weighs 18.2 lbs. Speed is T4.5 and close focus is 4 ft.

Table 7.78 Panavision T Series anamorphic zoom lenses

Panavision T Series Anamorphic Zooms		
Focal length	T-Stop	Close Focus m / Inches
AWZ2.3 37-85mm	2.8	0.84m / 33"
ALZ10 42-425mm	4.5	1.22m / 48"

Front Anamorphic Zooms – AWZ2 and ATZ

These anamorphic zoom lenses feature high contrast and resolution, minimal aberrations, and excellent field illumination, as well as low veiling glare, ghosting, distortion, and minimal breathing. The front anamorphic lens design substantially reduces stop loss, and produces superior image quality, with minimal aberrations and improved field illumination. They have a constant aperture at all zoom and focus positions, and constant focus at all zoom positions. Because of their high performance imaging, these zooms are not restricted to use only as variable primes but are fully usable as in-shot zooms. Performance and size makes these zoom lenses comparable to the E Series anamorphic primes.

Anamorphic Wide-Angle Zoom – AWZ2

Figure 7.254 Panavision anamorphic 40–80mm Wide-Angle Zoom.

Panavision's anamorphic wide-angle zoom is a T2.8, 40–80mm zoom with a close focusing distance of 3¼ feet. The lens is 10½ inches in length and weighs 10.4 lbs. This is the first zoom lens to use anamorphic elements at the front of the lens. The AWZ2 is known as the "Bailey zoom," after John Bailey, ASC, who was among the first cinematographers to ask Panavision to develop a wide-angle anamorphic zoom.

Anamorphic Telephoto Zoom – ATZ

Figure 7-255 Panavision anamorphic 70–200mm telephoto zoom.

The Panavision anamorphic telephoto zoom is a T3.5, 70–200mm zoom with a close focusing distance of 5½ feet. The lens is 15 inches in length and weighs12.75 pounds.

Anamorphic Telephoto Zoom – ATZ2

Figure 7.256 Panavision ATZ2 75–210mm T/2.8 Zoom Lens.

A second generation of ATZ is now available. It has a focal length range of 75–210mm T/2.8 and is designed to cover the full height of the new larger sensors. The ATZ2 has higher contrast and better horizontal breathing control over the ATZ. The ATZ2 retains all of the aesthetic characteristics associated with Panavision's front anamorphic optics. The ATZ2 comes with a round front element housing so there is no need for a special matte box adapter.

3:1 Primo Anamorphic Zoom – ALZ3

With rear-mounted anamorphic optics, the 3:1 spherical zoom lens can be converted to a 270–840mm, T4.5 anamorphic zoom with a close focusing distance of 8 feet 7 inches. As with the ATZ and AWZ2, this zoom lens is not restricted to be used only as a variable prime but is fully usable as an in-shot zoom.

11:1 Primo Anamorphic Zoom – ALZ11

By attaching rear-mounted anamorphic optics, the 11:1 spherical zoom lens can be converted to a 48–550, T4.5 anamorphic zoom lens with a close focusing distance of 4 feet 1 inch. As with the ATZ and AWZ2, this zoom lens is not restricted to be used only as a variable prime but is fully usable as an in-shot zoom.

Table 7.79 Panavision anamorphic zoom lenses

Focal Length	T-Stop	Close Focus inches/m
37–85mm	2.8	33"/83.8cm
40–80mm	2.8	39"/99.1cm
42–425mm	4.5	48"/122cm
48–550mm	4.5	49"/125cm
70–200mm	3.5	69"/175cm
270–840mm	4.5	103"/262cm

Panavision Ultra Vista Lenses

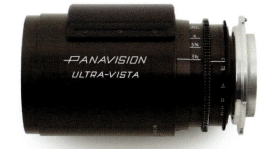

Figure 7.257 Panavision Ultra Vista Lens.

Taking advantage of the aspect ratio associated with the newer class of large format sensors, the Ultra Vista line of anamorphic optics evolved. The Ultra Vista anamorphic lenses have a 1.65x squeeze ratio and are designed to cover a 46.5mm diagonal. The Ultra Vista lenses maintain all of the attributes associated with other Panavision anamorphic lenses such as vertical bokeh, breathing control, horizontal flares, and disproportionate magnification that creates the mosaic out of focus qualities iconic with anamorphic photography.

The Ultra Vista come in focal lengths ranging from 35mm up to 180mm and have an aperture ranging from T/2.3 to T/2.8. The Ultra Vista lenses share many of the mechanical conveniences of the T-series anamorphic lenses. The Ultra Vista lenses come equipped with the Panavision System 65 mount and are compatible with all digital cameras.

The imaging characteristics of the Ultra Vista are similar to the E-series lenses and have a unique cylindrical prescription that reduces distortion and keeps the compression ratio consistent from the center of frame to the edge of the designed image diagonal. Because of the improvements in design, the Ultra Vista lenses are suitable for visual effects while maintaining their ability to produce the classic "blue line" anamorphic flares. The Ultra Vista lenses exhibit very little fall-off on the edge of the frame and the center to edge resolution flatness is excellent. The Ultra Vista lenses produce an overall image sharpness that is respectable, but they do not produce a look that can be interpreted as being too clinical or too sharp. The Ultra Vista lenses had been developed to complement volumetric image capture that is becoming popular in the effects industry.

Table 7.80 Panavision Ultra Vista lenses

Focal Length	T-Stop	Close Focus inches/m
35mm	2.5	42"/106.7cm
40mm	2.5	27"/68.6cm
50mm	2.5	27"/68.6cm
65mm	2.5	27"/68.6cm
75mm	2.5	27"/68.6cm
100mm	2.5	27"/68.6cm
150mm	2.8	42"/106.7cm

Specialty Anamorphic Lenses

Figure 7.258 Panavision Specialty Anamorphic 150mm Macro Lens.

In addition to the standard prime and zoom anamorphic lenses, Panavision has a wide ranging inventory of specialty anamorphic lenses

such as high speed, flare, portrait, macro, and telephoto lenses.

The high-speed anamorphic lens set includes a 24mm, 35mm, 40mm, 50mm, 55mm, 75mm, 85mm, and 100mm. These lenses have widest apertures ranging from T1.1 to T1.8 and close focusing distances from 4 feet 6 inches to 6 feet depending on which lens you are using. The high speed anamorphic lenses come in a variety of prescriptions that yield varied looks.

Anamorphic flare lenses differ from the spherical flare lenses in that they do not have the coatings removed and so do not have reduced overall contrast or veiling glare. They are modified to produce stronger anamorphic cylindrical "blue line" flares.

Anamorphic portrait lenses are available in a 40mm, 50mm, 75mm, and 100mm with apertures of T2.8. The 40mm has a close focusing distance of 3 feet 3 inches and the 100mm has a close focusing distance of 4 feet. The 50mm and 75mm portrait lenses have a close focus of 3½ feet. These lenses typically have a soft focus look around the edges of the frame, leaving the center of the frame sharp.

Anamorphic macro lenses are available in 55mm, 150mm, 200mm, and 250mm focal lengths and each is a T3.2. The 55mm utilizes a front anamorphic design and has vintage imaging characteristics. The 55mm macro has amber horizontal flares and a unique fall-off. The 150mm, 200mm, and 250mm utilize a rear anamorphic assembly. The 150mm has a close focus of 17 inches, the 200mm has a close focus of 18 inches and the 250mm has a close focus of 29 inches.

Telephoto anamorphic lenses are available in a 360mm, 400mm, 600mm, 800mm, 1000mm, 1200mm, 2000mm, and 2800mm. The widest aperture ranges from T3 to T9 and close focusing distances range from 5 feet 6 inches to 30 feet.

Table 7.81 Panavision super high speed anamorphic prime lenses

Panavision Super High Speed Anamorphics		
Focal length	Aperture	Close Focus Inches / cm
HS24 24mm	1.6	72" / 182.9cm
HS35 35mm	1.4	54" / 137.2cm
HS50 50mm	1.1	48" / 121.9cm
HS55 55mm	1.4	48" / 121.9cm
HS75 75mm	1.8	54" / 137.2cm
HS100 100mm	1.8	54" / 137.2cm

Panavision Legacy Primes		
Super Speed MKII		
Focal length	**Aperture**	**Close Focus Inches / cm**
SP24 24mm	2	24" / 61cm
SS28 28mm	2	24" / 61cm
SS35 35mm	1.6	24" / 61cm
SS50 50mm	1.4	27" / 68.5cm
SS55 55mm	1.1	30" / 76.2cm
Normal Speed MKII		
Focal length	**Aperture**	**Close Focus Inches / cm**
SPN8 8mm	2.8	12" / 30.5cm
SP8D 8mm	2.8	14" / 35.5cm
SP9.8 9.8mm	2.8	24" / 61cm
SP16 16mm	2.8	20" / 50.8cm
SP20 20mm	3 or 4	30" / 76.2cm
SP24 24mm	2.8	27" / 68.5cm

Table 7.82 Panavision close focus/macro panatar

Focal Length	Aperture	Close Focus inches/cm
AR90-SF 90mm	4.3	17"/43.2cm
MAP55 55mm	2.5	14"/35.56cm
MAP150 150mm	3.2	17"/43.2cm
MAP200 200mm	3.2	18"/45.7cm
MAP250 250mm	3.2	29"/73.7cm

P+S Technik Anamorphic Lenses

Figure 7.259
Source: www.pstechnik.de/lenses/.

Technovision 1.5X Anamorphic Lenses

Anamorphic origination has made a resurgence, and the Technovision Classic 1.5X anamorphic series is helping meet the demand for widescreen optics.

Figure 7.260 P+S Technik Technovision Classic 1.5X Anamorphic Lenses.

Available in 40mm, 50mm, 75mm, 100mm, and 135mm prime focal lengths and 35-70mm and 70–200mm zoom sizes as well. The Technovision Classic 1.5X anamorphic lenses are used for 16:9 image sensor capture, making use of the whole sensor. This maximizes the number of pixels used to put an anamorphic image onto a 16:9 frame with all the classic properties associated with front anamorphic elements, unique bokeh, anamorphic flares, pincushion distortion, shallow depth of field, and a wide field of view.

Technovision Classic series 1.5X anamorphic zooms and primes feature a 43.3 large format image circle. This large image circle means it will cover the most common image sensors today at all focal lengths with no vignetting, and the 70–200mm zoom will actually cover the ARRI ALEXA 65 image sensor. The Technovision Classic 1.5X series of lenses come in PL mount, LPL mount, and other options include an IMS interchangeable lens mount, EF-mount, e-mount, and MFT mount.

Table 7.83 P+S Technik Technovision Classic 1.5X anamorphic lenses

P+S Technik Technovision 1.5X anamorphic primes			
Focal Length	**T-Stop**	**Close Focus**	**Image Circle**
40mm 1.5x squeeze	T2.2	0.7m/2.3'	43.3mm LF
50mm 1.5x squeeze	T2.2	0.7m/2.3'	43.3mm LF
75mm 1.5x squeeze	T2.4	1m/3.3'	43.3mm LF
100mm 1.5x squeeze	T2.8	1m/3.3'	43.3mm LF
135mm 1.5x squeeze	T2.4	1m/3.3'	43.3mm LF

(Continued)

Table 7.83 (Continued)

P+S Technik Technovision 1.5X anamorphic zooms			
Focal Length	T-Stop	Close Focus	Image Circle
40–70mm 1.5x squeeze	T3.2	0.85m/2.8'	43.3mm LF
70–200mm 1.5x squeeze	T3.2	1m/3.3'	43.3mm LF

Evolution 2X Anamorphic Lenses

Evolution 2X anamorphic lenses are the P+S Technik lens rehousing of vintage Kowa anamorphic designs.

Figure 7.261 P+S Technik Evolution 2X Anamorphic Lenses.

The original KOWA anamorphic prime lenses were produced until the 1970s and four different primes were available: 40mm, 50mm, 75mm, and 100mm. P+S Technik added two additional focal lengths to the set, a 32mm wide-angle and a telephoto 135mm, which match the look of the original set. The optical design of the Evolution 2X lenses is based on the original KOWA optical design using front anamorphic elements. They are low in contrast and warm in color and flare in traditional anamorphic fashion.

The lenses are built in a compact, lightweight housing with modern cam driven internal focus mechanics. The focus throw has changed significantly compared to the originals. The Evolution lenses offer a 200° rotation of the focus ring and a 100° rotation of the aperture ring. The mod 0.8 pitch gears are in the same position of the gear rings throughout the set which integrates them well into a modern production environment. Standard 80mm front diameter for use with a clip-on matte box and a 77mm thread allows for screw-in filters. That makes the Evolution 2X useful for hand-held,

Steadicam, or drone camera work. Evolution 2X lenses are equipped with a standard mount PL-mount, options include an IMS interchangeable lens mount, EF-mount, e-mount, and MFT mount.

Table 7.84 P+S Technik Evolution 2X anamorphic lenses

Focal Length	T-Stop	Close Focus	Image Circle
32mm 2x Squeeze	T2.4	0.70m/2.3'	31.1mm
40mm 2x Squeeze	T2.4	0.86m/2.82'	31.1mm
50mm 2x Squeeze	T2.4	0.85m/2.78'	31.1mm
75mm 2x Squeeze	T2.5	0.86m/2.82'	31.1mm
100mm 2x Squeeze	T3.2	1.35m/4.43'	31.1mm
135mm 2x Squeeze	T3.5	1.5m/4.92'	31.1mm

P+S Technik – Skater Scope

The P+S Technik Skater Scope is a compact periscope that can be rotated through 360 degrees (driven by a standard 0.8 pitch gear) and tilted through +/–105 degrees. It has an open aperture of T5.6 covering a Super 35mm sensor with very flat field performance, and works with most PL, Panavision, Nikon, and B4 mount lenses.

Figure 7.262 P+S Technik Skater Scope.

P+S Technik – Lens Rehousing

P+S Technik also offer well designed, reliable, and sturdy rehousing for many of the classic lines of legacy cine lenses including Angénieux, Bausch and Lomb Super Baltar, Canon FD, Canon K35, Cooke Panchro, Kinoptik, Kowa, LEITZ-R, Meyer Görlitz, Schneider, and ZEISS High Speed MKI.

Schneider Cine Xenar Lenses

Figure 7.263
*Source:*www.schneideroptics.com/news/cine-xenar/
cine-xenar.htm.

Figure 7.264 Schneider Xenar III 18mm Prime Lens.

Schneider-Kreuznach Cine-Xenar Series (I, II and) III lenses feature fast T-stops and an iris with up to 18 blades for a pleasing bokeh effect. They are designed for digital cameras and come in PL mount for digital and 35mm film cameras, as well as Canon EF mount.

Image circle coverage is 33mm for use on S35 2K and 4K cameras, Canon 7D, and Canon 1D MKIV. Color matched telecentric optical design gives them good performance with digital cameras, low distortion, with good flare suppression through internal light traps and high performance coatings, and virtually no breathing.

Figure 7.265 The Schneider Xenar Family of Prime Lenses.

Table 7.85 Schneider Cine Xenar (I, II, and) III Prime Lenses

Schneider Cine Xenar Lenses			
Focal length	Aperture	Close Focus Inches / cm	Image Circle
T2.2/18mm	T2.2 - 16	11" / 26cm	S35 33mm
T2.2/25mm	T2.2 - 16	11" / 26cm	S35 33mm
T2.1/35mm	T2.1 - 16	13" / 33cm	S35 33mm
T2.0/50mm	T2.0 - 16	14" / 35cm	S35 33mm
T2.0/ 75mm	T2.0 - 16	18" / 45cm	S35 33mm
T2.0/ 95mm	T2.0 - 16	26" / 65cm	S35 33mm

Focus scales are easily interchanged to read in feet/meters; the lenses all have the same dimensions, so all focus and iris gears are in the same position, and lens motors need not be moved for lens changes. These lenses are robust and reliable, designed and built in Germany.

Schneider Full Frame Prime Lenses

Figure 7.266 Schneider Full Frame Prime Lenses.

The first focal lengths being introduced in the Xenon FF-Prime series are 35mm T2.1, 50mm T2.1, and 75mm T2.1. They are available in Nikon F, Canon EOS, or PL mounts with more focal lengths on the way.

Built for digital cinematography with today's HDSLR and other cameras, the new Xenon full-frame lenses are designed for 4K resolution They cover the full 45mm image circle that's usable on Canon 5D Mark III and Nikon D800 cameras. Each 3.3-pound lens offers all new optical and mechanical design for outstanding operation and performance as well as rugged reliability. The circular 14-blade aperture is specially engineered for a smooth and consistent bokeh. The precision constant volume focusing design ensures that breathing is minimized. With a 300-degree barrel rotation, the manual focus markings offer accuracy and repeatability, and all lenses are color-matched for consistency.

Engineered for compatibility with industry standard cine-style accessories like follow focus rigs and matte boxes, the Xenon FF-Primes feature identical external dimensions and positioning of focus and gear rings in each focal length. Oversized focus and distance scales are readable on both sides of the lens, and each lens has a 100mm front diameter with a standard 95mm thread.

Table 7.86 Schneider Cine Full Frame prime lenses

Focal Length	Aperture	Close Focus inches/cm	Image Circle
XN FF/18mm	T 2.4–22	16"/40cm	FF 36mm × 24mm
XN FF/25mm	T 2.1–22	12"/30cm	FF 36mm × 24mm
XN FF/35mm	T 2.1–22	13.8"/35cm	FF 36mm × 24mm
XN FF/50mm	T 2.1–22	19.7"/50cm	FF 36mm × 24mm
XN FF/75mm	T 2.1–22	30"/75cm	FF 36mm × 24mm
XN FF/100mm	T 2.1–22	3'3"/1m	FF 36mm × 24mm

Schneider Xenon FF Prime Cine Tilt Lenses

Figure 7.267 Schneider Full Frame Prime Cine Tilt 35mm Lens.

Schneider full-frame cine primes are also available with dynamic tilt/shift functionality. Their Full Frame Prime Cine Tilt lenses combine a similar form factor and capabilities as the standard Xenon FF-Primes with added tilt lens function up to +/– 4°. By sustaining the field of view during focus and tilt actions, the new cine-tilt design means that previously unimaginable images can be taken by moving and tilting the focus plane. These lenses make it possible to capture out-of-focus areas in the frame, especially when using tilt with a large aperture. A 4° tilt angle on the sensor plane corresponds to an 80° focal plane, which varies according to the selected focal length and aperture setting.

These color-matched prime lenses feature minimized breathing and a pleasing bokeh. The new design incorporates sophisticated mechanics for smooth and accurate dynamic tilt action, even while rolling. The tilt of the lens is controlled via a high-precision ring with 120° rotation that is as

intuitive to operate as pulling focus. Thanks to the common 0.8 module gear, the Cine Tilt can be used with standard follow-focus systems. With the tilt set at 0°, the Cine Tilt lenses provide identical images to the standard FF-Primes in focal lengths of 25 mm, 35 mm, 50 mm, 75 mm, and 100 mm, all at T2.1.

Service Vision Scorpio Anamorphic 2x Lenses

Figure 7.268
*Source:*www.servicevision.es/en/product-selling/scorpiolens-anamorphic-2x

Figure 7.269 Scorpio 2x Anamorphic Prime Lenses.

Scorpio 2x anamorphic lenses are small in size and lightweight, with consistent 95mm front so you can use them with standard matt boxes and filters. They have fast minimum apertures and minimal distortion or breathing. Available in PL Mount, with exchangeable focus scales in either feet or meters, and the internal focus mechanism keeps the external position of the lens constant.

Compatible with film and digital cameras, Scorpio anamorphics all cover up to ANSI super 35 Silent (31.14 mm diameter). They provide good close-up performance with no anamorphic compression in close proximity, you can focus close like spherical lenses, without any "mumps" effect. Floating elements, designs and multi aspheric telecentric design provides high resolution and contrast uniform quality over the whole field of view with consistent optical performance across the whole focus range.

Figure 7.270 Scorpio 2x Anamorphic Zoom Lens.

There is also a Scorpio anamorphic 2x zoom lens created to complement Scorpio anamorphic 2x primes, covering the longer focal ranges offering matching image quality with the same ease of use with the same front diameter, weight and size.

Table 7.87 Service Vision Scorpio anamorphic lenses

Service Vision Scorpio Anamorphic Lenses			
Focal length	T-Stop	Close Focus	Image Circle
20mm	T2.8	0.40 m / 15.75""	S35mm - 31.14mm
25mm	T2	0.45 m / 17.7"	S35mm - 31.14mm
30mm	T2	0.45 m / 17.7"	S35mm - 31.14mm
35mm	T2	0.45 m / 17.7"	S35mm - 31.14mm
40mm	T2	0.50 m / 19.68"	S35mm - 31.14mm
50mm	T2	0.55 m / 21.65"	S35mm - 31.14mm
60mm	T2	0.65 m / 25.6"	S35mm - 31.14mm
75mm	T2	0.75 m / 29.5"	S35mm - 31.14mm
100mm	T2	1 m / 39.37"	S35mm - 31.14mm
135mm	T2.8	1.3 m / 51.18"	S35mm - 31.14mm
150mm	T2.8	1.5 m / 59"	S35mm - 31.14mm
200mm	T2.8	1.8 m / 70.86"	S35mm - 31.14mm
250mm	T2.8	2.0 m / 78.75"	S35mm - 31.14mm
300mm	T2.8	2.5 m / 98.42"	S35mm - 31.14mm
Focal length	T-Stop	Close Focus	Image Circle
138-405mm 2 x Zoom	T4.3	1.52m / 60"	S35mm - 31.14mm

Sigma Cine Lenses

Figure 7.271
*Source:*www.sigma-global.com/en/cine-lenses/.

Sigma Cine Full Frame High Speed Prime Lenses

Figure 7.272 Sigma Cine Full Frame High Speed Prime Lenses.

Sigma High Speed zoom line is compatible with Super 35mm while the FF High Speed prime line and FF zoom line are compatible with cameras up to those requiring a larger full-frame image circle. The FF High Speed prime lenses and the 18–35mm T2 and 50–100mm T2 High Speed zoom lenses are available in PL, EF, and E mount. The 24–35mm T2.2 FF zoom lens is not available in PL mount, available lens mounts are the Canon EF mount and SONY E-mount. SIGMA makes a Mount Conversion Service available for its cine lenses that allows users to convert their lenses to and from EF and E-mounts (charges apply). Mount Conversion Service is not available for PL mount lenses.

Table 7.88 Sigma Cine High Speed Prime Lenses Full Frame

Focal Length	T-Stop	Close Focus m/inches	Image Circle
14mm	T2	0.27m/11"	Full Frame
20mm	T1.5	0.276m/11"	Full Frame
24mm	T1.5	0.25m/10"	Full Frame
28mm	T1.5	0.3m/12"	Full Frame
35mm	T1.5	0.3m/12"	Full Frame
40mm	T1.5	0.40m/1'4"	Full Frame
50mm	T1.5	0.40m/1'4"	Full Frame
85mm	T1.5	0.85m/2'10"	Full Frame
105mm	T1.5	1.0m/3'4"	Full Frame
135mm	T2	0.875m/2'11"	Full Frame

Sigma "Classic Art Prime" Full Frame Classic Prime Lenses

Figure 7.273 Sigma Cine Classic Prime Lenses.

The Sigma "Classic Art Prime" Full Frame Classic Prime Line set incorporates more non-coated optical elements to achieve a creative look. Classic Primes retain high resolution capability but also offer a combination of low contrast, artistic flare/ghosting in the image and beautiful bokeh.

FF Classic Prime Line has implemented newly developed coatings on the glass elements and offers consistent T stop across the lineup (14mm and 135mm at T3.2 and the rest of the lenses at T2.5). Sigma Cine Classic Full Frame lenses are compatible with Cooke /ĩ technology, ideal for shooting VFX. A special coating is implemented on the front and rear elements so that the lens durability is ensured as with all other cine lenses from SIGMA.

Table 7.89 Sigma Cine Classic prime lenses full frame

Focal Length	T-Stop	Close Focus m/inches	Image Circle
14mm	T3.2	0.27m/11"	Full Frame
20mm	T2.5	0.276m/11"	Full Frame
24mm	T2.5	0.25m/10"	Full Frame
28mm	T2.5	0.3m/12"	Full Frame
35mm	T2.5	0.3m/12"	Full Frame
40mm	T2.5	0.40m/1'4"	Full Frame
50mm	T2.5	0.40m/1'4"	Full Frame
85mm	T2.5	0.85m/2'10"	Full Frame
105mm	T2.5	1.0m/3'4"	Full Frame
135mm	T3.2	0.875m/2'11"	Full Frame

Sigma Cine Full Frame High Speed Zoom Lenses

Figure 7.274 Sigma Cine 24-35mm Full Frame Zoom Lens.

Color balance is standardized across the entire line, the lenses deliver sharpness combined with pleasing bokeh effect. Computer-assisted ray tracing has been used to minimize flare and ghosting and enhance contrast in backlit conditions. Ghosting has also been checked at every proto-

type stage, with its causes identified, assessed, and eliminated.

Selectable focus ring with feet or meter graduations, all markings on rings and elsewhere are laser engraved. The specification, gradation baseline, and lens change indications all feature luminous paint to aid in changing the lens in the dark and other tasks. Fully luminous versions of the lenses feature all numbers and gradations finished with luminous paint. Markings are durably painted so tape may be placed on gradations without stripping away paint when removed. All lenses feature dust-proof and splash-proof construction. Robust 100% metal barrel construction stands up to tough professional use over the long term.

Figure 7.275 Sigma Cine Full Frame High Speed Zoom Lenses.

The positions of the focus, iris, and zoom gears are standardized, eliminating the need to adjust the follow focus, motor unit, or accessories even when the lens changes. Cine standard 0.8M gear pitch provides for compatibility with existing accessories. The stops of each ring incorporate a damper for silent operation end to end. Focus ring rotates through 180°, zoom rotates through 160°, and the iris ring rotates through 60°. The linear iris ring gives users the same rotational angle per T-stop. Focus rings with either feet or meter graduations are available.

Table 7.90 Sigma Cine zoom lenses (full frame and high speed)

Focal Length	T-Stop	Close Focus m/inches	Image Circle
24–35mm Full Frame	T 2.2	0.28m/11"	Full Frame
18–35mm High Speed	T 2	0.28m/11"	S35 28.4mm
50–100mm High Speed	T 2	0.95m/3'2"	S35 28.4mm

A lens support foot comes as a standard accessory with all lenses which helps minimize load on the camera body while enhancing mount stability. The height of the seating surface is designed for compatibility with other accessories.

A USB dock accessory allows the user to connect lenses to a computer and update firmware, while the MOUNT CONVERTER MC-11 allows users to use SIGMA's Canon EF mount interchangeable lenses with a SONY E-mount camera body.

SIGMA Cine lenses are not complete until they undergo lens performance evaluation. SIGMA has developed their own A1 proprietary Modulation Transfer Function (MTF) measuring system using 46-megapixel Foveon direct image sensors. Each and every lens is thoroughly QC checked before shipping.

SONY CineAlta 4K Prime Lenses

SONY.

Figure 7.276

*Source:*https://pro.sony/ue_US/products/camera-lenses/scl-pk6-f

Figure 7.277 The SONY Cinealta 4K Prime Lens Family.

SONY's F65, F55, and F5 cameras are available with a PL lens mount for use with high-end cine-style lenses, and SONY has also created a line of six CineAlta T2.0 PL-mount lenses for the cameras in focal lengths of 20mm, 25mm, 35mm, 50mm, 85mm, and 135mm. These SONY PL mount prime lenses are SONY's second generation of cost-effective PL mount prime lenses, certified for 4K capture, carefully color matched, and designed to minimize geometric distortion, vignetting, and breathing.

A nine-blade iris delivers pleasing bokeh, and the focus rings rotate through a range of 240 degrees. For easy lens changes, each has the same T2.0 aperture, the same external diameter, matte box diameter, and gear locations for follow focus and aperture. Lenses can be ordered

with barrels marked in feet and inches or in meters.

Features include robust, metal housings, focal lengths are 20, 25, 35, 50, 85, and 135 mm, all with an aperture of T2. All lenses have the same front diameter and same lens length except the 135mm lens. Geared lens rings are all in the same relative locations. They each have a 9-bladed iris, and the focus ring rotates 240°.

Table 7.91 SONY CineAlta 4K prime lenses

Sony SCL-PK6/F Lenses			
Focal Length	T-Stop	Close Focus Inches / cm	Image Circle
20 mm	2	8" / 21cm	Super 35mm
25 mm	2	12" / 3cm	Super 35mm
35 mm	2	17" / 44cm	Super 35mm
50 mm	2	27" / 69cm	Super 35mm
85 mm	2	19" / 49cm	Super 35mm
135 mm	2	33" / 85cm	Super 35mm

Spirit Lab Al Full Frame Prime Lenses (Al and Ti)

SPIRIT LAB

Figure 7.278

*Source:*www.spiritlaboptics.com/.

Spirit AI cine lenses are actually larger than full frame, they actually will cover a 52mm image circle, and the 85mm, 100mm, and 135mm even cover a 65mm image circle.

Figure 7.279 Spirit Lab Al Prime Lenses.

Spirit Lab Prime provides high resolution 8K images, even in S35 cameras. Spirit Lab Prime AI lenses 52mm coverage circle covers sensors from ALEXA LF, RED Monstro, SONY VENICE 6K, and Canon C700. Spirit Lab Prime lenses use advanced techniques such as floating correction and displacement compensation to minimize breathing to an imperceptible level. Computer-assisted design has helped create large-diameter aspheric lenses and lens groups that significantly increase image quality and reduce the number of lens elements and minimize aberrations. Spirit Lab's Prime lens series offers image distortion at less than 1% level, allowing cinematographers to move the camera freely without visible distortion effects.

Spirit Lab lens are compact and lightweight, between 1240 and 1410 grams or 2.75 to 3.1 lbs.

Interchangeable mounts available are PL, LPL, L, E, EF, and easy to be changed by owners. The maximum apertures range from T1.3 to T2.2.

Table 7.92 Spirit Lab Prime AI lenses

Focal Length	T-Stop	Close Focus m/inches	Image Circle
15mm	T2.2–22	0.30m/11.8"	FF 52mm
24mm	T1.6–16	0.30m/11.8"	FF 52mm
35mm	T1.5–16	0.30m/11.8"	FF 52mm
50mm	T1.3–16	0.45m/17.7"	FF 52mm
85mm	T1.5–16	0.85m/33.46"	FF 52mm
100mm macro 1:1	T2.2–22	0.30m/11.8"	FF 52mm
135mm	T2.2–22	1.0m/39.37"	FF 52mm

Tokina Cinema Vista Full Frame Lenses

Figure 7.280
Source: www.tokinacinemausa.com/.

Tokina Vista Beyond Full Frame Lenses

Tokina Cinema have been manufacturing lenses for still photographers for many years, so in the new era of larger sensor cinematography,

it makes sense for them to enter the cinema market.

Figure 7.281 Tokina Vista Beyond Full Frame Lenses.

Tokina's newly designed large format cinema glass Vista Beyond Full Frame lenses feature fast T1.5 T stop, for good image character across the T1.5 through to T22 iris range, usable wide open. They are engineered with aspheric elements and modern coatings for low chromatic aberration and minimal breathing during focus pulls. With an image circle of 46.7mm they cover FF35, VistaVision, and RED Dragon 8K VV. Clearly marked focus and iris scales on both sides of the lenses, consistent 114mm front outer diameter and a 112mm screw-in filter size (not available on Vista 18mm) and consistent length of lenses, makes them efficient on set for quick lens changes. Consistent lens length during focus pulls means a swing away matte box stays put. Nine-bladed iris makes for nice rounded bokeh, robust construction materials, and shim adjustable mounts come in PL, Canon EF, MFT, and SONY E mount.

Tokina Cinema Vista One Lenses

Tokina Cinema Vista One lenses allow cinematographers to employ controlled contrast and flare with single coated aspheric front elements.

Figure 7.282 Tokina Cinema Vista One Lenses.

Tokina Cinema Vista One lenses feature single-coated front aspheric elements, with grey color painted lens barrel with blue accents, and fast T1.5 aperture with virtually no breathing,

8k resolution and coverage capability, low dispersion glass, low chromatic aberration, high resolution, and low distortion.

Construction features durable, all-metal cine-style housing, geared focus rotation angle of approximately 300 degrees focus, smooth, 9-blade, curved iris, 114mm front diameter, 112mm front filter thread and identical gear positions on all focal lengths.

Figure 7.283 Tokina Cinema ATX AT-X 100mm T/2.9 Macro Lens.

The Tokina Cinema AT-X 100mm T/2.9 macro is a 35mm, full-frame, 1:1 macro

close-up lens that achieves maximum magnification at a working distance of 11.8 inches (0.3 meters).

Tokina Cinema Zoom Lenses

Figure 7.284 Tokina Cinema 11–20mm T2.9 Zoom Lens.

The compact, lightweight Tokina Cinema 11–20mm T2.9 lens has been engineered it to provide 4K performance in a compact package. The 11–20mm

Table 7.93 Tokina Vista Beyond Full Frame Lenses

Tokina Vista Beyond Full Frame Cinema Prime Lenses			
Focal Length	T-Stop	Close Focus m/inches	Image Circle
18mm	T1.5	0.45m/17.7"	46.7mm Full Frame
25mm	T1.5	0.35m/13.86"	46.7mm Full Frame
35mm	T1.5	0.41m/16"	46.7mm Full Frame
50mm	T1.5	0.48'/19"	46.7mm Full Frame
85mm	T1.5	0.95m/37.5"	46.7mm Full Frame
105mm	T1.5	1.15m/45"	46.7mm Full Frame
135mm	T1.5	1.39m/4'7"	46.7mm Full Frame

Tokina Vista One Full Frame Cinema Zoom Lens			
Focal Length	T-Stop	Close Focus m/inches	Image Circle
18mm Vista One	T1.5	0.45m/17.7"	46.7mm Full Frame
25mm Vista One	T1.5	0.35m/13.86"	46.7mm Full Frame
35mm Vista One	T1.5	0.41m/16"	46.7mm Full Frame
50mm Vista One	T1.5	0.48m/19"	46.7mm Full Frame
85mm Vista One	T1.5	0.95m/37.5"	46.7mm Full Frame
105mm Vista One	T1.5	1.15m/45"	46.7mm Full Frame
135mm Vista One	T1.5	1.39m/4'7"	46.7mm Full Frame

Tokina Vista One Full Frame Cinema zoom lens			
Focal Length	T-Stop	Close Focus m/inches	Image Circle
100mm macro	2.9	0.3m/11.8" 1:1	46.7mm Full Frame

Vantage One4s cover from 48.5mm to 60mm with close focus ability and the familiar look of the Vantage One primes.

Figure 7.292 Vantage One4 80mm prime lens.

Table 7.96 Vantage One4 Spherical Prime Lenses

Focal Length	T-Stop	Close Focus m/ft	Image Circle
Vantage One4 22mm	T 1.4	0.25/10"	48.5mm
Vantage One4 27mm	T 1.4	0.3/1'	48.5mm
Vantage One4 35mm	T 1.4	0.3/1'	48.5mm
Vantage One4 50mm	T 1.4	0.35/1'2"	52mm
Vantage One4 65mm	T 1.4	0.40/1'3"	60mm
Vantage One4 80mm	T 1.4	0.50/1'7"	63mm
Vantage One4 105mm	T 1.4	0.70/2'3"	63mm

The Vintage Lens Co.: Neo Super Baltar Classics

Figure 7.293
Source: www.vintagelensco.com/.

Released in the early 1960s, Bausch and Lomb Super Baltars established themselves as the optics of choice for major motion pictures and television. Never manufactured in large numbers, original Super Baltars are now extremely rare, and the originals remain popular today.

Super Baltars were among the first cine lenses made with high-index rare earth glasses to control field curvature. Coupled with pre-computer design and single layer coatings they produce a vintage image that can't be duplicated with ultra-sharp modern optics. Glass types and coatings were painstakingly researched to ensure that the Neo Super Baltars would produce the same images as their namesake.

Figure 7.294 Neo Super Baltar Lenses.

Caldwell Photographic has resurrected these famous lenses from original Bausch and Lomb optical design blueprints to create the Neo Super Baltars. The only thing separating the Vintage Lens Co. Neo Super Baltars from the originals is availability.

For maximum versatility, the Neo Super Baltars will be available as lens cells with an iris, with external dimensions identical to the originals. They are ready for adaptation into high quality cine focusing mounts available from Van Diemen, P+S Technik, True Lens Services, and other rehousing specialists.

Key features include standard 110mm front diameter, 280 degree focus rotation, 45 degree iris rotation, PL mount, aircraft aluminum construction, dual cam focus drive optimized for modern motors, matching 0.8 standard gears across the range, and imperial or metric focus marks.

Each lens faithfully replicates the original Super Baltar optical design. Lenses feature the iconic styling from the original era that is both beautiful and functional, with raised grips for hand operation. In keeping with modern standards, lenses are equipped with stainless steel PL mounts that are easily collimated without using shims.

Table 7.97 Neo Super Baltar Prime Lenses

Focal Length	T-Stop	Close Focus	Image Circle
20mm	T2.3	0.28m/11"	Super 35mm
25mm	T2.3	0.23m/9"	Super 35mm
35mm LWD*	T2.3	0.33m/13"	39mm FF
35mm C**	T2.3	0.33m/13"	39mm FF
50mm	T2.3	0.36m/14.17"	38mm FF
75mm	T2.3	0.51m/20"	41mm FF
100mm	T2.3	1m/39.37"	42mm FF
152mm	T3.0	1.53m/60.25"	42mm FF
229mm	T4.4		42mm FF

* LWD – Long Working Distance
** C – Compact Version

Whitepoint Optics Lenses

W. WHITEPOINT OPTICS

Figure 7.295
Source: www.whitepointoptics.com/.

Whitepoint Optics TS Series Lenses

Whitepoint Optics manufacture high-quality cinema lenses for the motion picture industry using ZEISS and LEITZ glass housed in a custom barrels.

Figure 7.296 Whitepoint Optics TS Series Lenses.

Whitepoint Optics TS70 lenses are based on Hasselblad V-series glass, offering a unique bokeh from a 10 blade iris that is circular through all stops. Image circle is 82mm, so optics will cover Full Frame sensors, RED VistaVision and ARRI ALEXA 65, Super35, SONY VENICE, and other large format and full format imaging sensors without vignetting or distortion. Focus/

Iris ring locations are matched on each lens, and the front diameter of the lenses throughout the set maintains consistent 114mm for easy lens changes. Mounts are available in PL, LPL, EF, and E-mount in stainless steel.

Table 7.98 Whitepoint Optics TS70 Series Lenses

Focal Length	T-Stop	Close Focus	Image Circle
30mm	3.5	0.35m/13.8"	82mm
40mm	4	0.35m/13.8"	82mm
50mm	3.5	0.35m/13.8"	82mm
60mm	3.5	0.45m/17.7"	82mm
80mm	2.8	0.65m/25.6"	82mm
100mm	3.5	0.80 m/31.5"	82mm
110mm	2	0.80 m/31.5"	82mm
120mm	4	1.1m/43.3"	82mm
150mm	4	1.1m/43.3"	82mm
250mm	4	2.5m/98.42"	82mm
350mm	5.6	4.5m/177.17"	82mm
500mm	8	8m/315"	82mm

The HS series lenses are based on a same Hasselblad V-series glass as the TS70 lenses. Speed and focal length conversions are made with WPO 0.7x Speed Converter so the resulting HS- series image circle is 46mm. The converter is also sold separately so that a set of six TS70 lenses can be converted.

Table 7. 99 Whitepoint Optics HS Series Lenses

Focal Length	T-Stop	Close Focus	Image Circle
21mm	T2.5–16	0.35m/13.8"	46mm
28mm	T2.8–22	0.35m/13.8"	46mm
42mm	T2.5–16	0.45m/17.7"	46mm
56mm	T2–16	0.65m/25.6"	46mm
70mm	T2.5–16	0.80 m/31.5"	46mm
77mm	T1.4–16	0.80 m/31.5"	46mm
84mm	T2.8–22	1.1m/43.3"	46mm
105mm	T2.8–16	1.1m/43.3"	46mm
175mm	T4–16	2.5m/98.42"	46mm
245mm	T4–16	4.5m/177.17"	46mm
350mm	T5.6–16	8m/315"	46mm

An additional Tilt-Swing mechanism maximum of 9 degrees without vignetting or distortion on is simple to lock and release.

Figure 7.297 Whitepoint Optics 0.7x Speed Converter.

Whitepoint Optics 0.7x Speed Converter is available in PL, LPL, E, and EF – stainless steel.

Resulting image circle is 46mm for full frame coverage. The convertor increases the lens speed by almost 1 stop, reduces the focal length of the TS70 lenses by 0.7x, and is compatible only with WPO TS70 lenses.

Figure 7.298 Whitepoint Optics Tilt & Swing Adapter.

Whitepoint Optics Tilt & Swing Adapter is available in PL, LPL, E, and EF stainless steel lens mounts. Resulting image circle is 82mm with no vignetting or distortion, coverage is up to ARRI ALEXA 65 and is compatible only with WPO TS70 lenses.

XEEN Lenses

Figure 7.299

Source: www.rokinon.com/xeen/httprokinoncomxeenxeen-cine-system.

XEEN CF Prime Lenses

Figure 7.300 Xeen CF Prime Lenses.

Xeen's CF Cine Prime lenses are compatible with full frame image sensors with an image circle of 43.3mm. Compact and lightweight design, carbon fiber is used in the construction of the exterior lens barrels to reduce weight, making them ideal for use on Steadicam, drones, and gimbals. 8K resolution, X-coating technology, and a minimum aperture of T1.5 offer beautiful bokeh and good low light performance. Features include .9kg/2.0lbs. weight per lens, luminous glow in the dark focus markings, 11 blade iris, 200 degree travel of focus barrel, 40 degree travel of iris ring, unified focus and iris gear positions, and interchangeable lens mounts available in PL, Canon EF, and SONY E mounts.

Table 7.100 XEEN CF prime lenses

Focal Length	T-Stop	Close Focus m/inches	Image Circle	
16mm	2.6	0.3 m/12"	43.3mm	Full Frame +
24mm	1.5	0.25 m/9.8"	43.3mm	Full Frame +
35mm	1.5	0.33 m/13"	43.3mm	Full Frame +
50mm	1.5	0.45m/17.7"	43.3mm	Full Frame +
85mm	1.5	1.12 m/44"	43.3mm	Full Frame +

XEEN Prime Lenses

Figure 7.301 Xeen Prime Lenses.

Cinema lenses by Rokinon feature prime lenses at 14mm, 16mm, 20mm, 24mm, 35mm, XEEN 50mm, 85mm, and 135mm focal lengths. Compatible with full frame and Super 35 sensor cameras with coverage up to 24mm × 36mm. Lens elements feature X-Coating Technology and barrels are calibrated with focus scales in either metric or imperial units. Each lens features dual right- and left-side focus and T-stop scales. Aluminum construction to help withstand the rigors of daily production work, internal focus design minimizes the appearance of breathing when changing focus. Non-rotating front element and consistent front diameter allow for the use of optional clip-on matte boxes. Each lens in the Xeen series share common focus and iris gear ring positions enabling lens changes without repositioning follow focus unit. Interchangeable lens mounts available in PL, Canon EF, and SONY E, Nikon F and micro four thirds mounts. Non-PL mount lenses come with a tripod mounting foot with ¼" threaded mount hole.

Table 7.101 XEEN Prime Lenses

Focal Length	T-Stop	Close Focus m/inches	Image Circle
14mm	3.1	0.28 m/11"	43.3 mm Full Frame +
16mm	2.6	0.3 m/12"	43.3 mm Full Frame +
20mm	1.9	0.2 m/7.9"	43.3 mm Full Frame +
24mm	1.5	0.25 m/9.8"	43.3 mm Full Frame +
35mm	1.5	0.33 m/13"	43.3 mm Full Frame +
50mm	1.5	0.45m/17.7"	43.3 mm Full Frame +
85mm	1.5	1.12 m/44"	43.3 mm Full Frame +
135mm	2.2	0.8 m/31.5"	43.3 mm Full Frame +

ZEISS Lenses

Figure 7.302
Source: www.zeiss.com/camera-lenses/us/home.html.

ZEISS Supreme Primes

Supreme Prime lenses are the latest generation of ZEISS cinema lenses, purpose built for larger format digital cinema cameras.

Figure 7.303 ZEISS Supreme Prime Lenses.

ZEISS Supreme Primes give users consistent coverage, color rendering, aperture, size, weight, and ergonomics. All the lenses across the family cover full frame and larger sensors with an image circle of 46.2 mm. The Supreme Prime lenses are color matched across the full range and most feature a fast T-stop of T1.5. Smooth focus rotation of the Supreme Prime lenses even in extreme temperatures allows for smaller motors and easy setup.

The now decades old PL mount design left room for a spinning mirror reflex shutter that digital cameras don't have. Several camera companies are making the move to shorter flange depths as the lack of a mirror shutter offers more efficient lens design options. The new LPL mount is designed for large format and a shorter 44mm flange depth.

ZEISS eXtended Data technology offers lens metadata critical for VFX-intensive productions and workflows. The frame accurate focal length, focusing distance, T-stop, and depth-of-field data eliminates guesswork for the assistant, the VFX team and the DIT. ZEISS specific distortion and vignetting data accelerates compositing and stitching in post production.

Table 7.102 ZEISS Supreme Prime and Supreme Prime Radiance Lenses

Focal Length	T-Stop	Close Focus m/inches	Image Circle
15mm SP	1.8		LF 46.2mm
18mm SP	1.5	0.35m/14"	LF 46.2mm
21mm SP/SP Radiance	1.5	0.35m/14"	LF 46.2mm
25mm SP/SP Radiance	1.5	0.26m/10"	LF 46.2mm
29mm SP/SP Radiance	1.5	0.33m/13"	LF 46.2mm

(*Continued*)

ARRI/ZEISS Master Anamorphic Lenses

Figure 7.314 ARRI/ZEISS Master 2x Anamorphic 50mm Prime Lens.

ARRI/ZEISS Master Anamorphic lenses feature unique new optical technology, with optimized flare protection, 15-blade iris that renders pleasing bokeh as well as state-of-the-art lens barrels. Master Anamorphics are color matched to all other ZEISS primes and zooms, with a form factor that gives good balance, minimal weight, good optical performance, and virtually no breathing.

Table 7.105 ARRI/ZEISS Master Anamorphic prime lenses

Focal Length	Aperture	Close Focus m/ inches	Image Circle
MA 35 mm/T1.9	T1.9 to T22	0.75m/2'6"	Super 35mm
MA 40 mm/T1.9	T1.9 to T22	0.75m/2'6"	Super 35mm
MA 50 mm/T1.9	T1.9 to T22	0.75m/2'6"	Super 35mm
MA 60 mm/T1.9	T1.9 to T22	0.9m/3'	Super 35mm
MA 75 mm/T1.9	T1.9 to T22	0.9m/3'	Super 35mm
MA 100 mm/T1.9	T1.9 to T22	1.2 m/4'	Super 35mm
MA 135 mm/T1.9	T1.9 to T22	1.5m/5'	Super 35mm

ZEISS Compact Primes

Figure 7-315 ZEISS Compact Prime CP3 prime lenses.

The Compact family of lenses are full-frame (24 × 36 mm sensor coverage) cine lenses designed for all types of cameras from HDSLR to high-end digital movie cameras, all the way up to VistaVision. Compact Primes are very lightweight and small, but very sharp, sturdy, and well built, so are very well suited to Steadicam, handheld and drone work on almost any camera. The Interchangeable Mount System gives these lenses flexibility for present and future use in many situations and for a wide range of camera platforms.

ZEISS eXtended Data technology in CP3 XD lenses offers lens metadata critical for VFX-intensive productions and workflows. The frame accurate focal length, focusing distance, T-stop, and depth-of-field data eliminates guesswork for the assistant, the VFX team, and the DIT. ZEISS lens specific distortion and shading data accelerates compositing and stitching in post-production.

Table 7.106 ZEISS CP3 and CP3 XD Compact prime lenses

Zeiss Compact Primes CP.3 & CP.3 XD			
Focal length	T-Stop	Close Focus m / Inches	Image Circle
15mm CP.3 & CP.3 XD	T 2.9 to T 22	0.3 m / 12"	FF 24mm x 36mm
18mm CP.3 & CP.3 XD	T 2.9 to T 22	0.3 m / 12"	FF 24mm x 36mm
21mm CP.3 & CP.3 XD	T 2.9 to T 22	0.24 m / 10"	FF 24mm x 36mm
25mm CP.3 & CP.3 XD	T 2.1 to T 22	0.26 m / 10"	FF 24mm x 36mm
28mm CP.3 & CP.3 XD	T 2.1 to T 22	0.24 m / 10"	FF 24mm x 36mm
35mm CP.3 & CP.3 XD	T 2.1 to T 22	0.3 m / 12"	FF 24mm x 36mm
50mm CP.3 & CP.3 XD	T 2.1 to T 22	0.45m / 18"	FF 24mm x 36mm
85mm CP.3 & CP.3 XD	T 2.1 to T 22	1.0m / 3' 3"	FF 24mm x 36mm
100mm CP.3 & CP.3 XD	T 2.1 to T 22	0.7 m / 2' 6"	FF 24mm x 36mm
135mm CP.3 & CP.3 XD	T 2.1 to T 22	1.0m / 3' 3"	FF 24mm x 36mm

Table 7.107 ZEISS CP2 Compact Prime lenses

Zeiss Compact Primes			
Focal length	Aperture	Close Focus m / Inches	Image Circle
CP.2 15 mm/T2.9	T 2.9 to T 22	0.3 m / 12"	FF 24mm × 36mm
CP.2 18 mm/T3.6	T 3.6 to T 22	0.3 m / 12"	FF 24mm × 36mm
CP.2 21 mm/T2.9	T 2.9 to T 22	0.24 m / 10"	FF 24mm × 36mm
CP.2 25 mm/T2.9	T 2.9 to T 22	0.17 m / 7"	FF 24mm × 36mm
CP.2 25 mm/T2.1	T 2.1 to T 22	0.26 m / 10"	FF 24mm × 36mm
CP.2 28 mm/T2.1	T 2.1 to T 22	0.24 m / 10"	FF 24mm × 36mm
CP.2 35 mm/T2.1	T 2.1 to T 22	0.3 m / 12"	FF 24mm × 36mm
CP.2 50 mm/T2.1	T 2.1 to T 22	0.45 m / 18"	FF 24mm × 36mm
CP.2 85 mm/T2.1	T 2.1 to T 22	1 m / 3'3"	FF 24mm × 36mm
CP.2 100 mm/ T2.1 CF	T 2.1 to T 22	0.7 m / 2'6"	FF 24mm × 36mm
CP.2 135 mm/T2.1	T 2.1 to T 22	1 m / 3'3"	FF 24mm × 36mm
CP.2 50 mm/ T2.1 Macro	T 2.1 to T 22	0.24 m / 10"	FF 24mm × 36mm

ZEISS Compact Prime Super Speeds

ZEISS Compact Primes CP.2 Super Speeds are fast cine prime lens designed for filmmaking and video production applications that shoot remarkably well in low-light. Featuring great optics and mechanics, these lenses offer broad flexibility in the areas of camera compatibility featuring an interchangeable-mount system that is ensured to be compatible with future cameras.

Figure 7.316 ZEISS Compact Prime Super Speed 35mm Lens.

ZEISS Compact Prime Super Speed T1.5 performs well in low light, and night exteriors. The fast aperture additionally offers more creative possibilities when the cinematographer wants a shallow depth of field look. Compact Super Speeds incorporate aspheric lens elements and two special types of glass with abnormal partial dispersion that exceptionally corrects for chromatic aberration.

Figure 7.317 Compact Primes glass coatings.

ZEISS-famous T* anti-reflective coatings along with internal light traps provide advanced flare suppression. Fourteen high-precision iris blades open up consistently circular across all T-stops, allowing impressive highlights in out-of-focus areas and producing smooth bokeh. The CP.2 family provides coverage of full frame 24 × 36 sensors such as the Canon 5D and 1DC and the Nikon D800. Across the CP.2 family, the front diameter is consistent, focus and iris gears are standard, and the housing is cine-style, offering thus compatibility with all standardized follow-focus systems with a focus ring rotation of 300°. The entire CP.2 family is 4K-compatible, and is color matched with the rest of the CP.2 lineup. Sturdy construction and with durable optics promise future-proof compatibility.

Table 7.108 ZEISS Compact Prime CP2 Super Speeds

Zeiss Compact Prime CP2 Super Speeds			
Focal length	Aperture	Close Focus m / Inches	Image Circle
CP.2 35 mm Super Speed	T 1.5 to T 22	0.3 m / 12"	FF 24mm x 36mm
CP.2 50 mm Super Speed	T 1.5 to T 22	0.45 m / 18"	FF 24mm x 36mm
CP.2 85 mm Super Speed	T 1.5 to T 22	1 m / 3'3"	FF 24mm x 36mm
CP.2 50 mm/T2.1 Macro	T 2.1 to T 22	0.24 m / 10"	FF 24mm x 36mm

ZEISS Compact Zooms and Lightweight Zoom

Figure 7.318 ZEISS Compact Zoom 15–30mm.

Figure 7.319 ZEISS Compact Zoom 28–80mm.

Figure 7.320 ZEISS Compact Zoom 70–200mm.

Table 7.109 ZEISS Compact Zooms

Zeiss Compact Zooms CZ.2			
Focal length	Aperture	Close Focus m / Inches	Image Circle
CZ.2 15-30mm	T 2.9 to T 22	0.55 m / 22"	FF 24mm × 36mm
CZ.2 28-80mm	T 2.9 to T 22	0.83 m / 2'8"	FF 24mm × 36mm
CZ.2 70-200mm	T 2.9 to T 22	1.52 m / 5"	FF 24mm × 36mm

Compact Zoom CZ.2 lenses 15–30mm, 28–80 mm, and 70–200 mm support 4K cameras and offer full-frame coverage. Overlapping zoom ranges give the cinematographer a wide range of coverage in three small package lenses. A circular iris gives these lenses natural looking out of focus highlights, and beautiful bokeh. T* anti-reflex coating and internal light traps suppress flare for a sharp image with good contrast.

The ZEISS 15–30mm CZ.2 Compact Zoom lens is a short, wide-angle zoom lens color matched to intercut with ZEISS Master Prime, Ultra Prime, Compact Prime Lenses, and other CZ.2 zoom lenses. Almost 300° of focus rotation with easy to read focus scales calibrated in feet allows accurate focus pulls with minimal focus shift across the zoom range. Standard pitch gears on zoom, focus, and iris. Interchangeable Lens Mounts are available in Canon EF, Nikon F, MFT, and PL.

All three Compact Zoom lenses cover full frame sensors, and are available with interchangeable lens mount systems (PL, EF, F, MFT, E). CZ.2 lenses deliver excellent optical performance, solid mechanics, and great compact lightweight design. The family of Compact Zooms are color matched to intercut with ZEISS Master Prime, Ultra Prime, Compact Prime Lenses.

Figure 7.321 ZEISS Lightweight Zoom 15.5–45mm.

The Lightweight Zoom LWZ.2 15.5–45 mm is great for shooting in confined spaces like airplanes, car interiors, or elevators. Compact size and light weight makes this zoom great for hand-held or Steadicam. Features include interchangeable mount, full-frame coverage (36 × 24 mm), no focus shift over the zoom range, consistent aperture, and great flare. suppression.

Figure 7.322 ZEISS Lightweight Zoom 21–100mm.

The 21–100mm LWZ.3 has a longer focal range than the LWZ.2, and is also a good fit for steadicam, documentary and "run and gun" shooting situations. The 21–100 covers Super 35mm with minimal breathing, and weighs only 4.4 pounds.

Wide open, the 21–100 aperture-ramp is gradually reducing the T-stop all the way through the zoom range. T2.9 at 21mm, it continuously stops down to T3.9 at 100mm. The focus ring rotates 294° with clear, readable focus marks. The lens rings are geared with the standard 0.8mm film gear pitch for use with a follow focus or motorized FIZ control, and have rubberized rings on the focus and zoom that make it easy to find and grip the rings when shooting hand-held or documentary style.

The LWZ.3 is a very sharp lens edge to edge throughout the stop range, and holds and tracks center perfectly zooming in or out, with no drift. The 21–100mm is available in Canon EF, Nikon F, SONY E, MFT, or PL, and the mounts are field-switchable. It is solidly built, with full metal construction, and is described as having a "splash-proof," allowing cinematographers to continue shooting when the weather changes.

Table 7.110 ZEISS Lightweight Zooms

Zeiss Lightweight Zooms			
Focal length	Aperture	Close Focus m / Inches	Image Circle
LWZ.2 15.5-45mm	T 2.6 to T 22	0.45 m / 18"	FF 24mm × 36mm
LWZ.3 21-100mm	T2.9-3.9 to T22	0.8 m / 2′ 8"	Super 35mm

Notes

1. From Nikon USA.
2. Courtesy of Mitch Gross.
3. Courtesy of Christophe Casenave.

Chapter 8

Camera Issues

A wise old cinematographer once said, "Failing to prepare is preparing to fail." There are many areas of the technology of digital cameras wherein the cinematographer should have at least some working knowledge, if not a thorough understanding. Knowing the issues and concerns in advance helps us to prepare, and hopefully by preparing properly, to avert potential problems or failures down the road. An understanding of camera issues therefore seems to me to be essential to the job of the cinematographer.

Variety of Camera and Lens Package Configurations: Studio, Portable, Documentary, Steadicam, Crashcam, etc.

Most cameras can be outfitted to perform a variety of tasks, but rental houses charge for gear by the piece. While accessories are usually pretty cheap to rent, it all adds up, so when you are filling out the camera order, work from the script to determine what accessories you must have, and what you can live without. The difference between a correctly configured studio camera package and a correctly configured portable run-and-gun package can mean quite a difference in cost.

Similarly, consider the size of the lens package that you order. Lenses are the most expensive discretionary items on your list, and when you are searching for something to help you get down to the budget number your production has for cameras, look for redundancy in lenses.

Figure 8.1 There are a lot of lenses to choose from!

It helps to ask yourself realistically, "What lenses must I have every day, and what lenses must I have for special shots?" The first assistant director can add specialty camera item days to his breakdowns and call sheets so that they can be scheduled, or more importantly flagged when they are rescheduled! The camera rental company can then be informed on a day-to-day basis of special needs and short-term additions to the camera package.

Figure 8.2 Steadicam in action.

Steadicam work is very specialized, and most Steadicam operators are by necessity owner/operators; as such, they are usually very well equipped for the task. Most often their greatest need is for the time to prep properly and configure their rig for the cameras they will be using.

Figure 8.3 Crashcam housing.

Also keep in mind if you are doing action work or stunts, it might be necessary to bring in short-term extra cameras other than the main camera during the course of shooting. Consider that a dangerous car stunt might be better cost managed by using a cheaper camera in harm's way, perhaps a crashcam or DSLR camera if there is a chance of destroying the camera to get the shot.

"Ready to Roll" Capabilities, Boot-Up Time, Pre-Roll Management of Expectations on the Set

I begin every production I work on by reinforcing one important point to the camera crew. If the call time is 7 a.m. then the camera should be on the set, on the dolly or sticks, with a 35mm lens on it, booted up and ready to roll at 7 a.m. – no matter what! This policy has almost always resulted in the evolution of a little wagering game about where the first shot will be, but the result is that no one is waiting on camera when the day begins. The boot up time of some electronic cameras on set is not a trivial issue, and when the occasional battery death, power kickout or camera crash happens, director producer and studio can all quickly become very impatient. In some cases, this can become a consideration when choosing a camera, as some cameras reboot and restart much more quickly than others. Whatever the resulting choice of camera, it is important to gently let your director, producer and first assistant director know ahead of time that there are going to be some camera reboots, and especially to let them know how long restart routinely takes. It is similarly important to inform the first assistant director and the sound department if the camera being used requires a pre roll period at the start of each take.

Viewing the Image while Shooting

Viewing system concerns are a very big consideration when deciding which camera to use for a production. Both video viewfinders and on set monitors (of any size!) are notoriously difficult to use in judging critical focus, so choose carefully. No producer, director, or studio executive that I know of has ever been forgiving of an out-of-focus shot; there is nowhere to hide from bad focus. The viewfinder is the first line of defense against bad focus, so get the best viewfinder available for the camera you choose, and make sure that the operator understands the job of judging focus through that viewfinder.

Figure 8.4 ARRI ALEXA viewfinder.

Almost always during a shoot there will arise a need to move the viewfinder or reorient it into some awkward or nearly impossible configuration in order to get a shot, so it is important to be sure that the mounting hardware you will need is in the camera package on the truck. Never, ever, ever put yourself in the position of having to explain that you could not get a shot because you failed to bring along the equipment required.

Wireless video transmission technology has reached a point where it can work reasonably well on shoots. For example, if one is shooting to and from several boats in a scene, it is possible to broadcast video from one boat to another, enabling much better directorial control over what happens in the scene. Keep in mind that most such equipment is only usable for viewing, and NOT for actual recording!

Viewfinders: A Cautionary Note

In the heat of battle during production, many people may have the need to look through the camera viewfinder, which raises a non-trivial health issue. There are a number of communicable diseases that can be passed via direct contact with the viewfinder eyecup or a chamois eyecup cover, most frequently, "pinkeye." Encourage crewmembers to use the monitors whenever possible, and request extra eyecups and covers. A little hygienic caution can go a long way in preventing annoying and dangerous eye infections!

Weight and Balance Issues

If you are choosing a camera to do a studio production, shot on stage, where the camera lives on a dolly for most of the show, weight and balance might only be a minor part of the equation. But if the script dictates that you are going to be climbing rugged terrain, or fording streams, or hiking through jungles, it is worth considering that a lighter, more portable camera is more likely to get the crew to the place where the shoot is happening a little earlier in the day, and a little less out of breath.

Because one of the criteria by which a cinematographer is judged is the amount of work he or she can get done in a day, it becomes crucial to one's career success to make good judgments about what camera to use based on efficiency and the speed at which your crew can work. If the story dictates a lot of Steadicam, or hand-held work, it is important to pick a camera or cameras suited for that purpose, one that balances well on the operator's shoulder. A lighter camera with good ergonomics and comfortable shoulder mounts is essential for working hand-held day after day. If the story dictates a documentary style of shooting, one might choose a camcorder camera with onboard recording capability. A well-educated cinematographer can let the story inform the choice of cameras. Remember that not every script will lead you to the same camera every time.

Onboard Camera Controls vs. Outboard Camera Controls

Stage shoots, Steadicam shooting, crane shooting, hand-held work, and many other shoot parameters beg for camera remote control capability. In such cases, it is important to choose a camera that integrates with a good remote camera control unit, as well as remote focus, iris, and zoom controls. Interfaces with Preston, FIZ, C-Motion LDS, and other systems, multi-camera synchronizers as well as various lens data systems are important to test before leaving the rental house with a camera package.

Ease of Use of Camera Controls and Menus

One of the great success stories in camera design is that most camera menu systems and structures have become much simplified in the last few years. I said *most* menu systems, not *all*. Every camera available for digital cinematography is still to some degree a beta test site for the manufacturer, and they all have built in "gotchas" that can keep you from getting the shot your director wants. It is very easy to go out into the field and discover a new software or firmware bug, or to discover that the menu system is too complex to quickly accomplish a special shot, but there is NEVER any good way to explain yourself out of the situation. Part of preparing for a shoot is finding those cases in the script that will demand some deeply hidden or arcane camera menu function and testing those functions before the cameras leave the rental house. Many of the current generation digital cinematography cameras allow the user to build presets that include menu functions

Figure 8.5 VistaVision camera (circa 1956).

Figure 8.6 ARRI ALEXA mini camera head and lens.

from deep down in menu trees to be called upon using assignable preset function buttons.

Accessory Design: Focusers, Matte Boxes, etc.

There are generally two main standards for the design and manufacture of motion picture camera accessories: Panavision and ARRIFLEX. By and large, most camera rental companies and manufacturers alike have come to realize and value the simplicity of standardized common accessories.

Figure 8.7 ARRI accessories.

In many cases, ARRIFLEX accessory standards have become the de facto standard for the industry, simply because ARRI sell their accessories (and have been selling them for over 50 years!), whereas Panavision only rent theirs. Panavision has always built to its own standards, but there exists a multitude of solutions for using either standard of gear with the other. Nonetheless, it is still important to consider the multitude of accessories that go into the camera package in preparation for a shoot. There are innumerable filters and correctly or incorrectly sized filter trays, lens donuts to prevent reflections in filters from behind camera, rods and bridge plates to support lenses, camera baseplates, matte boxes and brackets, power adaptors and the myriad of cables that go into connecting everything, and any one of these accessories can keep you from getting a shot if lost or omitted from the camera package order!

In Camera, Behind-the-Lens Filtration

Many HD cameras feature onboard behind-the-lens filters in configurable filter wheels, some controlled manually and some controlled through menu functions.

Figure 8.8 Onboard camera ND filters.

Usually these consist of a series of neutral density filters, and sometimes color correction filters for a range of daylight to tungsten corrections, and clear filters (optically necessary when no other filtration is needed). While the default filters are well chosen to accommodate the needs of most productions, other filters can be substituted into the filter wheels. ALEXA XT and upgraded pre-XT camera systems provide for behind-the-lens ND filters where the spectral transmission of those filters (provided by ARRI) has no impact on color or resolution. Two cautionary notes must be given here: (1) Never attempt to open up the onboard filter wheel yourself – that is the work of trained professionals! (2) If you do change to your own custom menu of behind-the-lens filters, test, test, test them thoroughly for correct focus and to assure that you are getting the effect you think you are getting!

Cables, Cables, and More Cables

Some cameras are well packaged, well thought out, and well suited to moving quickly and efficiently in confined spaces. Others are not. As an example, it becomes very difficult to work efficiently inside a moving car if the camera you are using has wires and cables and brackets and accessories hanging off of it in every direction.

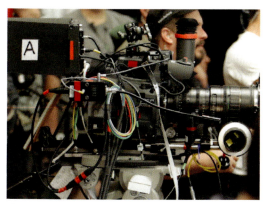

Figure 8.9 Wires, Wires, and More Wires!

Clutter on the camera is an invitation to failure. I have a slogan that I recite when a camera fails to give picture: "First check the cables – because it is *almost always* the cables that fail!"

Camera Power

Camera power is also a concern that should be addressed in camera prep. Camera batteries fail, so this is an area that needs constant attention by the camera crew, and this is not an area where you should look for savings. Bring enough batteries for the job and then bring spares, and always have an AC power supply available for each camera.

Figure 8.10 Batteries *are* included!

Batteries should be tested for charge level during prep, and monitored throughout the shoot. If a battery seems even slightly questionable, it is perfectly within etiquette to send it back to the rental house for immediate replacement. No one at any camera rental company will ever question the decision to exchange a camera battery. If a battery is questionable, place a big red tape "X" across the top, write a detailed description of the problem on

red tape on the top of the battery, and send it for a replacement.

Lens Mount/Chip Mount Optical Block Strong Enough to Eliminate Back-Focus Problems

Modern cine lenses can be quite heavy. For example, the Angenieux Optimo 24–290mm zoom lens weighs 24lbs and is over 17 inches long. The lens mount in most digital cameras is usually secured to a stainless steel optical block in the front of the camera by four to six small screws. A lens of that size and weight can exert enormous leverage on the lens mount.

Figure 8.11 A large zoom lens mounted on an ARRI ALEXA.

Consider that lens mounts are calibrated to lenses with accuracy measurable in thousandths of an inch; it only takes a microscopic change to the flange focus distance calibration to invalidate the focus marks on the lens barrel. It is very important to exercise caution when mounting large and heavy lenses to digital cameras, so as not to distort, stress, or break the components that secure the mount to the optical block. Large, or heavy lenses should always be supported by the hands of a camera assistant until a bridge support bracket has been correctly positioned and secured under the front lens support stud. A long and heavy unsupported zoom lens on a bumpy road is capable of ripping the entire lens mount right off of *any* camera!

Digital Still Cameras Used for Production Shooting

Cinematographers are creating a lot of interesting images for motion pictures and television work with DSLRs. There are many times when it helps to have stealth in your toolbox. If you want to work unnoticed in a public place, a bigger camera might attract attention, people might just stare into the camera, whereas if you are just shooting with a still camera on a tripod, you can grab an establishing shot of traffic going by for a movie or

From the Visible Dust kit, you can use the Arctic Butterfly Brush, the included green swabs, and Sensor Clean and Smear Away solvents. Swabs should be kept very clean and should be carefully and lightly moistened right at the edge with two drops of solvent in order to evenly wet the edge. Let the solvent soak in a minute or so before swabbing, careful not to squeeze out any liquid onto the sensor filter pack. Tilt the swab and drag it from one edge of the filter to the other with a light amount of pressure, and then turn it over and drag it back across the filter in the other direction, so the other side of the swab is being used. First use the Smear Away solvent, followed by the Sensor Clean solvent. The swabs may leave lint, so do another round of blowout with the bulb and another brush out with the brush if necessary. If a loop inspection tells you the filter seems clean, then shoot another test. If after several passes you are not successful, then a service visit to the rental house will be needed.

Dead or Lit Pixels

Dead pixels are not as frequently a problem with the current generation of digital cinema cameras, and most good rental houses test their cameras both before letting them out on rentals and upon return.

Figure 8.24 Dead pixels (30 minute exposure time to exaggerate!).

If you think you might have dead pixels, test by warming up the camera for a half an hour and then shooting frames of a gray card or a white (but not clipped white card), and by shooting some frames with the lens cap on. Shoot the white frames out of focus, evenly illuminated, and not exposed above clip level at the lowest compression ratio and highest resolution available on the camera. Shoot the black frames by placing the lens cap on the lens and setting the ISO level to the factory default. Using Adobe Photoshop or the software package of your choice, examine the full frame carefully and meticulously. Report any problems you find to the rental company and supply them with the frames in question.

Chapter 9

High Resolution Digital Motion Picture Cameras

Numerous cameras are built to deliver a high enough degree of performance to serve the purpose of acquiring motion pictures for the big screen. The cameras included in this chapter are chosen for inclusion by virtue of their high levels of performance and utility in making movies. If I were to include every camera that could shoot HD or 4K images, this chapter would easily be 300+ pages long. As a result, I have chosen to cover cameras in current common use and more or less current manufacture. I am also focusing on cameras that present themselves as serving the Digital Cinema market, but not cameras that advertise themselves for broadcast television. It is not my intent to invalidate the contribution of any of the cameras excluded from this section, nor is it my intent to help sell cameras for any manufacturer. If there is a great story being told on the screen, an audience doesn't care at all what cameras were used. I can only hope to provide a guide to quality for those who aspire to it, and to reinforce the caution that the cinematographer rarely succeeds by accident. Careful planning and preparation for shooting a project always pays dividends, and the well informed cinematographer can let the parameters of the story, the script, and the budget guide the decision what gear to use for any given task.

Figure 9.1

Source: www.ARRI.com/en/camera-systems/cameras

ARRI ALEXA Workflows

Codex High Density Encoding (HDE) uses lossless encoding to reduce ARRIRAW file sizes by around 40% during downloading or later in the workflow. High Density Encoding is a technique that is optimized for Bayer pattern images, completely lossless, so that when an HDE file is decoded, it is a bit-for-bit match to the original file. HDE lowers storage costs, shortens transfer times, and speeds up workflows. HDE is available free of charge for use with Codex Capture and Compact Drives, openly shared, and fast. ARRIRAW Open Gate 4.5K can be encoded at 24 fps on a modern MacBook Pro.

ALEXA also offers on-board recording of Apple ProRes in MXF and ProRes in Quicktime files onto SxS PRO cards, with codecs ranging from ProRes 422 (Proxy) all the way up to ProRes 4444XQ.

The ARRI Look Library supports 87 predefined creative color grades, each in three intensities and, all looks can be used as a basic to create new color grades.

ARRI ALEXA 65

Figure 9.2 ARRI ALEXA 65.

ARRI's ALEXA 65 system is available exclusively through ARRI's global network of rental facilities. A complete large-format solution for high-end motion pictures, television productions, and commercials, the system is based on a 65mm digital cinema camera, numerous custom-designed prime and zoom lenses, and efficient workflow tools. Capturing uncompressed 65 mm ARRIRAW images, ALEXA 65 is the flagship of the ALEXA camera platform.

An integral part of the ALEXA 65 system is a range of exclusive 65 mm prime lens series specifically designed to cover the full image area of the sensor. Lenses for the ALEXA 65 are covered elsewhere in this book, in the lens chapter.

The ALEXA 65 sensor is slightly bigger than a 5-perf 65mm film frame, and the 65mm format offers a distinct aesthetic for telling stories with images. With an open gate resolution of 6560 × 3100, ALEXA 65 offers the same sensitivity, high dynamic range and natural colorimetry as the rest of the ALEXA line, but at far greater spatial resolution.

Prime 65, Zoom 65, and Prime 65 S lenses utilize high-performance optics, housed in precision-engineered lens barrels that were co-developed with IB/E Optics. Featuring an XPL mount equipped with the ARRI Lens Data System (LDS), the lenses provide metadata about focus, iris, and zoom settings to be recorded with the image stream. This data can be used on set for wireless remote lens control, but it can also be used to help match a virtual lens with the recorded image in post production, reducing the time and cost involved in generating complex visual effects shots.

ALEXA 65 captures in the ARRIRAW format, unprocessed 12-bit log encoded raw Bayer data, a good fit for high quality visual effects production. ARRI Rental worked closely with Codex during the camera's development to create a high-performance workflow unique to the ALEXA 65. Depending on the shooting environment and location, ALEXA 65 workflows can run on either a purpose-configured ARRI Rental Vault S65 or the high performance ARRI Rental Vault XL65.

Commissioned and manufactured to design specifications by ARRI Rental, ALEXA 65 is a robust and relatively compact camera that can be operated under duress and in extreme conditions.

Table 9.1 ARRI ALEXA 65 specifications

ARRI	ALEXA 65
Camera type	65 mm format digital cinema camera
Sensor	ARRI A3X CMOS sensor
Image aperture	5-perf 65 mm (54.12 mm × 25.58 mm active image area)
Sensor resolution	6560 × 3100 (Open Gate – maximum recordable)
Lens mount	ARRI XPL mount with Lens Data System (LDS) functionality
Shutter	Electronic, 5.0° to 358.0°. Adjustable with 1/10° precision
Frame rates	20 to 60 fps (Open Gate)
Exposure index	EI 200 to EI 3200. Base sensitivity EI 800
Recording system	ALEXA 65 cameras feature only in-camera ARRIRAW recording – uncompressed 12-bit log without white balance or exposure index processing applied
Recording file format	Uncompressed ARRIRAW
Sensor crop modes	1.78 Crop Mode (5-perf 65 mm): 5120 × 2880 1.50 Crop Mode (8-perf 35 mm): 4320 × 2880 LF Open Gate: 4448 × 3096 4K UHD: 3840 × 2160* *Available with the release of software update SUP 3.0
Storage	Codex SXR Capture Drive 2000 GByte capacity Max. frame rate capability: 60 fps (Open Gate) Recording time: 43 minutes @ 24 fps Codex XR Capture Drive 480 GByte capacity/850 MByte per second data rate Max. frame rate capability: 27 fps (Open Gate) Recording time: 11 minutes @ 24 fps

ARRI	ALEXA 65
Viewfinder	Electronic color viewfinder ARRI EVF-1 with 1280 × 768 F-LCOS micro display (image: 1280 × 720, status bars: 1280 × 32 above and 1280 × 32 below image) and ARRI LED illumination. Image can be flipped for use of viewfinder on camera left or right. Viewfinder Mounting Bracket allows movement of viewfinder forward/backwards, left/right, up/down, 360 degree rotation and placement on camera left or right. EVF-1 controls: viewfinder and basic camera settings, ZOOM button (2.25x pixel to pixel magnification), EXP button (false color exposure check) and jog wheel.
Controls	Camera right: main user interface with 3" transflective 400 × 240 pixel LCD color screen, illuminated buttons, button lock, and jog wheel. Camera left: operator interface with illuminated buttons, button lock, and card swap button.
BNC connectors	4 × 3G SDI – MON (1) OUT: 2 × 3G SDI – MON (2) OUT: 2 × 3G SDI
SD card	For software updates and menu settings etc. as with ALEXA High speed operating mode for fast ARRIRAW frame grabs
Miscellaneous interfaces	Focus/iris/zoom motor control with full wireless lens control support 5 × RS 24V 1 × 12V TC I/O (5-pin Lemo) 1 × LDD 2 × LCS BAT and ACC connection
Monitoring	3 independent color outputs, all with optional overlays: EVF-1 OUT MON (1) OUT MON (1) OUT MON OUT assistive displays: Zoom, overscan, overlay info, frame lines, false color exposure check, peaking focus check
CDL	CDL server support is provided as ALEXA XT
In-camera playback	Playback via EVF-1, HD-SDI MON OUT including audio
Dimensions	Length: 387.8 mm | 15.3 in Width: 208.3 mm | 8.2 in Height: 163 mm | 6.4 in (body only with XPL mount)
Weight	10.5kg | 23.2lb

ARRI ALEXA LF and ALEXA Mini LF

ARRI ALEXA LF

Figure 9.3 ARRI ALEXA LF.

ARRI's large-format camera system consists of the ALEXA LF (large-format) camera, and the ALEXA LF Mini (combining compact size, lighter weight, the same recording formats, and the same large-format ALEXA LF sensor), ARRI Signature Prime lenses, LPL lens mount, and PL-to-LPL adapter. ALEXA LF's sensor is slightly larger than full frame, and the ALEXA LF camera records native 4.5K and supports all anamorphic de-squeeze ratios. ARRI's image quality allows film makers to capture large-format images with ARRI's natural colorimetry, high dynamic range, high sensitivity ARRI color science for natural skin tones, easy color correction, and clean VFX. ALEXA LF cameras are well suited for high dynamic range (HDR) and wide color gamut (WCG) acquisition. Versatile recording formats include efficient ProRes and uncompressed, unencrypted ARRIRAW up to 150 fps, for most on-set workflow requirements.

The camera, lens mount, and lenses and accessories are fully compatible with existing PL mount lenses and ALEXA accessories. A PL-to-LPL adapter offers backwards compatibility with all PL mount lenses, whether Super 35 or full frame. The adapter attaches securely to the LPL lens mount without tools, allowing crews to rapidly switch between PL and LPL lenses with complete lens metadata accessible from LDS-2, LDS-1 or /i lenses. For even further cross-system compatibility, an LPL lens mount can be fitted to existing ALEXA, ALEXA Mini, and AMIRA cameras, enabling ARRI Signature Primes and other future LPL mount lenses can to be used for both Super 35 and large format on productions combining the two systems.

ARRI ALEXA LF Workflows

ALEXA LF also offers fast and efficient workflows with internal recording to Codex Compact Drive Uncompressed and unencrypted MXF/ARRIRAW and MXF/Apple ProRes. Codex Compact Drive 1TB is small, durable, and cost-efficient. The Compact Drive Reader works without license or extra software, and is compatible with SXR Capture Drive Docks.

ALEXA LF and LF Mini feature the MVF-2 high-contrast 1920 × 108 HD OLED viewfinder with stable temperature-controlled color balance for optimal judgment of focus, dynamic range, and color. A flexible and reliable CoaXPress View Finder cable, extends up to 10m/33 ft. Menus or camera image can also be displayed on a 4" flip-out monitor.

Features include three internal, motorized large-format FSND filters: ND 0.6, 1.2, and 1.8, dedicated, regulated 12V and 24V accessory power outputs, SYNC IN and improved AUDIO connectors, and two built-in microphones. User features include six user buttons on camera's left side, one LOCK button each for camera and viewfinder, an additional external Wi-Fi antenna, and easier access to media, VF, and TC connectors.

ALEXA LF cameras are compatible with ARRI and cmotion wireless remote systems, and work with 12V and 24V on-board batteries (~65W power draw).

ARRI ALEXA Mini LF

Figure 9.4 ARRI ALEXA Mini LF.

The ALEXA Mini LF combines the ALEXA LF sensor with a compact size, lightweight body. The ALEXA Mini LF uses the same sensor as the ALEXA LF, the ALEV 3 A2X sensor, which has the same photosite size and type as Super 35mm ARRI digital cameras. It's 4.5k sensor has 4448 × 3096 photosites and measures 36.70 × 25.54mm. The ALEXA Mini LF has the same dimensions and the same mounting points as an ALEXA Mini except for the media bay on the camera left side. The body weighs 2.6kg/5.7lbs including the LPL lens mount and the MVF-2 viewfinder weighs 800g/1.7lbs. The ALEXA Mini LF uses the small and cost-effective Codex Compact Drive 1 TB. The Compact Drive has been specifically designed for the small form factor of the ALEXA Mini LF, using flash technology in a miniaturized tough casing. The ALEXA Mini LF accepts Compact Drives directly, without the need for an adapter. The Compact Drive 1 TB contains one industrial SSD and both ARRIRAW and ProRes recording can utilize the drive's full recording capacity of 960 GB. The drive is formatted by the ALEXA Mini LF in the UDF format for both ARRIRAW and ProRes, so both ARRIRAW and ProRes can be recorded onto the same media without reformatting or switching drives. The drive offers sustained write rates of up to 8 Gb/s. ALEXA LF or ALEXA SXT W do not support the Compact Drive.

Camera controls include the Wireless Compact Unit WCU-4 is a 3-axis hand unit for wireless remote lens and camera control. It includes an integrated lens data display and offers extended ALEXA camera control. Using the Multi Viewfinder MVF-2 with a 10m/33ft. VF cable to the ALEXA Mini LF, the viewfinder becomes a remote control for all camera functions as well as a monitor for the live image the camera is capturing. ALEXA Mini LF can be controlled over WiFi or by cable (ethernet connector) from a computer, tablet, or smart phone running a web browser with the web remote. Operator Control Unit OCU-1 is an addition to the WCU-4 lens control system on ALEXA Mini, ALEXA LF and ALEXA Mini LF that connects to the camera via an LBUS cable. The OCU-1 enables operators to over-ride and return focus, iris, and zoom controls at the touch of a button.

Table 9.2 ARRI ALEXA LF, ALEXA Mini LF specifications

ARRI	ALEXA LF/ALEXA Mini LF
Sensor	44.71mm format A3X CMOS sensor with Dual Gain Architecture (DGA) and Bayer pattern color filter array
Sensor Size	36.70 × 25.54mm 4448 × 3096, ø 44.71 mm Overall Dimensions (active imaging area)
Sensor Mode LF 16:9	31.68 × 17.82mm
Surround View	3840 × 2160, ø 36.35mm
ARRIRaw	3840 × 2160, ø 36.35mm
Sensor Mode LF 2.39:1	36.70 × 15.31 mm 4448 × 1856, ø 39.76mm
Exposure Index/ISO	EI 200 (+5.3/–8.7), EI 400 (+6.3/–7.7), EI 800 (+7.4/–6.6), EI 1600 (+8.4/–5.6), EI3200 (+9.4/–4.6)
Notable Features	Large Format (LF) digital camera with electronic viewfinder EVF-1 and built-in radios for ARRI Wireless Remote System, ARRI Wireless Video System and WiFi
Compatibility	All current ARRI ALEXA accessories, LPL lenses and PL lenses with PL-to-LPL adapter
Frame Rates ALEXA LF	Open Gate ARRIRAW: 0.75–90 fps, ProRes: 0.75 up to 60 fps LF 16:9 ARRIRAW: 0.75–90 fps, ProRes: 0.75–60 fps LF 2.39:1 ARRIRAW: 0.75–150 fps, ProRes: 0.75 up to 100 fps
Frame Rates ALEXA LF Mini	Open Gate ARRIRAW 4.5K: 0.75–40 fps ProRes 4.5K: 0.75–40 fps 16:9 ProRes HD: 0.75–90 fps 16:9 ProRes 2K: 0.75–90 fps 16:9 ProRes UHD: 0.75–60 fps 16:9 ARRIRAW UHD: 0.75–60 fps 2.39:1 ARRIRAW 4.5K: 0.75–60 fps 2.39:1 ProRes 4.5K: 0.75–60 fps
Shutter	5.0°–358.0°. Shutter angle setting precision: 1/10 degree.
Lens Mount	62mm LPL mount (LDS-1, LDS-2 and /ꞵ)
Flange Focal Depth	44mm
Viewfinder EVF-1	Low latency (≤1 frame delay) electronic color viewfinder ARRI EVF-1 with 1280 × 768 F-LCOS micro display (image: 1280 × 720, status bars: 1280 × 32 above and 1280 × 32 below image) and ARRI LED illumination. Image can be flipped for use of viewfinder on camera left or right. Viewfinder Mounting Bracket allows movement of viewfinder forward/backwards, left/right, up/down, 360 degree rotation and placement on camera left or right. EVF-1 controls: viewfinder and basic camera settings, ZOOM button (2.25× pixel to pixel magnification), EXP button (false color exposure check) and jog wheel.
Viewfinder EVF-2	Low latency (≤1 frame delay) electronic color viewfinder with 1920 × 1080 high-contrast OLED display. Eyepiece is based on the ARRICAM design and offers high contrast, low distortion, an evenly illuminated viewing area for a clean image and a wide exit pupil for greater freedom of movement for the operator. Image can be flipped for use of viewfinder on camera left or right. Surround view shows an area larger than that being recorded. The EVF-2 displays customizable frame lines, surround view, camera status, Lens Data System info, clip/reel numbers, false color, and peaking. Control of the basic viewfinder and camera

(Continued)

Table 9.2 (Continued)

ARRI	ALEXA LF/ALEXA Mini LF
	settings is possible through CAM and EVF on-screen menus. Display brightness is adjustable in three steps: 120, 200, and 300 nits. The color balance is stable at all display brightness settings, image brightness levels and from –20ºC to +45ºC (–4º F to +113º F). Compatible with ALEXA LF cameras with LF SUP 3.0 and later and Heated Eyecup HE-7. Not compatible with ALEXA Classic cameras
LF Controls	Wireless Compact Unit WCU-4 is a 3-axis hand unit for wireless remote lens and camera control. It includes an integrated lens data display and offers extended ALEXA camera control.
	Single Axis Unit SXU-1 controls a single lens axis. On set the SXU-1 complements the 3-axis WCU-4 as a separate iris control unit, or it can be used on its own
Mini LF Controls	Multi Viewfinder MVF-2 with a 10m/33ft VF cable to the ALEXA Mini LF, enables the viewfinder to become a remote control for all camera functions as well as a monitor for the live image the camera is capturing.
	ALEXA Mini LF can be controlled over WiFi or by cable (ETH connector) from a computer, tablet or smart phone running a web browser with the web remote.
	Operator Control Unit OCU-1 is an addition to the WCU-4 lens control system on ALEXA Mini, ALEXA LF and ALEXA Mini LF that connects to the camera via an LBUS cable. The OCU-1 enables operators to override and return focus, iris, and zoom controls at the touch of a button.
	General Purpose IO Box GBP-1 is a break-out box that works with ALEXA Mini, ALEXA Mini LF and AMIRA. It allows users to build custom button interfaces and electronic controls. The box can be connected to the camera EXT port which it also replicates. It provides protected input channels that can be mapped to various functions
Recording Codecs	ALEXA LF – MXF/ARRIRAW, QuickTime/ProRes (422, 422HQ, 4444, and 4444 XQ)
	ALEXA MINI LF – MXF/ARRIRAW, MXF ProRes (422, 422 HQ, 4444, and 4444 XQ)
Recording Resolutions	4.5K (sensor modes LF Open Gate and LF 2.39:1) UHD (sensor mode LF 16:9) 2K (in-camera downscale in sensor mode LF 16:9) HD (in-camera downscale in sensor mode LF 16:9)
Supported Media	SxS PRO+ 256 GB (ProRes) SXR Capture Drives 1 TB (ARRIRAW or ProRes) SXR Capture Drives 2 TB (ARRIRAW or ProRes)
BNC connectors	4x 3G SDI video. MON (2) OUT: 2 × 3G SDI
Miscellaneous interfaces	Focus/iris/zoom motor control with full wireless lens control support 5 × RS 24V 1 × 12V TC I/O (5-pin Lemo) 1 × LDD 2 × LCS BAT and ACC connection
Monitoring	EVF – 1 OUT MON OUT 1a, 1b, and 2: SDI 6G UHD or SDI 1.5G HD up to 30 fps MON OUT 3: SDI 1.5 G HD up to 30 fps, also wireless video Anamorphic de-squeeze for 1.25×, 1.3×, 1.5×, 2× lens squeeze ratios MON OUT assistive displays: Zoom, overscan, overlay info, frame lines, false color exposure check, peaking focus check

ARRI	ALEXA LF/ALEXA Mini LF
Image Processing	Internally represents linear data in 16-bit, LogC in 12-bit and can record 10-bit or 12-bit ProRes Target output color spaces: Log C, Rec 709, or Rec 2020 Supports ARRI Look File (ALF-2) with CDL values and a 3D LUT 3D LUTs available for SDR, HDR PQ, and HDR HLG
In-camera playback	Playback via EVF-1, HD-SDI MON Out including audio. ARRIRAW ProRes
Audio	1 × XLR 5-pin AUDIO IN for 2 channels, line level
SD Card	For importing ARRI Look Files, camera set up files, frame line files and feature licenses. Stores captured stills from the REC OUT image path in ARRIRAW (.ari, 12 bit), TIFF (.tif, 16 bit), DPX (.dpx, 10 bit) and JPEG (.jpg, 8 bit) format as well as logging files. Also used for software updates.
Synchronization	Master/Slave mode for precision sync of settings, sensor, processing, HD-SDI outputs and SxS recording for 3D applications.
Sound Level	Sound level ≤ 20 db(A) while recording LF Open Gate ProRes 4.5 K 4444 @ 30 fps and ≤ +30° Celsius (≤ +86° Fahrenheit), measured 1 m/3 feet in front of the lens
Power In	19.5 to 34V DC
Power Out	4× RS (24V), 1× 12V (12 V), 1× EXT (24V), 1× ETH (24V)
Weight	7.8kg/17.2lbs
Dimensions	Length: 364mm/14.33", width: 201mm/7.91", height: 158mm/6.22" (body only with XPL mount)

ARRI ALEXA SXT W

Figure 9.5 ARRI ALEXA SXT W.

ALEXA SXT W is an S35mm ALEXA camera with a built-in video transmitter which makes the camera smaller and lighter than it would be with an external transmitter attached. That means fewer cables around the camera and fewer associated problems, since cable failure is by far the most common technical hitch on set. Camera setup and power-up are quicker, and productions are able to move faster. The camera supports four independent monitoring outputs, EVF, and MON OUT 1–3, each independent in color space, surround view, and look.

Fourteen in-camera recording formats fulfill almost any production need with all sensor modes available in both ARRIRAW and ProRes. Four different types of media give the camera flexibility for rental houses and productions. Media options include CFast 2.0 Adapter 2 and CFast 2.0 card, SxS Adapter 2 and SxS PRO/SxS PRO+ cards, XR Adapter and XR Capture Drives, SXR Adapter and SXR Capture Drives.

The ALEXA SXT W is part of a complete ARRI Wireless Video System (WVS), along with a stand-alone video transmitter for use with other ARRI or third-party cameras, and a stand-alone video receiver that picks up signals from either transmitter. Integrated wireless video, ARRI ECS, and WiFi radios are small and light with external transmitters, fewer cables, and fewer cable problems, faster setup (power on and go). An extensive accessory range includes various mounting brackets, antenna extensions, and the handheld Director's Monitor Support (DMS-1), as well as a specially adapted transvideo monitor with a built-in receiver for the ARRI transmitters. Whether using this monitor or others, the modular system allows for a compact and efficient setup. An extra power-out on the video receiver permits a single on-board battery to power both the receiver and an attached handheld monitor. A higher input voltage range allows more flexibility on battery choice.

Table 9.3 ARRI ALEXA SXT W specifications

ARRI	ALEXA SXT W
Sensor Type	Super 35 format ARRI ALEV III CMOS sensor with Bayer pattern color filter array
Sensor Maximum Resolution and Size	3424 × 2202 28.25 × 18.17mm/1.112 × 0.715" ø 33.59mm/1.322"
Sensor Frame Rates	0.75–120 fps
Exposure Index	Adjustable from EI 160–3200 in 1/3 stops EI 800 base sensitivity
Shutter	Electronic shutter, 5.0°–358°
Photosite Pitch	8.25µm
Sensor Active Image Area (photosites)	16:9 ProRes HD: 2880 × 1620 16:9 ProRes 2K: 2880 × 1620 16:9 ProRes 3.2K: 3200 × 1800 16:9 Prores 4K UHD: 3200 × 1800 16:9 ARRIRAW 2.8K: 2880 × 1620 16:9 ARRIRAW 3.2K: 3168 × 1782 6:5 ProRes 2K Anamorphic: 2560 × 2146 6:5 ProRes 4K Cine Anamorphic: 2560 × 2146 6:5 ARRIRAW 2.6K: 2578 × 2160 4:3 ProRes 2.8K: 2880 × 2160 4:3 ARRIRAW 2.8K: 2880 × 2160 Open Gate ProRes 3.4K: 3424 × 2202 Open Gate ProRes 4K Cine: 3414 × 2198 Open Gate ARRIRAW 3.4K: 3424 × 2202
Sensor Active Image Area (dimensions)	16:9 ProRes HD: 23.76 × 13.37mm/0.935 × 0.526" 16:9 ProRes 2K: 23.76 × 13.37mm/0.935 × 0.526" 16:9 ProRes 3.2K: 26.40 × 14.85mm/1.039 × 0.585" 16:9 Prores 4K UHD: 26.40 × 14.85mm/1.039 × 0.585" 16:9 ARRIRAW 2.8K: 23.76 × 13.37mm/0.935 × 0.526" 16:9 ARRIRAW 3.2K: 26.14 × 14.70mm/1.029 × 0.579" 6:5 ProRes 2K Anamorphic: 21.12 × 17.70mm/0.831 × 0.697" 6:5 ProRes 4K Cine Anamorphic: 21.12 × 17.70mm/0.831 × 0.697" 6:5 ARRIRAW 2.6K: 21.38 × 17.82mm/0.842 × 0.702" 4:3 ProRes 2.8K: 23.76 × 17.82mm/0.935 × 0.702" 4:3 ARRIRAW 2.8K: 23.76 × 17.82mm/0.935 × 0.702" Open Gate ProRes 3.4K: 28.25 × 18.17mm/1.112 × 0.715" Open Gate ProRes 4K Cine: 28.17 × 18.13mm/1.109 × 0.714" Open Gate ARRIRAW 3.4K: 28.25 × 18.17 mm/1.112 × 0.715"
Recording File Container Size (pixel)	16:9 ProRes HD: 1920 × 1080 16:9 ProRes 2K: 2048 × 1152 16:9 ProRes 3.2K: 3200 × 1824 16:9 Prores 4K UHD: 3840 × 2160 16:9 ARRIRAW 2.8K: 2880 × 1620 16:9 ARRIRAW 3.2K: 3168 × 1782 6:5 ProRes 2K Anamorphic: 2048 × 858 6:5 ProRes 4K Cine Anamorphic: 4096 × 1716

ARRI	ALEXA SXT W
	6:5 ARRIRAW 2.6K: 2592 × 2160
	4:3 ProRes 2.8K: 2944 × 2176
	4:3 ARRIRAW 2.8K: 2944 × 2176
	Open Gate ProRes 3.4K: 3456 × 2202
	Open Gate ProRes 4K Cine: 4096 × 2636
	Open Gate ARRIRAW 3.4K: 3424 × 2202
Recording File Image Content (pixel)	16:9 ProRes HD: 1920 × 1080
	16:9 ProRes 2K: 2048 × 1152
	16:9 ProRes 3.2K: 3200 × 1800
	16:9 Prores 4K UHD: 3840 × 2160
	16:9 ARRIRAW 2.8K: 2880 × 1620
	16:9 ARRIRAW 3.2K: 3168 × 1782
	6:5 ProRes 2K Anamorphic: 2048 × 858
	6:5 ProRes 4K Cine Anamorphic: 4096 × 1716
	6:5 ARRIRAW 2.6K: 2578 × 2160
	4:3 ProRes 2.8K: 2880 × 2160
	4:3 ARRIRAW 2.8K: 2280 × 2160
	Open Gate ProRes 3.4K: 3424 × 2202
	Open Gate ProRes 4K Cine: 4096 × 2636
	Open Gate ARRIRAW 3.4K: 3424 × 2202
Recording Formats	ARRIRAW (.ari)
	Apple ProRes 4444 XQ
	Apple ProRes 4444
	Apple ProRes 422 HQ
	Apple ProRes 422
	Recording Media
	SXR Capture Drives
	XR Capture Drives
	SxS PRO+ Cards
	CFast 2.0 Cards
Recording Frame Rates	16:9 ProRes HD: 0.75–120 fps
	16:9 ProRes 2K: 0.75–120 fps
	16:9 ProRes 3.2K: 0.75–72 fps
	16:9 Prores 4K UHD: 0.75–50 fps
	16:9 ARRIRAW 2.8K: 0.75–120 fps
	16:9 ARRIRAW 3.2K: 0.75–120 fps
	6:5 ProRes 2K Anamorphic: 0.75–96 fps
	6:5 ProRes 4K Cine Anamorphic: 0.75–60 fps
	6:5 ARRIRAW 2.6K: 0.75–96 fps
	4:3 ProRes 2.8K: 0.75–60 fps
	4:3 ARRIRAW 2.8K: 0.75–96 fps
	Open Gate ProRes 3.4K: 0.75–60 fps
	Open Gate ProRes 4K Cine: 0.75–48 fps
	Open Gate ARRIRAW 3.4K: 0.75–90 fps
Recording Modes	Standard real-time recording
	Pre-recording (ProRes only)
	No Intervalometer

(*Continued*)

Table 9.3 (Continued)

ARRI	ALEXA SXT W
Viewfinder Type	Electronic Viewfinder EVF-1 F-LCOS viewfinder display
Viewfinder Resolution (pixel)	1280 × 784
Viewfinder Diopter	Adjustable from –5 to +5 diopters
Color Output	Rec 709 Rec 2020 Log C Custom Look (ARRI Look File ALF-2)
Look Control	Import of custom 3D LUT ASC CDL parameters (slope, offset, power, saturation)
White Balance	Manual and auto white balance, adjustable from 2000K to 11000K in 100K steps Color correction adjustable range from –12 to +12 CC 1 CC corresponds to 035 Kodak CC values or 1/8 Rosco values
Filters	Manual behind the lens FSND filters: Optical Clear, 0.3, 0.6, 0.9, 1.2, 1.5, 1.8, 2.1, 2.4 Fixed optical low pass, UV, IR filter
Image Outputs	1× proprietary signal output for EVF-1 viewfinder 4× MON OUT: 1.5G (SMPTE ST292-1) uncompressed HD video with embedded audio and metadata
Lens Squeeze Factors	1, 1.3, 2.00, 2.00 mag.
Exposure and Focus Tools	False Color, Peaking, Zoom
Audio Input	1x XLR 5-pin balanced stereo line in (Line input max. level +24dBu correlating to 0dBFS)
Audio Output	3.5mm stereo headphone jack SDI (embedded)
Audio Recording	2 channel linear PCM, 24-bit 48kHz
Remote Control Options	Web-based remote control from phones, tablets and laptops via WiFi and Ethernet WCU-4 hand unit with control over lens motors and operational parameters via built-in white radio Remote Control Unit RCU-4 via Ethernet
Interfaces	1× LEMO 5-pin LTC Timecode In/Out 1× BNC SDI Return In 1× LEMO 16-pin EXT for accessories and sync 1× LEMO 10-pin Ethernet for remote control and sync 1× SD Card (for user setups, look files etc.) 3× Fischer 12-pin connectors for CLM lens motors 2× Fischer 5-pin LCS Lens Control System connectors for hand units 1x LDD Lens Data Display connector
Wireless Interfaces	Built-in WiFi module (IEEE 802.11b/g) Built-in White Radio for ARRI lens and camera remote control Built-in Wireless Video System

ARRI	ALEXA SXT W
Lens Mounts	PL lens mount
	LPL lens mount
	Flange Focal Depth
	PL mount: 52mm
	LPL mount: 44mm
Power Input	1× Fischer 2-pin BAT connector (10.5–34 V DC)
	1× On-board battery interface (10.5–34 V DC)
Power Consumption	min. 88W
	max. 141W
	(Camera body with EVF-1)
Power Outputs	3× Fischer 3-pin 24V RS
	1x LEMO 2pin 12V
Power Management	Active ORing between BAT connector and on-board battery adapters
Measurements (HxWxL)	158 × 189 × 351 mm/6.22 × 7.44 × 13.82"
	(camera body with PL lens mount)
Weight	~7.4kg/~16.3lbs
	(camera body with PL lens mount)

ARRI ALEXA Mini

Figure 9.6 ARRI ALEXA Mini.

ARRI ALEXA Mini is compact, lightweight, sturdy, small, and versatile. The Mini is a Super 35mm format film-style digital camera, recording up to 200 fps with High Dynamic Range capability. Its symmetrical design permits filming in any orientation, including upside-down and in portrait mode, and multiple accessory points enable numerous mounting solutions

ALEXA Mini is a highly versatile tool on set. On some productions, the Mini is used as a second or third camera, while on others it can be used as the main camera throughout the shoot. ARRI has developed a studio set for ALEXA Mini. At its core is the ARRI Compact Bridge Plate CBP-1, a base plate with integrated sliding bridge plate and shoulder pad. This allows for rapid, tool-less transitions between configurations. The Rear Accessory Bracket RAB-1 offers flexible attachment options for the Power Splitting Box Mk II, a power distribution unit available in Gold Mount and V-Mount versions, while the Side Accessory Bracket SAB-1 provides a simple interface for mounting accessories towards the rear of the camera. Most previously released ARRI camera accessories for the ALEXA Mini are compatible with the studio set.

ALEXA Mini is available with a variety of rapidly interchangeable lens mounts that allow the use of B4 2/3" video-style lenses, an EF mount for compatibility with a wide range of still photography lenses, a PL mount for cine-style lenses (including those compatible with the ARRI Lens Data System), or even ARRI Signature Primes with an LPL mount.

Accompanied by a wide range of mechanical and electronic accessories for every use case, Easy, rapid, and tool-less transitions between configurations with built-in motorized FSND filters 0.6, 1.2, 2.1. For 360° VR shooting, 3D, and VFX applications the EXT SYNC mode permits synchronizing up to 15 ALEXA Minis with one master ALEXA Mini, allowing an entire multi camera setup to be operated as if it is one camera.

An ALEXA Mini can be operated in number of ways: by wireless remote control, as an A-camera with the ARRI MVF-1 multi viewfinder attached, or with an on-board monitor and controlled via the user button interface on the camera body. The Mini is light enough to be used in a hand-held rig, while its compact size also makes it ideal for tight shooting conditions, as well as shooting underwater, aerials, cars, action, and 3D shoots.

ALEXA Mini is stable in harsh environments from –20° to +45°C/–4° to +113°F with sealed electronics that are non-condensing, splash, and dust-proof.

Table 9.4 ARRI ALEXA Mini specifications

ARRI	ALEXA Mini
Sensor	35mm format ALEV III CMOS with Dual Gain Architecture (DGA) and Bayer pattern color filter array.
Sensor Size	28.25mm × 18.13mm overall dimensions
Photosites (16 × 9 Mode)	
Sensor Size	3424 × 2202 (1:55:1)
Surround View for monitoring	1760 × 980 (S16 HD) 3168 × 1762 (HD, 2K or MXF/ARRIRAW 2.8K), 3154 × 1764 (2K), 3424 × 1826 (4K UHD, 3.2K), 3424 × 2203 (Anamorphic), not available in Open Gate Mode
Open Gate (Mxf/ARRIRaw)	3424 × 2202 (1:55:1)
Anamorphic Mode (Mxf/ARRIRaw or ProRes)	3424 × 2202 (1:55:1)
4K UHD ProRes	3200 × 1800
3.2K ProREs	3200 × 1800
2.8K ARRIRAW/Mxf	2880 × 1620
2K ProRes	2868 × 1612
HD	2868 × 1612
S16 HD	1600 × 900
Recording Pixel Count	1920 × 1080 ProRes HD, MPEG 2 and HD outputs, 2048 × 1152 ProRes 2K, 3200 × 1800 ProRes 3.2K*, 3840 × 2160 Pro Res 4K UHD and UHD outputs* (* Requires installed 4K UHD License)
Exposure Index/ISO	EI 160 (+5.0/–9.0), EI 200 (+5.3/–8.7), EI 400 (+6.3/–7.7), EI 800 (+7.4/–6.6), EI 1600 (+8.4/–5.6), EI3200 (+9.4/–4.6)
Exposure Latitude	14 stops for all sensitivity settings from EI 160 to EI 3200, as measured with the ARRI Dynamic Range Test Chart (DRTC)
	Values behind the exposure index are the number of stops above and below 18% grey. These values are for Log C. Rec 709 and DCI P3 are the same except for 0.5 stops fewer in the low end at EI 160, 0.4 stops fewer in the low end at EI 200 and 0.2 stops fewer in the low end at EI 400.

ARRI	ALEXA Mini
Audio Recording	4 channels, 24-bit PCM, 48kHz
Integrated motorized ND Filters	Built-in motorized ND filters 0.6, 1.2, 2.1
Sound Level	< 20dB(A)
Notable Features	35mm format film-style digital camera with lightweight and compact carbon body, switchable active sensor area, support for ARRI MVF-1 viewfinder, built-in remote control capabilities via ARRI Electronic Control System and Wi-Fi, support for cforce motors, built-in motorized ND filters, interchangeable lens mounts and ARRI Lens Data System as well as Lens Data Archive.
Frame Rates	16:9 ProRes HD 0.75–200 fps ProRes S16 HD 0.75–200 fps ProRes 2K 0.75–200 fps ProRes 3.2K 0.75–60 fps ProRes UHD 0.75–60 fps MFX/ARRIRAW 16:9 2.8K 0.75–48 fps 4:3 ProRes 4:3 2.8K 0.75–50 fps 6:5* ProRes 2:39:1 2K Ana. 0.75–120 fps 8:9** ProRes HD Ana. 0.75–120 fps Open Gate MFX/ARRIRAW 3.4K Open Gate 0.75–30 fps * 4:3 cropped ** Center crop from anamorphic (1) Minimum frame rate is always 0.75 fps (2) The "recording resolution" determines the number of horizontal pixels that will be recorded (the number of vertical pixels is dependent on the recording file type and sensor mode)
Color output	Rec 709, custom look, or Log C
Recording formats	ProRes: S16 HD: 1920 × 1080 (up-sampled from 1600 × 900) HD: 1920 × 1080 2K Cine 16:9: 2048 × 1152 3.2K: 3200 × 1800 4K UHD: 3840 × 2160 (up-sampled from 3.2K) 4:3 2.8K: 2880 × 2160 (padded to 2944 × 2160) Anamorphic ProRes formats with 2x in-camera de-squeeze: HD Anamorphic: 1920 × 1080* 2.39:1 2K Anamorphic: 2048 × 858* MXF/ARRIRAW (in-camera recording to MXF-wrapped ARRIRAW files): 2.8K 16:9: 2880 × 1620** Open Gate: 3424 × 2202>> MXF/ARRIRAW Open Gate modes with active image area matching 4:3 ProRes modes: 4:3 2.8K (OG 3.4K): 2880 × 2160 (Recording in Open Gate 3.4K)>> 2.39:1 Ana. (OG 3.4K): 2560 × 2145 (Recording in Open Gate 3.4K)>> 16:9 HD Ana. (OG 3.4K): 1920 × 2160 (Recording in Open Gate 3.4K)>> *) requires ALEXA Mini 4:3 License Key, **) requires ALEXA Mini ARRIRAW License Key, >>) requires both ALEXA Mini 4:3 and ARRIRAW Licenses Keys
Recording codec	ProRes 4444XQ, 4444, 422 (HQ), 422, 422(LT), MXF/ARRIRAW
Look control	Import of custom 3D LUT, ASC CDL parameter (slope, offset, power, saturation)

(*Continued*)

Table 9.4 (Continued)

ARRI	ALEXA Mini
Adjustable Image parameters	Knee, Gamma, Saturation, Black Gamma, Saturation by Hue
Focus and exposure control	Peaking, Zebra, False color
Whitebalance	Manual and auto white balance
Wi-fi Camera Remote Control	Built-in Wi-Fi interface and web-based remote control from phones, tablets and laptops
Custom control	Optional GPIO interface for integration with custom control interfaces
Audio monitoring	Headphone output (mini jack)
Pre Record function	–
Intervalometer	Intervalometer
Multicam interface	Multicam interface
S16 lens mode	S16 lens mode
ARRI Look Library	–
1.3x Anamorphic Desqueeze	1.3x Anamorphic Desqueeze (Requires installed 4K UHD License)
Shutter	Electronic rolling shutter, 5.0°–356.0°, Shutter angle setting precision: 1/10 degree.
Lens Mount	Titanium PL mount with L-Bus connector and LDS EF mount PL mount with Hirose connector and LDS B4 mount with Hirose connector(A)
Viewfinder	AMIRA Multi Viewfinder MVF-1 (OLED and LCD) with flip-out LCD screen, Camera Control Panel (CCP-1) LCD control panel with option to daisy-chain MVF-1
Controls	Via ARRI ALEXA Mini LF Multi Viewfinder MVF-1 or MVF-2 multifunction units. MVF-2 can be used on either side of the camera. MVF-2 OLED EVF and monitor feature upgrades from the MVF-1, including the ability to detach the eyepiece from the monitor unit.
Onboard Recording	All ALEXA XT cameras feature in-camera ARRIRAW recording – ARRIRAW: 2880 × 1620, uncompressed 12-bit log without white balance or exposure index processing applied.
	Apple QuickTime/ProRes files or MFX/DNxHD files onto either one or two (Dual Recording) SxS PRO cards. All codecs legal range with embedded audio, timecode, and metadata.
	Codec: QuickTime/ProRes 4444
	Compression (1): 5:1
	Bit Rate in Mb/s at 30 fps: 330
	Bit Depth: 12
	Color Coding: 4:4:4 RGB
	Recording time in hrs:min (2): 0:22
	Application: High quality television or cinema applications requiring color correction and/or compositing.

ARRI	ALEXA Mini
	Codec: QuickTime/ProRes 422 (HQ)

Compression (1): 8:1

Bit Rate in Mb/s at 30 fps: 220

Bit Depth: 10

Color Coding: 4:2:2 YCbCr

Recording time in hrs:min (2): 0:34

Application: High quality television applications requiring color correction.

Codec: QuickTime/ProRes 422

Compression (1): 12:1

Bit Rate in Mb/s at 30 fps: 147

Bit Depth: 10

Color Coding: 4:2:2 YCbCr

Recording time in hrs:min (2): 0:52

Application: Basic television applications if images do not require adjustments in postproduction.

Codec: QuickTime/ProRes 422 (LT)

Compression (1): 18:1

Bit Rate in Mb/s at 30 fps: 102

Bit Depth: 10

Color Coding: 4:2:2 YCbCr

Recording time in hrs:min (2): 1:14

Application: On-set monitoring and proxy-editing when the master is captured with an external device.

Codec: QuickTime/ProRes 422 (Proxy)

Compression (1): 40:1

Bit Rate in Mb/s at 30 fps: 45Bit

Bit-Depth: 10

Color Coding: 4:2:2 YCbCr

Recording time in hrs:min (2): 2:42

Application: Same as above when a longer recording time is desired.

Codec: MXF/DNxHD 175x/185x/220x

Compression: 8:1

Bit Rate in Mb/s at 30 fps: 220

Bit Depth: 10

Color Coding: 4:2:2 YCbCr Recording time in hrs:min (2): 0:39 Application: High quality television applications requiring color correction.

Codec: MXF/DNxHD 115/120/145

Compression: 12:1

Bit Rate in Mb/s at 30 fps: 147

Bit Depth: 8

Color Coding: 4:2:2 YCbCr

Recording time in hrs:min (2): 0:59

Application: Basic television applications if images do not require adjustments in postproduction.

(1) Compression rate calculated based on 10-bit full HD RGB with 1.8Gbit/s

(2) Approximate time at 30 fps with SxS PRO 64 GB card

(*Continued*)

Table 9.4 (Continued)

ARRI	ALEXA Mini
Outputs Video	2x HD-SDI outputs: 1.5G, (dual) 3G, and (dual) 6G; uncompressed HD/UHD video with embedded audio and metadata
Inputs	SDI-Genlock (optional activation through ARRI Service), Timecode (in and output)
Other Interfaces	USB 2.0 (for user sets, looks etc.) Ethernet for service and web remote control EXT accessory interface w. RS pin and unregulated power output (outputs battery voltage)
Recording Media Supported CFast 2.0 memory cards	CFast 2.0 memory cards
Outputs Audio	3.5mm headphone jack, Bluetooth audio
Connectors	2× slots for CF cards 2× BNC recording out HD-SDI, 1.5G/3G switchable (REC OUT 1 and REC OUT 2) 1× BNC monitoring out HD-SDI 1.5G (MON OUT) 1× XLR 5-pin audio in (AUDIO IN) 1× BNC return signal HD-SDI, 1.5G (RET/SYNC IN) 1× BNC return signal/sync in HD-SDI 1.5G (RET/SYNC IN) 1× LEMO 16-pin external accessory interface (EXT) 1× Fischer 2-pin 24V power in (BAT) 2× Fischer 3-pin 24V remote start and accessory power out (RS) 1× LEMO 2-pin 12V accessory power out (12V) 1× LEMO 5-pin timecode in/out (TC) 1× TRS 3.5mm headphone mini stereo jack out (AUDIO OUT) 1× LEMO custom 16-pin electronic viewfinder (EVF) 1× LEMO 10-pin Ethernet with 24V power (ETHERNET)
SD Card	For importing ARRI Look Files, camera set up files, frame line files and feature licenses. Stores captured stills from the REC OUT image path in ARRIRAW (.ari, 12-bit), TIFF (.tif, 16-bit), DPX (.dpx, 10-bit) and JPEG (.jpg, 8-bit) format as well as logging files. Also used for software updates.
Synchronization	Master/Slave mode for precision sync of settings, sensor, processing, HD-SDI outputs and SxS recording for 3D applications.
Sound Level	Under 20 db(A) @ 24 fps and ≤ –20C–45C (–4F–113F) with lens attached and fan mode set to "Regular," measured 1m/3 feet in front of the lens. Silent operation at higher temperatures possible with fan mode set to "Rec low."
Power In	Three inputs: BAT connector, battery adapter back and battery adapter top. All accept 10.5 to 34V DC. 85W power draw for camera and EVF-1 in typical use recording 24 fps to SxS PRO cards, without accessories.
Power Out	Hirose 12-pin (for ENG type zoom lenses); 12V: D-tab, Hirose 4-pin, Lemo 2-pin; 24V: RS 3-pin
Weight	~ 2.3kg/5lbs (camera body with titanium PL lens mount)

ARRI	ALEXA Mini
Dimensions	Length: 185mm/7.3" Width: 125mm/4.9" Height: 140mm/5.5" (camera body with PL lens mount)
Environmental	–20° C to +50° C (–4° F to +122° F) @ 95% humidity max, non-condensing, splash and dust-proof through sealed electronics

ARRI AMIRA

Figure 9.7 ARRI AMIRA.

The ARRI AMIRA Camera features an ergonomic design well-suited for single-operator use or for extended shoulder-mounted operation. It includes the same 35mm sensor as the ALEXA and records 1080 HD images using a CFast 2.0 workflow.

AMIRA records 4K UHD 3840 × 2160 (with license), HD 1920 × 1080, Rec 709, ProRes recording on CFast 2.0 cards. It has a native ISO of 800, and the AMIRA can capture 200 fps slow motion. The AMIRA ARRIRAW License Key enables in-camera 16:9 2.8K (2880 × 1620) MXF/ARRIRAW recording at frame rates of up to 48 fps.

HD-SDI outputs on the AMIRA allow overlay of timecode and other information parameters seen in the optional viewfinder to also be seen on connected monitors. Choose between interchangeable lens mounts from PL, B4 2/3" or Canon EF, and ND filters 0.6, 1.2, 2.1 are built into the camera.

Sliding dovetails adjust shoulder balance so that the ARRI AMIRA can be ready to shoot straight out of the bag for documentary-style productions. The AMIRA also has a pre-record function which is an internal buffer to perpetually record a loop, so that the record button becomes a "cut" button.

The camera comes preloaded with numerous looks, including some 3D LUT-based looks to apply while filming. Cinematographers can either burn in the looks to recorded footage or apply looks only to monitoring.

The AMIRA includes sealed electronics for longevity and to protect against humidity and dust, and the camera boots up in about 13 seconds. An integrated thermal core produces efficient cooling. The solid internal skeleton gives the camera and lens stability, even as ARRI AMIRA is almost half the weight of the ARRI ALEXA. A Premium license enables WiFi remote control and Bluetooth audio capabilities.

AMIRA configures for handheld shooting with an optional ARRI MVF-1 or MVF-2 viewfinder, which combines a high-resolution OLED eyepiece with a fold-away LCD monitor for a live view or for access to camera controls and settings. MVF-1 features peaking functions, zebra and false color tools, and focus assist via easy-access buttons. MVF-2 allows the fold away screen to detach from the viewfinder for cabled remote use.

The OLED eyepiece is mounted to a rugged, lightweight sliding bar so operators can slide it forward and back and side-to-side. The fold-away LCD display is daylight visible and ideal for either a single-operator or as a monitor for a director or assistant. Its full-access to camera functionality permits quick changes to settings and configurable user buttons.

AMIRA supports workflows for live multi-camera productions in HDR according to BT.2100 Hybrid Log Gamma (HLG) or Perceptual Quantizer (PQ). It is suitable for a variety of productions, from TV drama and low-budget movies to nature films, sports coverage, commercials, reportage, branded content and multi-camera live TV. Multicam mode is a simple and flexible interface that can be used with live broadcast and transmission systems. It allows the image parameters of multiple AMIRA cameras, including iris setting, to be controlled remotely using SONY remote control panels (RCPs).

Table 9.6 (Continued)

ARRI	ALEXA, ALEXA XT, XT Plus, ALEXA XT M, ALEXA XT Studio, ALEXA FR
1.85:1 (4 × 3 Mode)	2880 × 1558
Sensor Size	3392 × 2200
Surround View	3168 × 2200
ARRIRaw	2880 × 2160
2.39:1 Flat	2880 × 1205
2.39:1 Scope	2581 × 2160
2.39:1 Scope 1.3x	2880 × 1567
1.85:1	2880 × 1558
Exposure Index/ISO	EI 160 (+5.0/–9.0), EI 200 (+5.3/–8.7), EI 400 (+6.3/–7.7), EI 800 (+7.4/–6.6), EI 1600 (+8.4/–5.6), EI3200 (+9.4/–4.6)
Exposure Latitude	14 stops for all sensitivity settings from EI 160 to EI 3200, as measured with the ARRI Dynamic Range Test Chart (DRTC)
	Values behind the exposure index are the number of stops above and below 18% grey. These values are for Log C. Rec 709 and DCI P3 are the same except for 0.5 stops fewer in the low end at EI 160, 0.4 stops fewer in the low end at EI 200 and 0.2 stops fewer in the low end at EI 400.
Notable Features	Spinning Mirror Optical Reflex Viewfinder available in ALEXA Studio Model, separate Optical Block and tethered Camera Body available in ALEXA M Model
	ALEXA XT Plus and ALEXA XT Studio models have an integrated wireless receiver for camera and lens remote control, built-in tilt and roll sensors and additional connectors for camera and lens control
	XT Models feature a 4:3 Super 35 sensor, LDS PL mount, improved viewfinder mounting bracket, included anamorphic de-squeeze and high speed licenses as well as a super silent fan. Additionally, the ALEXA XT Studio also has an internal motorized ND filter and a DNxHD license
	ALEXA XT Studio features an adjustable mirror shutter and an optical viewfinder that provides a real-time, high contrast image with true colors
Frame Rates	ProRes 422 (Proxy), 422 (LT), 422 and 422 (HQ): 0.75–60 fps
	ProRes 422 (Proxy), 422 (LT), 422 and 422 (HQ) with High Speed license: 0.75–120 fps
	Prores 4444 with 32 GB SxS PRO cards: 0.75–40 fps
	ProRes 4444 with 64 GB SxS PRO cards, SUP 5.0 or later: 0.75–60 fps
	DNxHD 145 and 220x: 0.75–60 fps
	DNxHD 145 and 220x with High Speed license: 0.75–120 fps
	HD-SDI: 0.75v60 fps
	ARRIRAW SUP 5.0 or later: 0.75 - 60 fps
	All speeds adjustable with 1/1000 fps precision
Shutter	Electronic rolling shutter, 0.75–60 fps: 5.0°–358.0°, 60–120 fps: 356°. Shutter angle setting precision: 1/10 degree.
Lens Mount	ARRI Exchangeable Lens Mount (ELM); ships with Lens Adapter PL Mount w/o LDS, 54 mm stainless steel PL mount, Super 35 centered
Viewfinder	Low latency (≤1 frame delay) electronic color viewfinder ARRI EVF-1 with 1280 × 784 F-LCOS micro display (image: 1280 × 720, status bars: 1280 × 32 above and 1280 × 32 below image) and ARRI LED illumination. Image can be flipped for use of viewfinder on camera left or right. Viewfinder Mounting Bracket allows movement of viewfinder forward/backwards, left/right, up/down, 360 degree rotation and placement on camera left or right. EVF-1 controls: viewfinder and basic camera settings, ZOOM button (2.25× pixel to pixel magnification), EXP button (false color exposure check) and jog wheel.

ARRI	ALEXA, ALEXA XT, XT Plus, ALEXA XT M, ALEXA XT Studio, ALEXA FR
Controls	Camera right: main user interface with 3" transflective 400 × 240 pixel LCD color screen, illuminated buttons, button lock and jog wheel. Camera left: operator interface with illuminated buttons, button lock and card swap button.
Onboard Recording	All ALEXA XT cameras feature in-camera ARRIRAW recording – ARRIRAW: 2880 × 1620, uncompressed 12 bit log without white balance or exposure index processing applied.

Apple QuickTime/ProRes files or MFX/DNxHD files onto either one or two (Dual Recording) SxS PRO cards. All codecs legal range with embedded audio, timecode and metadata.

Codec: QuickTime/ProRes 4444
Compression (1): 5:1
Bit Rate in Mb/s at 30 fps: 330
Bit Depth: 12
Color Coding: 4:4:4 RGB
Recording time in hrs:min (2): 0:22
Application: High quality television or cinema applications requiring color correction and/or compositing.

Codec: QuickTime/ProRes 422 (HQ)
Compression (1): 8:1
Bit Rate in Mb/s at 30 fps: 220
Bit Depth: 10
Color Coding: 4:2:2 YCbCr
Recording time in hrs:min (2): 0:34
Application: High quality television applications requiring color correction.

Codec: QuickTime/ProRes 422
Compression (1): 12:1
Bit Rate in Mb/s at 30 fps: 147
Bit Depth: 10
Color Coding: 4:2:2 YCbCr
Recording time in hrs:min (2): 0:52
Application: Basic television applications if images do not require adjustments in postproduction.

Codec: QuickTime/ProRes 422 (LT)
Compression (1): 18:1
Bit Rate in Mb/s at 30 fps: 102
Bit Depth: 10
Color Coding: 4:2:2 YCbCr
Recording time in hrs:min (2): 1:14
Application: On-set monitoring and proxy-editing when the master is captured with an external device.

Codec: QuickTime/ProRes 422 (Proxy)
Compression (1): 40:1
Bit Rate in Mb/s at 30 fps: 45-Bit
Bit-Depth: 10
Color Coding: 4:2:2 YCbCr
Recording time in hrs:min (2): 2:42
Application: Same as above when a longer recording time is desired.

Codec: MXF/DNxHD 175×/185×/220×
Compression: 8:1
Bit Rate in Mb/s at 30 fps: 220

(*Continued*)

Table 9.8 (Continued)

BLACKMAGIC	BLACKMAGIC Ursa Mini Pro 4.6k Camera G2
	2 × 3-Pin XLR Mic/Line Level (+48 V Phantom Power) Output 1 × 1/8" (3.5 mm) TRRS Headphone/Microphone Input/Output
	SDI Audio Output – 4 channels in HD-SDI 1 × BNC Timecode Input 1 × BNC Reference Input
	External Control – Blackmagic SDI Control Protocol. 2 × 2.5mm LANC for lens and record control.
	Lens Connector Hirose 12-pin
	USB 2.0 mini B port for software updates and configuration.
	1 × External 12V power supply. 12-pin molex connector on rear battery plate
Synchronization	Tri-Sync/Black Burst/Timecode
Audio	Integrated stereo microphone. Mono Speaker. 2 × XLR analog Audio Inputs switchable between mic, line and AES audio. Phantom power support. Analog Audio Outputs - 1 × 3.5mm headphone jack, supports iPhone microphone for talkback.
Power In	1 × 4-pin XLR port for external power or battery use. 1 × 12-pin molex connector on rear battery plate. Custom V-mount battery plate with D-tap +12V regulated output from camera. Rear camera mount compatible with industry standard V-mount or Gold Mount battery plates.
Weight	2.38kg/5.54lb
Dimensions	8.2 × 8 × 5.8"/21 × 20.1 × 14.7cm.

Figure 9.16

Source: www.usa.canon.com/cusa/professional/
products/professional_cameras/cinema_eos_cameras/

Canon C700, C700 GS (Global Shutter), C700 FF (Full Frame) Cine Cameras

Figure 9.17 Canon EOS C700, C700 GS, C700 FF.

Canon's EOS C700 Super35 format camera features the choice of one of two Super 35mm CMOS sensors. The EOS C700 is available in both EF and PL versions and features resolution up to 4.5K and Dual Pixel CMOS Automatic Focus (DAF). The PL mount only EOS C700 GS PL gives users up to 4.2K resolution and a Global Shutter.

The EOS C700 features both internal 4K ProRes and XF-AVC recording, and with the optional 4K Codex CDX-36150 recorder, the EOS C700 is capable of recording uncompressed RAW up to 120 frames per second. The C700 also includes a variety of 2K/HD recording options featuring frame rates up to 120 fps using the full frame of the sensor, and up to 240 fps in 2K crop mode.

The C700 camera's 4K Super 35mm CMOS sensor has ISO settings that range from ISO

160 to 25600 in normal operations or 100 to 102400 in extended range mode, with a native ISO rating of 800. Internal NDs from 2 to 10 stops are available on board. EVF menus will be familiar to users of other Canon Cinema EOS cameras, and the C700 FF also has a six-button side panel with a menu structure that will make sense to users of ALEXA, VariCam, and SONY F55.

An optional OLED HD electronic viewfinder (EVF-V70) offers additional versatility. The EVF itself has buttons for image magnification, false color, FUNC, the EVF menu button, and a SELECT wheel and SET button, joystick, and BACK button for menu navigation. Menus and settings can be accessed using the EVF's controls and display that can be echoed on the MON outputs, or on the side panel's controls and display. The EVF bracket adjusts laterally and the EVF can slide back and forth along it. The pivoting mounts on the EVF's arm allow rotation and vertical repositioning, but they don't allow the EVF to pivot to either side. There's a 1/4" socket under the EVF to mount it on a magic arm. The EVF feed can be shown full-screen with superimposed data. In Super 35mm mode, it can display a look around area marked by a 25%, 50%, or 75% dimming, or by a colored outline. Features include dual-level zebras or one of two peaking signals, each adjustable for color, gain, and frequency. There's a small WFM available showing line mode (normal), line select (showing a single line chosen from the image), field mode, RGB or YCbCr Parade, or Line+Spot. There's also a false-color mode for exposure confirmation in every mode.

Anamorphic desqueeze is supported at 1.3x and 2.0x squeeze ratios, or "use the lens's squeeze factor as defined in the metadata (Lens Squeeze Factor)", which users can set manually. Anamorphic desqueeze won't work on HDMI if HDMI is displaying 4K/UHD, nor will it desqueeze the image in Browser Remote.

Browser Remote is a web-based remote monitoring and control application, available over both the built-in wired networking or over Wi-Fi using an optional radio module. It doesn't require any special app, just a web browser, so it's accessible on iOS, Android, Mac, or PC.

Other options include Codex CDX-36150 recorder, a Canon shoulder Support Unit (shoulder pad, 15mm rail mounts, tripod quick-release wedge) SG-1 handgrip/controller, and a right-side OU-700 six-button side panel. The camera is available with a variety of lens mount configurations including EF, PL, and B4. The EF-mount version of the camera used with EF lenses, enables Canon's autofocus options and manual focus assist modes.

The Canon C700 FF is a full-frame version of the C700 that uses a larger 38.1mm × 20.1mm (17:9) sensor, with 5952 × 3140 active photosites. The C700FF is also available in both EF-mount and PL-mount versions. It records XF-AVC and ProRes internally on CFast cards, and offers an integrated raw recording option with a Codex CDX-36150 docking recorder. To record the full-frame 5.9k raw output, the Codex recorder is needed. SDI can be configured for a 4K raw output, but this is intended only for Canon monitors equipped to deBayer the raw output and apply LUTs for display.

The C700 FF shoots in full-frame mode, 4K/UHD Super 35mm crop mode, or 2K/HD Super 16mm crop. It offers slow & fast frame rates from 1 fps through 60 fps in full-frame, 72 fps in S35mm crop, or 168 fps in S16mm crop. These maximums are slightly lower than the S35mm-native C700, those cameras can capture at 120fps in S35 and 240fps in Super16mm.

The EOS C700 FF is capable of ProRes and XF-AVC internal recording up to 4K to CFast cards. With the optional Codex CDX-36150 recorder, the EOS C700 FF is capable of recording 5.9K RAW up to 60 frames per second. The C700 FF also has a wide array of 2K/UHD/HD recording options, including recording up to 168 fps in 2K RAW in Super 16mm (crop) mode.

Key features of the EOS C700 FF camera system include Canon Log 2 and 3, Slow/Fast Motion Recording, IP Streaming and support for ACES, SMPTE ITU-R BT.2100 (HDR) and User LUTs. All outputs can apply LUTs, BT.709, BT.2020, DCI, ACES proxy, HDR-PQ and HDR-HLG are built in, or choose from four user-loadable LUTs. All the outputs support embedded audio and timecode.

Table 9.9 Canon EOS C700, C700 GS, C700FF specifications

CANON	EOS C700 C700 GS C700FF
Sensor Size EOS C700, C700 GS	C700, C700 GS – Super 35 – 24.6 mm × 13.8 mm
Sensor Size EOS C700FF	C700FF – Full frame – 38.1mm × 20.1mm
Sensor EOS C700	Super 35mm CMOS image sensor with DAF Technology
Sensor EOS C700GS	Super 35mm CMOS sensor with Global Shutter
Sensor EOS C700FF	Full frame CMOS image sensor with DAF Technology
Photosites EOS C700	4622 × 2496, RAW Recording Photosites 4512 × 2376
Photosites EOS C700GS	4374 × 2496, RAW Recording Photosites 4272 × 2376
Photosites EOS C700FF	6062 × 3432, RAW Recording Photosites 5952 × 3140
Effective Sensor Resolution EOS C700, C700GS	4096 × 2160 when 4096 × 2160 or 2048 × 1080 is selected as the resolution, 3840 × 2160 when 3840 × 2160 or 1920 × 1080 is selected as the resolution
Effective Sensor Resolution EOS C700FF	5952 × 3140 when 4096 × 2160 or 2048 × 1080 is selected as the resolution, 5580 × 3140 when 3840 × 2160 or 1920 × 1080 is selected as the resolution
Exposure Index/ISO	160 to 25,600 (400 – 640 – 25600 – 102400) Native 100 to 102,400 Expanded
ND Filter	5 density settings (2, 4, 6, 8*, 10* stops) *when expansion is selected
Notable Features	EOS C700 (EF or PL mount) 4.5K, and EOS C700 GS PL 4.2K Global shutter, C700FF Full frame 5.9K Cinema raw capture – 4K, 2K multiple output formats Canon MPEG-2 4:2:2 50 Mbps XF Codec Canon 4K Super 35mm 16:9 CMOS sensor Canon Log Gamma 2 and 3 Fully compatible with a wide variety of PL-mount lenses, EF, B4 (with optional adapter) and anamorphic Terminal Connectors Full Manual Control Slow and Fast Motion WFT-E6 Wi-Fi unit with Remote Capabilities (optional)
Recording frame rate	59.94 Hz: 59.94i/59.94P/29.97P/23.98P (Depending on resolution selected) 50.00Hz: 50.00i/50.00P/25.00P (Depending on resolution selected 24.Hz: 24.00P
Internal Recording	CFast 2.0™ card × 2 for XF-AVC or Pro Res recording, SD card for XF-AVC Proxy recording SD card also used for Photo Storage (1920 × 1080) and firmware update, including firmware updates for CODEX CDX-36150 Recorder
Recording Formats	Canon RAW .RMF, XF-AVC Intra, XF-AVC Long GOP. XF-AVC Proxy ProRes, Apple Quick File Format 4444XQ/4444/422HQ/422
RAW Recording options C700, C700GS	Codex Drive: 59.94P/50.00P. 5952x3140/5952x2532:10bit 4096x2160/2048x1080:12bit 29.97P/23.98P/25.00P/24.00P. 5952x3140/5952x2532/4096x2160/2048x1080:12bit External Recorder via SDI: 59.94P/29.97P/23.98P/50.00P/25.00P/24.00P 4096x2160:10bit

CANON	EOS C700 C700 GS C700FF
RAW Recording options C700FF with Codex Recorder CDX-36150	Full frame 5.9K – 60 fps, 5.9K Cinescope – 60 fps, RGB Bayer RAWSuper 35mm crop – 72 fps, Super16mm crop –168 fps.
XF-AVC Recording Bit Rate/ Sampling (50Hz Mode) to CFast 2.0™ Card	XF-AVC Recording Bit Rate/ Sampling (50Hz Mode) To CFast 2.0™ Card 4096x2160 YCC422 10-bit/3840 × 2160 YCC422 10-bit 2048x1080 YCC422 10-bit/1920 × 1080 YCC422 10-bit 2048x1080 RGB444 12-bit/1920 × 1080 RGB444 12-bit 2048x1080 RGB444 10-bit/1920 × 1080 RGB444 10-bit Bit Rates: 810/440/410/310/225/210/170/160/ 90Mbps Intra-frame 50 Mbps Long GOP depending on Recording Mode
ProRes Recording Bit Rate/ Sampling (50Hz Mode) Max Frame Rate Capture Drive or CFast card	CFast 2.0™ or CDX-36150: Full frame Super 35mm (Crop) 4K/UHD ProRes 422HQ 10-bit 30 fps 2K/FHD ProRes 422HQ 10-bit 60 fps, ProRes 4444 12-bit 60 fps Super 16mm (Crop) 2K/FHD ProRes 422HQ/ ProRes 422 10-bit 168 fps CDX-36150 Full frame Super 35mm (Crop) 4K/UHD ProRes 422HQ 10-bit 60 fps 2K/FHD ProRes 4444XQ 12-bit 60 fps Super 35mm (Crop) 2K/FHD ProRes 422HQ 10-bit 72 fps
XF-AVC Proxy Recording Bit Rate/ Sampling (50Hz Mode) To SD Card	2048 × 1080 YCC420 8-bit/1920 × 1080 YCC420 8-bit Bit Rate: 24/35Mbps Long GOP
Slow/Fast motion	C700, C700GS, C700FF 1–168 fps, depending on shooting mode/resolution.
Shutter	C700, C700FF, Fast Scan Minimized Rolling Shutter 1/24 to 1/2000 sec. Angle from 11.25 to 360, C700GS CMOS Sensor with Global Shutter.
Lens Mount	Canon EF Mount with Cinema Lock/PL Mount (Cooke /$\mathbf{i}$ Technology compatible), B4 mount lens via adapter accessory.
Viewfinder	Optional FHD 1920 × 1080 OLED Electronic View Finder (EVF-V70) color 16:9 rotatable LCD Rotating LCD Screen Monitor Unit
Controls	Camera Setup Menu Audio Setup Menu Video Setup Menu LCD/VF Setup Menu TC/UB Setup Menu Other Functions Menu Configurable Custom Menus
Recording Outputs	HD/SD-SDI Terminal (with embedded audio) BNC Connector HD 8-bit 4:2:2 (YPbPr) 1920 × 1080: 59.94i/50i/23.98/24.00, 1280 × 720: 59.94p/50p/23.98/24.00 SD 8-bit 4:2:2 (YPbPr) 480: 59.94i, 576: 50i
Connectors	Timecode Terminals BNC (4) (input/output), Sync Out (BNC) External Audio Inputs: 2 – XLR inputs (Auto and Manual level settings) Recording Media CF 2.0 Card 2 slots (Movie files); UDMA supported SD Card: 1 slot: Still images, Custom Picture Data*, Clip Metadata and menu settings GENLOCK terminal (also serves as SYNC OUT terminal), TIME CODE terminal (input/output switching), REMOTE terminals (A/B), LENS terminal, Ethernet terminal, CTRL terminal Video Terminal Same as HD/SD-SDI Terminal Audio Terminal XLR 3-pin jack (2), Switchable between MIC/LINE HDMI Terminal (Type A), output only

(Continued)

Table 9.9 (Continued)

CANON	EOS C700 C700 GS C700FF
	AV Mini-terminal/Headphone Terminal 3.5mm stereo mini-jack
	WFT Terminal For compatible Wi-Fi Accessory
SD Card	SD Card (Still Images (JPEG), Custom Picture Data*, Clip Metadata, and menu settings); SD/SDHC/SDXC Supported; MMC Cards are not supported
Synchronization	Genlock Terminal BNC Connector (Input Only) Adjustment range: –1023 to +1023
	Timecode Terminals BNC Connector (Input and Output)
Power In	DC 7.4V (Battery Pack)/DC 8.4 V (DC In)
Power Out	DC 24V 2A Fisher 3-pin jack (output only),
	DC 12V 2A LEMO 2-pin jack (output only)/D-TAP
Weight	Approx. 3440g (7.6lb)
Dimensions	Approx. 6.6 × 6.1 × 12.9in (167 × 154 × 327mm)

Canon EOS C500Mark II, C500 Cine Cameras

Figure 9.18 Canon EOS C500MkII.

Canon EOS C500Mark II

Canon EOS C500 Mark II features a 5.9K (38.1 × 20.1mm) full-frame CMOS sensor. The sensor's gamut exceeds both ITU-R BT.2020 and DCI-P3, supports both SDR and HDR, and is capable of capturing footage in a variety of aspect ratios and formats, including DCI-4K, UHD, and Anamorphic Widescreen. The Cinema EOS C500 sensor supports both anamorphic and spherical lenses, and can also be paired with conventional Super

35mm and Super 16mm lenses using appropriate sensor crop modes. The EOS C500 Mark II uses a newly developed DIGIC DV 7 Image Processor that takes RAW data captured from the 5.9K sensor and processes it for on-board recording. DiG!C is the engine behind other features such as high frame rate recording, Dual Pixel Auto Focus, Cinema Raw Light Recording, HDR (PQ and HLG) output, electronic image stabilization, proxy recording and oversampling 5.9K processing. Users can upload and apply custom LUTs assigned to specific outputs or to the LCD or viewfinder, clients can be viewing one LUT, while production works from another.

Two CFexpress recording slots provide high write speeds for higher resolutions and frame rates. The dual card slots can be used to either create an instantaneous backup thorough simultaneous recording or extend record run time by relay recording. Cinema RAW Light (5.9K, 4K Crop, or 2K (Crop)) can be recorded to CFexpress card (Type B) while an XF-AVC 2K 4:2:0 8-bit Proxy can be recorded directly to an internal SD card. Cinema RAW Light file sizes are about 1/3 to 1/5 the size of Cinema RAW. When recording in 5.9K Cinema RAW Light, 60 fps is available, and in 2K (Crop) mode, frame rates up to 120 fps are available. Two function buttons; S&F (Slow and Fast Motion) and S&F fps (Slow and Fast Motion – Frames per Second) have been added for fast access to speed settings. The EOS C500 Mark II supports both Canon Log 2 and Canon Log 3 Gammas.

The EOS C500 Mark II ships with an EF Mount that can be changed to an optional locking EF or PL mount. Mounts swap easily by removing four M3 hex screws, and a shim set is provided with each mount kit to adjust back focus for focus accuracy. An optional B4 lens mount adapter is available for the either the PL or EF mount allowing 2/3" lenses to be used with the camera. The EOS C500 Mark II is the first Canon Cinema EOS camera to feature built-in five-axis electronic Image Stabilization that works with almost any lens including anamorphic. When operating with a lens that does have internal IS, the lens manages the Yaw and Pitch compensation while the camera deals with the Roll and Horizontal/Vertical (X/Y) movements.

The EVF-V50 OLED electronic viewfinder is a tilting 0.46" approx. 1.77 million dot OLED EVF that offers outstanding visibility for single-operator applications, such as documentaries and outdoor interviews. The LM-V2 4.3" LCD Monitor attaches to the EOS C500 Mark II and can be adjusted to different viewing positions for image framing and visual confirmation of camera settings.

The Expansion Unit 1 – EU-V1 extends connectivity that benefits both remote operation and live uses of the EOS C500 Mark II. This expansion adds genlock/sync out, remote B (RS422) and Ethernet ports ideal for multi-camera, streaming, and live television applications. The Expansion Unit 2 – EU-V2 adds two additional XLR audio inputs, Lens port, 24-volt DC out, and D-Tap power, in addition to Genlock, sync out, Remote B (422) and Ethernet port. It also allows the camera to be powered using industry standard v-lock batteries.

The C500 Mark II features Canon's Dual Pixel CMOS AF Technology. For DAF, each photosite in the camera's CMOS sensor is configured with two photodiodes. Two independent image signals can then be detected at each site and compared using phase-difference to provide autofocus with compatible lenses. DAF can survey the scene and recognize not only whether the subject is in focus or not, but also in which direction (near or far), and by how much.

Photodiode A — Photodiode B

The photodiodes are independent.
Each is able to capture light separately.

Figure 9.19 Dual photodiodes compare adjacent phase to determine focus.

DAF technology can also be used to aid in manual focus – called Focus Guide. Focus information is translated to an on-screen viewfinder guide that conveys to the operator the subject's current focus and direction to move in order achieve focus. When sharp focus is attained, the indicator turns green as a clear indication.

TDAF can simulate a focus pull using preset locations. After setting two separate focus locations on screen, the cameras set button can be used to alternate between the two focus points. The focus racking effect can be fine-tuned by adjusting AF tracking speed and response.

Table 9.10 Canon EOS C500 Mk II specification

CANON	C 500 Mk II
Sensor	Full-frame/Super 35mm (crop)/Super 16mm (crop)
	CMOS Sensor with DAF Technology
Total Photosites	Approx. 20.8 Megapixels (6062 × 3432)
Number of Effective Photosites	Approx. 18.69 Megapixels (5952 × 3140) When 4096 × 2160 or 2048 × 1080 is selected as the resolution
	Approx. 17.52 Megapixels (5580 × 3140)
	When 3840 × 2160 or 1920 × 1080 is selected as the resolution
ISO	160 to 25,600 (Native)100 to 102,400 (Expanded)
	100 to 102,400 (Expanded)
Lens Mount	EF models: Canon EF mount w/autofocus support

(*Continued*)

Table 9.10 (Continued)

CANON	C 500 Mk II
Exposure Modes	(1) Manual exposure based on shutter setting, iris setting, ISO/gain setting and ND filter setting (2) Push auto iris control, auto iris control
Shutter Setting	Speed, Angle, Clear Scan, Slow or Off mode selected Either 1/3 or 1/4 steps selected as speed increment
Iris Setting	Can be set to 1/2-stop, 1/3-stop or Fine (1) Push auto iris control (2) Auto iris control Lenses that support Auto Iris:
ISO	1 step, 1/3 step settings: 100* – 160 – 25600 – 102400* * When the sensitivity is expanded
ND Filter	5 density settings (2, 4, 6, 8*, 10* stops) * When expansion is selected
Focus Control/Assist	Dual Pixel CMOS AF (DAF), Manual Focus, One-Shot AF, Continuous AF, AF- Boosted MF, Face Detection AF* * Only lenses that support AF functions can be used in these modes
Focus Guide	Available; displays focus status or unfocused status using the AF signal. It is useful while MF or One-Shot AF is not being performed.
LCD Monitor	LM-V2 LCD Monitor
White Balance	AWB, Kelvin setting (setting range: 2000K–15000K), Daylight, Tungsten, Set (A/B)
Frame Rates	59.94 Hz mode: 59.94i/59.94P/29.97P/23.98P 50.00 Hz mode: 50.00i/50.00P/25.00P 24.00 Hz mode: 24.00P
Recording Media	
CFexpress™ Cards (2 slots)	Recording of movies (Cinema Raw Light/XF-AVC), custom pictures, metadata
SD Card	Recording of movies (XF-AVC (proxy)), photos (JPEG), custom pictures, metadata, menus and other data
Compression Formats	
Video	(1) XF-AVC: MPEG-4 AVC/H.264 (2) RAW: Cinema RAW Light
Audio	Linear PCM (24-bit – 48kHz; 4-channel recording)
XF-AVC (CFexpress™ cards)	
Resolution/Color Sampling	4096 × 2160/YCC422 10-bit 3840 × 2160/YCC422 10-bit 2048 × 1080/YCC422 10-bit 1920 × 1080/YCC422 10-bit
Bit Rate	810/410/310/160 Mbps Intra-frame
XF-AVC (SD card)	
Resolution/Color Sampling	2048 × 1080/YCC420 8-bit
Bit Rate	35/24 Mbps Long GOP
Cinema Raw Light (CFexpress™ cards)	
Bit Depth	12/10-bit

CANON	C 500 Mk II
Resolution	5952 × 3140 4096 × 2160 (cropped) 2048 × 1080 (cropped)
Time Code	Drop frame* or non-drop frame * Only in 59.94 Hz mode
Operation Mode	Rec Run, Free Run, Regeneration
Gamma	Canon Log 3, Canon Log 2, Wide DR, Normal 1, HDR-PQ, HDR-HLG
Color Space	Cinema Gamut, BT.2020 Gamut, DCI-P3 Gamut, BT.709 Gamut
LUT	BT.709/BT.2020/DCI/ACESproxy/HDR-ST2084 etc.
Other Features	Slow & Fast motion recording, pre-recording, relay recording, double slot recording, custom picture settings, color bar, peaking display, zebra display, My Menu settings, waveform monitor display, assignable buttons, key lock, marker display, enlarged display, custom display, control via browser remote, peripheral illumination correction, diffraction correction, built-in monaural microphone, fan control, geotagging, and other functions
Playback Operations	Normal playback, fast forward (at speeds of 5x), fast reverse (at speeds of 5x), frame forward, frame reverse, forward skip, reverse skip, rec review
Clip Display	3 × 4 (clip) index display (RAW, XF-AVC, XF-AVC proxy, photo index)
Clip Information Display	Clip metadata display, custom pictures data display
Edit	Clip deletion
Input	MIC jack, INPUT terminal (1/2)*, REMOTE terminal (A), USB
Output	HDMI, headphone jack, MON. terminal, SDI OUT terminal*, VIDEO terminal * 12G-SDI supported
Input/Output Control	TIME CODE terminal, Expansion System terminal, Expansion Unit connector* * For the EVF-V50, EU-V1 or EU-V2 Expansion Units
Power Supply	DC IN 12V jack (DC 11.5V–20V), Battery terminal (DC 14.4V), DC 12–20V* * When using a V-mount battery with the EU-V2 Expansion Unit
Image Processing Platform	DIGIC DV 7 Image Processor
IP Streaming	Streams video to decoder transmission device or computer over the network
Compression	MPEG-4 AVC/H.264 8 bit
Bit Rates	9 Mbps/4 Mbps (1920 × 1080)
Frame Rates	59.94p/59.94i/50.00p/50.00i
Audio	MPEG-2 ACC-LC 2ch
Audio Rate	256 KBbps
Transfer Media	Wi-Fi®, Ethernet
Protocols	(1) UDP: Prioritizes transfer speed, with no guarantees of reliability or correct order. Lost or lagging packets ignored. (2) RTP: Standard system for sending videos and audio online. Lost or lagging packets ignored. (3) RTP+FEC: Error correction (FEC) control during RTP transfer enables recovery of lost or corrupt packets on the receiving side. (4) RTSP+RTP: Real-time data streaming control via RTSP (Real Time Streaming Protocol) and transfer via RTP. The receiving side can start or stop streaming.

(*Continued*)

Table 9.10 (Continued)

CANON	C 500 Mk II
Others	Enabled in XF-AVC mode
Standards	Follows the specifications of WFT
Wi-Fi® Setup Methods	(1) WPS [Wi-Fi® Protected Setup] (push-button system, PIN code system)
	(2) Manual Setup
	(3) Search for Access Points
Authentication Systems	Open system, WPA-PSK, WPA2-PSK
Encryption Systems	WEP-64, WEP-128, TKIP, AES
IP Address Settings	Auto (automatic switching between DHCP and AutoIP), Manual
Dimensions (W × H × D)	Approx. 6.0 × 5.8 × 6.6 in. (153 × 148 × 168mm)
Weight	Approx. 3.8 lb. (1750g)

Canon EOS C500 (discontinued)

Figure 9.20 Canon EOS C500.

With a Super 35mm Canon CMOS sensor, Canon DIGIC DV III Image Processor and 50 Mbps 4:2:2 codec, the EOS C500 provides a modular, portable and adaptable system with the ability to output 4K (4096 × 2160 pixels) and Quad HD (3840 × 2160 pixels).

Frame rates are variable from one to 120 frames per second and the camera records HD internally to CF cards at 50 Mbps with 4:2:2 color sampling. HD and 2K pictures. C500 offers two forms of 4K origination; DCI, SMPTE 2048-1:2011 standard, at 4096 × 2160 pixels, or UHD, SMPTE 2036-1:2009 and ITU-R BT.1769 standards, at 3840 × 2160 pixels.

The EOS C500 records uncompressed Canon raw output for both 4K and 2K recording, raw output is delivered to external recording systems via built-in dual 3G-SDI ports. Dual uncompressed HD-SDI out ports supports external live monitoring. HD content can be written to dual onboard CF cards simultaneously to provide proxy video for offline NLE systems.

C500 is compatible with EF, EF-S, and EF Cinema lenses for Canon SLR cameras, while the C500 PL model is compatible with PL-mount EF Cinema lenses and other PL-mount lenses. The EF mount features a rotating collar to facilitate cine-style lens changes. Canon EF lens mount is compatible with all of Canon's latest EF Cinema lenses and current EF lenses, including compact primes, super telephotos, specialty tilt-shift, macro, and fisheye. The C500PL is compatible with all cine PL mount lenses. Designed within SMPTE HD production standards, the MPEG-2 codec is compatible with major NLE applications, and Canon Log integrates with existing production workflows including ACES.

Canon's CMOS sensor has an active image size of 24.4 × 13.5mm with 3840 × 2160 photosites. Proprietary technologies within the photosite simultaneously lower the image sensor noise floor while enhancing the photon capacity of the photodiode assuring good dynamic range. The image sensor employs an innovative readout technique that delivers full bandwidth individual RGB video components without the need for any deBayering algorithms in HD.

Table 9.11 Canon EOS C500 specifications

CANON	EOS C-500
Sensor	Super 35mm, 8.85-megapixel CMOS image sensor
Sensor Size	Super 35 (26.2mm × 13.8mm) (for 4KDCI)
Photosites	4096 × 2160
Exposure Index/ISO	ISO 640
Notable Features	4K, 2K Multiple Output Formats
	Cinema raw Capture
	Canon MPEG-2 4:2:2 50 Mbps XF Codec
	Canon 4K Super 35mm 16:9 CMOS Sensor
	Canon Log Gamma
	Fully Compatible with a Wide Variety of PL-mount Lenses
	4K/2K Workflow
	Terminal Connectors
	Full Manual Control
	Slow and Fast Motion
	WFT-E6 Wi-Fi® unit with Remote Capabilities (optional)
Frame Rates	4K raw
	4096 × 2160/3840 × 2160 Playback 60Hz/24:00 1–60
	4096 × 2160/3840 × 2160 Playback 50Hz/24:00 1–50
	4K raw
	4096 × 1080/3840 × 1080 Playback 60Hz/24:00 1–60. 62–120 in 2 frame increments
	4096 × 1080/3840 × 1080 Playback 50Hz/24:00 1–50. 52–100 in 2 frame increments
	2K RGB 4:4:4
	2048 × 1080/1920 × 1080 Playback 60Hz/24:00 1–60. 62–120 in 2 frame increments
	2048 × 1080/1920 × 1080 Playback 50Hz/24:00 1–50. 52–100 in 2 frame increments
	2K YCC 4:2:2 2048 × 1080/1920 × 1080
	Playback 60Hz/24:00 1–60. 62–120 in 2 frame increments
	Playback 50Hz 1–50. 52–100 in 2 frame increments
	50 Mbps
	1920 × 1080 29.97p/23.98p/24.00p 1–30 fps
	1920 × 1080 50i/25p 1–25
	1280 × 720 59.94p/29.97p/23.98p/24.00p 1–60
	1280 × 720 50p/25p 1–50
	35 Mbps
	1920 × 1080 29.97p/23.98p/24.00p 1–30 fps
	1920 × 1080 50i/25p 1–25
	1280 × 720 59.94p/29.97p/23.98p/24.00p 1–60
	1280 × 720 50p/25p 1–50
	25 Mbps 1440 × 1080 29.97p/23.98p 1–30
Shutter	Fast Scan Minimized Rolling Shutter
Lens Mount	EF, EF-S, and EF Cinema lens systems
Viewfinder	0.52-inch diagonal, color 16:9 rotatable LCD +2.0 to –5.5 diopter eye adjustment
	LCD Screen (Monitor Unit) Rotating 4-inch Wide Screen Color LCD Display (1,230,000 dots: 854 × 480) on detachable controller

(Continued)

Table 9.11 (Continued)

CANON	EOS C-500
Controls	Camera Setup Menu
	Audio Setup Menu
	Video Setup Menu
	LCD/VF Setup Menu
	TC/UB Setup Menu
	Other Functions Menu
	Configurable Custom Menus
Onboard Recording	CF Card (Type 1 Only); 2 Slots (Movie Files); UDMA supported
	SD Card (Still Images (JPEG), Custom Picture Data*, Clip Metadata, and menu settings); SD/SDHC/SDXC Supported; MMC Cards are not supported
	2K RGB 444 12bit 2048 × 1080/1920 × 1080 59.94p/29.98p/23.98p/50.00p/25.00p True 24 (24.00p)
	4K raw 10-bit 4096 × 2160/3840 × 2160 59.94p/29.97p/23.98p/50.00p/25.00p/24.00p
	4K raw 10-bit 4096 × 1080/3840 × 1080 62p up to 119.88p in 2 frame steps
	2K RGB 444 12-bit 2048 × 1080/1920 × 1080 59.94p/29.98p/23.98p/50.00p/25.00p True 24 (24.00p)
	2K RGB 444 10-bit 2048 × 1080/1920 × 1080 59.94p/29.98p/23.98p/50.00p/25.00p True 24 (24.00p)
	2K YCC 422 10bit 2048 × 1080/1920 × 1080 62p up to 119.88p in 2 frame steps
Recording Outputs	HD/SD-SDI Terminal (with embedded audio) BNC Connector
	HD 8-bit 4:2:2 (YPbPr) 1920 × 1080: 59.94i/50i/23.98/24.00, 1280 × 720: 59.94p/50p/23.98/24.00
	SD 8-bit 4:2:2 (YPbPr) 480: 59.94i, 576: 50i
Connectors	HDMI Terminal HD 8-bit 4:2:2 (YPbPr) 1920x1080: 60i/59.94i/50i, 1280 × 720: 60p/59.94p/50p SD 8-bit 4:2:2 (YPbPr) 480: 59.94i, 576: 50i
SD Card	SD Card (Still Images (JPEG), Custom Picture Data*, Clip Metadata, and menu settings); SD/SDHC/SDXC Supported; MMC Cards are not supported
Synchronization	Genlock Terminal BNC Connector (Input Only) Adjustment range: -1023 to +1023
	Timecode Terminals BNC Connector (Input and Output)
Power In	DC 7.4 V (Battery Pack)/DC 8.4 V (DC In)
Power Out	n/a
Weight	C500 Body: Approx. 4.0 lb. (1820 g)
Dimensions	6.3 × 7.0 × 6.7 in (160 × 179 × 171 mm)
User Manual URL	www.usa.canon.com/cusa/professional/products/professional_cameras/cinema_eos_cameras/eos_c500#BrochuresAndManuals

Canon EOS C300 Mark III

The Canon EOS C300 Mark III digital cinema camera features a Super 35mm Dual Gain Output sensor for superior HDR recording and low noise. The Canon EOS C300 Mark III digital cinema camera features a Super 35mm Dual Gain Output (DGO) sensor for superior HDR recording and low noise. The DGO Sensor is a newly developed imaging system that

Figure 9.21 Canon EOS C300 Mk III.

generates high dynamic range and maintains low-noise levels by reading out each photodiode with two different gains. It combines the two images with a saturation-prioritizing amplifier for bright areas, and a lower-noise, noise-prioritizing amplifier for darker areas. The sensor is paired with the Canon DiGIC DV7 image processor, which uses the sensor's raw information and processes it for various applications such as high frame rate recording, raw recording,

The camera records up to DCI 4K resolution video to dual CFexpress cards, and an SD card slot is available to record additional images. High frame rates up to 120 fps can be recorded in 4K raw, and up to 180 fps in 2K cropped mode. Canon's Cinema RAW Light and XF-AVC recording formats are supported, providing DCI 4K images with a 10-bit, 4:2:2 Long GOP codec, and editorial proxy recording is also supported. The camera also offers Canon's Log 2 and Log 3 gamma modes, which results in excellent tonal reproduction in the highlight and low-light regions of an image, and expanded dynamic range. EOS C300 Mark III can also simultaneously record 2K Proxy files. Cinema RAW Light can be recorded to the internal CFexpress card, while an XF-AVC 2K 4:2:0 8-bit proxy can be recorded directly to an internal SD card.

The C300 Mark III supports custom user LUTs that can be utilized on monitors, the LCD, or viewfinder to ensure accurate color. LUTs can

be assigned to specific output terminals, LCD, and viewfinder. The C300 Mark III can also apply LUTs to Proxy recording.

Canon's Dual Pixel CMOS AF (autofocus) provides accurate autofocus, and also features touch AF and face detection. EOS C300 Mark III includes the same built-in five-axis electronic Image Stabilization introduced with the EOS C500 Mark II that works with almost any lens, including anamorphic. The EOS C300 Mark III body has a remote A terminal (LANC) on the body and supports remote B (RS-422) in both expansion unit EU-V1 and EU-V2. Through these connectors, the EOS C300 Mark III can be completely remote-operated either by a standard LANC compatible cable or over longer distances via a serial connection.

The camera features up to 12G-SDI output over a single BNC cable, timecode I/O, and genlock input BNCs. It supports up to 4-channel audio using the internal mic, mini-mic input, and XLR ports, and an expansion unit can be added to support up to four XLR inputs. The body has a modular design that can either be stripped down completely or be built up using the included handle, 4.3" rotating touchscreen LCD unit with full controls, grip, and thumb rest.

Modular design allows productions to customize the EOS C300 Mark III to specific shooting needs. Accessories and expansion units can be easily attached to provide different levels of functionality. The camera is equally at home fully rigged with a large zoom lens, FIZ unit, audio accessories, and rangefinder as it is stripped down flying on a drone. The LM-V2 4.3" LCD Monitor is an easy-to-view touch panel with approximately 2.76 million dots. The monitor easily attaches to the EOS C300 Mark III using included accessories and can be adjusted to different viewing positions. The LCD monitor is capable of displaying both image framing and camera settings, and has a control interface to make it easy to access and change camera settings.

User interchangeable PL and EF lens mounts offer compatibility with Canon's DSLR lenses, EF-mount cinema prime, zooms, 2.0 and 1.33 anamorphic lenses, and an available B4 mount adapter. Each mount swaps by simply removing four M3 hex screws. A shim set is provided with mount kits in order to adjust back focus.

Table 9.12 Canon EOS C300 Mark III specifications

CANON	EOS C300 Mark III
Image Sensor Size	26.2 × 13.8 mm (Super35)
Sensor Type	CMOS
Sensor Resolution	Actual: 4206 × 2280 (9.6 MP)
	Effective: 4096 × 2160 (8.85 MP)
Pixel Pitch	6.4 µm
Color Filter	Bayer
ISO	100 to 102,400 (Expanded)
Gain	–6 to 54 dB (Native)
	–2 to 54 dB (Expanded)
Lens Mount	Canon EF, PL
Lens Communication	Yes, with Autofocus Support
Interchangeable Lens Mount	Yes
Shutter Speed	1/12 to 1/2000 sec (In 24p/60p Mode)
Built-In ND Filter	Mechanical Filter Wheel with 2 Stop (1/4), 4 Stop (1/16), 6 Stop (1/64), 8 Stop (1/256), 10 Stop (1/1024) ND Filters
Recording Media	2 × CFexpress Card Slots
	1 × SDXC Card Slot
Variable Frame Rates	1 to 180 fps
Recording Modes	MXF:
	4096 × 2160p (225 to 410 MB/s)
	3840 × 2160p (225 to 410 MB/s)
Audio Recording	2-Channel 24-Bit 48 kHz
Video Connectors	2 × BNC (3G-SDI) Output
	1 × HDMI Output
Audio Connectors	2 × 3-Pin XLR Mic Level (+48 V Phantom Power) Input
	1 × 1/8"/3.5mm Stereo Mic Level Input
	1 × 1/8"/3.5mm Stereo Headphone Output
Other I/O	1 × BNC Timecode Input
	1 × BNC Timecode Input/Output
	1 × 2.5mm LANC Control Input
Display Type	LCD
Screen Size	4"
Touchscreen	Yes
Screen Resolution	1,230,000 Dots
EVF	Optional, Not Included
Screen Size	.46"
EVF Resolution	1,170,000 Dots
Battery Type	Canon BP-A Series
Power Connectors	1 × 4-Pin LEMO Input
Accessory Mount	1 × 1/4" –20 Female
	1 × Cold Shoe Mount
Dimensions	5.9 × 7.2 × 7.2"/149 × 183 × 183mm (without grip)
	7.5 × 7.2 × 7.4"/19.1 × 18.3 × 18.8cm (with grip)

Canon EOS C300 Mark II

Figure 9.22 Canon EOS C300 Mk II.

The EOS C300 Mark II digital cinema camera is Canon's 2nd generation Cinema EOS 4K camera system with a range of improved features including 4K/2K/Full HD internal and external recording (including 4K RAW output), 10-bit Canon Log 2 Gamma, and ACES compatibility. The camera also features Canon's Dual Pixel CMOS Autofocus and focus assist engineering. Dual-Pixel CMOS AF capabilities of the EOS C300 Mark II are enabled by the AF motors in Canon EF lenses. The improved EF lens communication capabilities of the EOS C300 Mark II camera allow for the display of CN-E Cinema lens T-values, lens metadata acquisition, and chromatic aberration correction on the camera's LCD Monitor/EVF/Output display.

The EOS C300 Mark II digital cinema camera integrates a Super 35mm 16:9 CMOS image sensor that supports up to 4K (DCI) recording with a maximum resolution of 4096 × 2160 and a high-speed readout for reduced rolling-shutter distortion. In addition, the EOS C300 Mark II camera also incorporates a trio of XF-AVC H.264 codecs that enable in-camera 4K (DCI) recording to dual CFast card slots and 2K/Full HD recording to an SD card slot. For external recording and monitoring, twin 3G-SDI outputs capable of 4K RAW output are included on the rear of the camera body.

Operability improvements include full manual control, a High Resolution 1.77 Megapixel color OLED EVF with adjustable 60° tilting angle, a removable hand grip, an improved camera handle extension with additional attachment points, and a removable LCD Monitor and control panel with XLR inputs.

Canon's original EOS C300 camera features a Super 35mm Canon CMOS sensor, Canon DIGIC DV III Image Processor and 50 Mbps 4:2:2 codec. The EOS C300 has a Canon EF lens mount and is compatible with all of Canon's EF Cinema lenses and current EF lenses, including compact primes, super telephotos, specialty tilt-shift, macro and fisheye. The EOS C300 PL is a PL-mount camera, compatible with cine PL mount lenses. Designed within SMPTE HD production standards, the MPEG-2 codec is compatible with major NLE applications, and Canon Log integrates with existing production workflows including ACES.

Canon's CMOS sensor has an active image size of 24.4 × 13.5mm with 3840 × 2160 photosites each 6.4 × 6.4 micrometers in area and each photosite uses a microlens to ensure high efficiency light transfer to the individual photodiode. Proprietary technologies within the photosite simultaneously lower the image sensor noise floor while enhancing the photon capacity of the photodiode. The image sensor employs an innovative readout technique that delivers full bandwidth individual RGB video components without deBayering algorithms. Each of these components has a 1920 × 1080 sampling structure at up to 60 frames. From these original video components, a 1080-line 60i format or a 1280 × 720 at 60P HD format are selectively derived.

Canon EOS C300

Figure 9.23 Canon EOS C300.

Canon's EOS C300 camera provides a modular, portable, and adaptable system of cameras,

Table 9.13 Canon EOS C300 Mark II specifications

CANON	EOS C300 Mark II
Sensor	RGB Bayer Pattern CMOS with Dual Pixel AF, Super 35mm, Progressive
Sensor Size	26.2 × 13.8mm effective screen size (6.4 × 6.4 micrometer photosite pitch) (for 4K DCI)
Photosites	Effective Photosites – (3840 × 2160) Effective Photosites – (4096 × 2160) Total Photosites – (4206 × 2340)
Exposure Index/ISO	100 to 102400, 1-stop or 1/3-stop, Base ISO 800
Built-In ND Filter	Mechanical Filter Wheel with 2 Stop (1/4), 4 Stop (1/16), 6 Stop (1/64) ND Filters
Notable Features	New Canon 8.85 Megapixel CMOS Sensor Dual Canon DIGIC DV 5 Image Processors Canon Log Gamma 2 and 3 Fully Compatible with a Wide Variety of EF and PL-mount Lenses CF 2.0 Memory Card Recording Multiple Recording Formats and Advanced Recording Full Manual Control and Focusing Aids Wi-Fi for Remote LiveView Display and Camera Control (with optional WFT-E6A Wireless Controller) ACES 1.0 Output via SDI/HDMI
Recording frame rate	59.94 Hz: 59.94i/59.94P/29.97P/23.98P (Depending on resolution selected) 50.00Hz: 50.00i/50.00P/25.00P (Depending on resolution selected 24.Hz: 24.00P
Video Storage Media	CFast2.0™ and SD card supported. Simultaneous Recording to CFast2.0™ and External Device possible. VPG130 protocol for CFast2.0 card supported.
Recording file format	XF-AVC (Material eXchange Format (MXF))
Recording Standard	Video Compression: MPEG-4 AVC/H.264 Audio Recording: Linear PCM (16-bit/24-bit – 48kHz – 4ch) File Format: XF-AVC (MXF) Bit rate: Intra 410/225/220/110Mbps, Long GOP 50Mbps Long GOP: 35 or 24Mbps (for proxy recording on SD cards)
Frame Rates	59.94Hz:59.94P 2K (2048 × 1080/1920 × 1080) 1 to 60 fps 2K CROP (*1)(2048 × 1080/1920 × 1080) max 120 fps 29.97P 4K (4096 × 2160/3840 × 2160) 1 – 30 fps 2K (2048 × 1080/1920 × 1080) max 60 fps** 2K CROP * (2048 × 1080/1920 × 1080) max 120 fps ** 23.98P 4K (4096 × 2160/3840 × 2160 max 30 fps 2K (2048 × 1080/1920 × 1080) max 120 fps ** 2K CROP * (2048 × 1080/1920 × 1080) max 120 fps** 50.00Hz 50.00P 2K (2048 × 1080/1920 × 1080) 1 – 50 fps 2K CROP * (2048 × 1080/1920 × 1080) max 100 fps ** 25.00P 4K (4096 × 2160/3840 × 2160) 1 – 25 fps 2K (2048 × 1080/1920 × 1080) max 50 fps ** 2K CROP * (2048 × 1080/1920 × 1080) max 100 fpscz** 24.00Hz 4K (4096 × 2160/3840 × 2160) max 30 fps 2K (2048 × 1080/1920 × 1080) max 60 fps** 2K CROP * (2048 × 1080/1920 × 1080) max 100 fps**

CANON	**EOS C300 Mark II**
Shutter	Fast Scan Minimized Rolling Shutter 1/24 to 1/2000 sec. Angle from 11.25 to 360
Lens Mount	Interchangeable: EF mount with EF Contacts
Viewfinder	0.46" (1.18 cm on the diagonal), color organic EL display with a wide-screen 16:9 aspect ratio +2.0 to –5.5 diopter eye adjustment Adjustment of the viewfinder brightness, contrast, color, sharpness and luminance boosting (on/off) can be performed (using menu settings). Rotable
Controls	Camera Setup Menu Audio Setup Menu Video Setup Menu LCD/VF Setup Menu TC/UB Setup Menu Other Functions Menu Configurable Custom Menus
Video Storage Media	CFast2.0™ and SD card supported. Simultaneous Recording to CFast2.0™ and External Device possible. VPG130 protocol for CFast2.0 card supported.
Recording format: CFast 2.0™ Card	Intraframe recording Resolution: 4096 × 2160/3840 × 2160/2048 × 1080/1920 × 1080 Signal configuration: YCC422 10-bit/(*)RGB444 (12-bit/10-bit) (*) Only with 2048 × 1080 or 1920 × 1080; 29.97P, 23.98P, 25.00P and 24.00P Long GOP recording Resolution: 2048 × 1080/1920 × 1080 Signal configuration: YCC422 10-bit
Recording format: SD Card	Movies: Long GOP recording only (*) Resolution: 2048 × 1080/1920 × 1080 Signal configuration: YCC420 8-bit Photo: JPEG Resolution: 2048 × 1080/1920 × 1080 (*) Proxy recording using low bit rate
Recording Outputs	HD/SD-SDI Terminal BNC (output only), with embedded audio
Connectors	Timecode Terminals BNC (input/output), Sync Out (BNC) External Audio Inputs: 2 – XLR inputs (Auto and Manual level settings) Recording Media CF 2.0 Card 2 slots (Movie files); UDMA supported SD Card: 1 slot: Still images, Custom Picture Data*, Clip Metadata and menu settings *Custom Picture Data and settings are not compatible with data from other Canon models Video Terminal Same as HD/SD-SDI Terminal Audio Terminal XLR 3-pin jack (2), Switchable between MIC/LINE HDMI Terminal (Type A), output only AV Mini-terminal/Headphone Terminal 3.5mm stereo mini-jack WFT Terminal For compatible Wi-Fi Accessory
SD Card	SD Card: 1 slot: Still images, Custom Picture Data*, Clip Metadata and menu settings
Synchronization	Genlock Terminal BNC (input only)
Power In	7.4V DC (battery pack), 8.4V DC (DC-IN)
Power Out	n/a
Weight	EF Mount: 1770g (3.9lb) PL Mount: 2000g (4.4lb) EF Mount with Cinema Lock: 1850g (4.1lb)
Dimensions	Approx. 149 × 183 × 183 mm (5.9 × 7.2 × 7.2 in) [C300 Mark II + thumb rest]

lenses, and accessories with a Super 35mm Canon CMOS sensor, Canon DIGIC DV III Image Processor and 50 Mbps 4:2:2 codec. EOS C300 has a Canon EF lens mount and is compatible with all of Canon's EF Cinema lenses, including compact primes, super telephotos, specialty tilt-shift, macro, and fisheye lenses. The EOS C300 PL is a PL-mount camera, compatible with cine PL mount lenses. Designed within SMPTE HD production standards, the MPEG-2 codec is compatible with major NLE applications, and Canon Log integrates with existing production workflows including ACES.

Canon's CMOS sensor has an active image size of 24.4 × 13.5mm with 3840 × 2160 photosites, each photosite uses a microlens to ensure high efficiency light transfer to the individual photodiode. Proprietary technologies within the photosite simultaneously lower the image sensor noise floor while enhancing the photon capacity of the photodiode. The image sensor employs a readout technique that delivers full bandwidth individual RGB video components without the need for deBayering. Each of these components has a 1920 × 1080 sampling structure at up to 60 frames. From these original video components, a 1080-line

Table 9.14 Canon EOS C300 specifications

CANON	EOS C300
Sensor	RGB Bayer Pattern CMOS single sensor, Super 35mm, Progressive
Sensor Size	26.2 × 13.8mm effective screen size (6.4 × 6.4 micrometer pixel pitch)
Photosites	Effective Pixels – approx. 8.29 megapixels (3840 × 2160)
	Effective Pixels – approx. 8.85 megapixels (4096 × 2160)
	Total Pixels - approx. 9.84 megapixels (4206 × 2340)
Exposure Index/ISO	320 to 20,000, 1-stop or 1/3-stop, Base ISO 850
Notable Features	New Canon Super 35mm CMOS Sensor
	Canon DIGIC DV III Image Processor
	Canon XF Codec
	Fully Compatible with a Wide Variety of EF and PL-mount Lenses
	CF Memory Card Recording
	Multiple Recording Formats and Advanced Recording
	Full Manual Control and Focusing Aids
	WFT Wireless Remote Control over Wi-Fi
Frame Rates	NTSC: 59.94P, 59.94i, 29.97P, 23.98P
	PAL: 50P, 50i, 25P
	Film: 24P
Shutter	Fast Scan Minimized Rolling Shutter
Lens Mount	Interchangeable: EF mount with EF Contacts
Viewfinder	0.52-inch diagonal, color 16:9 rotatable LCD +2.0 to -5.5 diopter eye adjustment
	LCD Screen (Monitor Unit) 4-inch diagonal, 1.23 megapixel color 16:9 rotatable LCD 100% field of view adj. brightness, contrast, color, sharpness and backlight
Controls	Camera Setup Menu
	Audio Setup Menu

CANON	EOS C300
	Video Setup Menu
	LCD/VF Setup Menu
	TC/UB Setup Menu
	Other Functions Menu
	Configurable Custom Menus
Onboard Recording	NTSC and PAL
	Compression: 8 Bit MPEG-2 Long GOP
	Color Space: 4:2:2 at 50Mbps recording
	Maximum Bit Rate: 50Mbps (CBR)
	Canon Log Gamma: Available
	File Format: MXF (OP-1a)
	Recording Options:
	50Mbps (CBR) 4:2:2 422P@HL
	1920 × 1080: 59.94i/29.97p/23.98p; 50i/25p; True 24 (24.00)
	1280 × 720: 59.94i/29.97p/23.98p; 50p/25p; True 24 (24.00)
	35Mbps (VBR) 4:2:0 MP@HL
	1920 × 1080: 59.94i/29.97p/23.98p; 50i/25p
	1280 × 720: 59.94p/29.97p/23.98p; 50p/25p
	25Mbps (CBR) 4:2:0 MP@H14
	1440 × 1080: 59.94i/29.97p/23.98p; 50i/25p
Recording Outputs	HD/SD-SDI Terminal BNC (output only), with embedded audio
Connectors	Timecode Terminals BNC (input/output), Sync Out (BNC)
	LCD Screen (Monitor Unit)
	4-inch diagonal, 1.23 megapixel color 16:9 rotatable LCD
	100% field of view
	adj. brightness, contrast, color, sharpness, and backlight
	External Audio Inputs: 2 – XLR inputs (Auto and Manual level settings)
	Recording Media
	CF Card (Type 1 Only): 2 slots (Movie files); UDMA supported
	SD Card: 1 slot: Still images, Custom Picture Data, Clip Metadata and menu settings
	Custom Picture Data and settings are not compatible with data from other Canon models
	Video Terminal Same as HD/SD-SDI Terminal
	Audio Terminal XLR 3-pin jack (2), Switchable between MIC/LINE
	HDMI Terminal (Type A), output only
	AV Mini-terminal/Headphone Terminal 3.5mm stereo mini-jack
	WFT Terminal For compatible Wi-Fi Accessory
SD Card	SD Card: 1 slot: Still images, Custom Picture Data, Clip Metadata and menu settings
Synchronization	Genlock Terminal BNC (input only)
Power In	7.4V DC (battery pack), 8.4V DC (DC-IN)
Weight	EOS C300: 3.2lb/1430g
Dimensions	EOS C300 + Thumb Rest: 5.2 × 7.0 × 6.7 in/133 × 179 × 171mm

60i format or a 1280 × 720 at 60P HD format are selectively derived.

Canon EOS C200 Cine Camera

Figure 9.24 Canon EOS C200.

The EOS C200 digital cinema camera features a Super 35mm CMOS sensor with an active image size of 24.4 × 13.5mm with 4096 × 2160 resolution supporting Ultra HD 3840 × 2160, and Full HD 1920 × 1080. C200 features include an 8.85 Megapixel Super 35mm CMOS sensor, Dual Pixel CMOS Auto Focus, full

compatibility with Canon EF-mount lenses, and HDR capability.

The EF lens mount on the EOS C200 offers compatibility not only with Canon's existing broad range of DSLR lenses but also with their line of EF-mount CN-E cinema prime and zoom lenses. The Super 35mm sensor is paired with Canon's Dual DIGIC DV 6 image processor, allowing it to capture and record up to DCI 4K resolution.

The C200 comes with a built-in 1.23MP color electronic viewfinder and a 4-inch touch screen LCD monitor. The camera can record internal 4K RAW to a CFast 2.0 card in Canon's Cinema RAW Light format as well as 4K UHD and HD in MP4 format to SD cards. Canon's Cinema RAW Light codec allows users to record raw data internally to a CFast 2.0 card via the camera's single CFast card slot. UHD 4K and Full HD recording onto SD cards is available via the two SD card slots. Record options include slow-motion recording, pre-recording, frame recording, interval recording, relay recording, double slot recording, and High-Speed Shooting at 120/100p when recording in HD.

Output live video via the camera's SDI output, and built-in XLR connectors provide two channels of audio at line, mic, and mic+48V level. A built-in Ethernet connector provides input/output control.

Table 9.15 Canon EOS C200 specifications

CANON	EOS C200
Sensor	RGB Bayer Pattern CMOS single sensor, Super 35mm, Progressive
Sensor Size	26.2 × 13.8mm effective screen size (6.4 × 6.4 micrometer pixel pitch) (for 4K DCI)
Photosites	3840 × 2160 when 3840 × 2160 or 1920 × 1080 is selected as the resolution
	4096 × 2160 when 4096 × 2160 or 2048 × 1080 is selected as the resolution
	Total Photosites – 4206 × 2340
Exposure Index/ISO	320 to 20,000, 1-stop or 1/3-stop, Base ISO 850
Notable Features	Canon Super 35mm CMOS Sensor
	Canon Dual DIGIC DV 6 Image Processor
	Canon AVCHD Codec
	Fully Compatible with a Wide Variety of EF-mount Lenses
	SD Memory Card Recording
	Multiple Recording Formats and Advanced Recording
	Full Manual Control and Focusing Aids
	WFT Wireless Remote Control over Wi-Fi

CANON	EOS C200
Frame Rates	NTSC: 59.94P, 29.97P, 23.98P PAL: 50P, 25P Film: 24P
Shutter	Fast Scan Minimized Rolling Shutter
Lens Mount	Interchangeable: EF mount with EF Contacts Dual Pixel CMOS AF supported, Manual Focus, One-Shot AF, Continuous AF, AF-Boosted MF, Face Detection AF (only lenses that support AF functions can be used in any of these modes), Focus Guide
Viewfinder	0.46" (1.18 cm on the diagonal), color wide-screen organic EL display
Controls	Camera Setup Menu Audio Setup Menu Video Setup Menu LCD/VF Setup Menu TC/UB Setup Menu Other Functions Menu Configurable Custom Menus
Onboard Recording	NTSC and PAL Codec: Cinema RAW Light Resolution: 4096 × 2160 Bit Depth: 10-bit (59.94P/50.00P), 12-bit (29.97P/23.98P/25.00P/24.00P) Bit Rate: 1 Gbps Codec: MPEG-4 AVC/H.264 Resolution: 3840 × 2160/1920 × 1080 Bit Rate: 150 Mbps (3840x2160), 35 Mbps (1920x1080) Color Sampling: YCC420 8 bit MP4 Proxy Resolution: 2048 × 1080 Bit Rate: 35 Mbps
Recording Outputs	HDMI (Type A x1) SDI Out
Connectors	LCD Screen (Monitor Unit) 4-inch diagonal, 1.23 megapixel color 16:9 rotatable LCD 100% field of view adj. brightness, contrast, color, sharpness and backlight External Audio Inputs: 2 – XLR inputs (Auto and Manual level settings)
Recording Media	(1) CFast™ card (1 slot): RAW movies Only CFast™ 2.0 with VPG-130 is supported (2) SD card (2 slots): Recording of MP4 movies, photos (JPEG), custom pictures, menus, and other data possible HDMI (Type A x1) Ethernet terminal 3.5mm Headphone mini-jack (x1) High Speed Mini-B USB (input/output x1)
Power In	14.4 V DC (battery pack), 16.7 V DC (DC-IN)
Weight	Approx. 3.2 pounds (1430g)
Dimensions	Approx. 5.7 × 6.0 × 7.0 in. (144 × 153 × 179mm)
User Manual URL	

Canon EOS C100 Cine Camera (discontinued)

Figure 9.25 Canon EOS C100.

The Canon EOS C100 digital video camera features a Canon CMOS sensor, DIGIC DV III Image Processor, and EF lens compatibility in a smaller, lighter body. The C100's Super 35mm-sized sensor provides an angle-of-view and depth of field that equivalent to Super 35mm film with a native resolution of 8.3MP. C100 records at 24Mbps using an AVCHD codec and HDMI output with embedded timecode, support for external recorders, remote operation, and manual control over both video and audio recording.

C100 is compatible with the full range of Canon EF, EF-S, and EF Cinema lenses, from fish-eye to macro to super telephoto, and has been optimized for run-and-gun and one-man-band style shooting. It is about 15% smaller than the C300, and has a few features not found in the C300, like One Shot AF, Push Auto Iris, a built-in microphone, and uncompressed HDMI out with superimposed time code and 2:3 pull down marker. One-Shot AF makes focus adjustments with a dedicated button, and the Push Auto Iris button automatically adjusts the aperture of the lens to quickly set proper exposure. Both of these functions can be accessed while operating in manual mode.

Dual SDHC/SDXC memory card slots allow the C100 to record simultaneously to two memory cards, creating an instant back-up, or C100 can record HD footage to Slot A while simultaneously recording down-converted SD footage to Slot B. Canon Log preserves a high dynamic range and presupposes color grading in post production. Wide DR gamma setting is based on Rec 709, which offers a wide dynamic range and smooth gradations in highlights and shadow.

C100 features peripheral illumination correction, which automatically compensates for light fall-off in the corners of the image. The LCD screen features Edge Monitor Display, green waveforms display the overall focus of the scene and red waveforms provide focus feedback of the three focus check boxes visible on the LCD monitor.

Table 9.16 Canon EOS C100 specifications

CANON	EOS C100
Sensor	RGB Bayer Pattern CMOS single sensor, Super 35mm
Sensor Size	24.6 × 13.8mm effective screen size (6.4 × 6.4 micrometer pixel pitch)
Photosites	Effective Pixels – approx. 8.29 megapixels (3840 × 2160)
	Total Pixels – approx. 9.84 megapixels (4206 × 2340)
Exposure Index/ISO	320 to 20,000, 1-stop or 1/3-stop, Base ISO 850
Notable Features	Canon Super 35mm CMOS Sensor
	Canon DIGIC DV III Image Processor
	Canon AVCHD Codec
	Fully Compatible with a Wide Variety of EF-mount Lenses
	SD Memory Card Recording
	Multiple Recording Formats and Advanced Recording
	Full Manual Control and Focusing Aids
	WFT Wireless Remote Control over Wi-Fi (optional)
Frame Rates	NTSC: 59.94P, 59.94i, 29.97P, 23.98P
	PAL: 50P, 50i, 25P
	Film: 24P

CANON	EOS C100
Shutter	Fast Scan Minimized Rolling Shutter
Lens Mount	Interchangeable: EF mount with EF Contacts
Viewfinder	LCD: 3.5-inch, 920k dots, vari-angle (100% coverage) EVF: 0.24-inch with an equivalent of 1,560,000 dots (100% coverage)
Controls	Camera Setup Menu Audio Setup Menu Video Setup Menu LCD/VF Setup Menu TC/UB Setup Menu Other Functions Menu Configurable Custom Menus
Onboard Recording	NTSC and PAL Compression: 8 Bit MPEG-2 Long GOP Compression: MPEG-4, AVC/H.264 File Format: AVCHD Color Space: 4:2:0 SD down Conversion: MPEG2 Recording Options: 24Mbps LPCM: 1920 × 1080 at 60i, PF30, PF24, 24p, 50i, PF25 24Mbps: 1920 × 1080 at 60i, PF30, PF24, 24p, 50i, PF25 17Mbps: 1920 × 1080 at 60i, PF30, PF24, 24p, 50i, PF25 7Mbps: 1440 × 1080 at 60i, PF30, PF24, 24p, 50i, PF25
Recording Outputs	2 SDHC/SDXC card slots HDMI (Type A x1)
Connectors	LCD Screen (Monitor Unit) 4-inch diagonal, 1.23 megapixel color 16:9 rotatable LCD 100% field of view adj. brightness, contrast, color, sharpness and backlight External Audio Inputs: 2 – XLR inputs (Auto and Manual level settings) Recording Media SD Card × 2 (Video and Still images (JPEG), Custom Picture Data*, Clip Metadata, and menu settings); SD/SDHC/SDXC Supported; MMC Cards are not supported *Custom Picture Data and settings are not compatible with data from other Canon models HDMI (Type A x1) LANC Remote Connector 3.5mm Headphone mini-jack (x1) High Speed Mini-B USB (input/output x1)
Synchronization	n/a
Power In	7.4V DC (battery pack), 8.4V DC (DC-IN)
Power Out	n/a
Weight	Approximately 2.2lbs (1020g)
Dimensions	5.2 × 7.0 × 6.7in/133 × 179 × 171mm
User Manual URL	www.usa.canon.com/cusa/professional/products/professional_cameras/cinema_eos_cameras/eos_c100#BrochuresAndManuals

Canon ME20F-SH Cine Camera

Figure 9.26 Canon ME20F-SH.

Canon's ME20F-SH multi-purpose camera features a Canon 35mm full-frame 2.2MP (2160 × 1200) high sensitivity CMOS sensor to shoot 16 × 9 high definition color video in extreme low light conditions. The camera's 35mm full-frame CMOS sensor has an equivalent sensitivity in excess of 4,000,000 ISO, minimum illumination is 0.0005 lux or less (at 75dB, F1.2, 1/30s, 50IRE). The camera can be used for television, cinema, nature and wildlife, documentary production, astronomy, military, security, and law enforcement. ME20F-SH uses Canon Lenses EF, EF-S, and Cinema (EF).

Output resolutions include 1920 × 1080, 1280 × 720, and frame rates include 1920 × 1080 at 59.94P, 59.94i, 50P, 50i, 29.97P, 25P, 23.98P, and 1280 × 720 at 59.94P, 59.94P, 50P, 29.97P, 25P, 23.98P.

Canon ME200S-SH Cine Camera

Figure 9.27 Canon ME200S-SH.

The ME200S-SH multi-purpose camera is equipped with the advanced 16:9 Super 35mm Canon CMOS image sensor, the same sensor used in Canon's Cinema EOS cameras. Capable of 204,000 ISO,

the camera performs extremely well in low-light conditions. The camera's Dual Pixel CMOS AF (Auto-Focus) technology works well to focus on moving subjects, and rugged construction makes it able to withstand use in harsh environments.

The ME200S-SH Multi-Purpose camera's modular box design allows users to connect only the components needed. An HDMI terminal allows for connection to compatible third party external displays, and 3G/HD-SDI terminals allow for connection to compatible third party external displays and recording devices. The camera is compact (4.0" W × 4.6" H × 4.4" D) and lightweight (2.2lbs). Depending on the end user's needs, the ME200S-SH Multi-Purpose Camera can produce HD video at frame rates up to 60 fps, with selectable frame rates of 59.94P/59.94i/50.00P/50.00i/29.97P/25.00P/23.98P. The ME200S-SH camera features industry standard connection terminals allowing the camera to be used in a wide range of applications from recorded content to live broadcast. By employing 3G/HD-SDI and HDMI output terminals, Canon's ME200S-SH camera can output audio/video to peripheral equipment including external recorders and monitors. The camera is also equipped with Genlock input for camera switching in a multi-camera, live broadcast environment, and a 3.5mm stereo mini-jack that allows the camera to connect with an external microphone. Power can be provided through standard 12 volt, 4-pin XLR, as well as 2-pin connector for use in more permanent installations. Canon's RC-V100 Multi-Function Remote controller can be used to remotely control camera operation using the supplied 2.5mm stereo mini-jack or 8-pin jack for RS-422. Image quality and other settings can be adjusted when shooting from a crane, jib arm, or mounted remotely in some other inaccessible location.

Canon EOS-1D X Mark III Camera

Figure 9.28 Canon EOS-1D × Mark III camera.

The EOS-1D X Mark III uses a 20.1 Megapixel CMOS image sensor and a DIGIC X processor. Autofocus through the viewfinder has a 191-point AF module, and can operate from Ev-4 to Ev-21 (maximum). Head detection has been added as an alternative to face detection, and is useful in situations where faces become partially or fully obscured.

In image capture, the EOS-1D X Mark III adds a 10-bit HEIF codec. It also adds a C-RAW option to RAW, allowing smaller file sizes. HDR functionality for still photo shooting uses a standardized PQ system. Video OETFs include Canon Log to be compatible shooting within a Cinema EOS production. 5.5K RAW video can be internally recorded up to 60 fps. The full-frame sensor also creates uncropped 4K, offering a choice of either cinema-centric 4K DCI or broadcast television-centric 4K UHD, both exploit the full width of the sensor (the 16:9 UHD is cropped from the 17:9 DCI format). These are simultaneously recorded on a second memory card as YCbCr 4:2:2 at 10-bit at all of the standard frame rates up to 60P using the MPEG-4 HEVC/H.265 codec at high data when the Canon Log OETF is selected. They can alternatively be recorded as YCbCr 4:2:0 at 8-bit using the MPEG-4 AVC/H.264 codec when Canon Log is switched OFF. In addition, a cropped 4K DCI from the central portion of the image sensor can be created and recorded at frame rates up to 60P. Full 16:9 1080P HD, capitalizing on the full sensor width, can be recorded up to 120P.

Figure 9.29

*Source:*https://pro-av.panasonic.net/en/cinema_camera_varicam_eva/products/varicam_pure/

Panasonic VariCam Pure

Figure 9.30 Panasonic VariCam Pure.

VariCam Pure combines the VariCam 35 camera head with the Codex VRAW 2.0 recorder, giving VariCam users an uncompressed RAW recording solution. Acquisition functionality supports 4K/120fps RAW recording with Codex V-RAW2 Recorder and in-camera color grading. Using the Codex Virtual File system, during off load users can transcode to additional file formats, including Panasonic V-RAW, Apple ProRes, and Avid DNxHR.

The Panasonic VariCam Pure combines a native 4K Super 35 high resolution and wide dynamic range sensor in a more compact body (approximately 11lbs). In summary, it offers 4K RAW acquisition for 4K UHD TV (16×9) or 4K DCI (17×9) cinema deliverables, two native ISO settings: 800 and 5000, and integrated Codex recording.

Panasonic VariCam 35

Figure 9.31 Panasonic Varicam 35.

The VariCam 35 is equipped with a super 35 mm single-chip MOS sensor. It offers native 4K (4096 × 2160) and UHD (3840 × 2160) resolution, high sensitivity, low noise, wide dynamic range, wide color gamut, and cinematic depth of field.

It has two native ISO settings: 800 and 5000, allowing the VariCam 35 to achieve high sensitivity while maintaining a low noise level. The noise level at 5000 ISO is nearly identical to that seen at 800 ISO.

To achieve this function, two dedicated analog circuits are implemented on each photosite of the imager to avoid the noise that is normally introduced by gain amplification in digital cameras. This low light sensitivity and wide dynamic range assures accurate image rendering over the entire image area, from dark parts to highlights, even in dimly lit scenes.

The VariCam 35 is equipped with Panasonic "V-Gamut" color and "V-Log" encoding, extending dynamic range, and a built in V-709 LUT provides a pleasing look for monitoring on set. Custom LUTs can also be imported via SD Card as well as modified in camera with internal CDL controls.

The AU-VCVF2G Large-Diameter OLED Viewfinder has high-resolution (1920 × 1080), shows operators an adjustable view magnification from 6.2× to 9.7×. The large-diameter 38mm eyepiece lens minimizes vignetting for comfortable viewing and has an auto locking diopter to maintain settings. Additional diopter magnification can be simply added via the 52mm filter thread on the eyepiece.

VariCam 35 offers multiple recordings at the same time consisting of Main, Sub, and Proxy. In addition, two media slots are provided for continuous recording. The Main recording has two Express P2 slots and Sub recording uses two microP2 slots. The Main recording offers AVC-Intra recording in 12-bit or 10-bit in 4K, UHD, 2K, or HD. The main recording also supports all flavors of 2K/HD ProRes.

The sub recording supports AVC-Intra in 2K or HD 10-bit 422. Proxy is also available on the Sub recording as ¼ HD. If proxy is turned on, it is always saved to the microP2 slot.

Note, if shooing 4K DCI (17x9), the sub will be 2K, if shooting UHD (16×9), the sub will be HD.

Using one 512GB Express P2 card, you record approximately 200 minutes of AVC-4K422/24p video, 24-bit/48kHz/ 4-channel high-quality audio, and metadata.

The VariCam 35 also features an in-camera color grading function (3D LUT/CDL). This enables color tuning in the field, using the control panel of the VariCam or third party software. Dailies can be produced on-set with only the camera on the sub recording and proxy. Grading information, such as a 3D LUT file and CDL file, can be recorded together with the image data of the Main Recorder, Sub Recorder, and Codex V-RAW Recorder, allowing dailies to reflect what users saw on-site to the postproduction process. LUT and CDL files can also be applied to playback and output images from Ver. 5.0 onward. Current firmware versions are recommended as they have the lasted features and improvements.

The VariCam 35 has a modular design comprised of the AU-V35C1G 4K camera head module with PL lens mount and the AU-VREC1G recording module. The recorder docks to the camera head without any cable connection, and the rugged docking mechanism allows tools free docking and undocking in the field. Using the AU-VEXT1G Extension Module, the camera module and recording module can be separated by up to 20 meters to make is easier to mount the camera to a crane or rig. The removable control panel on the recording module has a built-in 3.5-type LCD display panel that can be used for menu operation and can be used as a live/preview monitor.

The illuminated keys and large jog dial are laid out around the display for quick and accurate operation so frequently used settings can be accessed directly.

The Codex V-RAW 2 Recorder for VariCam 35 can be docked to the rear section of the VariCam 35 head which turns the camera into the VariCam Pure. The Codex V-RAW2 Recorder supports uncompressed RAW recording with a frame rate up to 120 fps. Variable frame rate recording is enabled from a range of 1 fps to 120 fps, and the frame rate can be adjusted while shooting.

Note, when changing the fps during shooting (ramping), using SEC. instead of Degrees on the shutter will allow exposure tracking if desired. If flash frames or motion blur are desired, use Degrees on the shutter.

The camera head houses a rotary ND filter system with four filters (0.6ND, 1.2ND, 1.8ND, CLEAR) for easy switching. The lens mount section is made of stainless steel and designed to prevent flange back deviation due to temperature changes. The lens mount was designed so that the PL mount can be removed allowing Panavision to use their PV lens mount. The body is made of strong and rigid aluminum alloy with a cooling system designed for effective dissipation of heat from the circuitry section. VariCams are compatible with a wide variety of cine accessories, there are flat top and bottom panels with several mounting holes for easy installation of various plates. Mounting holes are also provided on the body right side and all sides of the handle for convenient mounting of accessories.

Panasonic VariCam LT

Figure 9.32 Panasonic VariCam LT Shown with EF Mount, PL mount is user changeable.

The VariCam LT is equipped with the same super 35mm single-chip MOS sensor developed for the VariCam Pure and VariCam 35, in a compact and lightweight magnesium body (approx. 6lbs). It offers native 4K (4096 × 2160) and UHD (3840 × 2160) resolution, with high sensitivity, low noise, wide dynamic range and cinematic depth of field. In addition to wide dynamic range, VariCam LT also features V-Gamut, a wide color gamut (exceeding BT. 2020) for 4K image acquisition, and has the same dual native ISO settings of 800 and 5000. Its size and design facilitate a wide array of shooting styles including handheld, shoulder mounted, Steadicam, and on gimbals and drones. Mounting holes are provided on the right side of the body, as well as on all sides of the handle. In addition, the top and bottom panels are flat with multiple holes for easy installation of accessories. Interchangeable stainless-steel EF and PL mounts connect to a flange also made of stainless steel designed to prevent deviation due to temperature changes. Like the VariCam 35, the LT also supports the Panavision PV lens mount.

The VariCam LT features the same in-camera color grading functions (3D LUT/CDL) as the VariCam 35 and Pure. Similar to the VariCam 35, the VariCam LT also has multiple codec recording function that allows the user to simultaneously record a primary codec and a proxy file. In addition to in-camera color grading function, the LT has six baked-in scene file options. This allows the VariCam LT to be used on sitcoms or other similar baked in color recording requirements. HLG (live HDR) recording and output are also provided.

To support live applications, remote operation is enabled with the optional AK-HRP200G, AK-HRP1000G, or AK-HRP1005G Remote Operation Panels (ROP) via LAN or WLAN connection. The wired/wireless LAN connection also enables on set and grading software to enable in-camera color grading by wired/wireless remote control.

Using the ROP panels listed above, the VariCam LT supports "CineLive." This allows full remote control for sitcoms or similar live venues. Return video, tally, record start/stop as well as other features are built into the latest software versions 6 or higher. It is recommended to use the latest posted version since this would have the latest features.

The internal recording is supported for AVC-Intra 4K (10 bit) through HD with a choice of codecs (10-bit or 12-bit) or ProRes in 2K or HD (10-bit or 12-bit). For Proxy files, the VariCam LT are 1080 G6 .MOV files and can record to an SD memory card, the main card or both. This feature lets the user record an ungraded 4K master with V-Log on the main express P2 card recorder while simultaneously recording a graded HD proxy file (in camera dailies) as the sub recording. The primary recording data is used to create deliverables while the proxy recordings are used for viewing or off-line editing, the file name and time code of each file will match.

VariCam LT encoded with Panasonic's V-Log gamma and V-Gamut, which exceeds BT. 2020 color space. The camera also equipped with a removable IR cut filter that allows cinematographers to capture infrared images for subjects such as nocturnal wildlife in extreme darkness. Note, removing the IR Cut adds 1 stop, making the LT a native ISO 10,000 in 5,000 base mode. When removing the IR Cut filter, a clear filter is provided with the camera to ensure consistent back focus. Note, only the VariCam LT has a removable IR Cut filter – *do not* remove the IR Cut filter on the VariCam 35 or Pure as damage will occur.

The VariCam LT maximum frame rate recording in 4K (4096 × 2160) or UHD (3840 × 2160) resolution is 60 fps. When shooting at 2K Crop (2048 × 1080) or HD Crop (1920 × 1080) resolution, high-speed 240 fps recording can be used to produce slow-motion by cropping (2×) the image sensor recording area. Variable frame rates are available from 1 to 120 fps in AVC-Intra 2K422 and from 1 to 240 fps in AVC-Intra 2K-LT, and frame rate can be changed while recording.

When shooting in 4K, the VariCam LT provides down conversion to HD via two 3G-SDI outputs and one VF output (BNC), and looks can be applied to each output. For external RAW recording, the 2 SDI output terminals can be switched to from 3G SDI to RAW Data. This enables RAW acquisition from third party RAW recorders such as select models from Atomos and Convergence Design. This allows 4K/60p uncompressed raw recording or 2K Crop up to 240fps uncompressed recording.

A detachable 3.5-inch LCD display panel can be used for menu operation or as a live/preview monitor. The illuminated keys and large jog dial are laid out around the display for quick and accurate operation. Frequently used settings can be accessed directly. VariCam LT has a regular BNC connector for the View Finder, so users can select from various HD monitors or viewfinders as an option to the Panasonic AU-VCVF20G OLED View Finder. Note, the Panasonic VF offers additional user buttons and full menu access.

Table 9.17 Panasonic Varicam Pure, Varicam 35, and Varicam LT specifications

Panasonic	Varicam Pure, Varicam 35, Varicam LT Specifications (subject to change)
Sensor	Super 35 mm MOS - Rolling Shutter
Image aperture	Super 35mm – 26.668mm × 14.184mm
Sensor resolution	Effective photosites 4096 × 2160
ND Filters	ND Filters: Clear/0.6/1.2/1.8
Lens mount	35mm PL mount, User changeable EF Mount is for LT only
Frame rates V35/Pure	Maximum Frame Rate 4K 120 fps uncompressed RAW or AVC-4K422 60 fps and AVC-422LT 120 fps
Frame Rates for LT	Maximum Frame Rate 4K 60 fps 2K/HD Crop Mode 240 fps
Exposure index	Dual Native ISO: 800, 5000 800 base: 200 – 4000 5000 base: 1250 to 12800
Shutter Speeds	[deg] mode: 1.0 deg to 358 deg (0.5 deg step) [sec] mode: 1/24 sec to 1/250 sec (for 24p mode)
Recording file format	Recording Formats 4K/UHD RAW, AVC-4K444, AVC-4K422, AVC-4KLT ProRes 2K/HD 4444 XQ ProRes 2K/HD 4444 ProRes 2K/HD 422 HQ, 422, LT
Sensor crop modes	VariCam LT offers 2X Crop to 2K/HD (max 240 fps)
Recording media	VariCam Pure: Codex Recording Media Capture Drive 2 VariCam 35 Main: Express P2 x2, Sub: microP2 x2 VariCam LT Main: ExpressP2 x1, Sub: microP2 or Class 10 x1 SD 64G Minimum required for Sub.
CODECS	
VariCam Pure	Codex V-RAW 2 4K (4096 × 2160) V-RAW 12 bit/10 bit uncompressed UHD (3840 × 2160) V-RAW 12 bit/10 bit uncompressed
VariCam 35 Main	Express P2 Card x2 4K/UHD (4096 × 2160 or 3840 × 2160) AVC-Intra4K444 4K/UHD (4096 × 2160 or 3840 × 2160) AVC-Intra4K422 4K/UHD (4096 × 2160 or 3840 × 2160) AVC-Intra4K-LT 2K (2048 × 1080) AVC-Intra2K444 2K (2048 × 1080) AVC-Intra2K422 HD (1920 × 1080) AVC-Intra444 HD (1920 × 1080) AVC-Intra200 HD (1920 × 1080) AVC-Intra422 HD (1920 × 1080) AVC-Intra100

Panasonic	**Varicam Pure, Varicam 35, Varicam LT** Specifications (subject to change)
	2K/HD (2048x1080 or 1920 × 1080) ProRes 4444XQ 2K/HD (2048x1080 or 1920 × 1080) ProRes 4444 2K/HD (2048x1080 or 1920 × 1080) ProRes 422HQ 2K/HD (2048x1080 or 1920 × 1080) ProRes 422 2K/HD (2048x1080 or 1920 × 1080) ProRes 422LT
VariCam 35 Sub+	microP2 Card x2 (64G required to support cine file naming) 2K (2048 × 1080) AVC-Intra2K422 +¼ HD Proxy option HD (1920 × 1080) AVC-Intra422+¼ HD Proxy option HD (1920 × 1080) AVC-Intra100+¼ HD Proxy option HD (1920 × 1080) AVC-LongG50+¼ HD Proxy option HD (1920 × 1080) AVC-LongG25+¼ HD Proxy option
VariCam LT Main	Express P2 Card x1 4K/UHD (4096 × 2160 or 3840 × 2160) AVC-Intra4K422 4K/UHD (4096 × 2160 or 3840 × 2160) AVC-Intra4K-LT 2K (2048 × 1080) ACV-Intra444 2K (2048 × 1080) AVC-Intra422 HD (1920 × 1080) AVC-Intra444 HD (1920 × 1080) AVC-Intra200 HD (1920 × 1080) AVC-Intra422 HD (1920 × 1080) AVC-Intra100 HD (1920 × 1080) AVC-LongG50 HD (1920 × 1080) AVC-LongG25 2K/HD (2048 × 1080 or 1920 × 1080) ProRes 4444XQ 2K/HD (2048 × 1080 or 1920 × 1080) ProRes 4444 2K/HD (2048 × 1080 or 1920 × 1080) ProRes 422HQ 2K/HD (2048 × 1080 or 1920 × 1080) ProRes 422 2K/HD (2048 × 1080 or 1920 × 1080) ProRes 422LT
VariCam LT Proxy	Record to Sub Slot: microP2 64G ×1 or SD Card 64G Class 10, Main Slot (Express P2) or both. Proxy is always HD (1920 × 1080) AVC-LongG6 .MOV
System interfaces	Extension Module (AU-VEXT1G) Removable LCD Control Panel, 3.5-type QHD /color monitor
Viewfinder	Display Panel: OLED, 0.7-type, approx. 2.76 million dots Signal Input:1080/59.94p, 1080/50p, 1080/60p, 1080/23.98psF, 1080/24psF, 1080/25psF, 1080/29.97psF, 1080/59.94i, 1080/50i
Controls	Removable Display Panel: LCD, 3.5-type QHD color monitor
Additional Meta Data	Lens Data Capture ARRI LDS, Cooke /ℤ, B4 and EF for LT Color Control CDL Server Dynamic Metadata Capture User Defined Shot Metadata

(*Continued*)

Panasonic	Varicam Pure, Varicam 35, Varicam LT Specifications (subject to change)
BNC connectors	• HD/3G SDI 4K QUAD Output (BNC) for V35/PURE only • HD/3G SDI Monitor Output (BNC × 2) All Models • HD/3G SDI VF SDI Output (BNC × 1) All Models
Misc. Interfaces	V35 AUDIO Input 3-pin XLR × 2 LINE/MIC/MIC+48V/AES LT AUDIO Input 3-Pin XLR × 2 LINE/MIC/MIC+48V PURE/V35/LT MIC Input 5-pin XLR × 1 Stereo mini jack Speaker: 20 mm diameter, round GENLOCK IN: HD-SDI (1.5G) /3G-SDI, 0.8 V[p-p], 75 Ω TC IN/OUT: BNC × 1, I/O menu switchable IN: 0.5 V[p-p] to 8 V[p-p], 10 kΩ OUT: 2.0 V ± 0.5 V[p-p], low impedance V35/LT DC IN XLR 4-pin, DC 12V (DC 11.0 V to 17.0 V) V35/LT DC OUT/RS: 4-pin, DC 12V 1A V35/Pure Camera Head DC OUT: 2-pin, DC12V 1A PURE DC IN 2-pin Fisher DC 24V PURE DC OUT/RS 3-pin Fisher 24V x3 60W total LENS: 12-pin Hirose × 1 PURE/V35 VF: 14-pin LT VF: BNC plus 4-pin Hirose for data/power V35/LT LAN: 100BASE-TX/10BASE-T PURE LAN: 100BASE-TX/10BASE-T LEMO USB2.0 (device): Type B connector, 4-pin (Service Use Only) USB2.0 (host): Type A connector, 4-pin (for Wi-Fi Dongle) V35 EXT: 50-pin, exclusive for VREC or Codex Rec Modules.
Monitoring	4K SDI OUT: QUAD 3G-SDI, 0.8 V[p-p], 75 Ω V35/Pure MON OUT1: HD (1.5G)/3G-SDI, 0.8 V[p-p], 75 Ω MON OUT2: HD (1.5G)/3G-SDI, 0.8 V[p-p], 75 Ω VF SDI: HD (1.5G)/3G-SDI, 0.8 V[p-p], 75 Ω
CDL	In-camera color grading functions (3D LUT/CDL)
Weight	Pure 5.15kg (11.35lbs) V35 5kg (11.2lbs) LT 2.7kg (6lbs)
Dimensions WxHxD	
Pure	180.2 × 236.3 × 314mm 7 3/32 × 9 19/64 × 12 23/64in.
VariCam 35	179 × 230.5 × 347mm 7 1/16 × 9 3/32 × 13 21/32in.
VariCam LT	184.0 × 230.5 × 247.0mm 7 1/4 × 9 3/32 × 9 3/4in.
Power Consumption	V35 = 69w body only, 99w max. LT = 47w body, 77w max. PURE = DC 24V 105w

Panasonic AU-EVA1

Figure 9.33 Panasonic AU-EVA1.

Panasonic's AU-EVA1 Compact 5.7K Super 35mm cinema camera features Dual Native ISO technology that uses switchable alternate circuitry (rather than adding gain or shifting the gamma of the original signal) to increase sensitivity while maintaining a high signal-to-noise ratio. The standard native ISO is 800, which can be switched to 2500 when shooting in low light settings.

An EF lens mount supports a wide range of interchangeable lenses, and behind the mount is an electronically controlled ND filter wheel offering 2, 4, and 6 stops of light attenuation. The lens mount features electronic contacts for communication with compatible lenses and enables one-push autofocus. The IR-cut filter can also be actuated out electronically, allowing for night vision and unique photographic effects.

Panasonic's 5.7K sensor provides over-sampled 4K footage, and video is recorded on widely available SD cards, providing high-quality recording on accessible, industry-standard media. The full active resolution of the 5.7K sensor can also be output via the SDI port as a 10-bit raw data stream for external recording by a compatible recorder in Panasonic V-Log and V-Gamut to enable wide exposure latitude in a wide color palette.

The EVA1 can record in several formats and compression rates, and offers up to 10-bit 4:2:2 sampling at bit rates up to 400 Mb/s, even at 4K resolutions. For in-camera recording, you can capture in SDI 4K (4096 × 2160), UHD 4K (3840 × 2160), 2K (2048 × 1080), Full HD (1920 × 1080), and HD (1280 × 720). For high-

speed capture, the EVA1 offers up to 59.94 fps for 4K, up to 120 fps for 2K and Full HD, or 240 fps with an image sensor crop. EVA1 uses relatively affordable SDXC memory to record video. V60-rated SD cards support all internal recording modes, including the 10-bit 4:2:2 4K modes and dual card slots can continuously record from card to card, or record to both cards simultaneously for a backup.

Tactile controls and I/O connections provide good ergonomics for any shooting scenario whether operating hand-held or locked down atop a tripod. The HDMI and SDI video outputs are 4K-capable and can each be adjusted separately, allowing for HD to be fed to a viewfinder or other third-party monitor while 4K is sent to an outboard recorder or monitor. The camera is also equipped with timecode I/O, EVA1 imaging tools including Peaking, Image Zoom, Waveform, Zebras, and Spotmeter (Y-Get). The EVA1 autofocus utilizes Focus Squares which enable automated critical focus. Included with the EVA1 is the AG-VBR59 battery for approximately an hour and a half of continuous operating time.

Figure 9.34
*Source:*www.panavision.com/home

Panavision Millennium DXL 2

Figure 9.35 Panavision DXL2.

Combining Panavision's inventory of large-format and anamorphic optics, a 16-bit color pipeline from Light Iron and the Red Monstro 8K VV sensor, the Panavision Millennium DXL2 offers native ISO of 1600 and full-frame 8K at up

Table 9.18 Panasonic AU-EVA1 camera specifications

Panasonic	AU-EVA1 Specifications (subject to change)
Image Sensor Size	Super35
Sensor Resolution	6340 × 3232 (20.49 MP)
Effective Sensor Resolution	5720 × 3016 (17.25 MP)
ISO	800 (Native)
	200 to 2000 (Expanded)
	2500 (Native)
	1000 to 25,600 (Expanded)
Gain	–12 to 8 dB (Native)
	–8 to 20 dB (Expanded)
Lens Mount	Canon EF
Lens Communication	Yes
Shutter Speed	1/24 to 1/8000 sec
Shutter Angle	1 to 358°
Built-In ND Filter	Mechanical Filter Wheel with 2 Stop (1/4), 4 Stop (1/16), 6 Stop (1/64) ND Filters
Recording Media	2 × SDXC Card Slots (V60 or faster cards recommended)
Internal Recording	
Recording Modes	**MOV 4:2:2 10-Bit:**
	4096 × 2160 at 23.98/24/25/29.97 fps (400 Mb/s)
	4096 × 2160 at 23.98/24/25/29.97 fps (150 Mb/s)
	3840 × 2160 at 23.98/25/29.97 fps (400 Mb/s)
	3840 × 2160 at 23.98/25/29.97 fps (150 Mb/s)
	2048 × 1080 at 50/59.94 fps (200 Mb/s)
	2048 × 1080 at 23.98/24/25/29.97/50/59.94 fps (100 Mb/s)
	2048 × 1080 at 23.98/24/25/29.97 fps (50 Mb/s)
	1920 × 1080 at 50/59.94 fps (200 Mb/s)
	1920 × 1080 at 23.98/25/29.97/50/59.94 fps (100 Mb/s)
	1920 × 1080 at 50/59.94 fps (100 Mb/s)
	1920 × 1080 at 23.98/25/29.97 fps (50 Mb/s)
	1920 × 1080 at 50/59.94 fps (50 Mb/s)
	MOV 4:2:0 8-Bit:
	4096 × 2160 at 50/59.94 fps (150 Mb/s)
	4096 × 2160 at 23.98/24/25/29.97 fps (100 Mb/s)
	3840 × 2160 at 50/59.94 fps (150 Mb/s)
	3840 × 2160 at 23.98/25/29.97 fps (100 Mb/s)
	2048 × 1080 at 50/59.94 fps (150 Mb/s)
	2048 × 1080 at 23.98/24/25/29.97 fps (100 Mb/s)
	1920 × 1080 at 50/59.94 fps (100 Mb/s)
	1920 × 1080 at 23.98/25/29.97 fps (50 Mb/s)

Panasonic	**AU-EVA1** Specifications (subject to change)
External Recording	
Video Output	4:2:2 10-Bit via SDI/BNC: 4096 × 2160 at 23.98/24/25/29.97 fps 3840 × 2160 at 23.98/24/25/29.97 fps 1920 × 1080 at 23.98/24/25/29.97/50/59.94 fps 1920 × 1080 at 50/59.94 fps 1280 × 720 at 50/59.94 fps 4:2:2 10-Bit via HDMI: 4096 × 2160 at 23.98/24/25/29.97/50/59.94 fps 3840 × 2160 at 23.98/24/25/29.97/50/59.94 fps 1920 × 1080 at 23.98/24/25/29.97/50/59.94 fps 1920 × 1080 at 50/59.94 fps 1280 × 720 at 50/59.94 fps 720 × 576 at 50 fps 720 × 480 at 59.94 fps 4:2:0 8-Bit via HDMI: 4096 × 2160 at 50/59.94 fps 3840 × 2160 at 50/59.94 fps
Raw Output	**SDI/BNC:** 5760 × 3072 10-Bit at 23.98/24/25/29.97 fps 4096 × 2160 10-Bit at 23.98/24/25/29.97/50/59.94 fps 2048 × 1080 10-Bit at 23.98/24/25/29.97/50/59.94 fps
Interfaces	
Video Connectors	1 × BNC (6G-SDI) Output 1 × HDMI (HDMI 2.0) Output 1 × HDMI Output
Audio Connectors	2 × 3-Pin XLR Input
Other I/O	1 × USB Type-A 1 × 40-Pin Monitor Output 1 × BNC Timecode Input/Output 1 × 2.5 mm LANC Control Input
Display	
Display Type	LCD
Screen Size	3.5"
Touchscreen	Yes
Screen Resolution	1,150,000 Dots
Power	
Battery Type	Panasonic AG-VBR Series
Power Connectors	1 × Barrel Input
Power Consumption	19 W
Environmental	

(*Continued*)

Table 9.18 (Continued)

Panasonic	AU-EVA1 Specifications (subject to change)
Operating Temperature	32 to 104°F/0 to 40°C
Storage Temperature	–4 to 140°F/–20 to 60°C
Operating Humidity	10 to 85%
General	
Accessory Mount	1 × 1/4" –20 Female 1 × Cold Shoe Mount
Dimensions	6.7 × 5.3 × 5.2"/17 × 13.5 × 13.3 cm (without protrusions)
Weight	4.5lb/2.1kg

to 60 fps. DXL2 was designed from the ground up specifically for the needs of the professional cinema industry.

The sensor color calibration through to the display output transforms have been designed along with Light Iron creating a more cinematic image straight out the camera. The image pipeline is based off of an industry standard log pipeline allowing for traditional on-set workflows. Display transforms are publicly available for all standard displays allowing DXL2 to work in any post pipeline.

Panavision has a wide variety of lenses available for large format coverage including the Primo 70 series, Sphero 65 lenses, Ultra Panavision 70, and more. With 5µ (micron) pixel pitch and a sensor diagonal of 46.31mm (40.96mm × 21.60mm), the DXL2's sensor covers anamorphic, available through many of Panavision's large format anamorphic lens options, like the Pana Ultra 70 with 1.25x squeeze as well as many series of traditional 2x anamorphics.

Sixteen-bit RedCode can be captured in 8K full sensor raw at up to 60fps. For slow motion effects 7K at up to 72 fps, 6K at up to 80 fps, 5K at up to 96 fps, 2K at up to 300 fps. ProRes and Avid DNxHR capture are available in 4K or 2K with metadata synchronized to the raw files to be used as simultaneous proxies available out of the camera.

At a base weight of 10lbs, the DXL2 has been designed modularly with compartmentalized, independent electronics. Full camera controls can be customized to either side. Panavision has configured the Millennium DXL2 with

interchangeable modules that allow users to switch from studio mode to hand-held or even a gimbal and Steadicam mode. The camera has integrated and interchangeable MDR modules for wireless lens control, including an option for the DXL2's Preston Module, an integrated 3-axis, 3-channel version of the Preston MDR3. For single or multiple cameras, the DXL2 Control iOS app provides full menu access, real time histogram, and remote program for up to eight shortcuts. A cheek pad module can be replaced with soft pad for hand-held work. In addition to a secondary power port and primary 24v power port on the camera, the DXL2 has a Hot Swap Module with two 24v and three 14v ports plus USB.

Panavision Genesis

Figure 9.36 Panavision Genesis.

Table 9.19 Panavision Millennium DXL2 specifications

Panavision	Millennium DXL2
Sensor	16-bit, 35.4 Megapixel CMOS
Sensor Size	40.96mm × 21.60mm (Diagonal: 46.31mm)
Photosites	8192 × 4320 photosites
Exposure Index/ISO	Nominal 1600
Notable Features	
	16bit, 1600 native ISO Color Profile Light Iron Color 2 (compatible with all popular gamuts and transfer curves)
	Modular Design Interchangeable modules for customization and field serviceability
	DXL2 is a dual-recording system allowing proxy files a faster and more streamlined workflow for editorial. DXL2 has 3 options for recording codecs so users can decide exactly which file type fits their editorial pipeline. When editing is complete, proxy file metadata matches RAW file metadata for a simple and streamlined final conform in 2K, 4K, or 8K.
	Ability to utilizes entire Panavision lens portfolio including Primo70, Sphero65, Ultra Panavision 70, Super Panavision 70 and System 65 lenses and more
Frame Rates	60 fps at 8K Full frame (8192 × 4320), 75 fps at 8K 2.4:1 (8192 × 3456)
	http://panalab.panavision.com/sites/default/files/docs/documentLibrary/DXL%20Quick%20Guide%20V_5_35_5.pdf?_ga=2.34889249.1438488492.1530923401-818661899.1530923401
Shutter	Electronic, Continuously Variable from 3.8 degrees to 360 degrees
Lens Mount	Native SP70 Large Panavision Mount, adapters available to PV35, PV65, PL
Viewfinder	Panavision Primo HDR 600 nit Electronic Viewfinder
Controls	Both sides user interface Camera LCD display provide user- definable access to all camera functions RCP via Wi-Fi, Ethernet, and RS232
Onboard Recording	SSD (up to 1 hour on a single magazine)
	r3d (supported in RED SDK)
	Light Iron Color (compatible with all popular gamuts and transfer curves, including RAW, ACES, selectable)
External Recording Outputs	Single-Link 6G 4K HD-SDI output (with supplied interface box) BNC type x2
Connectors	Genlock video input BNC type ×1, 1.0 Vp-p, 75 Ω LCD/EVF (3×) Timecode in/out USB Power Out SDI output BNC ×3, 3G HD-SDI SDI output BNC ×2, 6G/3G HD-SDI DC input Lemo 4-pin (Male) ×2, DC 11.5V to 17V DC aux output DC 14V 2-pin Lemo DC aux output DC 24V 3-pin Fischer RJ-45 GigE Ethernet Communication Aux power out Return HD SDI In

(Continued)

Table 9.19 (Continued)

Panavision	Millennium DXL2
	SDI ports output two (2) channels of 24-bit 48KHz uncompressed, embedded digital audio
Synchronization	Genlock Video In BNC type ×1, 1.0 Vp-p, 75 Ω
Power In	DC 11.5V to 17V
Power Out	5V, 12V and 24V outputs
Weight	10lbs
Dimensions	13.95" Depth × 8" Height × 6.5" Width
Manual URL:	https://panalab.panavision.com/sites/default/files/docs/documentLibrary/Millennium%20DXL%20Operation%20Guide%20V_05_35_5.pdf

The Panavision Genesis employs a single Super 35mm 5760 × 2160 photosite CCD striped array sensor to create 4:4:4 and 4:2:2 1920 × 1080 HD images. The sensor records the same number of color samples for each of the primary colors, and the CCD active area of 23.622mm (.930 inches) × 13.2842mm (.523 inches), outputs 1920 × 1080 from 12.4 million photosites that are sampled 3x in horizontal and 2x in vertical. Onboard digital lateral color aberration compensates for improved image quality. Both vertical and horizontal resolution are oversampled and then reduced to 1920 × 1080.

Genesis has a standard Panavision lens mount and uses all existing 35mm Panavision Primo and PVintage series spherical lenses. It uses the same accessories as Panavision's film cameras, and runs at speed of 1–50 fps at 4:4:4, with an ASA/ISO rating of EI 400.

Extended range Panalog encoding records 10-bit PANALOG and transforms the 14-bit per color linear output of the Genesis A/D converters into a quasi-log 10-bit per color signal that enables the RGB camera signal to be recorded to either the Panavision Solid State Recorder SSR-1, or to a SONY SRW-1 videotape recorder and both units can dock directly to the camera, giving complete portability without cables running to an external recording device. Genesis can also be recorded by other HD capable recorders. The SSR-1 can capture up to 42 minutes of uncompressed 4:4:4 HD footage, and the SRW-1 deck can record up to 50 minutes on an HDCam SR tape.

The Genesis offers dual electronic viewfinder outputs, integrated lens control for focus, zoom, and iris, user-selectable menu terminologies such as shutter angle or shutter speed and camera control via on board camera LCD display panel, Panavision RDC (Remote Digital Controller), or SONY MSU (Master Setup Unit), or RMB (HD Remote Control Unit) series controllers. All functions such as record start/stop and format options can be controlled directly from the camera control panel or from remote control units.

Camera shutter angles range from 3.8° to 360° and frame rates from 1 to 50fps. The 360° shutter is new territory for film cinematographers, yielding one more stop of exposure, with increased motion blur. The nominal EI 400 sensitivity can be extended to EI 1600 and above for low light situations, by the judicious use of shutter and gain. Frame Rates range from 23.98, 24, 25, 29.97 30 50, 59.94, 60 fps at either 4:2:2 or 4:4:4 sampling, and from 1–29.97 fps at 4:2:2 or 4:4:4, 1–50 fps at 4:2:2 variable as well.

RED Digital Cinema

Figure 9.37

Source: www.red.com/

Table 9.20 Panavision Genesis specifications

	Panavision Genesis
Sensor	1-chip Super 35mm type Progressive CCD 1920 × 1080 RGB Output
Sensor Size	CCD active area .930 in. × .523 in.
Photosites	12.4 megapixel stripe array CCD chip, 5760 × 2160 photosites
Exposure Index/ISO	Nominal 400
Notable Features	14-bit A/D converter
	Panalog Gamma Correction Curve
	customizable gamma curve
	1 to 50fps Variable Speed with either Shutter Angle or Gain Exposure Compensation for Programmable Ramping
	Utilizes all existing spherical 35mm lenses, including Primo Primes and Zooms
Frame Rates	23.98PsF 4:2:2 YCbCr or 4:4:4 RGB
	S23.98PsF 4:2:2 YCbCr or 4:4:4 RGB
	24PsF 4:2:2 YCbCr or 4:4:4 RGB
	S24PsF 4:2:2 YCbCr or 4:4:4 RGB
	25PsF 4:2:2 YCbCr or 4:4:4 RGB
	S25PsF 4:2:2 YCbCr or 4:4:4 RGB
	S30PsF 4:2:2 YCbCr or 4:4:4 RGB
	29.97PsF 4:2:2 YCbCr or 4:4:4 RGB
	S29.97PsF 4:2:2 YCbCr or 4:4:4 RGB
	50P 4:2:2 YCbCr or 4:4:4 RGB
	S50P 4:2:2 YCbCr or 4:4:4 RGB
	S59.94P 4:2:2 YCbCr or 4:4:4 RGB
	59.94I 4:2:2 YCbCr or 4:4:4 RGB
	50I 4:2:2 YCbCr or 4:4:4 RGB
	S60P 4:2:2 YCbCr or 4:4:4 RGB
	1 to 29.97fps YCbCr or 4:4:4 RGB
	1 to 50fps YCbCr
Shutter	Electronic, Continuously Variable from 3.8 degrees to 360 degrees
Lens Mount	Panavision Mount/Optional PL Mount
Viewfinder	Panavision Electronic Viewfinder
Controls	Assistant side main user interface Camera LCD display provides user-definable access to all camera functions
	Compatible with Panavision RDC (Remote Digital Controller)
	Compatible with SONY MSU (Master Setup Unit)
	Compatible with RMB (HD Remote Control Unit) series controllers.
Onboard Recording	Dockable SSR-1 or SONY SRW-1 VTR (no cables) on rear or top
	10-Bit HDCAM SR Tape
	10-Bit Uncompressed or 12-Bit – w/Panavision SSR Recorder
Recording Outputs	Dual-Link HD-SDI output (with supplied interface box) BNC type x2
Connectors	Genlock video input BNC type x1, 1.0 Vp-p, 75 Ω
	Audio CH1/CH2 input (with supplied interface box) XLR-3-31 type (Female), line/mic/mic +48 V selectable

(Continued)

Table 9.20 (Continued)

	Panavision Genesis
	Test output BNC type x1, VBS/HD Y
	Dual-Link HD-SDI output (with supplied interface box) BNC type x2
	Monitor output BNC type x2, HD-SDI (4:2:2)
	DC input Lemo 8-pin (Male) ×1, DC 10.5V to 17V,DC 20V to 30V
	DC input (with supplied interface box) XLR-4-pin type (Male) ×1
	DC output DC 12V: 11-pin ×1, max. 4 A DC 24V: 3-pin ×1, max. 5.5 A
	Remote 8-pin ×1
	Viewfinder 20-pin ×2
	External input/output Lemo 5-pin (Female) ×1
	Network RJ-45 type ×1, 10BASE-T/100BASE-TX
SD Card	SD Memory Stick
Synchronization	Genlock Video In BNC type ×1, 1.0 Vp-p, 75 Ω
Power In	DC 10.5V to 17V 58 W (without lens, viewfinder, at 23.98PsF mode)
Power Out	12V and 24V outputs
Weight	11lb (5.0kg) Body Only
Dimensions	8.97" Depth × 8.07" Height × 9.01" Width
Genesis Operators Manual URL:	www.panavision.com/sites/default/files/Genesis%20Users%20Manual.pdf

RED RANGER and DSMC2 Camera Bodies

RED MONSTRO, HELIUM, GEMINI, and DRAGON Sensors

Figure 9.38 RED RANGER camera body.

Figure 9.39 DSMC2 camera body.

The modern RED digital cinema ecosystem is very similar to the traditional film camera configuration. Two distinct bodies, RANGER and DSMC2, can be coupled with four distinct imagers, MONSTRO, HELIUM, GEMINI, or DRAGON, much the same way one would choose a film camera and a film stock.

RED designed the DSMC2 camera body to be modular and fit a wide range of production workflows. Smaller and lighter than the original DSMC design, when stripped down to the camera body itself, users have a high-resolution gimbal, Steadicam, or drone camera. DSMC2 can be fitted a MONSTRO, HELIUM, GEMINI, or DRAGON sensor depending on the desired image. Add DSMC2 modules to the rear to add more I/O connections and battery power – the DSMC2 BRAIN can be built as small or as big as needed for the production. Many other parts of the DSMC2 system design are meant to be user-interchangeable. Users can swap out the lens mounts, or exchange the included standard OLPF (optical low-pass filter) for alternative image renderings at the sensor level (www.red.com/dsmc2-low-light-optimized-olpf).

The DSMC2 BRAIN itself does not have a DC IN power port. A port expander or power module is required to power the camera. To construct a working configuration of any camera, RED sells an expander, batteries, lens mounts, displays, and media.

Mount an EVF without cables, or use a separately available adapter to attach RED LCDs via LEMO cable. The DSMC2 form factor is standardized, so accessories for this DSMC2 body will work with any other DSMC2 body.

Contrary to RED's DSMC2 design, the RANGER is designed to be an integrated camera body with built-in I/O and power management that weighs around 7.5 pounds (depending on battery mount), supports wide input voltage (11.5V to 32V), features more independent SDI and AUX power outputs and an integrated XLR audio input. It also has a larger fan for quieter and more efficient temperature management.

RED RANGER is available with three difference sensor options: MONSTRO, HELIUM, and GEMINI, with the older DRAGON sensor being left off the compatibility list. All three sensors deliver very high resolution and image quality. The MONSTRO and HELIUM sensors take the next step in resolution to 8K. While 8K exhibition is not yet mainstream, the extra recorded resolution is helpful for acquiring a pristine 4K delivery by overcoming the inherent resolving issues of Bayer-pattern sensors, for VFX artists, and for future-proofing productions for a time when 8K becomes standardized.

The technical processing capabilities of RANGER and DSMC2 camera bodies are equal, with full support for 3D LUTs, in-camera proxies, and up to 8K 60P capture when using MONSTRO or HELIUM sensors. All sensors allow for 5K 96P, and 4K 120P capture as well. Both cameras capture identical forms of RED's proprietary REDCODE RAW format.

RED Camera Models: History

In 2009, RED began building cameras with a form factor updated from the RED One, called DSMC which stands for "Digital Stills and Motion Capture." The first camera released for this system was their EPIC-X, a digital stills and motion capture camera with interchangeable lens mounts. After that a camera line called SCARLET was introduced that provided lower end specifications at a more affordable price. Initially equipped with a 5K imaging sensor, upgrades were later offered to a 6K sensor with higher dynamic range called "DRAGON."

The DSMC2 style of cameras was introduced in 2015 with unified form factor, all with varying sizes of the same DRAGON sensor. The WEAPON 8K VV and WEAPON 6K were the first two cameras announced, and then followed by the RED RAVEN 4.5K and SCARLET-W 5K. In 2016, a new 8K sensor called "HELIUM" was introduced with two cameras RED EPIC-W and WEAPON 8K Super 35mm. It should be noted that nomenclature such as EPIC and WEAPON are no longer part of RED's modern camera lineup.

I am covering the RED camera section as a modular system, in accordance with the evolution of their designs, with individual data on DSMC legacy cameras.

RED Sensors

DRAGON

The DRAGON sensor was once RED's flagship sensor, but since has given way to the more modern sensors with improved architecture. However, demand from the market for the "look" that DRAGON provided drove RED to reintroduce

Table 9.21 RED cameras and sensors progression chart

RED Digital Cinema DSMC Model	Sensor	Active Photosite Area	Active Imaging Area	Imaging Area Diameter	Format
SCARLET M-X 5K	MYSTERIUM-X 5K	5120 × 2700	27.7mm × 14.6mm	31.4mm	Acad 35mm
SCARLET DRAGON 6K	RED DRAGON 6K	6144 × 3160	30.7mm × 15.8mm	34.5mm	Super 35mm
EPIC M-X 5K	MYSTERIUM-X 5K	5120 × 2700	27.7mm × 14.6mm	31.4mm	Acad 35mm
EPIC M-X 5K MONOCHROME	MYSTERIUM-X 5K MONOCHROME	5120 × 2700	27.7mm × 14.6mm	31.4mm	Acad 35mm
EPIC DRAGON 6K	RED DRAGON 6K	6144 × 3160	30.7mm × 15.8mm	34.5mm	Super 35mm
EPIC DRAGON 6K MONOCHROME	RED DRAGON M	6144 × 3160	30.7mm × 15.8mm	34.5mm	Super 35mm
EPIC DRAGON 6K CF	RED DRAGON 6K	6144 × 3160	30.7mm × 15.8mm	34.5mm	Super 35mm

RED Digital Cinema DSMC2 Model	Sensor	Active Photosite Area	Active Imaging Area	Imaging Area Diameter	Format
RED RAVEN 4.5K	RED DRAGON 4.5K	4608 × 2160	23.04mm × 10.80mm	25.5mm	Acad 35mm
SCARLET-W RED DRAGON 5K	RED DRAGON 5K	5120 × 2700	25.60mm × 13.50mm	28.9mm	Acad 35mm
SCARLET-W RED DRAGON 5K MONOCHROME	RED DRAGON 5K M*	5120 × 2700	28.9mm × 13.5mm	28.9mm	Acad 35mm
RED EPIC-W GEMINI 5K S35	GEMINI 5K S35	5120 × 3000	30.72mm × 18mm	35.61mm	Super 35mm
RED EPIC-W HELIUM 8K S35	HELIUM 8K S35	8192 × 4320	29.90mm × 15.77mm	33.80mm	Super 35mm
DSMC2 GEMINI 5K S35	GEMINI 5K S35	5120 × 3000	30.72mm × 18mm	35.61mm	Super 35mm
DSMC2 DRAGON 6K S35 (Carbon Fiber/Magnesium)	RED DRAGON 6K	6144 × 3160	30.72mm × 15.8mm	34.5mm	Super 35mm
DSMC2 DRAGON-X 6K S35	RED DRAGON-X 6K	6144 × 3160	30.72mm × 15.8mm	34.5mm	Super 35mm
DSMC2 HELIUM 8K S35,	HELIUM 8K S35	8192 × 4320	29.90mm × 15.77mm	33.80mm	Super 35mm
DSMC2 HELIUM 8K S35 MONOCHROME	HELIUM 8K S35 M*	8192 × 4320	29.90mm × 15.77mm	33.80mm	Super 35mm
DSMC2 DRAGON 8K VV	RED DRAGON 8K VV	8192 × 4320	40.96mm × 21.60mm	46.31mm	Full frame
DSMC2 MONSTRO 8K VV	MONSTRO 8K VV	8192 × 4320	40.96mm × 21.60mm	46.31mm	Full frame

the sensor into the modern DSMC2 camera line up. DRAGON, now with the benefits of the newer processing provided by DSMC2, allows users to achieve their desired look with the added benefit of coming in at a lower cost due to its relative age.

GEMINI

For more flexibility, GEMINI is RED's highest sensitivity sensor to date, offering increased performance in low-light settings and improved performance in shadows. It is also RED's only non-17:9 sensor, adding additional height to make it similar to 4-perf motion picture film and ideal for anamorphic shooting.

The GEMINI 5K Super 35mm sensor features dual sensitivity modes. Standard mode is for conventional shooting scenarios, Low Light mode for increased sensitivity and improved noise floor. In addition to the increased sensitivity, the signal is manipulated to increase shadow reproduction. Unlike other dual sensitivity sensors on the market, GEMINI shifts the dynamic range of the image two stops in favor of the shadows, allowing for a more subtle and detailed shadow reproduction.

HELIUM

HELIUM is an 8K Super 35mm format solution for high-end production use. HELIUM allows for high-resolution 8K recording while using classic cinema lenses designed for the Super 35 film format. The high pixel density of HELIUM allows for capture of subtle detail, and the additional resolution is often used to expand the coverage of a shot by cropping in post to produce two angles, or is used to stabilize a shot.

By nature, HELIUM packing 35 million pixels onto a Super 35mm sized chip results in smaller photosites than any other sensor in RED's lineup, which can result in less lowlight performance than GEMINI or MONSTRO. However, when delivering a 4K file from the 8K sensor, the oversampling provides a much smaller and subtler noise pattern.

MONSTRO

MONSTRO is an 8K sensor like HELIUM; however, it is a much larger format at 40.96 × 21.6mm. Considered a full frame sensor, it is actually larger than the traditional full frame 43mm diagonal, coming in at 46.31mm. Like most of RED's sensors, MONSTRO is a 17:9 or 1.89:1 native aspect ratio. This means that compared to more traditional 36 × 24mm full frame sensors, the MONSTRO has a much larger image circle when delivering in traditional 17:9 or 16:9 aspect ratios, the full 46.31mm compared to a 40mm diagonal of a 1.89 extraction from a 36 × 24mm sensor.

MONSTRO is RED's current flagship sensor, and it is the same sensor that can be found in the Panavision DXL2 which was built in collaboration between Panavision and RED Digital Cinema.

The MONSTRO allows for full frame 8K capture, as well as Super 35mm 6K capture. This flexibility allows filmmakers to choose their format as needed for the shot, deciding when to use the large format look or the Super 35mm look all while still acquiring well above the minimum 4K requirement of many production companies.

Because of MONSTRO's large photosites and higher resolution, it is a good lowlight performer as well.

Table 9-22 RED DSMC2 Monstro, Helium, Gemini and Dragon-X camera specifications

Sensor Type	MONSTRO 35.4 Megapixel CMOS	HELIUM 35.4 Megapixel CMOS*	GEMINI 15.4 Megapixel Dual Sensitivity CMOS	DRAGON-X 19.4 Megapixel CMOS
Effective Photosites	8192 × 4320	8192 × 4320	5120 × 3000	6144 × 3160
Sensor Size	40.96mm × 21.60mm (Diagonal: 46.31mm)	29.90mm × 15.77mm (Diagonal: 33.80mm)	30.72mm × 18.0mm (Diagonal: 35.61mm)	30.7mm × 15.8mm (Diagonal: 34.5 mm)
Dynamic Range	17+ stops	16.5+ stops	16.5+ stops	16.5+ stops
Max Frame Rates	60 fps at 8K Full Format (8192 × 4320), 75 fps at 8K 2.4:1 (8192 × 3456)		75 fps at 5K Full Height 1.7:1 (5120 × 3000)	75 fps at 6K Full Format (6144 × 3160), 100 fps at 6K 2.4:1 (6144 × 2592)
Max Frame Rates	60 fps at 7K Full Format (7168 × 3780), 75 fps at 7K 2.4:1 (7168 × 3024)		96 fps at 5K Full Format (5120 × 2700), 120 fps at 5K 2.4:1 (5120 × 2160)	96 fps at 5K Full Format (5120 × 2700), 120 fps at 5K 2.4:1 (5120 × 2160)
Max Frame Rates	75 fps at 6K Full Format (6144 × 3240), 100 fps at 6K 2.4:1 (6144 × 2592)		120 fps at 4K Full Format (4096 × 2160), 150 fps at 4K 2.4:1 (4096 × 1728)	120 fps at 4K Full Format (4096 × 2160), 150 fps at 4K 2.4:1 (4096 × 1728)
Max Frame Rates	96 fps at 5K Full Format (5120 × 2700), 120 fps at 5K 2.4:1 (5120 × 2160)		150 fps at 3K Full Format (3072 × 1620), 200 fps at 3K 2.4:1 (3072 × 1296)	150 fps at 3K Full Format (3072 × 1620), 200 fps at 3K 2.4:1 (3072 × 1296)

(Continued)

Table 9.22 (Continued)

Sensor Type	MONSTRO 35.4 Megapixel CMOS	HELIUM 35.4 Megapixel CMOS*	GEMINI 15.4 Megapixel Dual Sensitivity CMOS	DRAGON-X 19.4 Megapixel CMOS
Max Frame Rates	120 fps at 4K Full Format (4096 × 2160), 150 fps at 4K 2.4:1 (4096 × 1728)		240 fps at 2K Full Format (2048 × 1080), 300 fps at 2K 2.4:1 (2048 × 864)	240 fps at 2K Full Format (2048 × 1080), 300 fps at 2K 2.4:1 (2048 × 864)
Max Frame Rates	150 fps at 3K Full Format (3072 × 1620), 200 fps at 3K 2.4:1 (3072 × 1296)			
Max Frame Rates	240 fps at 2K Full Format (2048 × 1080), 300 fps at 2K 2.4:1 (2048 × 864)			
Max Data Rates	Up to 300 MB/s using RED MINI-MAG (480GB and 960GB)			
	Up to 225 MB/s using RED MINI-MAG (120GB and 240GB)			
Project Timebase	23.98, 24, 25, 29.97, 47.95, 48, 50, 59.94, 60 fps, all resolutions			
REDCODE Settings	5:1 REDCODE for 8K Full Format (8192 × 4320) at 24 fps		3:1 REDCODE at 5K Full Height (5120 × 3000) and 24 fps	3:1 REDCODE at 6K Full Format (6144 × 3160) and 24 fps
REDCODE Settings	12:1 REDCODE for 8K Full Format (8192 × 4320) at 60 fps		6:1 REDCODE at 5K Full Height (5120 × 3000) and 60 fps	7:1 REDCODE at 6K Full Format (6144 × 3160) and 60 fps
REDCODE Settings	2:1 REDCODE for 4K Full Format (4096 × 2160) at 24 fps		2:1 REDCODE at 5K Full Format (5120 × 2700) and 24 fps	2:1 REDCODE at 4K Full Format (4096 × 2160) and 24 fps
REDCODE Settings	3:1 REDCODE for 4K Full Format (4096 × 2160) at 60 fps		8:1 REDCODE at 5K Full Format (5120 × 2700) and 96 fps	6:1 REDCODE at 4K Full Format (4096 × 2160) and 120 fps
REDCODE Settings			2:1 REDCODE at 4K Full Format (4096 × 2160) and 24 fps	
REDCODE Settings			6:1 REDCODE at 4K Full Format (4096 × 2160) and 120 fps	
REDCODE Settings	8K Full Format (8192 × 4320), 2:1, 2.4:1, 16:9, 14:9, 8:9, 3:2, 6:5, 4:1, 8:1, and Ana 2×, 1.3×, 1.25×		5K Full Height 1.7:1 (5120 × 3000), 5K Full Height 6:5 (3600 × 3000), and Ana 2×, 1.3×	6K Full Format (6144 × 3160), 2:1, 2.4:1, 16:9, 3:2, 6:5, 4:1, 8:1, and Ana 2×, 1.3×, 1.25×
REDCODE Settings	7K Full Format (7168 × 3780), 2:1, 2.4:1, 16:9, 8:9, 6:5, 4:1, 8:1, and Ana 2×, 1.3×		5K Full Format (5120 × 2700), 2:1, 2.4:1, 16:9, 4:1, 8:1, and Ana 2×, 1.3×	5K Full Format (5120 × 2700), 2:1, 2.4:1, 16:9, 4:1, 8:1, and Ana 2v, 1.3×
REDCODE Settings	6K Full Format (6144 × 3240), 2:1, 2.4:1, 16:9, 8:9, 3:2, 4:3, 6:5, 4:1, 8:1, and Ana 2×, 1.3×, 1.25×		4K Full Format (4096 × 2160), 2:1, 2.4:1, 16:9, 3:2, 4:3, 5:4, 6:5, 4:1, 8:1, and Ana 2×, 1.3×	4K Full Format (4096 × 2160), 2:1, 2.4:1, 16:9, 3:2, 4:3, 5:4, 6:5, 4:1, 8:1, and Ana 2×, 1.3×
REDCODE Settings	5K Full Format (5120 × 2700), 2:1, 2.4:1, 16:9, 8:9, 6:5, 4:1, 8:1, and Ana 2×, 1.3×		3K Full Format (3072 × 1620), 2:1, 2.4:1, 16:9, 3:2, 4:3, 5:4, 6:5, 4:1, 8:1, and Ana 2×, 1.3×	3K Full Format (3072 × 1620), 2:1, 2.4:1, 16:9, 3:2, 4:3, 5:4, 6:5, 4:1, 8:1, and Ana 2×, 1.3×
REDCODE Settings	4K Full Format (4096 × 2160), 2:1, 2.4:1, 16:9, 8:9, 3:2, 4:3, 5:4, 6:5, 4:1, 8:1, 1:1, and Ana 2×, 1.3×		2K Full Format (2048 × 1080), 2:1, 2.4:1, 16:9, 3:2, 4:3, 5:4, 6:5, 4:1, 8:1, and Ana 2×, 1.3×	2K Full Format (2048 × 1080), 2:1, 2.4:1, 16:9, 3:2, 4:3, 5:4, 6:5, 4:1, 8:1, and Ana 2×, 1.3×

Sensor Type	MONSTRO 35.4 Megapixel CMOS	HELIUM 35.4 Megapixel CMOS*	GEMINI 15.4 Megapixel Dual Sensitivity CMOS	DRAGON-X 19.4 Megapixel CMOS
REDCODE Settings	3K Full Format (3072 × 1620), 2:1, 2.4:1, 16:9, 3:2, 4:3, 5:4, 6:5, 4:1, 8:1, and Ana 2×, 1.3×			
REDCODE Settings	2K Full Format (2048 × 1080), 2:1, 2.4:1, 16:9, 3:2, 4:3, 5:4, 6:5, 4:1, 8:1, and Ana 2×, 1.3×			
Apple ProRes	ProRes 422 HQ, ProRes 422 and ProRes 422 LT at 4K (4096 × 2160) up to 30 fps			
Apple ProRes	ProRes 4444 XQ and ProRes 4444 at 2K (2048 × 1080) up to 120 fps			
Apple ProRes	ProRes 422 HQ, ProRes 422 and ProRes 422 LT at 2K (2048 × 1080) up to 120 fps			
Avid Codecs	DNxHR HQX at 4K (4096 × 2160) 12-bit up to 30 fps			
Avid Codecs	DNxHR HQ, SQ and LB at 4K (4096 × 2160) 8-bit up to 30 fps			
Avid Codecs	DNxHR 444 at 2K (2048 × 1080) 12-bit up to 120 fps			
Avid Codecs	DNxHD 444 and HQX (1920 × 1080) 10-bit up to 120 fps			
Avid Codecs	DNxHD HQ, SQ and LB (1920 × 1080) 8-bit up to 120 fps			
Construction	Aluminum Alloy			
Weight	3.35lbs (BRAIN with Integrated Media Bay)			
Operating Temp	0°C to 40°C (32°F to 104°F)			
Storage Temp	–20°C to 50°C (–4°F to 122°F)			
Relative Humidity	0% to 85% non-condensing			
Color Management	Supports 33×33×33, 32×32×32, 26×26×26, and 17×17×17 3D LUTs			
Color Management	Variable number of 3D LUT outputs with DSMC2 expander module			
Color Management	User programmable shaper 1D LUTs			
Color Management	Tetrahedral interpolation, 16-bit processing			
Audio	Integrated dual channel digital stereo microphones, uncompressed, 24-bit 48 kHz			
Audio	Optional 2 additional channels with DSMC2 expander module, uncompressed, 24-bit 48 kHz			
Remote Control	Integrated R.C.P. WiFi antenna Ethernet, RS232, and GPI Trigger with DSMC2 expander module			
Monitor Outputs	3G-SDI (HD-SDI) and HDMI with DSMC2 expander module 1080p RGB or 4:2:2, 720p RGB or 4:2:2 480p RGB or 4:2:2 (HDMI only) SMPTE Timecode, HANC Metadata, 24-bit 48 kHz Audio			
Monitor Options	DSMC2® Touch 7.0" Ultra-Brite LCD (Direct Mount), DSMC2® RED Touch 4.7" LCD, DSMC2® RED Touch 7.0" LCD and DSMC2® RED EVF (OLED) with cable-free connection. RED Touch 9.0" LCD, RED Touch 7.0" LCD, RED Touch 5.0" LCD, RED PRO 7" LCD, DSMC2 Touch 7.0" Ultra-Brite LCD, BOMB EVF (OLED) and BOMB EVF (LCOS) compatible with DSMC2 LCD/EVF Adaptor A or DSMC2 LCD/EVF Adaptor D, and LCD/EVF cable.			
REDcine-X Delivery Formats	4K: DPX, TIFF, OpenEXR (.RED via RRencode plugin)			
REDcine-X Delivery Formats	2K: DPX, TIFF, OpenEXR (.RED via RRencode plugin)			
REDcine-X Delivery Formats	1080p RGB 4:2:2, 720p 4:2:2 : QuickTime, JPEG, AVID AAF, MXF			
REDcine-X Delivery Formats	1080p 4:2:0, 720p 4:2:0 : H.264, .MP4			
Video Editing Software Compatibility	Adobe Premiere Pro, AVID Media Composer, DaVinci Resolve, Edius Pro, Final Cut Pro, Vegas Pro			

RED Digital Cinema KOMODO 6K

At the time of publication, RED DIGITAL CINEMA introduced their new RED KOMODO 6K Global Shutter camera with image stabilization.

> Sensor – KOMODO 19.9 MP Super 35mm Global Shutter CMOS
> Effective Photosites – 6144 (h) × 3240 (v)
> Sensor Size – 27.03 × 14.26mm (Diagonal 30.56mm)

Lens Mount Type – RF mount – Accepts Canon RF mount-based lens adaptors for diverse lens choices, supports Canon EF with full electronic communication via compatible, Canon RF mount adapters, and supports mechanically operated RF lenses (electronic control of Canon RF lenses not supported at this time)

> Recording Max Data Rates – Up to 280 MB/s using RED Pro CFast and qualified CFast 2.0 memory cards
> REDCODE Raw Max Frame Rates – 40 fps at 6K 17:9 (6144 × 3240), 50 fps at 6K 2.4:1 (6144 × 2592), 48 fps at 5K 17:9 (5120 × 2700), 60 fps at 4K 17:9 (4096 × 2160), 120 fps at 2K 17:9 (2048 × 1080)
> Playback Frame Rates – Project Time Base: 23.98, 24, 25, 29.97, 30, 50, 59.94, 60 fps, all resolutions

Best Available REDCODE Settings:

> REDCODE HQ, MQ and LQ at 6K 17:9 (6144 × 3240) up to 40 fps
> REDCODE HQ, MQ and LQ at 4K 17:9 (4096 × 2160) up to 60 fps
> REDCODE HQ, MQ and LQ at 2K 17:9 (2048 × 1080) up to 120 fps
> REDCODE Raw Acquisition Formats
> 6K 17:9 (6144 × 3240) 2:4:1 and 16:9
> 5K 17:9 (5120 × 2700)
> 4K 17:9 (4096 × 2160)
> 2K 17:9 (2048 × 1080)
> Apple Prores
> 4K (4096 × 2160) at ProRes 422 HQ and ProRes 422 up to 60 fps
> 2K (2048 × 1080) at ProRes 422 HQ and ProRes 422 up to 120 fps

Color Management – Image Processing Pipeline (IPP2), Supports 33×33×33 3D LUTs, Supports import of CDLs
    Remote Control – Wi-Fi for camera control via interchangeable antenna with SMA connection, Genlock, Timecode-in, GPIO, and Ctrl (RS232)

via the integrated 9-pin EXT port, Wired control via KOMODO Link Adaptor, using USB-C or Gigabit Ethernet (compatible USB-C to Ethernet adapter required) allowing camera control and live MJPEG preview video feed

Monitor Outputs
    Integrated 12G-SDI with 6G-SDI and 3G-SDI modes:

> 12G-SDI: Up to 4096 × 2160 4:2:2 for 60p
> 6G-SDI: Up to 4096 × 2160 4:2:2 for 30p
> 3G-SDI: Up to 2048 × 1080 4:2:2 for 60p
> 1.5G-SDI: Up to 2048 × 1080 4:2:2 for 30p, 24p
> SMPTE Timecode, HANC Metadata, 24-Bit 48kHz Audio

Monitor Options – Integrated 2.9 1440 × 1440 touchscreen LCD with 720p preview and camera control, Wireless live preview video feed via 2.4Ghz/5Ghz WiFi for framing.

REDCODE RAW

REDCODE RAW is the format of choice for DSMC2 and RANGER cameras. RED's versatile raw codec uses wavelet compression with ratios ranging from 2:1 to 22:1, to reduce data rates while maintaining a visually lossless image rendering. R3D files can be edited on many available NLE software programs including Adobe Premiere Pro, Blackmagic Design DaVinci Resolve, Apple Final Cut Pro, and Avid Media Composer without transcoding, and if productions prefer a proxy workflow, ProRes or DNx files can be recorded simultaneously to the MINI-MAG media. Lowering the recording resolution allows the sensor to capture higher frame rates for dramatic slow-motion footage. The DSMC2 and RANGER cameras use sensor windowing to record slow motion in lower resolutions, requiring wider or smaller-format lenses to compensate for the additional crop. Recording rates range from 12 fps and up, including 24/25/30/48/50/60 fps and higher.

RED Digital Cinema IPP2 Color Science

RED's IPP2 color science overhauled the RED image processing pipeline. IPP2 impacts camera firmware, REDCINE-X PRO, and RED's third-party Software Development Kit. Because RED's on camera image processing hardware has been revamped in IPP2, only DSMC2 and RANGER camera bodies benefit from these in-camera features. However, all R3D files can benefit during post-production.

Edge-of-gamut or out-of-gamut colors no longer become overly saturated or intense near the boundaries of a color space. In practice, this means that things like neon signs, tail lights, police lights and lens chromatic aberrations appear more pleasingly saturated and less often as solid blocks of out of gamut color. Highlight roll-off is now adjustable and can be made to be smoother and less abrupt compared to other film or cinematic styles, and better corresponds with maximum pixel intensity under a wide range of ISO speeds. In practice, this is most apparent with clipped background highlights, strong reflections, and shots containing the light source itself. Mid-tone colors become less susceptible to hue shifts during operations such as color space conversion or white balance adjustment. Shadow detail is also better preserved while retaining overall image contrast.

RED converts red, green, and blue photo-site values from the RAW sensor data into full color pixels using a high-quality deBayer or "demosaicking" algorithm that achieves a good combination of detail, low-noise, and speed. IPP2 improves the deBayer algorithm to achieve higher detail at the same pixel resolution.

IPP2 menu function now separates out technical controls that are standardized references that rarely change from the creative controls, which are unique to the colorist/production and which change with every shoot or clip. This allows RED to move toward industry-standard color spaces (such as Rec 709 or Rec 2020), which are better understood and more compatible with a wide variety of workflows. It also allows the creatives to maintain their look in both SDR and HDR without building multiple LUTs. Other unfamiliar controls have either been renamed or removed, such as FLUT (which becomes Exposure Adjustment) or DRX (which is now hidden and enabled by default).

RED's color science previously required specifying both a proprietary color space and gamma, such as REDgamma4 plus DRAGONcolor2. IPP2 is based on a single REDWideGamutRGB (RWG) and Log3G10 specification that remains the same regardless of any downstream changes.

IPP2 supports ASC CDL controls of slope, offset, power, and saturation. Color corrections made with one device can be applied or modified by other devices, on devices from different manufacturers and using different standards.

Apple ProRes and Avid DNx Formats

For projects requiring proxy files or quicker turnaround times than raw files permit, Apple ProRes or Avid DNx formats can be recorded at 4K and 2K resolutions directly to the onboard MINI-MAG media. Since these deBayered video files can be recorded alongside the raw files, no extra time is required for transcoding the proxies. Bring the deBayered files straight into an NLE and begin editing.

Color Management

DSMC2 and RANGER supports 33×33×33, 32×32×32, 26×26×26, and 17×17×17 3D LUTs, with a variable number of 3D LUT outputs using the DSMC2 expander module. Technology employs user-programmable shaper 1D LUTs and Tetrahedral interpolation, 16-bit processing. IPP2 Color Management is also available in camera for the ability to work in SDR and HDR space while leveraging the same creative looks.

Legacy Product Overview

RED WEAPON Dragon (Carbon Fiber/ Magnesium) and SCARLET W Cameras

Figure 9.40 RED WEAPON Dragon 6K brain.

The RED WEAPON 6K boasts features that include blazing fast data transfer rates up to 300 MB/s, and the freedom to simultaneously record in REDCODE® RAW and Apple ProRes or Avid DNxHR/HD file formats.

RED WEAPON 6K with Dragon Sensor is engineered to capture motion and stills in 6K 2.4:1 at up to 100 fps, or 6K full frame at 75 fps. Manufactured with ultra-lightweight carbon fiber – the WEAPON delivers intuitive control and ergonomic design. With the best aspects from EPIC and SCARLET WEAPON features performance enhancements such as on-board Apple ProRes and Avid DNxHR/HD recording, as well as limited 3D LUT support in a smaller modular package.

High Speed up to 100 fps in 6K, 120 fps in 5K and up to 300 fps in 2K, RAW recording at 16-bit, Features include ProRes Recording at 4K and 2K with RAW and ProRes Recording Simultaneously, 3D LUT, 1D LUT capabilities, interchangeable OLPF, Automatic Sensor Calibration (Black Shading), an improved cooling system for quieter camera, two LCD/EVF outputs, and built-in microphones. Improvements in color science render better color reproduction for skin tones, extended highlights, soft roll-off for easier correction of over/underexposure, and improved noise performance.

Table 9.23 RED WEAPON 6K and SCARLET W specifications

RED Digital Cinema WEAPON 6K and SCARLET W

	WEAPON 6K (Carbon Fiber)	SCARLET-W
Sensor	19.4 Megapixel RED DRAGON™	13.8 Megapixel RED DRAGON™
Pixel Array	6144 (h) × 3160 (v)	5120 (h) × 2700 (v)
S/N Ratio	80db	80db
Dynamic Range	16.5+ stops	16.5+ stops
Sensitivity	ISO 250 – 2000 Base Range	ISO 250 – 2000 Base Range
	ISO 250 – 12800 (Metadata)	ISO 250 – 12800 (Metadata)
Lens Coverage	30.7mm (h) × 15.8mm (v) × 34.5mm (d)	25.6mm (h) × 13.5mm (v) × 28.9mm (d)
Lens Mounts	PL	PL
	Canon EF/EF-S	Canon EF/EF-S
	Nikon AF-D/AF-S	Nikon AF-D/AF-S
	Leica M	Leica M
	Motion Mount PL and Canon EF/EF-S	Motion Mount PL and Canon EF/EF-S
Film Format	S35+	
	S35	S35
	A35	A35
	S16	S16
Acquisition Formats	ANAMORPHIC 1.3x and 2x with each format	ANAMORPHIC 1.3x and 2x with each format
	6K RAW	
	5.5K RAW	
	5K RAW	5K RAW
	4.5K RAW	4.5K RAW
	4K RAW	4K RAW
	3.5K RAW	3.5K RAW
	3K RAW	3K RAW
	2.5K RAW	2.5K RAW
	2K RAW	2K RAW
	4K Apple ProRes 422 HQ, up to 29.97 fps	
	4K Apple ProRes 422, up to 29.97 fps	
	4K Apple ProRes 422 LT, up to 29.97 fps	
	2K Apple ProRes 4444 XQ, up to 120 fps	
	2K Apple ProRes 4444, up to 120 fps	
	2K Apple ProRes 422 HQ, up to 120 fps	2K Apple ProRes 422 HQ, up to 60 fps
	2K Apple ProRes 422, up to 120 fps	2K Apple ProRes 422, up to 60 fps
	2K Apple ProRes 422 LT, up to 120 fps	2K Apple ProRes 422 LT, up to 60 fps
	Avid DN×HR (coming soon)	Avid DN×HR (coming soon)
	Avid DN×HD (coming soon)	Avid DN×HD (coming soon)

RED Digital Cinema WEAPON 6K and SCARLET W

	WEAPON 6K (Carbon Fiber)	SCARLET-W
Project Frame Rates	23.98, 24, 25, 29.97, 48, 50, 59.94, all resolutions	23.98, 24, 25, 29.97, 48, 50, 59.94, all resolutions
Recording	REDCODE RAW + QuickTime ProRes simultaneous REDCODE RAW only QuickTime ProRes only	REDCODE RAW + QuickTime ProRes simultaneous REDCODE RAW only QuickTime ProRes only
Max Data Rates	300 MB/s using RED MINI-MAG® (512GB & 1TB) 225 MB/s using RED MINI-MAG (120GB & 240GB)	140 MB/s using RED MINI-MAG®
Max Frame Rates	75 fps at 6K FF and 9:1 REDCODE 100 fps at 6K 2.4:1 and 9:1 REDCODE 96 fps at 5K FF and 8:1 REDCODE 120 fps at 5K 2.4:1 and 8:1 REDCODE 100 fps at 4.5K FF and 7:1 REDCODE 120 fps at 4.5K 2.4:1 and 7:1 REDCODE 120 fps at 4K FF and 6:1 REDCODE 150 fps at 4K 2.4:1 and 9:1 REDCODE 150 fps at 3K FF and 5:1 REDCODE 200 fps at 3K 2.4:1 and 5:1 REDCODE 240 fps at 2K FF and 4:1 REDCODE 300 fps at 2K 2.4:1 and 4:1 REDCODE	50 fps at 5K FF and 9:1 REDCODE 60 fps at 5K 2.4:1 and 9:1 REDCODE 100 fps at 4.5K FF and 14:1 REDCODE 120 fps at 4.5K 2.4:1 and 13:1 REDCODE 120 fps at 4K FF and 13:1 REDCODE 150 fps at 4K 2.4:1 and 15:1 REDCODE 150 fps at 3K FF and 10:1 REDCODE 200 fps at 3K 2.4:1 and 11:1 REDCODE 240 fps at 2K FF and 8:1 REDCODE 300 fps at 2K 2.4:1 and 8:1 REDCODE
REDCODE Settings **Range from 2:1 up to 22:1**	3:1 REDCODE for 6K (6144 × 3160) at 24 fps 7:1 REDCODE for 6K (6144 × 3160) at 60 fps 2:1 REDCODE for 5K (5120 × 2700) at 24 fps 5:1 REDCODE for 5K (5120 × 2700) at 60 fps 2:1 REDCODE for 4K (4096 × 2160) at 24 fps 3:1 REDCODE for 4K (4096 × 2160) at 60 fps	5:1 REDCODE for 5K (5120 × 2700) at 24 fps 9:1 REDCODE for 5K (5120 × 2700) at 48 fps 3:1 REDCODE for 4K (4096 × 2160) at 24 fps 7:1 REDCODE for 4K (4096 × 2160) at 60 fps
Delivery Formats	4K: DPX, TIFF, OpenEXR (RED via RRencode plugin) 2K: DPX, TIFF, OpenEXR (RED via RRencode plugin) 1080p RGB or 4:2:2, 720p 4:2:2: Quicktime, JPEG Avid AAF, MXF. 1080p 4.2.0, 720p 4:2:0: H.264, .MP4	4K: DPX, TIFF, OpenEXR (RED via RRencode plugin) 2K : DPX, TIFF, OpenEXR (RED via RRencode plugin) 1080p RGB or 4:2:2, 720p 4:2:2: Quicktime, JPEG Avid AAF, MXF. 1080p 4.2.0, 720p 4:2:0: H.264, .MP4
Program Output	HD-SDI Clean Feed 2K RGB, 1080p RGB or 4:2:2 720p 4:2:2 SMPTE Timecode, HANC Metadata 24-bit 48Khz Audio	HD-SDI Clean Feed 2K RGB, 1080p RGB or 4:2:2 720p 4:2:2 SMPTE Timecode, HANC Metadata 24-bit 48Khz Audio
Monitor Output	3G-SDI (HD-SDI) and HDMI® with DSMC² expander module 1080p RGB or 4:2:2, 720p RGB or 4:2:2 480p RGB or 4:2:2 (HDMI Only) SMPTE Timecode, HANC Metadata, 24-bit 48 kHz Audio	3G-SDI (HD-SDI) and HDMI® with DSMC² expander module 1080p RGB or 4:2:2, 720p RGB or 4:2:2 480p RGB or 4:2:2 (HDMI Only) SMPTE Timecode, HANC Metadata, 24-bit 48 kHz Audio

(Continued)

Table 9.23 (Continued)

RED Digital Cinema WEAPON 6K and SCARLET W

	WEAPON 6K (Carbon Fiber)	**SCARLET-W**
Digital Media	RED MINI-MAG SSD: 512GB & 1TB, 300 MB/s RED MINI-MAG SSD: 120GB & 240GB, 225 MB/s	RED MINI-MAG SSD: 120GB, 240GB, 512GB, 1TB
Monitoring Options	DSMC RED Touch 7.0" Touch LCD DSMC RED Touch 4.7" Touch LCD DSMC RED EVF(OLED) RED Pro 7" LCD" RED Touch 5", 7", 9" LCD BOMB EVF (LCOS) High Definition Viewfinder BOMB EVF (OLED) High Definition Viewfinder	DSMC RED Touch 7.0" Touch LCD DSMC RED Touch 4.7" Touch LCD DSMC RED EVF(OLED) RED Pro 7" LCD" RED Touch 5", 7", 9" LCD BOMB EVF (LCOS) High Definition Viewfinder BOMB EVF (OLED) High Definition Viewfinder
Color Management	Supports 33×33×33, 32×32×32, 26×26×26, and 17×17×17 3D LUTs Variable number of 3D LUT outputs with DSMC²™ expander module User programmable shaper 1D LUTs Tetrahedral interpolation, 16-bit process	Supports 17×17×17 3D LUTs Variable number of 3D LUT outputs with DSMC²™ expander module User programmable shaper 1D LUTs Tetrahedral interpolation, 16-bit processing
Audio	Integrated dual channel digital stereo microphones, uncompressed, 24-bit 48 kHz Optional 2 channels with DSMC² expander module, uncompressed 24-bit, 48KHz	Integrated dual channel digital stereo microphones, uncompressed, 24-bit 48 kHz Optional 2 channels with DSMC² expander module, uncompressed 24-bit, 48KHz
Remote Control	Integrated REDLINK® WiFi Ethernet, RS232, GPI Trigger	Integrated REDLINK® WiFi Ethernet, RS232, GPI Trigger
Weight	3.3lbs (BRAIN® with Integrated Media Bay)	3.5lbs (BRAIN® with Integrated Media Bay)
Construction	Carbon Fiber, Magnesium, Aluminum Alloy	Aluminium Alloy

Legacy Product Overview

RED Epic Dragon 6K and SCARLET Dragon Cameras

Figure 9.41 RED Epic Dragon 6K BRAIN.

RED Epic Dragon offered increases in both resolution dynamic range and low light capabilities. Improved low-light capabilities that allow cinematographers to shoot at ISO 2000 and still produce a clean image fit for theatrical exhibition. Improved color science renders skin tones that are softer, and primary colors that are more saturated.

The Epic-M weighs in at 5lbs with a 6k Dragon sensor and an advanced image processor. The camera has even more dynamic range available in the HDRx mode. In this mode, the camera captures two simultaneous images of identical resolution and frame rate, but at different shutter angles. One image protects highlights; the other protects shadows.

The camera comes with a 5" touchscreen monitor, and an intuitive graphic user interface. Assistants can control the camera with the REDmote (a controller that can be wirelessly operated or docked on the camera). It records on RED Mini-Mag SSD digital media; camera speeds up to 100 fps in 6K, 120 fps in RAW Recording 16-bit at 5K, and up to 300 fps in 2K.

Table 9.24 RED Epic Dragon and SCARLET Dragon specifications

	RED Digital Cinema Epic Dragon and SCARLET Dragon	
	Epic Dragon	**SCARLET Dragon**
Sensor	RED DRAGON	RED DRAGON
Pixel Array	6144 (h) × 3160 (v)	6144 (h) × 3160 (v)
S/N Ratio	80db	80db
Sensitivity	ISO 250 – 2000 Base Range ISO 250 – 12800 (Metadata)	ISO 250 – 2000 Base Range ISO 250 – 12800 (Metadata)
Lens Coverage	30.7mm (h) × 15.8mm (v) × 34.5mm (d)	30.7mm (h) × 15.8mm (v) × 34.5mm (d)
Lens Mounts	PL Canon EF/EF-S Nikon AF-D/AF-S Leica M Motion Mount PL and Canon EF/EF-S	PL Canon EF/EF-S Nikon AF-D/AF-S Leica M Motion Mount PL and Canon EF/EF-S
Depth of Field	Equivalent to S35mm (Motion) APS-H (Still) lenses Equivalent to 16mm (Motion) in 2K RAW	Equivalent to S35mm (Motion) APS-H (Still) lenses Equivalent to 16mm (Motion) in 2K RAW
Acquisition Formats	6K RAW 5.5K RAW 5K RAW 4.5K RAW 4K RAW 3.5K RAW 3K RAW 2.5K RAW 2K RAW	6K RAW 5K RAW 4K RAW 3K RAW 2K RAW
Project Frame Rates	23.98, 24, 25, 29.97, 48, 50, 59.94, all resolutions	23.98, 24, 25, 29.97, 48, 50, 59.94, all resolutions
Delivery Formats	4K: DPX, TIFF, OpenEXR (RED Ray via optional encoder) 2K: DPX, TIFF, OpenEXR (RED RAY via optional encoder) 1080p RGB or 4:2:2, 720p 4:2:2: Quicktime, JPEG Avid AAF, MXF. 1080p 4.2.0, 720p 4:2:0: H.264, .MP4	4K: DPX, TIFF, OpenEXR (RED Ray via optional encoder) 2K: DPX, TIFF, OpenEXR (RED RAY via optional encoder) 1080p RGB or 4:2:2, 720p 4:2:2: Quicktime, JPEG Avid AAF, MXF. 1080p 4.2.0, 720p 4:2:0: H.264, .MP4
Program Output	HD-SDI Clean Feed 2K RGB, 1080p RGB or 4:2:2 720p 4:2:2 SMPTE Timecode, HANC Metadata 24-bit 48Khz Audio	HD-SDI Clean Feed 2K RGB, 1080p RGB or 4:2:2 720p 4:2:2 SMPTE Timecode, HANC Metadata 24-bit 48Khz Audio
Monitor Output	HD-SDI and HDMI with Frame Guides and Look Around 2K RGB 1080p RGB or 4:2:2 720p RGB or 4:2:2 SMPTE Timecode HANC Metadata 24-bit 48Khz Audio	HD-SDI and HDMI with Frame Guides and Look Around 2K RGB 1080p RGB or 4:2:2 720p RGB or 4:2:2 SMPTE Timecode HANC Metadata 24-bit 48Khz Audio

(Continued)

Table 9.24 (Continued)

	RED Digital Cinema Epic Dragon and SCARLET Dragon	
	Epic Dragon	**SCARLET Dragon**
Digital Media	RED MINI-MAG SSD: 512GB (fastest media, less compression at high fps) REDMAG 1.8" SSD Module: (48, 64, 128, 240, 256, 512GB Media)	RED MINI-MAG SSD: 512GB (fastest media, less compression at high fps) REDMAG 1.8" SSD Module: (48, 64, 128, 240, 256, 512GB Media)
REDCODE™	16-bit RAW:	16-bit RAW:
fps	Compression choices of 18:1 to 2:1 1–100 fps 6K 1–110 fps 5.5K 1–120 fps 5K 1–134 fps 4.5K 1–150 fps 4K 1–172 fps 3.5K 1–200 fps 3K 1–237 fps 2.5K 1–300 fps 2K	Compression choices of 18:1 to 2:1 6K FF: 12 fps (in Burst mode) 5K FF: 48 fps 4K FF: 60 fps 3K FF: 80 fps 2K FF: 120 fps 5K 2.4:1: 60 fps 4K 2.4:1: 75 fps 3K 2.4:1: 100 fps 2K 2.4:1: 150 fps
Audio	2 channel, uncompressed, 24 bit, 48KHz Optional 4 channel and AES/EBU digital audio	2 channel, uncompressed, 24-bit, 48KHz Optional 4 channel and AES/EBU digital audio
Monitoring Options	RED LCD 5", 9" Touchscreen Display BOMB EVF™ High Definition Viewfinder	RED LCD 5", 9 Touchscreen Display BOMB EVF™ High Definition Viewfinder
Remote Control	REDLINK Wireless, Ethernet, RS232, GPI Trigger	REDLINK Wireless, Ethernet, RS232, GPI Trigger
Weight	5lbs Body only	5lbs Body only
Construction	Aluminium Alloy	Aluminium Alloy

Legacy Product Overview

RED Epic Mysterium-X Cameras: Epic M-X, Epic M-X Monochrome

Figure 9.42 RED Epic Mysterium-X camera.

RED Epic M-X is a Super 35mm 4520 × 2540 photosite sensor camera that can shoot up to 120 fps at 5k raw Bayer resolution and up to 300 fps at 2k raw Bayer resolution. HDRx mode allows cinematographers to dial in up to six more stops of highlight protection above the native range of the camera. REDCODE 12:1 allows the cinematographer to shoot two hours of 5k raw material on a 256gb SSD drive, while REDCODE 3:1 yields visually lossless raw. Adobe Premiere, After Effects, and SONY Vegas allow drag and drop editing of raw files, while Apple Final Cut requires transcoding to ProRes codec. RED Epic's acquisition formats include 4.5K (at 2.4:1), 4K (at 16 × 9, 2:1, and Anamorphic 2:1), 3K (at 16 × 9, 2:1, and Anamorphic 2:1), and 2K (at 16 × 9, 2:1, and Anamorphic 2:1). Its delivery formats include full 4K 4:4:4 RGB, 1080P, 720P and all other standard formats available in supported post-production software.

Epic accepts most ARRI PL mount lenses and ARRI accessories interchangeably with a titanium PL mount. Depth of field is equivalent to S35mm film with cine lenses, (or S16mm with windowed sensor at higher frame rates).

Epic has two monitoring options, either the RED-LCD High Resolution Monitor, or RED-EVF color electronic viewfinder. Viewing options include video preview, HD-SDI and HDMI preview including Look Around, 1280 × 720 progressive, 4:2:2.

Electronic shutter is adjustable from 1/6000th second to 360 degrees variable, and available frame rates are up to 30 fps at 4K, up to 60 fps at 3K (windowed sensor area), and up to 120 fps at 2K (windowed sensor area).

The camera records to proprietary Redmag (SSD) digital magazines or Redflash (CF) options, which require compatible software for download and implementation.

Epic Mysterium-X is also available in a monochrome version.

Legacy Product Overview

RED SCARLET M-X Camera

Figure 9.43 RED SCARLET M-X camera.

Table 9.25 RED Epic M-X and SCARLET M-X specifications

	RED Digital Cinema Epic and SCARLET M-X	
Sensor	Epic Mysterium-X (Super 35mm)	SCARLET Mysterium-X (Super 35mm)
Pixel Array	5120 (h) × 2700 (v)	5120 (h) × 2700 (v)
S/N Ratio	66db	66db
Sensitivity	ISO 800 Base ISO 250 – 12800 (Metadata)	ISO 800 Base ISO 250 – 12800 (Metadata)
Lens Coverage	27.7mm (h) × 14.6mm (v) × 31.4mm (d)	27.7mm (h) × 14.6mm (v) × 31.4mm (d)
Lens Mounts	PL Canon EF/EF-S Nikon AF-D/AF-S Leica M	PL Canon EF/EF-S Nikon AF-D/AF-S Leica M
Depth of Field	Equivalent to S35mm (Motion) APS-H (Still) lenses Equivalent to 16mm (Motion) in 2K RAW	Equivalent to S35mm (Motion) / APS-H (Still) lenses Equivalent to 16mm (Motion) in 2K RAW
Acquisition Formats	5K RAW 4K RAW 3K RAW 2K RAW 1K RAW	5K RAW 4K RAW 3K RAW 2K RAW 1K RAW
Project Frame Rates	23.98, 24, 25, 29.97, 48, 50, 59.94, all resolutions	23.98, 24, 25, 29.97, 48, 50, 59.94, all resolutions
Delivery Formats	4K: DPX, TIFF, OpenEXR (RED Ray via optional encoder) 2K : DPX, TIFF, OpenEXR (RED RAY via optional encoder) 1080p RGB or 4:2:2, 720p 4:2:2 : Quicktime, JPEG Avid AAF, MXF. 1080p 4.2.0, 720p 4:2:0 : H.264, .MP4	4K: DPX, TIFF, OpenEXR (RED Ray via optional encoder) 2K : DPX, TIFF, OpenEXR (RED RAY via optional encoder) 1080p RGB or 4:2:2, 720p 4:2:2 : Quicktime, JPEG Avid AAF, MXF. 1080p 4.2.0, 720p 4:2:0 : H.264, .MP4
Program Output	HD-SDI Clean Feed 2K RGB, 1080p RGB or 4:2:2 720p 4:2:2 SMPTE Timecode, HANC Metadata 24-bit 48Khz Audio	HD-SDI Clean Feed 2K RGB, 1080p RGB or 4:2:2 720p 4:2:2 SMPTE Timecode, HANC Metadata 24-bit 48Khz Audio

(Continued)

Table 9.25 (Continued)

	RED Digital Cinema Epic and SCARLET M-X	
Sensor	**Epic Mysterium-X** (Super 35mm)	**SCARLET Mysterium-X** (Super 35mm)
Monitor Output	HD-SDI and HDMI with Frame Guides and Look Around	HD-SDI and HDMI with Frame Guides and Look Around
	2K RGB 1080p RGB or 4:2:2	2K RGB 1080p RGB or 4:2:2
	720p RGB or 4:2:2	720p RGB or 4:2:2
	SMPTE Timecode	SMPTE Timecode
	HANC Metadata	HANC Metadata
	24-bit 48Khz Audio	24-bit 48Khz Audio
Digital Media	REDMAG 1.8" SSD Module: (64, 128, 256, 512GB Media)	REDMAG 1.8" SSD Module: (64, 128, 256, 512GB Media)
REDCODE™	16-bit RAW: Compression choices of 18:1 to 3:1 1–120 fps 5K 1–120 fps 4K 1–160 fps 3K 1–300 fps 2K 1–400 fps 1K	16-bit RAW: Compression choices of 18:1 to 3:1 1–12 fps 5K FF 1–30 fps 4K 1–48 fps 3K 1–60 fps 1080p HD 1–120 fps 1K
Audio	2 channel, uncompressed, 24-bit, 48KHz Optional 4 channel and AES/EBU digital audio	2 channel, uncompressed, 24-bit, 48KHz Optional 4 channel and AES/EBU digital audio
Monitoring Options	RED LCD 5", 9" Touchscreen Display BOMB EVF™ High Definition Viewfinder	RED LCD 5", 9" Touchscreen Display BOMB EVF™ High Definition Viewfinder
Remote Control	REDLINK Wireless, Ethernet, RS232, GPI Trigger	REDLINK Wireless, Ethernet, RS232, GPI Trigger
Weight	5lbs Body only	5lbs Body only
Construction	Aluminium Alloy	Aluminium Alloy

The RED SCARLET-X camera has the ability to capture 5K stills and 4.5K motion, utilizing HDRx and interchangeable lens mounts. Capture with 5K burst modes that snap up to 12 frames per second and 4K reaching up to 30 frames per second. HDRx technology yields up to 18 stops of dynamic range, broadening exposure latitude in challenging lighting conditions.

RED's SCARLET-X comes standard with Canon EF and PL mount options, providing convenient access to a familiar arsenal of lenses. SCARLET-X makes it easy to stay sharp with interchangeable lens mounts, so Leica, Canon, and even Nikon lenses will all be available for use.

Redmag SSD provides media solutions with storage capacities from 32GB to 512GB. Capable of reaching speeds up to 180 MB/s, Redmag media

is 2 times faster than traditional CF cards – making it easier to offload the 160,000+ REDCODE Raw frames captured with one SSD.

SONY

Figure 9.44

*Source:*https://pro.sony/ue_US/products/digital-cinema-cameras

SONY VENICE

Figure 9.45 SONY VENICE.

SONY VENICE features a full-frame 36 × 24-mm sensor that captures images up to a maximum resolution of 6048 × 4032. In full-frame mode the 6048 photosite width of the sensor accommodates shooting modes at 3:2, 2.39:1, 1.85:1, 17:9, and 16.9 for shallow depth of field and use of super wide angle lenses.

VENICE is capable of High Dynamic Range imaging, and its sensor color capability exceeds ITU-R-BT.2020 color space, wider than DCI-P3 to reproduce very saturated colors. This also provides the broad palette in the grading suite using the established workflow of SONY's third-generation LOG gamma encoding (S-Log3) and ultra-wide color space (S-Gammut3). VENICE's high-speed readout sensor minimizes rolling shutter jello effect typical in CMOS sensors.

VENICE has a Dual ISO feature. A Low ISO of 500 provides the optimal dynamic range for typical cinematography applications with on-set lighting. A secondary High Base ISO of 2500 excels in low-light high dynamic range capture, useful when using slow lenses or shooting dimly lit environments (a firmware update may be required to activate this feature).

VENICE comes stock with a PL lens mount. It is compatible with all Super 35mm and full-frame PL mount lenses, spherical and anamorphic (with additional license). The lens mount includes contacts that support /i Technology. Lens information is recorded as metadata frame by frame. Cinematographers can also choose E-mount lenses and, via third-party adaptors, the world of SLR and rangefinder lenses. Standard Lever Lock E-mount operation provides added security with large lenses, and in most cases lens support rigs don't need to be removed when changing lens. Users can switch from Lever Lock E-mount to PL Mount by removing six hex screws. E-mount

lens iris operation is controllable with an assignable button.

The full 6K resolution of the camera can be recorded directly in X-OCN (16-bit eXtended tonal range Original Camera Negative) file format onto AXS Memory cards. Also, XAVC 4K can be captured onto SxS cards while still sampling from the full 6K resolution of the sensor.

VENICE uses a fully modular design and even the sensor block is interchangeable. In order to maintain ergonomic balance for operators, the top handle and viewfinder are adjustable. As the height of the camera from the bottom to the optical center of the lens mount is the same as the F55, base plates and other accessories used for the F55 can be used with VENICE. The AXS-R7 recorder can be attached to VENICE with four screws.

VENICE features a servo-controlled 8-step mechanical ND filter mechanism built into the camera chassis that offers an ND range of 0.3 (1/2 = 1 stop) to ND2.4 (1/256 = 8 stops) and that increases flexibility when being controlled remotely on drones and cranes, or in an underwater housing.

Control buttons are positioned for intuitive operation and illuminated for easy use on dark sets. There are control panels on both sides of the camera, with the main display positioned on the camera outside for fast access to redesigned camera menus by the camera assistant while shooting. A select fps function lets cinematographers choose frame rates from 1 frame per second to 120 fps (requires separate license), depending on imager mode. The camera operator's OLED mini display allows intuitive control of commonly accessed features, and on-set monitoring operation benefits from an extra HD output alongside the standard 12G-SDI (capable of 4K content on a single BNC cable). VENICE provides up to 4.0× high resolution magnification of the viewfinder image for best focus accuracy. In Surround View mode, the viewfinder and on-set monitors can display a 5% look around margin around the area being recorded. Surround View is available on 3.8K 16:9, 4K 17:9, and 4K 4:3 imager modes on VF, SDI 1/2/3/4, and HD monitor outputs. Maximum supported frame rates are up to 29.97 fps (project) and 48 fps (variable).

The DVF-EL200 1920 × 1080 OLED viewing panel enables precise, high-resolution focusing and framing, including false color display. A rotary encoder provides access to brightness, peaking contrast, and VF menu setting. An ergonomic design allows for quick, tool-free attachment/detachment and reconfiguring. The industry-standard LEMO connector offers exceptional durability.

VENICE can load and store up to 16 user-generated LUTs (Look Up Tables, 33 grids cube file). High key/low key viewing mode makes it easy to judge exposure settings by using an assigned button to cycle in Base ISO 500 from normal exposure to 64 EI to 1000 EI, and also to cycle in Base ISO 2500 from normal exposure to 320 EI to 5000 EI and then back to normal on the VF and monitor.

Wired or wireless LAN control the VENICE from a PC or Mac using a web browser and ethernet cable or USB dongle adaptor, CBK-WA02. To control multiple cameras, add an ethernet router. Users can control Record Start/Stop, Assignable Buttons and Frames per Second, Exposure Index, Shutter, ND Filter White Balance and all menu settings.

Internally, VENICE supports XAVC, ProRes or MPEG HD recording onto an SxS memory card. Additionally, by using the AXS-R7 recorder, it can record 16-bit RAW or X-OCN (16-bit eXtended tonal range Original Camera Negative) onto AXS memory card. XAVC is the most high performance implementation of H.264/AVC intra-frame coding. VENICE supports XAVC Class 480, the highest bitrate and quality available. Apple ProRes and ProRes 422 proxy formats are popular in postproduction and are supported by VENICE and can be transcoded directly from the camera. 16-bit eXtended tonal range Original Camera Negative (X-OCN) linear RAW format preserves all the information captured in 6K or 4K. 16-bit X-OCN offers significant file size reduction, which makes working with full resolution content from VENICE's 6K sensor more practical in terms of file transfer times and storage requirements. X-OCN is supported by leading non-linear editing software tools such as Adobe Premiere CC, AMA plug-in for AVID now provided by NABLET, Blackmagic DaVinci Resolve, Colorfront OSD, FilmLight Baselight, and others.

VENICE is capable of simultaneous recording using two record media. For example, a production could use RAW/X-OCN data recorded by AXS-R7 for online editing and also use XAVC, Apple ProRes or MPEG HD for offline editing without waiting for any file conversion. VENICE can also record XAVC 4K and RAW/X-OCN simultaneously. Another option would be to use XAVC 4K for quick turnaround production while using simultaneous recording RAW/X-OCN as a future-proof archive suitable for high quality HDR applications. Even without using AXS-R7, VENICE itself can record XAVC 4K and Apple ProRes 422 Proxy simultaneously.

Table 9.26 SONY VENICE specifications

SONY	VENICE MPC-3610
Sensor	Full-frame CMOS image sensor
Sensor Size	36.0 × 24.0mm. 43.3mm (diagonal).
Photosites	24.8M (total), 24.4M (effective)
Gamma Curve	S-Log3
Built-In ND Filters	Clear, 0.3(1/2), 0.6(1/4), 0.9(1/8), 1.2(1/16), 1.5(1/32), 1.8(1/64), 2.1(1/128), 2.4(1/256)
ISO Sensitivity	ISO 500, and ISO 2500
White Balance	2000~15000Kelvin and Green/Magenta adjust, AWB
Lens Mount	E-mount (lever lock type, without supplied PL lens mount adaptor)
Select fps	Imager mode:
	4K 2.39:1 1–120 fps, 4K 17:9 1–110 fps, 3.8K 16:9 1–60 fps
	4K 4:3 1–75 fps, 4K 6:5 1–30 fps
	6K 2.39:1 1–90 fps, 6K 17:9/1.85:1 1–72 fps, 5.7K 16:9 1–30 fps
	6K 3:2 1–60 fps
Recording Formats (Video)	XAVC 4K Class480: 23.98p, 24p, 25p, 29.97p
	XAVC 4K Class300: 23.98p, 24p, 25p, 29.97p, 50p, 59.94p
	XAVC QFHD Class480: 23.98p, 25p, 29.97p
	XAVC QFHD Class300: 23.98p, 25p, 29.97p, 50p, 59.94p

SONY	VENICE MPC-3610
	MPEG HD422(1920x1080): 23.98p, 24p, 25p, 29.97p, 50i, 59.94i
	HD ProRes 422HQ*: 23.98p, 24p, 25p, 29.97p, 50p, 59.94p, 50i, 60i
	HD ProRes 422*: 23.98p, 24p, 25p, 29.97p, 50p, 59.94p, 50i, 59.94i
	HD ProRes 422 Proxy*: 23.98p, 24p, 25p, 29.97p, 50p, 59.94p, 50i, 59.94i
	HD ProRes 4444: 23.98p,24p,25p,29.97p
Recording Format (RAW/X-OCN) *required AXS-R7	RAW SQ:
	4K 17:9 (4096 × 2160): 23.98p, 24p, 25p, 29.97p, 50p, 59.94p
	3.8K 16:9 (3840 × 2160): 23.98p, 24p, 25p, 29.97p, 50p, 59.94p
	X-OCN XT/ST/LT:
	6K 3:2 (6048 × 4032): 23.98p, 24p, 25p
	6K 2.39:1 (6048 × 2534): 23.98p, 24p, 25p, 29.97p
	6K 1.85:1 (6054 × 3272): 23.98p, 24p, 25p, 29.97p
	6K 17:9 (6054 × 3192): 23.98p, 24p, 25p, 29.97p
	5.7K 16:9 (5674 × 3192): 23.98p, 24p, 25p, 29.97p
	4K 6:5 (4096 × 3432): 23.98p, 24p, 25p, 29.97p
	4K 4:3 (4096 × 3024): 23.98p, 24p, 25p*, 29.97p*
	4K 17:9 (4096 × 2160): 23.98p, 24p, 25p, 29.97p, 50p, 59.94p
	4K 2.39:1: 23.98p,24p,25p,29.97p,50p,59.94p
Recording Format (Audio)	LPCM 4ch , 24-bit 48-kHz
SDI Output	BNC×4, (12G, 6G, 3G, 1.5G-SDI)
HD MONI Output	BNC×1 (3G, 1.5G-SDI)
HDMI Output	Type A ×1
VF Output	LEMO 26pin
Audio Input	XLR-type 5pin (female) x1 (LINE/ AES/EBU/MIC/MIC+48V selectable)
Timecode Input	BNC ×1
Genlock Input	BNC ×1
AUX	LEMO 5pin (female) ×1 (Timecode Output)
Remote Connector	8-pin ×1
Lens Connector	12-pin ×1
Lens Mount Hot Shoe	4-pin ×2, conforming to Cooke /ï Intelligent Electronic Lens System
Network	RJ-45 type ×1, 10BASE-T, 100BASE-TX
USB	USB host, type-A x1
Media type	ExpressCard/34 SxS Pro+ & SxS PROX ×2
	SD card slot ×1
Power Requirements	DC12V (11~17.0V)
	DC24V (22~32.0V)
DC Input	XLR-type 4-pin (male)
DC Output	12V: Hirose 4pin x1
	24V: Fischer 3pin x2
Weight	Approx. 3.9kg (8lb 10oz) (without lens, handle, VF attachment expansion bottom plate and accessories)
Dimensions	158 × 147 × 235 mm (6 1/4 × 5 7/8 × 9 3/8 inch) (excluding protrusions)

SONY F65

The F65 was designed with 8K resolution and 16-bit linear raw recording F65's sensor has 20 million photosites. Where the typical 4K sensor has half as many green photosites as there are 4K output pixels, the F65's sensor has a one-to-one ratio: one green photosite for each pixel of the 4K output image. This "Zig-Zag" sampling structure results in greater image sharpness, including full 4K resolution on the all-important green channel.

The F65's raw files contain full bandwidth data from the camera's sensor, and 16-bit linear recording equates to 65,536 shades each of the red, green, and blue channels. The F65 was built from the ground up to work in a 16-bit half-float ACES pipeline. The F65's raw recording maintains all the potential of the latent image and preserves the integrity of the camera master all the way into the archive, where the images will retain the resolution and color they had when captured. The SONY F65 features a proprietary color management system so that the F65 exceeds the gamut for color negative film in every direction.

The ACES workflow protects color integrity with a series of open source, non-destructive, unambiguous transforms. The input device transform (IDT), look modification transform (LMT), reference rendering transform (RRT), and output device transform (ODT) components of ACES all work together to reliably convey the cinematographer's intent from acquisition through post production and into distribution.

The F65's raw files maintain flexibility in output resolution. F65 super sampled images deliver higher contrast at high frequencies, for a noticeably sharper picture. F65 can deliver a super-sampled HD master with detail far beyond the reach of conventional HD cameras, with 20 million photosites, the F65 records a tremendous overhead in resolution. From the original image, the cinematographer can "punch in," reframing a shot after the fact to remove stands, cards, and mic booms. For shots marred by camera shake, cinematographers can use the extra resolution to perform image stabilization or extract high quality 2K and HD quadrants from anywhere within the 4K picture.

The F65 records to SONY's SRMASTER platform that includes field recorders, studio decks, a transfer station and SRMemory cards. About the size of a smart phone, the SRMemory card delivers a sustained write speed of 5.5 Gbps at a maximum capacity of 1 Terabyte and is also available in capacities of 256 GB and 512 GB. The SR-R4 dockable recorder for the F65 is part of a comprehensive workflow system that includes a studio deck and transfer stations as well as SRMemory cards.

The F65 acquires at the native 1.9:1 aspect ratio of the DCI projection standard (4096 × 2160 or 2048 × 1080). This format enables a choice of picture composition from 1.85:1, 1.78:1, 1.66:1, 1.33:1, 2.35 spherical, 1.3× anamorphic, or 2× anamorphic cropped.

To support slow motion and fast motion, the F65 provides over and under cranking at frame rates of 1 to 60 frames per second (4K×2K resolution), and up to 120 frames per second, and in both modes, users get high-speed shots without a "windowing," crop factor or change of effective focal length.

CMOS sensor cameras are frequently prone to rolling shutter artifacts, where the exposure timing of each row of pixels is slightly offset from the next. Rolling shutter artifacts are especially troublesome in 3D mirror rigs, where one camera shoots through a beam splitter and the other camera shoots a reflection off of the beam splitter. When artifacts in the left camera don't match those in the right, the disparities can make the resulting 3D images painful to watch. Rolling shutter also incurs "flash banding" where a strobe light illuminates only a horizontal band across the frame. As with other SONY cameras, the F65 uses an advanced CMOS design to reduce rolling shutter artifacts to a bare minimum, and the F65 mechanical shutter eliminates rolling shutter artifacts entirely.

Table 9.27 SONY F65 specifications

SONY	F65
Sensor	Super 35-mm CMOS image sensor
Sensor Size	17:9 – 24.7 × 13.1mm (1" × 1/2"), diagonal 28.0mm (1 1/8")
Photosites	8192 × 2160 – 20 million photosites
Exposure Index/ISO	Native ISO800
	Assignable; 200EI, 250EI, 320EI, 400EI, 500EI, 640EI, 800EI, 1000EI, 1250EI, 1600EI, 2000EI, 2500EI, 3200EI
Notable Features	Mechanical Shutter
	Internal ND Filters
	S-LOG gamma and 709 (800%) gamma for monitors
	Built to monitor output to 16 bit ACES proxy and ACES RRT
	Wide Gamut Primaries beyond the capabilities of film
	Compatible with film-camera accessories
	Viewfinder contrast function remaps viewable exposure range for low light or high light viewing
Frame Rates	1 to 60 fps (4K × 2K resolution), 1 – 120 fps (4K × 1K resolution)
	Progressive Mode23.98p, 24p, 25p, 29.97p, 59.94p
Shutter	4.2° to 360° (Electrical shutter), 11.2° to 180° (Mechanical rotary shutter)
Lens Mount	PL Mount, 52mm flange depth (±0.04 mm adjustable in 0.01 mm increments by shim replacement)
Viewfinder	DVF-EL100, 0.7" 1280 × 720 OLED
	DVF-L350, 3.5" 960 × 540 LCD
	DVF-L700, 7" 1920 × 1080 LCD
Controls	Basic settings of the camera settings can be performed using subdisplay. Items set on the subdisplay can also be set using the VF menu.
	If camera is used with optional Wi-Fi adapter, menus can be displayed on a tablet device, such as an iPad, via a wireless LAN. The settings displayed are almost identical to the display in the viewfinder or on a monitor.
	Video format, Shutter value, ND filter, Sensitivity (EI value), Highlight latitude, Color temperature, Look-up table (LUT)
Onboard Recording	SR-R4 SRMASTER Memory recorder
	16-bit linear raw recording
	12-bit SR Codec recording 880 Mbps (4:4:4 RGB HQ mode) of 1080p high definition
	10-bit SR Codec recording of 1080p high definition
	880 Mbps (4:4:4 RGB HQ mode)
	440 Mbps (4:2:2 YCbCr and 4:4:4 RGB SQ mode)
	220 Mbps (4:2:2 YCbCr SR Lite mode)
	Selectable fps (Slow & Quick motion)
	4Kx2K (4096 × 2160): up to 60 fps
	4Kx1K (4096 × 1080): up to 120 fps
Connectors	BNC (×2), HD-SDI signal, 4:2:2, BTA-S004A-compliant, 75 Ω, 0.8 Vp-p, 1.485 Gbps BNC (×1), 75 Ω, 1.0 Vp-p BNC (×1)
	HD-Y OUT BNC type (1), 75 ohms, 1.0 Vp-p
	Viewfinder 20 pin (×1)
	Lens12-pin (×1)
	Lens Mount Hot Shoe 4-pin (2), conforming to ARRI LDS (Lens Data System) and Cooke /ᵢ Intelligent Electronic Lens System

(*Continued*)

Table 9.27 (Continued)

SONY	F65
	Type A, USB2.0 Hi-Speed (2)
	Network RJ-45 type (1), 10BASE-T, 100BASE-TX
	REMOTE 8-pin (1)
SD Card	Supports "Memory Stick Duo", "Memory Stick PRO Duo" Supports SD memory cards, SDHC memory cards up to class 10
GENLOCK IN	BNC type (1), 75 ohms, SMPTE 274M
	HD 3-level sync, 0.6 Vp-p
	Or HD-SDI
Power In	LEMO 8-pin male (×1), DC 10.5V to 17V, 20V to 30V
Power Out	12V: 11-pin (×1), DC 12V, 4 A maximum 24V: 3-pin (×1),
	DC 24V, 4 A maximum (The usable current may be limited depending on the load and input conditions.)
Weight	11lbs (5.0kg) without included accessories. 14lbs 5oz (6.5kg) with included accessories.
Dimensions	W226.7 (9) × D254.5 (10 1/8) × H203 (8) without included accessories.

SONY PMW-F55

Figure 9.47 SONY F55.

The SONY PMW-F55 camera gives cinematographers options for HD, 2K, or 4K acquisition and production with a 4K Super 35mm image sensor with 4096 × 2160 resolution without an external recorder. Its 4K image sensor incorporates an electronic global shutter removing CMOS rolling shutter artifacts. The F55 offers modular design, OLED viewfinder and PL lens mount. This multi codec camera from SONY offers a diversity of recording modes, integrating an XAVC codec for 4K and HFR shooting as well as the HD422 50Mbps HDTV standard. It also features 16-bit linear raw for 2K/4K recording and high-speed shooting at up to 240fps.

F55 offers multi-codec support featuring SONY's XAVC MPEG-4 AVC/H.264 format, the SR codec (MPEG4 SStP) and the industry-standard High Definition XDCAM 50Mbps 4:2:2 codec. In-camera recording is on SONY's SxS media, SxS PRO+ (Plus), which can be used to record XAVC in HD High Frame Rate and in 4K at up to 60 fps in the PMW-F55.

In addition to on-board recording onto SxS PRO+, the PMW-F55 can be connected to the AXS-R7 and the AXS-R5 raw recorder. Slow-motion imagery at up to 240 fps can be captured as 2K raw files on AXS memory cards. F55 can capture up to 120 fps in 4K mode when connected to the AXS-R7.

The PMW-F55 camera includes a PL-mount adaptor so that users can choose cinematic lenses from suppliers such as Angenieux, ARRI, Canon, Carl Zeiss, Cooke, FUJIFILM, and Leica. Removing the supplied PL-mount adaptor reveals the native FZ mount that makes it easy to use adaptors for third-party lenses, including Canon EF, Canon FD, Nikon DX, Nikon G, Leica M, and even 2/3-inch B4 lenses. Another option is the use of SONY FZ-Mount lenses with auto focus, servo, and zoom.

PMW-F55 uses SONY OLED and LCD viewfinders. The DVF-EL100 OLED viewfinder measures 0.7-inches with 1280 × 720 HD resolution. The DVF-EL200 OLED viewfinder measures 0.7-inches with 1920 × 1080 HD resolution. The DVF-L350 3.5-inch LCD viewfinder offers 10 times the contrast of previous SONY LCD viewfinders, with a flip-up eyepiece for direct monitoring. A fourth option is the full HD DVF-L700. This compact 7-inch LCD viewfinder enables high resolution when shooting in 2K and 4K, with pixel-to-pixel 1920 × 1080 representation of HD images.

AXSM Access Memory System for 2K/4K raw recording is based on SONY's recording technology with AXSM memory cards (512 GB capacity, model AXS-A512S48), using the generic file system exFAT. Users can record 4K raw data up to 120 fps and 2K raw up to 240 fps, with 600 MB/s sustained transfer speed. PC-friendly operation is enabled through use of the AXS-CR1 card reader, offering a USB 3.0 interface and the AXS-AR1 card reader, offering a Thunderbolt 2 interface. The AXS-R5 and AXS-R7 raw recorder directly docks onto the PMW-F55, for 2K and 4K raw recording.

Table 9.28 SONY PMW F55 specifications

SONY	PMW-F55
Sensor	Super 35-mm CMOS image sensor
Sensor Size	23.6mm × 13.3mm
Photosites	4096 × 2160
Exposure Index/ISO	1250 in S-Log3
Notable Features	Internal 4K/2K/HD Recording
	Optional AXS-R5/AXS-R7 dockable Recorder
	Wider Color Gamut than Film
	Internal ND filters
	SxS Pro+ Media Cards
Frame Rates	High Frame Rate 4K/QFHD XAVC up to 60p
	High Frame Rate 2K/HD XAVC up to 180p
	2K XAVC: 1-180 fps internal, 2K raw: 1-240 fps with AXS-R5/R7 outboard recorder
	XAVC HD: 1-60p
	XAVC 4K: 4096 × 2160 at 23.98p, 25p, 29.97p, 50p, 59.94p
	XAVC QFHD: 3840 × 2160 at 23.98p, 25p, 29.97p, 50p, 59.94p
	XAVC 2K: 2048 × 1920 at 23.98p, 24p, 25p, 29.97p, 50p, 59.94p
	XAVC HD: 1920 × 1080 at 23.98p, 25p, 29.97p, 50p, 59.94p
	MPEG4 SStP: 1920 × 1080, 23.98p/24p/25p/29.97p
	MPEG2 HD: 1920 × 1080 at 50i, 59.94i, 23.98p, 25p, 29.97p
Shutter	Electronic Global Shutter 1/24s to 1/6,000s 4.2 – 360°(electronic shutter)
Lens Mount	Native FZ-mount (includes PL Mount adapter)
Viewfinder	DVF-EL100, 0.7" 1280 × 720 OLED
	DVF-EL100, 0.7" 1920 × 1080 OLED
	DVF-L350, 3.5" 960 × 540 LCD
	DVF-L700, 7" 1920× 1080 LCD
Controls	F55 simplified interface for a range of controls with direct, one-touch access to key shooting parameters – frame rate, shutter speed, color temperature, ISO sensitivity and gamma, with assignable buttons
Onboard Recording	Using SxS Pro+ Media Cards
	4K XAVC 422 10-bit (intern)
	QFHD XAVC 422 10-bit (intern)
	2K XAVC 422 10-bit
	HD MPEG2 422 8-bit
	HD XAVC 422 10-bit
	HD SR SStP 444/422 10-bit
	SxS Pro+ Media Cards

(Continued)

Table 9.28 (Continued)

SONY	PMW-F55
	Using AXS Memory cards
	4K raw 16-bit linear with AXS-R5/R7
	2K raw 16-bit linear with AXS-R5/R7
Recording Outputs	4K 3G-SDI × 4 (square division or 2SI) up to 60p
	4K HDMI × 1 (1.4a) up to 60p
Connectors	HD-Y or HD Sync (tri-level) V1.0
	Analog Composite (VUP)
	HD-SDI Output HD mode: SDI 1/2 Line Output, SDI 3/4 Monitor Output (character on/off)
	4K mode: SDI 1/2/3/4 Line Output (character on/off), HD-SDI/3G-SDI switchable
	Timecode TC IN or OUT switchable (×1)
	Genlock BNC input (×1)
	HDMI A Type output (×1)
	Audio Input: XLR-type 3-pin with Line/Mic/Mic +48V/AES/EBU selectable (×2, female)
	Audio Output: phono jack (CH-1, CH-2)
	Speaker: Monaural
	USB device, Mini-B (×1)
	USB host, type-A (×1)
	Wi-Fi
	DC Output 4-pin (×2), 11 V to 17 V DC (MAX 2.0A) using the battery adapter
	Remote 8-pin (×1)
SD Card	SD card slot (×1)
Synchronization	HD-Y or HD Sync (tri-level) V1.0
	Timecode
	Genlock BNC × 1
Power In	DC 12V (11 V to 17.0 V)
Power Out	DC Output 4-pin (×1), 11 V to 17 V DC (MAX 2.0A) w/ battery adapter
Weight	4lb 14oz (2.2 kg)
Dimensions	7 1/8" × 7 7/8" × 12 1/4" (151mm × 189mm × 210 mm)

SONY FX9

Figure 9.48 SONY FX9.

The SONY FX9 shoots both full-frame and Super35 in a modular package roughly the size and weight and shape of its Super35 predecessor FS7M2. Frame rates are variable from 1 up to 60 fps for quick and slow-motion footage. The FX9 also offers a quality priority setting that maximizes full HD slow-motion image quality with advanced oversampling technology. FX9 has a variable electronic neutral density filter that can be controlled from a hard dial on the side of the camera. Designed with hybrid technologies from the SONY VENICE and the SONY A9, the FX9 has roughly the same basic "run and gun" form factor body as the previous FS7 and FS7M2 cameras, with an E-mount lens mount and quick menu options on the side of the camera that cover functions for customizable ND filter presets, 4-channel audio adjustment, iris control, white balance, and shutter.

SONY FXW-FX9 utilizes a full-frame 6K Exmor R image sensor that oversamples 6048 × 4032 resolution to create 4K images capable of full HDR. The Exmor R sensor has a dual base ISO option at ISO 800 and ISO 4000. In full-frame mode the active sensor area is 35.7mm × 18.8mm yielding a 1.89:1 aspect ratio. The Exmor R sensor is back-illuminated sensor, an innovative design that increases quantum efficiency by placing the wiring that removes the signal from individual photosites on the back side of the sensor.

Figure 9.49 SONY Exmor R CMOS back illuminated sensor.

SONY also incorporated the fast hybrid AF phase-detection and contrast autofocus system from their Alpha a7 and a9 series cameras with 561 focus points covering 94% in the horizontal and 96% in the vertical in full-frame mode. They also enable face detection to give the camera the ability to choose and track a subject by setting it with the touchscreen LCD. Artificial intelligence keeps focus sharp in face priority AF, face only AF, and face registration. There are seven AF transition speeds from fast-switching between subjects as quickly as possible to slow, where speed is reduced to fit a more measured shooting style.

Advanced image stabilization metadata means even handheld footage can be transformed with SONY Catalyst Browse/Catalyst Prepare software in post-production to look as smooth as if it were shot from a gimbal. Unlike in-camera or lens stabilization, metadata generated by the FX9's built-in gyro allows users to choose a balance between the level of shake compensation and the resolution of trimmed 4K imagery. This feature is also compatible with any E-mount lens and allows for far faster processing than conventional NLE stabilization workflows.

The FX9 is capable of recording modes at 6K full-frame oversampling QFHD (3840 × 2160) recording at 24p/25p/30p or S35 QFHD (3840 × 2160) recording at 24p/25p/30p/60p. A firmware update will add 4K (4096 × 2160) and 60 fps in 5K cropped full-frame oversampling mode and in S35 it includes 24p/25p/30p/60p at 4096 × 2160. High frame rates of 100/120fps are supported in 1080p full frame and S35. In a future update, 150/180fps will be added in 1080p. SONY plans for future updates that will include 16-bit RAW output, 4K60p recording in 5K cropped full-frame mode, full HD 180 fps, and DCI 4K recording, and the FX9 camera is Netflix approved. XAVC Proxy Rec is also available, offering a up to 9 Mb/s small size proxy file which will be easily sent via a network, and a 28-second Cache Rec is available to prevent missing any shot. FX9 encoding options include S-Log 3 and S-Gamut 3 Cine, but SONY added a mode called S-Cinetone to the FX9, intended to produce more accurate color and skin tones.

The XDCA-FX9 extension unit to the back of the FX9 adds advanced networking for streaming/file transfers and a slot-in for a wireless audio receiver. The extension kit output features include genlock and timecode when using a multicamera setup, TC in/Out and Gen-Lock In/Ref out, is on the body of the camera. Future firmware updates will enable 16-bit raw 4K/2K output to compatible external recorders. RAW output won't be enabled at launch but will come in a future update. Other refinements include genlock and timecode in/out. Electronic viewfinder can be changed to have a sunshade and the grip is more compact, the basic body weighs 2kg (4.4lb). A locking E-mount reduces lens play and allows use of most 35mm lenses including PL, EF, Leica, and Nikon via optional adapters. This stronger E-mount is also handy for using heavier-long cine-zooms without having to add additional lens support. The FX9 comes with a wide range of expansion features including compatibility with the UWP-D series of wireless microphones via Multi Interface Shoe™ (MI Shoe) with digital audio interface. The XDCA-FX9 has a compatibility with SONY BP-GL and BP-FL series batteries, D-Tap, RJ-45 interface and stable "Dual Link" streaming by using two carrier lines, as well as DWX slot-in type digital wireless receiver commonly used in broadcasting settings.

Table 9.29 SONY FX9 specifications

SONY	PXW-FX9 XDCAM Specifications
Sensor Resolution	Effective: 3840 × 2160
Sensor Size	35.7 × 18.8 mm (Full-frame)
ISO	800 to 4000 (Native)
Signal-to-Noise Ratio	57 dB
Lens Mount	SONY E-Mount
Shutter Speed	1/1 to 1/8000 sec
Built-In ND Filter	4 to 128 Stop Electronic ND Filter
Recording Media	2 × XQD Card Slots
	1 × SDXC/Memory Stick PRO Duo Hybrid Card Slot
Internal Recording	XAVC-I 4:2:2 10-bit:
	3840 × 2160p at 23.98/25/29.97/50/59.94 fps (240 to 600 Mb/s)
	1920 × 1080p at 23.98/25/29.97/50/59.94/100/120 fps (89 to 222 Mb/s)
	1920 × 1080i at 50/59.94 fps (112 Mb/s)
	XAVC-L 4:2:2 10-bit:
	3840 × 2160p at 23.98/25/29.97/50/59.94 fps (100 to 150 Mb/s)
	1920 × 1080p at 25/29.97/50/59.94/100/120 fps (25 to 50 Mb/s)
	1920 × 1080i at 50/59.94 fps (50 Mb/s)
	MPEG HD422 4:2:2 10-bit:
	1920 × 1080p at 23.98/25/29.97 fps (50 Mb/s)
	1920 × 1080i at 25/50/59.94 fps (50 Mb/s)
	XAVC Proxy 4:2:0 10-bit:
	1920 × 1080p (9 Mb/s)
	1280 × 720p (6 to 9 Mb/s)
	640 × 360p (3 Mb/s)
Gamma Curve	SONY S-Log 3
Audio Recording	XAVC: 4-Channel 24-bit 48 kHz LPCM Audio
	Proxy: 2-Channel AAC Audio
Built-In Microphone	Mono
Video Connectors	1 × BNC (12G-SDI) Output
	1 × BNC (3G-SDI) Output
	1 × HDMI (HDMI 2.0) Output
Audio Connectors	2 × 3-Pin XLR Mic/Line Level (+48 V Phantom Power) Input
	1 × 1/8"/3.5mm Stereo Headphone Output
Other I/O	1 × BNC Genlock Data Input
	1 × BNC Timecode Data Input/Output
	1 × 2.5mm LANC Control
	1 × USB Micro-B USB 3.1 Gen 1 Data
Wireless Interfaces	2.4 GHz, 5 GHz Wi-Fi
EVF	Included
EVF Display Type	LCD
Screen Size	3.5"
EVF Resolution	2,760,000 Dots
Battery Type	SONY BP-U Series
Power Connectors	1 × Barrel (19.5 VDC) Input
Power Consumption	35.2W

SONY	PXW-FX9 XDCAM Specifications
Accessory Mount	1 × Multi-Interface Shoe
	1 × 1/4"–20 Female
Dimensions	5.75 × 5.61 × 9.02"/146 × 142.5 × 229 mm
Weight	4.4lb/2kg

SONY PXW-FS7M2

Figure 9.50 SONY FS7 M2 camera.

The SONY PXW-FS7M2 XDCAM S35mm camera is designed for shooting "Cinéma Vérité" style documentaries, reality TV, commercial, and corporate applications. It features a Super 35mm sized sensor that allows cinematographers to capture images with cinematic depth of field. The camera incorporates a locking E-mount that is compatible with E-mount lenses, and supports all electronic connections. The locking mount reduces lens play, and allows use of most 35mm lenses including PL, EF, Leica, and Nikon with optional adapters. Just behind the lens mount an electronic variable ND system provides a clear filter and three user definable preset ND filters that can be adjusted to provide between 2 and 7 stops of ND. The camera can capture footage to optional on-board XQD media cards in either DCI 4K (4096 × 2160) or UHD 4K (3840 × 2160) at up to 59.94 fps or HD at up to 180 fps.

The 4K Super 35mm EXMOR sensor features a wide color gamut. The FS7M2 offers a choice of XAVC or MPEG-2 codecs. The XAVC codec can be used for 4K and HD recording, while MPEG-2 is limited to HD recording. XAVC comes in two flavors, XAVC INTRA, and XAVC Long, allowing users to encode from HD to 4K DCI 4096 × 2160 using Intra-Frame or Long GOP compression with 10-bit 4:2:2 for HD and the choice of 10-bit 4:2:2 or 8-bit 4:2:0 for UHD. XAVC intra compression is very efficient, recording at modest bit rates and XAVC Long also substantially extends the recording time while attaining very high quality and low noise. The camera incorporates Dual XQD media card slots that support simultaneous or relay recording.

The camera supports two signal processing modes: Cine-EI and Custom. Cine-EI offers three color grading spaces for electronic cinematography production. The Custom mode supports Rec-709 and Rec BT-2020 at UHD 3840 × 2160 with YCbCr color subsampling. Set the PXW-FS7M2 to record onboard and monitor on a BT 2020 compliant monitors via HDMI 10-bit 4:2:2 or SDI at 10-bit 4:2:2 with a 709 monitor LUT applied.

The PXW-FS7M2 is equipped with a locking E-mount that provides improved stability and strength compared to a standard E-mount. It features a safety interlock system that helps prevent accidental disengagement of the lens from the camera body. The locking mount also reduces lens play compared to a standard E-mount and the locking mount is strong enough to support long cine and ENG zooms that normally require a lens support. The shallow flange distance of the E-mount allows mounting most 35mm lens types such as PL, Canon EF, Leica, Nikon, as well as many others with simple mechanical adapters.

Behind the lens mount sits a retractable clear filter. When engaging the internal ND filters, the clear filter retracts and a stepless electronic ND filter drops into place maintaining the proper flange focal distance. Program the electronic ND filter to act as three individual filters and rotating the filter knob will step between these presets.

Cinematographers can manually adjust the density of the filter from 2 to 7 stops. One of the advantages of the electronically variable ND filter is that the operator can use the iris on the lens to set a preferred depth of field, and then make exposure adjustments with the ND, as it does not introduce any color shift as the strength of the ND changes.

The camera includes an ergonomic handgrip that SONY calls a SmartGrip, which features zoom, start/stop, and assign controls. The SmartGrip facilitates camera operation with the right hand, leaving the left hand free to operate the lens. Both the arm and handgrip can be positioned at different angles permitting great flexibility, and it has been re-designed for additional extension adjustment.

The PXW-FS7M2 viewfinder and mic holder mount have been repositioned. It also incorporates a shoulder pad designed to sit on the operator's shoulder by extending the support arm of the SmartGrip, which allows the camera to be held in front of the operator without requiring a support rig. The viewfinder and mic holder attach to a 15mm rod. This allows the user to swap out the included rod with a longer rod, and to move the position of the viewfinder

or mic holder relative to the camera. Adjust the position of the viewfinder so a left-eye shooter can use the left eye, while the camera is resting on the right shoulder. The viewfinder also rides on a square mounting rod that ensures level operation.

The PXW-FS7M2 records internally in both DCI 4K and UHD 4K at up to 59.94 fps, and in HD up to 180 fps using XAVC-I or up to 120 fps with XAVC-L. DCI 4K (4096 × 2160) can be recorded internally without the need of an external recorder. The camera features two XQD media slots that support simultaneous or relay recording. The XQD card slots are shallower on the PXW-FS7M2 compared to the FS7, making inserting and removing media cards easier. Genlock and timecode breakout are available with an optional XDCA-FS7, which allows for RAW and ProRes recording. The camera body is made from magnesium, so the camera body weighs only four pounds.

SONY FX6

At the time of publication, SONY Electronics Inc. announced the FX6 (model ILME-FX6V) camera, the latest addition to SONY's Cin-

Table 9.30 SONY FS7M2 specifications

SONY	PXW-FS7M2
Sensor Resolution	Effective: 4096 × 2160
Image Sensor Size	Super35
Sensor Type	CMOS
Signal-to-Noise Ratio	57 dB
Lens Mount	SONY E-Mount
Shutter Speed	1/3 to 1/9000 sec
Built-In ND Filter	Internal ND filters
	CLEAR: OFF
	1: 1/4ND
	2: 1/16ND
	3: 1/64ND
	Linearly variable ND: 1/4ND to 1/128ND
Recording Media	2 × XQD Card Slots
	1 × SD Card Slot
Internal Recording Modes	XAVC-I 4:2:2 10-bit:
	3840 × 2160p at 23.98/25/29.97/50/59.94 fps (240 to 600 MB/s)
	XAVC-L 4:2:0 8-bit:
	3840 × 2160p at 23.98/25/29.97/50/59.94 fps (100 to 150 MB/s)

SONY	PXW-FS7M2
Gamma Curve	SONY S-Log 3
Audio Recording	4-Channel 24-bit 48 kHz
External Recording Raw Output with XDCA-FS7	SDI/BNC:
	4096 × 2160 12-bit
	2048 × 1920 12-bit
Video Connectors	2 × BNC (3G-SDI) Output
	1 × HDMI (HDMI 2.0) Output
Other I/O	1 × BNC Genlock Data Input
	1 × BNC Timecode Data Input/Output
	1 × 2.5 mm LANC Control Input
	1 × USB Mini-B Data Input/Output
	1 × 2.5 mm LANC Control Input
Display Screen Size	3.5"
Screen Resolution	1,560,000 Dots
Battery Type	SONY BP-U Series
Power Connectors	1 × Barrel (12 VDC) Input
Power Consumption	19 W
Accessory Mount	1 × Multi-Interface Shoe
	1 × Extension unit connector
Dimensions	6.14 × 9.41 × 9.72"/156 × 239 × 247mm
Weight	4.7 lb/2.0kg

ema Line. The FX6 leverages technology from SONY's VENICE cinema camera and marries it with the best of SONY's innovative Alpha mirrorless camera technology.

The FX6 features a 10.2 MP full-frame back-illuminated Exmor R™ CMOS sensor with high sensitivity and low noise. FX6's base sensitivity is ISO 800 with an enhanced sensitivity setting of ISO 12,800 – expandable up to 409,600 – for shooting in low and very low light conditions. It is capable of recording in XAVC all Intra 4:2:2 10-bit depth with stunning image quality in DCI 4K (4096 × 2160 – up to 60p), QFHD 4K (3840 × 2160 – up to 120p) and FHD (1920x1080 – up to 240p) for incredibly detailed slow motion. When more convenient file sizes are needed, FX6 can record in XAVC Long GOP 4:2:0 8-bit QFHD 4K (3840 × 2160 – up to 120p) and 4:2:2 10-bit FHD (1920 × 1080 – up to 240p). FX6 also includes a BIONZ XR™ image processing engine, first used in the new SONY Alpha 7S III camera.

FX6 offers advanced cinematic color science including S-Cinetone™ as well as S-Log3,

S-Gamut3, and S-Gamut3 cine for post-production flexibility. FX6's cinematic color science is optimized for premium applications by capturing the maximum dynamic range from the sensor and providing creative freedom. FX6 allows productions to match footage with other cameras in the SONY Cinema Line.

FX6 offers fast hybrid AF by combining 627-point focal plane phase-detection AF with face detection and real-time eye AF in high frame rates with continuous AF, allowing camera operators to track fast-moving subjects in slow motion without losing focus. Fast hybrid AF works with over 50 native E-mount lenses. The camera can also capture up to five times slow-motion with 4K (QFHD) 120 fps.

The new FX6 also offers internal electronic variable ND filters for easy and seamless control of the camera's filter density. Users can set variable ND to auto or adjust the filter density manually in smooth increments from 1/4 to 1/128 for perfectly exposed images without affecting the depth of field or shutter angle, even during changing lighting conditions. Combined with the camera's ultra-high sensitivity, the electronic variable ND filter provides users with outstanding creative control in almost any shooting environment.

SONY PXW-FS5M2

Figure 9.51 SONY PXW-FS5M2.

SONY's PXW-FS5M2 4K XDCAM Super 35mm compact camcorder features Hybrid Log Gamma, enabling both an HDR (high dynamic range) and SDR (standard dynamic range) in-camera workflow for flexibility in post and delivery. The FS5M2 offers high frame rate (HFR) cache recording at full HD 10-bit 4:2:2 image quality, and a frame rate of up to 240 fps 8-second cache recording on to SDXC cards. The FS5M2 also records continuous 120 fps internally in full HD, and higher frame rates of 480 fps and 960 fps are possible at specific resolutions.

The FS5M2 delivers slow-motion imagery, including four seconds of 120 fps in 4K and continuous 240 fps in 2K raw when used with a compatible third-party external recorder such as the ATOMOS Shogun and Convergent Design® Odyssey 7Q.

FS5 II is built around a high-sensitivity 4K Super35 "Exmor" CMOS sensor that offers all the benefits of a large format sensor in combination with the exceptional image readout speeds required for 4K motion-picture shooting and super slow

motion. SONY's Exmor CMOS design provides high-speed full-pixel read-out capability (without pixel binning) and sophisticated camera processing to ensure aliasing and Moiré are minimized.

A built-in electronic variable neutral density (ND) filter expands depth of field capability of the large format sensor. The electronic ND filter can be controlled from 1/4 to 1/128 ND continuously, and ND filters can also be set to auto, obviating the need to change filters as lighting conditions change.

FS5M2 supports ten picture profiles, including ones customized for S-Log2, S-Log3, Hybrid Log Gamma, and a profile specifically tuned to provide vibrant, high contrast visuals for creators who desire a DSLR-style look. Profiles can be individually adjusted to suit specific requirements and switched between in seconds.

SONY's α mount system is compatible with both SONY and third-party lenses. FS5 II's E-mount can take cinema lenses and SLR lenses with a third-party adapter, as well as SONY's E-mount and A-mount lenses. FS5II is available on its own (PXW-FS5M2) or with lens SELP18105G (PXW-FS5M2K).

SONY's proprietary clear image zoom technology can enlarge the image by an additional 200% in full HD and 150% in 4K. It is also compatible with fixed focal length lenses, so you can zoom into a scene while using a prime lens.

A high resolution 0.39-inch OLED viewfinder enables accurate manual focus and is offset for either right-eye or left-eye viewing. A 3.5-inch LCD screen can be attached in nine different locations: three on top of the handle and another six on top of the body, and positioning of the screen can be adjusted beside the camera body or along the axis of the lens.

Networking features allow live streaming over Wi-Fi or built-in wired LAN, and control of the camera from a smartphone or tablet; built-in NFC supports one-touch authentication possible with appropriate devices. GPS function automatically records GPS data.

Table 9.31 SONY PXW-FS5M2 specifications

SONY	PXW-FS5M2 XDCAM
Image Sensor	Super 35mm Single-Chip 11.6MP Exmor CMOS
Sensor Resolution	Actual: 4096 × 2160
	Effective: 3840 × 2160
ISO	2000
Gain	0 to 30 dB (Native)

SONY	PXW-FS5M2 XDCAM
Lens Mount	SONY E-Mount
Lens Communication	Yes
Shutter Speed	1/6 to 1/10,000 sec
Built-In ND Filter	Mechanical Filter Wheel with 2 Stop (1/4), 4 Stop (1/16), 6 Stop (1/64) ND Filters and a 1/4 to 1/128 Stop Electronic ND Filter
Recording Media	1 × SDXC/Memory Stick PRO Duo Hybrid Card Slot 1 × SDXC Card Slot
Internal Recording Recording Modes	XAVC 4:2:0: 3840 × 2160p at 23.98/25/29.97 fps XAVC 4:2:2: 1920 × 1080p at 50/59.94 fps (50 Mb/s) 1920 × 1080i at 50/59.94 fps (50 Mb/s) 1920 × 1080p at 23.98/25/29.97 fps (50 Mb/s) 1280 × 720p at 50/59.94 fps (50 Mb/s) AVCHD: 1920 × 1080p at 50/59.94 fps (28 Mb/s) 1920 × 1080i at 50/59.94 fps (24 Mb/s) 1920 × 1080p at 23.98/25/29.97 fps (24 Mb/s) 1920 × 1080i at 50/59.94 fps (17 Mb/s) 1920 × 1080p at 23.98/25/29.97 fps (17 Mb/s) 1280 × 720p at 50/59.94 fps (24 Mb/s)
Gamma Curve	SONY S-Log 2, SONY S-Log 3
External Recording Raw Output	SDI/BNC: 4096 × 2160 10-bit at 60 fps
Video Connectors	1 × BNC (3G-SDI) Output 1 × HDMI Output 1 × Multi/Micro-USB A/V Output
Audio Connectors	2 × 3-Pin XLR Mic/Line Level (+48 V Phantom Power) Input
Built-In Microphone Type	Stereo
Other I/O	1 × RJ45 LAN 1 × 2.5mm Control
Wireless Interfaces	2.4 GHz Wi-Fi, NFC
Display Type	LCD Touchscreen
Screen Size	3.5"
Screen Resolution	1,560,000 Dots
EVF Display Type	OLED
Screen Size	.39"
EVF Resolution	1,440,000 Dots
Battery Type	SONY BP-U Series
Power Connectors	1 × Barrel Input
Power Consumption	≥12.6 W
Operating Temperature	32 to 140°F/0 to 60°C
Accessory Mount	1 × Multi-Interface Shoe
Tripod Mounting Thread	1/4"–20 Female
Dimensions	4.38 × 5.07 × 6.79"/111.3 × 128.7 × 172.4 mm (With Protrusions)
Weight	1.83lb/830g

SONY PXW-FS5

Figure 9.52 SONY PXW-FS5.

SONY's PXW-FS5 XDCAM Super 35 camera captures UHD video using a Super 35mm-sized sensor with a smaller, hand-held form factor similar to SONY's line of digital cinema cameras. The camera's E-mount is machined from stainless steel and allows use of E-mount lenses and most 35mm lenses with the use of adapters, including PL, EF, Leica, and Nikon lenses. A built-in, electronic, variable ND system allows users to dial in anywhere from 1/4 to 1/128th ND filtration in the camera body, and also features four preset positions; off, 1/4, 1/16, and 1/64.

It incorporates two SD media card slots that support simultaneous or relay recording of XAVC-L or AVCHD. The XAVC codec can be used for 4K and HD recording, while MPEG-2 is limited to HD recording. The XAVC Long allows you to encode from HD to UHD using intra-frame or long GoP compression with 10-bit 422 for HD and 8-bit 420 for UHD. The camera features two SD media slots that support simultaneous or relay recording. One of the two SD slots also accepts memory stick-type media.

The camera includes an ergonomic positionable handgrip that SONY calls a SmartGrip, which features zoom, start/stop and assign controls. The SmartGrip facilitates camera operation with the right hand, leaving the left hand free to operate the lens. All input, output connectors feature covers for dust protection, and the media card slots and multi-terminal are similarly protected from dust by a swing-away door. The camera includes a removable top handle that incorporates a second XLR 3-pin audio input that compliments the 3-pin XLR input incorporated into the body. Both audio inputs feature a selector switch for line/mic/mic+48. The top handle allows users to attach the LCD viewfinder to the camera, providing a choice of using the camera's built-in EVF, or a larger LCD viewscreen.

Outputs include both HDMI and SDI and SONY's proprietary multi-terminal. The body also incorporates an ethernet connector, headphone jack, and XLR audio inputs. One SDI connector provides HD 10-bit 422 output. In addition, one A-type HDMI 2.0 provides 4K and HD output. Both the SDI and HDMI ports can output REC trigger and time code. There are two Rec s/s buttons: one on the camera grip, the other on the camera handle. The PXX-FS5 is also capable of simultaneously recording proxy files with the same name and time code as the main recordings. A paid upgrade allows users to record 12-bit 4K and 2K RAW to external recorders. This supports 4K up to 60p and 120p for 4 seconds to the camera's buffer. You can also record 2K up to 240p to an external recorder without being limited by a buffer limit.

The PXW-FS5 records to XAVC-L QFHD 8-bit 420 (up to 30fps) and HD 10-bit 422 (up to 60fps) internally, and mirror or back-up recording is assignable. PXW-FS5 has simultaneous-recording capability with individual Rec trigger, and the target SD card slot for each trigger is assigned in the recording menu. The camera has built-in Wi-Fi capabilities that enable live streaming to PCs, tablets, and smart phones. Recorded movie files can be transferred via network to a designated FTP server. The following file formats are available for FTP: XAVC Proxy files, XAVC-L recorded files (4K(QFHD) and HD), AVCHD files (only m2ts stream files). When using content browser mobile, the user can control the camera wirelessly. One ethernet connector located on the rear panel of the camera provides connection when a reliable Wi-Fi link is not available.

Table 9.32 SONY PXW-FS5 specifications

SONY	PXW-FS5 XDCAM
Imaging System	Super 35mm Single-Chip 11.6MP Exmor CMOS
Effective Picture Size	3840 × 2160
ND Filter	Variable: 1/4 to 1/128
	Presets: Clear, 1/4, 1/26, 1/64

SONY	PXW-FS5 XDCAM
Sensitivity	ISO Rating: 3200 (S-Log3 Gamma)
	Lux: 2000 lx, 89.9% reflectance
	Video Gamma: T14(3840 × 2160 @ 23.98p mode, 3200K)`
Min. Illumination	60i: 0.16 l× (iris f/1.4, gain auto, shutter speed 1/24)
	50i: 0.18 l× (iris f/1.4, gain auto, shutter speed 1/25)
S/N Ratio	57 db (Y) (typical)
Recording Format	XAVC Long
	100 Mb/s: 3840 × 2160p 29.97/25/23.98
	60 Mb/s: 3840 × 2160p 29.97/25/23.98
	50 Mb/s: 1920 × 1080p 59.94/50/29.97/25/23.98
	50 Mb/s: 1920 × 1080i 59.94/50
	50 Mb/s: 1280 × 720p 59.94/50
	35 Mb/s: 1920 × 1280p 59.94/50/29.97/25/23.98
	25 Mb/s: 1920 × 1080i 59.94/50
	XAVC Proxy
	H.264/AVC
	4:2:0 8-bit
	MP4 wrapper
	1280 × 720: 3 to 6 Mb/s
	640 × 360: 1 to 3 Mb/s
	AVCHD
	28 Mb/s (PS): 1920 × 1080p 59.94/50
	24 Mb/s (FX): 1920 × 1080p 29.97/25/23.98
	24 Mb/s (FX): 1920 × 1080i 59.94/50
	24 Mb/s (FX): 1280 × 720p: 59.94/50
	17 Mb/s (FH): 1920 × 1080p 29.97/25/23.98
	17 Mb/s (FH): 1920 × 1080i 59.94/50
	17 Mb/s (FH): 1280 × 720p: 59.94/50
	9 Mb/s (HQ): 1280 × 720p: 59.94/50
Gain	0 to 30 dB
Signal-to-Noise Ratio	57 dB
Audio Recording Format	XAVC Long
	Linear PCM 2 ch, 24-bit, 48kHz
	AVCHD
	Linear PCM 2 ch, 16-bit, 48kHz
	Dolby digital 2ch, 16-bit, 48kHz
Shutter Speed	60i: 1/8 to 1/10,000
	50i/24p:1/6 to 1/10,000
Gain Selection	0, 3, 6, 9, 12, 15, 18, 24,27, 30dB, AGC
Lens Mount	SONY E-Mount
Gamma Curve	Selectable
Shutter Speed	1/6 to 1/10,000 sec
White Balance	Preset
	Memory A
	Memory B (1500K-50000K)/ATW

(Continued)

Table 9.32 (Continued)

SONY	PXW-FS5 XDCAM
Slow & Quick Motion Function	3840 × 2160 30p: Frame rate selectable 1, 2, 4, 8, 15, 30
	3840 × 2160 25p: Frame rate selectable 1, 2, 3, 6, 12, 25
	1920 × 1080 60i: Frame rate selectable 1, 2, 4, 8, 15, 30, 60
	1920 × 1080 50i: Frame rate selectable 1, 2, 3, 6, 12, 25, 50
Built-In ND Filter	2 to 7 Stop Electronic ND Filter
Super Slow Motion	60i: Frame rate selectable (120, 240, 480, 960)
	50i: Frame rate selectable (100, 240, 400, 800)
Recording Media	2 × SDXC Card Slots
WiFi Compatible	Format: IEEE 802.11 b/g/n
	Frequency Band: 2.4 GHz
	Security: WEP/WPA-PSK/WPA2-PSK
	NFC: NFC Forum Type 3 Tag Compliant
LCD Monitor	3.5"/8.8 cm
	Approx.: 1.56M dots
Viewfinder	0.39"/0.99 cm OLED
	Approx.: 1.44M dots
Media Card Slots	1 × MS/SD (dual Memory Stick/SD)
	1 × SD
Audio I/O	2 × 3-pin XLR
	Line/mic/mic +48
SDI Output	1 × BNC HD/3G-SDI SMTPE292M/424M/425M
HDMI 2.0	1 × Type A
USB	1 × Multi/Micro (composite video integrated into Multi/Micro USB jack)
Headphone	1 × Stereo mini jack
Wired LAN	1 × RJ-45 (100Base-TX/10Base-T
Remote	Stereo mini jack (Φ2.5 mm)
Accessory Shoe	Multi-Interface (MI) shoe
Recording Modes	XAVC-L:
	3840 × 2160p at 23.98/25/29.97 fps (60 to 100 MB/s)
	1920 × 1080p at 23.98/25/29.97/50/59.94 fps (35 to 50 MB/s)
Power Requirement	Battery Pack: 14.4 VDC
	AC Adapter: 12 VDC
Audio Recording	2-Channel 24-Bit 48 kHz
Power Consumption	NTSC: Approx. 11.8W
	PAL: Approx. 11.5W
	Note: While recording with LCD on, EVF off, when external device connector is not used.
Temperature	Operating: 32 to 104°F/0 to 40°C
	Storage: –4 to 140°F/–20 to 60°C)
Interfaces	
Dimensions	Body Only: 4.50 × 5.13 × 6.88"/11.43 × 13.02 × 17.46 cm (approx.)
	Body, Lens, and Accessories: 7.38 × 8.63 × 6.88"/18.73 × 21.91 × 17.46 cm (with 18 to 105mm lens, lens hood, large eyecup, LCD viewfinder, top handle, grip)

SONY	PXW-FS5 XDCAM
Video Connectors	1 × BNC (3G-SDI) Output
	1 × HDMI (HDMI 2.0) Output
Audio Connectors	2 × 3-pin XLR Mic/Line Level (+48 V Phantom Power) Input
	1 × 1/8"/3.5 mm Stereo Headphone Output
Other I/O	1 × USB Micro-B Data, Monitor Input/Output
	1 × 2.5 mm LANC Control Input
	1 × RJ45 LAN
Wireless Interfaces	2.4 GHz Wi-Fi Control
Battery Type	SONY BP-U Series
Power Connectors	1 × Barrel Input
Power Consumption	11.8 W
Operating Temperature	32 to 104°F/0 to 40°C
Accessory Mount	1 × 1/4"–20 Female
	1 × Multi-Interface Shoe
Dimensions	Body Only: 4.50 × 5.13 × 6.88"/11.43 × 13.02 × 17.46 cm (approx.
	Body, Lens, and Accessories: 7.38 × 8.63 × 6.88"/18.73 × 21.91 × 17.46cm (with 18 to 105mm lens, lens hood, large eyecup, LCD viewfinder, top handle, grip)
Weight	Body Only: 29.2oz/827.8g
	Body, Lens & Accessories: 4.9lb/2.23kg (with 18 to 105mm lens, lens hood, large eyecup, LCD viewfinder, top handle, grip)

SONY FS7/FS7 M2

SONY NEX-FS700U

Figure 9.53 SONY NEX-FS700U.

The SONY NEX-FS700U Super 35 camera uses a native 4K Super 35 CMOS resolution sensor compatible with cine-style film lenses. FS700 offers cinematic depth of field, high sensitivity in low light, low image noise, and exceptional dynamic range.

Capable of 1080p video in a range of frame rates up to 60p, the FS700 provides the option of recording AVCHD footage onto SD card/memory stick or via the FMU (flash memory unit) port, or it can output 4:2:2 video via HDMI 1.4 or 3G/HD-SDI to an external recording unit, with simultaneous recording to both media.

A unique feature of the FS700 is its ability to record bursts of super-slow motion video at rates up to 960 fps ranging from 8 to 16 seconds, depending of the frame rate. Full-resolution recording is possible at up to 240 fps, and at 480 and 960 fps, resolution is reduced.

The 3G/HD-SDI port will soon have expanded capability when a firmware upgrade will allow 4K output via the BNC out as a data stream, which can be recorded to an optional SONY 4K recorder.

Table 9.33 SONY NEX-FS700U specifications

SONY	NEX-FS700U
Sensor	Exmor Super 35 4K CMOS sensor
Sensor Size	24 × 12.7 mm
Photosites	11.6 million photosites
Exposure Index/ISO	ISO 500 in Standard Gamma
Notable Features	Low priced high-frame-rate imaging
	Uses a new 4K "Exmor" Super 35 CMOS sensor (total 11.6 million pixels) features high sensitivity, low noise and minimal aliasing. NEX-FS700 outputs a 4K raw bit-stream data over 3G HD-SDI when used with an optional recorder
	Slow motion capability of up to 10x slow motion at full HD resolution or up to 40× slow motion at a reduced resolution.
	Four Built-in, ultra-thin ND Filters: Clear; 2, 4, and 6 Stop
	A 3G-SDI output enables easy integration with highest quality recording formats.
	Up to 99 camera profile settings can be stored, allowing rapid adaptation to multiple shooting environments. Settings are also easily shared in multi-camera productions.
Frame Rates	1 to 960 fps
	Auto: 1/60–1/2000, 30p: 1/30–1/2000, 24p: 1/48–1/2400
	Manual:60i/30p/60p: 1/3–1/10000, 24p: 1/3–1/10000
	Manual:60i/30p/60p: 1/3–1/10000, 24p: 1/3–1/10000
	60Hz System:
	REC. Frame rates: 1080/60p, 1080/30p, 1080/24p
	Camera capture: 960 fps, 480 fps, 240 fps, 120 fps, 60 fps, 30 fps, 15 fps, 8 fps, 4 fps, 2 fps, 1 fps
	50Hz System:
	REC. Frame rates: 1080/50p, 1080/25p
	Camera capture: 800 fps, 400 fps, 200 fps, 100 fps, 50 fps, 25 fps, 12 fps, 6 fps, 3 fps, 2fps, 1 fps
Shutter	Electronic Rolling; Auto: 1/60–1/2000, 30p: 1/30–1/2000, 24p: 1/48–1/2400 Manual:60i/30p/60p: 1/3–1/10000, 24p: 1/3–1/10000
Lens Mount	SONY E-Mount interchangeable lens system
Viewfinder	LCD Screen 3.5 inch-type, XtraFine LCD, approx. 921,600 dots(1920 × 480), 16:9 aspect
Controls	SONY Standard Full Function Onboard Menu Controls
	AUTO, ONE PUSH AB, INDOOR (3200K),
	OUTDOOR (5800K±7 positions),
	MANU WB TEMP (2300K~15000K, 100K step)
Onboard Recording	HD: HD MPEG-4 AVCHD
	SD: MPEG-2 PS (Same as DVD)
	HXR-FMU128optional 128 GB Memory Module
	SD/SDHC/SDXC Memory Card
	Memory Stick PRO Duo Mark2
	Memory Stick PRO-HG Duo
	Memory Stick PRO-HG Duo HX
	AVCHD Recording Modes (1080 59.94i)
	HD-FH
	HD-FX
	HD-HQ
	HD-LP
	PS 1920 × 1080 60P (59.97P)
Recording Outputs	SDI Out 3G HDSDI BNC ×1
	Component Out HDMI 1.4 RCA Type (×1)
	Video Out RCA Pin ×1

SONY	NEX-FS700U
Connectors	Audio In XLR 3-pin (female) (×2), LINE/MIC/MIC with selectable attenuation and +48V phantom power
	Audio Out 2 RCA L&R
	Component Out HDMI 1.4 RCA Type (×1)
	RCA Type (×3) via Mini-D jack
	Composite Video Out RCA Type (×1)
	Earphone 3.5mm Stereo
	Lens Connector E-Mount Hot Shoe
	MIC In Two 3-Pin XLR with selectable attenuation and phantom power
	Monitor Speaker
	Remote LANC type 2.5mm Stereo mini-mini jack (ø2.5 mm) ×1
	SDI Out 3G HDSDI BNC
	TC Out HDMI 1.4/ 3G HDSDI (embedded SMPTE TC Out)
	Test Out Via HDMI 1.4
	USB mini-AB/Hi-Speed (x 1)
SD Card	MS PRO Duo, SD/SDHC/SDXC compatible ×1
Synchronization	Not available
Power In	DC7.2 V (Battery Pack) DC7.6 V (AC-DC adaptor)
Power Out	Not available
Weight	3lbs 2oz
Dimensions	5" × 4" × 7 5/8" (126.5mm × 101.5mm × 193.5 mm)

SONY PMW-FS5/FS5M2

Figure 9.54 SONY F5 camera.

SONY PMW-F5 gives cinematographers options for HD, 2K, or 4K acquisition and production. The camera features a 4K Super 35mm image sensor for 4096 × 2160 resolution.

The F5 are the next generation after the F3, offering modular design, OLED viewfinder and PL lens mount. This multi codec camera offers a diversity of recording modes, integrating XAVC codec for 4K and HFR shooting as well as the HD422 50 Mbps HDTV standard.

It also features 16-bit linear raw for 2K/4K recording, and high-speed shooting at up to 180fps.

F5 offers multi-codec support featuring SONY's XAVC MPEG-4 AVC/H.264 format, the SR codec (MPEG4 SStP) and the industry-standard high definition XDCAM 50Mbps 4:2:2 codec. In-camera recording is on SONY's SxS media, SxS PRO+ (Plus), which can be used to record XAVC in HD High Frame Rate and in 4K at up to 60fps, and XAVC HD High Frame Rate.

In addition to on-board recording onto SxS PRO+, the PMW-F5 can be connected to the AXS-R5 raw recorder. Slow-motion imagery at up to 120fps can be captured as 2K raw files on recently developed AXS memory cards. The F5 can capture up to 60fps in 4K mode when connected to the AXS-R5.

F5 includes PL-mount adaptors so that users can choose cinematic lenses from suppliers such as Angenieux, ARRI, Canon, Carl Zeiss, Cooke, FUJIFILM and Leica. Cinematographers on a budget can use high-quality still camera lenses by removing the supplied PL-mount adaptor to reveal the native FZ mount. This makes it easy to accept commercially available adaptors for third-party lenses, including Canon EF, Canon FD, Nikon DX, Nikon G, Leica M, and even 2/3-inch B4 lenses. Another option is the use of SONY FZ-Mount lenses with auto focus, servo, and zoom.

PMW-F5 users can use high-quality OLED and LCD viewfinders. The DVF-EL100 OLED viewfinder measures 0.7-inches with 1280 × 720 HD resolution. The DVF-L350 3.5-inch LCD viewfinder offers 10 times the contrast of previous SONY LCD viewfinders, with a flip-up eyepiece for direct monitoring. A third option is the full HD DVF-L700. This compact 7-inch LCD viewfinder enables high resolution when shooting in 2K and 4K, with pixel-to-pixel 1920 × 1080 representation of HD images.

AXSM Access Memory System for 2K/4K raw recording is based on SONY's recording technology with AXSM memory cards, using the generic file system exFAT. Users can record 4K raw data up to 60 fps and 2K raw up to 240 fps, with 300 MB/s sustained transfer speed. PC-friendly operation is enabled through use of the AXS-CR1 card reader, offering a USB 3.0 interface for high speed transfers. The AXS-R5 raw recorder directly docks onto the PMW-F5 for 2K and 4K raw recording. Both cameras support SONY's high-speed, enhanced versions of its SxS PRO memory cards.

Table 9.34 SONY PMW F5 specifications

SONY	PMW-FS5/FS5M2
Sensor	Super 35-mm CMOS image sensor
Sensor Size	24 × 12.7mm
Photosites	4096 × 2160
Exposure Index/ISO	2000 in S-Log2
Notable Features	Internal 4K/2K/HD Recording
	Optional AXS-R5 "Bolt-on" Recorder RAW Output
	Wider Color Gamut than Film
	SxS Pro+ Media Cards
Frame Rates	2K raw 1–180 fps, 1–240 fps with AXS-R5 outboard recorder and upgrade
	XAVC HD: 1–180p (NTSC)
	XAVC HD: 1–150p (PAL)
	XAVC 2K: 2048 × 1920 at 23.98p, 24p, 25p, 29.97p, 50p, 59.94p
	XAVC HD: 1920 × 1080 at 23.98p, 25p, 29.97p, 50p, 59.94p
	MPEG4 SStP: 1920 × 1080, 23.98p/24p/25p/29.97p
	MPEG2 HD: 1920 × 1080 at 50i, 59.94i, 23.98p, 25p, 29.97p
	MPEG2 HD: 1280 × 720 at 50p, 59.94p
Shutter	CMOS Rolling Shutter 1/24s to 1/6,000s 4.2 – 360°(electronic shutter)
Lens Mount	E mount, alpha mount, FZ-mount (includes PL-mount adaptor)
Viewfinder	DVF-EL100, 0.7" 1280 × 720 OLED
	DVF-L350, 3.5" 960 × 540 LCD
	DVF-L700, 7" 1920 × 1080 LCD
Controls	F5 interface for a range of controls with direct, one-touch access to key shooting parameters – frame rate, shutter speed, color temperature, ISO sensitivity and gamma, assignable buttons
Onboard Recording	Using SxS Pro+ Media Cards
	2K/4K RAW 16-bit
	2K/4K XAVC 422 10-bit
	HD MPEG2 422 8-bit
	HD XAVC 422 10-bit
	HD SR SStP 444/422 10-bit
	SxS Pro+ Media Cards

SONY	PMW-FS5/FS5M2
Recording Outputs	External Recording with AXS-R5
	2K/HD XAVC up to 180p
	2K raw up to 120p (w/AXS-R5)
Connectors	HD-Y or HD Sync (tri-level) V1.0
	Analog Composite (VUP)
	HD-SDI Output HD mode: SDI 1/2 Line Output, SDI 3/4 Monitor Output (character on/off)
	Timecode TC IN/OUT switchable (×1)
	Genlock BNC input (×1)
	HDMI A Type output (×1)
	Audio Input: XLR-type 3-pin with Line/Mic/Mic +48V/AES/EBU selectable (×2, female)
	Audio Output: phono jack (CH-1, CH-2)
	Headphone: Stereo mini jack (×1)
	Speaker: monaural
	USB device, Mini-B (×1)
	USB host, type-A (×1)
	Wi-Fi
	DC Output 4-pin (×2), 11 V to 17 V DC (MAX 2.0A) using the battery adapter
	Remote; 8-pin (×1)
SD Card	SD card slot (×1)
Synchronization	HD-Y (out) or HD Sync (tri-level) V1.0
	Timecode (In or Out)
	Genlock BNC × 1
Power In	DC 12 VDC (11V to 17.0V)
Power Out	DC Output 4-pin (×1), 11 V to 17 V DC (MAX 2.0A) w/ battery adapter
Weight	4lb 14oz (2.2kg)
Dimensions	7 1/8' × 7 7/8' × 12 1/4" (151mm × 189mm × 210 mm)
User Manual URL	https://pro.sony/en_GB/support-resources/pmw-f5/manual

SONY F35

Figure 9.55 SONY F35.

The SONY F35 employs a single Super 35mm RGB CCD striped array image sensor (not a Bayer pattern sensor) to create 4:4:4 and 4:2:2 1920 × 1080 HD images. The F35 camera offers a Super 35mm-sized monoplanar CCD sensor with 14-bit A/D converter and advanced digital signal processing, and a ø54mm PL lens mount for working with 35mm film lenses. It can use many of the same accessories as ARRI or Panavision film cameras, and runs at speed of 1–50 fps at 4:4:4, with an ASA/ISO rating of EI 640.

The F35's Super 35mm-sized CCD sensor provides an extensive range of depth-of-field controls, dynamic range, and wide color gamut. The CCD active area of 23.6mm × 13.3mm, yields a 1920 × 1080 output from a 12.4 million photosite RGB line array sensor.

The F35 allows direct top or rear docking with SONY's SRW-1 portable HDCAM-SR recorder. When used with the SRW-1 recorder, F35 supports multiple output formats including 24P,

50P, and 59.94P, plus variable frame capability, for over-cranking and under-cranking and ramping from 1 to 50 fps in 1 fps increments. F35 is compatible with SR Motion; interval recording, select fps, slow shutter and digital accelerating, decelerating, and linear speed ramps.

The cinematographer can use numerous color curves including five preset hyper gamma response curve settings, user definable custom gamma curves using the CVP File Editor Software, and a 10-bit S-Log gamma for very wide latitude.

Table 9-35 SONY F35 specifications

	SONY F35 Specifications
Sensor	Single chip Super 35 mm type Progressive CCD 1920 × 1080 RGB Output
Sensor Size	CCD active area 23.6 mm × 13.3 mm
Photosites	12.4 megapixel stripe array CCD chip, 5760 × 2160 photosites
Exposure Index	ISO 640
Notable Features	14-bit A/D converter and advanced DSP LSI
	S-LOG gamma
	HyperGammas 1 to 8
	customizable User gamma curve
	1 to 50 fps Variable Speed with either Shutter Angle or Gain Exposure Compensation for Programmable Ramping
Frame Rates	23.98PsF 4:2:2 YCbCr or 4:4:4 RGB
	24PsF 4:2:2 YCbCr or 4:4:4 RGB
	25PsF 4:2:2 YCbCr or 4:4:4 RGB
	29.97PsF 4:2:2 YCbCr or 4:4:4 RGB
	50P 4:2:2 YCbCr or 4:4:4 RGB
	59.94I 4:2:2 YCbCr or 4:4:4 RGB
	50I 4:2:2 YCbCr or 4:4:4 RGB
	1 to 50 fps YCbCr or 4:4:4 RGB
Shutter	Continuously Variable from 3.8 degrees to 360 degrees
Lens Mount	ø54 mm PL mount
Viewfinder	HDVF-C35W LCD Color Viewfinder
Controls	Assistant side main user interface with 3" transflective 400 × 240 pixel LCD color screen, illuminated buttons, button lock and jog wheel. Camera left: operator interface with illuminated buttons, button lock and card swap button.
	Compatible with SONY MSU (Master Setup Unit)
	Compatible with RMB (HD Remote Control Unit) series controllers.
Onboard Recording	10-bit HDCAM SR Tape with SRW-1
Recording Outputs	Dual-Link HD-SDI output (with supplied interface box) BNC type ×2
Connectors	Genlock video input BNC type ×1, 1.0 Vp-p, 75 Ω
	Audio CH1/CH2 input (with supplied interface box) XLR-3-31 type (Female), line/mic/mic +48V selectable
	Test output BNC type ×1, VBS/HD Y
	Dual-Link HD-SDI output (with supplied interface box) BNC type ×2
	Monitor output BNC type ×2, HD-SDI (4:2:2)
	DC input Lemo 8-pin (Male) x1, DC 10.5V to 17V, DC 20V to 30V
	DC input (with supplied interface box) XLR-4-pin type (Male) x1
	DC output DC 12V: 11-pin ×1, max. 4 A DC 24V: 3-pin ×1, max. 5.5 A
	Remote 8-pin ×1
	Viewfinder 20-pin ×2
	Network RJ-45 type ×1, 10BASE-T/100BASE-TX

SONY F35 Specifications	
SD Card	Memory StickTM PRO
Synchronization	Genlock Video in BNC type ×1, 1.0 Vp-p, 75 Ω
Power In	DC 10.5V to 17V 58W (without lens, viewfinder, at 23.98PsF mode)
Power Out	DC12V: 11-pin ×1, max. 4 A
	DC 24V: 3-pin ×1, max. 5.5 A
Weight	11 lb (5.0kg)
Dimensions	7 7/8" (199.3mm) × 7 7/8" (199.3mm) × 8 5/8" (219mm) Body Only

SONY PMW-F3

Figure 9.56 SONY PMW-F3.

SONY's PMW-F3 is equipped with an Exmor CMOS Super 35mm sensor which has been designed to fit the optical performance of 35mm Cine lenses. The F3's sensor technologies provide an excellent sensitivity of ISO 800 and a signal-to-noise ratio of 63 dB. SONY minimizes CMOS rolling shutter artifacts by giving each column of photosites its own, dedicated A to D converter, minimizing the rolling shutter effect. The resulting high-speed transfer enables the F3 to read every photosite, even when overcranking at 60 frames per second, with no sacrifice in resolution. The Exmor sensor design also significantly shortens analog signal paths for an extra reduction in image noise.

Cinematographers can customize the F3 with different picture profiles for various lighting scenarios, such as interior day, exterior night, and fluorescent. One can store custom matrices, detail, knee, and gamma. The camera saves picture profiles internally, and displays them on the LCD panel at the touch of a button. In addition, share any picture profile by saving it onto an SxS card and copying from camera to camera. Picture profiles can also be saved to a computer and e-mailed and archived.

To accommodate corrected viewing, S-Log mode allows for the use of look up tables or LUTs. The F3 comes with four preset LUTs, and additional LUTs can be created using SONY's CVP File Editor software. One of the camera's built-in LUTs converts S-Log gamma to conventional Rec 709 video for real-time monitoring on the set and offline recording onto SxS memory cards, which allows recording of the S-Log Signal onto an external recorder such as the SR-R1 while recording Rec 709 to the internal SxS Cards.

The PMW-F3 is supplied with a PL Mount Adapter for compatibility with the enormous range of existing 35mm cine lenses. There are also lens mount hot shoe interfaces for Cooke /i and ARRI LDS. The PMW-F3K also comes with three high-quality SONY lenses, including 35mm, 50mm, and 85mm focal lengths and all at T2.0.

The PMW-F3 can capture images at frame rates selectable from 1 to 60 fps in 720P mode and from 1 to 30 fps in 1080P mode and in increments of 1 fps onto a single card.

When over cranking or under cranking, images are recorded natively without interpolating frames. The quality of these slow and off speed images is exactly the same as images captured at normal speed. Slow and fast motion images can be played back immediately after shooting, without using any converter or processing on nonlinear editing systems. The F3 offers a slow shutter function, which accumulates from two to eight frames, integrating them and recording them as one. This not only increases camera sensitivity but also produces an interesting "ghost-like" high-speed blurring of moving subjects. The F3 also shoots using time lapse. The interval recording function captures individual frames at preset intervals from 1 to 10, 15, 20, 30, 40, and 50 seconds, from 1 to 10, 15, 20, 30, 40, 50 minutes, and from 1 to 4, 6, 12, 24 hours.

The PMW-F3 camcorder records 1920 × 1080 HD images using an MPEG-2 Long GOP codec, which conforms to the MPEG-2 MP@ HL compression standard. MPEG-2 Long

GOP enables users to record high-quality HD footage with efficient, reliable data compression. The F3 comes equipped with a wide range of interfaces including dual HD-SDI outputs, down-converted SD-SDI output, i.LINK (HDV) input/output, USB2 and analog composite output. The Dual-Link HD-SDI output option enables 10-bit RGB 4:4:4 at 23.98, 25, and 29.97PsF, or 10-bit 4:2:2 at 50P and 59.94P for uncompressed external recording. The PMW-F3 also supports selectable Gamma, four levels of Hyper Gamma and S-Log for a wide range of shooting conditions from standard to wide latitude.

Using the 3D Link option users can synchronize time code, genlock, and control functions with a single cable, locking the left and right cameras together to simplify 3D acquisition. Another XDCAM EX recording option is SONY's PHU-220R professional hard disk recorder, which plugs directly into one of the two SxS card slots. This high-quality, shock-resistant module captures up to 12 hours of content at 35 Mbps.

Table 9.36 SONY PMW F3 specifications

	SONY PMW F3K
Sensor	Super 35mm size single chip Exmor CMOS image sensor
Sensor Size	23.6 × 13.3mm
Photosites	Approx. 3.5M pixels
Exposure Index/ISO	ISO 800
Notable Features	Slow Shutter
	Over- and Undercranking
	Selectable gamma curves standard gamma ×6, CINE gamma ×4, S-Log gamma
	Uncompressed 4:4:4 RGB 10-bit output with CBK-RGB013E
	Uncompressed 4:2:2 10-bit output
	3D-Link upgrade with CBK-3DL01
	S-Log EI mode
	S-Log 4:2:0 capture to XDCAM EX internal recording
	S-Log 4:2:2 external recording via Link A HD-SDI output
	S-Log 4:4:4 external recording via Dual-Link HD-SDI
	S-Log 4:2:2 1080/60p external recording via Dual-Link HD-SDI
	Simultaneous S-Log recording to HD-SDI output and LUT applied to XDCAM EX internal recording
	Simultaneous S-Log recording to HD-SDI A output and 4:2:2 monitor LUT to SDI output
	Simultaneous S-Log recording to Dual-Link HD-SDI or 3G-SDI output at 4:4:4 and 4:2:2 monitor LUT to SDI output
Frame Rates	720P: 1–60fps selectable (17–60 fps when HD-SDI Dual Link active) •
	1080P: 1–30fps selectable (17–30 fps when HD-SDI Dual Link active)
	NTSC: HD HQ mode: 1920 × 1080/59.94i, 29.97p, 23.98p,
	1440 × 1080/59.94i, 29.97p, 23.98p, 1280 × 720/59.94p, 29.97p, 23.98p HD SP mode: 1440 × 1080/59.94i, 23.98p
	SD mode: 720 × 480/59.94i, 29.97p
	PAL: HD HQ mode: 1920 × 1080/50i, 25p,
	1440 × 1080/50i, 25p, 1280 × 720/50p, 25p HD SP mode: 1440 × 1080/50i
	SD mode: 720 × 576/50i, 25p
Shutter	Shutter speed 1/32–1/2000 sec
	Slow Shutter (SLS) 2, 3, 4, 5, 6, 7, 8 frame accumulation
Lens Mount	PL mount (with supplied lens mount adapter)
Viewfinder	Viewfinder: 0.45", Aspect Ratio 16: 9

	SONY PMW F3K
	Built-in LCD monitor: 3.5", 16: 9, Hybrid (semi-transmissive) type
Controls	SONY Standard Full Function Onboard Menu Controls
Onboard Recording	MPEG-2 Long GOP
	Media: ExpressCard/34 slot (×2)
	VBR, maximum bit rate: 35 Mb/s, MPEG-2 MP@HL
	HD SP mode: CBR, 25 Mb/s, MPEG-2 MP@H-14
	SD mode: DVCAM
Recording Outputs	Composite output: BNC (×1), NTSC or PAL, S-Video output;
	SDI output: BNC (x1), HD-SDI/SD-SDI selectable
	HD-SDI Dual Link Out: BNCx2 4: 2: 2 1080 50/59.94P 10bit output
	i.LINK: IEEE1394 S400 Connector
Connectors	HD/SD SDI OUT BNC (×1) (HD-SDI/SD-SDI switchable)
	HD-SDI Dual Link OUT BNC (x2) 4:2:2 1080 50/59.94p
	10 bit output; 4:4:4 1080 25/29.97p 10 bit output
	VIDEO OUT BNC (×1) (HD-Y signal or Composite signal)
	HDMI OUT HDMI connector (Type A) (×1)
	i.LINK IN/OUT IEEE1394 S400 4-pin Connector (×1)
	AUDIO INXLR Type 3-pin (female) (×2), LINE/MIC/MIC+48 V selectable
	AUDIO OUT RCA (×2)
	GENLOCK IN BNC (×1)
	TC IN/OUT BNC (×1 each)
	Stereo Mini Jack (×1)
	DC IN XLR type 4-pin (male) (×1)
	REMOTE 8-pin (×1)
	USB Mini TypeB connector (×1)
	PHONES Stereo Mini Jack (×1)
Synchronization	Timecode In: BNC (×1); Timecode Out: BNC (×1); Genlock In: BNC (x1)
Power In	DC 12V; DC input: XLR type 4-pin (male)
Weight	body only: Approx. 2.4kg (5lb 4.7oz) (without accessories)
Dimensions	151mm × 189mm × 210mm

SONY F23

The SONY F23 uses three 2/3" progressive CCD sensors to generate a 1920 × 1080 HD picture in Rec. 709 video mode, Hyper Gamma, or S-log mode recorded on a 10-bit in either 4:2:2 or 4:4:4 to the dockable HDCAM SR SRW-1 VTR. For aerial and underwater shooting applications, the SRW-1 can be connected to the F23 using dual-link via a pair of coax cables or a single SMPTE fiber cable. Any 2/3" lens can be mounted to the F23's reinforced B4 lens mount which eliminates back-focus issues. The "Assistant's Control Panel" duplicates all the camera controls and indicators on the camera body. The F23 is compatible with most ARRIflex film camera accessories, matte boxes, and the ARRI wireless remote control unit WRC-2.

Figure 9.57 SONY F23.

The F23 is equipped with a specially made prism that allows the camera to capture a wide color gamut, known as S-Gamut which is then processed by the camera's 14-bit A/D converter and unique DSP. F23 shoots full-bandwidth RGB 4:4:4 at a resolution of 1920 × 1080 in multiple formats including: 24P, 50P, and 59.94P, plus variable frame capability, for over-cranking and under-cranking and ramping from 1 to 60 fps in 1fps increments, even 4:4:4 mode. The cinematographer can use numerous color curves including five preset hyper gamma settings, user-definable custom gamma curves (using SONY's free CVP File Editor Software), and "S-Log" for very wide latitude.

Table 9.37 SONY F23 specification

	SONY F23
Sensor	3-chip 2/3-inch type Progressive CCD 14-bit A/D convertor
Sensor Size	3 × 8.80mm × 6.60mm 11mm diagonal
Photosites	2/3" CCD 1920 × 1080 × 3 = 6,220,800 photosites
Exposure Index/ISO	430 ISO
Exposure Latitude	12+ stops
Notable Features	Onboard Filters; A: 3200K, B: 4300K, C: 5600K, D: 6300K, E: ND0.3 (1/2ND) 1: Clear, 2: ND0.6 (1/4ND), 3: ND1.2 (1/16ND), 4: ND1.8 (1/64ND), 5: CAP
	1 fps to 60 fps in 4:4:4 mode
	S-LOG gamma
	HyperGammas 1 to 8
	Customizable user gamma curve
Frame Rates	23.98PsF 4:2:2 YCbCr or 4:4:4 RGB
	24PsF 4:2:2 YCbCr or 4:4:4 RGB
	25PsF 4:2:2 YCbCr or 4:4:4 RGB
	29.97PsF 4:2:2 YCbCr or 4:4:4 RGB
	50P 4:2:2 YCbCr or 4:4:4 RGB
	59.94I 4:2:2 YCbCr or 4:4:4 RGB
	50I 4:2:2 YCbCr or 4:4:4 RGB
	1 to 59.94fps YCbCr or 4:4:4 RGB
	1 to 60fps YCbCr
Shutter	Continuously Variable from 3.8 degrees to 360 degrees
Lens Mount	Bayonet mount (B4)
Viewfinder	HDVF-C35W LCD or HDVF-C30WR Color Viewfinder
Controls	Assistant side main user interface with 3" screen, illuminated buttons, button locks and jog wheel. Camera left: operator interface with illuminated buttons, button locks.
	Compatible with SONY MSU (Master Setup Unit)
	Compatible with RMBSeries Remote Controllers.
Onboard Recording	10 Bit HDCAM SR Tape with the SRW-1
Recording Outputs	Dual-Link HD-SDI output (with supplied interface box) BNC type x2
Connectors	HD SDI Out BNC type ×2
	Monitor Out HD-SDI 4:2:2, BNC type (2)
	Audio Input XLR-3-31 type (Female) line/mic/mic +48 V selectable (via supplied interface module)
	DC IN Lemo 8-pin (Male) x1, DC 10.5V to 17V, DC 20V to 30V
	DC IN XLR-4-pin type (Male) ×1 (via supplied interface module)
	Genlock/Return IN BNC type ×1, 1.0 Vp-p, 75 ohms
	Remote 8-pin
	VF1 Viewfinder 20-pin

SONY F23	
	VF2 Viewfinder 20-pin
	Test Out BNC type ×1, VBS/HD Y
	Network RJ-45 type (1), 10BASE-T, 100BASE-TX
Memory Card	Memory Stick Pro Media
Synchronization	Genlock/Return IN BNC type ×1, 1.0 Vp-p, 75 ohms
Power In	DC 10.5V to 17V
Power Out	DC 12V: 11-pin ×1, max. 4 A
	DC 24V: 3-pin ×1, max. 5.5 A
Weight	Approx. 11lb (5.0kg)
Dimensions	7 7/8" (199.3mm) × 8 5/8" (219mm) × 8 5/8" (219mm) Body Only

Vision Research Phantom High Speed Cameras

Figure 9.58

Source: www.phantomhighspeed.com/products/cameras/4kmedia

Vision Research Phantom Flex4K

Figure 9.59 Vision Research Phantom Flex4K

The Phantom Flex4K is a full-featured digital cinema camera, capable of speeds from 23.98 to over 1000 fps at 4K and up to 2000 fps at 2K resolution. Flex4K combines features found in the latest cinema cameras with those found only in specialty cameras.

With the option to record either uncompressed raw or with industry-standard compression, the workflow is now just as flexible as the camera's frame rate. The latest in non-volatile storage technology is implemented to move data quickly, while a complete on-camera control menu eliminates the need for a computer on set.

At 4K resolution the Flex4K offers super-35mm depth of field. The 10-megapixel sensor captures intricate detail with good dynamic range and low noise, featuring excellent image quality and low-light performance. Intelligent temperature control and advanced mechanical design provides quick to shoot capability with a very stable image. Control the Phantom Flex4K with an on-camera control interface for both basic and advanced camera operation, and set up universal capture and recording parameters before the shoot, while retaining access to the more commonly adjusted parameters like frame rate and exposure time. Capture, trigger, playback, and save controls can be found on both sides of the camera in order to provide a seamless workflow for different shooting environments. Remote control is also possible with a hand-held Phantom RCU, which can be connected to the camera via a cable or built-in Bluetooth connection at a distance up to 100 meters.

The Phantom Flex4K is available with up to 64 Gigabytes of internal RAM. "Loop mode" gives users the fastest high-speed workflow. Loop mode records into the RAM buffer at the camera's top speeds. Once the camera is triggered, the files can be quickly offloaded to an installed Phantom CineMag IV, available in sizes up to 2TB. For longer record times use run/stop (R/S) mode to record directly to the CineMag IV at speeds over 100 4K frames-per-second and record for several minutes. This is a good option when ultra high-speed is not required, at 24 fps users can record more than an hour of raw 4K footage directly to a 1TB CineMag IV.

Vision Research Phantom VEO 4K 990 and 590

Figure 9.60 Vision Research Phantom VEO 4K-PL and 590 models.

The Phantom 4K camera can be set to write either raw or compressed files directly to the CineMag. Cine Raw files are uncompressed and maintain the most information for processing, and they are compatible with several post processing and color grading systems. They can also be converted to a variety of formats using software provided with the camera. Users can also choose to save compressed files directly to the CineMag IV. While not as fast as working with raw files, this workflow increases record time and decreases

file size, and simplifies the process straight out of the camera. A third workflow option is recording the HD-SDI video playback with a video-based field recorder, taking advantage of the camera's in-camera video scaling to 4:4:4 1080p or 4:2:2 4K video via the 2× 3G-SDI outputs.

Vision Research Phantom VEO 4K PL-RLS

Figure 9.61 Vision Research Phantom VEO 4K PL.

Camera synchronization and 3D recording uses a single cable connection between cameras. Advanced video monitoring includes 2× 3G HD-SDI outputs, and 1× return, customizable for monitoring with adjustable frame guides, and/or a clean output for use with HD-SDI field recorders. Both HD-SDI outputs support video scaling for a sharp 1080p output of the camera's full sensor. The 2× 3G-SDI outputs can also be combined to monitor the full resolution on 4K production monitors. Zoom, focus, and exposure assist functions are all included.

Table 9.38 Phantom 4K camera family specifications combined

Vision Research Phantom Flex4K and VEO4K		
	Flex4K	**VEO4K**
Overview	The Flex4K is rolling shutter only. The Flex4K-GS additionally incorporates a global shutter mode, which reduces dynamic range but may be necessary for certain subject matter. Both Flex4K models work with CineMag media for the fastest on-set workflow.	Most VEO4K models work in both rolling shutter and global shutter modes (switchable). The VEO4K-PL is a black housing with PL mount, the VEO4K 590 runs at 1/2 speed and is in a white housing. RLS versions are rolling-shutter only. The VEO4K is about half the size of Flex4K.
Sensor Specifications	CMOS	CMOS
Maximum Resolution	4096 × 2304	4096 × 2304
Bit Depth	12-bit	12-bit
Pixel Size	6.75μm	6.75μm
Sensor Size	27.6mm × 15.5mm	27.6mm × 15.5mm
Native ISO	320D Rolling Shutter, 640D Global Shutter (Color)	320D Rolling Shutter, 640D Global Shutter (Color)

Vision Research Phantom Flex4K and VEO4K

	Flex4K	VEO4K
Exposure Index Range	800–1000 Color; 4000-8000 Mono	800–1000 Color; 4000-8000 Mono
Dynamic Range	12-stop Rolling Shutter, 9-stop Global Shutter	12-stop Rolling Shutter, 9-stop Global Shutter
Throughput/Speed		
Throughput	9 Gpx/sec	9 Gpx/sec 4K-PL and 990 models; 5 Gpx/sec 4K-590
Full resolution Max frame rate	938 fps at 4096 × 2304	4K-PL and 990 = 938 fps 4K-590 = 530 fps
4096 × 2160 Max frame rate	1000 fps	4K-PL and 990 = 1000 fps.4K-590 = 570 fps
2048 × 1080 Max frame rate	1977 fps	4K-PL & 990 = 1977 fps 4K-590 = 1130 fps
Exposure		
Minimum exposure	5µs to 1/frame rate	5µs to 1/frame rate
	Can be set in degrees or microseconds (µs)	Can be set in degrees or microseconds (µs)
	Rolling shutter scan time =1-millisecond	Rolling shutter scan time =1-millisecond
Memory		
RAM Buffer	RAM = 64GB or 128GB	RAM = 36GB or 72GB
Removable Media	CineMag V media 2TB or 8TB	Cfast 2.0 card media (not for direct record)
Record Times		
to RAM	10 seconds at max fps 128GB RAM	4K-PL & 990 = 6 seconds at max fps 72GB; 4K-590 = 11 seconds
Direct record to media	2TB CineMag holds 2 hours of raw 4K playback at 24P	
Special Features		
	Integrated on-camera control menu system for complete control	10Gb Ethernet option for camera body for fastest transfer out of RAM
	ProRes HQ recording support with CineMag IV and CineMag IV-PRO	
Triggering		
	Programmable Trigger Location (pre/post recording)	Programmable Trigger Location (pre/post recording)
Software Trigger	Software trigger from button on camera body or over ethernet	Software trigger from button on camera body or over ethernet
Hardware Trigger	Hardware trigger from Sync port or 3-pin accessory ports	Hardware trigger from BNC on camera body
Timing and Synchronization		
Frame Sync	Frame sync to internal or external clock	Frame sync to internal or external clock
Timecode	IRIG in/out timecode with SMPTE time code support	IRIG in/out timecode with SMPTE time code support
Misc.	Genlock available through HDSDI	
Signaling		
Most signals	Sync connector for Trigger, time code, F-sync, AES/EBU Audio (via MiniBob or Capture cable)	Programmable I/O allows for signals to be assigned and defined. Accessed from BNC ports on camera body
Unique port	Remote port for RCU/serial control	Range Data

(Continued)

Table 9.38 (Continued)

Vision Research Phantom Flex4K and VEO4K

	Flex4K	VEO4K
Connectivity		
Standard	Gb Ethernet from camera body	Gb Ethernet from camera body
10Gb	10Gb Ethernet on CineStation IV only	10Gb Ethernet from camera body optional
Camera Control		
	PCC software (Phantom camera control)	PCC software (Phantom camera control)
	on-camera menu system	on-camera controls for basic commands
	3rd party Mac-software (such as Glue Tools Séance)	3rd party Mac-software (such as Glue Tools Séance)
Video Out		
Ports	3G-SDI - 4 BNC ports	3G-SDI 1 BNC, 1 DIN and 1 HDMI
Supported formats	1080p, psf, and i standard rates up to p60. 2160 up to p30	1080p, psf, and i standard rates up to p60
SDI features	Versatile Dual-SDI where one port is always live and others switch to playback	N/A
Lensing		
Standard mount	PL-mount standard	PL-mount standard on VEO4K-PL, Nikon standard on other models
Mount options	Nikon F/G mount optional	Canon EF mount optional
Mount options	Canon EF mount optional	C-mount optional
Supported File Formats		
	Cine RAW is primary format	Cine RAW is primary format
	Convert to many other industry standard formats using PCC or 3rd party software	Convert to many other industry standard formats using PCC or 3rd party software
	ProRes recording support with CineMag IV PRO only	
Power		
Voltage Range	12-28V; 280 Watt power supply included	16-32V; 85 Watt power supply included
Power Draw	Power draw ~ 150Wh	Power draw ~ 75Wh
Battery options	Optional battery backs for V-Lock, Gold Mount (high capacity batteries only) or 26V Hawk-Woods.	12V input via capture port, supports V-Lock or Gold mount battery mounts

Vision Research Phantom v2640 Onyx

Figure 9.62 Vision Research Phantom V2640 Onyx.

The v2640 Onyx is a special model Phantom camera that is only available on a rental basis through Vision Research and select partners in different regions. Adapted from a Vision Research v2640 scientific camera, the Onyx is the fastest 4 Mpx camera available to the media and production industry. The v2640 is capable of 6,600 fps at its full resolution of 2048 × 1952.

Image quality for media and production is of the highest importance and the Phantom v2640 Onyx has multiple features that aid in producing pristine images. Onyx employs an optical low pass filter (OLPF) to reduce aliasing artifacts caused by the sensor's Bayer pattern CFA. The very low noise rating of 7.2e- (the lowest of any Phantom camera) and 64dB of dynamic range (the highest of any global shutter Phantom camera) work well together making the Onyx a good choice for high-speed VFX production.

Interchangeable lens mounts increase flexibility by adapting to Nikon, PL, C, and Canon EF with electronic control. Correlated double sampling (CDS) in standard mode provides clean image with dark regions.

Table 9.39 Phantom v2640 Onyx specifications

Phantom	v2640 ONYX
Sensor Specifications	
	CMOS Sensor
	2048 × 1952 pixels
	13.5μm pixel size
	27.6mm × 26.3mm;
	Super-35mm wide; 38.2mm diagonal
	12-bit depth
	TE and heat pipe cooled
	CAR in 128 × 8 increments,
	Standard Mode:
	ISO Color 3,200D,
	E.I. range 3,200-16,000D;
	High Speed Mode:
	ISO Color 3,200D,
	E.I. range 3,200–16,000D
Throughput/Speed	
	26 Gpx/second
	Max speed at full resolution of 2048 × 1952 is 6,600 fps.
	Minimum frame rate is 100 fps
Exposure	
	1μs minimum exposure standard,
	499ns min. exp. in Standard
	142ns min. exp. in HS with FAST option
	Global electronic shutter
	Auto Exposure
	Shutter Off mode for PIV
Memory	
	144 GB standard RAM
	288 GB optional RAM.
	CineMag IV and V for non-volatile storage (up to 8TB)
Record Times	
	3.9 seconds at max fps, 12 bits, 2048 × 1952 resolution and into 144GB RAM.
	Longer times available when recording directly to a CineMag at lower frame rates
Special Features	
	10Gb Ethernet standard
	Segment memory up to 63 times
	Continuous recording
	Memory gate
	Event marking
	Frame timestamp
	IRIG In (modulated and unmodulated)
	IRIG Out (unmodulated)

(*Continued*)

In Phantom HQ Mode, Vision Research's image enhancement results in more stable blacks, lower noise, higher dynamic range, and repeatable shots over the full range of supported resolutions, frame rates and temperatures without the need for pre-shot black references. Maximum frame rates in HQ mode are about half those in Standard Mode, which means that in HQ Mode the Phantom Flex captures images at speeds up to 1,275 fps at 1920 × 1080 or 2,640 fps at 1280 × 720.

The Phantom Flex supports both a raw digital workflow, and a video workflow, or a combination of both. With a video workflow, the Flex offers a video signal on the dual-link HD-SDI ports independent of the camera resolution. Set the resolution to 2560 × 1440 (16:9), and the camera will automatically scale the oversampled image when rendering the video signal. This technique increases the dynamic range in the video signal and eliminates edge artifacts sometimes seen in other Bayer pattern cameras.

Phantom Flex accepts a wide range of industry standard lenses. 35mm (PL, Canon EOS, Nikon F Panavision, Super 16mm and 2/3" lenses are all compatible with the Flex.

Table 9.40 Phantom Flex specifications

	Vision Research Phantom Flex
Sensor	Vision Research CMOS
Sensor Size	25.6mm × 16.0mm 10μm pixel size
Photosites	2560 × 1600 photosites
Exposure Index/ISO	ISO 1200 color
Exposure Latitude	10 stops
Notable Features	12-bit pixel depth
	Dual shooting modes:
	Standard mode for highest frame rates
	HQ mode for ultimate image quality
	Segment memory for up to 63 scenes in multi-cine mode
	Continuous recording
	Frame rate profile
	Frame timestamp
	IRIG in/out (modulated and unmodulated)
	Programmable trigger location (pre/post trigger recording) Trigger from software Hardware trigger BNC Trigger inputs also available on Aux ports
Frame Rates	Up to 1455 fps @ Standard Quality 725 fps @ HQ – 2560 × 1600
	Up to 2570 fps @ Standard Quality 1275 fps @ HQ – 1920 × 1080
	Up to 5350 fps @ Standard Quality 2640 fps @ HQ – 1280 × 720
	Up to 10750 fps @ Standard Quality 5285 fps @ HQ – 640 × 480
	6 Gpx/second
	Max speed at full resolution of 2560 × 1600 is 1455 fps in Standard mode and 725 fps in HQ mode
	At 1920 × 1080, max speed is 2570 fps in Standard mode and 1275 fps in HQ mode
	Record direct to CineMag at up to 800 Mpx/second
Shutter	Global electronic shutter
Lens Mount	645, PL, Super-PL Panavision, Canon EOS, and F-mount lens mounts
	Super 16mm and 2/3" lenses are all compatible
Viewfinder	Viewfinder port

	Vision Research Phantom Flex
Controls	External trigger signal on camera connector panel and both 12VDC power ports
	Phantom Camera Control (PCC)
	On-Camera Controls
	Remote Control Unit (RCU), connects direct to camera
	Phantom Application (legacy)
	Selectable auto-scaling of 2560 × 1440 to 1920 × 1080 or 1280 × 720 on video out
	Brightness
	Gain
	Gamma
	Saturation
	Hue
	White Balance
	Color interpolation algorithm
	Filters
	Color matrix
	Image flip and rotate
	Crop
	Scale
Onboard Recording	8GB, 16GB, 32GB high-speed internal RAM
	CineMag for non-volatile storage (128GB, 256GB, 512GB)
Recording Outputs	2 × 4:2:2 HD-SDI video ports, can be configured as dual-link 4:4:4 video (4:4:4 not available at 60 fps video formats)
Connectors	Dual-link HD-SDI
	Genlock BNC
	FSYNC BNC
	Trigger BNC
	Timecode In BNC
	Timecode Out BNC
	Remote (RCU) port
	Viewfinder port
	Two 12VDC (1.5A) Aux ports (with trigger signal available)
	Gb Ethernet for both control and data
SD Card	n/a
Synchronization	SMPTE in/out
	Genlock for synchronizing video playback – essential for 3D video workflows
Power In	20–36 VDC battery input
	Two power connectors for hot-swapping battery power or having battery backup when on AC power
Power Out	Two 12VDC (1.5A) Aux ports (with trigger signal available)
Weight	(without lens or CineMag): 11.75 lb; 5.33 kg
Dimensions	(without lens, CineMag or handle): 11.5 × 5.5 × 5.0 inches (L × W × H); 29.2 × 14 × 12.7 cm

Vision Research Phantom 65 4K

Figure 9.64 Vision Research Phantom 65 4K – legacy.

The Phantom 65 Gold delivers nearly 10 megapixel resolution at speeds of up to 144 frames per second, plus shutter speed control down to 1/500,000 second, giving precise control over the amount of blur or clarity in each scene. Exposure time can also be set in increments of one microsecond. The excellent sensitivity of the CMOS sensor and user determined contrast ratio combine to give very good image quality.

The Phantom 65 Gold is compatible with numerous formats, 65mm, 1080 HD, UHD (3840 × 2160) and 35mm film scanned, and this camera is compatible with almost all 35mm accessories. The Phantom 65 Gold can be configured for "live" broadcast or studio production using the 4:2:2 output and provides a continuous video output that conforms to HD-SDI (720p, 1080p, 1080psf, 1080i) standards. Phantom 65 Gold is compatible with many HD viewfinders and monitors making operation easier and more efficient. Many Bayer pattern high-speed cameras require rendering; with Phantom 65 users can immediately see the results of the shot. The camera records to an internal RAM memory that can then be downloaded to a laptop computer. The Phantom 65 Gold is available in 4, 8, 16 or 32 GB memory models. Phantom Cine Mags provide hot-swappable, solid-state recording in 256 and 512GB models.

Phantom 65 has multiple triggering and recording modes that can be tailored to the application. Camera setup and image file downloads using a common Gigabit Ethernet connection are accomplished using a PC and Phantom software. Image files can easily be converted to TIFF stacks, DNG, DPX, or MOV formats using the included software package.

Table 9.41 Phantom 65 4K specifications

	Vision Research Phantom 65
Sensor	Vision Research CMOS
Sensor Size	52.1mm × 30.5 mm 12.5μm pixel size
Photosites	4096 × 2440 photosites
Exposure Index/ISO	ISO 600 color
Notable Features	1.4 Gpx/second
	Max speed at full resolution of 4096 × 2440 is 140 fps
	Max speed at reduced resolution of 256 × 256 is 1340 fps
	At 1920 × 1080, max speed is 320 fps
	Record direct to CineMag at up to 1 Gpx/second
	Minimum frame rate of 10 fps
	Segment memory for up to 63 scenes in multi-cine mode
	Continuous recording
	Frame rate profile
	Frame timestamp
	IRIG in/out (modulated and unmodulated)
	Programmable trigger location (pre/post trigger recording) Trigger from software Hardware trigger BNC Trigger inputs also available on Aux ports
Frame Rates	Up to 141fps @ 4096 × 2440
	Up to 150fps @ 4096 × 2304 (4k 16:9)
	Up to 202fps @ 4096 × 1712 (65mm 2.40)
	Up to 160fps @ 3840 × 2160 (UHD)
	Up to 169fps @ 2048 × 2048
	Up to 313fps @ 2048 × 1104 (2k 1.85)

Vision Research Phantom 65	
	Up to 396fps @ 2048 × 872 (2k 2.35)
	Up to 320fps @ 1920 × 1080 (HDTV 16:9)
	Up to 288fps @ 1632 × 1200
	Up to 431fps @ 1280 × 800
	Up to 479fps @ 1280 × 720 (HDTV 16:9)
	6 Gpx/second
	Max speed at full resolution of 2560 × 1600 is 1455 fps in Standard mode and 725 fps in HQ mode
	At 1920 × 1080, max speed is 2570 fps in Standard mode and 1275 fps in HQ mode
	Record direct to CineMag at up to 800 Mpx/second
Shutter	Global electronic shutter
Lens Mount	Mamiya, Super PL, and F-mount lens mounts
Viewfinder	Component viewfinder port
Controls	Phantom Camera Control (PCC)
	On-Camera Controls
	Remote Control Unit (RCU), connects direct to camera
	Phantom Application (legacy)
	Brightness
	Gain
	Gamma
	Saturation
	Hue
	White Balance
	Color interpolation algorithm
	Filters
	Color matrix
	Image flip and rotate
	Crop
	Scale
Onboard Recording	8GB, 16GB, 32GB high-speed internal RAM
	CineMag for non-volatile storage (128GB, 256GB, 512GB)
	Cine Raw Format
Recording Outputs	4:2:2 HD-SDI
Connectors	Dual-link HD-SDI
	Genlock BNC
	FSYNC BNC
	Trigger BNC
	Timecode In BNC
	Timecode Out BNC
	Remote (RCU) port
	Viewfinder port
	Two 12VDC (1.5A) Aux ports (with trigger signal available)
	Gb Ethernet for both control and data
SD Card	n/a
Synchronization	SMPTE in/out
Power In	20–36 VDC battery input
	Two power connectors for hot-swapping battery power or having battery backup when on AC power
Power Out	Two 12VDC (1.5A) Aux ports (with trigger signal available)
Weight	12.1lbs, 5.5kg
Dimensions	5.47 × 7.62 × 12.13 in (L, W, H) 13.97 × 19.4 × 30.8cm

Vision Research Phantom HD GOLD

Figure 9.65 Vision Research Phantom HD Gold – legacy.

Phantom HD GOLD is a high-speed camera that gives the cinematographer 35mm filmic depth of field at HD or 2K resolutions. If a cinematographer is shooting TV commercials, music videos, documentaries, a motion picture, or monitoring a rocket launch, and needing a slow motion look to tell the story, the Phantom HD GOLD can provide the footage.

Phantom HD GOLD is capable of resolution above 2K, with frame rates in excess of 1000 fps at 1080p and 1500 fps in 720p, from 1 to 1,000 fps in increments of one

frame-per-second at HD resolution. Phantom HD GOLD's shutter is variable to 1/500,000 second, giving the cinematographer control of the duration, speed and time of a story element.

The camera has a sensitivity of ISO 640, making it useful under normal lighting conditions. The GOLD upgrade means improved overall camera performance with increased latitude, stable black balance, improved thermal stability, and a video encoder that provides additional HD-SDI formats.

The camera records to an internal RAM memory that can then be downloaded to a laptop computer so users can immediately see the results of a shot. Phantom Cine Mags provide hot-swappable, solid-state recording in 256 and 512GB models. The Phantom HD GOLD also allows the user to "play" the contents of the memory module over single (4:2:2) HD-SDI outputs on the docking station to a recorder, disk array, or other HD-SDI capture device.

Accessories like the Phantom Breakout Box (12v power distribution system), and JuiceBox, (400 watt power supply), make electronic accessorizing easier. The camera is compatible with many HD viewfinders and monitors making shooting any subject easier and more precise. The monoplanar CMOS imager achieves 35mm depth-of-field, and the camera is fully compatible with all 35mm accessories like matte boxes and follow focus.

Table 9.42 Phantom HD Gold specifications

	Vision Research Phantom HD GOLD
Sensor	Vision Research CMOS
Sensor Size	25.6mm × 25.6mm 12.5µm pixel size
Photosites	2048 × 2048 pixels
Exposure Index/ISO	ISO 600 color
Exposure Latitude	10 stops
Notable Features	2.3 Gpx/second
	Max speed at full resolution of 2048 × 2048 is 555 fps
	Max speed at reduced resolution of 256 × 256 is 4,400 fps
	At 1920 × 1080, max speed is 1050 fps
	Record direct to CineMag at up to 1 Gpx/second
	Minimum frame rate of 10 fps
	Segment memory for up to 63 scenes in multi-cine mode
	Continuous recording
	Frame rate profile
	Frame timestamp
	IRIG in/out (modulated and unmodulated)
	Programmable trigger location (pre/post trigger recording)

	Vision Research Phantom HD GOLD
	Trigger from software
	Hardware trigger BNC
	Trigger inputs also available on Aux ports
Frame Rates	Up to 555fps @ 2048 × 2048
	Up to 1029 fps @ 2048 × 1104 (2k 1.85)
	Up to 1302 fps @ 2048 × 872 (2k 2.35)
	Up to 1052 fps @ 1920 × 1080 (HDTV 16:9)
	Up to 946 fps @ 1632 × 1200
	Up to 1419 fps @ 1280 × 800
	Up to 1576 fps @ 1280 × 720 (HDTV 16:9)
	2.3 Gpx/second
	Max speed at full resolution of 2048 × 2048 is 555 fps
	Max speed at reduced resolution of 256 × 256 is 4,400 fps
	At 1920 × 1080, max speed is 1050 fps
	Record direct to CineMag at up to 1 Gpx/second
	Minimum frame rate of 10 fps
Shutter	Progressive electronic shutter
	2μs minimum exposure
Lens Mount	PL-mount standard
	Nikon F-mount optional
Viewfinder	Component viewfinder port
Controls	Phantom Camera Control (PCC)
	On-Camera Controls
	Remote Control Unit (RCU), connects direct to camera
	Phantom Application (legacy)
	Brightness
	Gain
	Gamma
	Saturation
	Hue
	White Balance
	Color interpolation algorithm
	Filters
	Color matrix
	Image flip and rotate
	Crop
	Scale
Onboard Recording	8GB, 16GB, 32GB high-speed internal RAM
	CineMag for non-volatile storage (128GB, 256GB, 512GB)
	Cine RAW Format,
Recording Outputs	Analog video (NTSC or PAL) on capture cable
	4:2:2 HD-SDI
Connectors	4:2:2 HD-SDI
	Analog video (NTSC or PAL) on capture cable
	Hardware trigger BNC
	Timing & Synchronization
	Frame synchronization to internal or external clock (FSYNC)
	IRIG in/out (modulated or unmodulated)
	Ready output

(Continued)

Table 9.42 (Continued)

	Vision Research Phantom HD GOLD
	Strobe output
	Signaling
	Strobe, Ready, Video, IRIG on capture cable
	Viewfinder
	20–36 VDC battery input
Synchronization	Frame synchronization to internal or external clock (FSYNC)
	IRIG in/out (modulated or unmodulated)
	Ready output
	Strobe output
Power In	20–36 VDC battery input
Power Out	n/a
Weight	12.1lbs, 5.5kg
Dimensions	5.47 × 7.62 × 12.13in (L, W, H) 13.97 × 19.4 × 30.8cm

WEISSCAM HS-2

Figure 9.66

*Source:*www.weisscam.com/highspeed-cameras/
weisscam-hs-2/

Figure 9.67 WEISSCAM HS-2.

The WEISSCAM HS-2 is an uncompressed high speed digital camera used for shooting at frame rates up to 4,000 fps. Workflows include two shooting modes, raw and HD via HD SDI, in two aspect ratios (4:3 + 16:9). The WEISSCAM HS-2 has a Super35 CMOS sensor with a global shutter and uses an Interchangeable Lens Mount System (IMS) from P+S Technik. Cinematographers can use a wide variety of lenses with the camera: PL Mount, Nikon F-Mount, Panavision Mount; the lens mount can be changed in a few seconds.

The output of the WEISSCAM HS-2 offers two different output signals and uses the HD SDI interface for either signal. Weisscam's raw HD SDI mapping enables transport of raw files via standard HD SDI single and dual link interfaces. The HD stream offers YCbCr in 4:2:2. Very fast boot up time allows the camera to be ready for shooting in less than 7 seconds.

Menus allow choice between standard curves like ITU-R 709 or a log curve for higher dynamic range within the HD SDI image. The raw stream is a 12-bit uncompressed Weisscam raw file and gives users the freedom to deBayer in post production. In conjunction with the WEISSCAM DIGIMAG DM-2, users are able to record both formats via HD SDI: YCbCr and raw.

Numerous accessory mounting positions allow the user to connect additional accessories like onboard monitor, lens control system, etc. and power them from several outputs of the DC/DC board. Intelligent master/slave DC/DC power management prevents any short circuit or incorrect battery connection, and makes it unnecessary to shut down the camera for a battery change.

Table 9.43 Weisscam HS-2 specifications

	WEISSCAM HS-2 High Speed Camera
Sensor	CMOS Sensor, Global shutter
Sensor Size	22.18 × 22.18mm/31.36mm diagonal
Photosites	2016 × 2016 pixels max. recording in IT mode. 2048 × 1536 pixel max. recording over HD SDI. To achieve 2048 pixels, HD SDI format will be framed by vertical black bars on both the left and right sides.
Exposure Index/ISO	600 ASA
Notable Features	5 different trigger modes:
	Ringbuffer continuously record in a loop to the internal memory
	Sequence the camera begins to record by pressing REC – and stops automatically when RAM is full
	70/30 trigger
	50/50 trigger
	30/70 trigger
	3 – 5 are mixtures of sequence, ringbuffer and center trigger.
Frame Rates	up to 1,500 fps in 2K
	up to 2,000 fps in 1080p
	up to 4,000 fps in 720p
Lens Mount	Interchangeable Mount System (PL, Panavision, BNC-R, Professional, Nikon F, Canon EF, Canon FD, Leica-R, Leica-M)
Viewfinder	Weight (with holder): 770 grams
	Dimensions (with holder): L = 125mm W = 175mm
	Diameter of Eyepiece: 65mm
	Resolution: 800 × 600 pixel
	Light source: OLED Technology
	Connectors: Power connector: 4-pin Lemo Video connector: VGA (use with DVI to VGA Adapter)
Controls	Ring Buffer
	Sequence Mode
	Trigger Mode: 70/30, 50/50, 30/70
	Direct Recording (immediate playback without RAM-buffering)
Onboard Recording	RAW Signal: 12-bit uncompressed WEISSCAM RAW
	HD Signal: 10-bit YCbCr 4:2:2
	Digimag DM-2 via HD-SDI or onto PC via GigE or USB 2.0
Recording Outputs	HD
	1:1 mode ("STANDARD RAW MODE SL")
	Standard transfer (single link)
	1280 × 720p: 50p
	1920 × 1080: 23.98psf, 24psf, 25psf, 29.97psf, 30psf
	2K: 25psf (1920 × 1080 Preview)
	2:1 mode ("FAST RAW MODE SL")
	Single Link: 1080: 50i, 59.94i, 60i
	Dual Link: 1080: 50p, 59.94p, 60p
	RAW
	1:1 mode ("STANDARD RAW MODE SL")
	1280 × 720: 50p
	1920 × 1080: 23.98p, 24p, 25p, 29.97p, 30p
	2K: 25p

(Continued)

Table 9.43 (Continued)

	WEISSCAM HS-2 High Speed Camera
	2:1 mode (FAST RAW MODE SL):
	1280 × 720: 100p
	1920 × 1080: 50p, 100p, 60p, 120p
	2K: 50p
Connectors	Power connector: 4-pin Lemo
	Video connector: VGA (use with DVI to VGA Adapter)
Synchronization	n/a
Power In	24V DC, Fischer 2-pin
Power Out	12V/0.5A DC OUT: Connector type 4-pin Lemo
	12V/3A DC OUT: Connector type 4-pin Lemo
	24V/3A DC OUT: Connector type 3-pin Fischer
	WEISSCAM power supply: Socket type 4-pin XLR
Weight	6.8kg
Dimensions	Height: 210.4mm, Length: 315.9mm, Width: 200.7mm

Chapter 10

Camera Setup and Operation

Bars and Tone

Bars and tone are used to calibrate the video and the audio levels properly. In the absence of a calibration probe they can quickly tell you whether your monitors are set up correctly. It's good practice to include 60 seconds of bars and tone at the beginning of your tape or digital mag (even if only once or twice a day). It gives post production a fighting chance to know where to begin with picture and sound levels throughout the image pipeline.

Figure 10.1 Association of Radio Industries and Businesses SMPTE Standard Dynamic Range (SDR) color bars.

The Society of Motion Picture and Television Engineers (SMPTE) have standardized HD digital test color bars as SMPTE RP 219-2002. In this pattern, the top two-thirds contains nine vertical bars of 75% video intensity: gray, white, yellow, cyan, green, magenta, red, blue, and 40% gray again. Vector scopes are marked with graticule boxes showing the target regions where the traces from red, green, blue, yellow, cyan, magenta and white are meant to land if the signal is properly calibrated.

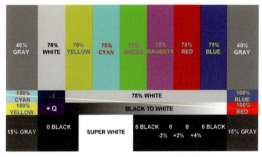

Figure 10.2 SMPTE ARIB Standard Dynamic Range (SDR) color bars with labels.

Below the main set of nine bars are two short strips of patches. There is a small 100% cyan bar, a 100% yellow bar. There is a section that contains a patch of very dark blue, and a patch of very dark purple, these are the –I and +Q broadcast test chrominance patches used to tell engineers whether a display is properly demodulating color sub carrier. Then there are wide rectangles containing 75% white and a ramp from black to 100% white, and at the right there are 100% blue and red patches.

The bottom row of the test pattern (from left to right) contains a square of 15% gray, a rectangle of 0 black, a rectangle of 100% white, a rectangle of 0 black, a series of narrow black PLUGE bars, another square of 0 black and another square of 15% gray. The small set of black PLUGE bars are a "Picture Line-Up Generation Equipment" pattern. These five small bars from left to right have values of –2% black level, 0 black level, +2% blacklevel, 0 black level, and +4% black level. The PLUGE pulse is useful for correctly adjusting the black level of a display. When a monitor is properly adjusted, the right PLUGE bar should be just barely visible and the +2% and –2% bars should appear identically black.

Figure 10.3 All PLUGE bars are visible – too bright, +4% PLUGE bar barely visible – Correct.

Using Color Bars to Set Up a Monitor

To use color bars to adjust a monitor, begin by turning the chroma (color) in the monitor all the way down so that the picture becomes monochrome. Then adjust brightness until the center PLUGE bar becomes the same black value as the left PLUGE bar, and the right PLUGE bar is still just visibly different. Then adjust contrast (or picture adjustment) until the white patch at the bottom left center is white, but not so bright as to change the relationship of the PLUGE bars. Then adjust color (chroma) until they are saturated but not bleeding into adjacent bars, and then adjust hue (or tint) until the yellow and magenta bars look correct. Yellow has a tendency to turn orange or green when set incorrectly, magenta has a tendency to turn red or purple when set incorrectly.

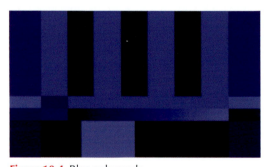

Figure 10.4 Blue only mode.

An alternate method for adjusting chroma is available if your monitor has a "blue only" mode. In this mode, adjust the chroma until the top left and top right bars are the same brightness. Then adjust the hue until the cyan and magenta bars either side of the center green bar are also the same brightness. Switch out of the blue only mode and the monitor color should be correct.

SMPTE Time Code

In 1967, the Society of Motion Picture and Television Engineers standardized a system to label individual frames of video or film with a time code in their SMPTE 12M specification, and revised the standard in 2008, turning it into a two-part document: SMPTE 12M-1 and SMPTE 12M-2.

Time code is used to synchronize video, film, audio content, and music, and to provide a time reference for video tape editing, eventually leading to the invention of non linear edit systems such as Avid and Final Cut Pro.

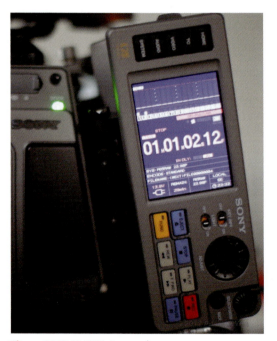

Figure 10.5 SMPTE time code.

The timing data in SMPTE time code is based on an eight digit, 24-hour clock. The count runs from 0 to 59 seconds, 0 to 59 minutes, and 0 to 23 hours. The second is subdivided into a number of frames, which varies depending on regional acquisition frame rates. In the United States and the Americas, timecode runs at 29.97 fps in video (30 ÷ 1.001 fps) for ATSC (Advanced Television Systems Committee) broadcast, and 23.976 fps for films. Even though we always shot on film at an even 24 fps, for the purposes of using timecode to sync to audio throughout post production, most digitally acquired projects are shot at 23.976 fps. In Europe and many other markets the television frame rate is 25 fps, while films are acquired at 23.976, 24 fps and, 25 fps.

Time Code on Set

When shooting video, time code is normally recorded onto the camera, even if audio is recorded separately. Jam-syncing (where sync is carried to each camera manually for the camera to pick up and carry forward) all of the time codes can take care of basic sync. In addition to jam-sync, use a time code slate for matching up picture with audio. One possible solution is to have all cameras and audio recorders hard wired to gen-lock so they are always in phase, but that requires cables running to every device, usually awkward.

The portable battery powered Ambient Clockit family of time code products can provide mobile time code that, based on a very accurate, temperature compensated crystal oscillator, can be calibrated in the field to a reference deviation of less than .2ppm or less than 1 frame per day.

Figure 10.6 Ambient lockit time code box.

This allows for a sync without hard-wiring or relying on problematic RF transmission. Clockit units support all SMPTE TC modes, including pull up/down and drop rates, and time code over ASCII.

Figure 10.7 Denecke time code slate.

A standard of the industry is the Denecke "smart" slate, with a sync box that can be easily jam-synced to the audio recorder, holding sync for half a day. Jam-syncing the time code is easy, so there is no reason to wait that long.

Give every tape, mag, or roll a unique sequential number based on the camera (roll A42, B27). As long as the tape number, scene, and take correspond to the scene, take, camera, and roll in the script supervisor's notes, then time code should be accurate no matter what method used. Well managed on set time code will be useful to sync audio and to conform media for output.

When tapes or rolls or digital mags are ingested into an Avid or FCP, the tape number must be logged as well. A good protocol is to number the tapes sequentially, be sure no two tapes have the same number, and correctly enter the tape or roll number into the edit system in preparation for the edit. When you re-conform the footage for the online edit, the edit system will ask you for the correct tape number as it drops the shot into the timeline.

Most post houses have their own tape cataloging system with a 5, 6, or 7 digit bar code numbering system – so that if used correctly, many productions can be edited in the same building without the tapes getting mixed up.

When doing sync playback, as in a music video, the time code slate needs to display the code of the soundtrack being played back, so the slate must function as a "dumb" slate and receive a time code feed from the playback source. This feed can come either via a connecting cable or a transmitter.

How Time Code Is Carried

The audio sync tone version of SMPTE is called linear or Longitudinal Time Code or LTC, and is recorded on an audio channel. To read LTC, the recording must be moving; LTC doesn't work when the recording is stopped or significantly slowed.

Vertical Interval Time Code or VITC is recorded directly into the vertical blanking interval of a video signal on each frame of video. The advantage of VITC is that, since it is a part of the playback video, it can be read when the tape is stationary.

Control Track Longitudinal Time Code is embedded in a videotape's control track.

Visible Time Code (Burnt-in Time Code) or BITC refers to the numbers that are burned into the video image so that humans (users?)

can easily read the time code. Videotapes that are duplicated with these time code numbers are known as window dubs.

Keycode can also carry time code information in film applications.

29.97 Frames per Second?

In 1941, the American monochrome television standard had a frame rate of 30 fps at 525 lines. The audio signal was combined with the video signal by modulating an audio sub carrier at a frequency of 4.5 MHz. In 1953, the American NTSC (National Television System Committee) added a color television standard that it hoped would be backward compatible with existing black and white television sets.

Figure 10.8 1950s Philco black and white Predicta television.

Two new chrominance components were combined with the original black and white luminance signal by adding two sub carrier frequencies. Engineers discovered an interference between the line frequency and both sub carrier frequencies, so they changed the frame rate by 0.1%, resulting in a frame rate of (30 × 1000/1001) fps, or 29.97 fps, resulting in an interlace field rate of 59.94 Hz. This historical artifact has given us the requirement to shoot projects in the US market at fractional frame rates: 29.97 fps and 23.976 fps. Shooting at integer frame rates of 24 fps and 30 fps dictates a re-parse of the footage (and resampling of the audio) to the standardized fractional frame rates for broadcast.

Drop Frame and Non Drop Frame Time Code

Black and white broadcasting was based on non drop frame time code that assumed a frame rate of 30 fps, so programming broadcast at 29.97 fps created a problem; a one hour program was now longer than an hour of clock time by 3.59 seconds, leading to an error of almost a minute and a half over a day. To correct this error, Drop Frame Time Code was invented. No picture frames are deleted using drop frame time code, but rather, some of the numerical time code labels are dropped. In order to make an hour of time code match an hour on the clock, drop frame time code drops frame numbers 0 and 1 of the first second of every minute, except when the number of minutes is divisible by ten. This creates a drop frame rate of 18 frames each ten minutes, and very closely compensates for the difference in frame rate, leaving a residual timing error of roughly 86.4 milliseconds per day.

If you are shooting digital for cinema in the United States, the correct camera time code frame rate is either 23.976 fps (*not* 24 fps) or 29.97 fps to sync to audio recorded at 29.97 fps, both non drop frame.

The correct frame rate for recording audio that will be synced to true 24 fps shooting is 30 fps, regardless of whether the camera is running at 24 fps or 30 fps. This is because the audio does not have to correspond to the film speed but rather to the video speed, and the editing is being done in video. Unless otherwise instructed, use non-drop time code on true 24 fps and 30 fps shoots.

Five Running Modes for Generating Time Code

1. The most basic setting is Free Run/Time of Day, where the internal time code generator is like a clock, showing the actual time of day. The clock runs continuously, whether the capturing device is recording or not. Time code errors between the slate and the recorder are easy to detect. This setting is useful when the actual time of day is important to know for each shot.

2. Free Run/User Set is similar to Free Run/ Time of Day, except that the starting time is chosen by the user and does not necessarily correlate to the actual time of day.

3. Record Run time code means that the time code generator stops when the recording stops. Numbers increment during the Record mode, but remain frozen in time during pause or stop. The elapsed time code is sort of like a tape counter, and

is an indication of how many minutes have been recorded. Most camcorders and disk recorders have a Resume Record Run Function to re-cue for continuous record numbers after reviewing shot footage.

4. External time code refers to continuously reading time code from an External source and re-generating it onto the recorder. If the External code should stop or be intermittent, the code being recorded would also be in error.

5. Jam-sync means that the recorder synchronizes its internal time code generator to match the starting numbers from an External source, such as a "Lockit" box. When the connection to External is released, the internal code will keep in step with the external time code source for a few hours or longer, depending on the accuracy of the time code generators in question (recorder and source). Of course, jam-sync only makes sense in the Free-Run time code modes.

Shutter/Exposure Time

Digital cinematography cameras can be confusing in their expressions of exposure time. Some cameras' Sync Scan functions read exposure time as a function of fractional time, such as 1/48, 1/96, 1/125, 1/250, 1/500, 1/1000, while others read in frames per second and shutter angle, while still others read in decimal fractional time, or in milliseconds (thousandths of a second).

Exposure Time: Speed vs. Shutter Angles

Let's examine as an example the mathematics of exposure times expressed in fractional terms like 1/48th of a second as opposed to 24 fps at a 180 degree shutter angle.

To accurately convert shutter speed to shutter angles at 24 fps the formula is (24 × 360)/Time Fraction, or 8640/xx where "xx" is 1/xx sec), so the equivalent shutter angle for 1/50 sec shutter speed is 8640/50 = 172.8 degrees.

To find a shutter speed that relates to a known shutter angle, do the math in reverse. At 24 fps the equation is (24 × 360)/Shutter Angle, or 8640/xx where "xx" is xx degrees, so the shutter speed for 144 degrees at 24 fps is 8640/144 = 60 (1/60th of a second).

Similarly, to convert shutter speed to shutter angles at 30 fps the formula is (30 × 360)/Time Fraction, or 10800/xx where "xx" is 1/xx sec.

I have not included charts or calculations for 23.976 fps or 29.97 fps fractional frame rates because the difference between those speeds and 24 fps or 30 fps is such a small fraction as to be insignificant.

Table 10.1 Exposure time expressed in fractions of a second, degrees at FPS, and decimal time

FOR 24 fps				
Time Expressed in Fractions of a Second		Shutter Angle Expressed in Degrees @ 24 fps		Time Expressed as a Decimal
1/32	=	270	=	0.03125000
1/48	=	180	=	0.020833333
1/50	=	172.8	=	0.02000000
1/60	=	144	=	0.01666666
1/96	=	90	=	0.01041666
1/120	=	72	=	0.00833333
1/198	=	45	=	0.00505050
1/200	=	43.2	=	0.00500000
1/348	=	22.5	=	0.00287356
1/500	=	17.28	=	0.00200000
1/696	=	11	=	0.00143678
1/1000	=	8.6	=	0.00100000

FOR 30 fps				
Time Expressed in Fractions of a Second		Shutter Angle Expressed in Degrees @ 30 fps		Time Expressed as a Decimal
1/30	=	360	=	0.033333333
1/48	=	225	=	0.020833333
1/50	=	216	=	0.02000000
1/60	=	180	=	0.01666666
1/96	=	112.5	=	0.01041666
1/120	=	90	=	0.00833333
1/198	=	54.5454	=	0.00505050
1/200	=	54	=	0.00500000
1/348	=	31.0344	=	0.00287356
1/500	=	21.6	=	0.00200000
1/696	=	15.5172	=	0.00143678
1/1000	=	10.8	=	0.00100000

Going Beyond 180 Degree Maximum Shutter Angle

In order to understand how varying the shutter angle works in digital, it is important to review how cinema shutter angles work in historical context. Film cameras have almost always employed a physical shutter to prevent light from exposing the film during the period while an unexposed frame of film is being shuttled into the aperture. Thomas Edison relied on a shooting frame rate of up to 46 fps with a pull down cycle of 10% of the per frame exposure cycle to lessen the streaking effect until a mechanical shutter was later added.

Figure 10.9 The Edison Kinetoscope.

Most film cameras employ a shutter that is basically half a circle. Shutter angle refers to the amount of the 360 degree shutter circle that is open. This has historically been in the neighborhood of 180 degrees resulting from the nature of the mechanics involved in alternately shuttling a new frame into the aperture and then registering that frame for exposure.

Flange focal distances for cinema lenses have for many years been dictated by the use of spinning mirror reflex systems for direct reflex viewing through the taking lens of motion picture cameras. The ARRI IIc and the Mitchell BNCR both employed 180 degree opening spinning mirror shutters interposed at a 45 degree angle between the lens and the film plane in order to simultaneously relay the image to an optical viewfinder system while also covering the film plane during the film pull down cycle. Advances in image processing have reduced the latency of live images from digital sensors to electronic viewfinders, obviating the need for reflex viewing systems. One result of this evolution is that lens new designs based on shorter flange focal depths are greatly increasing optical performance in lenses.

Figure 10.10 180 degree physical shutter from an ARRIflex film camera.

The resulting exposure cycle at 24 fps is 180/360; one half of 1/24th of a second = 1/48th of a second exposure time. Engineering a film shuttle movement for a 180 degree exposure cycle followed by 180 degree film shuttle cycle was much easier than engineering any other relationship of the pull down and exposure cycles.

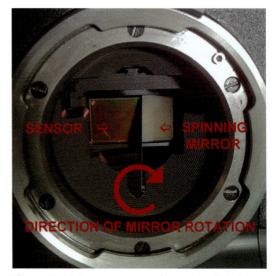

Figure 10.11 Spinning mirror shutter in a digital camera.

The only variations on the 180 degree shutter came in the form of adding a second leaf to the shutter that could be rotated against (alongside, as an extension of) the original shutter to reduce the exposure time.

Electronic Viewfinders

In the age of electronic cameras, spinning mirror reflex viewing systems have been all but eliminated. Because of the advances in image processing that have reduced the latency of live images from digital sensors to electronic viewfinders, the need for sharp, bright, reliable electronic viewfinders is critical. Video viewfinders can vary wildly in quality and resolution. Choosing a viewfinder may not seem like a very important area of concern, but the first time you get a phone call from an editor or a studio to discuss out of focus dailies it will become the number one topic on your agenda! Brightness, resolution, exit pupil size, color, and ease of use are all important to consider in choosing a viewfinder for your shoot. Take the time to fully learn to use all the onboard tools that a good viewfinder affords.

Figure 10.12 ARRI EVF-1 F-LCOS viewfinder.

Figure 10.13 SONY OLED DVF-EL100 viewfinder.

Viewfinder Magnification

Magnifying the image is extremely useful for setting and checking critical focus marks. Many well designed viewfinders give the operator the ability to magnify the viewing image 2× or 4×. Just remember to reset the viewfinder back to normal before starting a take!

Figure 10.14 Viewfinder in normal viewing mode.

Figure 10.15 Viewfinder in magnified viewing mode.

Shutter Angle and Motion Blur in Digital Cameras

Temporal resolution refers to the discrete resolution of a sampling system with respect to time. In some applications, temporal resolution may be equated to the sampling period, or its inverse, the refresh rate, or the update frequency in Hertz, of a sensor or camera or display.

The primary result of the issues of the mechanics of pulling film into and out of the film gate on a frame to frame basis has been that we have become accustomed to the look of motion images acquired with a 180 degree shutter. Images with smaller shutter angles have been used to great effect in story telling such as the narrow shutter angle images used to accentuate the stacatto feel of the battle scenes in *Saving Private Ryan*. Narrowing the shutter angle decreases the amount of light being captured, requiring exposure compensation by decreasing the frame rate or opening the iris.

Motion blur is the streaking of sequential frames that results when the objects being recorded move during the exposure, or when the camera itself is moved. Usually at 24 frames per second at 180 degree shutter the exposure time is brief enough that the image captured is not perceptibly blurred, but fast moving objects, or a moving camera, may result in increased image blurring along the direction of relative motion.

When one considers the pace of the films we make today, it is hard to imagine making a movie without moving the camera. Panning, tilting, rolling, dollying, and craning the camera are essential to the vocabulary of modern story telling. It is important that cinematographers understand the effect of camera movement on images. If (for example) the cinematographer has made efforts to assure sharply detailed images by shooting in 4K, 5K, or even 8K with very sharp lenses, he or she should understand and appreciate that those efforts are only evident to the audience while the camera is at rest. Once the camera is put in motion, the apparent resolution is determined by the amount of motion displacement in the scene while the shutter is open. Shooting at high resolution still has value, *especially* when doing visual effects, but a firm understanding of the relationship between shutter open time and apparent resolution is still essential.

Figure 10.16 Magnified portion of a static shot with no motion blur.

Figure 10.17 Magnified portion of a subsequent frame with camera panning and dollying – horizontal motion blur is very evident.

Widening the shutter angle even slightly for adding exposure time in film cameras was only achieved by Herculean engineering effort, such as in the Panaflex R200, which boasted a 200+ degree shutter opening.

Figure 10.18 The Panavision R-200 camera.

Because electronic cameras are not constrained by the necessity of mechanical shutters, we are now free to explore the new creative territory of wider shutter angles, but we are not used to seeing images with that look, so our first steps out of that box are cautious and hesitant. The look of 360 degree shutter opening seems foreign to the traditional look and feel of motion pictures, and many cinematographers and directors rebel against it.

In order to illustrate what 360 degree shutter means, I have captured single frames from moving footage of a Mini Maglight flashlight bulb waving around in the dark. I overlaid multiple frames in sequence to show the effect of shutter angle opening on the amount of blur in consecutive images. I set the shutter at a variety of angles in order to illustrate the differences. In the first example, the shutter was set to 11 degrees, meaning that the shutter was open for 11 degrees out of a 360 degree cycle, and closed for 349 degrees of the 360 degree cycle. Notice that the flashlight bulb appears as a sharp, recognizable, crisp shape, and consecutive frames indicate the distance the bulb has traveled from one frame to the next frame of the 24 fps sequence.

Figure 10.19 Sequence of four consecutive 24p frames at an 11 degree shutter opening.

Observing all seven frames integrated into one picture shows the distance the bulb traveled while the shutter was open, and the space between exposures shows the distance the bulb traveled during the time the shutter was closed. An 11 degree shutter opening produces a relatively sharp image of the bulb, with no motion blur or streaking, which results in a staccato look when played back in real time.

Now let's open the shutter to 45 degrees out of 360.

Figure 10.20 Sequence of four consecutive 24p frames at a 90 degree shutter opening.

When all five consecutive frames are integrated into one picture, we can see that the flashlight is streaked, and there is still a substantial gap between images. The streaks represent the 90 degrees of shutter open time, one quarter of the 360 degree exposure cycle, and the gaps between exposures make up the remaining 270 degrees, or three quarters of the cycle. Now let's examine frames that were taken at a 180 degree shutter opening.

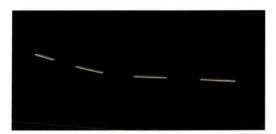

Figure 10.21 Sequence of four consecutive 24p frames at a 180 degree shutter opening.

The 180 degree shutter is the look that we have been accustomed to seeing since the advent of motion pictures. This is the amount of streak that has always resulted when objects moved across the frame at this relative speed. This relationship of shutter open time to shutter closed time is the basis for all of the panning speed tables and image strobing recommendations that have been written for film.

Now we are getting into new and uncharted territory …

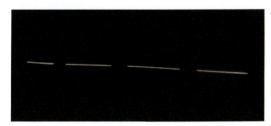

Figure 10.22 Sequence of four consecutive 24p frames at a 270 degree shutter opening.

I opened the shutter to record a sequence of four consecutive 24p frames at a 270 degree shutter opening, and it is easy to see that the amount of streaked exposure time is three times the amount of interval between exposures.

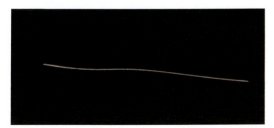

Figure 10.23 Sequence of four consecutive 24p frames at a 355 degree shutter opening.

Then I opened the shutter to its maximum opening and integrated a sequence of four consecutive 24p Frames at a 355 degree shutter opening. There is hardly any shutter closed interval at all. A tiny interval can be seen between frames, and there is almost no missing image data. Fast pans and especially circular dolly shots exposed this way exhibit no judder and can look very interesting.

There is a growing movement toward high frame rate (HFR) acquisition, which affords many new options for the cinematographer.

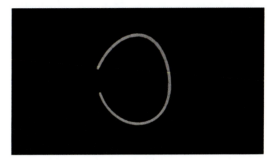

Figure 10.24 Sequence of 20 Consecutive 120p Frames at a 355 degree shutter opening.

I have included a sample to show the amount of blur in 120 fps HFR material shot with a 355 degree shutter opening. Note that there is almost no gap between consecutive images, but the amount of blur in each image is comparable to the amount of blur we saw in each image of the 24 fps 90 degree shutter opening material. Judder and strobing are effectively eliminated, and individual frames are sharp and crisp. The decision to shoot at this combination of frame rate and shutter angle is partly a matter of taste and partly a technical decision based on the kind of content you are shooting. Many film cinematographers, critics, and movie-goers disdain this look, but at the same time, others find it clearer, more resolved, and more satisfying for shooting fast action content.

Some cinematographers assert that 360 shutter is not cinematic and should be avoided, but I have used it for very satisfying results in a number of cases. Several years ago, I photographed a circular dolly shot around an actor in a medium shot, and by opening the shutter to 360 degrees I was able to focus on the actor without any distracting judder of the out of focus background. Because the actor was stationary in the middle of the frame and because his image was not physically displacing appreciably from one frame to the next, the effect of the wide shutter angle could not be detected at all on him, but without using a 360 shutter I would have been forced to do the dolly at a *much* slower speed in order to avoid the sickening juddering background effect that would have occurred with a 180 degree shutter opening. I could not have done the same shot on film, and this was the first time I have ever done a circular dolly shot that I felt really worked. When used properly, a 360 degree shutter can be an amazing tool!

Additionally, I find it very useful to gain an extra bit of exposure in very low light situations by opening up to a 270 or even 360 degree shutter to gain a half stop to a stop of light. If the action and camera movements are not fast and the story allows, wide shutter openings can often give a pleasing and gentle look to a scene. Wide shutter angle is a useful tool that should always be considered as an option, and as the technology of DCP playout in theaters improves, it should soon be possible to create Digital Cinema Packages that can switch frame rates on the fly. This would eventually give creatives the option to shoot quieter, more static dramatic scenes at 24 fps at 180 degree shutter for a traditional cinematic feel, combined with action sequences, car chases, and fight scenes at 120 fps 360 shutter to eliminate motion judder.

Camera Setup and Operation: Menus

Manipulating the color and contrast of images on set using on board camera controls should only be attempted after much deliberation and testing. In cameras that acquire RGB images, adjustments made in camera are "baked" into the image and for the most part difficult if not impossible to undo. (This usually is not true in cameras that shoot raw images.) There are only a few things that can be done in the camera that can't be done better in post production. If you set your stop correctly, and white and black balance carefully, you can generally achieve success. If you feel you must manipulate the image on set through the use of camera menu functions, the best advice I can offer is test, test, and test again! Review the results on the biggest screen possible, and share the results with your postproduction department.

White Balance

Most cameras that record RAW images do not "bake in" the white balance, but rather, they carry the setting as metadata embedded in the image

stream. That does not excuse the cinematographer of the duty to white balance the camera. As the color of daylight changes throughout the day, or as you move from exteriors to interiors white balance affects the color balance of images and eventually shows up to cost time and money in color correction during post production. When using cameras that provide for baked in white balance adjustment, it is always advisable to white balance your camera to accommodate varying color temperatures in lighting, *but remember*, you are color correcting the overall bias of the image on set when you white balance, and it is a color decision that you will have to live with. If you don't have a budget for spending time color correcting or changing the white balance metadata of your images in post, white balance *carefully* and *judiciously*! Test, test, test!

Figure 10.25 ARRI ALEXA with optimo zoom white balanced at 5600 kelvin.

Figure 10.26 The same scene white balanced at 3200 kelvin.

It can be painful to watch a scene that is not color corrected and which bounces from one color temperature to another from shot to shot. When the sun is setting and you are struggling to get a reverse on an actor, keep in mind that the color temperature is changing quickly and radically, and the reverse that you shoot at magic hour probably won't match the color of the master you shot an hour ago unless you are diligent in white balancing.

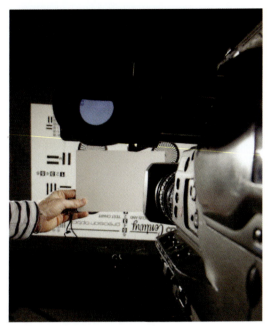

Figure 10.27 Setting white balance.

White balance following the menu path for the particular camera in question, set the gain to zero, check that you have the proper filter (if any) in place for the color temperature of light on set, and use a good standard white balance card or 18% gray card that is evenly illuminated to match the predominant set lighting color balance. Exercise caution, not all chart lights are created equal. Tungsten lights are often 3,000K, tungsten balanced Kino Flo bulbs are 3,200K, which is technically correct but reads cooler than tungsten by comparison, HMI lights in good working order run around 5600K, clear sky daylight is 6500K, and fluorescent and LED practicals may be wildly unpredictable in color temperature. It helps to have a color temperature meter or better, a spectroradiometer handy to (approximately) measure the color temperature of the lamp being used to white balance.

Fill as much of the center of frame as possible with the white card, be sure not to have anything else in the frame that competes with the card for white value. Set the iris so that the card reaches peak white value and then execute the balance operation.

If you absolutely cannot white balance, I recommend setting the camera to its default 3200 white balance setting for tungsten lit interiors or to 5500 white balance for exteriors, then use camera the filter wheel to accommodate your shoot conditions according to the on set color temperature, and then color correct the material later.

Black Balance

Some cameras almost never require black balance, some require infrequent black balance, and some cameras (such as Vision Research Phantom cameras) should be black balanced frequently.

Figure 10.28 Black frame from a camera in need of black balance.

On cameras that require black balance adjustment, follow instructions to black balance menu, remember to close the lens iris or preferably cap the lens with an opaque black cap, and adjust black balance:

When you start your shooting day.
When the camera has been in use for some time.
When the ambient temperature has changed, for example after sunset or sunrise, or after a lunch break.
When you change your gain setting.
When you change camera frame rate.

Black balancing an HD camera will reduce the amount of noise in the blacks, so don't be shy, black balance liberally on cameras that require it!

Gamma γ A Video Power Function

Gamma adjustment in digital cameras and in color correction is used to modify the non-linear manner in which humans perceive light. It adjusts the power function of code values *between* white and black without modifying blackest black and whitest white.

Figure 10.29 11 Step crossed gray with normal gamma.

Figure 10.33 11 Step crossed gray with gamma down.

Figure 10.30 Waveform RGB parade representation of 11 step crossed gray with normal gamma.

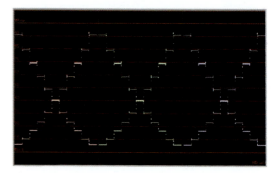

Figure 10.34 Waveform RGB parade representation of 11 step crossed gray with gamma down adjustment.

Gamma sets the overall contrast curve of the camera from black through gray to white. It can be used very effectively to reallocate the mid tones of the camera to various exposure levels. Gamma can be used to preserve detail in dark areas of the frame, midtone, or brighter areas of the frame. Think of gamma almost like the bellows of an accordion, where the ends can be held constant, but the middle is variable. Depending on the subject matter in front of the camera, gamma can be used to preserve detail in selected tonal regions for manipulation in post production and color correction. Once again, test, test, test!

Figure 10.31 11 Step crossed gray with gamma up.

Gain

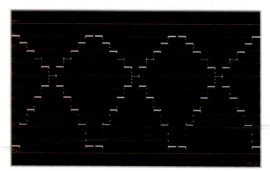

Figure 10.32 Waveform RGB parade representation of 11 step crossed gray with gamma up adjustment.

Figure 10.35 11 step crossed gray with normal gain.

Figure 10.36 Waveform RGB parade representation of 11 step crossed gray with normal gain.

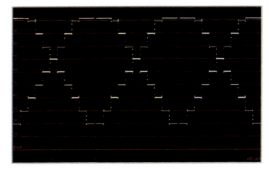

Figure 10.40 Waveform RGB parade representation of 11 step crossed gray with gain up beyond clipping.

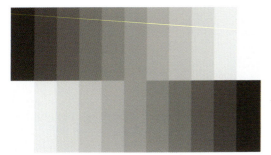

Figure 10.37 11 step crossed gray with gain up.

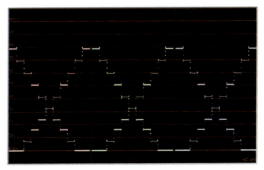

Figure 10.41 11 step crossed gray with gain down crushing black values.

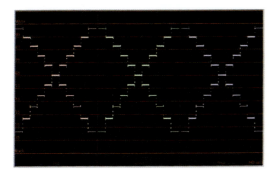

Figure 10.38 Waveform RGB parade representation of 11 step crossed gray with gain up.

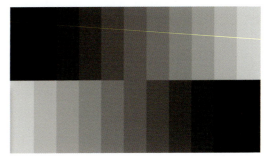

Figure 10.42 Waveform RGB parade representation of 11 step crossed gray with gain down crushing black values.

Figure 10.39 11 step crossed gray with gain up beyond clipping.

In some cameras, a gain menu control can set the overall Exposure Index or ISO rating of the camera by changing the analog gain or ADC operation, in other cameras changing the EI only changes the metadata interpretation of the sensor data.

In cameras where the gain control affects the actual analog amplifiers, I recommend that this be left set to zero to prevent noisy pictures.

As we have seen in previous chapters, when we increase the gain of the sensor, we pay a price in image noise. When more sensitivity is needed, gain can be set to +3db, +6db, or even +9db to get more exposure, but usually at the cost of increased noise in the pictures. Gain lifts the blacks, white, and midtones by the same amount – exercise caution as it is easy to add noise to the blacks or clip the bright areas using gain.

Knee

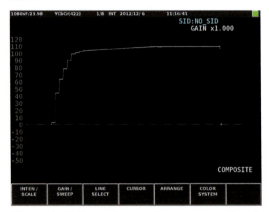

Figure 10.43 Composite waveform representation of knee function curve.

Knee is a video function that can be used to capture more highlight detail when the subject matter has a contrast range and brightness that exceeds the dynamic range of your camera. It generally gives a somewhat "video" look, but when used judiciously it can put more picture on the screen. A number of parameters can be used to tune the knee setting to a scene:

> Knee Point – Sets the brightness level at which the master knee point hinges.
> Knee Slope – Sets the slope level of the knee curve, affecting how the knee rolls off to white clip.
> White – Sets the white clip level of the knee function.
> Knee Saturation – Sets the amount of color saturation inside the bright area affected by the knee correction.

Master Black

On cameras that provide this function, master black sets an absolute minimum black level for the camera.

Master Black Gamma

Sets a curve affecting how dark exposure rises from deepest black level.

White Clip

This toggles the white clip function on and off; white clip can sometimes be effective and sometimes it clearly squashes highlights, so use with caution.

Detail

Figure 10.44 Section of 11 step crossed grayscale with no sharpening.

Figure 10.45 Same crossed grayscale with sharpening applied – note the resulting edge artifacts.

On cameras that have this feature, the detail function defines a minimum and maximum range of "sharpening" that can be applied. This detail function actually only increases the *acutance* of the image. Acutance describes a subjective perception of sharpness related to the edge contrast within the image. An image with higher acutance can appear sharper to the human visual system even when there is no more resolution in the image. In the example image, acutance was artificially increased by the detail function by adding a darker border on the dark side of an edge and a brighter border on the bright side of the edge. The actual sharpness of the image is unchanged, but the increase in acutance gives a sense of more apparent sharpness.

Artificially increased acutance has drawbacks. As a general rule, this detail setting should be dialed down when shooting bluescreen or greenscreen, as it can create matte lines in compositing. There are several detail menus available in some cameras, general detail, fine detail, and even skintone detail which sometimes helps make fleshtones in faces look much gentler. Exercise caution when using any of the detail circuits on cameras that have them, as this is another one of those on set menu selectable functions that can be accomplished better in a post suite.

In REDCine X there is a menu devoted entirely to this function called "unsharp mask," which can be applied when transcoding. I recommend shooting sample images and experimenting with this setting before trying to use it on a production … test, test, test!

De-Bayer Sharpening: ALEXA Mini and AMIRA Scaler Parameters

In HD, 2K, or UHD recording on the ALEXA MINI and the AMIRA, users can control the sharpness through two settings in: MENU>>System>>Sensor>>, which can be used to manipulate perceived sharpness, dedicated to internal recording.

Sharpness controls the amplification of micro contrast in the image. The acutance is controlled by the parameter sharpness. Even more confusing is the fact that the detail parameter influences acutance too.

Frequency (detail) controls the smallest detail that is reproduced by the filter. The Detail parameter influences acutance too. The detail parameter of the scaler controls the resolution by adjusting the frequency where the transfer function of the filter becomes zero, or very small.

The feeling of general sharpness in images increases when sharpness and frequency are increased, leading to greater *perceived sharpness* to differentiate it from the parameter sharpness.

ADA5e-HW is the current internal RAW de-Bayer algorithm in both the ALEXA Mini and in the AMIRA cameras. Both cameras have a menu adjustment called Scaler that adjusts sharpness and frequency (detail). The Scaler camera menu parameters range from –5 to +5 for both frequency and sharpness, and the default setting is zero. Both frequency and sharpness adjustment are available in the ALEXA Mini and AMIRA cameras in HD, 2K, and UHD. In 3.2K in the AMIRA, only the sharpness is enabled. In ALEXA Mini this setting allows adjustment of frequency, but does not allow adjustment of sharpness. These parameters are not available in other ALEXA camera models.

ADA5-SW is the de-Bayer algorithm used in the ARRIRAW Converter (ARC) software and in the ARRI software development kit. In the ARC, Scaler adjusts both sharpness and frequency (detail) to fine tune the relative sharpness of the red, green, and blue channels individually in the de-Bayer process. The default of sharpness in RGB is 100-100-50 which means that the blue high pass filter is reduced compared to red and green. The ADA5-SW is a more complex de-Bayer algorithm, too computationally intensive to be implemented in hardware and is only available in the ARRIRAW software (ARC or SDK). These parameters are only available for the ALEXA Mini.

A deeper discussion of the parameters of de-Bayering and their effects on images can be found at this location: www.afcinema.com/Debayering-special-report.html?lang=fr.

Matrix

Handle with care, the camera's color matrix is the heart of the color engine on cameras that allow you to manually change it. The color matrix is an overall colorimetry correction for adjusting various output color settings such as CCD prism block filtering, CMOS color filter array filtering, or target display device output. It usually does not affect the grey scale, gamma, or overall color temperature, only the hue, saturation, and overlap of colors. Usually the matrix menu provides a selection of preset color matrices, conforming to various international standards such as SMPTE-240M, ITU-709, SMPTE Wide, NTSC (National Television System Committee), EBU (European Broadcast Union), and ITU-609. ITU-709 is normally used for broadcast HD.

If your master black and white levels are correct, the vectorscope can serve you in adjusting the camera's color matrix, color phase, color balance, and overall gain levels. The vectorscope has three primary red, green, and blue target boxes and three secondary yellow, cyan, and magenta target boxes arranged in a circular pattern, clockwise from red, magenta, blue, cyan, green, yellow, and completing the circle, back to red; the middle of the vectorscope is white.

Figure 10.46 What the vectorscope shows.

Adjustment of the matrix (on cameras that allow access to this setting) varies from camera to camera, but one thing is constant in all cameras; any adjustment to the matrix in one direction affects every other aspect of the matrix – it's a little like oil-wrestling an anaconda! If you must adjust the matrix of the camera, take your time, and work in close proximity to a good video engineer. And learn how to reset to factory preset when you paint yourself into the inevitable corner.

Figure 10.47 Vectorscope representation of color.

Matrix can be used to alter the colorimetry of the camera, and can give some interesting looks, but anything that can be done with custom matrix adjustment can usually be done better on a color corrector in post. Changes in the matrix can be very difficult to UNDO in post. I have spent many hours experimenting with pulling and tugging at individual colors in matrix settings, usually to discover that any gain had in one area invariably causes a loss in some other part of the matrix. I have gotten some very interesting looks out of this function, but I generally reset the matrix to default, relying on the color corrector in post production instead.

Hue

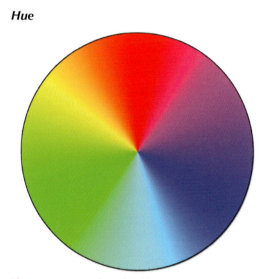

Figure 10.48 A color wheel before hue adjustment.

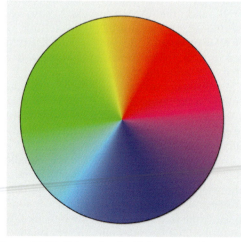

Figure 10.49 Color wheel with hue rotated 45 degrees clockwise.

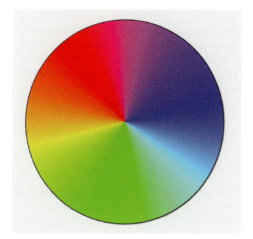

Figure 10.50 Color wheel with hue rotated 45 degrees counter clockwise.

Hue control rotates all of the color vectors of the camera matrix simultaneously. Notice how the entire color wheel rotates globally as hue is rotated. Once again, exercise caution! Much the same as Matrix, adjustments of Hue can almost always be done better in post production.

Saturation

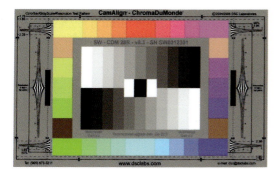

Figure 10.51 Chroma Du Monde chart at normal color saturation.

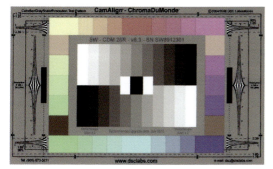

Figure 10.52 Chroma Du Monde chart at decreased color saturation.

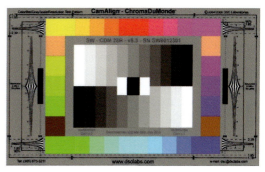

Figure 10.53 Chroma Du Monde chart at increased color saturation.

Saturation is the colorfulness or vividness of a color relative to its own brightness, and this control increases or decreases the color saturation or color intensity of the entire camera color matrix simultaneously. Unless it's a specific look you are going for, oversaturation can bleed colors, draw attention, and potentially not pass broadcast standards. Use with caution.

Lens Shading

Figure 10.54 Shading error due to lens camera mismatch.

Figure 10.55 Shading error due to lens falloff and sensor issues.

Lens shading is used to correct an incorrect green to red graduation of color from top to bottom of the image that results from a mismatch of the lens to the camera, or to correct uneven field illumination by a lens. This effect varies with different types of lenses and cameras, and most camera manufacturers have provided adjustments to compensate for those differences. To adjust for lens shading in camera settings, you'll need a very clean and VERY evenly lit white card to fill the frame. You will also need a good wave form vector scope and a good viewing monitor. The viewing monitor should be set to max contrast and chroma, the luminance of the monitor may need to be adjusted to a gray level to best see the color shading.

If a shading error is observed on a camera with no adjustment, shoot a very evenly lit clean white card at 80% exposure for wide open on the lens for use in creating a global correction in post production.

In cameras with no auto shading function, save the original camera shading values named with the make and model of your original lens before you begin. Open the engineering menu and navigate to the menu pages containing the parameters for color shading adjustment for red, green, and blue. Adjust the signals in each page, green, red, and blue, always starting with green first. Adjust horizontal shading using HSAW – left/right, adjust horizontal parameters using HPARA – middle to edge, adjust vertical shading using VSAW – upper/lower, and vertical parameters using VPARA – middle upper/middle lower. Save the new values named for the new lens on a separate memory stick.

Saving Camera Settings

Figure 10.56 Memory stick to save camera settings.

In the few cameras equipped with a lens file mode that allows you to save lens settings, there is also an auto shading mode. Put the lens being shaded on the camera and point it at a *very* evenly lit white card. The card should be lit to a level that results in approximately 80% levels

on a waveform monitor for a wide open stop on the lens. Go to the LENS FILE page and select a file number that has no info stored, and name it with the make and model of the lens you are setting up. Open the MAINTENANCE menu and go to the WHITE SHADING page, select V MOD – ON, and then perform a camera white balance. Switch to vectorscope mode and adjust calibration to variable, expand the view until the white dot in the vector scope center becomes large enough to see well. Go to the WHITE SHADING menu page, and find the V MOD adjustment for R, G, B, and M. While watching the white dot on the vectorscope, adjust only V MOD – MASTER until the white dot becomes as round as possible, as opposed to oval. Go back to the LENS FILE page and store the newly named file.

Gamut

There are three discreet color values for each pixel, red, green, and blue (RGB), which relate to the amounts of the three primary colors that are mixed to create a color. The spectral sensitivities of camera sensors combine with the dyes used in the Bayer pattern mask are very carefully calculated to result in camera primary colors. These primary colors are used to make up the color gamut, which is a subset of all humanly visible colors. A gamut includes only the colors that fall

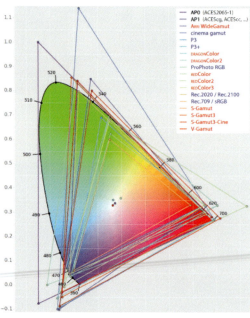

Figure 10.57 CIE chromaticity diagram with multiple gamuts overlaid.

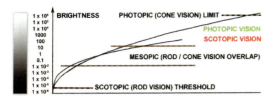

Figure 10.58 Human visual system response resembles exposure response

within the bounds of a triangle formed by connecting the primary color points with straight lines.

In images captured from digital camera sensors, the values of the primaries relate to the amount of light seen through red, green, and blue color filter pigments on the Bayer color filter array. Cameras do not have a gamut per se, so it does not make sense to talk about the gamut of a camera, but it is very important to specify a color space container into which colors from cameras are to be encoded. Camera encoding gamuts are selectable in many cameras, but exercise caution, consult your lab, and test, test, test!

The location of the three primary colors defines the outer boundaries of a gamut.

- ALEXA wide gamut is the color encoding space used in combination with ARRI Log C.
- Canon cinema gamut is used to encode log images from Canon cinema cameras.
- RED color, RED DRAGON color, RED DRAGON color2, RED DRAGON color3, are all RED digital cinema camera color encoding spaces.
- REDWideGamutRGB is designed to encompass the colors a RED camera can generate without clipping any colors.
- Panasonic V-Gamut encodes wide color from Panasonic Varicam cameras by optimizing the on-chip filter characteristics for splitting light into RGB.
- SONY S-Gamut3 color space is wider than S-Gamut3.Cine. SONY S-Gamut3 color space covers the same range as S-Gamut, but has improved color reproduction
- SONY S-Gamut.Cine color space is slightly wider than DCI-P3. Combining S-Gamut3. Cine with S-Log3, which has gradation characteristics similar to those of scanned negative film, makes SONY camera images easier to grade.

- SONY S-Gamut color space is wider than S-Gamut3.Cine.

Log Output Signals

As we have learned, the practice of encoding images with a log function evolved out of the early days of scanning film to 10-bit log Cineon digital files. Film has a logarithmic, non-linear response to light, and an increase exposure of one stop requires twice as much light and human perception also functions in a similarly *non-linear* way.

This response can be closely reproduced by either a logarithmic encoding function, or a power function so that approximately the same numerical interval represents the same change in exposure no matter where on the exposure curve it happens.

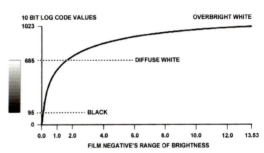

Figure 10.59 Cineon film curves map light to digital code values.

The enormous dynamic range of film could not be preserved through the post process without characterizing the response of film with its unique exposure shoulder and toe, and log encoding it, so the Cineon Log encoding curve was devised by Eastman Kodak to preserve the maximum latitude from film scans for digital manipulation into a 10-bit log file. Notice that black is mapped to Cineon code value 95 (out of 1024) instead of 0. In this way, Cineon *files store* both blacker-than-black values and whiter-than-white values in order to emulate film's latitude and response characteristics. When a film negative is printed up, the blacker-than-black information can reveal itself, when a film negative is printed down, it can reveal overbright details. The Cineon standard code white value is 685, and everything above is considered overbright.

In the early days of log encoding of digital cameras, there was a common misconception

RED digital cinema advocates essentially the same strategy: "A good way to balance between noise and clipping protection is with the ISO setting. ISO doesn't actually change the raw image data, but it does change how the image is displayed, how it is viewed, and how the cinematographer is likely to set the stop."

"For most scenes and uses, exposing with an ISO of 640-2000 strikes the best balance between highlight protection and low image noise. If one ventures outside this range, exposure needs to be much more precisely controlled, and has much less margin for error. When in doubt, ISO 800 is a good start, but the optimal setting will also depend on image content. For example, lower contrast scenes generally don't need as much highlight protection, and may therefore benefit more from ISO settings as low as ISO 320."

As less light is received, image noise increases. This happens throughout an image with less exposure, but also within darker regions of the same image for a given exposure. Decrease the ISO rating and the solution becomes obvious to the cinematographer – open up the stop.

In a brightly lit scene, if too much light is received, otherwise continuous tones hit a digital wall and clip. Increase the ISO rating and the solution again becomes obvious to the cinematographer – stop down to protect highlights.

The exposure goal is to strike an optimal balance between the disadvantages of too little light and too much light; between noise and clipping. In general, some underexposure is acceptable and recoverable, and some overexposure can contribute to a beautiful shot, but remember, overexposure to the point of clipping isn't recoverable.

Figure 10.65 Backlight is beautiful!

Even in a dark scene strong highlights or backlight can help define the shapes in the image, and can even help bring a round, natural-looking depth to the composition, enhancing the dramatic effect of your image. Direct reflections and

other specular highlights make some clipping unavoidable. In high contrast scenes with low-key lighting, some regions will often remain virtually solid black. That is the beauty of cinematography. Remember the very first sentences in this book. Cinematography is the art of capturing, recording, and manipulating motion pictures on a medium such as film or a digital image sensor. The discipline that underlies cinematography is the mastery of the science of matching the tonal range of scenes in front of the lens to the capability of the sensor medium behind the lens in order to artistically capture and record that tonal range.

ARRI Log C

ARRI Log C is a logarithmic encoding of the ALEXA camera's scene data where the relationship between exposure (measured in stops) and the signal is constant over a wide range. Each stop of exposure increases the signal by the same amount. The overall shape of the Log C curve is similar to the exposure curves of film negative.

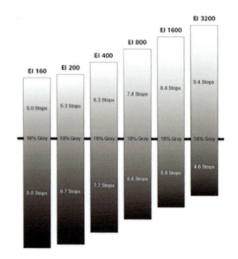

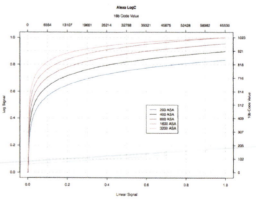

Figure 10.66 ARRI Log C response changes as exposure index changes.

Because of fundamental differences between the ARRI ALEXA sensor and negative film, the color and contrast characteristics are quite different. Log C actually is a set of curves for different exposure index values or ASA ratings. Each curve maps the sensor signal corresponding to 18% gray to a code value of 400/1023 (i.e. code value 400 in a total code value range of 0–1023 i.e. a 10-bit signal). The maximum value of each Log C curve depends on the EI value. When the lens is stopped down by one stop, the sensor will capture one stop more highlight information. Since the Log C output represents scene exposure values, the maximum value increases.

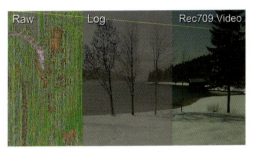

Figure 10.67 Raw Bayer pattern data, log output, and Rec 709 output from one image, compared.

Because Log C is an in-camera de-Bayered log output from the sensor, it cannot be correctly viewed on a Rec 709 HD monitor. ARRI and numerous other on-set look management software packages provide a robust set of tools for correcting Log C for on set monitoring and for generating color corrected "looks" to be forwarded to editorial and to form the basis of post production color correction.

SONY S-Log

S-Log is a logarithmic encoding of SONY digital cinematography camera's scene data that is optimized for digital motion picture cameras, as opposed to broadcast Rec 709 HD cameras.

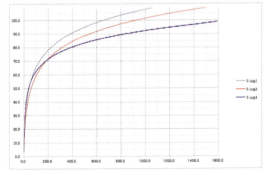

Figure 10-.68 SONY S-Log curves.

The S-Log gamma function was designed for post-processing in a digital film style workflow by analyzing the noise floor characteristics and the tonal reproduction of SONY sensors to preserve the greatest amount of scene reproduction data possible into post production. Since negative film stock and the CCD or CMOS imager respond differently to incoming light, especially in the low-light and highlight region, the S-Log curve differs from log curves designed for film images. CCD or CMOS sensors respond to incoming light in a far more linear fashion than film, there is no toe or shoulder in the response curves of digital imagers. The S-Log curve provides sufficient quantization bits to offer exceptional tonal reproduction in both the low light and highlight regions.

Figure 10.69 Log C image on a Rec 709 monitor compared to a Rec 709 Gamma corrected image on the same monitor.

Log images can be viewed on HD monitors by applying the appropriate display look-up table (LUT) to correct to emulate film print or Rec 709. If no LUT is applied, the log picture will appear gray and washed out; Rec 709 monitors cannot display large bit depth images.

The SONY VENICE has a base ISO of 500 to optimize camera dynamic range for typical cinematography applications with on-set lighting. A second, high base ISO of 2500 excels in low-light high dynamic range capture, with an exposure latitude from 6 stops over to 9 stops under 18% middle gray, for a total of 15 stops.

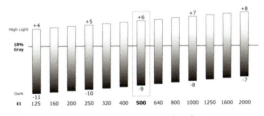

Figure 10.70 SONY VENICE latitude of exposure at ISO 500.

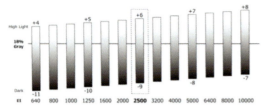

Figure 10.71 SONY VENICE latitude of exposure at ISO 2500.

The cinematographer can use the same counterintuitive exposure strategy to protect against underexposure and highlight clipping. By raising the ISO on an already bright scene and exposing for the brighter image displayed from the viewing output, the cinematographer stops down so that less light is received, protecting highlights. In a brightly lit scene, if too much light is received, otherwise continuous tones hit a digital wall and clip. Increase the ISO rating and the solution again becomes obvious – stop down to protect highlights. Similarly, when the cinematographer decreases the ISO rating for a predominantly dark scene the output display solution becomes obvious – open up the stop.

The exposure goal is to strike an optimal balance between the disadvantages of too little light and too much light; between noise and clipping. In general, some underexposure is acceptable and recoverable, and some overexposure can contribute to a beautiful shot, but remember, overexposure to the point of clipping isn't recoverable.

Hyper Gamma Curves

HyperGamma is a set of SONY digital cinematography camera encoding functions similar to log encodings that are designed to maximize exposure latitude, especially in highlights. Hypergamma curves apply parabolic shaped curves to the gamma correction function to maximize the dynamic range of SONY cameras without the need to adjust any other settings in the camera.

Because this approach does not use any knee, the non linear part of the transfer characteristic in HyperGamma is a smooth curve. This smooth curve prevents the traditional issues of non-linear tonal response in skin tones when using knee corrections.

There are four HyperGamma curves as standard: two are optimized for 100% white clip in a TV workflow (HyperGamma 1 and 2), and two are optimized for 109% white clip generally used in a film style workflow (HyperGamma 3 and 4).

HD-SDI Outputs

HD-SDI is the digital standard used to send data from cameras to recorders and through out the entire signal chain over BNC connected HD-SDI RG59 cables with 75 ohm impedance. These are the main output connections on most digital cinematography cameras. High definition serial digital interface is standardized in SMPTE 292M to transmit high definition images at a data rate of 1.485 Gbit/s.

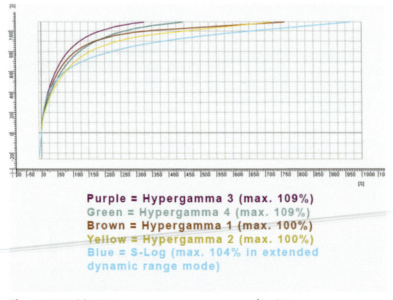

Purple = Hypergamma 3 (max. 109%)
Green = Hypergamma 4 (max. 109%)
Brown = Hypergamma 1 (max. 100%)
Yellow = Hypergamma 2 (max. 100%)
Blue = S-Log (max. 104% in extended dynamic range mode)

Figure 10.72 SONY Hyper gamma curves compared to S-Log.

Figure 10.73 HD SDI outputs.

Dual link high definition serial digital interface consists of a pair of SMPTE 292M links, and is standardized in SMPTE 372M to provide a 2.970 Gbit/s interface for use in applications that require greater bandwidth than standard single link 292M can provide. In digital cinematography cameras that provide for both single and dual link out from two adjacent BNC connectors; the A link of dual link is usually the number 1 link, and the B link is the number 2 link. Exercise caution in connecting to dual link, as the two links are not interchangeable, and if they are accidentally connected backward, the signal cannot be recorded correctly, and is not useable! High-end ultra high definition cameras and systems are now being designed to employ Quad Link HD SDI and Eight Link HD-SDI for signal transmission.

The 6G-SDI and 12G-SDI standards were published in 2015. These standards are used for passage and transmission of uncompressed digital video signals including embedded audio and time code.

Cautionary note: users and the manufacturing community have recently discovered a 6G and 12G SDI port vulnerability. This problem affects all cameras and all accessories with SDI I/O, but specifically with 6G or higher output. On camera batteries supply up to10 amps, and if cables are connected to the camera's SDI connections, the BNC cable can complete the camera power circuit to ground, if only for a nanosecond, potentially destroying camera and accessories alike. This was much less a problem with 1.5G and 3G SDI connectors, but has become a serious problem with 6G and 12G. It's easier to protect 1.5G or 3G SDI than its higher-bitrate counterparts. To avoid this problem, *always* plug in your camera/accessories power sources before connecting your BNC (SDI) cables, and then remove the SDI cables before unplugging the power. If you don't, you'll run the risk of frying your SDI circuit.

Many manufacturers are now recommending use of shielded power cables. The metal shell of the connector can then provide a path to ground via the shield, if the positive pin connects before the negative pin. Panavision and ARRI both use 3-Pin XLR connectors for connection to their 24 volt batteries, but with REVERSE POLARITY from each other, so Pana and ARRI cables are not interchangeable, as many an unfortunate Camera Assistant has discovered.

Here is a link to ARRI's white paper about this issue: www.arri.com/resource/blob/194752/26e7a4ca07e7a8f0ce038b23109b216c/download-technical-information-data.pdf.

Here is a link to RED DIGITAL CINEMA's discussion about the issue: https://support.red.com/hc/en-us/articles/360057166453-Preventing-Damage-to-KOMODO-SDI-Outputs.

Raw Output

Some cameras output Raw Bayer pattern sensor data as files to be offloaded and manipulated in post, but currently, only some ARRI ALEXA cameras transmit Raw data out of the camera in real time.

ARRIRAW T-Link is a legacy method of transporting the ARRIRAW data over a standard dual link HD-SDI connection. The ARRIRAW T-Link Certificate allows simple identification of other ARRIRAW recorders that are compliant. This signal output type is very rarely used because Codex on-board recorders now very efficiently record ARRIRAW signals. In post production ARRIRAW files can be de-Bayered into the file format of choice or used natively by a number compliant applications, allowing for high image quality resolution and postproduction flexibility.

Viewing Output: A Cautionary Tale

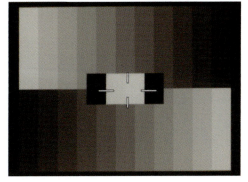

Figure 10.74 Crosshairs in the viewfinder output.

The viewing output of many cameras is actually a recordable ITU 709 HD signal which can easily be confused with HD/SDI out. *Always check* that you have correctly connected to the proper output connectors if you are attempting to record on a separate recorder. I once answered a day call to consult for a producer to determine if it was possible to help him to remove camera crosshairs from an entire day of his master tapes.

Sync/Black Burst

There are many times when it is imperative to synchronize multiple cameras, recorders, projectors, or other imaging devices. In 3D Cinematography, synchronizing the stereo camera pair is crucial to the success of the effect. In live multi-cam broadcasting, all the cameras must be synchronized to accommodate live switching from one camera to another.

Figure 10.75 Camera sync connector.

Genlock (generator locking) is a common technique where a reference signal from a video signal generator or a video output from another video source is used to synchronize several sources together. When video devices are synchronized this way, they are said to be generator locked, or genlocked.

Black burst refers to an analog sync generator lock signal consisting of vertical and horizontal synchronizing pulses together with chrominance phase reference color burst with no picture.

Tri-level sync is a very accurate reference sync signal that goes from 0 volts DC to –300mV, then to +300mV, before returning to zero volts DC again.

These signals are generally either generated by the camera internally as clock functions to drive the image sampling process, or provided externally to synchronize multiple cameras to each other for switching or acquiring precise time critical images.

Test Signal Outputs

Camera test signal and maintenance outputs are reserved for technical staff at the camera rental house and are not generally of any concern to production camera crews. In rare instances production camera staff may be asked to use these outputs under the direction of a trained camera technician.

Exposure Metrics

Waveform Monitor and Vectorscope

When television began in the United States it was black and white. Analog video was controlled by engineers at every step of production, post production, and delivery. The rules of video were very strict to assure that video signals met the technical requirements of broadcasting. A video testing and analysis oscilloscope called a waveform monitor was devised to measure video signals so that adjustments and verifications could be made.

When color came along in the late 1950s another instrument called a vectorscope had to be developed to adjust and verify the color portion of the video signal. Together these two scopes comprise the best way we have to understand that things are technically correct in video images.

There are a variety of ways that these specialized oscilloscopes can be used with different testing signals. Generally, they are used to display and understand color bars, either from a camera for system alignment or from video playout to adjust the deck's processing amplifier to verify that the video output is correct. Waveform monitors and vectorscopes are also very useful for evaluating video signals from a camera pointed at an actor on a set. Just keep in mind that when using a waveform monitor, the scales and graticules are all in the language of video, and to make judgments about log signals is still difficult. No waveform monitor in current manufacture accommodates a meaningful analysis of log curves such as ARRI Log-C, SONY S-Log or any of the other log encodings in standard dynamic range. Leader Zen Series of waveform monitors with the SER23 HDR software license does allow you to display S-Log3, C-Log, and LogC waveforms in high dynamic range.

The waveform monitor is used to evaluate the brightness of your image. The scale of a waveform monitor is from 0 to 100 IRE. IRE is a video metric that represents the scale invented by the Institute of Radio Engineers. This scale was designed to match the capabilities of early CRT televisions to display an image. Anything at 0 is completely black, with no detail, and anything above 100 will be clipped and white, with no detail. The waveform monitor produces a number of possible abstract views of the image. From left to right the waveform mirrors the image, making it easy to reference the brightness of specific areas of the image/frame. From top to bottom it displays the intensity or brightness of the picture. It can display the luminance filling the scope from left to right across the entire picture, it can display each color in an RGB parade view, and it can display luminance and individual RGB channels in yet another parade view – YRGB.

With modern displays (especially with HDR displays) it is now possible to exceed the standard dynamic range 100 IRE threshold and not clip highlights. Luminance values found in this region are called super whites.

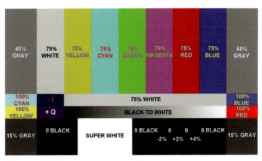

Figure 10.77 Association of Radio Industries and Businesses standard dynamic range color bars labeled with explanation of values.

The color patches are arranged in four rows. The top row begins with a 40% gray strip followed by 75% white, 75% yellow, 75% cyan, 75% green, 75% magenta, 75% red, 75% blue, and 40% gray again. These are the three primary colors (red, green, and blue) and the three secondary colors (yellow, cyan, and magenta), often referred to as the additive and subtractive colors, surrounded by gray strips.

The second row includes 100% cyan, –Inphase (for broadcast signals), 75% white and 100% blue. The third row includes 100% yellow, +Q Quadrature patch (also for broadcast signals), to evaluate color demodulation, a black to white graduation, and 100% red. These are used for calibrating monitors.

The bottom row shows a dark gray patch, a black patch, then 100 IRE white, then black, then five small strips of black called a PLUGE ("Picture Line-Up Generation Equipment"), another black patch, and then another dark gray. On a waveform monitor the luminance signal from the ARIB chart looks like Figure 10.78.

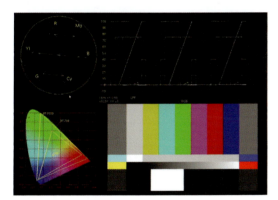

Figure 10.76 Vector scope, waveform monitor RGB parade mode view, CIE chart, and RGB screen of camera color bars in standard dynamic range (SDR).

The illustration in Figure 10.76 is a multi-view screen showing a vector scope (top left), waveform monitor RGB parade view (top right), CIE chart (bottom left) and RGB picture displaying camera color bars, a subset of the ARIB color bars. The most prominent markings are the horizontal lines that go from 100 at the top to –10 at the bottom with a heavy subdivided line about at 0 on this scale.

Color bars are the standard test signal used for calibrating cameras and monitors. There are many different variations of color bars that have been used over the years, but the most common version of color bars is the SMPTE RP 219-2002 Association of Radio Industries and Businesses (ARIB) bars.

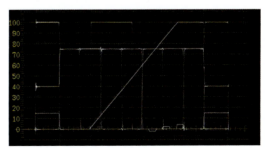

Figure 10.78 Waveform luma view representation of standard dynamic range ARIB bars.

This is the luminance waveform display for ARIB color bars. This view makes it easy to show the full range of white and black levels and the PLUGE patches, which are the critical parts that one needs to set up monitors correctly.

The white patch in the bottom left of the SMPTE color bar signal is sitting right on the 100 IRE line and the black patches are right on the 0 IRE line. This represents a correctly adjusted video signal. When playing back color bars from a camera, tape or file, this is what the bars should look like.

Digital does NOT use 7.5 IRE setup, and HD black levels go to 0 IRE. There are lines above 100 up to 109 IRE called the Superwhite area, where really strong light peaks (glints of the sun off shiny objects, for instance) may travel. What we perceive as white on a monitor is not 100 IRE but is actually around 75 to 85 IRE depending upon the visual content of the picture. Cinematographers consider highlights at 100 IRE and above not as white but as hot highlights that are a normal part of the picture.

Now let's look at a vector scope graticule. On a vector scope, the ARIB color bars signal looks like this;

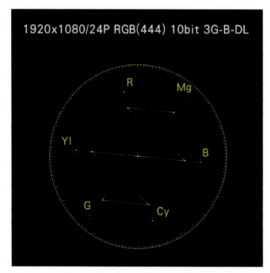

Figure 10.79 ARIB SDR color bars vectorscope screen.

On a vector scope there are a number of color vector targets, the ones we are most concerned about are the crosshairs in the center and the six targets that are the aim points for the three primary and three secondary colors. The larger circle surrounding the target represents the acceptable limit of color saturation. (Note: The vector trace can be within the circle graticule and still be illegal from an FCC broadcast legal gamut standpoint.) Note where the 75% color patch vector lines land. 100% saturation lands at the target squares.

Now let's look at a DSC Chroma Du Monde test chart exposed properly in Figure 10.80.

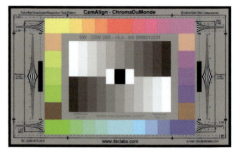

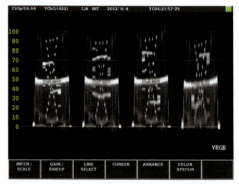

Figure 10.80 DSC Chroma Du Monde color chart yields saturation of 50%.

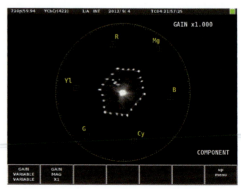

Figure 10.81 Chroma Du Monde SDR waveform RGB parade view.

In this waveform display we see a parade view that separates the red, green, and blue channels into side by side waveforms. The test chart signal that has 11 crossed grayscale steps from 0 to about 100 IRE. The lines of grayscale values appear linear, and intersect at about 50% on the IRE scale. That intersection is NOT 18% middle gray! The nearest patches to 18% gray are the slightly darker patches below and at either side of the "X" intersection on the scope. The perimeter colors on the chart appear as lines of color values across the middle regions of the scope at about 50% saturation.

Figure 10.82 Chroma Du Monde vectorscope representation.

The Chroma Du Monde displays a linear pattern of 50% saturated colors along the graduations between primary colors and the secondary colors between the primaries. (The colors are at 50% saturation because the chart is a reflective chart.) The color wheel starts with red at the top, then clockwise shows that red plus blue yields magenta between, then blue plus green yields cyan between, green plus red yields yellow between. Complementary colors all fall opposite each other across the color wheel.

Each color on the Chroma Du Monde color chart can be clearly seen on the vector scope. If you needed to match that color to some other object then you could compare its vector scope reading and see what the differences are. If you are shooting a blue screen or green screen, levels and color can be confirmed.

A vector scope is also good for confirming white balance, if you fill the frame with a white or gray card then it should look something like Figure 10.83.

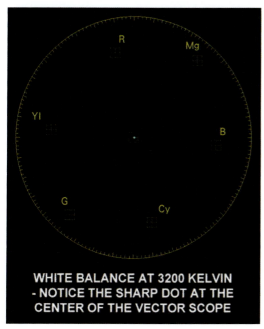

Figure 10.83 Vectorscope representation after white balance at 3200 kelvin.

When everything is clustered in the exact center of the graticule, you are properly white balanced. You can white balance to numerous color temperatures, but after correct white balance the vector scope should display a centered dot. If it is off center then you need to re white balance. But remember, use the wave form monitor to set exposure level.

Now let's see what a real-world camera signal looks like.

Figure 10.84 Original camera image.

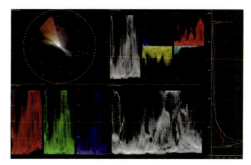

Figure 10.85 (Clockwise from top left) SDR vectorscope representation, $Y'C_BC_R$ representation, histogram, SDR composite representation, and SDR RGB parade representation (from a BaseLight color corrector).

The image in Figure 10.84 has areas that are at both the top and bottom of the range of contrast. The black hats are very dark, and the sparkler is clipped at the top of the exposure range. In order to understand the waveform scope view of the image, you must know a few things about waveform representations.

Figure 10.86 Night scene luminance levels on a waveform monitor.

The waveform monitor shows the video level (essentially exposure) for every line in the image raster all at once. In other words, all of the lines from top to bottom are piled on top of one another to form the waveform image.

Waveform monitors can show both the black and white (luminance) portion of the signal *and* the color (chrominance) portion (vectorscope) superimposed on top of one another. Zero luminance (black) values are at the bottom, 100% luminance (white) values are at the top, and in between are all the mid tones.

Caucasian skin tones will be at about 60 to 70 IRE on a correctly exposed camera. Black and Hispanic skin tones will be darker and vary greatly depending on the darkness of the subject's skin. There are pale skinned people who are correctly exposed at 75 or 76 IRE. This varies, but 65 IRE is about average for Caucasian skin.

White is *not* 100 IRE. White is actually about 80 IRE or so and is more defined as the absence of color on the vector scope than it is level on the waveform monitor. White is also perceived relative to the rest of the picture. A white tablecloth in a very dark restaurant might be only 70 IRE or less whereas in a brightly lit restaurant it might be 85 to 90 IRE. The sparkler in the picture is super white and reaches 100%.

As you approach 0 and 100 IRE detail diminishes. Fully black and fully white portions of the picture have no detail information at all, so there is nothing that can be "brought out" in post. You can raise the blacks or lower the whites all you want, but there still won't be any details there. If you want all the beautiful beadwork and lace in that gorgeous wedding gown to be seen you'd better not let it get very far above about 80 IRE.

Peak whites, like sunlight off a chrome bumper, are actually details themselves if they are small enough. Don't worry if they go up to or even over 100 IRE. Exposure is set by the overall brightness of the scene or by human skin if that is available, especially the face. If you have tiny pieces of peak white, remember, those are just details and aren't the measure to set your exposure by.

Cameras output color images in RGB form, monitors, and TV systems display images in RGB form, but television transmission systems use $Y'C_BC_R$ to transmit those images. When acquiring RGB images that are meant to be converted to $Y'C_BC_R$ for broadcast, it is important to monitor both the RGB and $Y'C_BC_R$ representations of those images, as there are legal value combinations in $Y'C_BC_R$ that result in illegal RGB values that can be over or under range, and which can create color artifacts either in the dark areas or highlights. The $Y'C_BC_R$ representation is at the upper middle left

in the scope capture and it shows the monochrome luminance of the signal reaches full band width but the C_B and C_R reach much lower levels.

The waveform monitor is one of many tools that you should use to adjust exposure. The main metric is your eye, viewing a correctly calibrated reference video monitor, NOT a television or computer monitor. There are huge differences between displays, and you should only trust a calibrated HD video monitor to evaluate the image results. During shooting, a vectorscope isn't as much help as a waveform monitor except for achieving a precise color match.

Figure 10.87 Diamond view for detecting RGB gamut errors.

Waveform monitors display this view to detect valid signal limits and gamut errors for RGB encoding. Displays are designed to accept RGB values within a given dynamic range, and light producing displays cannot make negative light, so no negative values of RGB are processed. The Diamond display is the most reliable and useful R'G'B' gamut violation indicator available for several reasons. Because the top diamond in the Diamond display indicates levels of blue and green signal components, while the bottom diamond displays only red and green, it is easy to identify which channel or channels are in error when manipulating the R'G'B' signal. The Diamond display shows neither false alarms nor allows severe gamut errors to slip by without being displayed. Another important advantage of the Diamond display is its ability to be used as a subjective measure of the severity of a gamut violation.

Leader Instruments[1] waveform vectorscopes have a screen view called a 5-bar display, which is used for determining whether luminance or color gamut is within legal range, and whether the analog output version of those images is within legal range.

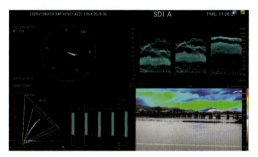

Figure 10.88 Leader Instruments combined vectorscope, waveform, CIE Chart, 5-bar gamut screen and HDR zone false color image.

The bottom right quadrant in Figure 10.88 shows a real HD picture with false color superimposed. The 5-bar display at bottom center shows when color exceeds the broadcast legal range of between 7.2 IRE and 109.4 IRE. Using this function, broadcast gamut errors can be avoided on set, instead of having to be corrected or adjusted in post production manually, or by the use of a video legalizer.

Waveform Monitoring for Log Signals

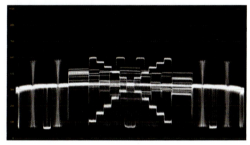

Figure 10.89 SDR log signal of Chroma Du Monde Chart Viewed on a waveform monitor set to Rec 709.

Figure 10.89 illustrates that a waveform monitor presented with a log signal while set to Rec 709 mode presents a picture that is difficult to comprehend. White values are nowhere near the top of the scale, black values do not reach the bottom of the scale, and middle gray lands arbitrarily somewhere in between. For a correct Rec 709 SDR signal read from a monitor output, white levels from the chart should be up at about 90% to 100%, and black should read close to zero, while middle gray should read 40.9%. Wave form monitors are not scaled to read log encoded signals in standard dynamic range. Using middle gray to set exposure from a log signal on a wave form monitor is only possible if the cinematographer is familiar with the 18% gray level of each log function. If one trusts the Rec 709 transform in the camera, then middle gray can be set at 40.9%, but that places the cinematographers trust entirely in that camera's internal Rec709 transform.

Gray cards and grayscales can yield a wide variety of waveforms and values when viewed uncorrected and unlutted on a Rec 709 waveform monitor. In Chapter 15 of this book there are numerous plots of log encodings with insights into how to understand the varied proprietary log encodings. It is valuable to closely examine the portion of those log plots where the values cross the 18% middle gray line. A closer graph of log encoding functions shows that for the various encodings, 18% reflectance varies widely in luminance.

Also, exposing a green or blue screen for a middle gray value optimizes color saturation for the green record on a green screen, or the blue record on a blue screen. Darker than that increases the amount of noise in the mattes, and brighter than that increases the amount of red and blue contamination in a green screen, or green and red in a blue screen. The idea of color difference matting is to minimize noise and maximize color difference, and middle gray is that crossover point for either a blue screen or a green screen. For true Rec 709, that crossover point is 40.9%, and for log encodings it varies

Table 10.3 A guide to gray values for a variety of log encodings when viewed on an SDR waveform monitor set to Rec 709

Stop	Linear Light (% Reflectance)	ARRI LogC	Canon Log	Canon Log2	Canon Log3	DJI Dlog
0	0.1800	38.3540%	32.7954%	39.2026%	31.3435%	39.2621%

Panasonic Vlog	Rec709	RED Log3G10	REDlohfilm	Sony S-Log	Sony S-Log2	Sony S-Log3
42.1287%	40.9008%	31.6210%	46.0992%	37.6074%	32.3062%	40.6393%

from camera to camera depending on the log encoding being used.

Waveform Monitoring for High Dynamic Range (HDR)

The new high dynamic range (HDR) standards for broadcast and motion pictures dictate new tools for measuring digital picture signals. In order to understand the metrics of HDR and brightness, it is first important to be familiar with the unit of emissive display brightness, the nit. The nit is defined as one candela per square meter, indicated by the symbol cd/m^2. As a measure of light emitted per unit area, nits are used to quantify the brightness of a display device. In real-world terms, digital cinema projection has been standardized for many years at 14 foot lamberts, which equates to 48 nits, standard Rec 709 broadcast video extends to 100 nits, and Dolby Vision cinema projection increased cinema brightness to 32 foot lamberts, which equates to 108 nits. HDR professional reference monitor nit levels run from 1,000 to 2,000, and 4,000 nits with new electro optical transfer functions (EOTF) specified. Using an HDR monitor on set is vital to ensuring the results, and using an HDR waveform vector scope also helps to assure correct signal levels.

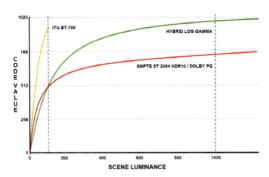

Figure 10.90 HDR electro optical transfer functions.

Hybrid Log Gamma (HLG)

Hybrid Log Gamma ITU.BT2100 was jointly developed as a high dynamic range broadcast standard by the BBC and NHK. HLG is an open source royalty-free standard which specifies system parameters essential for extended image dynamic range in television broadcast including system colorimetry, signal format and digital representation. Hybrid Log Gamma specifies a nominal peak luminance of 1,000 nits (cd/m^2) and a system gamma value that can be adjusted depending on background luminance.

HDR10 and HDR10+

HDR10 is an open source standard for high dynamic range video broadcast and display. Every TV that is HDR-capable is compatible with HDR10, it is the minimum HDR specification. HDR 10 is a de facto standard, i.e. there is not a specification document that defines the system. The difference between HDR10 and HDR 10+ is metadata, additional info that gets transmitted along with an HDR movie or TV show that controls brightness and contrast. Metadata tells your TV how to modulate high dynamic range content. HDR10 has static metadata, one setting for the entire program. HDR10+ and Dolby Vision incorporate dynamic scene to scene, shot to shot metadata. The idea with HDR10+ and Dolby PQ dynamic metadata is that the creative film maker can specify how to show each shot or scene.

Dolby Vision Perceptual Quantization (PQ)

Dolby Vision PQ perceptual quantization (SMPTE ST 2084) is a standard that uses the SMPTE 2084 electro optical transfer function (EOTF) with ranges of 1,000, 2,000, and 4,000 nits specified for mastering and viewing. Dolby Vision employs dynamic metadata which controls how HDR looks from scene to scene, or even on a frame to frame basis. This extra level of control lets film makers decide how a movie should look on your TV.

Next generation waveform monitors now support the emerging standards for high dynamic range and wide color gamut acquisition. A new range of metrics is required to analyze video, metadata, and audio from the SDI data stream. HDR waveform monitors support video formats ranging from SD up to 4K/UHD at frame rates up to 60Hz and color spaces from BT.709 up to BT.2020 color space. Additional tools such as BT.2020 color space waveform displays, histograms, false color brightness displays and CIE chromaticity charts are now available to ensure that BT.2020 color space rendition of the image is correct.

Figure 10.91 Leader Phabrix HDR false color display.

Leader and Phabrix both feature false color displays for checking HDR brightness. This feature superimposes user adjustable false colors directly on the picture.

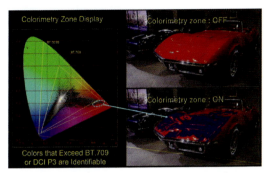

Figure 10.92 Leader Rec 2020 scene wide color chromaticity map.

Leader has a colorimetry zone option (SER31) which combines the function of the CIE chart with a false color confirmation on the picture. The colorimetry zone display helps to check chroma levels beyond BT.709 or DCI-P3 color space, or to identify errors when converting content from BT.2020 to narrower color spaces.

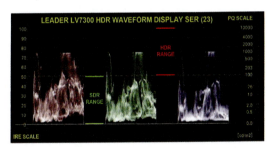

Figure 10.93 HDR (and SDR) waveform monitor levels – PQ scaled.

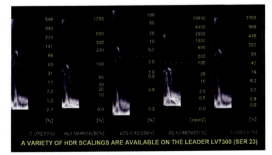

Figure 10.94 HDR waveform monitor scales.

Leader's high dynamic range wave form monitor displays HDR levels with scales for C-LOG,

Hybrid Log Gamma, LOG-C, perceptual quantization up to 10,000 nits and S-LOG encodings.

European Broadcast Union Hybrid Log Gamma (HLG) Color Bars

https://tech.ebu.ch/publications/tech3373

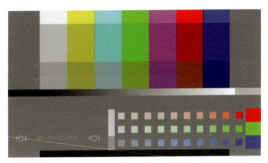

Figure 10.95 European Broadcast Union Hybrid Log Gamma (HLG) Color Bars.

EBU Hybrid Log Gamma color bars are designed to help ensure production equipment is correctly configured when shooting in HLG. Values for the EBU color chart are given for ITU-R BT.2100 HLG R'G'B' 10-bit narrow-range signals, designed to work correctly with Y'CbCr 4:2:2 color sampling. The color bars can identify HDR to SDR conversion problems, monitor limitations, undesired signal clipping, and even disconnected or swapped SDI cables.

The color bar signals are comprised of 100% (the top row of color bars) and 75% ITU-R BT.2100 HLG color bars (the second row from the top), and color bars which will correctly convert to ITU-R BT.709 75% bars when converted using the scene-light and display-light mathematical transforms defined in ITU-R BT.2408. The display light (DL) color bars (the horizontal row just above the center of the chart) should appear correctly on an ITU-R BT.709 vectorscope following a display-light conversion from ITU-R BT.2100 HLG to ITU-R BT.709. The scene light (SL) color bars (the horizontal row just below the center of the chart) should appear correctly on an ITU-R BT.709 vectorscope following a scene-light conversion from ITU-R BT.2100 HLG to ITU-R BT.709.

The Luma Ramp test signal (just below center of the chart) is designed to measure the effect of processing on the luma (Y') signal. The HLG luma signal is linear. Tone-mapping operators will affect the linearity of the signal and this can be measured on a waveform monitor. Video processing may also limit the range of the signal, causing clipping of highlights and shadows; this can also be measured on a waveform monitor.

The linear ramp covers all values which are legal within a SMPTE SDI signal, i.e. 4–1019. The linear ramp for UHD is 3 × 1015 pixels wide and for HD is 1.5 × 1015 pixels wide. The ramp increments linearly and is converted from double precision floating point to integer using a floor function.

The ramp is centered in the test card and the space to the left of the signal is achromatic at code level 64 and to the right is achromatic at code level 721. One-pixel wide tick marks appear at the values 64, 721 and 94

The two sample interleave test pattern section (at bottom left) has several letters displayed (A, B, C, D). If cable A is disconnected, the letter A will not be displayed on the monitor, if cable B is disconnected, the letter B will not be displayed on the monitor, etc. A further technical fault that can be detected is a cable swap, e.g. cable A being plugged into input B and cable B being plugged into input A. In use, this manifests itself as very slight misalignment of pixels on edges and looks like coding noise or aliasing.

A near-black test signal across the bottom of the charts used to check that sub-blacks are not removed by equipment in the production chain (e.g. by a legalizer). This test signal is not to be used for setting the black level control (brightness) of a monitor.

The color squares (just above bottom, on the right) are test patterns used for visualizing hue shift in a broadcast monitor or television. The test patterns show a linearly increasing value for saturation of red, green and blue; 100% saturation is ITU-R BT.2100 HLG primary.

Dolby Laboratories HDR Alignment Frame

HDR test frames such as the image from Dolby in Figure 10.96 will help you align your monitors for high dynamic range work. www.dolby.com/us/en/technologies/dolby-vision/dolby-vision-for-creative-professionals.html

Figure 10.96 Dolby Vision HDR alignment frame.

The Dolby Vision alignment frame is meant to be used to verify the signal path from the playback device/color corrector, scope settings, and display setup/calibration. It has features that can be used in both SDR and HDR. There are currently versions for HD (1920 × 1080) and UHD (3840 × 2160) in 16-bit Tiff and 12-bit DPX. This frame must not be scaled as this will introduce rounding errors and/or create false results especially for the 422/444 test patch.

The bottom row contains eight luminance patches which are only valid in PQ EOTF. The patches should measure (from left to right) 48, 108, 600, 1000, 2000, 4000, 8000, and 10,000 nit. (There are currently no displays with a luminance higher than 4000 so the 8000 and 10,000 patches will not produce a reading). Below the patches are printed the code-values in 10-bit, 12-bit, % luma, and nit. They also act as patches to measure the white-point of the display/projector and can be used for PQ and gamma encodings.

The next row contains 100% red, green, and blue patches to measure the gamut of the set color space. The printed values are given in x y coordinates for DCI P3 and Rec 2020, and can also be used for PQ and gamma encodings. To measure the white-point, use the luminance patches.

On the right side are two patches that can be used in SDR to verify the full/legal range settings of the video signal. If the signal is set to legal then the inner squares are not visible. The values in the squares are the 10bit values for the legal signal range of 64–940. The grey ramp goes from 4095 to 0 in 12 bit. It can be used to visualize clipping or banding. Also, it can be used to verify the signal path to the waveform monitor. It should appear as a straight line.

The step ramps can be used to verify scope settings. There are two scales: 25%, 50%, 75%, 100%, and 100, 200, 300, 400, 500, 600, 700 mV. Depending on the presets of the scope these values should align with the lines in the scope. There are also two sets of PLUGE patches. The right set is to be used for PQ and consist of three areas: 0.1, 0.2, 0.4 nit. The other set is for gamma encoding and is located between the 100–700mV ramp and the 0.1, 0.2, 0.4 nit PLUGE set.

The 422/444 patches are in the right upper corner and can be used to verify the chroma sub-sampling setting (can be used for PQ and gamma). If a 422 signal is used then the detect patch in upper right quadrant should have a red tint and match the patch with 422 printed on. If a 444 signal is used then the detect patch in the upper right quadrant should look gray and match the patch with 444 printed on it showing a 444 signal.

How and Why to Use Color Charts[2]

Now that the industry has fully embraced the digital workflow for cinematography, charting your camera's capabilities has never been more essential to creating the images to fulfill the Director's or Cinematographer's intent. In this section I will strive to offer simple guideline for the calibration and customization of your camera system, however due to the vast issues involved with the plethora of camera models available to the professional user, I will not offer specifics for individual cameras.

Camera calibration, using a color chart, like those from DSC Labs, allows users to define your camera's photometric sensitivity, modify the gamma, exposure, and even dynamic range. Charts are used to calibrate cameras to an established baseline or standard, whether that be for color matching, matching scenes under diverse lighting, maintaining critical focus, or properly aligning 3D stereoscopic camera systems.

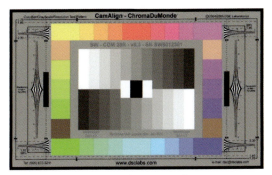

Figure 10.97 DSC extended gamut chart.

The process of calibration allows a user to adjust detail, match color, correct for focus error, and determine the resolving power of the lens and camera combination being tested, even when matching cameras of varying models and manufacture. Other uses for charts include white balance, forensics analysis, or to establish a baseline for VFX workflows when using mixed or complicated lighting, or for green screen compositing of multiple characters or sources into a single image.

There are essentially two ways of charting your camera, one is for camera calibration, the other is devised to offer a scenic baseline for post production. The latter often is little more than capturing a few seconds of your chart in the same lighting being used on set, thereby offering your post production guidance by using a known color and gamma reference.

FRAMING GUIDES   **NEUTRAL GRAY BG**   **RESOLUTION TRUMPETS**

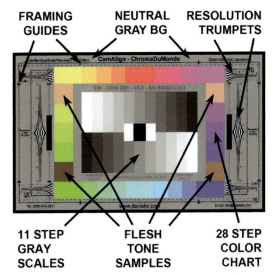

11 STEP GRAY SCALES   **FLESH TONE SAMPLES**   **28 STEP COLOR CHART**

Figure 10.98 Chroma Du Monde_28r with call-outs.

Calibrating a camera requires more effort and can take a considerable amount of time if you plan on establishing a baseline on multiple cameras or if customized looks are being created for your production. Specific charts are available to determine focus, skin tone, detail settings, color calibration, general and 3D alignment, EFX, and even for the extended color and gamut ranges found in the latest digital cameras.

Charts like DSC Lab's Chroma Du Monde 28R offer multiple calibration tools in a single setup, with resolution trumpets, framing lines for both 16 × 9 and 4 × 3 aspect ratios, 4 common skin tone swatches, 24 Rec 709 specific color chips, as well as two crossed grayscales. This allows one chart to be used for gamma, color, alignment, and resolution, the most common calibrations issues confronting users. (Author's note: the grayscale cross does *not* intersect at 40.9% middle gray! The gray patches next down the "X" from the center crossing point are nearly at middle gray.)

Calibrating starts with proper setup of both the camera and chart; they should be level and properly aligned to each other.

The chart should be lit evenly, within 1/10 of a stop accuracy whenever possible. DSC Lab's CDM28r has a highly reflective surface that forces lighting accuracy to eliminate surface reflections and its glossy surface offers deeper reference black than is possible with a matte surface. The chart is designed so that the opposing grayscales on the chart will appear as a distorted "X" pattern when viewed on a waveform monitor if the lighting is not falling evenly across the face of the chart. The crossed grayscale is also used for exposure, gamma, and dynamic range calibration as well as making sure the R, G, and B outputs fall in the same position on a waveform monitor.

Then establish a proper white balance, noting that using common paper or a painted wall for the white balance may induce unwanted color bias due to chemical fluorescence of the dyes and bleaches that cannot be corrected in post.

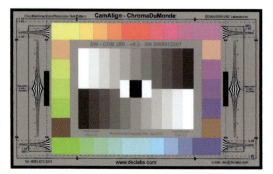

Figure 10.99 Chroma Du Monde 28r chart with grayscale.

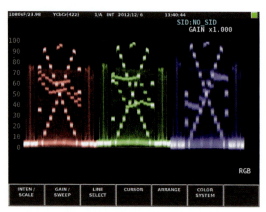

Figure 10.100 Chroma Du Monde 28r chart 4:2:2 waveform representation.

Now comes the challenge of color. Every camera created is different, even two cameras of the same type and manufacture will offer differing spectral responses of the same scene. Adding to that, the human eye is ineffective at determining subtle differences between light and or color sources as well as being susceptible to color blindness (a predominately male trait); it is suggested not to ever rely on your eyes for calibration. A vectorscope monitor offers the fastest and easiest way to see and control the modifications made to the colorimetry of your camera.

Few people realize that the sensitivity of the color matrix for some digital cameras is set at the factory at between 70% and 75% saturation levels;

this is a carry over from the early digital cameras designed for broadcast. This limits the true color capacity of an imaging system but maintains colors well within the SMPTE Rec 709 color and luma standards for broadcast television.

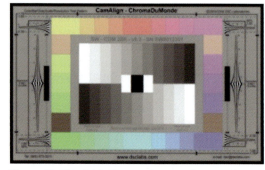

Figure 10.101 DSC Chroma Du Monde 75% chart .

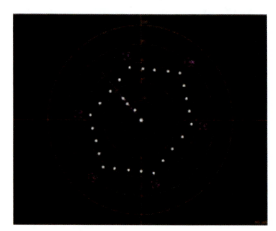

Figure 10.102 DSC Chroma Du Monde 75% vector representation.

Using DSC Lab's CDM 28r as our reference chart we are able to view 24 separate vector colors as uniquely plotted points around the six designated targets on a vectorscope. Each chip is individually calibrated, ensuring the highest accuracy when mapping or modifying your camera's color matrix and with three additional chips mapped between each primary vector, you are provided with the tools to do precision matrix tuning of your camera's color profile.

Modification of the camera's internal color matrix settings offers the user the ability to expand the recorded color space to the full Rec 709 specifications, create custom color looks that can be baked in (on cameras without Log or LUT support), or correct for spectral response errors under adverse or non-continuous lighting.

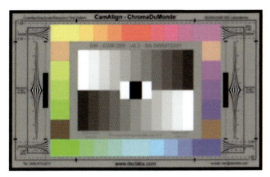

Figure 10.103 DSC Chroma Du Monde 100% chart.

Figure 10.104 DSC Chroma Du Monde 100% vector representation.

the company's technical capabilities with projects such as the BBC Test Card 60 (TC-60), a sine wave resolution test pattern for the BBC and ITVA. They introduced their rear-lit Ambi/Combi System in the 1990s and later that decade, CamAlign front-lit test charts. DSC continues to develop premium test charts today, expanding its existing product lines for HD production. Over the past 10 years, Chroma Du Monde, "The impossible test chart," has become the Hollywood "standard" used in digital cinema and HD/SD television production. They make charts to test every aspect of color, resolution, and dynamic range, and at DSC, if you don't see what you want, ask them and they will probably make it for you.

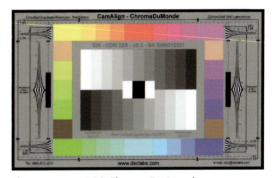

Figure 10.105 DSC Chroma Du Monde.

As part of the controls on this chart, swatches of the four most common skin tones are also included as reference. Skin tones always fall into a consistent pattern centered between the red and yellow primary vector points, providing a guide to ensure skin tone is not contaminated (i.e.: green) during the color matrix adjustments.

As camera technology advances, the ability of a camera sensor to capture greater and greater levels of color and detail is advancing exponentially. Using a calibrated camera chart will simplify and accelerate the setup and process of optimizing your camera, whether it is for a basic setup or to create customized looks for your work.

While camera matching can be a tedious task, with the proper tools and training, it becomes a simple process to setup a variety of cameras to create the imagery as you intend it.

Contributed by Gary Adcock

DSC Color Charts

http://dsclabs.com/

David and Susan Corley have been making test and alignment charts at DSC Labs for many years. During the 1980s, broadcast test patterns stretched

The Chroma Du Monde chart is designed to generate a precise hexagonal shaped vectorscope display for Rec 709 HD, and SD images and is available in different combinations of colors from 12 to 72. CDMs include a precision crossed grayscale for quick adjustment of gammas. This CDM 12 features six primaries plus six intermediate colors and hyperbolic resolution trumpets up to 1200 TV LPPH (15 MHz), for checking camera and monitor resolution.

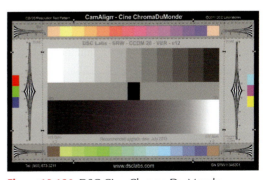

Figure 10.106 DSC Cine-Chroma Du Monde.

The Cine-ChromaDuMonde is designed for digital cinema workflows with 24 CDM Rec 709 colors, DSC's four skin tones, six super saturated colors, an 11-step neutral grayscale plus LOG ramp, cavity black for critical digital cinema work, 18% and DSC step 6 gray background references.

Figure 10.107 DSC Chroma DuMonde Galaxy.

Chroma Du Monde Galaxy Gradient Rec 709 colors join vectorscope primaries, four DSC ethnic skin tone patches, 11-step crossed grayscale, corner focus fans to 1600 LPPH, and resolution trumpets.

Figure 10.108 DSC Northern Lights.

The Northern Lights chart combines the 28 popular Chroma Du Monde REC 709 colors, 11-step crossed grayscale, hyperbolic resolution wedges (DSC's trumpets), advanced electronics, and extreme saturation primary colors. These colors have a gamut so saturated they almost fall off the edge of the visual spectrum. Northern Lights also features upper and lower 18% gray strips that provide assurance that the test target is evenly illuminated.

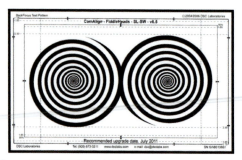

Figure 10.109 DSC FiddleHeads.

The FiddleHeads chart features a double spiral designed that produces what has been described as a visual "pop" at the precise point of optimum focus. It includes framing lines for 2.35, 1.85, and 90% of 1.85.

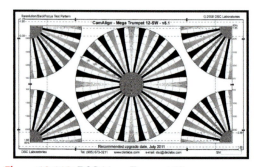

Figure 10.110 DSC Mega Trumpet 12.

The Mega Trumpet 12 chart features 16 hyperbolic resolution trumpets 500 to 2000 TV LPH, 16 solid black wedges interspersed with hyperbolics (checking back focus), and corner wedges for checking resolution and chromatic aberration.

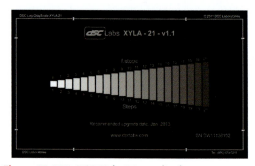

Figure 10.111 DSC Xyla-21 rear lit chart.

The Xyla-21 rear lit dynamic range chart is designed to measure 20 f-stops of dynamic range (21 steps), comes with a fully enclosed voltage regulated light tight backlight source, and a shutter system that allows users to isolate and evaluate individual steps. The stepped xylophone shape minimizes flare interference from brighter steps.

Image Engineering TE269 V2 D Dynamic Range Chart

www.image-engineering.de/products/charts/all/406-te269

Image Engineering manufactures image quality test charts, analysis software, measurement, and illumination devices that provide users with the means to accurately test and evaluate the image quality of cameras and lenses. Image Engineering charts measure factors such as camera resolution, texture loss, distortion, flare, and noise (among many other metrics) that play a vital role in determining the overall quality of an image.

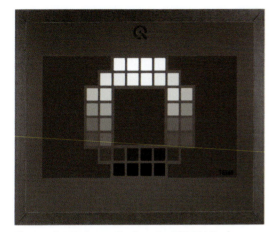

Figure 10.112 Image Engineering TE269 V2 chart.

Their 36 patch OECF TE269 V2 chart is a transparent grayscale test chart used to determine the OECF, noise, SNR, and dynamic range of digital high dynamic range digital cameras, measuring high dynamic ranges up to 1.000.000:1/120 dB.

X-Rite Macbeth ColorChecker

www.xrite.com/categories/calibration-profiling/colorchecker-targets

Figure 10.113 X-Rite Macbeth ColorChecker.

The X-Rite Macbeth ColorChecker chart has been the standard color chart for many years. It consists of 24 patches in a 4 × 6 grid, the bottom

six of the patches form a uniform grayscale from patch 19 white at 90%, patch 20 neutral (value 8) 59.1%, patch neutral 21 (value 6.5) at 36.2%, patch neutral (value 5) at 19.8%, patch neutral (value 3.5) at 9.0%, and patch 24 black at 3.1%. None of the patches is precisely at 18% middle gray. The next six above that are the primary and secondary colors typical of digital and photochemical processes: red, green blue, cyan, magenta, and yellow. The other colors include medium light and medium dark flesh tones, blue sky, the front of a typical leaf, and a blue chicory flower. The rest were chosen arbitrarily to represent a gamut "of general interest and utility for test purposes," though the orange and yellow patches are similarly colored to typical oranges and lemons. For a guide to spectral reflectance values of the ColorChecker please refer to the website of Charles Poynton (www.poynton.ca).

Focus Assist, Crispening, and Peaking

Crispening is used to accentuate high frequency areas in frame, and can be set to shimmer slightly on areas that are in sharp focus. Video viewfinders take a bit of getting used to for novices, so learn to use this function as a high priority.

Figure 10.114 Crispening for focus assist on an Atomos Samarai recorder.

Judging critical focus in digital cinematography is always a serious challenge, and crispening can help in the critical operator task of judging whether or not images are in good sharp focus!

Peaking is a circuit that emphasizes sharp edges on the picture to check if your subject is correctly focused. When you turn up peaking, sharp high frequency edges on the image get a bright outline when they come into crisp focus.

Most electronic viewfinders also allow for adjustment of brightness, contrast, and operator comfort. A diopter on the viewfinder can be adjusted to suit your eyesight by turning the diopter focusing ring.

Red tally lights at the front of the viewfinder light to indicate that the camera is recording. A tally switch can be used to disable or enable the tally light.

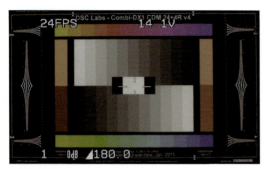

Figure 10.115 Data displayed on screen over picture in viewfinder.

Most viewfinders also provide for the ability to display real time camera information such as record indicator, gain setting, tape status, battery status, on board filter setting, iris setting, zoom position, zebra pattern enable setting, white balance, framing markers, safe area markers, and cross hairs.

Zebras

Zebras are a quick and dirty tool for exposure control. By setting the user configurable video levels at which multiple zebras are activated, the animated diagonal stripes they generate superimposed on the image can indicate areas of the frame to see where predefined exposure levels are being met or exceeded.

Figure 10.116 Exposure zebras on an Atomos Samarai recorder.

Many cameras/monitors allow you to set your luminance threshold and many systems have two sets of zebras (opposite diagonal lines) to indicate two different luminance thresholds. In cameras that allow flexibility in zebra settings, it is generally useful to set one lower zebras level at 80% to judge safe exposure and another zebra pattern at 95% in order to judge when bright areas in frame are edging toward clipping, but zebra levels are infinitely configurable according to the scene being photographed.

False Color

Historically, the term "false color" describes what radio astronomers did to make sense of grayscale images by assigning a rainbow spectrum ranging from red for the most intense radio emission and blue to the least intense emission recorded on the image. Intermediate colors (orange, yellow, and green) were assigned to the intermediate levels of radio intensity. This technique has been very effectively adopted in digital cinematography to measure luminance and control exposure. RED Digital Cinema pioneered equipping their cameras with false color tools, and the use of false color is now becoming commonplace throughout digital cinematography.

Figure 10.117 False color mode on the Atomos Samarai recorder.

The range of color used in false color Atomos displays assigns yellow to show the brightest areas leading to red to show areas leading to peak exposure and clip, gray occupies the middle of the false color scale, and can be very effective to judge correct exposure of skin tones. Caucasian skin at normal exposure levels lands at 50–70% reflectance on a grayscale. Black skin under normal exposure lands at about 15–35% reflectance on a grayscale. These two gray ranges can be very effectively used to set proper exposure for skin tones. Greens and blues usually occupy the lower end of the exposure scale leading to violet for the darkest areas of the image, but it is *always* important to familiarize yourself with the range of colors that the device you are using employs in false color mode. There is no standard set for this tonal mapping, and different manufacturers vary widely in the color mapping used to portray the range of exposures! Clip Guides are a simplified version of false color where the only areas indicated are those that fall below 0 IRE and above 100 IRE.

Color	Level	Description
red	99 – 100%	White clipping
yellow	97 – 99%	Just below white clipping/white shoulder
pink	52 – 56%	One stop over medium gray (Caucasian skin)
green	38 – 42%	18% neutral gray
blue	2.5 – 4.0%	Just above black clipping/black slope
purple	0 – 2.5%	Black clipping

Figure 10.118 ARRI ALEXA false color mode legend.

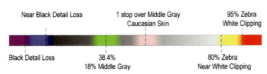

Near Black Detail Loss   1 stop over Middle Gray   95% Zebra
Caucasian Skin   White Clipping

Black Detail Loss   38.4%   80% Zebra
18% Middle Gray   Near White Clipping

Figure 10.119 Blackmagic design false color mode legend.

Panasonic	When [MAIN COLOR] is [V-Log]		False Color Exposure Guide
Color	**Level**		**Description**
Red	White clip –3% or more		White-level clip
Yellow	White clip –6% to White clip –3%		Lower area of the white-level clip
Pink	48.7% - 51.8%		One stop over neutral gray
Green	40.5% - 43.6%		18% neutral gray
Blue	10.3% - 13.2%		Upper area of the black-level clip
(Purple)	7.3% - 10.3%		Black-level clip

The white clip level will differ according to the [EI] and [MAIN CODEC] settings.

	When [MAIN COLOR] is not [V-Log]	
Color	**Level**	**Description**
Red	White clip –1% or more	White level clip
Yellow	98% - 100%	100% level of video output
Blue	2.5% - 4.0%	Upper area of the black-level clip
Purple	0% - 2.5%	Black-level clip

The white clip level will differ according to the [EI] and [MAIN CODEC] settings.

Figure 10.120 Panasonic Varicam LT false color legend.

Near Black Detail Loss   Caucasian Skin   Clipping
BlueTeal   Pink   White

Purple   Green   Straw Yellow Orange
Black Detail Loss   18% Middle Gray   Near White Clipping

Figure 10.121 RED Video Mode false color mode legend

Color	IRE Level	Description
Red	105.4% and higher	White Clipping
Yellow	102.4 - 105.4%	Just below white clipping
Pink	41.3 - 45.3%	One stop over 18% gray on S-Log2
Green	30.3 - 34.3%	18% gray on S-Log2
Blue	2.5 - 4.0%	Just above black clipping
Purple	0.0 - 2.5%	Black clipping

Figure 10.122 SONY F55 false color mode for Slog2

Histograms

Log encodings generally allocate more code values per channel to the bright end of the tonal scale, so it makes sense to use this section of the scale to record the most visible details of the picture. This has led to the practice of "exposing to the right" using camera histograms. If a face is the subject in a generally dark scene with no highlights, the cinematographer can afford to shift the dynamic range of the scene to the right in the histogram judiciously, exercising caution so as not to lose any highlights. This gives more exposure to the dark parts of the scene, and reduces noise in those areas. When there are bright highlights to preserve, the cinematographer should

Figure 10.123 Day interior image shot on film.

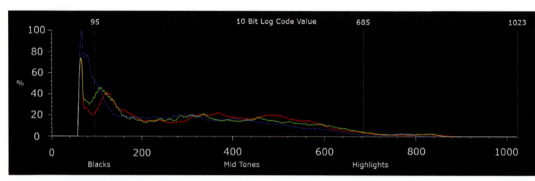

Figure 10.124 Histogram of the day interior image.

shift the dynamic range of the scene to the left in the histogram accordingly.

A color histogram is an intuitive graphical representation of the distribution of colors in an image. Histograms represent luminance values within the image on a "bell curve" with shadows and dark areas to the left and highlight information to the right. Most histograms represent only luminance values, but some histograms can separate out RGB values. For digital images, a color histogram represents the relative number of pixels that have the colors in each of a fixed color range that spans the image's color encoding range.

A histogram is scaled so that greatest number of pixels at any single value is set at 100%, and all of the other values are scaled relatively across the range of 10-bit log code values. Histograms can be used to portray luminance, RGB, or both. If we look at a histogram and the majority of the display is all the way over to the left or all the way over to the right, this indicates that most of the image is either very dark or very bright.

A waveform monitor will allow us to see which part of the image is above 100 IRE, allowing us to identify hot spots or exposure issues. The histogram shows a rough percentage of where the image is exposed. To get the most out of a histogram, the cinematographer has to consider the shot itself. If it is a night scene that is supposed to be mostly dark with a few highlights, then having the majority of the histogram values to the left side makes sense. If the image is an intentionally bright desert shot, then it would also make sense that the majority of the histogram values are to the right. In either of those scenarios, it might make sense to adjust the exposure a bit toward the middle and leave some room to adjust in post.

A histogram depicts the relative fraction of an image (vertically) that comprises each tonal level (horizontally). Further to the left represents deeper shadows, and similarly, further right represents brighter highlights.

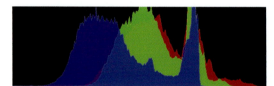

Figure 10.125 Shadows at left, midtones at center, highlights to the right.

RED cameras show separate overlaid histograms for each of the red, green, and blue color channels. All three histograms are useful for assessing clipping risk in those channels, but the green histogram can also give a rough approximation of overall image brightness. In general, RGB histograms only truly represent brightness when all three histograms correspond. As specific regions of these histograms diverge, the more saturated and colorful those tones will often appear, and the less those regions of the histogram will represent brightness.

Images usually appear correct whenever the tonal distribution within the histogram reflects the tones which are perceived in the scene. For standard scenes with a predominance of mid tones, this usually means the histogram will have a "mountain in the middle" with a decline toward the sides. If the histogram piles up toward the left or right, the image will often appear too dark or bright.

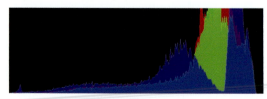

Figure 10.126 Histogram values weighted to the right in a bright scene.

Some advocate a strategy called "expose to the right," where the principle is to record as much light as possible without clipping. This approach works well with still photography, but it greatly increases the likelihood of clipped highlights with video footage, as lighting conditions are often more dynamic.

"Expose to the right" can be a misleading strategy, since the live histogram of a RED camera doesn't represent raw image data. An "expose to the right" strategy that doesn't pay attention to the goal posts runs a risk of overexposure, especially at lower ISO settings. Instead of recording as much light as possible, we should instead only record as much light as necessary to meet the goals for reducing image noise, but not more than that, all while paying attention to the goal posts and traffic lights in addition to the histogram.

Additionally, always aiming for a centered histogram would be a mistake especially with high and low-key scenes. For example, a centered histogram would cause a snow scene to appear too dark, and a nighttime cityscape to appear too bright. Histograms cannot be treated as the equivalent of a digital light meter since they represent reflected, not incident light.

Figure 10.127 High key scene with its histogram.

Histograms alone don't indicate proper exposure, they just affect how the on-screen preview will appear using the current ISO and look settings. An optimal exposure could easily have a sub-optimal histogram, and vice versa. Trying to achieve a centered histogram at the lowest ISO speed could still lead to overexposure, for example even if the on-screen preview appears correct because highlight clipping will become much more likely. Ultimately, the raw image data is what determines whether an exposure is optimal.

Goal Posts

Goal posts are an additional feature to an RGB histogram which indicates what percentage of the image is likely to contain noise (underexposed)

or likely to be clipped (overexposed). In order to quickly balance the competing trade-offs of noise and highlight protection, RED cameras also have indicators at the far left and right of their histogram. Unlike the histogram though, these are not affected by the ISO speed or look setting, and instead represent raw image data. The indicators are depicted as vertical bars to each side of the histogram, and are often referred to as the "goal posts," since the aim is usually to achieve a histogram which doesn't adversely hit either side.

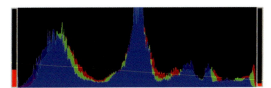

Figure 10.128 Goal posts at far left and far right.

The height of each goal post reflects the fraction of overall pixels that have become either clipped (on the right), or near the capabilities of the camera to discern real texture from noise (on the left). The full scale for each goal post represents a quarter of all image pixels. In general, the left goal post can be pushed up to about 50% height and still give acceptable noise, but even a small amount on the right goal post can be unacceptable, depending on where this clipping appears in the image.

Traffic Lights

Traffic lights are an additional indicator tool that notes when one (or more) of the color channels has hit a point of clipping (overexposed).

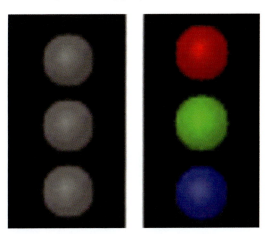

Figure 10.129 Dark means no clipping, illuminated means that channel is clipping.

Sometimes the goal posts alone don't provide enough information about how an image is clipped. RED cameras also indicate which color channels have become clipped (to the right of the histogram). These indicators appear as a red, green, and blue dot for each color channel – and are therefore often referred to as the "traffic lights." When a colored light is illuminated, that color channel contains overexposed areas. If the lights are not lit, there is no clipping in that channel.

When about 2% of the image pixels for a particular color channel have become clipped, the corresponding traffic light will turn on. This can be particularly helpful in situations where just the red channel has become clipped within a skin tone, for example. In that case, the right goal post would be much lower than it would appear otherwise, since all three channels haven't become clipped.

The "One Eyed Jack" Exposure Ball

I have my own personal metric for determining exposure levels in digital work using a wave form scope and a photopic white ball.

When setting critical backlight, I frequently use a tool I call "One Eyed Jack," a 90% diffuse reflective white ball (five stops above middle gray) with a hole in one side to adjacently reveal a flat black interior cavity. The "one eyed jack" ball is a hollow sphere about 16 inches in diameter, painted with a very smooth coat of diffuse reflective white paint on the outside, with a 4-inch hole cut in one side to reveal the far inner surface flat black painted interior in the ball.

This tool enables simultaneous evaluation of brightest highlights and darkest blacks in one waveform vector scope picture. Diffuse reflections off of the white surface create spikes in the wave form picture that help the cinematographer set the intensity of the backlight and ultimately the *f*-stop. The body of the ball gives an indication of how to expose non-clipped white levels, and the black cavity inside the hole on the side gives a good indication of the blackest black level available on the set.

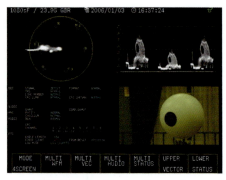

Figure 10.131 One-Eyed Jack with waveform and vector representations.

When the ball is placed on a C-Stand on set where an actor has been marked for a shot, the round white exterior surface gives a good indication of overall exposure levels, the edges of the sphere help to factor in exposures from hot backlights, and the hole in the side gives a cavity black reading directly adjacent to the other white level readings. Acknowledgment must be given here to film maker Joe Di Gennaro, who has also long been a proponent of the "One-Eyed Jack" exposure method and who helped evolve the use of this tool.

Chrome and Gray Balls

Chrome and gray balls are frequently used on sets in scenes and shots which will have CGI objects added later. The technique of lighting CGI objects with scene lighting is called Image Based Lighting, or IBL. The technique is predicated on lighting computer generated objects with high dynamic range lighting from a light probe (most often a chromed silver ball) to reproduce a greater dynamic range than is possible from cameras used in normal cinematography. The aim is to present a similar range of luminance as that of the human visual system.

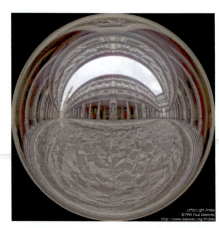

Figure 10.132 Light probe image courtesy of Dr. Paul Debevec.

Figure 10.130

High dynamic range images can capture and reproduce a wider range of luminance levels from very bright, direct sunlight to deep shade. The technique involves capturing and then integrating several exposures of a reflective silver sphere by tone mapping multiple bracketed exposures into one high dynamic range spherical image.

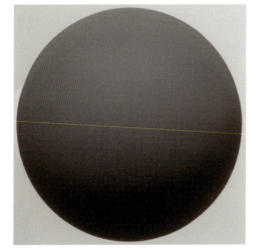

Figure 10.133 18% gray ball for lighting reference.

It is frequently helpful in tone mapping to also shoot an 18% gray ball in the same environment to help balance color from the environment. That reflected spherical high dynamic image is scaled to surround the CGI object and to project light on the object from the same direction and with the same intensity as the light the object would have received if it had been placed in the scene where the high dynamic range light probe image was obtained.

Image-based lighting (IBL) is the process of illuminating scenes and objects (real or synthetic) with images of light from the real world. It evolved from the reflection-mapping technique in which we use panoramic images as texture maps on computer graphics models to show shiny objects reflecting real and synthetic environments. IBL is analogous to image-based modeling, in which we derive a 3D scene's geometric structure from images, and to image-based rendering, in which we produce the rendered appearance of a scene from its appearance in images. When used effectively, IBL can produce realistic rendered appearances of objects and can be an effective tool for integrating computer graphics objects into real scenes. The basic steps in IBL are:

1. capturing real-world illumination as an omni-directional, high dynamic range image;
2. mapping the illumination onto a representation of the environment;
3. placing the 3D object inside the environment; and
4. simulating the light from the environment illuminating the computer graphics object.[3]

www.elsevier.com/books/high-dynamic-range-imaging/reinhard/978-0-12-374914-7

www.elsevier.com/books/high-dynamic-range-imaging/reinhard/978-0-12-374914-7?countrycode=US&format=print&utm_source=google_ads&utm_medium=paid_search&utm_campaign=usashopping&gclid=CjwKCAiAkJKCBhAyEiwAKQBCknvJ1dfwvbCraN4vxcsoCwCDYQSoFzkMi6qExERVhqFZldDpcCtRFxoCZooQAvD_BwE&gclsrc=aw.ds.

Datacolor Spyder Cube HDR Reference Target

https://spyderx.datacolor.com/?gclid=CjwKCAjwsMzzBRACEiwAx4lLG0EzPHHi4yXghmqcg1r2o6ciq2I7dbDY-wprM2lRCox6ohFHYJoAoxoCa-kQAvD_BwE

Datacolor's SpyderCube 3D Cube for RAW color calibration is a small digital color balancing tool that enables you to correct color temperature, exposure, brightness, and black point in images. It is very handy to keep in your kit when shooting for HDR, and can tell you a lot about the dynamic range of a scene when viewed on an HDR monitor on set.

Figure 10.134 Datacolor Spyder Cube light probe.

Place the Spyder Cube in the lighting conditions under which you will be shooting. Orient the cube so that the lower black face, containing the black trap, is at the bottom front and the two split white/gray faces are both visible. Take a photograph that includes the cube. It makes several measurements that make it possible for you to be confident that your colors are accurate, your shadows and highlights are properly exposed, and your image is adjusted to the ideal density, regardless of the lighting conditions.

Notes

1. www.leader.co.jp/en
2. This section is an original contribution from Gary Adcock, to whom the author extends special thanks.
3. Courtesy of Dr. Paul Debevic.

Chapter 11

Prep, Testing, and Problem Solving

Failing to Prepare Is Preparing to Fail

Every ounce of preparation before the shoot is worth a pound of cure during the shoot. If you have thoroughly thought out everything that you need to make the shots, scenes, and the project work in every stage or location where you are shooting, or moreover, if you have thought out everything that could possibly go wrong as well, then fewer surprises can spoil your day.

Prep Begins with Understanding the Final Deliverables

The specification of final deliverables determines everything that goes into making a project. Prep should begin with an understanding of the production's delivery contract with distributors or broadcasters and work backwards from there. Here is a checklist of parameters to understand in determining how to prep:

- What is the final frame size and resolution – 4K cine, 4K UHD, 2K cine, HDTV, commercial, internet streaming?
- Does the delivery spec require a high dynamic range finish, standard dynamic range, digital cinema P3, Rec 709, all of the above?
- What is the final frame rate for exhibition – 23.976 fps, 24 fps, 25 fps, 29.97 fps?
- Will there be any high speed overcranked shooting, undercranked shooting, time lapse?
- What is the final aspect ratio – 16 × 9, Widescreen 2.39, 2K cine, 16 × 9 UHD, 4K cine?
- What recording file type best accommodates the workflow through deliverables – ProRes, DN × HD, HD, RAW ?
- What sensor mode best accommodates the finished framing – 16 × 9, 4 × 3, open gate?
- What lens type best accommodates the finished framing – spherical, anamorphic?

- During prep, the cinematographer and the director should discuss all the relevant questions regarding camera and workflow parameters with the producer and the post production supervisor of the project in order to define and agree upon a workflow.
- During prep, the cinematographer and the director should discuss the intended look of the production with the production designer and costume designer of the project. It is important to invite the designers to participate in testing, especially in casting, wardrobe, location, and set testing.
- The cinematographer and the digital imaging technician should meet with the sound engineer to discuss acquisition frame rate, dailies workflow, and lab delivery procedures.

Sharing a Visual Language with Your Director

I always start a project by chatting with the director about favorite movies and images. By renting a stack of Blu-ray disks or DVDs and watching them with your director, you can foster a discussion about likes and dislikes that helps to create a visual language between you, and that creates a personal bond as well. The creative look of the project can be collaboratively evolved in an enjoyable and relaxing way by sharing time watching films together and comparing notes.

Create a "Look Book"

ShotDeck

Figure 11.1

Source: https://shotdeck.com/

ShotDeck is a time-saving resource and collaborative tool to help cinematographers create look books for their directors, producers, and studios. ShotDeck is a library of meticulously tagged still images by film title, keyword, location, color, or a dozen other criteria to quickly find the exact "shots" needed to create "decks" of images for presentations or for sharing with your clients and crews.

Cinematographers can search and find the perfect images, save them to a deck, download them to use in a pitch or presentation, embed them in an article, or use an iPad on set and flip through reference images for a scene. Every image in Shot-Deck's library is BluRay quality and color correct. ShotDeck have hand-tagged every single image with everything imaginable and relevant. Not just the obvious things like a car or a gun, but also everything about the image including lighting, location, frame size, composition, and even the emotions on a person's face. Finding, capturing, and tagging key images from every film in history is an arduous and over-whelming task, but it is what ShotDeck have set out to do. ShotDeck currently have over 150,000 images from over 1,500 films and that number will grow every day. They add new films as they are released and continue cataloging important films from the past century. If there is a film you need images from but don't see it, just ask and they will work on adding that film to our library of images in the future.

Breaking Down the Script

When going through a script, I always begin by having the script printed on 11" × 17" paper, with the text regular size in the left half of the page. This gives me lots of room to make notes, draw pictures, tape in reference photos and draw circles and arrows.

This is good a way to get all of one's thoughts down on paper quickly, in one place, and directly related to the written words. I might make a dozen passes through the script, re-reading for details and things I might have missed. I take note of where a crane shot might be useful, where I might need a specialty lens like a super long zoom or a low angle prism, where I will need to silk the scene from overhead, when I might need a smoke machine, what the look of each scene could be, every detail I can possibly derive from the words on the page. Then I go through my notes with the director. Then I go through them by myself again. From this hodge-podge of scribbling, I organize and compile all of my notes into a presentable form, and I price out the costs of the gear that it will take to achieve what's on the list. This process usually takes two or three revisions in collaboration with the director and the producers, and when it has been refined and approved, I go over it with the first assistant director to incorporate the notes into the technical schedule. When my notes have been integrated by page number and scene number, the schedule serves as notification when specialty items will be needed, so that the production doesn't incur the expense of carrying gear that will be used once or twice for the full run of the shoot, and so that the production has official notice of what specialty gear needs to arrive for each scene. As the schedule changes, the notes linked to individual scenes or shots change along with the schedule, automatically.

Location Scouting

Depending on the budget and schedule, location scouting can begin far in advance of the shoot, or just as the shoot is about to begin. Obviously, the

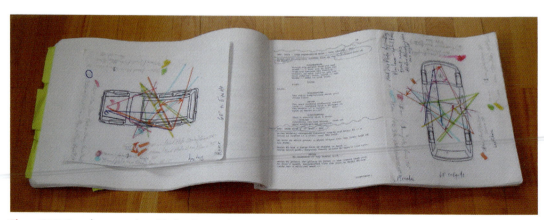

Figure 11.2 Sample prep script with drawings and notes.

Figure 11.3 A panoramic photo of the Merderet River and the La Fière Causeway, St. Mère Eglise, France.

Figure 11.4 Another panoramic photo of the same location.

more time one has to react to the circumstances dictated by the locations the better, but any lead time is better than none.

The Tools of Location Scouting

Whenever I go out on a location scout I bring a defined set of tools:

1. A good still camera with some video capability and a tripod with a small lateral slider under the camera for taking 3D pairs.
2. An iPhone or iPad with a variety of apps for cinematography: pCam Film + Digital Pro, Artemis Director's Viewfinder, Helios Sun and Moon Position Calculator, Sun Surveyor, Cine Meter II, Field Monitor, Clinometer, Google Maps and Apple Maps and a host of other apps I will detail below.
3. A Mac laptop loaded with the Full Adobe Creative Suite of applications. Especially important to me is the automated photo stitching utility in LightRoom.
4. A 50' Rabone cloth measuring tape (a good Rabone is hard to find, but classy – any model will do) and a goniometer for measurement of angles, such as the pan angle looking across two actors in a car when doing background plates for driving shots.

A good still camera, a solid tripod and a Nodal Ninja head help me to visually record the proposed location specifically for shoot planning. In addition to lots of photos of details in the location, I always do numerous 360 degree panoramic

panels to be stitched together later, in order to fully establish the geography of the location.

With the camera on a tripod, take well-framed sequential panels of the location that overlap by at least 10% at the edges. Don't change the tilt angle substantially through the panels, or if you have to, take a panel at the same tilt angle as the rest of the panels, and then take another panel tilted up or down as needed. Don't change focal length during the process or the panels will be impossible to stitch together. If it is a wide, flat area, take the panels on a longer lens and take more of them, if the location is crowded with close in detail use a wider lens to be sure to get good detail in any potential areas of interest. A full 360 degree panoramic can come in very handy for discussing which direction to shoot with your Director, or even for discussing where to park production vehicles with your transportation captain.

pCam Film + Digital Pro

Figure 11.5 pCam Film + Digital Pro app.

The pCam Film + Digital Pro app for iPhone, iPad, iPod Touch provides information on depth of field, field of view, angle of view, sensor sizes, focal length matching, exposure, shooting to screen time, HMI flicker-free speeds, color correction, diopters, time lapse, underwater distance, beam intensity, light coverage, conversion calculator, insert slate, focus chart, and more. This app is absolutely mandatory for the cinematographer's kit.

Artemis Director's Viewfinder

Figure 11.6 Artemis Director's Viewfinder app.

Artemis Director's Viewfinder for iPhone, iPad, and Android is an app for setting user configurable frame line markings for framing, blocking, location scouting, and making storyboards. Artemis Pro allows you to input a specific sensor, choose lenses, and see an accurate field of view. The virtual stand in feature allows users to place a silhouette of a subject in the frame and size them up relative to the sensor size and lens. Exposure and LUT emulations create looks with controls over exposure, contrast, tint, or choose from a set of preprogrammed looks. Features include image store and video recording, broadcast picture to on-set monitors and devices; overlay frame lines and mask off the areas outside of the frame lines at varying opacities from 0 to 100%, create custom aspect ratios, and stitch wide-angle shots together.

Figure 11.7 Artemis Prime director's viewfinder.

Artemis Prime is a physical director's viewfinder that attaches a lens mount (PL, LPL, PV, SP70), to mount any lens, spherical or anamorphic of any squeeze ratio, and virtually all camera formats, film and digital. The Mark II version is now available for all formats including full-frame cameras (DXL, LF, VENICE and Monstro), with an XL version in the works for use with ARRI ALEXA 65.

Helios Sun and Moon Position Calculator

Figure 11.8 Helios Sun and Moon position calculator.

Helios Sun and Moon position calculator for iPhone, iPad, iPod Touch has seven modes to track the sun. HelioMeter represents the direction of the sun on a compass dial, also indicating elevation and shadow length, Virtual Sun View shows the sun's path overlaid onto the live camera image, Sun Path view shows the path of the sun the old-fashioned way, Map View shows the direction of the sun overlaid onto a map of the location, Sky View is a representation of the sun's path across the sky, Inclinometer determines at which times the sun will be at a certain elevation, and Compass shows the azimuth of the sun in both degrees and time of day.

For landscapes Helios creates a 3d mesh of the surrounding terrain to show how the light will change throughout the day across the hills, mountains, and valleys. For city photographers Helios downloads OpenStreetMap building data and renders a 3d reconstruction of the buildings and streets. The milky way section gives you three different ways of visualizing the stars at any location. The days of the month run along the bottom and the hours of the day on the left-hand side. The yellow, white, and blackcurrant overlays show when the sun, moon, and Milky Way are in the sky. A light pollution map shows the likelihood that light from surrounding houses and cities will disrupt your view of the night sky for a particular location. Across the bottom runs the color scale that tells you how polluted the sky is likely to be.

Sun Surveyor

Figure 11.9 Sun Surveyor app.

The Sun Surveyor app helps plot the track of sunlight across a location, including time of sunrise and time of sunset. This will tell you how long your day will be on that location, how long you have to make all of your shots for the day, and how long "magic hour" will be. 3D compass, live camera view, and interactive map help you quickly determine the ideal lighting for your shoot. Use the augmented reality to view projections of the sun and moon path. You can plan for the time the sun will be at a certain location in the sky so you won't have a problem getting your talent ready and in place for a sunset shot

Cinematography Electronics FLICKERfree Calculator

Figure 11.10 FLICKERfree Calculator app.

Cinematography Electronics has created the FLICKERfree Calculator iPhone app, a free

downloadable tool to calculate camera speed and shutter angle combinations for FLICKERfree film or digital cinematography.

Cine Meter II

Figure 11.11 Cine Meter II app.

Cine Meter II for iPhone, iPad, and Android provides waveform monitor and false color display, shutter angle, ND filter compensation, and arbitrary filter factors; use the front-facing camera for "light meter selfies." The spot meter zooms in up to 15×, and there's the option to add a Luxi photosphere for incident-light readings. Cine Meter II doesn't require a Wi-Fi connection, nor does it use any of your phone's data.

FieldMonitor

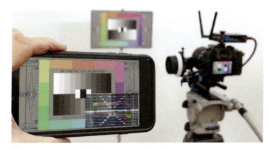

Figure 11.12 FieldMonitor wireless camera monitoring app.

FieldMonitor wireless camera monitoring turns your iPhone, iPad, or iPod Touch into a wireless picture monitor/waveform monitor/vectorscope/ histogram. See what your camera is doing, without tethering your camera to a hardwired monitor and set of scopes. FieldMonitor generates a full range of onscreen markers frame lines and masks with adjustable safe areas and aspect ratios, grids, center markers, and a customizable crosshair.

Features include focus assist with variable sensitivity and two display modes, 3D LUTs to view camera images; use the built-in VLog-to-V709 LUT or import your own .cube LUTs (camera sources only). On modern iDevices, you can also see a fully adjustable false-color overlay for direct exposure verification. It also provides H and V Image Flip, anamorphic desqueeze support for 1.33×, 1.5×, 1.8×, and 2.0× lenses. With a compatible camera you also get start/stop, exposure, color balance, and focus controls, so you can maintain essential control even while recording.

Clinometer

Figure 11.13 Clinometer app screen and bubble level feature.

The "Clinometer app" by Plaincode is very useful for a variety of measurements including measuring the tilt angle of a camera for a visual effects shot, or for determining whether the camera or set is level.

AJA DataCalc

AJA Data Calc for iPhone, iPad, iPod Touch allows you to enter your camera settings and calculate your storage requirements. Enter the time you need in days, hour, seconds, then enter the format you are shooting (RAW, ProRes, etc.) and the resolution (720, 1080, 4K) and the calculator will determine how many GB or TB of storage you will need.

Digital Cinema Pocket Guides

Digital Cinema Pocket Guides for 30 different cameras are full of charts, text, graphics, and diagrams that take complicated camera systems and make them easy to understand. They are designed to fold from a full sheet of paper into a small "book" that fits inside a toolbag, frontbox, or a pouch.

Figure 11.14 AJA Data Calc app

Figure 11.15 Digital Cinema Pocket Guides.

The pocket guides are PDF files with tablet and mobile formats for use on many platforms including iOS, Android, Windows, or OS X devices or Kindle. Significant research went into the pocket guides, from manuals, white papers, brochures, and third-party data. If a camera's firmware is updated, its pocket guide will get updated, and users receive emails whenever a pocket guide gets updated.

Google Street View

Google Street View is very useful for finding locations, and you can now create 360-degree panoramas. Scout your location virtually, take a 360-photo, and the app will index your photo and the location. The app is also compatible with Google's Cardboard VR viewer giving you instant virtual-reality locations.

Apple Maps

Apple's "Maps" app is useful for specifying the exact spot of the location scouted, especially if you are scouting in the middle of nowhere, and it is additionally useful for finding that spot on Google Maps in order to generate aerial and street views of a location.

Figure 11.16 Google Street View app

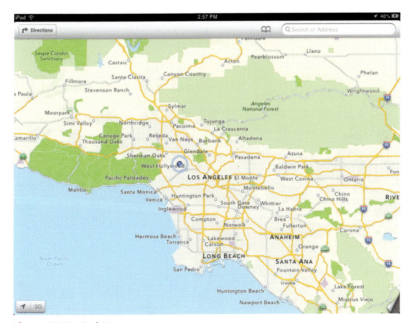

Figure 11.17 iPad Map screen.

Stellar App by ARRI

ARRI's Stellar app is an intelligent app for professional lighting control available for iPhones and iPads. Stellar manages DMX settings making connecting ARRI SkyPanel and L-Series fixtures to the app simple and straightforward.

Stellar creates project files and scenes to organize your lighting setups, automatically discovers ARRI fixtures using RDM, automatically manages DMX modes and addresses, controls CCT, HSI, RGBW, x, y coordinates, gel selection, source matching and lighting effects, and selects gel and source matching colors for the L-Series panels. It imports a light plot diagram to visually lay out fixtures, assigns names to fixtures for easy referencing, groups fixtures to control them at the same time, manages look creation to store scene color settings, changes settings of individual fixtures, controls the master intensity of all fixtures, and handles Art-Net compliant nodes and complex DMX networks.

ARRI Photometrics

The ARRI Photometric app gives you the ability to quickly reference the photometric characteristics of all of the ARRI light fixtures. The app

Figure 11.18 ARRI's Stellar app.

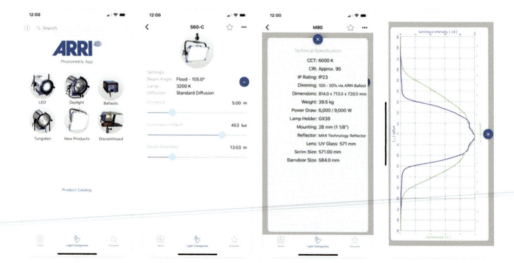

Figure 11.19 ARRI Photometric app

provides information on luminous output, beam diameter, beam angle, flood, middle and spot photometrics, luminous distribution graphs, camera exposure, and aperture information. Light properties data includes color temperature, CRI, protection rating, dimming, dimensions, weight, power draw, lamp holder type, mounting, reflector type, lens type, and scrim size, metric and imperial units. Create projects and save preset fixtures. Includes info on bulb selection, lampheads, DMX implementation tables, DMX conversion calculator, CCL calculator and electronic ballast Information.

The Grip App

The Grip app is a guide to all things related to the grip department, their equipment and tools. Compatible with iPhone, iPad, and iPod Touch.

Some other useful apps for cinematographers are:

VUER

VUER is for wireless monitoring of Teradek client on set video assist monitoring and recording.

iMovie

iMovie is for general movie editing needs.

Magicplan

Magicplan is for quickly drafting and plotting accurate drawings of rooms and locations.

LUTCalc

LUTCalc – 1D and 3D Cube LUT Calculator, very quick way to create LUTs and transforms.

Adobe Suite

My trusted Mac laptop equipped with Adobe Creative Suite allows me to previsualize looks, stitch and doctor photos right on the spot, always useful for making a visual point to your director or to the production.

Adobe Photomerge can help you to assemble your panoramic photos before you leave the location for the next location thirty miles away! During scouting, a picture is worth a *billion* words.

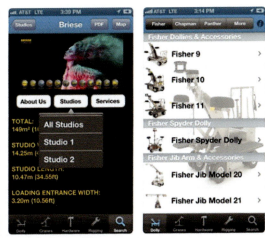

Figure 11.20 The Grip app.

QTake Monitor

QTake Monitor is for wireless monitoring of QTake client on set video assist monitoring and recording.

The LEE Diffusion app

The LEE Diffusion app is also useful for understanding different diffusion options.

Focus Chart

Focus Chart – to quickly grab a slate or check focus.

Figure 11.21 Adobe Creative Suite software.

Other Tools

Figure 11.22 Rabone 50′ cloth measuring tape.

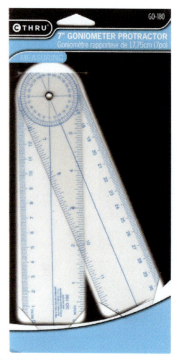

Figure 11.23 Goniometer.

I just bought another Rabone 50 foot cloth tape measure to replace my old one. Rabone tapes are hard to find now, the company went out of business years ago, but Rabone cloth tapes are an industry tradition. A goniometer is an invaluable tool for measuring camera pan angles across a car for background plates for a green screen driving shot.

Crew Size for Shooting Digital

For most narrative production, the crew size for shooting digital should be virtually the same size as for shooting on film. The cinematographer

frequently has the option of operating a camera himself, and that can have its plusses and minuses. It can be very difficult to work on setting up a difficult dolly shot while also quickly lighting a scene, it is usually best to use an operator in the interest of moving very quickly. The cinematographer should assign one operator to each camera, one first assistant camera person to each camera, and the proper number of second assistant camera persons to accommodate the number of cameras being used. The loader position has been replaced by the more highly qualified digital imaging technician, and on multi camera shoots there may be additional data wranglers or digital utility persons.

Hire a Great Gaffer

A good gaffer is usually your first hire for a project; the Electrical Department has the longest lead time of any department in your control. Planning, rigging, wiring, and hanging lighting is tedious and heavy labor. The bigger the project, the heavier the lifting. If your gaffer can be there to hear the creative look discussions with the Director, that is even better. Generally, the more shortcuts to achieving the desired look that you can create during preparation, the easier and more productive the shoot can be.

Lighting Plots for Sets

Once the production designer and art director have begun drawing, the cinematographer and the gaffer can begin planning the lighting of the sets. If this process can happen interactively with the art department, it should. The interaction allows the cinematographer and gaffer to suggest places to put lights, and ways to hide them that enhance the overall lighting greatly. From the drawings the art department generates, the cinematographer and the gaffer can create lighting diagrams of which lights to hang, how many of them to set, and where to hang them. Once the lighting diagrams are refined, they can be used to determine the amount of cable and number of generators needed, and the overall power requirement.

Hire a Great Key Grip

The gaffer sets the lights. The grips set the shadows. The grips also set up all of the scaffolding, green beds and rigging that holds the lights. A good key grip needs to be included once the lighting plans starts to solidify. Cranes, overhead blacks or silks, and all kinds of specialty rigging are handled by the grip department, so the best key grip you can find should be your second production hire.

Hire the Best Focus Puller You Can Get!

As you start to approach the shoot, your next hire should be the best focus puller you can find. Don't ever underestimate the value of a skilled focus puller, if your dailies come back soft or out of focus, you will have nowhere to hide!

Your first assistant camera will help you to assemble a camera package order that is thorough, but economical, and he can begin the work of prepping the gear for the shoot. Working with the first AC, the cinematographer can generate preliminary camera and lens package lists for bidding by rental vendors, and as the list evolves, the producer's and production managers can gain confidence in the numbers and in the support that they will receive. By the time the camera and lens lists have been passed back and forth between the rental house and the production enough times to finalize the list, a degree of confidence will likely have been built. The cinematographer and first assistant camera person's confidence in the camera package will give you both confidence in the shoot.

Get to Know Your Colorist

The dailies colorist is responsible for providing dailies services and deliverables to clients, and is the cinematographer's eyes and ears in the creation of editorial proxies. The digital intermediate colorist will eventually be responsible for color correcting the final picture. In the best circumstance, both jobs should be performed by the same person. The cinematographer and the digital imaging technician should meet with the dailies colorist during pre-production to talk through the workflow, the desired look of dailies, and the eventual final look of the project. A good relationship with the dailies colorist can help the cinematographer deliver a consistent look to the footage from day to day. The dailies colorist should also be included in the process of aligning on set monitors for color and contrast, shooting framing charts, writing lookup tables for on set use, and grading pre-production test footage.

During production, the dailies colorist's job duties include ingesting camera original picture and sound via mags, cards, and drives, data management, syncing audio to picture, QC of image and audio, checking camera, sound, and script supervisor reports, spotting soft focus or exposure problems, and reporting to the cinematographer and dailies producer. The dailies colorist checks for digital artifacts, missing frames, missing picture, failed checksums, and checks vector scope and waveform monitor to recognize exposure and technical concerns to ensure the technical accuracy and quality of work.

Equipment Lists

As the electrical department, the grip department, and the camera department begin their work, lists of gear to be rented will begin to flow. It is very important to constantly collaborate with the producers and production managers throughout this process in order to keep the costs of renting gear within the budget parameters that they have set. Yes, film making is an art, but it is primarily a business, so pay great attention to the business aspects of the job through this part of the process.

The lighting, grip and camera department equipment lists generated can be incorporated into the technical schedule being generated by the first assistant director, so that specialty items such as cranes, specialty lights, specific lenses, or filters and extra camera bodies can be brought in specifically for the scenes and shots where they are needed, and saving the expense of carrying un-needed gear on days when it won't be used.

Digital Imaging Technician

The digital imaging technician (or DIT) assists cinematographers in workflow, record and viewing systems, image integrity, and look management to achieve the desired look from digital motion picture cameras. The DIT frequently manages the settings of digital cameras to help the cinematographer creatively or technically manipulate the image. Many times the DIT serves as the on set colorist, creating looks and LUTs. It may also be the responsibility of the DIT to transfer, manage, and archive the digital data, to create dailies from the raw footage and to prepare digital images for post production.

Digital imaging technician is a relatively new position on a motion picture set, and there is some contention as to which department or union this position belongs. It is my assertion that this position is a camera department hire. The cinematographer must conduct the interviews for this position, it is the cinematographer that needs to trust the person hired in this position, it will be the cinematographer that directs the person doing this work, and the DIT answers directly to the cinematographer for direction; therefore, this is a camera department position. The position was created as a response to the transition from the long established film medium into digital cinema. The DIT's job is to work with the cinematographer and help in monitoring exposure, setting up "look-up tables" (LUTs), camera settings, and media management.

I believe that every narrative digital cinema project should have a DIT. Narrative film making presents so many challenges to the cinematographer on a moment to moment basis, that the extra set of hands is always useful, and under duress or when things break, essential.

Test Test Test!

The 2009 Camera Assessment Series

www.**youtube**.com/watch?v=HhHdRUs2Jn4

In 2009, there was an urgent need for a camera assessment test for feature motion picture production, so the ASC Technology Committee designed and conducted the ASC/PGA "Camera Assessment Series" (CAS), to quantify the characteristics of high-end digital cinematography cameras for use in feature motion picture production, as compared to film. Digital camera development had, by then, reached a point where many pictures were being shot digitally, and almost all studio level feature motion pictures were being completed through a 10-bit log digital intermediate workflow. For either film or digital origination, the 10-bit DPX Cineon print density workflow was and still is the de facto industry standard for feature motion picture finishing, so the Camera Assessment Series ran all of the cameras through the same 10-bit DPX Cineon print density workflow, using the film print look as the reference for all of the digital cameras.

In January of 2009 CAS shot side by side and round robin setups with a film camera and seven digital cameras for two days on the "Desperate Housewives" standing sets (Wisteria Lane) on Universal's back lot. A team of about 250 crew, cast, and manufacturers' representatives worked in five location teams and eight camera teams. Each location team was anchored by an ASC cinematographer and each camera team was anchored by a manufacturer-approved cinematographer and appropriate crew. The film camera was an ARRI 435 with 5207, 5217, and 5219 stocks, the digital cinematography cameras used were SONY F23, SONY F35, Panasonic AJ-HPX3700, ARRI D-21, Panavision Genesis, the RED One, and the Thomson Viper. Several setups were designed to test color, contrast,

sensitivity, and resolution of the cameras in comparison to film.

Figure 11.24 Night interior with a range of colors and skin tones.

Figure 11.25 Night interior with a range of colors and skin tones.

Figure 11.26 Close extreme contrast interior with a bare light bulb as a single source.

Figure 11.27 Wider extreme contrast interior with a bare light bulb as a single source.

Figure 11.28 Early morning day exterior with flame and water elements.

Figure 11.29 Day interior shot with bright specular highlights.

Figure 11.30 Day interior with widely differing skintones and a bright contrasty scene outside.

The ASC/Producer's Guild of America "Camera Assessment Series" in 2009 was completed all the way through film print and DCP using a 10-bit log DPX workflow at Laser Pacific Media in Los Angeles. The ASC, Revelations Entertainment, and the PGA Motion Picture Technology Committee (MPTC) presented the finished CAS results at the PGA's "Produced By" Conference in June 2009, and subsequently at the Academy of Motion Picture Arts and Sciences, the ASC, the National Association of Broadcasters (NAB) convention, and the International Broadcast Convention (IBC).

The 2012 Image Control Assessment Series

www.youtube.com/watch?v=aSQ1SB8JK7Y

In 2012, the ASC decided to do another camera assessment to accommodate the numerous new cameras brought onto the market subsequent to the 2009 assessment. Partly as a result of what was learned from the 2009 CAS, and partly to provide for future workflow improvement, the "Image Control Assessment" was conceived. Over 150 participants from the Producers Guild, the American Society of Cinematographers, Revelations Entertainment, and the production community at large converged on the Warner Bros. lot to conduct a two-day shoot for the ICAS. Organized by the ASC and PGA, this large-scale industry effort was designed to examine the next generation of digital cinematography cameras and the latest in digital workflow. The project incorporated the use of AMPAS' Academy Color Encoding Specification (ACES), aimed at maintaining consistent color throughout post production through to digital intermediate, at 4K, for output to film and digital cinema package.

This time the testing encompassed two "cinematic" scenes: "Serious News," a daytime, harshly lit interior/exterior scene designed to test the contrast range and resolution of each digital camera to film, and "Cinema Italiano," a night exterior in the rain that was designed to test each digital cameras sensitivity, color, contrast range and resolution compared to film.

Figure 11.31 Late afternoon day exterior with fine detail and wide range of contrast.

Figure 11.32 "Cinema Italiano" night wide shot (from ICAS tests).

Figure 11.33 "Serious News" day wide shot (from ICAS tests).

Each new digital cinematography camera was again tested in round robin order and shown dual stimulus fashion against the industry benchmark of film. Side by side tests included the ARRI ALEXA Studio, Canon's C300, RED Epic, SONY's PMW-F3 and SONY's F65, as well as an ARRI 435 film camera. ICAS was finished using the Academy Color Encoding System (ACES) workflow at SONY Colorworks in Culver City, and the results were shown at the Producer's Guild of America "Produced By" conference, at the Academy of Motion Picture Arts and Sciences, at the American Society of Cinematographers, and at the Directors Guild of America.

These tests have been informative both for me personally, but also for the community of cinematographers in general. We get to learn hands on, we get to discover the strengths of each camera, and we get to try out new products and workflows outside of the stress of a production environment. I participate in this sort of community based testing whenever my schedule allows as it gives me not only a deeper understanding and appreciation of the cameras being tested, but also very good insight into *how to test cameras, and how to evaluate camera tests.*

In addition, this sort of work builds comradery with other cinematographers and it builds trust between cinematographers and the manufacturing community.

Camera Prep Tests and Tasks Summary[1]

For a camera or recording system that you have used before, shoot the following tests:

- Lenses choice tests – spherical or anamorphic testing focus marks, collimation, lens projection, lens to lens matching in a set, and mechanical issues.
- Set camera parameters, active sensor area, gamma encoding, record mode, and other camera settings defined by production or by deliverables.
- Start a Camera Department Production Report. This log should be a record of every camera and lens ordered, received, and shipped in and out, and of what equipment was used on a shot by shot basis.
- Camera temperature – warm the camera up thoroughly before beginning all tests!
- Check camera serial numbers and maintenance menu – how many hours does the camera have in its internal diagnostics log?
- Check current software versions in all cameras – it is wise to "version lock" all camera firmware on the same version before beginning a production. Do not upgrade firmware during a production if it can be helped, and check any newly arriving cameras for firmware version during production.
- Check camera license to know the camera's capabilities and any licenses included (or not included) in the camera.
- Check the camera's cooling fan.
- The first test to shoot is an internal ND filter test to check the sensor and filter wheels for dirt or mechanical issues. Shoot an evenly lit white card on a long lens at T22. Visually check the clear flat filter and each ND filter for dust.
- Perform a lens collimation calibration test. Use a flange depth controller for PL-mount tolerance is between –3 and –5/100 mm. This test becomes more important in multi camera

shooting. The rental house should keep a record of your camera's reference flange depth in case you need to rent another camera or extra lenses during the shoot.

Figure 11.34 Denz FDC classic – flange depth controller for PL-mount.

- Normal (sensor flatness) – place resolution stars or charts at the center and corners of frame and shoot wide open with the camera perfectly perpendicular to the sharpness chart to assure that the sensor holds the same focus at all four corners of the frame as at the center of the frame. Shoot with a high speed lens, wide open, and check on a reference display.

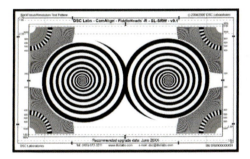

Figure 11.35 DSC labs FiddleHeads resolution chart.

- Shoot black level tests on a well warmed up camera with lens cap on for noise level, "lit," or dead pixels.

Figure 11.36 Lit pixels show up as multi color dots in the picture.

- Gamma Encoding tests can determine whether the camera encoding exhibits any color or tonal banding or aliasing in smooth gradations of tones from bright to dark. This test will also reveal workflow problems that might result in aliasing or color banding.

Figure 11.37 Quick test for gamma encoding or workflow quantizations.

- Shoot Keylight tests to evaluate ISO, creative latitude of exposure.
- Shoot Keylight reference tests for ISO and creative range of exposure, clip, and noise levels evaluation.
- Shoot Display/Monitoring tests for calibrating monitors, writing LUTs, applying LUTs on set, and sending them to and from the dailies lab. These tests can frequently be done at or near the dailies lab so that on set monitors can be checked for color consistency against the monitors being used in the lab for grading.
- Shoot Keylight reference tests with aspect ratio framing charts for editorial and sharpness check for the dailies lab!

For a camera or recording system that you have *not* used before, in addition to the tests above, shoot the following additional tests:

- Shoot Keylight tests through plus/minus 6 stops for evaluation of clip levels and noise levels for camera ISO rating evaluation
- Color temperature tests to determine the effects of tungsten, daylight, and mixed light on the camera ISO.
- Shoot indoor/outdoor, day/night tests.
- Shoot a greenscreen test.
- Shoot lenses calibration/lens shading tests.
- Shoot any other mechanical or digital tests that pertain to the particulars of the shoot, such as rain vibration, heat, cold, etc.

Contributed by Phillippe Ros AFC

Makeup Tests

It is *very* important to do makeup tests in pre-production. The cinematographer should shoot and view tests of all of the makeup "looks" for specific scenes. Be sure to test blend areas around wardrobe and hairline. If there are prosthetics or appliances, wigs or fake beards being used, be sure to shoot test footage to determine how close these can be framed before the illusion is destroyed. Nothing takes the audience out of a scene like a badly shot fake beard!

One issue frequently encountered in cinematography is the contrast difference between dark skin actors and light skin actors together in the same shot. Testing your actors together can give the cinematographer a measure of how much to compensate for dark skin tones alongside light skin tones before the shoot begins. Keep testing these scenarios until you have devised a plan for lighting, framing, composing and exposing to solve these problems!

Figure 11.38 Different skin tones in the same frame (from ICAS tests).

Another issue frequently encountered is dark skin tones framed against bright or blown out backgrounds. Keeping the contrast under control means having the correct lighting and filtration tools on hand. Contrast control filters like Tiffen Pro Mist and other beauty filters can help, and sometimes a polarizer can change the reflections and colors off skin. Testing beauty filters during prep is important, even if the VFX department sometimes won't allow you to use them in VFX shots. Beauty filter tests can give the colorist a guide for look or de-sharpening control in dailies and final digital intermediate. It can also prevent bad reactions from actors, directors, producers and actors agents.

Color lighting gels can also help with darker faces, so be sure to have the gaffer bring his "party gel" collection for the makeup testing sessions. Both Rosco and Lee (Panavision) manufacture a huge variety of diffusion, color correction, and party color gels.

https://us.rosco.com/en/products/family/filters-and-diffusions

www.panavision.com/lee-filters

It is also very helpful to have a variety of small lighting units, both snooted hard light and soft light to test when shooting widely differing skin tones on the same shot. Lighting the darker skin tones with colored light, magenta, gold, or green are interesting choices to test, strong back light can be very helpful on darker skin tones, and partial or full silhouette lighting is also an option when the background of the shot will be very bright. One benefit of adding extra light to dark skinned actors is the extra eye light that results.

These tests also give the cinematographer and the director a chance to test height, distance, angle, and lens to use when shooting closeups, especially for the ladies!

Makeup tests should be viewed on the biggest screen possible, or at least on the biggest screen the project is ever likely to be viewed on.

Wardrobe Tests

Wardrobe is another area of concern to the cinematographer during preproduction. Light fabrics and dark fabrics in the same scene can pose contrast problems. A pure white fabric can overpower skin tones and distract the viewer from focusing on the intended purpose of the scene. Frequently the costume department can tea dye white or very light colored fabrics to subtly blend them into an acceptable contrast range. Conversely, black fabrics can also pose contrast problems. It is normally better to work with fabrics and wardrobe that are not absolutely blackest dark black, so that a little bit detail can be held to separate characters from very dark backgrounds.

Some fine pattern fabrics can cause odd and annoying patterns to appear in your images. This is called a Moiré or alias effect and it is usually filtered out by the optical low pass filter over the sensor in the camera. Nonetheless, some patterns can still cause problems, so it is always recommended to test the wardrobe and fabrics to be used on screen to determine whether there will be any problem.

Figure 11.39 Fabric exhibits a Moiré or alias effect.

Figure 11.40 Fabric exhibits no Moiré or alias effect.

To test for Moiré begin by hanging the fabric against a neutral background. Put a sharp normal focal length lens like a 50mm on the camera, then dolly in and out from close up to very wide. Play the footage back on a good monitor and watch for any sign of Moiré. If something *does* show up, select frames where the effect can be clearly seen and put them into a computer to examine them more closely. Sometimes a scaler in a monitor or some other device in the signal path can show a false positive result for Moiré. The costume designer and the wardrobe department should participate in these tests, and should absolutely be invited to any screenings of the footage. Sometimes it is helpful to shoot wardrobe against a small greenscreen (foldable) to give the costume designer the opportunity to make composite photos which can be used to match with scouting location photos or drawings of production designs. This footage can be also sent to the colorist or production designer to help build the look of the film.

Infrared Filter Tests

Additionally, it is important to test dark or black fabrics under a variety of lighting conditions, but especially outdoors in sunlight with the full complement of neutral density filters for infrared contamination.

Figure 11.41 Black fabric with no infrared contamination.

Figure 11.42 Black fabric with pinkish infrared contamination.

Depending on which specific camera and which specific neutral density filters, infrared contamination can turn a black suit into a dark pink suit or a green army uniform into a brown one!

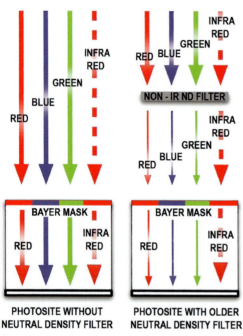

Figure 11.43 Older film style ND filters do not attenuate Infra Red light

Digital cinema camera sensors can be especially sensitive to infrared and near infrared light; the neutral density filter solution for these issues varies from camera to camera. There are now many manufacturer options available for IRND filters, and the technology of IRND filters has advanced rapidly. New Filters include Formatt ProStop IRNDs, Schneider Optics Platinum IRNDs, HMIRNDs, ARRI Full Spectrum ND Filters, Panavision Pana ND filters (ProGlass Cine IRND filters from Panavision/Lee) and Tiffen Full Spectrum IRND filters. Filter manufacturers have now caught up to the changing filter needs of digital cinematography, but here I must urge once again – test, test, test!

It never hurts to test all of the wardrobe for a project, especially specific colors being featured in scene to scene color correction. The costume designer and the wardrobe department should participate in these tests, and should absolutely be invited to any screenings of the footage.

I once shot a scene in which one character was wearing a light lavender sweater that seemed at first glance to be a harmless, innocuous color. Over the course of doing the digital intermediate

for the movie, my director became focused on precisely matching the sweater color from scene to scene, making it difficult to globally alter the overall levels of the scene. Any adjustment to the overall level of individual shots caused the color of the sweater to saturate and desaturate, creating a noticeable color mismatch in the color of the sweater from scene to scene that ultimately partially dictated the look of the scene! Test, test, test!

Lighting Tests

Lighting faces for close-up always dictates doing lighting tests before going into production. The human face reflects light in some very interesting and occasionally not so flattering ways. Better to learn well before going on stage or location if your leading lady looks great from her left side and not so great from her right side. Some lighting instruments can look fantastic on one face and not so pleasing on another. There are a wide variety of books and reference materials on lighting faces, so I will not go into great detail here, except to say the digital cinematography cameras have different spectral sensitivities to color than film. It is always advisable to test faces alongside known color charts such as a Macbeth or DSC Chroma Du Monde in order to quantify the spectral power distribution of the digital cinema camera that you intend to use for your project.

Color Temperature Is Not the Same Thing as Spectral Power Distribution

In 2012, the Academy of Motion Picture Arts and Sciences Science and Technology Council identified a need for an unbiased investigation of solid state lighting (SSL) technologies, including LED emitters, for motion picture production. Issues with SSL have been identified regarding its ability to supplement and integrate with existing lighting technologies such as tungsten, fluorescent, HMI, and Xenon that are currently used in the production of motion pictures. The primary purpose of this investigation is to provide the industry with data needed to properly evaluate the impact of using SSL, as well as to provide a framework for the evaluation of future light emitting technologies as they are developed. I believe that is essential for every cinematographer working with digital cameras to see the results of this study and to understand them thoroughly! For more informarion see www.oscars.org/science-technology/sci-tech-projects/solid-state-lighting, www.oscars.org/science-technology/projects/spectral-similarity-index-ssi, and www.youtube.com/watch?v=X8DtE1eh7PQ.

Spectral power distribution in light sources is important for the cinematographer to understand. The color temperature or color rendering index (CRI) of a light source does not tell the entire story of the spectral power distribution of the source. Color temperature is only an *average* color temperature of the light the source emits.

Color temperature does not tell you anything about the deficiencies in the spectrum of a light source. If the source with which you light your subjects is missing or deficient in a specific wavelength of light, then it follows your subject cannot reflect that color of light.

Figure 11.34 shows some sample spectral power distribution graphs for illuminants commonly used in motion picture lighting. I have included a common household fluorescent source to help the viewer understand why we use purpose built fluorescent lights with greatly enhanced spectral power distribution for photographic applications.

In the case of solid state lighting such as LED panels, these deficiencies coincide very closely with human flesh tones. The missing spectral components yield (in some cases) some

Color Temperature

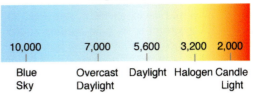

Color Rendering Index

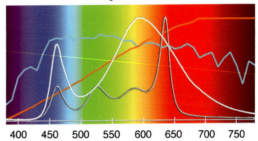

Figure 11.44 Color temperature is not the same as spectral power distribution.

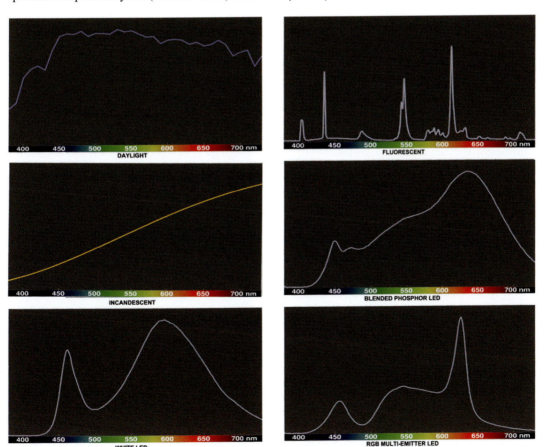

Figure 11.45 Graphic plots of the spectral power distribution of several common light sources.

perplexing and not so pleasing results. The good news is that, as a result of these studies, the manufacturing community has awakened to the need for research and development in this area, and new wide spectrum solid state lighting sources that are designed for photographic use are now making their way to the market. As a cautionary note, the cinematographer cannot take for granted the claims of sales brochures or internet blogs. Test, test, test if you want to be sure of the spectral power distribution of the lights you want to use on your project.

Spectroscopes

Figure 11.46 Eisco Spectroscope.

I highly recommend that cinematographers should go to Amazon.com and search for an Eisco Spectroscope.

This compact little box contains a diffraction grating with a scale that reads from 400 to 700 nanometers. They are usually priced at about $10 or under, and if you line up the slit at the far end of the device on a lamp, you can very quickly make a quick and rough assessment of the spectrum of any lamp.

Location Tests

When shooting on exterior locations, scouting and testing become urgent necessities. Cinematographers should conduct 360 degree lighting testing to learn which direction to shoot to make the most of back light or front light conditions, to determine what the time of year conditions might be. Winter conditions, snow, ice, rain,

clouds, harsh sunlight, wind, mosquitos, or other conditions might affect the efficiency of shooting on a given location. It is also very important to do a sun plot and to consider the length of the day, anticipated weather and the terrain and accessibility of a location. It is urgent to scout what kind of power is available on a location, and whether it is sufficient and usable for shooting. Night shoot locations should be thoroughly scouted and tested for flicker issues. Increasingly signage, display street lights, store lighting, and even home lighting are moving to LED light sources. The only way to know whether an LED light source is going to flicker is to test it. When testing for flicker, don't rely solely on the image in the viewfinder or on a monitor, also take a look at the signal on a waveform monitor and watch for subtle fluctuations in video levels. Flicker can be very difficult to "fix in post."

The production designer and the costume designer should participate in these tests, and should absolutely be invited to any screenings of the footage.

Flicker Tests

Flicker is defined as a condition where light sources or illuminants vary rapidly in brightness. The intensity of flicker depends on camera frame rate and shutter angle, the type of light source and the frequency of the power supply. If your camera shutter is open for exactly the same time as exactly one or more complete half cycles of the power supply sine wave, there will be no image flicker. Flicker can usually easily be seen on a waveform monitor, and sometimes an undetected flicker can become visible when image contrast is increased during color grading. A good starting point for eliminating an annoying flicker is to set the shutter angle to 144 degrees in 60hz line power, or to 172.8 degrees for 50hz line power. It is also frequently useful to set the shutter angle at two times those normal shutter angles if you need a little extra stop; 288 degrees in 60hz line power, or to 345.6 degrees for 50hz line power.

A quick and dirty field test can determine how badly a lamp flickers. Set a still camera to a modestly slow exposure and take a photo of the lamp,

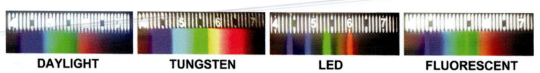

DAYLIGHT   **TUNGSTEN**   **LED**   **FLUORESCENT**

Figure 11.47 Approximate illuminant spectra compared.

street light, or neon sign while waving the camera rapidly left and right, or up and down.

Figure 11.48 Flickering LEDs create intermittent dashes of light.

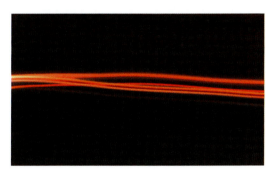

Figure 11.49 A non flickering light source creates long continuous streaks .

If the source shows up as continuous streaks it is probably not flickering. If the source shows up as a series of streaked dashes, it is flickering. If it shows up as a series of dots with a lot of space between them, it is flickering badly.

When shooting with non-flicker-free light sources, the cinematographer must adjust the frame rate and the shutter angle to the mains frequency so that no flicker is visibly detectable. Light intensity pulses at double the line frequency or, in other words: one time every half-cycle. To expose all frames equally and therefore flicker-free, you need to expose every frame to exactly the same amount of light. One approach is to adjust frame rate and shutter angle so that one or more entire half-cycles of the power sine wave is exposed. The exposure does not depend on an exact starting point during the sine wave half-cycle. Another approach is to set the camera speed to precisely match the power supply frequency so that the exposure always starts at the exact same point of the sine wave. The camera speed and the power frequency must be very accurate, as any drift in frequency between the two will result in a slow, pulsing flicker.

Nearly no illuminant made emits constant power light when supplied with sine wave alternating current. The intensity of flicker from any given light source depends on the supply voltage and frequency, and the persistence of the illuminant. In the continental United States, standard 117 volt power changes polarity 60 times per second. A lamp pulses in time with the power supply frequency, at greater or lesser intensity depending on the illuminants response time.

Tungsten light sources buffer the intensity of their flicker by virtue of the persistence of a white-hot filament that responds very slowly to changes in supply voltage. Smaller tungsten lights are more prone to flicker, larger units with more massive filaments are less prone to flicker.

HMIs are discharge lamps that respond very quickly to changes in supply power. When driven by magnetic ballasts, they flicker very strongly, and when driven by "flicker-free" electronic ballasts their flicker is greatly reduced. An electronic ballast transforms sine wave line voltage into square wave, so the arc in an HMI extinguishes just for a very short time during change of direction in the alternating current, and stays constant during the rest of the cycle. When an HMI bulb gets old, the electrode gap widens, and it can begin to flicker. Sodium vapor lamps used for street lighting, in factory buildings and shops, are similar to HMIs. They can also be driven by either magnetic ballasts or electronic ballasts. It is always prudent to test any intermittent light source either on camera or with a frequency meter before to shooting. Fluorescent lamps are also very responsive to changes in supply power and flicker strongly unless driven by high frequency flicker-free electronic ballasts.

Light emitting diode (LED) brightness responds to current changes at the speed of light. Even though the LEDs themselves are direct current devices, they can still flicker depending on the type and frequency of their AC to DC converting power supply. LED sources used in architectural and general illumination can flicker when photographed at a variety of combinations of frame rates and shutter angle combinations. Household screw-base LED replacement bulbs often flicker at 50 or 60hz. A good AC to DC power supply that generates a continuous stabile voltage can power LEDs to produce flicker-free light. Unfortunately, most LED power supply lights flicker intensely, at frequencies that range from 20hz to 300hx and up. Nearly all dimmable and/or variable-color LED fixtures are controlled using pulse width modulation (PWM) by which the DC current fed to individual LED emitters or groups of emitters is turned into pulses of various time durations. While the frequencies are usually higher than cinema frame rates, flicker can manifest itself at some intensity or color settings and disappear at others depending on how the timing and duration of particular pulses interact with the shutter speed and shutter angle. Fixtures manufactured specifically for motion picture use generally work at very high frequencies which helps to avoid flicker for normal shooting, but for high speed photography cinematographers should either test or use constant current LED fixtures. If LED lights in your shot don't seem to obey the rules of known 50 cycle or 60 cycle shutter angles, then a little experimentation can usually find a compromise shutter angle that will mitigate the flicker, but no one wants to conduct such experiments with a producer, a director and an entire shooting crew watching. The same holds true for shooting monitors and projection screens. The usual frame rates and shutter angles normally work, but some displays clock at 60hz, some clock at 90hz and some clock at odd frame rates. Preproduction is for testing! Test, test test!!!

Figure 11.50 Cinematography Electronics FLICKERfree Calculator app.

As I mentioned earlier in this chapter, Cinematography Electronics has created the FLICKERfree Calculator iPhone App, a free downloadable tool to calculate camera speed and shutter angle combinations for FLICKER-free film or digital cinematography. Their website also features downloadable HMI Flickerfree Filming Speeds reference cards. Their app calculates camera speed in frames per second (fps) and

camera shutter angle in degrees for selectable line frequency, either 50 Hz or 60 Hz. For example, for 50hz mains power at 24fps use a 172.8 degree shutter, and for 60hz mains power at 25fps use a 150 degree shutter. The colors on the calculator, burgundy (50 Hz) or blue (60 Hz), also match the colors on their pocket reference cards.

Workflow Tests

The final step in designing a workflow for a shoot is to put that workflow into action. Workflow tests should be conducted far enough in advance of the shoot that inevitable adjustments in the workflow plan can be made without the duress of an impending start date. Post production, editorial, and the lab are all necessary participants in the testing process, and the cinematographer must enlist their participation, critique, and comments as one of the duties of the job. The workflow for any given show can only succeed if the cinematographer has generated buy-in from the entire production.

Filmout Tests

Filmouts, obviously, are quickly becoming a thing of the past. As of 2020, about 30% of worldwide screens are still film projection screens. In the United States only 15% of the 42,803 are still film screens. With studio mandates to migrate to full digital releases by the end of 2014 – this last 15/30% will probably disappear quickly.

On projects where there is to be a theatrical film release, the final step for any workflow test is to take the material all the way through the imaging chain to film print and digital cinema package (DCP). It is vital to undertake this process in a timely fashion; it is not easy and takes quite a bit of time, so leave room in the schedule to react to all of the steps along the way. Your workflow plan is going to change, no matter how solidly you plan, so leave some time to adjust without the duress and time pressure of last minute changes.

Camera Tests, Lens Tests/Lens Projection

It is the camera department's responsibility to thoroughly prep and test the lenses and the entire camera package before signing it out of the rental company. Prep can take anywhere from a few days to a few weeks on a large production. On a tight budget the production may balk at paid prep time, but the cinematographer has a responsibility to the production and to their insurance policy to assure the condition of the equipment to be used.

60 Hz CINEMATOGRAPHY electronics

HMI FLICKERFREE FILMING SPEEDS

Speed (fps) At Any Shutter Angle		With Specific Shutter Angles		
		fps	Shutter Angle	
120.000	6.666	66.667	200°	
60.000	6.315	65.000	195°	
40.000	6.000	63.333	190°	
30.000	5.714	57.600	172.8°	
24.000	5.454	56.667	170°	
20.000	5.217	55.000	165°	
17.143	5.000	53.333	160°	
15.000	4.800	50.000	150°	
13.333	4.000	48.000	144°	
12.000	3.750	46.667	140°	
10.909	3.000	45.000	135°	
10.000	2.500	43.333	130°	
9.231	2.000	36.667	110°	
8.571	1.875	35.000	105°	210°
8.000	1.500	33.333	100°	200°
7.500	1.000	26.667	80°	160°
7.058		25.000	75°	150°

ALWAYS USE FILM TESTS TO VERIFY RESULTS

5321 Derry Ave., Suite G, Agoura Hills, CA 91301 USA
Phone (818) 706-3334   Fax (818) 706-3335
E-mail: info@CinemaElec.com
Website: www.CinematographyElectronics.com

© 2000 Cinematography Electronics Inc.

50 Hz CINEMATOGRAPHY electronics

HMI FLICKERFREE FILMING SPEEDS

Speed (fps) At Any Shutter Angle		With Specific Shutter Angles		
		fps	Shutter Angle	
100.000	5.555	55.556	200°	
50.000	5.263	54.167	195°	
33.333	5.000	52.778	190°	
25.000	4.761	48.000	172.8°	
20.000	4.545	47.222	170°	
16.666	4.347	45.833	165°	
14.285	4.166	44.444	160°	
12.500	4.000	41.667	150°	
11.111	3.333	40.000	144°	
10.000	3.125	38.889	140°	
9.090	2.500	37.500	135°	
8.333	2.000	36.111	130°	
7.692	1.250	30.556	110°	
7.142	1.000	29.167	105°	
6.666		27.778	100°	200°
6.250		24.000	86.4°	172.8°
5.882		22.222	80°	160°

ALWAYS USE FILM TESTS TO VERIFY RESULTS

5321 Derry Ave., Suite G, Agoura Hills, CA 91301 USA
Phone (818) 706-3334   Fax (818) 706-3335
E-mail: info@CinemaElec.com
Website: www.CinematographyElectronics.com

© 2000 Cinematography Electronics Inc.

Figure 11.51 Cinematography Electronics FLICKERfree 60hz table.

Figure 11.52 Cinematography Electronics FLICKERfree 50hz table.

In camera prep it is essential to assure that the camera body to be used has been thoroughly and correctly set up for collimation, sensor flatness, back focus, and flange depth. The first step in prep testing is usually to perform a black level test. Cold boot the camera, leave the port cap on the camera, and shoot a few seconds of black. Then allow the camera to warm up for at least a half an hour and then shoot the same test again. Shoot multiple takes of this test throughout an entire prep day. Then (on cameras that provide for it) perform a black balance operation and shoot a few more seconds of footage. This footage can be compared before and after to inform the crew whether the camera chosen will require frequent black balance, and this will also tell you whether the sensor has any "lit" or dead pixels.

Remember that as you test cameras, you are also testing codecs and recording systems, and any screenings of test footage will also serve to evaluate not only cameras and lenses, but also the file type to be recorded, the recording system, and the entire workflow through post production.

The rental company should provide a good selection of primes and zooms to choose from in all the selected focal lengths, as many as they reasonably can. These lenses should be checked for correct focus markings, sharpness, and contrast marking on a large flat lens chart with Siemens stars at center and in the corners, that completely fill the frame to evaluate sensor flatness alignment.

Then check the lenses on a lens projector. Projecting a lens chart on a wall in a dark room allows the camera assistant to evaluate each lens for color, astigmatism, chromatic aberration, flare, and sharpness across the field of view. Lens projection is covered in more depth in the lens chapter of this work. Camera assistants sometimes construct large collage lens test charts from magazine pages with lots of very sharp small print and details for testing lenses. Shooting footage of such collages makes it easy to see the color, sharpness, and resolution differences between lenses when projected on a big screen or large monitor.

Resources for Creative Lens Tests

Creative choices of lenses and lens types is the duty of the cinematographer. Vintage lenses can give footage a period feel. Softer lenses can give scenes a romantic feel, and very sharp, contrasty lenses can convey a sense of tension. Lenses are one of the principle creative tools for setting the mood and tone of the project.

Figure 11.53

One of my personal favorite resources for quickly evaluating a wide variety of lenses (old *and* new) in one place is at a website setup by a company called Old Fast Glass. They are a Los Angeles based cinema lens rental company, founded by a group of passionate young film makers, and specializing in renting both vintage and modern lenses. They have been researching, testing, collecting and, shooting with vintage lenses for years.

www.oldfastglass.com/lens-tests/

https://blog.sharegrid.com/ultimate-vintage-cinema-lens-test

Don't let the name fool you; they hold their rental lenses to high standards, they are serviced regularly, and they have multiple replacement sets of lenses in their inventory in the event that a lens needs service or replacement. They can provide lenses that cover full-frame sensors, lenses designed for the Super 16 format, and specialty optics. They also offer full camera package and accessory rentals as well.

Shoot Framing Charts!

Shooting framing charts is a very important part of the camera prep. The ability to ensure every department is working with the same frame with accuracy is very valuable.

The lab uses framing charts to compose dailies and mask excess picture area. It is also common to display multiple framing charts inside the viewfinder. For example, the cinematographer might superimpose both a 2.39:1 framing chart and a

1.79:1 framing chart with a common top line to dictate correct framing headroom of actors and to accommodate staging and framing of shots for two different aspect ratio deliverables.

If (for example) you are shooting at a high resolution like 4K or 5K and you are delivering the finished movie at 1920 × 1080, you could afford yourself the luxury of a small percentage of *safety area* inside the original image. This additional recorded image area outside the intended composition can allow the editor to slightly reframe, punch in, or to stabilize shots. A framing chart for this case would include frame lines for both the intended finished frame, and for the extra image area outside the frame, with both frame lines clearly labeled.

When the VFX department receive plates, they need to know precisely what the delivery frame area is so that they do not waste time on manipulating picture area that will never be seen in the finished product. In conform and color correction, the post facility also needs to know how to crop and re-frame the image. The goal is to ensure that every department will be looking at and working to the same frame.

ARRI Frame Line and Lens Illumination Tool

www.arri.com/en/learn-help/learn-help-camera-system/tools/frame-line-lens-illumination-tool

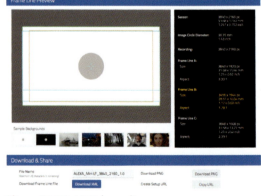

Figure 11.54 ARRI frame line composer.

The ARRI frame line composer is a web-app that lets you customize frame lines on a computer, export them to the camera via SD card or save them as images. This XML can be given to your lab and they can then take these numbers and make a pixel accurate leader within Photoshop.

Every aspect of the frame lines can be manipulated on the composer tool: multiple aspect ratio framings, common top offsets for multiple aspect ratios, surround view, the amount of shading in the surround view, how far the pillarbox lines extend if you choose to have a second aspect ratio.

Flesh Tone and Color Tests

Given the diversity of flesh tones and skin colors that cinematographers face in lighting actors in a scene, it is wise to audition stand-ins for a project by employing them to shoot flesh tone and skin color tests. By shooting stand-ins whose flesh tones closely match the principal actors, cinematographers can anticipate any issues of lighting and color correcting a variety of lighting scenarios.

Figure 11.55 Skin tone testing.

By testing several actors or stand-ins of varying skin tones in the same scene, the cinematographer can work with the DIT and gaffer to develop strategies for flattering all of the talent performing face to face, scene to scene.

Camera Noise/Exposure Latitude Tests

It is very important to the cinematographer to know first-hand what the exposure latitude and dynamic range of a camera is. This can be discovered by shooting dynamic range exposure tests. This testing informs what the cinematographer's *creative* range of exposure can be, how much overexposure or clip can be tolerated, and how much noise to expect in dark areas of the frame.

Image Engineering TE269 V2 D Dynamic Range Chart

www.image-engineering.de/products/charts/all/406-te269

Image Engineering manufactures image quality test charts, analysis software, measurement, and illumination devices that provide users with the means to accurately test and evaluate the image quality of cameras and lenses. Image Engineering charts measure factors such as camera resolution, texture loss, distortion, flare, and noise (among many other metrics) that play a vital role in determining the overall quality of an image.

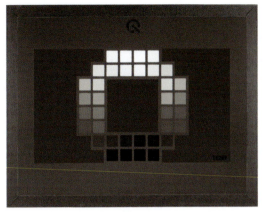

Figure 11.56 Image Engineering TE269 V2 dynamic range test chart.

Their 36 patch OECF TE269 V2 chart is a transparent grayscale test chart used to determine the OECF, noise, SNR, and dynamic range of digital high dynamic range digital cameras, measuring high dynamic ranges up to 1.000.000:1/120dB.

DSC XYLA 21: 20 Stop Grayscale Chart

http://dsclabs.com/

Cinematographers can accurately measure dynamic range using the DSC Labs XYLA21. With a built-in light source, the XYLA 21 displays photometrically neutral steps to measure 20 stops of dynamic range.

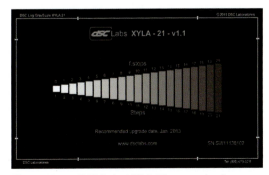

Figure 11.57 DSC Labs XYLA 21 grayscale chart.

Both the TEC 269 and Xyla 21 charts are rare and expensive pieces of gear, and moreover, they produce a very scientific result that can be unsatisfying to the artistic cinematographer, his director, and his producers.

Dynamic Range and Exposure Latitude

The dynamic range (or tonal range) of a scene is the ratio of the maximum and minimum light levels in the scene.

The dynamic range of a camera is the ratio of number of stops of latitude a sensor is capable of recording.

The exposure latitude of a camera is the range of tones that the camera can accurately capture from dark to light that will produce an image that is acceptable in color and tone without clipping highlights and with an acceptable noise level in dark areas of the frame.

The discipline that underlies cinematography is the mastery of matching the tonal range of scenes in front of the lens to the capability of the sensor medium behind the lens in order to artistically capture and record that tonal range.

Dynamic range and exposure latitude are intimately intertwined. The latitude of a sensor changes in distribution of the number of stops above and below middle gray as one alters the ISO rating. The cinematographer can rate a sensor's ISO higher and reduce the number of stops above middle gray, or rate the sensor ISO lower to prevent excessive noise in dark areas of the frame. In one type of project, the creative team might take great precautions to suppress and minimize noise in images while another type of project might use noise as a creative tool. These are among the many creative choices cinematographers have in telling stories. Just remember to let everyone involved in the project know when these choices are being made. It is urgent to have the producers, the director and the studio all involved in such a choice so that the decision doesn't come back to haunt during post production or quality control. Digital noise reduction is an expensive and time consuming post production process. Noise can be a subjective creative tool, but one that must be used with caution – your mileage may vary. The best advice is to do tests. Test to confirm that the manufacturers ISO rating of the camera is realistic, test to determine what noise floor is acceptable for the production, and test to learn at what level the sensor clips or loses the ability to reproduce color correctly. These tests will enable the cinematographer to expose with confidence on the set.

Dual Native ISO Cameras

Dual ISO cameras can capture at two ISO settings, a normal ISO, or a higher ISO for lower light levels. The standard signal path in a digital camera runs a photosite's output through an analog amplifier, then through an analog to digital converter, then the signal passes through a digital gain amplifier and finally through noise reduction. Dual ISO sensors provide a second parallel signal path that can change the amount of amplification being applied to the analog signal from photosites. When the higher ISO circuit is chosen, the signal is routed through a higher gain analog amplifier before it gets converted by the analog to digital convertor. The new signal path also then engages a different noise reduction algorithm, resulting in a higher base ISO, and this stronger noise reduction can reduce fine detail in darker parts of the frame. Raising the ISO essentially reallocates the dynamic range of the camera, increasing low light sensitivity while reducing the number of stops of highlight headroom, and altering the light level that the camera sees as middle gray. This higher ISO signal path is optimized for lower-light shooting, resulting in lower noise floor than just increasing gain in a camera or lifting light levels in color correction. Just remember to closely monitor highlights when using the higher ISO setting in a dual ISO camera, as highlights will clip sooner!

Practical Dynamic Range and Exposure Latitude Testing

In the absence of a XYLA 21, dynamic range can be measured using multiple side by side Macbeth charts or grayscale charts lit to different brightnesses. Hang three Macbeth color checker or grayscale charts side by side from C-stands with black flags between them to isolate the lights that will be separately illuminating them. Light the center chart with a medium tungsten unit from very near the camera, either from over or under the camera, so that the chart is evenly lit with no hot spot or sheen. The middle chart exposure should be lit, lit to T8 when using a lens with a range of T2.8 to T22, or to T5.6 when using a lens with a stop range of T2 to T16. The left-most chart should be lit with a large tungsten unit from far enough away that there is no falloff of exposure from one side of the chart to the other, and at such an angle that there is no sheen or hot spot reflecting from the lamp off of the chart. Light the right chart with a very small tungsten unit from about the same distance at a complementary angle to the large lamp. Flag the light from each lamp so that each chart receives light from only the lamp intended to light it. Use spot/flood and single/double nets on the lamps to set the exposure so that the left-most chart is three stops hotter than the center chart, and the right most chart is three stops darker than the center chart. Do not use neutral density filters to vary the exposure, either on the lens or on the lamps. Not all neutral density filters are created equal. The permutations of various neutral density filters on the lens in combination with the wide variety of camera sensors can sometimes skew colors and contribute a pink cast to the overall image. Similarly, neutral density gel for lamps will attenuate the visible spectrum, but is transparent to infrared light, which can result in images heavily contaminated with a pink cast in the blacks, green becomes brown, blue becomes lavender, red and orange become oversaturated.

Using this method, one can shoot bracket frames at every stop on the lens, either by varying the T-stop, by varying frame rate, or by varying the shutter angle, so that you are assured to have chart frames that range from at least three stops overexposed through at least three stops underexposed for a total range of about 14 to 15 stops.

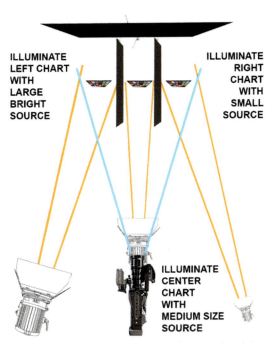

Figure 11.58 Lighting diagram for shooting dynamic range charts with three charts and three lamps.

Figure 11.59 Charts exposed at T2.8: left chart is very overexposed, center chart is overexposed, right chart is correctly exposed.

Figure 11.60 Charts exposed at T4: left chart is very overexposed, center chart is slightly overexposed, right chart is slightly underexposed.

Figure 11.61 Charts exposed at T5.6: left chart is overexposed, center chart is slightly overexposed, right chart is underexposed.

Figure 11.62 Charts exposed at T8: center chart is correctly exposed, left chart is overexposed, right chart is underexposed.

Figure 11.63 Charts exposed at T11: left chart is slightly overexposed, center chart is slightly underexposed, right chart is very underexposed.

Figure 11.64 Charts exposed at T16: left chart is slightly underexposed, center chart is underexposed, right chart is very underexposed.

Figure 11.65 Charts exposed at T22: left chart is correctly exposed, center chart is underexposed, right chart is very underexposed.

ILLUMINATE LEFT CHART WITH LARGE BRIGHT SOURCE

ILLUMINATE RIGHT CHART WITH SMALL SOURCE

ILLUMINATE CENTER CHART WITH MEDIUM SIZE SOURCE

With these charts exposed this way, a cinematographer can go into a color correction suite and attempt to correct over- and underexposures to compare the results to the normal exposure side-by-side. Lifting the underexposed charts up will reveal the noise floor of the camera, and will show the consequences of using color correction to lift darker areas of a frame. Similarly, by darkening the overexposed frames, the cinematographer can reveal where highlight clipping occurs and adjust his or her ISO and exposure strategy so as not to unintentionally clip highlights for any given camera.

Figure 11.66 Side-by-side split screen of normal, under- and overexposed charts with attempted exposure color correction.

In the illustration above, the center chart was correctly exposed, the left chart was grossly overexposed, the right chart was grossly underexposed, and correction has been attempted on both the overexposed (left) and underexposed (right) charts. Color correction of both the left and right charts clearly shows failure to reproduce both color and contrast. The left chart shows evidence of highlight clipping in the grayscale, and the right chart exhibits extreme digital noise. An in-depth examination of such test frames can inform the cinematographer about the exposure latitude, dynamic range, and reasonable ISO rating of a digital cinema camera for a variety of exposure strategies. By evaluating the number of stops above and below middle gray for any given ISO rating, the cinematographer can determine native ISO from a real data set.

The following is a proposal for an updated definition of dynamic range in digital cinema, contributed by Imaging Scientist Tony Davis of Tessive LLC.

A Proposed Definition of Dynamic Range in Digital Cinema Cameras

Introduction

For a phrase with relatively well-understood meaning and implications, "dynamic range" has been an unfortunately difficult metric to pin

down. To help understand it, let's start with the simplest expression of what it is supposed to represent and expand from there.

A sensor's "dynamic range" is the ratio between the brightest and dimmest measurable illumination.

This is a straightforward sentence, but each word and phrase immediately raises questions. When we say "sensor," are we referring to the whole sensor or just a part? Can sensor parameters change between the brightest and dimmest illumination? How is the ratio expressed? What do we mean by "measurable"? Depending on how these are interpreted, the resulting answer may change dramatically, and different measurements performed by different groups will not be comparable.

We propose to lock down the specific meanings of these phrases in a way most suitable for digital cinema measurement so that dynamic range measurements can be easily understood and measured reliably, and such that the resulting values have real-world utility.

Defining Terms and Making Choices

For each part of this definition, we need to make a choice and justify it somehow. Let's tear the phrase apart and analyze each aspect.

A sensor's "dynamic range" is the ratio between the brightest and dimmest measurable illumination.

Sensor

It's important to start by defining what the system under test really is. This may seem obvious, but it really isn't. Many parts of the optical system can determine the dynamic range, and also it is important to define the operating conditions under which the sensor is running. Do we mean "camera," including the lens? Do we mean entire sensor? Or do we mean each photosite on the sensor?

We propose "sensor" in the case of measuring cinema camera response should mean "the linear luminance or a color channel value of a single delivered pixel." This means that what we will measure is the response of a single delivered color or grayscale pixel value as acquired by the camera and processed by any necessary demosaic or rendering software.

For analysis, the value will be linearized, and the details of this will be expanded upon later. The important point is that the measured "sensor" is a color pixel as delivered. The measured dynamic range can be for the luminance response, or for the red, green, and blue channels.

Other options could be that the dynamic range should be for a single photosite of the mosaiced sensor, but this option is not available for every camera and ultimately doesn't provide direct information about how the camera will respond to the end-user. Alternatively, this could be an entire sensor measurement, using averaged information from all the photosites together, but that measurement is nearly meaningless from a resolving standpoint. We propose that it is important to be able to know what a single delivered pixel's response is when making decisions about lighting or image resolution.

It is apparent that camera settings as well as rendering software (if any) settings will have an impact on dynamic range, sometimes with the ability to improve dynamic range at the expense of other, desirable metrics. For example, under this definition, a digital softening filter in the rendering software could dramatically increase dynamic range at the expense of image sharpness. Also, under this definition, fine-pixel-pitch sensors will almost certainly have lower dynamic range per pixel than coarse-pitch sensors. Any dynamic range measurement would have to be considered in conjunction with the camera settings as well as the overall resolution of the delivered image. However, if the definition is clearly understood to be for a single delivered pixel, it should be easy to understand the relative trade-offs for different camera and software settings or different delivered resolutions.

Optically, those aspects which are to be included in the definition of "sensor" are non-removable items such as any microlens arrays or optical lowpass filters. Lenses and external filters are not to be included in the definition of "sensor." Therefore, any measurement technique should not return a different result for "dynamic range" if a different lens or lens setting is used.

Ratio

If the high value that can be measured by the sensor is A and the low value is B, then the ratio is obviously A/B. The presentation of the resulting number, however, is not always agreed upon. Some of the options are: decibels (power or energy), as a two-number ratio, as a single linear value, or in stops.

Decibels (power): $10 * \log_{10}\left(\dfrac{A}{B}\right)$

Decibels (energy): $20 * \log_{10}\left(\dfrac{A}{B}\right)$

Two-number ratio: "A:B" or "A/B" presented with both numbers visible Linear value: Simply dividing A/B = C, presenting "C"

Stops: $\log_2\left(\dfrac{A}{B}\right)$, which also can be approximated as $3.322 * \log_{10}\left(\dfrac{A}{B}\right)$

For cinematography use, we propose using stops for presentation of the ratio of the high to low illumination values. This corresponds to most widely understood practices in lighting and exposure, as well as previous understandings of film exposure.

Measurable

A key piece of the metric is the definition of what is measurable. If we depend upon visual inspection, there is too much room for subjective interpretation. Also, any criteria for "measurable" signals should be performed at a per-pixel level, without visually aggregating adjacent pixels in the determination.

There are lots of possible definitions of "measurability," so the best we can do is to try to make some logical definition that is mathematically stable, understandable, and relatively easy to determine from real-world data. Our proposal starts with the premise that an illumination value can be correctly measured if the resulting measurement is almost always within one stop of the correct value and not clipped. By almost always, we mean 99.9999% of the time, or five sigma (standard deviation).

In one sense, this is a very strict requirement. Five sigma is a tight limit, with only about 1 in 1.7 million measured values allowed to be outside the range. In another sense, this is a very loose requirement, as the measured value needs to be only within plus or minus a single stop of the correct value, i.e. doubled or halved.

This criterion for measurability is based on the Rose Criterion, which says that for something to be considered identifiable in a single measurement, it has to have a difference threshold to standard deviation ratio of five or greater. This is the five sigma requirement for detectability. In our case, we're defining the difference to be only one stop, so it's a very loose standard for the measurable threshold. Combining these ideas gives us a baseline for detectability.

This means that at a given illumination, we say that illumination level has been accurately measured by the pixels if the mean value is correct and fewer than 1 in 1.7 million measured values are less than 2× the mean or greater than ½ the mean value.

At the lower illumination limit (the darkest measurable value), the lower threshold (50% of the current illumination level) is the harder to avoid, since the image noise is generally an additive function. The result is that we consider that a detector can "measure" a given dark illumination level if the mean to standard deviation ratio (a measure of signal-to-noise) is 10 or greater.

The upper illumination limit (the brightest measurable value) is usually determined by the clipping of the A/D converter, as the signal statistics are almost always improving with image brightness. Our criterion for measurability says that only 1 in 1.7 million measurements may be clipped for a given brightness to be considered measured.

In practice this may be a tricky threshold to directly measure. As illumination levels increase and more pixels reach saturation, the standard deviation will necessarily decrease as many values are identical, which gives the impression of improving signal to noise ratio when in fact the overall deviation is increasing because the mean is not correct for the real illumination. A quick and fairly correct solution would be to accept the brightest illumination step level where no pixel values are in saturation.

This maximum measurable illumination value under this criterion is almost always less than the maximum A/D value. It takes into account the image noise in bright images and accepts as "measured" only those average values which do not saturate to a five-sigma tolerance.

For a step chart image, it is easy to take the pixel values for each illumination step and compute the mean versus standard deviation. If the result is greater than ten, then we can say that the imager correctly measured that illumination value.

In Figure 11.67, a simulated step chart is shown with fairly typical dark and photon noise for a modern cinema camera. A line profile (on a semi-log scale) through the image shows the increasing noise toward the lower illumination levels.

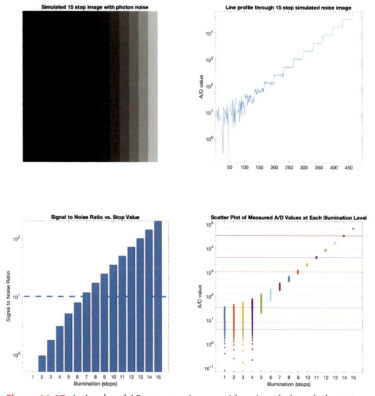

Figure 11.67 A simulated 15 stop step image with noise (dark and photon). In the line profile through the image, the noise can be seen to obscure correct identification of illumination values in darker regions. The measured signal-to-noise ratio for each step is shown in the lower left. A scatter plot of values at each stop is shown in the lower right, showing that stop #7 is the lowest illumination level where the measured values are within one stop (plus and minus) of the correct value.

Each step in the image is one stop darker than the step to its right. Visually, we can easily identify about 12 or 13 bars in the image. In the line profile, we're visually confident to about ten stops.

The bar chart in the lower left shows the signal-to-noise ratio (mean pixel value divided by the standard deviation) for each illumination step. Our criterion of ten is shown as a blue line. According to this threshold, only nine stops are accurately measured. If we look at the scatter plot on the lower right, we can see that stop 10 is the last illumination level that does not have significant overlap with the next lower values. Below that, the illumination levels are quite muddled together.

With features as large as steps, our eyes aggregate many pixels together to see the illumination change. In a line profile, we've removed one of the two dimensions, so our ability to average together adjacent data is diminished. For our measurement, however, we're interested not in groups of pixels, but in the response of single pixels. If we were allowed to consider many adjacent pixels when determining measurability, then the resolution of the system would necessarily be degraded.

To show this effect, look at Figure 11.68. A resolution target shows that a sensor's ability to represent detail degrades as the noise level increases. What this really means is that

statistically speaking, dynamic range improves if adjacent pixel information can be used. But when adjacent pixels need to show something different because the image resolution is high, then this sort of adjacent averaging isn't possible. This is why it is important to consider each pixel's individual ability to represent correct illumination when discussing dynamic range.

This criterion, which is based on measurability of individual pixels, is much stricter than is sometimes used. For example, some very simple definitions of dynamic range may simply divide the maximum A/D value by the standard deviation of the dark noise. This is based on modeling the noise as only dark noise (excluding photon statistic noise), and setting the threshold for detectability at a signal to standard deviation ratio of 1. By this standard, the simulated camera in our example would have 13 stops of dynamic range, and by our new criterion it only has nine.

The advantage of this proposed method is that it very strictly enforces that the dynamic range is of a single pixel, not of an aggregated sensor or area of a sensor, and it takes into account photon noise and any other noise source that may be present. The criterion is based on an understandable, practical, and lenient range of acceptable values for a given illumination (+/– 1 stop), and couples this with a tight statistical requirement for repeatability.

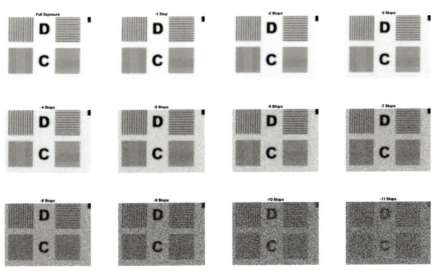

Figure 11.68 A resolution target imaged with decreasing illumination. As the illumination decreases, so does the sensor's ability to properly represent high-resolution information.

Summary of the Proposed Dynamic Range Metric

In summary, the proposed definition of dynamic range is: A value in stops defined as the log base 2 of the ratio of the maximum measurable value of a single pixel at clipping to the lowest illumination value when the mean to standard deviation ratio is ten or greater.

For measured, linear (colorspace gamma removed, linear with respect to incoming photon count) pixel values V, V_{max} is the largest value such that its mean is five-sigma below A/D saturation. V_{min} is the lowest pixel value V such that the ratio of the mean illumination to the standard deviation at that illumination level is at least ten.

$$V_{max} = \max\left(V \left| \frac{V}{\sigma_V} \leq V_{sat} - 5\sigma_V \right.\right)$$

$$V_{min} = \min\left(V \left| \frac{V}{\sigma_V} \geq 10 \right.\right)$$

$$DR = \log_2\left(\frac{V_{max}}{V_{min}}\right)$$

The measurement is performed on a per-pixel basis after demosaicking (if necessary), and unless otherwise specified, is computed using the luminance of the pixel as defined in the color space of the data. It can also be computed per color channel, and the resulting value would be identified with the color channel for which it has been computed.[2]

Notes

1. This section was contributed by Phillippe Ros, AFC.
2. This section was contributed by Tony Davis – Tessive LLC.

Chapter 12

The Shoot

Set Etiquette

As cinematographer, you drive three departments: camera, lighting, and grip. It is your job to know what is next up for all three departments at all times. Your job is to translate the director's intent on a scene by scene basis to the camera operator(s), the gaffer, the key grip, and the dolly grip(s). The cinematographer sets the lens, camera height, framing, and camera movement while lighting and grip departments light the scene. Equally common would be for the cinematographer to supervise lighting and grip as the camera operator finesses the camera to the cinematographer's shot description. You drive a shared vision that you and the director have negotiated. It should come from your heart rather than be passing along a message from the director.

By staying in close communication with the first assistant director, the cinematographer can always be one step ahead of the director in setting up the next shot, scene, or location. An efficient first assistant director is worth his weight in gold, and together, the two of you can be the best of friends and the producer's heroes if you communicate well. The first AD always knows what the next setup will be and when you will be moving to it. He knows when everybody on the set goes into overtime, and he always has a sense of where you are in the day's work, so the AD can help the cinematographer to move things forward on a minute to minute basis. Communicate with the first AD, the operator, and your gaffer, and always look forward to the next setups to be prepared ahead of time. On set, the cinematographer's mantra should be "What are we doing next?"

As the head of the camera department I always instruct the camera assistants to have the camera(s) on set or near set, powered, booted, and viewable, with fresh media and a lens, and ready to shoot – at call time every day. Keep the camera out of the way for rehearsals. I prefer to watch rehearsals with the director, the camera operator, the script supervisor, and the actors.

The digital imaging technician should have monitoring and record capabilities live and ready at call as well. Avoid camera reboots whenever possible, but also let the director and first assistant director know what to expect from the camera being used, in terms of reboot time, media or D-mag changes, pre roll, and any other special camera needs. I have many conversations with the operator(s) about framing, and camera movement based on the discussions I have had with the director during our prep time together. Frequently the operator(s) will wear headsets so that the cinematographer can whisper framing and composition comments to them as a shot is being made. I prefer not to abort takes if something is wrong in front of the camera when shooting digitally. On film shoots, this was common practice if something went badly wrong in front of the camera, such as a bump in the dolly track or a fallen flag, but when shooting digitally, the imperative to save money by cutting is not as strong, and I prefer to let the action play out on the off chance that a happy accident might occur in the scene. If, after the scene is over, I am convinced that the take is unusable, I always have a conversation about it with the director and the script supervisor so that bad takes do not end up cut into the finished project.

I like to give the lighting and grip departments constant information about what is happening next; they always appreciate as much time as you can give them to drag heavy cable, lights, scaffolding, or dollies. It is important to check the technical schedule frequently to remind lighting and grip of special equipment needs, and give them as much prep time as you can for specific setups.

Be prepared to have a continuous conversation with the gaffer and key grip about pre-lighting and prerigging the next scene, the next day's work, or even next week's work. In television, this can be imperative in staying on schedule. Have a similar continuous conversation with the camera operator and first assistant, so that they can prepare the camera for the next setup, or place orders for the additional gear needed for tomorrow.

Most of all, while shooting, try to keep cool, calm, and dispassionate about the chaos around you. Try to develop a zen for being in the moment of shooting, to be one with the confusion and let the chaos flow through you. Stay focused on the work, stay focused on the director's needs, and stay in communication with the first assistant director. If you have prepared thoroughly, chosen the right people, the right equipment and the right workflow, the shoot should be a joyful and fulfilling experience, so treasure that experience and try to find ways to let it be enjoyable.

Look Management, Monitors, Tents, and Directors

I prefer to have at least one control monitor in a light controlled environment or a dark tent, and that monitor is my private monitor. The director can share, or preferably have his own hi quality monitor on the set, close to the action. I like to allow the rest of the crew access to camera and monitors as much as possible within reason, but I try to discourage too much conversation and "contribution" to the image on set. It's fine to spot a mistake like a coffee cup or plastic water bottle left behind on the set, but it's not okay for random members of the crew to give "artistic" lighting or framing tips.

During takes, I like to watch the shot at the best monitor that I can get. The monitor should be calibrated regularly so as to match the DIT monitor and the monitor the colorist will use to make dailies at the lab. If you are shooting for a high dynamic range finish, it is imperative to have the biggest HDR monitor that can be practically used on the set. HDR can only be properly managed by monitoring in HDR on set!

Well color-corrected dailies and look-managed images will embed a familiarity of the eventual desired look in the minds of the director, the producers, the studio, the editors, and everyone involved in a project. This is an urgently important first step in arriving at a final look that reflects the cinematographer's intent! Once the creative team have wed themselves to the look of the dailies, making changes in that look

frequently becomes an uphill battle! It frequently happens that a cinematographer may not be available for or invited to attend final color correction, so attention to look management during production is a very good step toward assuring the look of the final image.

I watch focus as closely as I can without distracting myself from lighting and framing. Focus is the area of greatest concern to me on set when working digitally. Very small errors in focus can be very hard to detect when working digitally, the bigger the monitor, the easier it is to catch bad focus. I also appoint the digital imaging technician to help scrutinize focus for me, and to report quietly to me (and me only) if there is ever any problem.

During the shoot, I prefer not to engage the actors in conversation unless they come to me. The process of acting in front of the camera is a delicate one, and I am trying to assist the director in getting the best performance possible, so I try to hold my interactions with the actors to the mechanics of getting the shot or scene.

You Are the Producer's Business Partner

Part of the cinematographer's job is balancing the demands, hopes, dreams, and wishes of the director with the money available to do the job. This is a delicate dance, and ultimately the cinematographer walks a diplomat's tightrope in balancing what the director wants with what the producer will let you give him. This part of the job has always been the most stressful to me, but I find it useful to keep in mind that one must be diplomatic, but at the same time be resourceful and unreasonable. Resourcefulness is always rewarded in the process, and making the effort to save money will buy you favor and credibility with the producer and the studio, but at the same time, being unreasonable in the pursuit of the director's vision will create a bond that pays off in loyalty and creativity in the work you share.

You Are the Director's Hardest Working Best Friend

The cinematographer's job is ultimately awarded by the director. Yes, the producer and the studio have a say so in the matter, but if your director wants you on the job, he or she will usually get their way. Directors have widely varying styles and interests. I have worked with directors that have little or no interest in camera placement or lens selection, lighting and composition, and I have worked with directors that will say "put the camera right here with a 50mm on it and dolly slowly to over there on this line in the script." Every director has a different style and focus, and it is up to you to learn and accommodate for each style. One helpful tip is to begin the prep exercise by watching movies together and talking about them as a way to formulate a look and style for the project you are doing together. Directors *always* have favorite movies and they *always* have a movie to point to as a way of explaining their wants and expectations. It is up to you to realize those expectations, so you must translate the director's intent on a scene by scene basis to the rest of your crew: your operator(s), your gaffer, your key grip, and your dolly grip(s).

The Studio: What Time Did You Get the First Shot of the Day?

It is important to remember that someone is putting up a lot of money and taking a lot of risk to make a movie. You have a responsibility to make the best effort to see that risk rewarded. Bring honesty and integrity to your work as a cinematographer, be open and communicative and the studio can be your friend. They want to know what is happening all day, every day on the set. They want to know what time you got the first shot, how many shots you got by the time the crew broke for lunch, how many shots you got in your day, whether you got every shot that was on the call sheet, and whether any overtime was incurred by the crew. The studio does not like to hear about upsets on the set. If by example you can run a calm, easygoing set (in spite of whatever chaos may be happening around you), it puts everybody at ease, allowing for a more creative mood and better work, and that may be what gets you your next job.

Making a Shot

The ritual of the shoot day was taught to me by several mentors, in particular, Phil Lathrop ASC who was always a gentleman on set, and by Roger Corman, who mentored many famous directors and cinematographers. It is a well-evolved ritual that can work to perfection when followed.

Before beginning your production day, have a good breakfast, and then be sure to arrive on set well before shooting call. The cinematographer cannot be late to the shoot – *ever*. Find a second assistant director and get a set of sides (miniature script pages and a daily schedule for the day's work) and then make your rounds. Have conversations with the gaffer, the first assistant director, the first assistant cameraman and your director. Begin the preparation for the first shot of the day well before you go on the clock.

Generally the lighting for a new scene will have been "roughed in" by the lighting department rigging crew, based on a description of the scene by the cinematographer and the director.

The director, the AD, and the cinematographer confer to determine the order in which to shoot the scene, then the director describes the specific shot he wants to the cinematographer. As the director blocks the scene, the actor stand ins, cinematographer, the gaffer and the first assistant camera watch quietly to determine camera placement, movement, lighting, and focus marks. As the scene blocking solidifies, the first AC begins setting focus marks for rehearsal with stand-ins. The cinematographer confers with the gaffer and key grip and to begin lighting and camera placement. The stand-ins move in for lighting work while the actors are sent for their final hair, makeup, and wardrobe checks. The cinematographer sets the lens, camera height, framing, and camera movement while lighting and grip departments light the scene. When the actors return from makeup, rehearsals resume until the director is satisfied with the action.

When I trained under my original mentor Phil Lathrop ASC, he always had a small bicycle horn hanging by the camera, and everyone knew when he was ready to shoot the shot when he honked the horn. This is the signal for the AD to walk the actors onto set and do a last rehearsal. When the rehearsal and last looks by hair, makeup, wardrobe and lighting departments are complete, the cinematographer sets the stop and shooting begins.

If there are SPFX, smoke or rain or fire, those are set, the first AD locks up the set and stops any traffic that must be held for the shot. The first AD calls "roll," and the sound man acknowledges when he is at speed, the AD calls "roll camera" and each camera position acknowledges when they are rolling, the Operator calls "marker" and the second AC claps the sticks, calling out the scene and take per the script supervisor. The first AD calls "background action," and either the first assistant director or the director calls "action." When the scene is over the director calls "cut." The first AD calls "reset" or "back to one" and the next take is prepared. When the scene has been completed, the first AD will frequently call "We are on the wrong set!" or "Company moves!" At the end of the day, the AD might call out that a shot is the "Abby Singer," which means that you are on the second to the last shot of the day, and after that, he will call everybody's favorite – "That's a wrap!"

Picking up the Pieces at the End of the Day: The Crew

The time after wrap is called should be spent preparing for tomorrow's work. Find a second assistant director and get a call sheet for tomorrow and then make your rounds again. Have conversations with the gaffer about prelighting tomorrow's first scene, or even the entire next day's work. Chat with first assistant director, the first assistant cameraman and your gaffer and your key grip so that they can anticipate equipment and manpower needs. Begin the preparation for the first shot of the next day before you leave the set. Be sure to ask about the status of each department: camera, lighting, and grip. Were there any upsets? Were there any problems? Is there any discontent? Amateur psychiatry is little known and underappreciated part of the job description of the cinematographer. Smooth over the events of the day and sympathetically hear out any complaints, beefs, or injustices before you leave the set to watch dailies. At the end of each day remind yourself of your passionate need to create beautiful, but appropriate work – that's what ultimately drives you to endure the stress.

Dailies

Dailies are usually an uncut, one light sync sound version of the previous day's work screened for the director, the cinematographer and other invited crew members, with synched sound and a look applied. Dailies may be distributed as DVDs or BluRays, but if possible, I recommend viewing the material on as big a screen as possible. This makes it much easier to detect technical problems such as focus issues or flickering lights, but a larger screen can also give the director a better impression of the performances that the actors are giving. It is not unusual for actors to view the dailies as a measure of how their performances are progressing. Only the director can decide whether the actors should see their performance, and under no circumstance should the cinematographer or camera crew share the dailies with anyone – especially with actors. In traditional dailies, a representative of the editorial department will be there to take notes and comments on the work from the director and the cinematographer. Once dailies have been seen, the cinematographer should have a conversation with the colorist and/or the digital imaging technician about the work to make any necessary adjustments to color, contrast, and overall look. Then, off to bed for a good night's sleep to be rested, smiling, and ready for the next day.

While this is intended to be an advanced look at the equipment, technology, and practices of digital cinematography, I feel that I must give a little friendly advice here. At this point in the work, all the preparation and study should enable the cinematographer to focus on the task at hand: photographing a beautiful movie. This is the moment you have worked so hard for, so *relax, stay focused on making beautiful images*, and *enjoy the moment* that you have worked so hard to create!

Chapter 13

Workflow, Data, and Color Management

Workflow

Workflow is the managed process or mechanism by which images acquired on set make their way to editorial, through post production, visual effects, color correction, archival, and onto the screen. It is as the process whereby images, audio, and metadata are recorded, backed up, distributed, and safeguarded. In a digital cinema workflow, the full dynamic range of the uncorrected wide gamut images should be recorded, along with ASC CDLs (Color Decision Lists) and/or 3DLUT(s) as a metadata recipe for post color correction, which can then be used nondestructively to apply the cinematographer's "look" to the original camera images as displayed on a calibrated monitor or digital projector.

This discussion of workflow is specific to digital cinematography and is essential to the success of acquisition and postproduction. The cinematographer must help the production determine well in advance of the commencement of principal photography in collaboration with the post production department, the editorial department, the producers, and sometimes even the completion bond company and the insurance company, what the workflow of the project will be. Remember as you design your workflow, do not under staff or under equip the project's workflow, as this may violate the terms of a completion bond or violate the terms of the production insurance policy!

Workflow for a project is dictated in large part by the deliverables and by the market that is the ultimate target for the project, which in turn dictates the camera and equipment chosen for the shoot, and the equipment available within the budget. By gathering at a white board with dry erase markers, the cinematographer, the digital imaging technician, the colorist, the post producers or post supervisors (from either the production or the post facility), the editors and the camera rental house can answer a number of specific questions.

Be prepared to provide a copy of the workflow diagram to a completion bond company or a production insurance company before commencement of principal photography. Be prepared to create a color pipeline specification document for editorial, visual effects vendors, and laboratory facilities that clearly defines color space, file formats, code ranges and best practices for managing color on the project.

No doubt you have seen innumerable workflow diagrams on the internet or in camera sales brochures, and the inevitable spider web of overlapping data pathways in the diagrams can become impenetrable. There are infinite combinations of hardware and software that can be used for these purposes. Rather than write another bewildering workflow diagram that concatenates the several distinct tasks, I will try to distill, separate and simplify the five basic separate tasks of a workflow:

- Assessing the contract deliverables in order to determine camera, lenses, resolution, compression, and framing.
- Color correcting images for on set viewing
- Making secure and reliable backups of the footage and data
- Syncing audio and picture files to create editorial dailies
- Managing the look of images through post and into final color correction.

The factors and deliverables to consider in the equation of whether to generate dailies on set or near set are numerous. In prep, before shooting begins, the producer, the cinematographer, the editor, and the post producer should discuss and agree on a number of workflow considerations.

A Checklist for Defining a Workflow

- What are the deliverables? Is the project being made for HDTV? For 4K UHDTV? For 2K cinema? For 4K cinema? A commercial? For streaming?
- What sensor mode will be employed for shooting?
- What will be the original acquisition format and resolution?
- Will you be acquiring ProRes? Recording across HD SDI? RAW? MXF?
- What will be the original acquisition resolution? HD? 2K? 3K? UHD? 4K? 4.5K? 4.6K? 5K? 6K? 8K?
- What will be the original acquisition frame rate? 23.976 fps? 24 fps? 25 fps? 29.97 fps? 48 fps? 50 fps? 60 fps? 102fps?
- How will the image be viewed on set? Will there be HDR viewing on set?
- How is the "look management" of the images going to be accomplished?
- Who is creating viewing LUTs and CDLs?
- How are viewing LUTs and CDLs being created, assessed, approved, and tested throughout the planned workflow?
- What metadata is being collected on set and how is it being collected, preserved, and forwarded?
- How is the project going to be recorded, to what recorder system, and at what data rate?
- How soon after acquisition can the material be redundantly backed up?
- How and where will verified checksum backup and QC of the media be done, and by whom?
- Who has permission to delete camera original material, and under what conditions?
- How will the physical backup copies be created, safely shipped, stored, and vaulted?
- Who is making dailies, and where, when and how are they making them? Will a lab be employed to make dailies, or will the production generate dailies on set or near the set?
- Will dailies be screened? If so, how often? What kind of projector will be used to show dailies? What type of media will be shown? Who will be invited to see the dailies?
- Will a dailies service such as DAX or PIX or MOXION or DRYLAB be used?
- Will laptops, projectors, and monitors be calibrated so that everyone will be seeing the same color and contrast?
- Who is in charge of dailies QC and producer interface?
- What deliverables will be required from the footage and who will generate them?
- How will sound be recorded, how will syncing sound for dailies be done, when and by whom?

- How is the material from set being checked for quality control, and by whom?
- How will CDLs, LUTs, and metadata be handled and distributed, and by whom?
- Where will final color correction be done?
- What is the copy speed (and therefore time per mag) of the system used to make multiple redundant backups, and what software/hardware will be used for the task?
- What is the render speed of the system being used to generate dailies and editorial proxies?
- What non-linear edit system and which editorial codec will be used?
- Will editorial proxies be generated in an Avid DNx format (DN×36, DN×100, DN×145, DN×200, etc.), or in a Quicktime ProRes format (422proxy, 422LT, 422, 422HQ, 4444, 4444XQ)? Less compressed formats look better in screenings!
- Will the production and /or the studio require H.264 files or H.265 files? Will a cloud dailies system such as PIX or DAX be used for producers and studio execs to access footage? What material is uploaded – selects only, or all footage? What is the release authorization process?
- Will there be a "film out" of the final project?
- Will there be a high dynamic range (HDR) deliverable?
- Who is responsible to assure that all original data has been deleted from D-Mags, disks, cards, and media before that equipment is returned to rental houses?

One cautionary note is needed here: camera rental companies have begun instituting policies of *automatically* deleting media from returned cards, disks etc. in order to eliminate any implied liability for unauthorized dissemination of your content. You *must* take responsibility for properly backing up your data, and you *must* take responsibility for deleting your data from rented media before returning it to the rental house. *Never* rely on the rental company to rescue or delete any data from record media after you have returned it!

Sample Workflows

Baked in Look vs. Full Range Data

In a "baked in" Rec 709 video workflow, the approach is to try to obtain the best result possible on set using the digital image processing tools available in the camera. Various gamma curves (such as hypergamma curves), knee circuits, matrices, detail enhancement, and color balance processes can be used to pre-condition the signal during acquisition to adjust the image for the desired result. In a traditional video workflow where signal processing such as knee circuit clip image information from highlights, matrix, and gamma modify the color space, and when baked in, these decimations of image data cannot be undone. The practice of color correcting to achieve the final look while shooting is an outgrowth of the limitations of the first generation of HD cameras. The cameras and workflows being used today in digital cinema have almost completely obsoleted that approach.

In digital cinema style acquisition, the camera captures as much data as possible without decimation of the original log or Raw wide gamut camera signal, the full exposure range is preserved for postproduction. In post-production this higher dynamic range original is then graded to give the desired results according to the delivery medium, whether that is for theatrical presentation or for HDTV, UHDTV, and Rec 2020 for broadcast.

Digital cinema style acquisition means that nothing done within the camera will change the material recorded, the only adjustments are LUTs to guide the final look, and T stop, focus, filtration, and composition of the shot.

Shooting Log

Directors, producers, and studio execs generally have no idea what they are looking at when shown log images. Because log images do not look like the finished product, it is very nearly impossible to satisfactorily explain to non-technical viewers why log images look the way they do. It is always safer just to use some kind of on-set look management system to allow directors, producers, and studio execs to view color corrected images so that no one has to imagine what the final look might be or to accept your word that the final look will be ok.

Figure 13.1 Log and custom look compared.

It is risky to show log images on set. To the uninitiated, log images look like a mistake. Sometimes when talking with actors, directors,

producers, and studio executives, it can be helpful to say that the log image is the digital equivalent of camera negative – you don't judge color from it, but you can tell if your exposure is OK.

The value of acquiring images in raw format and log encoding is not in dispute. The technology offers substantial increases in color latitude and image control in post production. The understanding of how to view and use log or raw images is a matter of education. This book addresses recording and post production of raw/log images in other chapters, but the issues of viewing those images on set must be addressed here as a camera issue.

Look Management: Color Correcting the Images for On Set Viewing

Well color corrected dailies and look managed images embed a familiarity of the eventual desired look in the minds of the director, the producers, the studio, the editors, and everyone involved in a project. This is an urgently important first step in arriving at a final look that reflects the cinematographer's intent! Once the creative team have acclimated to and wed themselves to the look of the dailies, making changes to that look frequently becomes an uphill battle!

Look management generally refers to the use of color grading applications and tools either on-set or near-set during pre production and principal photography to set creative look references for scenes that can be applied to dailies and editorial media. These creative look references travel along with the original media as metadata that can then be used as a starting point for the final color grading.

The ASC CDL (American Society of Cinematographers Color Decision List) is frequently used in look management because of its convenient (non destructive) cross platform implementation of simple primary RGB color grading parameters: slope, offset, power, and a global saturation parameter. ASC CDLs are simple global RGB adjustments, and are not capable of carrying secondary color corrections.

Look-up tables (LUTs) can also be used for this purpose. A LUT is a portable mathematical conversion from one set of RGB pixel values to another. Unlike CDLs, LUTs are capable of carrying limited secondary color corrections. A LUT is *not* a *transform*, which *more accurately*, *smoothly*, and *explicitly* transforms color from one set of RGB pixel values to another.

Both CDLs and LUTs are very small files that are easily emailed or carried on a USB thumb drive. The point is to make color calibration and look management portable and consistent throughout your imaging workflow.

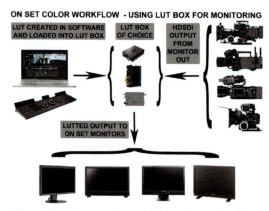

Figure 13.2 On set color workflow using a LUT box for monitoring.

LUTS can also be loaded to separate LUT boxes that take a signal from the camera, apply the look as a non-destructive in line transform, and pass a color corrected picture to on-set monitors through wired and/or wireless transmission.

Figure 13.3 On set color workflow using camera LUTs for monitoring.

Many newer camera workflows allow for use of onboard storage of viewing CDLs or LUTs, which can be generated by a variety of on set or post production color correction utilities to be detailed later in this chapter.

LUTs can also be loaded directly on a variety of monitors detailed in the monitoring section of this work. Color correction information generated on set can also be saved as non-destructive ASC CDLs, or Color Decision List files, which can be used to transmit on set corrections to post-production to be used in grading on almost any color corrector (rather than "baking in" a look on set). A colorist can either use these CDLs as a starting point for the grade, or as a reference to be matched using their own grading techniques.

Uncorrected log footage typically looks gray and washed out. It is usually a bad idea to show uncorrected log images to clients, directors, and studio executives. Dailies and editorial proxies should be generated by applying LUTs used while shooting, so that post production can see what the director and cinematographer saw on set. LUTs can be non-destructively applied either in camera or by using a LUT box to approximate what the footage will eventually look like after grading. Cinematographers can use LUTs to view a saturated and colorful image on set, while still recording in log. It's important to note that you are just viewing through a LUT not "baking it in," to approximate the eventual artistic look of the footage. There are other advantages to using LUTs – added contrast and saturation helps the cinematographer judge critical focus.

Much of the work of look management can (and whenever possible should) be done in pre production and testing. Tests of the lighting and filtration parameters of the shoot, makeup tests, wardrobe tests, location tests, and set tests should be used to develop looks that can be carried to the set and modified there.

When shooting single camera style, as lighting tweaks are done frequently between setups, and especially when the weather and time of day also play their part in look management on location shots, it can become difficult to manage scene to scene color correction. Continuity is a large part of what post production color correction is all about, the fine work of scene to scene correction can be done on set, but is usually best left for post production. Use look management on set to trim and shape the look of dailies, but a workflow that records raw output can efficiently leave the fine tweaking and final color correction to be done in post. Don't distract yourself from the real work by trying to create something too elaborate on set, but rather, just be sure to capture the greatest range of values in the scene, and allow look management to create a solid guide for dailies and post production color correction.

It is usually important for the DP, the director, the producer and script supervisor to own the shooting work as a group effort. This keeps the cinematographer in the creative loop, in communication with the creative intent of the picture. Spend time in the DIT tent, for sure, and guide the look of the picture diligently, but remember, this is only one part of the cinematographer's work on set.

In a digital cinema workflow, the full dynamic range of the uncorrected wide gamut images should be recorded, along with ASC CDLs (Color Decision Lists) and/or 3DLUT(s) as a metadata recipe for post color correction, which can then be used non-destructively to apply the cinematographer's "look" to the original camera images as displayed on a calibrated monitor or digital projector.

No matter what package is used to create the necessary transforms, or what hardware is used to view those transformed images, a thoroughly tested and proven on-set viewing workflow implementation is essential to correctly display log images for general consumption. If there is to be a high dynamic range deliverable, on set viewing and look management become even more critical.

Creating, Storing, and Recalling Camera Settings

One of the features afforded by many digital cinema cameras is the ability to create, upload, and select scene files, which control the settings for many user adjustable parameters.

Figure 13.4 SONY memory stick for saving camera settings.

On some cameras, an onboard memory card slot provides for the ability to save and load scene files or looks for a multitude of shooting situations. With these quick setup adjustment files, a user can quickly switch between a tungsten-balanced setting to a daylight setting to wild or fantastic look setting within seconds. In cameras using raw workflow, these looks can be saved as ASC CDLs or embedded as metadata to be applied in post-production. One word of caution in using cameras that allow deep menu

manipulation of look, color and contrast, once baked into the image, such looks cannot be undone in post!

The DIT Tent, Viewing Environment, and Monitor Calibration

Setting up a quality critical viewing environment on a movie set, or worse, on a far-flung location is challenging and difficult in these days of very tight budgets and "run and gun" schedules. In order to make best use of an on-set viewing environment, it is important to isolate the monitor (and the director of photography's eyes) from sunlight, ambient light, and set lights. For this purpose, *all* digital imaging technicians carry a viewing tent as part of their kit. Entry into the DIT tent is usually by invitation only.

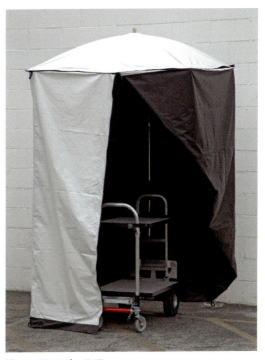

Figure 13.5 The DIT tent.

It is also equally important to assure that the critical viewing monitor has been calibrated, so that what the cinematographer is seeing on set is the same thing that the colorist sees when he applies a LUT or an ASC CDL from set to begin color correcting dailies for editorial and the studio.

If the prep schedule for a project allows, I highly recommend taking the actual monitor or monitors to be used on set into the lab or color suite where the dailies will be color corrected for comparison to the projector or monitors that will be used for the production. This can reassure everyone from the director to the producer to the studio that while you are shooting, what you see is what you will eventually get.

The DIT tent can and should be the director of photography's sacred space, a refuge from the chaos and tumult of the set. It is also the place where responsible, critical decisions about exposure and lighting are made. A preproduction conversation with the DIT can and should set the tone for how privacy is enforced in the DIT tent. All DITs know the value of the DIT viewing space to the director of photography and they are usually equipped to set boundaries around that space.

High Dynamic Range Monitoring On Set

If you are shooting for a high dynamic range (HDR) delivery, it is absolutely urgently necessary to monitor for HDR on set! This means equipping the DIT tent with the image processing equipment and especially monitor(s) that can display the signal, and controlling the viewing environment.

There are a number of constraints to consider when gearing up for viewing HDR on set. Most HDR capable consumer televisions cannot be used for on-set monitoring. They receive their HDR signals over an HDMI connection, which also carries Dolby or HDR10 metadata that maps the HDR image to fit the television's display capabilities. In the absence of that HDR mapping metadata, consumer televisions usually default to standard dynamic range (SDR). Professional HDR OLED monitors work well in darkness. Professional HDR LCD monitors work well in low ambient light. The very slightly lifted blacks of an LCD display can fairly accurately display shadow detail in situations with low ambient viewing environment light.

If you are shooting for an HDR deliverable, always monitor in the widest gamut available on the monitor, in a color gamut not less than DCI P3. Always set the camera to record the widest color gamut available and the lowest compression available. When composing shots, avoid bright background areas; over-bright windows, cloudy skies, and large expanses of daylight exterior can distract from the foreground action and therefore from the story being told. Large bright areas in shots can push a monitor beyond its maximum frame average light level (MaxFALL) and cause it to automatically dim. This limit varies from monitor to monitor, and automatic dimming can either be avoided by limiting the maximum scene brightness to a small percentage of the screen area, or by slightly raising fill light levels. HDR is a wonderful new creative tool, but it can become an assault on your audience when pushed too far.

Video Village

The phenomenon of "Video Village" has been a subject of controversy since the pioneering days of HD. There are as many opinions about the Video Village phenomenon as there are film makers. Make yourself equally comfortable with either incorporating a Video Village viewing system into your methodology or not incorporating it.

Figure 13.6 Video Village.

The subject of the Video Village is an area where you must have a well thought out answer to your director and producers whichever way they are leaning. Accommodate the directorial interface as your first priority; it is the director that gives you the job, and he is your first master. If in the course of preparing for the shoot, the producers or the studio call the size and scope of the directorial viewing environment into question, always make the decision a group decision in collaboration with your director.

Making Secure and Reliable Data Backups of the Footage

Until data backups are made, it is important to remember that there is *only one copy of the data* – the original. Backups should be made as quickly as possible after acquisition. There should always be *at least* two copies of the original material created as soon after acquisition as possible, and the second copy should be made from the original, and not made from the first copy. There have been numerous examples of workflows where a second copy made from the first copy simply duplicated an error that occurred when the first copy was being made. Both copies should be individually made from the original data and checksum verified to assure they are identical in order to avoid this known failure point!

Copies can be made to either two different RAID arrays of disk drives striped to a redundant failure proof RAID level, or to LTO (linear tape open source) backup tapes written in LTFS (linear tape file system) and vaulted in separate secure and fireproof locations. This operation might be performed on set, near set, or at a laboratory.

Production insurance companies have now had enough experience with digital production to know that they must issue written policies covering secure data management before insuring a production. They require redundant backups that have been checksummed, verified; LTO backup tape archives are required in addition to magnetic spinning disk drives, and archives must be updated redundantly on a daily basis including CDLs, LUTs, EDLs, AAFs, XMLs, reports, and paperwork. Camera magazines and cards are not permitted to be reformatted until all backups have been completed and verified.

DATA BACKUP WORKFLOW - REDUNDANT BACKUPS OF RAW DATA

Figure 13.7 Media/data backup workflow diagram.

In a videotape based workflow, images are recorded to tape on set, those image sequences are then ingested into edit system from a playback deck, where they are converted into files. The original tapes are then vaulted for protection.

In a file-based workflow, digital video is recorded as digital files onto random-access media or memory-based digital "magazines." These files are then copied to another storage device, typically to a server connected to an editing system. Before the original data on the digital magazines is erased, an LTO protection tape backup copy of the data is usually made, confirmed, and then vaulted.

LTO/LTFS Offline/Online, Conform from LTO[1]

The volume of data on digital productions has exploded, fueled by advanced capture formats such ARRIRAW, SR-Master, R3D, HFR, and the trend of increasing shooting ratios. Major productions can shoot 500GB–60TB per day, resulting in Petabytes of material in total. Storing this material for the entire production/post on spinning disk (SAN/NAS) can be a serious expense in hardware and power consumption.

Productions have been archiving to LTO (linear tape open) since the format's introduction in 2000 as a completion bond or studio requirement. Storage DNA's "DNA Evolution" provides the asset management for camera master data to be securely archived to LTO/LTFS and for the data to be conformed back from LTO for VFX/DI – a simple offline/online workflow like video tape but using all the advantages of modern data tape. A production will need enough storage for initial QC and dailies creation, typically 1–2 shooting weeks' worth, then, with the material confirmed to be safely on LTO, earlier material can be deleted from the temporary storage. For VFX turnovers and DI, editorial simply export an EDL, AAF, or XML of the sequence, which DNA Evolution uses to restore only the clips used in sequence from LTO. The restored data is then relinked in the grading system.

Features with a significant volume of VFX shots can justify keeping camera master files (or film scans) online using NAS or an automated LTO library that can quickly supply VFX Turnovers using an EDL. The automation system will pull the shots, apply the agreed transform and typically supply DPX or OpenEXR sequences delivered securely using a client pre-approved and tested method. This VFX turnover request process can be automated using VFX management software such as Shotgun. The request can be automatically fulfilled by the post facility's system such as MetaTrack (Deluxe/CO3/eFilm) or fulfilled manually.

Contributed by Jonathan Smiles CSI – Independent Workflow Consultant

There are numerous reliable tools for the work of creating data backups. ShotPut Pro from Imagine Software is a popular package for making checksummed backups and LTO tapes, YoYotta features powerful database tools and also manages LTO tape backups, ALEXA Data Manager is specific to ALEXA camera files, Double Data from NightSky Software is also popular. There are other tools for this task on the market, but these are the tools most widely used for making backups by the DITs that I have worked with.

The files from either media are then either converted to lower resolution or more compressed proxy formats for editing and viewing, or sometimes they are edited directly at full bandwidth. After editing is completed, the editorial timeline is output to a file sequence, or to another master tape, to be pushed to final color correction. The color corrector outputs a number of finished files: a digital cinema display master (DCDM), a Rec 709 master for television or Blu-ray use, to be stored either as a file or on another tape, and sometimes a filmout pass corrected for print density for use on a film recorder to create a negative for duplication for theatrical exhibition.

Delivering Materials from Acquisition to Editorial

It is not enough for the cinematographer to light and shoot the project and then ignore the needs of editorial or post production. The cinematographer's job description weaves through the post process all the way into digital intermediate and delivery in order to assure that the original creative intent from the set gets carried through all the way to the finished product on screen. Before taking on any project, it is important to consider the list of deliverables that the cinematographer is responsible for passing on from acquisition to every phase of finishing the project.

It is now also more important than ever for the cinematographer to have a good working relationship with the editor of a project, a relationship grown out of mutual respect. The cinematographer must be educated and aware of the deliverables above and beyond just picture and sound that are needed from the production set. The cinematographer is responsible for delivery of the day's footage, but also assuring that QCed backups are done, and that look management data, CDLs, and LUTs are correctly distributed and applied.

Marrying Audio and Picture Files to Create Editorial Dailies

Before beginning a production, it is important to decide how dailies creation will be handled. A show being both shot and edited on a distant and remote location might be more likely to create their own dailies and deliverables than a show being shot on stage in a major production city. In either case, there are many reliable tools available to create an economical and efficient custom workflow.

Many workflow combinations of software and hardware exist for productions that want to do color correction, create editorial proxy materials, and create quality dailies either on set or near set. I will outline some of the software and hardware available for the tasks later in this chapter.

Whether employing a lab to create editorial dailies or making them on set/near set, the tools workflows available are accessible to even lower budget projects.

Figure 13.8 Lab created dailies workflow diagram.

Working in a scenario where the lab will be creating dailies and deliverables using LUTs and/or CDLs from the set, it is recommended that screenshots should be taken of every setup to accompany the footage and LUTS or CDLs applied in lab breakoffs during the day and at wrap. The aim is to automate the process of communicating the look from set to lab as much as possible.

Figure 13.9 On set/near set dailies creation workflow

If dailies are being generated on set or near set, the first step is always to create and verify checksummed backups of all camera cards or mags. The digital imaging technician (DIT) or a data management technician (DMT) then imports the files into an on-set color grading application to color correct each setup with input from the director of photography.

As LUTs and/or CDLs are applied to the footage, a DaVinci Resolve project file should be generated and included with the LUTs, CDLs, footage, audio files, and other materials sent to the lab at footage break-off points during the day, and at wrap.

Managing the Look of Images from Set through Post and Final Color Correction

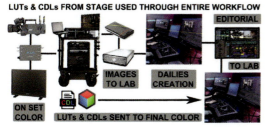

Figure 13.10 Color through the entire workflow.

The need for look management arises out of the use of non-Rec 709 wide color gamut cameras and log image encoding for acquisition of motion pictures. This creates a disconnect between the cinematographer on set, the editorial department, post production, the director and the studio. In order to communicate artistic intent from the set through to the post process and finishing, it becomes essential to be able to meaningfully communicate and propagate color and contrast adjustments for the generation of proxy editorial materials. LUTs and CDLs carry all the way through to final color correction and serve as rough guides to help communicate the original creative intent of the cinematographer from the set.

The Warner Brothers Next Generation Production Report

In 2011, a study of digital production workflow was conducted for Warner Bros. Emerging Technology division called the Next Generation Production Workflow Report or NGP Report. The report set out to explore major options available at the time for digital workflows, and the conclusions are still valid today. The process began with a five-camera test shoot. The parameters of the workflow analysis were intended to mirror real world conditions. After creating the test content, over 40 vendors participated to create 20 unique workflows that were evaluated

each on their own merits. These were divided into three categories:

1. "Custom Configured" – multi-vendor solutions where a production chooses different vendors for different tasks inside the workflow.
2. "Plug and play" – single box solutions where one package is chosen to handle all the tasks of a workflow.
3. "Facility provided solutions" – with traditional vendors such as Deluxe and Technicolor supplying and supporting equipment as needed in the workflow.

For each workflow, schematics were drawn, and notes taken.

Representative Samples of Workflow Diagrams

Category 1: "Custom Configured" Workflow

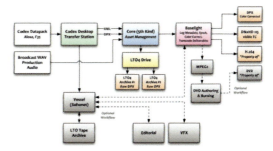

Figure 13.11 Custom configured workflow.

Category 2: "Plug and Play" Workflow

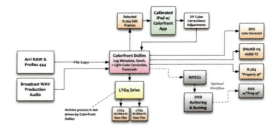

Figure 13.12 Plug and play workflow.

Category 3: "Facility Supplied" Workflow

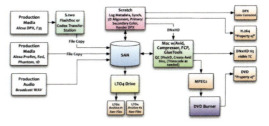

Figure 13.13 Facility supported workflow.

In addition to traditional workflows, we looked at 3D, the cloud, and ACES, as well as asset management. The studio concluded that there were a lot of options out there and they had a valuable chance to take a good look at many of them, as well as a chance to strategize about how to handle digital production in the future.

LUTs: A More Granular Examination

Cameras recording log images preserve the maximum amount of dynamic range, but uncorrected, they output a flat, grey, low-contrast picture. Directors, DPs, and producers prefer to have a sense of what the final product is going to look like while on set, which frequently dictates the use of LUTs. A LUT (look-up table) is a portable mathematical transform from one set of RGB pixel values to another. LUTs are matrices that frequently utilize keypoint math, and dependent on how they are generated and used, may not result in smooth transitions across gradients in color and contrast. A LUT is *not* a mathematical *transform*, which *explicitly* and *smoothly* transforms color from one set of RGB pixel values to another by a mathematical equation. LUTs are used in several ways: for mapping a source signal to a different color space, for emulating a particular film stock, or for making a creative look for your footage. LUTs are very small files that are easily emailed or carried on a USB thumb drive. The point is to make color calibration and look management portable and consistent throughout your imaging workflow. LUTs are most often used non-destructively, that is, not baked into the image.

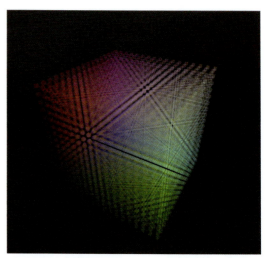

Figure 13.16 Pre LUT input RGB 3D color cube graph.

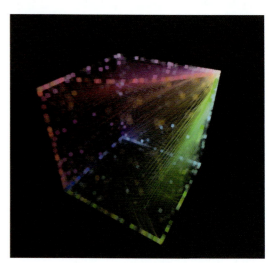

Figure 13.17 Post LUT output RGB 3D color cube graph.

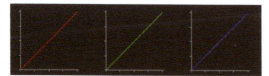

Figure 13.14 Pre LUT input RGB Channel Graphs where x is luminance and y is code value

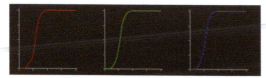

Figure 13-15 Post LUT Output RGB channel graphs where x is luminance and y is code value.

A 1D LUT transforms each color, red, green, and blue separately, which is usually sufficient for making simple color and contrast adjustments. For serious grading work, we use 3D LUTs.

A 3D LUT maps color values in a three-dimensional cube rather than using matrices. A 3D LUT uses input and output points for each color axis, in between colors are interpolated by the system. The greater the number of points, the greater the accuracy. The most common LUT resolution is a 17 × 17 × 17 3D cube.

Shaper LUTs

Before we can create a LUT to view linear-light images, it's important to understand shaper

LUTs. LUT formats generally require input values in the 0.0 to 1.0 range, and such a LUT would be unsuitable for use in transforming linear-light values input images where values exceed 1. To address this issue, some LUT formats contain a 1D preLUT or shaper LUT before the main LUT. This is a linear-to-log type transform used to transform the input values into a 0–1 range. The shaper LUT transforms values from input space to shaper space, then the main LUT transforms values from shaper-space to output space.

Calibration LUTs

A calibration LUT is used to correct color and contrast in displays. By applying a calibration LUT to each monitor, you assure that all the monitors in the workflow are displaying images consistently and accurately way from the set to editorial to the grading suite.

Display LUTs

A display LUT is used to convert from one color space to another, and is essential for on-set monitoring of log footage. Rather than viewing flat, desaturated log images on set, the display LUT maps the log footage to the color space of the monitor, letting you view images with contrast and saturation resembling the final product. For monitors that don't support LUTs, you can interpose a LUT into an incoming source signal using an external device like an AJA LUT-box or Teradek Colr LUT box or other similar in line color transform device.

Creative LUTs

A creative LUT goes beyond normalizing the footage to a specific color space by also making creative adjustments. DP, director and colorist often work together to create custom creative LUTs before production begins to monitor what the final images will look like. The same LUT can also be applied to dailies and then brought back into the mix during post production to serve as a starting point for the final grade. Creative LUTs should be camera-specific.

Emulation LUTs

Emulation LUTs are used when printing to film for distribution. By applying the LUT in combination with a display LUT, it will allow you to see how the film will look once the images are printed to the film stock you will be using.

Display and creative LUTs can be created on set using real-time LUT creation DIT software such as DaVinci Resolve Live, Lattice, LUTCalc, or Pomfort Live Grade (among others).

There are also numerous downloadable display LUTs on camera manufacturers' websites, and pre-built packages of camera-specific LUTs from third-party companies.

Table 13.1 LUT and Look file formats

3D LUT Formats	Extension	1D LUT Formats	Extension
Apple Color 3D LUT	.mga	AJA 1D LUT	.txt
ARRI Look	.xml	Blackmagic Design 1D LUT	.ilut
ARRI Look File 2	.aml	Blackmagic Design 1D LUT	.olut
Autodesk 3D LUT	.3dl	Colorfront 1D LUT	.1dlut
CDL Correction	.cc, .cdl, .ale, .edl	CSV 1D LUT	.csv
Cinetal 3D LUT	.clt	CTL LUT	.ctl
CMS Test Pattern Image 3D LUT	.tiff, .tif	Cube LUT	.cube
Colorfront 3D LUT	.3dmesh	Discreet 1D LUT	.lut
Convergent Design 3D LUT	.cdlut	FSI 1D LUT	.lut
CTL LUT	.ctl	IO Industries 1D LUT	.lut
Cube LUT	.cube	Iridas ITX LUT	.itx
DaVinci 3D LUT	.davlut	Lattice LUT	.lattice
DVS Clipster 3D LUT	.xml, .txt	Lightroom Preset Curve	.lrtemplate
eeColor 3D LUT	.txt	Nucoda CMS LUT	.cms
FSI DAT 3D LUT	.dat		
Hald CLUT	.tiff, .tif		

(Continued)

Table 13.1 (Continued)

3D LUT Formats	Extension	1D LUT Formats	Extension
ICC Profile	.icc, .icm, .pf, .prof		
Iridas ITX LUT	.itx		
Iridas Look	.look		
Lattice LUT	.lattice		
Nucoda CMS LUT	.cms		
Panasonic VLT 3D LUT	.vlt		
Pandora 3D LUT	.m3d	**Look Files**	**Extension**
Quantel 3D LUT	.txt	ARRI Look	.xml
Resolve DAT 3D LUT	.dat	CDL Correction	.cc, .cdl
Unwrapped Cube Image 3D LUT	.tiff, .tif	AMPAS / ASC CLF	.xml

Academy ASC Common File Format for Look-Up Tables

https://acescentral.com/t/aces-documentation/53

Recognizing a need to reduce the complexity of interchanging LUTs files, the Science and Technology Council of the Academy of Motion Pictures Arts and Sciences and the Technology Committee of the American Society of Cinematographers sponsored a project to bring together interested parties from production, postproduction, and product developers to agree upon a common LUT file format. This document is the result of those discussions. In their earliest implementation, LUTs were designed into hardware to generate red, green, and blue values for a display from a limited set of bit codes. Recent implementations see LUTs used in many parts of a pipeline in both hardware devices and software applications. LUTs are often pipeline specific and device dependent. The Common LUT File format is a mechanism for exchanging the data contained in these LUTs and expects the designer, user, and application(s) to properly apply the LUTs within an application for the correct part of a pipeline. All applications that use LUTs have a software or hardware transform engine that digitally processes a stream of pixel code values. The code values represent colors in some color space which may be device dependent or which is defined in image metadata. For each pixel color, the transform engine calculates the results of a transform and outputs a new pixel color. Defining a method for exchanging these color transforms in a text file is the purpose of this document. Saving a single LUT into a file to send to another part of production working on the same content is expected to be the most common use of the common LUT file format.

From the Academy of Motion Picture Arts and Sciences ACES Documentation Site

LUTs (Look-Up Tables), Exchange Spaces, and Working Spaces[2]

The process of importing digital camera files of any kind or from any digital motion picture camera into digital workflows for motion picture work requires a clear definition of the color space in which workflow components expect the image data to be encoded, and a mechanism for transforming the output of the digital camera into that color space. The color space in which the handoff occurs between the digital camera system and the downstream system is called an *exchange space*; this may or may not be the same as the downstream application's *working space*, in which it makes its actual image modifications.

The process of converting from one color space to another can be done, if the transformation is very straightforward, by a simple mathematical transform, such as the application of a 3×3 matrix. Often the transformation is not at all straightforward, and so the transformation of the input is accomplished with a color look-up table (or LUT).

A LUT is a table of correspondences (for X color input value, produce Y color output value) for transforming digital input color values from one color space to another. In some cases, the set of possible input values is very small, and a LUT can have an output correspondence for every possible input value. In other cases, the set of possible input values can be fairly large, and so the program using the LUT will deduce the correct corresponding output values by interpolating between the correspondences used for input values that are "neighbors" to an input value for which no explicit correspondence exists.

LUTs can be used to transport on-set color correction adjustments to post production for color grading. By employing an on-set color transform or "LUT box," it is possible to generate viewing LUTS for use on set that can be carried into post production as a preliminary or even final grade of the material. The only caveat with using LUTs in this way is that there are 60+ formats, defined by vendors, or standards bodies, or post-production houses, that are typically similar but not quite alike. Getting one color system to understand a LUT from another can be complex and frustrating.

LUTs may be used as a destructive transform of color data, or stored as non-destructive metadata. In the non-destructive case, the LUT functions as a comment as to how the original data is to be modified at some later time and place.

All applications that use LUTs employ a "transform engine" (either in software or hardware) that digitally processes a stream of pixel code values. The code values entering the transform engine represent colors in a color space that may be device dependent or which is defined in image metadata. For each pixel, the transform math calculates a calibrated device signal and outputs new pixel code values that will produce the desired color on the target viewing device.

Recent trends in color management systems have led to an increasingly important role for LUTs in production workflows. One very common use of LUTs is the transformation of color information from vendor-specific color spaces or wide-gamut "exchange spaces," where the color information is encoded as 16-bit or 10-bit log to preserve as much color and luminance detail as possible to the smaller color space and lesser color resolution of 8-bit viewing monitors calibrated to the Rec 709 or sRGB standards. Such LUTs are sometimes implemented in hardware, or sometimes in software.

LUTs are very often pipeline-specific and frequently device- or application-dependent. With a large number of product developers providing software and hardware solutions for LUTs, there has been an explosion of unique vendor-specific LUT file formats which are often only trivially different from each other.

One application of LUTs that has recently come under great scrutiny as a result of the ASC/PGA Camera Assessment Series is the input device transform (IDT), used as part of workflows built around ACES, the Academy Color Encoding System. In that system, the IDT is sometimes implemented as a LUT that transforms the vendor-specific recorded output of a digital camera into the ACES color space. Here ACES functions as an exchange space, where imagery can be passed back and forth between production, VFX, and color correction.

The work of developing ACES IDTs for cameras is arduous and painstaking. The sensor response of the camera in question must be carefully measured well beyond the latitude of the sensor, and this means exposing the camera to carefully controlled stimuli using specialized equipment, covering a very wide range of luminances and chromaticities. The data thus gathered are then very carefully analyzed, and used to write either a translating equation or a LUT to transform digital camera code values into ACES relative exposure values for use in a digital post production pipeline.

Before the advent of ACES, this characterization work has traditionally been done by each and every post house, for each and every digital camera, for each and every post production workflow, usually at great effort and expense, and on a proprietary basis. It is therefore, no surprise that the work of characterizing any given digital camera for import into a visual effects or color correction pipeline has produced expensive and well guarded "secret sauce" at every post house that has invested in doing the detailed work. Therein lies the most difficult part of digital workflow in post production ... the *secret sauce* of successful commercial color correction in the digital age!

The color science of camera transforms must eventually become an open source freely supplied data set, with characterizations of all of the individual cameras supplied by their manufacturers as a free download from their corporate website. This move away from "secret sauce" to open standards has been one of the primary goals of the ACES effort.

Contributed by Joseph Goldstone – ARRI

ASC CDL: A More Granular Examination

ASC Color Decision List (ASC CDL)[3]

The American Society of Cinematographers Technology Committee, DI subcommittee – with participants from the ASC, color correction system vendors, post production facilities, and color scientists – created the ASC Color Decision List (ASC CDL) to allow basic primary color correction data to be interchanged between color correction systems made by different manufacturers. This standardized interchange, when accompanied by good communication and consistent viewing conditions, can create the same results on multiple systems, substantially improving the consistency and quality of the resulting images while also increasing efficiency and reducing cost. The ASC CDL is widely used in motion picture production, television production, and in VFX. The ASC CDL is the primary look modification transform (LMT) used to express artistic intent in the wide gamut, high dynamic range Academy Color Encoding System (ACES).

The ASC CDL defines a small set of operations – transfer functions – that provide the most basic set of color correction operations – operations that can be implemented in all color correction vendors' systems. They are Slope, Offset, and Power that are applied to each of the R, G, and B signals independently, and Saturation which operates on R, G, and B in combination. Thus, ten parameters describe any ASC CDL color correction.

Most color correction systems natively provide vendor-specific Lift, Gain, and Gamma functions. Slope, Offset, and Power are similar but mathematically purer functions. In most cases, vendor-specific Lift, Gain, and Gamma can be easily translated into some combination of Slope, Offset, and Power for interchange between systems.

The ASC CDL defines mathematical operations that are applied to all image data, regardless of the format/encoding of that data. The ASC CDL defines the math, not the encoding-specific interpretation of that math. Each of the operations will have quite different results on log data than on "linear" data. For example, a Gain of 2.0 multiplies the image code values by 2.0. If the image data is linear, that will brighten the image by one stop. If the image data is log, a Gain of 2.0 will double the contrast of the image.

And a correction applied to the right data in the right way on two systems must still be viewed on calibrated displays with the same characteristics and in very similar viewing conditions to communicate the intended look. Coordination of data metrics and viewing conditions is also outside the scope of the ASC CDL and must be handled elsewhere in a project's workflow.

Although the ASC CDL functions are intended for purposes of interchange – to communicate basic color correction operations from set to facility and between systems from different vendors – many vendors also provide user level controls that operate on ASC CDL functions directly.

In a workflow, the set of ten ASC CDL parameters for a correction is interchanged via ASC CDL-defined XML files, by new fields in ALE and FLEx files, or special comments in CMX EDL files. Most often the formats shown in Figure 13.8 will be used, but the exact methods used will be facility- and workflow-dependent.

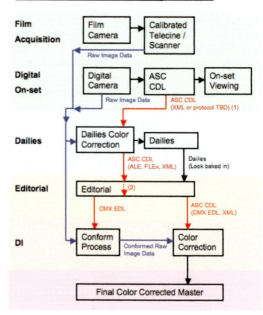

Figure 13.18 ASC CDL workflow.

1. Currently this communication is performed via the ASC CDL XML format or various vendor specific methods.
2. Editorial maintains association of ASC CDL parameters and shot. ASC CDL parameters are passed through editorial unchanged other than copying from one file format to another.

ASC CDL corrections are metadata that are associated with shots. Unlike LUT corrections, the ASC CDL corrections are *not* baked in to the image. Because of this approach, corrections later in the workflow can be based on earlier ASC CDL corrections without modifying the image data multiple times – yielding highest possible image quality. And sharing an ASC CDL correction gives information about how the earlier corrector was thinking about the look. Corrections implemented with LUTs are fixed – they can be viewed, or additional corrections can be layered on, but they cannot practically be adjusted or tuned.

The ASC CDL supports only the most basic color correction operations. Not all operations of interest (e.g. log/linear conversions, 3D LUTs, windowing, tracking) can be expressed with these operations. It is possible that future releases will support a somewhat expanded set of inter-changeable operations.

The ASC CDL does not handle everything necessary to communicate a look. A project must manage and communicate basic and critical information like color space, data representation format, display device, and viewing environment. To communicate a look between on-set and post or between post facilities absolutely requires that information be shared and used intelligently.

ASC CDL Transfer Functions

Although generally similar to the common *Lift*, *Gain*, and *Gamma* operations (which, incidentally, vary in detail from system to system and manufacturer to manufacturer), the ASC CDL defines a set of three transfer functions with unique names and simple definitions.

The ASC CDL's three basic transfer functions are *Slope*, *Offset*, and *Power*. They are applied in that order – *Slope* then *Offset* then *Power* – and are sometimes referred to collectively as *SOP*. The transfer functions are in RGB color space and are applied independently to each color component. These three transfer functions for the three color components (assuming the current trichromatic systems) can collectively be described by nine parameters.

The vendor-specific *Lift*, *Gain*, and *Gamma* operations found on most systems, individually or in combination, can be translated into *Slope*, *Offset*, and *Power*.

The *Saturation* function was added to the ASC CDL in release 1.2. Unlike the *Slope*, *Offset*, and *Power* functions, *Saturation* operates on all three color channels in combination. The ASC CDL uses a common industry definition for *Saturation* ("Rec. 709" weightings). *Saturation* is applied after *Slope*, *Offset*, and *Power*.

Vendors may still have their own proprietary saturation algorithms, but they must support the ASC CDL Saturation algorithm when they are operating in "ASC CDL mode."

Slope
Slope (see Figure 13.19) changes the slope of the transfer function without shifting the black level established by *Offset* (see next section). The input value, *slope*, ranges from 0.0 (constant output at *Offset*) to less than infinity (although, in practice, systems probably limit at a substantially lower value). The nominal *slope* value is 1.0.

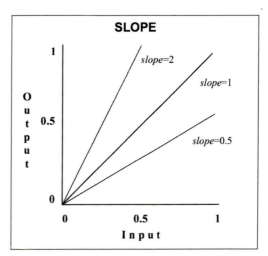

Figure 13.19 out=in*slope 0≤slope<∞.

Offset
Offset (see Figure 13.20) raises or lowers overall value of a component. It shifts the transfer function up or down while holding the slope constant. The input value, *offset*, can in theory range from –∞ to +∞ although the range –1.0 to 1.0 will fit most traditional use. The nominal *offset* value is 0.0.

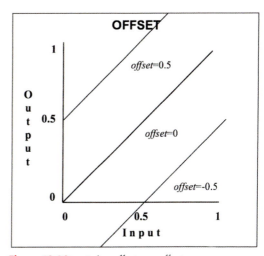

Figure 13.20 out=in+offset -∞<offset<∞.

If the underlying data is log, then *offset* is an interpretation of *printer points* – the most common method of color correction in film lab work.

Power
Power (see Figure 13.21) is the only non-linear function. It changes the overall curve of the transfer function. The input value, *power*, ranges from greater than 0.0 to less than infinity. The nominal *power* value is 1.0.

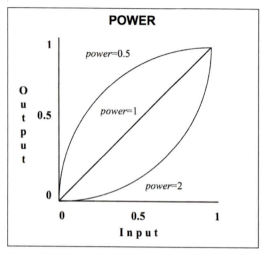

Figure 13.21 out = in ^ power (where ^ is "raised to the power") 0 < power < ∞.

Saturation

Saturation provides a weighted average of the normal color (*saturation* 1.0) and all gray (fully de-saturated, *saturation* 0.0) images. The saturation operation modifies all color components. Color components are weighted by the values used in most Rec 709 implementations of saturation. *Saturation* values > 1.0 are supported. Values > 4 or so will probably only be used for special purposes.

Saturation is applied after the *SOP* (*Slope, Offset, Power*) operations.

sat is the user input saturation parameter. *inR* is the input red color component value, *G* green, and *B* blue. *outR* is the output red color component value, *G* green, and *B* blue. *gray* is the fully desaturated gray value, based on the color component weightings.

$$gray = 0.2126 * inR + 0.7152 * inG + 0.0722 * inB$$
$$outR = Clamp(gray + sat * (inR - gray))$$
$$outG = Clamp(gray + sat * (inG - gray))$$
$$outB = Clamp(gray + sat * (inB - gray))$$
$$0 \leq sat < \infty$$

Behavior for Different Image Encodings

The ASC CDL operations perform the same math regardless of the encoding of the image data to which they are being applied. The resulting modifications to the image will vary a great deal for different image data encodings. Management of the image encoding and appropriate application of the ASC CDL operations is the responsibility of the project/show and outside the scope of the ASC CDL.

Video-Gamma and Linear (Gamma 1.0)

ASC CDL operations will have similar effects on images in the common encodings that are generally linear. Those encodings include linear light (photon count or energy) often used in CGI such as open EXR, Academy ACES scene-referred linear which will be showing up more often in both film and digitally originated material, and video signals which are linear but always have a gamma (power function) applied – nominally 2.2 but numbers vary in practice. Some custom "linear" encodings may have special handling near toe (blacks/crush) or shoulder (whites/roll-off). In those cases, the interaction of ASC CDL operations and the non-linear regions will have to be evaluated on a case-by-case basis.

Slope
For linear encodings, Slope controls the brightness of the image while maintaining contrast – like adjusting the *f*- or T-stop.

Offset
For linear encodings, Offset controls the overall "base fog" of the image. The values of the entire image are moved up or down together, affecting both brightness and contrast. This is not traditionally a common operation for linear data.

Power
For linear encodings, Power controls the contrast of the image.

Saturation
For all encodings, including linear, Saturation controls the saturation – intensity of the color of the image.

The old telecine Lift function – raising or lowering the darks while holding the highlights constant – can be achieved via a combination of Offset and Slope. Similarly, the telecine Gain function can also be achieved via a combination of Offset and Slope.

Video-Gamma Examples

Figure 13.22 ASC CDL slope RGB all 0.5.

Figure 13.23 ASC CDL slope normal RGB all 1.0.

Figure 13.28 Power – RGB all 1.5.

Figure 13.24 ASC CDL slope RGB all 1.5.

Figure 13.29 Power – RGB all 1.0.

Figure 13.25 Offset RGB all 0.2.

Figure 13.30 Power – RGB all 0.5.

Figure 13.26 Offset normal RGB all 0.0.

Figure 13.31 Saturation RGB all 0.5.

Figure 13.27 Offset RGB all 0.2.

Figure 13.32 Saturation RGB all 1.0.

Figure 13.33 Saturation RGB all 2.0.

Log

ASC CDL operations will have similar effects on images in the common encodings that are generally log. Those encodings include printing density (e.g. Cineon, DPX), commonly seen from film scanners and created or imitated by other sources; and the various log modes output by various digital cameras to present a more film-like response with a wider dynamic range (at least until cameras put out the high dynamic range Academy ACES "scene-referred linear" floating point format). Some "log" encodings have special handling near the toe (blacks/crush) or shoulder (whites/roll-off). In those cases, the interaction of ASC CDL operations and the special regions will have to be evaluated on a case-by-case basis.

In digital intermediate, log images will usually have a film print emulation applied as an output display transform in order to see the color corrected images as they will be theatrically projected. For this workflow, the ASC CDL is applied before the film print emulation. (This procedure was applied to the example log images shown here.)

Slope
For log encodings, Slope controls the contrast of the image.

Offset
For log encodings, Offset controls the brightness of the image while maintaining contrast – like adjusting the *f*- or T-stop. This is essentially the same as Printer Lights but with different values/units.

Power
For log encodings, Power controls the level of detail in shadows vs. highlights. This is not traditionally a common operation for log data.

Saturation
For all encodings, including linear, Saturation controls the saturation – intensity of the color of the image.

Log Examples

Figure 13.34 ASC CDL slope RGB all 0.75.

Figure 13.35 ASC CDL slope normal RGB all 1.0.

Figure 13.36 ASC CDL slope RGB all 1.25.

Figure 13.37 Offset RGB all –0.1.

Figure 13.38 Offset normal RGB all 0.0.

Figure 13.39 Offset RGB all 0.1.

Figure 13.40 Power – RGB all 1.25.

Figure 13.41 Power – RGB all 1.0.

Figure 13.42 Power – RGB all 0.75.

Figure 13.43 Saturation RGB all 0.5.

Figure 13.44 Saturation RGB all 1.0.

Figure 13.45 Saturation RGB all 2.0.

ASC CDL Interchange Formats

The ASC CDL allows basic color corrections to be communicated through the stages of production and post production and to be interchanged between equipment and software from different manufacturers at different facilities. The underlying color correction algorithms are described above.

When ASC CDL color correction metadata is transferred from dailies to editorial and from editorial to post production, provided that data representation, color space, and viewing parameters are handled consistently, the initial "look" set for dailies (perhaps from an on-set color correction) can be used as an automatic starting point or first pass for the final color correction session. ASC CDL metadata is transferred via extensions to existing, commonly used file formats currently employed throughout the industry: ALE, FLEx, and CMX EDL files. There are also two ASC CDL-specific XML file types that can be used to contain and transfer individual color corrections or (usually project-specific) libraries of color corrections.

ALE and FLEx files are used to transfer information available at the time of dailies creation to the editorial database. New fields have been added to these files to accommodate ASC CDL color correction metadata for each shot.

CMX EDL files are output from editorial and used primarily to "conform" the individual shots into the final edit. As there is a convention to include shot specific metadata as comment fields after the associated "event" in the EDL file, it made sense to use this mechanism to attach ASC

CDL parameters to each "event". There are two ways of specifying this in an EDL file – either "inline" or "via XML reference."

Many vendors are currently using XML to support their internal data structures. The ASC CDL includes a hook so that CDL parameters can reside in simple XML text files that can be referenced by the CMX EDL format or other vendor-specific formats. The two types of XML files are:

1. Color Decision List (CDL) files that contain a set of color decisions (a color correction with a reference to an image) and that may also include other project metadata.
2. Color Correction Collection (CCC) files which solely contain one or more color corrections.

Each and every color correction defined in these files has a unique Color Correction ID. Any specific color correction defined in these XML files can be referenced by its unique Color Correction ID.

Contributed by David Reisner and Joshua Pines

On-Set Look Management Hardware and Software

On set look management is the process whereby the finished look of individual shots and/or the entire project are anticipated and defined by the cinematographer and the director from the set, with the flexibility to interactively modify those looks throughout the entire production, editorial, post production, visual effects, and color correction processes. Many sophisticated look management applications and supporting hardware devices have been introduced as on-set or near-set options for establishing creative look references that can be applied to dailies, as well as to create metadata that can provide reference for final color grading. What follows is a summary of hardware and applications designed to generate LUTs and CDLs for conveying on set creative intent and look management downstream from the set, into editorial, through post and visual effects work, and into color correction and digital intermediate.

Color Correction and Look Modification Tools

Assimilate Scratch

www.assimilateinc.com/products/

Figure 13.46 Assimilate scratch.

Assimilate Scratch is a full function color correction system that can also be used on set to grade frames copied from the digital disk recorder, video tape recorder, or digital stills, allowing cinematographers to create and share non-destructive "looks" using familiar color corrector grading tools. Scratch is ASC-CDL compliant, and also exports standard LUT files for use by editorial, post production, and digital intermediate.

Scratch features include real-time full resolution, native playback of all popular camera formats including REDCODE .r3d with support for multiple RED Rocket cards, ARRI, SONY, Phantom high speed cameras, Panasonic, Canon and Canon 5D and 7D, GoPro, and may others. It is a real-time, non-destructive primary and secondary color grading system, with support for Avid Artist Color panel series or Tangent panels. Grading features include source-side adjustments for mixed color space workflows, match and auto grading, 2D and shape tracking, keying based on vector, chroma, or luminance, integrated histogram, waveform, vectorscope and color curve views, group shots, copy/paste color grades and reference libraries, key frames and animation curves, and import and save 1D and 3D LUTs based on primary color grades.

Scratch provides real-time data management to dailies playback and review, flexible conform, advanced color grading, and mastering to a variety of formats, real-time tools for frame-rate conversion, image-resolution scaling and frame-accuracy to monitors, projectors, and tape decks using both DVI and SDI interfaces. It integrates via XML with other tools such as Nuke, Shotgun, Avid, and Final Cut Pro, and supports QuickTime, DPX, ACES and over 50 additional formats, and blends color correction with 3D compositing and VFX tools in one unified, real-time system. Scratch can be used to create multiple deliverables and alternate versions in different resolutions, image formats, and framing, all from a single source, the CONstruct manages multiple versions of the same 2D or 3D shots within the same timeline for easy comparison.

Figure 13.47 Assimilate Player Pro.

Assimilate also recently released Play Pro, their Universal Player and Essential Media Tool kit supporting 16 camera specific format players/transcoders. Play Pro is a responsive player with modest hardware requirements. Play Pro supports look management, metadata management, dual screen/SDI output and rendering, ProRes, H.264 up to 8k and 12 bit H.265, all on either OS X or Windows. Other features of the Player include single view, dual view, split view, A-B view, SDI output via Blackmagic, AJA, Bluefish444 cards, range view, channel selectors, playback 360/180 equirectangular, VR headset support, and audio monitoring, routing and millisecond accurate slipping.

Source Media supported formats include uncompressed media; DPX, TIFF, TGA, SGI JPEG, JPEG2000, BMP, PNG files from digital, tape, or scanned sources, and OpenEXR uncompressed 16/32-bit format support.

Camera format support includes:

- SONY F65/F55/F5 RAW, XAVC 4K, X-OCN, SONY SR File (SStP) MXF
- Canon C200/C500/C700 RAW (RMF and CRM), C100/C300/C500 MPEG2, XF-AVC MXF, XF-HEVC MXF, EOS 1D/5D/7D
- Panasonic AVC-Intra MXF, Varicam V-RAW
- RED REDCODE RAW (R3D) support incl. Weapon, Helium, Monstro and Gemini 8K, ARRI RAW (ARI, ARX and MXF), DNxHD/HR and Apple ProRes

- Phantom Flex 4K .cine RAW
- Blackmagic RAW
- Apple ProRes RAW
- Cineform RAW
- CODEX RAW
- AVCHD (MTS and M2TS)
- Kinefinity RAW (DNG and KRW)
- Cinema DNG (incl. Blackmagic, AJA, AATON, Bolex, Kinefinity, Ikonoskop)
- Panasonic, Pentax, and DJI
- DSLR Raw Photo formats
- H.264 (MP4, MOV, and MXF up to 10-bit 4:2:2)
- H.265/HEVC (up to 12-bit)

Grade and Look management features include basic CDL grading, importing 1D and 3D LUTs (.lut, .xml, .txt, .3dl, .cube), importing CDLs (.cdl, .cc), CTL (.ctl), exporting 1D and 3D LUTs, exporting CDL as separate file or included in an ALE, and clip versioning.

Review and QC features include, vector scopes, histogram, curves, waveforms, multiple colored annotations per shot, and metadata management including additions/updates.

Section 1.01 HDR supports HLG, PQ, HDR10, generation of mastering report, including Max FALL/CLL, and Play Lists – start Play Pro with a (*.splx) playlist file.

Output encoding formats include Apple ProRes 4444XQ, ProRes 4444, ProRes 422 HQ, Proxy, LT, H.264 in 8- and 10-bit up to 8K, and H.265/HEVC (in up to 12-bit); publishing to SCRATCH Web/YouTube/Facebook/Vimeo. Other features include report generator, ALE metadata export, and export timeline including grade to SCRATCH.

VR features support includes 3D180/360 support, HMD support (Oculus Rift, HTC Vive, all Steam VR based headsets), Ambisonic Audio support, and publishing to FB/YouTube 180/360.

Black Magic DaVinci Resolve/Resolve Live

www.blackmagicdesign.com/products/davinciresolve

Figure 13.48 Blackmagic DaVinci resolve.

Blackmagic DaVinci Resolve is one of the oldest names in color correction, it is available as a full bandwidth software based post production color corrector, or for use as an on set portable color management tool for generating LUTs or ASC CDL files to be exported for use through post. For on set editing and grading, DaVinci Resolve Live includes dailies tools for syncing audio and to manage and edit metadata. The one click sync links full quality camera images with system audio for quick on set grading, preview, and render. In recent versions DaVinci has also added extensive post production tools and capabilities including offline/online editing, visual effects, and sound mixing.

DaVinci Resolve uses node based processing where each node can have color correction, power windows and effects, join unlimited nodes sequentially, or in parallel to combine grades, effects, mixers, keys, and custom curves. Resolve has a powerful primary color corrector for setting lift, gamma, and gain with the control of YRGB color space. Primary control includes shadows, midtones, and highlight log controls with offset. Resolve has precise specific secondary color qualification that lets you target colors with clean edges.

DaVinci Resolve supports HDR source images with real-time display, and also supports 16-bit floating point ACES colorspace for full quality and dynamic range. Resolve also supports open standard .cube files, add 1D and 3D LUTs for input, output, and display, or even a LUT for every node. DaVinci Resolve supports ASC CDLs including full slope, offset, power, and saturation metadata. All CDL events are synchronized with EDL events including additional support for stereoscopic 3D size data.

Custom curves let users define a custom gamma curve that's applied for your corrections. This can be ganged for all channels or set per channel. Custom curves also support YSFX luminance and saturation effects. Control high and low clip per node, and set high and low clip softness. For extreme looks and innovative creative styles, DaVinci Resolve supports RGB mixer grading to control individual red, green, and blue gain for each color channel, blend and mix channels. Resolve also includes texture control using a texture equalizer operator.

DaVinci Resolve features unlimited power windows with circle, linear, polygon, and Power Curve shapes. Windows have mask control with inside and outside grading and full multi point tracking, digital noise reduction for removing

noise in digital cameras, and noise reduction within Power Windows.

Store and export stills in Resolve's gallery to compare shots to keep grades consistent. Copy grades to any clip, or even a range of clips, and even copy camera raw metadata.

Colorfront: Transkoder, QC Player, On-set Dailies, and Express Dailies

www.colorfront.com/

Figure 13.49 Colorfront.

Colorfront Express Dailies is a powerful and easy to use mobile post-production system for transcoding, archiving, QC, and deliverables. Express Dailies aids DITs in the grading, data wrangling, and encoding workflow for commercials, film, and television production. Colorfront Express Dailies accommodates real-time RED R3D playback, HDR-X support, and RED stereoscopic 3D support. It also supports optimized high quality real-time deBayering; ARRIRAW playback for pixel-to-pixel, ARRIRAW playback for stereo 3D playback in 2K, ARRIRAW playback at 48 fps playback in real-time, and ARRIRAW playback for high end VFX shows.

Colorfront also supports Codex VFS on the Mac, real-time ARRIRAW playback directly from Codex data pack, ACES workflow with 16-bit floating-point wide-gamut light-linear color workflow (with 32-bits per channel internal processing), Open EXR support for both playback and rendering. In addition it offers optimized QuickTime handling for ALEXA ProRes, Timecode support for Canon 5D/7D/1D cameras, improved Phantom material handling, and ASC CDL compatibility.

FilmLight Truelight

www.filmlight.ltd.uk/products/truelight/overview_tl.php

Figure 13.50 FilmLight Truelight.

Truelight On-Set enables the cinematographer to view and manage the look of shots on-set on a calibrated display (whatever the camera or color space), and to easily determine exposure levels. The cinematographer can also review shots and set the "look" of the show, generating basic color correction on set, insuring a clear and accurate workflow for conveying the calibrated "look" through post production and into digital intermediate color correction. Truelight On-Set is simple to operate with a familiar interface, allowing cinematographers to use the tool set without specialized training.

When used for monitoring while shooting, Truelight On-Set can apply a color transform between the camera and monitors. Color grades, LUTs, and CDLs can be applied and modified during shooting.

Truelight On-Set integrates calibrated profiles of cameras and displays with color correction in ASC CDL standard format. Timecode-based events can be generated automatically, each with its own specific grade, then changed and visualized in real-time. Color decisions made on-set can easily be transferred to other ASC CDL compliant devices in post production. Codex recorder systems can be configured to grab CDL information from the Truelight On-Set system to include in their clip metadata.

When reviewing dailies or generating looks on set, primary color corrections can be reviewed and adjusted on the Truelight On-Set system and then conveyed to the post production colorist by a LUT or an ASC CDL. This allows for the ability to clearly communicate creative intent back and forth between production and post production teams.

Truelight On-Set also provides the ability to apply 3D color transforms on both input and output. This flexibility allows a range of color

workflows, including those built around ACES, which provides an unambiguous open source set of transforms for standardized color workflow. It also enables, with the additional use of a Truelight probe and the supplied software, the ability to calibrate any monitor to any desired color space standard.

FilmLight Prelight

Figure 13.51 FilmLight Prelight.

Prelight allows images to be color corrected interactively, by live updating LUT boxes, cameras or monitors directly, and by processing RAW files. Looks can be created and previewed on set or in down time on imported image files. Prelight supports the full set of Baselight primary and secondary grading tools including spatial operations and mattes. Looks developed in prep and test-shoots can be imported into Prelight and further refined on set using real-time grading tools. Looks created in Prelight are then exported back to grading and applied to the raw camera footage to reproduce looks for the final grade; look data and LUTs can be imported directly into Daylight and Baselight. Export standard ASC CDL lists and third-party formatted 3D LUTs integrate Prelight into any post-production workflow.

Prelight can connect to supported cameras, such as the ARRI ALEXA SXT, by Wi-Fi or Ethernet. The logging system can then extract ANC data from the camera's SDI monitoring output (for SDI devices that support this functionality), including the record flag (so it automatically detects when a shot is recording), timecode (either from the camera itself, or via its own internal timecode generator) and tape name. Prelight can also grab a thumbnail for each shot; this is then used as the BLG poster frame, if you're working with BLG files.

Prelight ON-SET channels provide an intuitive and flexible way to link input and output devices together so that you can easily set up different color spaces and apply different looks to each "set" of devices. When you apply a look in the library, or change the grade in the grade view, it applies it to all devices in the active channel. When using an ARRI ALEXA SXT with Prelight ON-SET the DIT can save both the 3D LUT preview of the grade, and the complete grading parameters directly inside the data recorded by the camera. Connecting Prelight ON-SET to the ALEXA SXT sends a 3D LUT representation of the look which can be used on the electronic viewfinder (EVF) and monitoring outputs of the ALEXA SXT. It also creates BLG, which describes the grading parameters and color space transformations that were used to create the look and 3D LUT. This information is automatically saved, non-destructively, inside the ARRIRAW files and ProRes files recorded by the Alexa SXT. Load these files into Baselight or Daylight and the software will recreate the grading stack used on set.

Reference stills can be imported from any RAW or other file format that is supported by full Baselight systems using the same decode methods, deBayer parameters and processing as the final grade. Reference images can be color corrected and saved in any image format supported by the Baselight software. Prelight ON-SET provides comprehensive logging capability, creating one log entry for each recorded shot. This entry tracks the look associated with that shot, then looks can be exported and automatically correlated with each shot in Daylight or Baselight. If you are not working with BLG files, you can export the log as an ALE or EDL to use in other workflows. The DIT can enter or edit information in the log manually, including capturing the poster frame for the shot, which updates any underlying BLG files automatically.

FotoKem nextLAB

http://fotokem.com/#/production

Figure 13.52 Fotokem nextLAB.

FotoKem's nextLAB mobile software was created to bring many lab and post resources for features, television, and commercial dailies and finishing to the set. nextLab streamlines the dailies process and standardizes file-based post workflow. Processing camera media as "original negative," the software securely ingests media, archives it to LTO, and provides QC tools. The ability to utilize metadata, sync audio, color, and transcode brings established lab dailies workflows to a mobile unit, on set. New workflows using digital cameras, multiple formats and codecs, and multiple frame rates create the need for numerous software solutions; nextLAB mobile fills those needs in a location portable system.

Color management tools provide LUT application and management, ASC CDL compatibility, full color correction control including RGB offsets, lift, gamma, gain, and curves with Euphonix MC color panel integration. The cinematographer can create and save color look presets, and accumulate a history custom looks.

Features of nextLAB include media management, and the ingest of camera original material to RAID storage with checksum; productions can utilize and track camera metadata within source files, tag files by shoot day and source device, and create accurate reports for media size, duration, and quality control. Audio sync functions automatically synchronize broadcast WAV audio to the source video, slip sync/offsets audio easily for sub-frame accuracy, and provides multi-channel playback and transcode capability. Dailies Creation application transcodes to Avid DNxHD .mxf or ProRes Quicktime for editorial, or to uncompressed media for DI conform. Calibrated iPads and monitors provide on-set viewing with Fotokem Cineviewer 4K, and new features automate integration with PIX System cloud dailies. nextLAB provides circled take and wild track management, creates H.264 proxies for viewing dailies or uploads to digital dailies systems, creates virtual tapes for Windows Media, IMX, or for DVD creation. Security features include window and watermark burn-ins for editorial or security, and an archival function features mirrored LTO archive with redundancy check, with standard TAR (tape archive) format for international compatibility, and EDL support for retrieving online clips.

Gamma and Density 3cP/Image Control

http://3cp.gammadensity.com/

Gamma and Density Image Control for Mac, iOS, or iPhone is a workflow solution for creating deliverables necessary for production and post by generating offline dailies, with the DP's custom look

Figure 13.53 Gamma and Density Image Control.

applied. Create dailies ready to edit in Avid, Final Cut Pro, Adobe Premiere, or create .DPX deliverables for visual effects and other departments.

Using Image Control, with an external LUT Box, the DP and/or DIT can create and load real-time color grades to a live SDI feed coming from the camera to the on-set monitor. This allows directors, producers, clients and the rest of "video village" to see the director of photography's creative intent, through a non-destructive color correction of the log or raw image being recorded in camera.

Use integrated color correction controls to create a custom LUT and export it as one of more than ten different types of LUTs, 3D LUT, or ASC CDL compatible with nearly every post production system. The same LUTs used for on-set monitoring can also be applied to dailies and sent on to post production. Import 3D LUTs (.cube and .3dl) directly into Image Control as a custom look. Tools include color wheels, curves, RGB sliders, printer lights, extended range test instruments, timecode, and manual audio syncing utility. Image Control also includes a utility for secure, verified footage offloads to three separate destinations simultaneously, and offers secure MD5 Checksum verification.

Image Control is available for purchase as a time controlled licensed subscription, and will work on nearly any Apple Laptop or Desktop, with no extra hardware required.

Lattice

https://videovillage.co/lattice/

Figure 13.54 Lattice color science and LUT laboratory.

Lattice by Video Village is a powerful LUT building too that has many features and capabilities to offer. It is compatible with OS X 10.9 Mavericks or later, with a simple Mac interface. Lattice uses custom visualization tools to see how a LUT modifies colors.

It applies LUTs to images in 16-bit color, with the ability to drag-and-drop images to see the LUT applied, or see a LUT applied to video in real-time. Lattice also allows users to preview on DPX files and other production image formats.

Lattice's advanced tools manipulate LUTs colors with 64-bit floating point precision:

- Convert color space: change color spaces and gamma curves
- Isolate color: get just the color transform of a LUT, without affecting contrast
- Convert: easily convert between 1D and 3D transformations
- Mix curves: adjust and swap curves
- Combine LUTs: merge multiple LUTs into one
- Isolate contrast: get just the contrast of a LUT, without affecting colors
- Convert to monochrome: make a LUT that isolates a single channel, or an average of channels
- Resize: change the cube or curve size
- Extended to legal/legal to extended conversions
- And more (limit, clamp, change color temperature, change opacity, invert colors, scale output).

Lattice reads and writes common LUT formats:

- FSI 3D LUT (.dat)
- DaVinci Resolve 1D and 3D Cube LUT (.cube)
- DaVinci Resolve DAT 3D LUT (.dat)
- Autodesk 3D LUT (.3dl)
- Nucoda CMS 1D and 3D LUT (.cms)
- Quantel 3D LUT (.txt)
- DVS Clipster 3D LUT (.xml, .txt)
- DaVinci 3D LUT (.davlut)
- Unwrapped Texture LUT Image (.tiff)
- CMS Test Pattern LUT Image (.tiff)
- DaVinci Resolve 1D LUT (.ilut, .olut)
- Discreet 1D LUT (.lut)
- ARRI Look 1D tone map only (.xml).

It also imports other formats as 3D LUTs:

- ARRI Look (.xml)
- ICC/ColorSync Profiles (.icc, .icm, .pf, .prof).

LUTCalc: 1D and 3D Cube LUT Calculator

https://apps.apple.com/us/app/lutcalc/id1000409621?mt=12

https://cameramanben.github.io/LUTCalc/LUTCalc/index.html

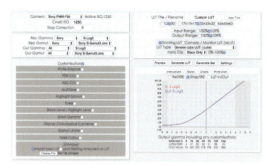

Figure 13.55 LUTCalc user interface.

LUTCalc is an app for generating, analyzing, and previewing 1D and 3D look-up tables (LUTs) for video cameras that shoot log gammas.

LUT Generator features:

- LUTCalc understands almost all log flavors in use today, plus standard gammas such as Rec 709 and manufacturer-tuned versions. Log and conventional gamma data has been taken from manufacturer-published documentation or standards papers.
- LUTCalc can produce accurate exposure adjustment LUTs for use in post where a simple tool is often not currently available, such as with SONY's CineEI.
- Converts between any of the included log and conventional gammas or to one of a number of creative looks modeled after those available in camera, either as a 1D tone curve only conversion, or as a full 3D color space conversion.
- Changes the input settings but not the output settings as a base when working with different camera models on a multi camera shoot.
- Customizes looks to taste, from simple black level and saturation adjustments to more complex effects such as desaturating specific color ranges.
- Adjusts color temperature either by CTO/CTB as with gels or by source and desired color temperature.
- Plus Green/Minus Green slider to correct for fluorescent lighting.
- Takes white balances from test images.
- Outputs to any of a number of common LUT formats, automatically adjusted for the intended use (MLUT or specific post software).
- Produces MLUTs suitable for loading directly into SONY's cameras (as user 3D MLUTs), with other in-camera options in development.

LUT Analyzer features:

- LUTCalc provides detailed exposure information about any look it generates, such as the recorded levels for absolute black, a correctly exposed 18% grey card or 90% white card and others. It takes

into account any adjustments and tweaks that have been made. The levels would ensure that when working to a monitor LUT the log recording would be correctly exposed as designed.

- Charts show the tone curves for the recording and the output, plus indicate the absolute dynamic range of the camera – black clip and white clip – where it is known.
- The "LUTAnalyst" tool can read LUTs in a number of formats. Where the recorded log and color space flavors it is designed for are known, it will attempt to convert them for use as with any of the built-in options, and provide the same exposure and tone curve information.
- A "false color" option can be used to generate accurate, log-curve specific exposure assistance MLUTs where not available in camera.
- Full instructions and details of all options are provided.

LUT Visualizer includes:

- LUTCalc includes a number of built-in test images with charts such as high contrast and low contrast, greyscale, and full color gamut along with the option to load a .png, .jpg or .bmp.
- Waveform, vector scope, and RGB parade scopes.
- xy/uv Chromacity preview image displays the recorded and output gamut triangles and white points, incorporating adjustments.
- Tone curve charts as stop in/recorded level out, linear in/linear out, and LUT in/LUT out.
- Provides 10-bit RGB readings from the Preview image.

A free online version is available at www.lutcalc. net for testing in any recent browser. File saving options are limited and there is no capability for running offline and quickly from disk, but all the base capabilities are there for testing.

MTI Film Cortex Control Dailies

www.mtifilm.com/cortex

Figure 13.56 MTI Film Control Dailies.

MTI's Cortex dailies system is a complete solution from set to delivery that includes tools for on-set playback, color correction, metadata management, checksumming, and transcoding. The system can run on a number of hardware configurations for use anywhere from a laptop to a DIT cart to a post facility, and provides a streamlined workflow for the production of dailies editorial and screening media.

Cortex applications share a common SQL database format where all project metadata is stored. Control dailies can play back media from any camera in real time, easily mixing clips from different cameras. It offers full control of camera-specific display options for cameras including RED, SONY, Panasonic, and ARRI. Common formats for editorial and finishing are supported as well. Create everything from Avid DNxHD and Apple ProRes to DPX and OpenEXR – even fully authored DVDs and Blu-rays.

Cortex Color Control Dailies lets the cinematographer set looks using printer lights or lift, gamma, gain. Import and export CDLs, LUTs, and ACES transforms for color management, and export stills and metadata for use downstream in post.

Cortex detects dead pixels in clips and compositions, and generates a manifest for processing on a CORTEX Enterprise workstation. It generates graphs for all video levels including SDR, HDR, SMPTE, and full scaling, 10-bit code values, bit rates. Full support of scopes for IRE, code values, NITs with automatic switching between HDR and Dolby Vision Content Mapping. Users can switch between VectorScope and Color Gamut Display and choose to view "out of gamut" zebra pattern in active picture, and outputs up to 4K HD-SDI and HDMI with Dolby Vision Tunneling.

Pomfort LiveGrade Pro

http://pomfort.com/livegrade/

Figure 13.57 Pomfort LiveGrade.

LiveGrade gives full control of the color of live SDI signals from digital film cameras, and assists in look and color management on set, supporting the exchange of ASC-CDLs, ALEXA Looks, 3D LUTs, ICC profiles, and more. It offers a unique visualization of the resulting color transformations as a three-dimensional cube, and assists in interactively manipulating colors of an SDI signal while visualizing the changes in code values.

LiveGrade supports grading modes tailored to specific camera setups and workflow environments. "CDL Grade" offers ASC-CDL controls for use with SDI signals from various cameras. It supports import and export of ASC-CDL files and allows to import 3D LUTs for custom log-to-video conversions. The "ALEXA Looks" grading mode offers the color controls for use with Log-C SDI signals coming from an Alexa camera and supports import and export of ALEXA Look files. Includes camera-specific gamma curve presets for various log signals such as Log-C, SLog, CineStyle, C-Log, or RED and more.

LiveGrade can manage up to eight LUT boxes on one computer. Each device can be configured for Legal-Range or Extended-Range SDI input and output. It can also manage several Pandora Pluto devices, and each Pluto device can store up to 16 3D LUTs internally using flash memory, which can be updated from LiveGrade PRO.

Pomfort LiveGrade supports both Avid Artist Color panels and Tangent Element and Wave grading panels to control all color correction and grading tasks.

RED Cine-X

www.red.com/downloads

Figure 13.58 REDCINE-X PRO.

REDCINE-X PRO is a free application from RED that allows users to view .r3d files natively on a Mac or windows computer. REDCINE-X PRO is a first light grading tool and batch conversion application designed specifically for transcoding and pre-editorial image manipulation of REDCODE R3D footage. It is a non-destructive application, enabling users to make image adjustments while preserving the original RAW format, giving the user the ability to return to the original files at any time for transcoding, scaling, cropping, or correcting color.

REDCINE-X PRO converts selected RAW files to RGB color space using de-mosaicing and color matrix algorithms. Timecode, white balance, and other metadata is maintained during RAW to RGB conversion. RMD file is a RED Metadata file created from R3D clips in REDCINE-X PRO.

REDCINE-X Pro toggles between REDs legacy and IPP2 workflows. With IPP2, R3D files go through a new standardized, three-step process: Image Primary (look independent controls, such as exposure and white balance), Image Grading (creative coloring decisions, including 3D LUTs and CDLs), and Image Output Transform (output-specific settings, such as SDR and HDR).

RED's IPP2 is a new workflow designed for HDR from the ground up with an industry-standard naming convention and standardized color space and gamma. IPP2 enhancements include better management of challenging colors, improved shadow detail, smoother highlight roll-off, and more accurate midtone hues. An improved demosaicking algorithm gives higher detail at the same pixel resolution.

RED recommends using a system that integrates their software development package which can read R3D files natively for final grades.

Technicolor DP Lights

www.technicolor.com/create/dp-lights

Figure 13.59 Technicolor DP Lights.

Technicolor DP Lights is a high quality on-set color primary grading toolset that creates looks in real time during production, and allows the DP to adjust to the look for dailies, VFX plate photography, and editorial materials, while simulating film print viewing.

DP Lights is compliant with the ASC CDL, offering an efficient post production workflow by delivering accurate color looks from color corrected dailies to final movie. DP Lights is easy to set up wherever you shoot, and easy to use for immediate color correction and pre-visualization or for matching set lighting.

The system is TrueLight compatible, allows wide variety of camera and monitor choices, and is designed to handle all types of source materials. Different looks can be saved during production and adjusted, even offline to give the DP the final look, and looks can be adapted to stills imported within the system for comparison to a live image.

The "LUTher" Color Space Converter accepts any color space in and converts to any color space out, employing 1D and 3D LUTs for on-set color correction. A standard color corrector panel can drive LUTher box adjustment of ASC CDL functions or Digital Printer Lites color corrections. This gives the user traditional "lift," "gain," "gamma" telecine style controls, ASC CDL controls, and RGB digital printer light emulation for film printing using print emulation LUTs.

Data Management/Checksum Software

Codex Digital

https://codex.online/products/vault-hardware/xl-series

Figure 13.60

Codex Digital introduced a device named Vault-XL, which follows their concept of the digital lab on the set, but with support for SXR/XR capture drives, SxS cards as well as CFast 2.0 cards. The fully featured version is a powerful standalone unit that handles a secure data transfer, can be used to directly playback or export dailies. It provides a data management and a metadata server. It also supports backup on parallel two or parallel four LTO-7 tapes. The XL-Series harnesses the benefits of network storage – faster access to files, simple configuration, and easy administration – and bolts on the power of Codex's Vault Platform so that whatever files you need are available on demand whenever you need them.

The XL-Series can be integrated into a facility using 40 GigE for fast connectivity. It is a parallel processing appliance, combining high quality processing, image science and automated efficiency. It includes 2 × Xeon E5-2690 v4 processors, 28 core.

Dailies can be generated in faster than real-time, with multiple LUTs and burn-ins applied. There's also a software only version available called Codex Production Suite.

Double Data

www.doubledata.biz/

Figure 13.61

From on set, to editorial to archiving, Double Data provides a way to verify that all the footage is correctly copied and rendered. Double Data keeps track of where data went, when, what its transfer status was, and its checksum. At the end of a day's work, it generates a report to send to editorial of all the files copied.

Scroll back and make sure all rolls were copied, and check their status. Double Data knows the difference between an error in a MOV or R3D® file and an error in a XML or RMD file. One is expected to change, one should never change. Double Data will warn when non-essential files have changed, but error when essential files don't match. For some cameras, Double Data can attempt a file recovery to recover files that may have been accidentally deleted. We currently support the Red® family of cameras, support for more cameras will come soon. It may take a while, but Double Data will try and save your shots.

Copy multiple rounds or multiple layers of copies automatically. When Double Data detects something is wrong, it will let you know via definitive red X in the main window, email and text notifications, and iOS notifications. Double Data can automatically start a copy as soon as it detects new camera media attached, and follow it through to every destination that you set up.

Drylab

www.drylab.io/

Figure 13.62

Drylab Viewer is designed to manage distribution of clips and metadata. Script supervisors and DITs should spend as little time as possible worrying about written reports, and as much time as possible on helping make the movie. Drylab's workflow integrates with industry standards such as Pomfort's Silverstack, in a simple and non-distracting background operation, and allows dailies and metadata distribution that works both with and without an Internet connection, both on- and off-set.

Drylab assists in preparing dailies and managing metadata. It integrates the other onset tools of dailies creation into the process of dailies distribution. Simple to use; ingest footage with Pomfort Silverstack, transcode with Silverstack Lab, Resolve, or the software of your choice, connect metadata and clip folder to Drylab Creator for processing and Drylab Creator automatically and securely distributes clips and metadata to authorized team members, directly on set using Wi-Fi, or via the Internet to remote users. Drylab will allow the DIT to load and securely store material on iPads and iPhones for instant access while offline. User permissions are added, managed, and removed using an online Admin system.

Pomfort Silverstack

http://pomfort.com

Figure 13.63

Pomfort Silverstack +XT or Silverstack LAB is a professional software for DITs with all necessary functionalities to create verified data copies that are checksum verified. The program keeps all copied files in a database, can edit and export the metadata, can create clip reports as PDF, and provides a simple interface for quality control. This program also has the ability to clone to multiple destinations. Transfer footage to multiple hard drives or to LTO tape with one action. Pomfort is a mainstay of on-set data and look management, handling all the tasks of on-set workflows, offloading, quality checking, reporting, transcoding, metadata transfer and conform.

Shot Put Pro

www.imagineproducts.com/product/shotput-pro

Figure 13.64

Shot Put Pro is another must have utility on set for copying and backing up shot data, audio, CDLs, and LUTs. Drag and drop ease saves files and folders into the "offload from" section, then choose your destination or "offload to" location that already exists. If you want to create a new folder for the offloads you will want to use the traditional ShotPut Pro view – preset mode. Mobile High Definition Link (MHL) reporting adheres to the standard naming conventions.

Generate PDF reports including metadata captured on the report and designate first frame for PDF thumbs or percentage sampling. Customize report names or use the job identifier for more organization. There are many report formats for all your workflow needs. This program also has the ability to clone to multiple destinations. Transfer footage to four different hard drives with one action.

Yoyotta

https://yoyotta.com/

Figure 13.65

YoYotta stores full media metadata including codec, resolution, and duration. It's quick to locate media and you can see where it's stored. Open a virtual folder showing all the media from your search in one place. Make PDF reports from searches, handy to give the producer a list of shoot durations for each media type.

As soon as camera cards or drives are connected they will appear in the media table. Source drives are mounted read-only preventing accidental erasure. YoYotta calculates both MD5 and xxHash checksum while copying, then verifies the copies using the checksum and delivers a PDF audit of the files copied.

Cards can be copied to multiple backup destinations simultaneously. Copy multiple cards at once, or add them to a card for sequential copies. Limited only by the speed of connected storage. Stop an import and pickup later. Span large jobs across multiple volumes, disks, and tapes. Start a large job that won't fit on a single volume. YoYotta will intelligently fill each volume without splitting shots. Keep adding volumes until the job is complete. The reports and the database will keep track of where the shots are archived. YoYotta LTFS will span the job across multiple tapes, and each backup is independently verified.

YoYotta creates a PDF report that can be automatically emailed to all team members without needing to set up any email software. The report contains the media checksums for future reference along with media codec, duration, and resolution. This metadata is also in the database and stored as extended attributes in the file directory.

If you need to copy multiple high speed cards to the same RAID, then it's often quicker to process them sequentially rather than simultaneously. YoYotta will offer to add the jobs into a queue, letting you know as each copy completes.

LUT Boxes

AJA LUT Box

www.aja.com/products/lut-box

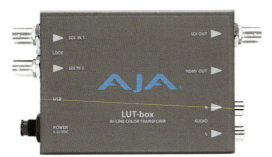

Figure 13.66 AJA LUT box.

Working with log encoded source material outside the normal Rec 709 video color space can cause confusion both on set and in the edit suite from colors that are not properly displayed. Load 3D LUTs or CDLs into the AJA LUT box to adjust the color look for any source signal with simultaneous outputs to HDMI and SDI monitors from a single LUT box. LUT box ensures that every monitor is showing the correct color "look" for any source signal without altering the original file color.

LUT box supports 16-point and 17-point 3D LUTs with 12-bit processing for accurate color representation. Multiple LUT formats are supported including .3dl, .lut, .txt, and .cube. In addition, a 10- or 12-bit 1D LUT can also be applied prior to the 3D LUT to allow for additional calibration or image enhancement before being processed by the 3D LUT.

AJA's free Mini-Config software can be used with any USB-enabled AJA Mini-Converter and provides a graphical interface with detailed information about the current input and output formats, controls all the parameters of any supported AJA Mini-Converter, as well as loading firmware updates from AJA that add new features and functionality.

AJA Mini-Converters are small enough to fit behind a monitor, in the back of a rack or directly on a camera rig. A locking power connector can't accidentally pull loose and an optional P-TAP power cable allows for battery power in remote locations.

Blackmagic Teranex Mini

www.blackmagicdesign.com/products/teranex mini8k

Figure 13.67 Blackmagic Teranex Mini.

Teranex Mini SDI to HDMI 8K HDR is an 8K monitoring solution for large screen televisions and video projectors. The front panel LCD provides confidence monitoring with images and accurate audio level meters. On-screen scopes can be switched between WFM, Parade, Vector, and Histogram, and 3D LUTs can be enabled in menus. The audio meters can be switched between VU or PPM ballistics. HDMI lock can be enabled to assure that the HDMI display locks instantly if the input video has been interrupted. There are settings for configuring scopes, their on-screen location and opacity, and for viewing and editing network settings.

Teranex Mini SDI to HDMI 8K HDR uses 33-point 3D LUTs for creating looks or to compensate for the colorimetry of the connected display. Teranex Mini can use calibration probes to align connected displays for precise color; calibrate a second connected display by connecting a third party USB color probe. SpectraCal C6, X-Rite i1 Display Pro, or the Klein K10-A probes are supported and plug into USB at the front of the converter. Use Teranex Mini SDI to HDMI 8K HDR to analyze a monitor or generate a 3D LUT to correct for color differences between two displays. Two independent 3D LUTs can be loaded and selected from the front panel. 3D LUTs use standard file formats so you can load LUTs generated by software such as DaVinci Resolve.

Teranex Mini SDI to HDMI 8K supports HDR workflows. Static metadata PQ and Hybrid Log Gamma (HLG) formats in the VPID are handled according to the ST2108-1, ST2084 and the ST425 standards. Teranex Mini SDI to HDMI 8K HDR handles ST425 which defines two new bits in the VPID to indicate transfer characteristic of SDR, HLG,or PQ. ST2108-1 standard defines how to transport HDR static or dynamic metadata over SDI, and there is support for ST2082-10 for 12G SDI as well as ST425 for 3G-SDI sources. Both Rec 2020 and Rec 709 color spaces are supported and 100% of the DCI-P3 format.

Box IO: Flanders Scientific

http://flandersscientific.com/boxio/

Figure 13.68 Flanders Scientific BoxIO LUT box.

BoxIO supports real-time LUTs over IP allowing for direct integration with popular on-set color management tools like Pomfort LiveGrade Pro, QTAKE Grade module, FilmLight Prelight, and FireFly Cinema FireDay and FirePlay.

Both 3D and 1D LUTs and can be used for calibration, on set grading, and in line viewing of LUT operations. BoxIO interfaces directly with monitor calibration software solutions for simple and accurate 3D LUT based display alignment. It is equipped with an integrated test pattern generator allowing for manual test patch generation from the BoxIO Utility or automated test pattern generation from calibration software like LightSpace or CalMAN. Users can upload LUTs generated from LightSpace CMS and Cal-MAN software directly to BoxIO without exiting or running additional programs.

TV Logic IS Mini LUT Box

https://wonderlook.net/en/product/isminix.php

Figure 13-69 TV Logic IS Mini LUT box

The IS-miniX 3D LUT box allows users to display a graded an image live on set. It connects between the camera and monitor, or to a computer via USB interface. The included WonderLookPro software allows for capture and grading of the live image, for saving the look for use in post later, and for generating shooting reports.

Send an image to the IS-miniX to view a creative look via SDI. Capture continuously, viewing real time live images on a computer and also monitor waveform or vectorscope displays. Other features include on-board test pattern generation and one-click white balance. The IS-miniX can provide ancillary information which included WonderLookPro software interprets as metadata. Exposure info and lens settings can be read from supported cameras and used for shooting reports.

IS-miniX is capable of displaying frame lines, three sets of frame lines are available to choose from, line width and line colors can additionally be adjusted. Send a logo or subtitle images to the IS-miniX to composite with a live image, or within a selected chroma range, and Chroma Key compositing allows pixels to be replaced from the live image.

LUT Processing includes 1D (1024 steps) +3D (26 × 26 × 26) + 1D (1024 steps).

Pandora Pluto LUT Box

https://pandoratek.global/products/pluto/

Pandora Pluto LUT box is a multi-purpose display management system designed for use on set and in post production, a hardware platform from which a 3D and 1D LUT manager, an ASC CDL manager, a stereoscopic processor, and a cursor generator application can be loaded and used.

Figure 13.70 Pandora Pluto.

PLUTO features twin HDSDI 3G connections and can be used to transcode from dual link 4:4:4 to single link 4:2:2 and or RGB/YUV color space. Additional output options provide HD-SDI to HDMI conversion. "Dual head" mode allows a single Pluto board to be used with two independent single link monitors with separate LUTs for each display for 16 or 17 point cubes only. Alternatively the device can be used in dual link mode with a single monitor in which case 16/17/32/33 point cubes are possible. Pluto has twin 3G-SDI channels with the ability to apply 1D and 3D LUTs and ASC-CDL color corrections to SDTV, HDTV, and 4K images in real-time. Adding a trackball mouse allows ASC CDL grading parameters to be updated in real-time. There is support for all common LUT file formats with ethernet connection for upload and full remote control. SMPTE 352 ANC Timecode reader allows CDL adjustments to be logged and exported as an EDL or ALE file.

The Pluto has a control wheel interface and on-screen menu for local control; also full remote control operation via 100BaseT ethernet. Up to 16 1D and or 3D LUTs can be stored internally using flash memory and can be uploaded using the software utility provided. Access to all stored LUTs, test patterns, and a safe area marker is available directly from the front panel. Multiple Plutos can be named and grouped together, and new LUTs can be uploaded simultaneously to all or to each unit individually. It is also possible to read the status of all units on the network so that engineering can ensure that the correct LUTs are applied in each area.

Software is provided to read LUT files in multiple formats and is fully compatible with PomFort LiveGrade, THX Cinespace, Light Illusion Light-Space CMS, and TruLight color management tools with support for 16,17,32,33 point cubes, and built-in test pattern and color tile generators.

A 1 unit rack mount model can house two Pluto Boards to provide 4K or 4-Channel operation. Twin channels can be used independently (even in different video standards) or together for stereo image processing. Stereoscopic processing modes include Anaglyph and Side by Side. A special software version allows Pluto to be used for Dolby Stereo Processing and theater screen management.

Teradek Colr/Colr Duo

https://teradek.com/collections/colr

Figure 13.72 Teradek Colr Duo LUT box, bridge and cross convertor.

COLR is a real-time LUT box, camera control bridge, and HDMI/SDI cross-converter in one tiny package. COLR integrates with Pomfort LiveGrade Pro, allowing DITs and colorists to display graded looks in real time. It also functions as a wireless controller for ethernet cameras.

Multiple presets, combining CDLs and 3D LUTs can be stored on the device for quick conversion or custom looks. COLR live converts RAW and LOG signals for monitoring.

COLR Duo offers two fully configurable SDI outputs, allowing you to display two independent 33pt 3D LUTs or even the same LUT across two monitors.

COLR supports 10-bit color, simultaneous HDMI and SDI outputs from almost every camera manufactured, is compatible with virtually all monitors, and is part of the Teradek Connected Set workflow.

Additional Useful Resources

AJA

www.aja.com/en/
AJA is a company that manufactures flexible and reliable hardware for acquisition, input/output,

editorial, and format conversion. AJA makes the KiPro recorder, it builds a family of I/O boards including Kona, IO, and T-Tap, and they manufacture a very large selection of small but rugged format convertors, frame synchronizers, streaming convertors, synchronizers, image analyzers, routers, and distribution amplifiers. Their products are well built, well supported, and give great value for the price.

Blackmagic Design

www.blackmagicdesign.com/products

Blackmagic Design builds a wide variety of products for both high end and budget conscious filmmakers. In addition to the Blackmagic Cinema Camera and the Hyperdeck family of digital disk recorders, they also manufacture I/O cards, format converters, switchers, routers, synchronizers, distribution amplifiers, streaming and encoding boxes, monitors, and test equipment. In addition, they are the manufacturing source for DaVinci color correction systems, Ultimatte keyers, Cintel film scanners, and Teranex 2D and 3D format processors.

DAX® Production Cloud and PIX Systems

Both DAX® Production Cloud and PIX Systems are online collaboration services for filmed entertainment that organize and secure media in a central location to provide access for sharing media, metadata, and production information. Both systems allow users to log in to securely access, upload or download media.

DAX® Production Cloud

www.primefocustechnologies.com/blog/dax-production-cloud-one-software-to-manage-dailies-and-post-servicing-workflows/

DAX (digital asset exchange) is a cloud-based production workflow application used to collaborate on content created throughout the course of motion picture and television production, as well as for marketing and distribution of the final product. DAX is used for storage, review, and distribution of digitized production elements and assets, including video, audio, photography, and documents such as screenplays, legal contracts, budgets, schedules, and basic text documents.

DAX® Digital Dailies Player/Viewer uses Wowza streaming technology (adaptive streaming, frame accuracy) and DAX® iDailies is an application that allows video to be viewed on mobile devices such as the iPad and iPhone.

DAX® Production Cloud allows clients to use the same system for both dailies and post servicing workflows. The entire production supply chain: editorial, VFX, marketing, localization vendors, and distribution all collaborate on the same software, handling high-res files with security, providing access to content at all times with Metadata access across the content life cycle.

Key features include the production servicing module, for single file ingest, transcode, watermark, distribution of multiple formats to production users, pre-production tools and services (on-set distribution, content engine, script ratings), support for mezzanine files and essences, adaptive, multi-bitrate streaming, advanced permissions and administration modules, DRM, and forensic watermarking.

DAX® login uses email and SMS 2-factor authentication. DAX® is MPAA® audited, SOC2, ISO 27001 (2013) certified, the home page shows an activity feed of all recent account events (uploads, edits, shares, etc.), customizable dashboard of reporting / analytics widgets and a permissions engine allows multi-level permissions management down to the folder level, including advanced auditing and reporting of all user actions and system events.

PIX System and Fotokem nextLAB®

https://pix.online/

PIX System provides film professionals with secure access to production content on mobile devices, laptops, or TVs from offices, homes, or while in transit. PIX System's secure digital collaboration platform is widely used on feature and television productions by filmmakers, motion picture studios, and television networks. Productions use the PIX service to view, manage, and collaborate on their media during various phases of production and marketing.

FotoKem's nextLAB® is an on-set and near-location solution for file-based workflows that supports productions from camera to color through editing and archive. The latest version of FotoKem's nextLAB® software for media management automates the transfer of dailies to PIX System's digital collaboration service. nextLAB® was designed to identify, capture, carry, and manage media and information throughout the workflow from dailies to archive. The metadata gathered in nextLAB® can be automatically shared through PIX for easy viewing, commenting, collaborating, and manipulating the data on set, at the studio, in editing rooms, at visual effects houses, or by other important stakeholders of a production. nextLAB® transcodes the source media files, and uploads the material and over 60 fields of searchable metadata per take directly into PIX.

Users can view and send clips or images, exchange notes or markups, approve takes and send play lists to collaborators. Secure on line viewing eliminates the risks associated with mailed DVDs, FTP sites, and hard copies. Material is watermarked in real time with the user's name, IP address, and time of access. All connections are secured and files are individually encrypted. Customizable privileges control access to every item in the system, restricting users' access to a specific IP address, administrators can disable a user's access to specific files, or the entire service, if necessary. Audit trails are automatically generated with detailed logs and usage reports.

Moxion

www.moxion.io/about/

Moxion provides another option for secure access to production content on mobile devices, laptops, or TVs from offices, homes, or while in transit. Moxion's secure digital collaboration platform is widely used on feature and television productions by filmmakers, motion picture studios, and television networks. Productions use the PIX service to view, manage, and collaborate on their media during various phases of production and marketing. Sharing footage on and off set, across multiple units enables collaboration from production designers to directors to cinematographers. Directors can pick up any missing shots or re-shoot scenes while the talent and set are still in place, reducing reshoots and pick-ups.

Moxion's platform is constantly evaluated by the world's top security teams. Features like MPAA compliance, Watermarking, Multi Factor Authentication, and full Digital Rights Management are just the start. A secure platform with data protection, Moxion works on browsers, desktop, iPhone, iPad, and secure streaming via the Moxion app for Apple TV.

Moxion enables users to track, control and share footage, with user access only via Moxion accounts; it offers dailies in HDR through Moxion Immediates so any project stakeholder with credentialed access can view footage (complete with metadata).

Moxion dailies platform is built inside a cloud-based ecosystem for the secure viewing, sharing, and editing of footage through a major studio-approved security environment, with features like DRM, screener, and access control that protects a project's assets.

Notes

1. The following three paragraphs were contributed by Jonathan Smiles CSI – Independent Workflow Consultant.
2. The following section is an original contribution from Joseph Goldstone, at ARRI; the author extends special thanks to Mr. Goldstone and ARRI.
3. The following section was contributed by David Reisner and Joshua Pines.

Chapter 14

Displays and Recorders

Displays

This chapter cannot go into tremendous detail on monitors and displays, as they change models and specs on a weekly basis. Rather, I will try to give a basic understanding of what to expect from current technology. Readers will discover many tried and true favorites and "old reliables" in the rental market, but this is a market sector where the technology changes very rapidly. For the purposes of digital cinematography there are four basic types of displays to concern yourself with.

A Brief History of Display Technologies

CRT – Cathode Ray Tube Monitors

The cathode ray tube monitor (CRT) was the original television picture tube technology. The de facto standard monitor for critical viewing of Rec 709 video material and for judging color correction in digital intermediate was, until recently,

Figure 14.1 Discontinued SONY broadcast video monitor.

one of SONY's BVM Reference HD monitors. This display was generally paired with a DCI compliant digital cinema projector for judging final color output in almost every color correction suite in the world.

In 2008, SONY announced the end of all production of its traditional-style cathode ray tube televisions and monitors. SONY had sold over 280 million CRT televisions and monitors since 1965, at the peak of their popularity, and production of cathode ray tubes for TVs monitors and computer monitors had topped 20 million units a year in 2000.

Unfortunately, at the time SONY discontinued manufacture of reference broadcast video monitors, no suitable replacement had been invented yet. The manufacturing community has responded to that need in the years since, and numerous products have emerged to replace the BVM. The evolution of display technology has moved on since the demise of the CRT, and new technologies are attempting to rise to the task of reference viewing as they mature. The issues manufacturers face in replacing the CRT are not easily overcome though – few monitors yet offer the contrast range, deep blacks, and consistency of calibration that made CRT the pillar of high end color correction.

LCD – Liquid Crystal Displays

Liquid crystal display (LCD) technology uses a matrix of tiny liquid crystal windows that change color under electrical charge to filter a backlight source creating RGB pixels. Laptops have used LCD screens almost exclusively, and LCD monitors are the most common display type for desktop computers.

LCD monitors have generally exhibited lower contrast, poor black reproduction, limited angle for optimal viewing, and are difficult to calibrate to a reference standard. In addition, they are generally inconsistent between different manufacturers' models.

LED – Light Emitting Diode Displays

Light emitting diode (LED) display is a technology that uses groups of tiny RGB-emitting semiconductor diodes to create individual pixels. Many colors can be generated based on the material used for the tips of the probes. LEDs last for decades and are virtually indestructible. In addition, white or red, green and blue LEDs are frequently used as backlight source lighting on many LCD displays. Aluminum indium gallium phosphide (AlInGaP) is used for red and yellow. Indium gallium nitride (InGaN) is used for green and blue, and with the addition of phosphor, for white light as well. Nonetheless, LEDs are deficient in some areas of spectral reproduction, and LED displays are not capable of reaching the kind of contrast ratios that are required of reference viewing monitors.

Gas Plasma Displays

Gas plasma displays work by sandwiching neon gas between two plates. Each plate is coated with a conductive print. The print on one plate contains vertical conductive lines and the other plate has horizontal lines. Together, the two plates form a grid. When electric current is passed through a horizontal and vertical line, the gas at the intersection glows, creating tricolor pixels. You can think of a gas-plasma display as a collection of very small neon bulbs. Plasma displays generally exhibit better contrast than LCD displays.

OLED – Organic Light Emitting Diode Displays

OLED (and it's more modern variant, active matrix OLED) is another light-emitting diode technology that integrates LEDs into the actual display panel substrate, yielding bright, colorful images with a wide viewing angle, low power, high contrast ratio, and fast response time. Because OLEDs do not require additional backlights, the screens can be ultra thin.

Active matrix OLED is an organic LED (OLED) display technology that drives each pixel separately. The typical AMOLED pixel uses two transistors and one capacitor. Contrasted with a "passive matrix OLED" (PMOLED), which drives the pixels by row and column (x-y) coordinates, active matrix OLEDs work on the same principle as active matrix LCDs (AMLCDs), and PMOLEDs are like passive matrix LCDs (PMLCDs).

In 2007 SONY introduced the first active matrix OLED TV, but with only an 11" screen. Significant progress has been made in the technology since then, giving the technology increased contrast, deeper blacks, and enabling the manufacture of larger screens.

OLEDs can be transparent, enabling them to function in heads-up displays and as window shades that react to sunlight. OLED's color, speed, thinness, transparency, and flexibility would seem to make it the display technology of the 21st century.

Calibration

In order to assure yourself that what you are seeing on your on-set monitor is what the editor, the director and the studio will see in dailies it is urgent to assure that your on-set displays are properly calibrated. There are a number of useful applications for this purpose. Whenever possible, the best way to double check agreement between on set displays and the color suite is to perform the calibration in the DI color suite. Most labs and digital intermediate houses will agree to this within the constraints of their schedule, and it is well worth the effort, even if it means the cinematographer has to do the work after hours or on a weekend. The confidence that this gives the cinematographer in the tools on set cannot be undervalued. Here are some of the options available for use in calibration of displays.

Manual Standard Dynamic Range Monitor Calibration

Figure 14.2 ARIB color bars labeled with values.

Many cameras can output color bars. The user can quickly set up a monitor or viewfinder from these color bars. Start by adjusting the contrast control to increase brightness until the 100% super white square is at peak white on the monitor – you will know you are there when the white box stops getting perceptibly brighter. Once it reaches its maximum brightness, back the contrast level down until you can just perceive the brightness change on the screen. Once this is set you can use the PLUGE bars to set up the black level. The PLUGE bars are the narrow near black bars marked as –2% +2% and +4%. Using the brightness control adjust the screen so that you can't see the –2% bar but can just see the +2% bar. The 4% bar should also be visible, separated from the 2% bar by black. Next watch the 100% color patches, two thirds of the way down the pattern, cyan and yellow on the left, blue and red on the right, and use saturation control to increase the color level until the saturation of the outer boxes stops increasing, then back the level down again until you can just start to perceive the color decreasing. Chroma adjusts color saturation of the image when using composite or Y Cb Cr inputs. It should not change the picture if the input is RGB or XYZ. Saturation can be calibrated by setting the display in "Blue Only" mode. Watch the top and middle bars second from the left (White and Blue), to adjust saturation until the middle bars are at the same level.

This "quick and dirty" procedure will usually produce an acceptable result for most cases except for critical viewing. A more thorough guide to setting up a monitor by eye can be found at the beginning of Chapter 10 of this book. For more critical calibrations, the use of a calibration probe is recommended.

When a monitor must be calibrated more critically, other calibration tools are available, at different price levels. Colorimeters use a set of filters designed around the CIE 1931 standard observer, whereas spectroradiometers use individual sensors to detect specific parts of the visual spectrum.

Display Calibration Tools

Portrait Displays CalMAN

https://store.portrait.com/professional-software.html

CalMAN is available in a variety of different configurations ranging from the DIY user to the full time calibration professional.

Figure 14-3 CalMAN software and hardware.

CalMAN 5 calibrates grayscale and gamut, and performs saturation and luminance sweeps, reading saturations at 20% intervals and luminance at 10% intervals. Numerous charts are available including the Gretag Macbeth color checker chart. CalMAN reports can be used in different workflows, users can get the same data out if using a standard workflow, a custom workflow, or an AutoCal workflow. CalMAN 5 offers improved device and meter support, so more meters are supported, and more features of those meters are supported. Additional displays can also be directly controlled to allow for AutoCal of ISF Day and Night modes, as well as custom adjustments. CalMAN 5's improved interface and workflow makes it easier to use and get good results.

Datacolor Spyder

https://spyderx.datacolor.com/

Datacolor's Spyder Studio Color Calibration package gives users tools to achieve reliable color calibration. This kit offers professional results and is easy-to-use.

Figure 14.4 Datacolor Spyder color calibration screen.

The Spyder 4 Elite USB colorimeter automates and simplifies display calibration. The sensor measures a series of colors on your screen and creates a profile that brings your display to reference state.

A patented, full-spectrum 7-color sensor accurately characterizes a variety of wide gamut and normal gamut displays.

Calibration determines the colors output by the red, blue, and green channels of the display, and how the light output of channels varies as the pixel value is changed from 0 to 255. Once the software knows how the display is behaving, it corrects by loading curves into the video card or to the monitor to produce a smooth tone curve and neutral greys. This step also adjusts the monitor to the correct gamma setting and color temperature.

X-Rite

www.xrite.com/categories/calibration-profiling/i1display-pro

On set color grading of footage creates the necessity for accurate color representation on screen. With the included broadcast video standards support for NTSC, PAL SECAM, and ITU-R Rec.BT.709, what you see is what you get throughout a digital video workflow. X-Rite i1Display Pro is a calibration and profiling system for displays and projectors. The i1Display features i1Profiler software for calibrating and profiling all modern display and projector technologies, including LED and wide gamut LCDs. The system incorporates three functions – ambient light measurement, monitor profiling, and projector profiling. A custom-designed RGB filter set provides accurate color measurements, while the optical design allows for high repetition on the same display and across different display types for more consistent color matching. Rotating diffuser arm and integrated tripod mount is made for projector profiling.

Figure 14.5 X-Rite menu screens.

Control white point, luminance, contrast ratio, gamma, as well as multiple monitor and workgroup profiling. Intelligent iterative profiling is an adaptive technology that measures and analyzes the color capabilities of each unique display for increased profile accuracy. Create unique patch sets for optimal results in your profiling.

Flare Correct measures and adjusts display profile for reduced contrast ratios caused by glare falling on the surface of your display. Three patch set sizes – small, medium, or large – allow you to increase your profile accuracy by measuring a higher number of patches. Automatic display control (ADC) technology automates the adjustment of your display's hardware, including brightness/backlight, contrast, and color temperature, in order to speed up the profiling process and eliminate manual adjustments.

Before and after images show instant results, and a profile reminds when it's time to re-profile a display. The system can perform visual validation using pre-defined and user defined images. Additionally, the i1Display Pro features color accuracy trending over time. For a display uniformity test, measure white point and luminance uniformity over nine locations on your display, and take control with user defined PASS/FAIL tolerance.

PR 735 Spectroradiometer

www.jadaktech.com/products/photo-research/

Figure 14.6 Photo Research PR-735 spectroradiometer.

A spectroradiometer is an instrument for measuring the radiant-energy distribution in a spectrum. It is the ideal instrument for contrast and brightness measurements of digital cinema projectors and display panels, and a wide variety of other target devices. Expect to see one of the units measuring the projection screen at the beginning of a session at any professional digital intermediate house. Spectroradiometers measure the absolute spectral quantity of light radiance by breaking up the broadband incoming optical signal into its component parts by means of a diffraction grating – much like a prism. The PR-735 uses 512 detectors to sample the emitted spectrum from 380 to 780nm yielding a resolution of 0.781 nm/pixel. Data is reported every 1nm. Spectral range of the PR-735 is 380 to 1080nm for a resolution of 1.348 nm/pixel and reported in 2nm increments.

Up to eight measuring apertures can be supplied on the instrument providing spot size and sensitivity flexibility. The PR-735 can measure as low as 0.0001 foot lamberts (0.0003 or 0.00015 cd/m²), and the PR-735 has variable bandwidth between 2, 5, 8nm spectral bandwidths to insure the optimum conditions for virtually any sample.

Waveform Monitors and Vectorscopes

The fundamental tools of shooting digitally are the waveform monitor and the vectorscope. Even in the most extreme "run and gun" shooting situations or under the worst budget pressure, don't consider sacrificing these essential tools, even if they are only displayed as an overlay on a picture monitor.

A vectorscope is a specialty oscilloscope used in video to display an X/Y plot of color signals, revealing details about the relationship between these signals. Vectorscopes have purpose designed graticules, and accept HD television or video signals as input, demodulating and demultiplexing the picture components to be analyzed internally.

A wave form monitor is typically used to measure and display the voltage of a video signal with respect to time. The level of a video signal usually corresponds to the brightness, or luminance of the image. A waveform monitor can be used to display the overall brightness of the picture, or it can zoom in to show one or two individual lines of the video signal. It can also be used to visualize and observe special signals in the vertical blanking interval of a video signal, as well as the color burst between each line of video.

Waveform monitors are used in the manufacture and calibration of cameras, to align multiple cameras to each other, and as a tool to assist in telecine, scanning, color correction, and visual effects work.

Cinematographers use waveform monitors and vectorscopes to monitor signals to make sure that neither the exposure levels or the color gamut are exceeded, and for setting the exposure levels of video and digital cinema cameras.

Additionally, waveform monitors and vectorscopes are used to diagnose and troubleshoot equipment in a television broadcast facility, to install and align equipment in a facility, and to determine the commissioning or certification of a facility.

Leader/Phabrix

www.leader.co.jp/en/
https://phabrix.com/products/

Figure 14.7 Phabrix QxL rasterizer screen.

Figure 14.8 Leader LV 5600 7" Waveform Monitor/ Vectorscope.

Phabrix

Phabrix Sx portable test and measurement devices offer advanced capabilities including hybrid IP/SDI performance and physical layer testing, rugged design, and exceptional ease of use. Phabrix rack-mounted Rx series offers advanced 2K/3G/HD/SD signal generation, analysis and monitoring for compliance testing, and fault diagnosis of video and audio. The Phabrix Qx line provides hybrid IP/SDI test and measurement tools required for next generation video formats, including instruments for fault diagnosis, compliance monitoring and product development. Current Phabrix products include Rx2000, Rx1000 and Rx500 rasterizers, and Sx TAG, SxE, SxA and SxD hand-held waveform video and audio signal analyzers and generators.

Leader

Leader Electronics specializes in measuring instruments for high definition, 4K and 8K video for television, motion pictures, and broadcasting. Leader's full line of waveform monitors are equipped with liquid crystal monitors for checking the quality of video signals and audio signals. Leader rasterizers are measuring instruments for checking the quality of video signals and audio signals. Their thin rack mount instruments display measurement results on an external monitor. Current Leader products include the LV5900, LV5600, LV5300, LV5350, LV5383 waveform monitors and LV7600 and LV7300 rasterizers.

Tektronix

www.telestream.net/video/waveform-monitors.htm

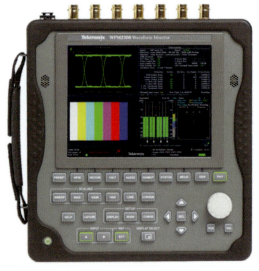

Figure 14.9 Tektronix WFM2300 Portable Waveform Monitor.

Figure 14.10 Tektronix WFM/WVR5200 Waveform Monitor.

WFM/WVR5000 series offers full HD/SD support and the capability to handle 3G-SDI (WFM/WVR5200) and HDMI (WFM/WVR5250).

The WFM2200A and WFM2300 are portable tools for measurement and analysis in field

applications for broadcast engineers and technicians in the field or stationed at remote locations within a facility. These instruments provide a full range of video, audio, and ancillary data measurements to verify performance or trace problems to their root cause.

The WFM2200A, WFM2300, WFM/WVR5200, and WFM/WVR5250 all come complete with a full set of physical interfaces and measurement components to address a wide range of broadcast issues. The basic waveform functions can be easily augmented with a full suite of tools to perform measurements as diverse as evaluating physical layer margins on long SDI runs or providing a known "good signal" to check AV delay or audio loudness.

Monitors/Monitor Recorders for On Camera/Near Camera Displays

This section will cover on set and near set displays in alphabetical order, from small to large. I have surveyed a number of DITs and colorists on the subject of displays in hope of covering the most widely used brands and models currently available for sale and rental at the time of this writing.

Atomos

www.atomos.com/
    Models include Shinobi/Shinobi SDI Monitor, Ninja V – (5" HDR Pro Monitor-Recorder), Ninja Inferno – (7" HDR Pro Monitor-Recorder), Shogun Inferno - (7" HDR Pro/Cinema Monitor-Recorder), Shogun 7 – (7" HDR Pro/Cinema Monitor-Recorder-Switcher), Shogun Flame, Shogun Studio – (Rack Mount), Sumo 19/Sumo 19M, and Neon Series.

Blackmagic Design

www.blackmagicdesign.com/products/black magicvideoassist
    Models include: Video Assist 7" 12G HDR, Video Assist 5" 12G HDR.

Figure 14.11 Blackmagic Design Video Assist 5" 12G HDR Monitor/Recorder

Figure 14.12 Blackmagic Design Video Assist 7" 12G HDR Monitor/Recorder

Convergent Design

www.convergent-design.com/products.html
Models include: Odyssey7Q+, Odyssey Apollo.

Figure 14.13 Convergent Design Odyssey7Q+ Monitor/Recorder

Figure 14.14 Convergent Design Odyssey Apollo Monitor/Recorder

IKAN

https://ikancorp.com/product-category/monitors/

Models include: IKAN S7C , 7P, DH7-V2, DH5e/DH5e-V2 D7C, S7H-V2, VK5, FM-055F.

Small HD

www.smallhd.com/
Models Include: 500 Series, 702 Touch, Cine 7, Wireless Series – Cine 7 500 TX/Cine 7 500 RX/Cine 7 500 SK RX, Focus 5 Series, Focus 7 Series, Ultrabright Series, 702 Bright/702 Black, and 702-OLED.

Transvideo

www.transvideo.eu/store/StarliteHD
Models include: StarliteHD-m Metadator, Transvideo StarliteHD+, Transvideo StarliteRF-a V2, CineMonitor UHD Evolution Monitors 8", 10", 12", 15" eSBL, 6" SBL+, and 8" X-SBL.

Figure 14.15 Transvideo StarliteHD-m Metadator 5" Monitor/Recorder.

StarliteHD-m gathers Cooke /i or Zeiss eXtended lens metadata through serial link and gives access to focus and zoom metadata, shading, distortion map, inertial data, timecode, and illumination tables through a direct serial connection. Files are written to an SD card and are immediately available to be processed through the plugins developed by the lens manufacturer.

TV Logic

www.tvlogic.tv/
Models include: VFM-055A, F-5A, F-7H mk2, F-10A, and LVM-075A.

Monitors for Use on Set/Near Set/DIT Cart/Director Viewing

Canon

www.usa.canon.com/internet/portal/us/home/products/list/reference-displays/4k-uhd-reference-displays/4k-uhd-reference-displays

Models include: DP-V3010, DP-V2420 HDR, DP-V2421, DP-V2411, DP-V2410, DP-V1711, and DP-V1710.

EIZO

www.eizo.com/products/coloredge/
Models include: CG3145 HDR, CG319X, CG248-4K, CG279X, CG248X, CG277, CG2730, CS2420, CG3145 HDR, CG319X, CG248-4K, CG279X, CG248X, CG277, CG2730, CG2420, and CS2420.

Flanders Scientific FSI

www.flandersscientific.com/
Models include: AM210, BM090, BM210, BM240, DM170, DM240, XM-310K, XM311K, XM551U, and XM651U.

LG

www.lg.com/us/tvs/lg-OLED55B6P-oled-4k-tv
LG C9PUA 55" OLED HDR UHD.

Panasonic

www.panasonic.com/in/business/broadcast/professional-monitors.html
Model currently available: BT-LH1770P.

SONY

https://pro.sony/ue_US/products/broadcast-monitors
Models currently available include: BVM-HX310 HDR, BVM-E251 OLED, BVM-E171+ HDR License BVML-HE171 HDR, PVM-X2400 HDR, PVM-X1800 HDR, LMD-A240 v3.0 HDR, LMD-A220 v3.0 HDR, LMD-A170 v3.0 HDR, LMD-B240, and LMD-B170.

TV Logic

www.tvlogic.tv/
Models currently available include: F-10A, LVM-095W-N, LVM-170A, LVM-171A, LVM-171S, LVM-171G, LVM-212W, LVM-232W-A, LVM-241S, LUM-242G, LUM-242H, LVM-246W, LUM-313G, LUM-318G, LUM-310R Rev 2, LUM-310X, and LVM-328W.

Monitors for DI Suite/Mastering

Canon DP-V3120 31-inch 4K HDR Reference Monitor

www.usa.canon.com/internet/portal/us/home/products/details/reference-displays/4k-uhd-reference-displays/dp-v3120

The Canon DP-V3120 31-inch 4K HDR Reference Monitor features 4096 × 2160 native resolution with standard 100 cd/m² brightness levels, as well as HDR productions with its peak 2000 cd/m², at 2,000,000:1 contrast ratio. It incorporates four 12G-SDI inputs and four 12G-SDI pass-through outputs. The monitor displays a 4K image from any one of its inputs, or you can use two inputs to create a dual view, or all four of the inputs to create a quad view on the monitor. You can also input an 8K image over the four 12G-SDI inputs, which the monitor will scale to 4K for display.

Figure 14.16 Canon DP-V3120 31-inch 4K HDR Reference Monitor.

Wide viewing area and anti-glare coating provide an image that can be viewed in less than ideal conditions and from off-axis without significantly compromising the image's contrast. The monitor supports ITU-R BT.2020, as well as ACES2065-1, and it exceeds the requirements for Dolby Vision-certified facilities. A LAN interface allows for control of the monitor's settings remotely. A built-in mode allows the monitor to automatically turn off its internal fan for a period of time when connected to a compatible camera, which makes the monitor suitable for on-set as well as post production work.

SONY BVM-HX310 30-inch 4K LCD Master Monitor

https://pro.sony/en_GB/products/broadcast promonitors/bvm-hx310

Figure 14.17 SONY BVM-HX310 30-inch 4K OLED Master Monitor.

The BVM-X300 30-inch 4K OLED Monitor for cinema applications and 4K color grading offers excellent black performance, accurate color reproduction, quick pixel response and wide viewing angle. BVM-X300 supports color gamuts including S-GAMUT3.cine and S-GAMUT3, DCI-P3, and most of the ITU-R BT.2020 standard, and S-Log3 which is optimized for live HDR production.

SONY's OLED panel resolution is 4K (4096 × 2160) pixels. The BVM-X300 can display formats including 4K, 2K, UHD, and HD at various frame rates. 3G/12G/HD-SDI quad link and dual link are supported for 4K/UHD and 3G/HD-SDI Single link and dual link supported for 2K/HD. XYZ signals as well as RGB and Y/CB/CR are also supported.

The BVM-X300 monitor can display an aspect marker, safe area marker, and center marker. When Rec 2020 colors out of Rec 709 or DCI-P3 color gamuts are detected, the monitor indicates them with a zebra pattern over the relevant area of the picture. Relative contrast modes (1/2, 1/3, and 1/4) allow HDR images to be monitored with higher peak luminance.

The BVM-X300 supports HDMI and both 2 Sample Interleave (2SI) and Square Division signals on SDI. HDMI support HD signals and 4K/UHD signals up to 50p 60p YCbCr 4:2:2 12-bit. It also supports HD signals including 3G-SDI single link for 1920 × 1080/50p 60p, YCbCr 4:2:2 10-bit, and 3G-SDI dual link for 1920 × 1080/50p 60p, 4:4:4 12/10-bit. 3G/HD-SDI quad link and dual link are supported for 4K/UHD and 3G/HD-SDI single link and dual link are supported for 2K/HD. XYZ signals as well as RGB and Y/CB/CR are supported. The BVM-X300 offers an interlace display feature for 1080i input. This enables the input to be presented as a true interlace display. As with the native scan function, interlace display mode offers faithful reproduction of the input signal, and the displayed interlace fields are free from the picture degradation that can occur as a result of typical I/P conversion processes.

Dolby Professional Reference Monitor PRM-4220

www.dolby.com/us/en/professional/cinema/products/prm-4220.html

Figure 14.18 Dolby® Professional Reference Monitor PRM-4220.

The Dolby® Professional Reference Monitor PRM-4220 displays the full dynamic range that the latest digital cameras can capture. It renders true blacks, accurate dark detail, and maintains linearity across the entire grayscale. The PRM-4220 displays DCI P3, all high-definition formats over HD-SDI, and 2K video content for accurate viewing of all image details in both the darks and highlights. It supports 10-bit video formats and emerging 12-bit formats without dithering or downscaling of the color gamut. As a color-grading monitor, the Dolby Professional Reference Monitor uses 3D LUTs to emulate the gamut and contrast ratio of film, as well as the color profile of digital cameras, making DCI P3 color grading possible without the use of a digital projector.

The 42-Inch flat panel display with 1920 × 1080 pixel resolution supports high frame rates (HFR) at 48 fps and 60 fps, delivers a wide viewing angle of 90 degrees horizontal (45 degrees on either side of the center point) and a refresh rate of 120 Hz. An external remote gives menu access to all features, functions, and parameters. Light Illusion© LightSpace Color Management System validates calibration, generates test patterns, and creates and loads 1D and 3D LUTs into the monitor via ethernet for monitor-matching, previs looks, and other LUT uses.

Digital Projection for Dailies, Previews, and Digital Cinema

It is always recommended to view dailies from shooting, the bigger the better. Projected dailies on a big screen can give the cinematographer and director needed feedback on exposure, noise floor, critical focus, framing, and performance. Projected dailies should always be viewed on a calibrated projector that is at least HD resolution, in a properly set up screening room, and on a cinema quality projection screen. There is an enormous selection of projector choices that serve this purpose, so it does not serve the reader of this book to recommend specifics beyond saying that cinema quality projectors are widely available. There are numerous manufacturers who have been building cinema quality digital projectors for many years. Here is a very small sampling of projector manufacturers making projectors for both location based dailies viewing, and for high end DCI compliant digital intermediate color correction. There are *many* projectors available for this work!

Barco Projectors

www.barco.com/en/products/cinema-projectors
Current models available include: UDX-4K26, UDX-W22, UDX-W40, UDX-4K40, UDX-U40, UDX-4K22, UDX-W22, UDX-W26, UDX-4K32, UDX-W32, and XDL-4K60.

Christie Projectors

www.christiedigital.com/products/projectors/cinema/
Current models available include: CP4450-RGB, CP4440-RGB, CP4330-RGB, CP4320-RGB, CP4315-RGB, CP2320-RGB, CP2315-RGB, CP2309-RGB, CP4230, CP4220, CP2230, CP2220, CP2215, CP2308, and Christie Duo.

NEC Projectors

www.nec-display.com/ap/en_projector/dlpcinema/index.html
Current models available include: NC1000C, NC1200C, NC1201L-A, NC1700L, NC1802ML, NC2000C, NC2002ML, NC2041L, NC2402 ML, NC3200S, NC3240S-A, NC3540LS, and NC3541L.

Panasonic Projectors

https://panasonic.net/cns/projector/products/lineup/

Current models include PT-RQ50K, PT-RQ32K, PT-RZ31K Series, PT-RQ22K, PT-Rz21K Series, PT-RQ13K/RZ12K Series, and PT-DZ21K2 Series.

SONY Projectors

https://pro.sony/en_GB/products/4k-digital-cinema-projection
Current models include: SRX-R815P, SRX-515P, SRX 510P, and 3D dual projector packages of each.

Recorders

Here is a short product survey of many of the choices of recorders and record media currently available for use in digital motion picture production.

AJA Ki Pro

www.aja.com/family/digital-recorders

Figure 14.19 AJA Ki Pro GO Recorder Multi Channel H.264 Recorder.

Figure 14.20 AJA Ki Pro Ultra Plus Multi-Channel HD Recorder 4K / UltraHD / 2K / HD Recorder and Player.

Figure 14.21 AJA Ki Pro Rack File Based 1RU Recorder and Player.

Blackmagic Design

www.blackmagicdesign.com/products

Figure 14.22 Blackmagic Design UltraStudio Mini Recorder.

Figure 14.23 Blackmagic Design HyperDeck Shuttle 2 Recorder.

Figure 14.24 Blackmagic Design HyperDeck Studio Recorder.

Figure 14.25 Blackmagic Design Hyperdeck Studio Pro Recorder.

Figure 14.26 Blackmagic Design Hyperdeck Studio 12G Recorder.

Figure 14.27 Blackmagic Design Hyperdeck Extreme 8K Recorder and Control.

Codex Digital

https://codex.online/products/media

Codex recorders are high-resolution media recording systems, designed to capture pictures and sound from digital cinematography cameras. Codex products used a touchscreen interface and removable "data packs" containing up to 10TB of RAID array disk storage. Codex XR capture drives historically captured data at up to 800MB/s, and the technology has subsequently been upgraded to support the requirements of the ALEXA 65 camera, with Codex SXR capture drives able to sustain 2500MB/s. Codex uses a "Virtual File System" meaning that when the recorded files are accessed, they can be viewed in a number of different resolutions and formats.

Codex supports ARRI cameras with built-in recording solutions, and they also recently partnered with Canon on an integrated recording solution for the Canon C700 camera and with Panasonic on the VariCam Pure camera.

Figure 14.28 Canon CDX-36150 Codex Digital RAW Recorder for EOS C700.

Figure 14.29 Codex partnered with Panasonic on the AU–VCXRAW2 Codex Digital RAW Recording solution for Varicam Pure offering uncompressed RAW on-board recording.

Figure 14.30 Codex Digital Capture Drives, Compact Capture Drives, and Capture Drives SXR.

Figure 14.31 Codex Digital Capture Drive Dock.

Figure 14.32 Codex Digital Compact Capture Drive Dock.

Figure 14.33 Codex Digital Transfer Drive Dock.

Figure 14.34 Codex Digital Capture + Transfer Drive Dock.

Figure 14.35 Codex Digital Compact Drive Reader.

Figure 14.36 Codex Digital Capture Drive Adapter for Compact Drive.

Panasonic Recorders

Panasonic P2 Media
https://pro-av.panasonic.net/en/products/accessories/memory_card.html

| 512GB B Series | 256GB B Series | 256GB A Series | microP2 64G |
| AU-XP0512BG | AU-XP0256BG | AU-XP0256AG | AJ-P2M064B |

Figure 14.37 Panasonic P2 Solid State Memory Media Cards.

Introduced in 1994, Panasonic P2 Solid State Memory Media Cards P2 (Professional Plugin) cards are a professional solid-state digital recording storage media.

- ExpressP2 for recording 4K and high frame rates.
- MicroP2 for Sub recording.
- B Series offer a 4× faster off load vs. A Series when used with the AU-XPD3 Reader.
- Standard reader AU-XPD1 USB3 support.
- High Speed Offload Reader AU-XPD3 Thunder Bolt 3 support.

It is recommended to write protect the P2 media before mounting in a computer! Always format cards in camera. Do not use any media cards smaller than 64G. This is required to support cine file naming structure.

RED Mini Mag

www.red.com/

RED DIGITAL CINEMA RED MINI-MAGs have 960GB record capacity. They are compatible with most RED cameras and on select cameras can attain write speeds as high as 300 MB/s. The RED MINI-MAG can support simultaneous R3D and Apple ProRes recording, when used with DSMC2 camera systems. RED MINI-MAGs are encased in aluminum and offer a compact form factor compatible with DSMC2 camera systems, the RED MINI-MAGs require a RED MINI-MAG Side SSD Module for use with RED EPIC or SCARLET BRAIN. The RED MINI-MAG system requires DSMC firmware v5.1.34 or later.

Figure 14.38 Red Mini Mag Media and Red Station Reader.

SONY On Camera Recorders

https://pro.sony/ue_US/products/broadcast-and-production

Figure 14.39 SONY SRR4 Dockable Memory Recorder for the SONY F65.

Figure 14.40 SONY AXS-R7 RAW Recorder for SONY PMW-F55 and F5

Figure 14.41 SONY SR-R1 Portable Memory Recorder for HD-SDI Cameras.

SONY SxS Cards

https://pro.sony/ue_US/products/memory-card

Figure 14.42 SxS and AXS Solid State Memory Cards

SxS cards are a flash memory card ExpressCard standard record media. According to Sandisk and SONY, the cards have transfer rates of 800 Mbits/second and burst transfer rate of up to 2.5 Gbits/second. SONY uses these cards as the storage media for the XDCAM EX line of cameras, and ARRI use SxS Pro cards for their onboard Pro Res compressed recording solution.

The XDCAM EX series of cameras originally adopted the SxS memory card as its recording media. This is an ultra-compact nonlinear medium using flash memory, compatible with the Express-Card/34 standard (most new Macintosh and PC computers are equipped with ExpressCard slots), and they use the PCI Express interface for a high data transfer speed. SxS PRO+ is a faster version of SxS designed for the recording of SONY 4K resolution cameras, the SONY PMW-F55, and SONY PMW-F5. SxS Pro+ has a guaranteed minimum recording speed of 1.3 Gbits/second and an interface with a theoretical maximum speed of 8 Gbit/s. The XAVC recording format can record 4K resolution at 60 fps with 4:2:2 chroma subsampling at 600 Mbit/s. A 256 Gigabyte SxS PRO+ media card can record up to 40 minutes of 4K resolution XAVC video at 60 fps, up to 80 minutes of 4K resolution XAVC video at 30 fps, and up to 240 minutes of 2K resolution XAVC video at 30 fps.

SONY's AXS Memory A-Series Cards are designed for use with CineAlta PMW-F55, Cine-Alta PMW-F5, PXW-FS7, and NEX-FS700 cameras, and with their AXS-R7 4K Portable Memory Recorder, AXS-R5 2K/4K Raw Recorder, AXS-CR1 USB 3.0 AXS Memory Card Reader using the AXS Memory Card Adapter, and AXS-AR1 Thunderbolt card Reader. Capable of capturing 4K and 2K 16-bit linear raw video, 512GB and 1TB AXS Memory A-Series Cards deliver write speeds of 4.8 Gb/s, and are able to capture high frame rate (HFR) video up to 120 fps in 4K and up to 240 fps in 2K when used with the AXS-R7 Portable Memory Recorder and the CineAlta VENICE and PMW-F55.

Sound Devices Pix 270i

www.sounddevices.com/product/pix-270i/

Figure 14.43 Pix 270i Recorder.

Vision Research CineMag and CineStation

www.phantomhighspeed.com/products/toolsandaccessories/cinemagandcinestation

The CineMag V is a proprietary storage device incorporating secure, removable, non-volatile flash memory for high-speed Phantom raw footage. At speeds up to 1.4Gpx/sec the CineMag V is the fastest data transfer solution for Phantom cameras. Users can record into camera RAM and then upload the recording to the CineMag, eliminating camera down time between shots. If an application demands longer record times, then the CineMag can be used in Run/Stop (R/S) mode, allowing for several minutes of record time at lower frame rates. CineMag Features include Loop Mode, Auto-Save, Direct-Record (Run/Stop) Mode, and Playback over SDI.

The Phantom CineStation is the download station for the CineMag. CineStation connects to a PC running Phantom PCC software via Gb or 10Gb Ethernet. The user can view each Cine stored on the CineMag, set in- and out-points to trim the Cines, and save the files to a connected hard drive.

Figure 14.44 Vision Research CineMag V and Vision Research CineStation.

Chapter 15

File Formats, Log Encoding, Data, and Compression

Motion Picture Image File Types

Cineon/DPX

The Cineon project was responsible for the creation of the Cineon (.cin) 10-bit log file format, designed to hold individual digital film frames. The Cineon file format became the basis for the later SMPTE standardized Digital Picture Exchange (.dpx) format. The Cineon image file format is very similar to the ANSI/SMPTE DPX file format, and they are for all intents and purposes used interchangeably. Both file formats have variable metadata header (headers are the part of a picture file that contain the metadata about what the file is and how to use it) lengths and share the same format for the image data. However, the format of the headers is different. DPX file headers are more flexible, allowing variable image headers to accommodate the needs of different industries by carrying more information about the picture, while the Cineon file format is more specific to digital film scanned images. Neither Cineon nor DPX is considered a container. When Cineon or DPX files are enclosed in a folder, a software player can play them out in numerical order as a series of single frames.

OpenEXR

OpenEXR is a high dynamic range single frame file format released as an open standard along with a set of software tools created by Industrial Light & Magic (ILM), under a free software license. It is notable for supporting multiple channels of potentially different pixel sizes, including 32-bit unsigned integer, 32-bit and 16-bit floating point values, as well as various compression techniques which include lossless and lossy algorithms. OpenEXR is the file format used in an ACES environment.

A full technical introduction of the format is available on the OpenEXR website. OpenEXR is broadly used in the computer-graphics industry, both in visual effects and animation. OpenEXR's multi-resolution and arbitrary channel format makes it appealing for compositing; as it can store arbitrary channels – specular, diffuse, alpha, RGB, normals, and various other types – in one file, it takes away the need to store this information in separate files. OpenEXR's Application Programming Interface makes tools development easy for developers. Since there are almost never two identical production pipelines, custom tools always need to be developed to address problems, e.g. image manipulation issues. OpenEXR's library allows quick and easy access to the image's attributes such as tiles and channels.

RAW File Formats

A camera RAW image file contains minimally processed image data from a Bayer pattern image sensor in a digital motion picture camera. RAW files are not yet ready to be viewed or edited until the image is processed by a RAW converter into a wide-gamut internal color space where precise adjustments can be made before deBayering into a usable image file format. There are dozens of raw formats in use by different manufacturers of digital image capture equipment.

A RAW digital image usually holds a wider dynamic range and color gamut than the resulting deBayered frame it will parent; the purpose of RAW image formats is to save, with minimum loss, the data obtained from the sensor. Raw image formats are intended to capture the scene-referred radiometric characteristics of the scene, the physical information about the light intensity and color of the scene, at the highest level of the camera sensor's performance.

RAW files contain a file header which conveys the byte ordering of the file, a file identifier and an offset into the main file data, camera sensor size, and color profile map of the Bayer pattern Color Filter Array (CFA) required to assign discrete colors to the sensor image data. They also contain image metadata required including exposure settings, camera and lens model, date, time, and place, authoring information, and an image thumbnail (a JPEG or other temp conversion of the image), which is used to view the file on the camera's viewfinder.

TIFF – Tagged Image File Format

TIFF is an image file format for storing raster graphics images, popular among graphic artists, the publishing industry, and photographers. TIFF is widely supported by many graphics applications and in digital motion picture production. Several Aldus or Adobe technical notes have been published with minor extensions to the format, and several specifications have been based on TIFF 6.0. TIFF is a flexible, adaptable file format for handling images and data within a single file, by including the header tags (size, definition, image-data arrangement, applied image compression) defining the image's geometry. A TIFF file, for example, can be a container holding JPEG (lossy compressed) and PackBits (lossless compressed) images. A TIFF file also can include a vector based clipping path (outlines, croppings, image frames). The ability to store image data in a lossless format makes a TIFF file a useful image archive, because, unlike standard JPEG files, a TIFF file using lossless compression (or none) may be edited and re-saved without losing image quality. This is not the case when using the TIFF as a container holding compressed JPEG. Other TIFF options are layers and pages. TIFF offers the option of using LZW compression, a lossless data-compression technique for reducing a file's size. TIFF file formatted images are used in the creation of a digital cinema package (DCP).

Log Functions

As we learned in Chapter 1, our eyes perceive brightness differently than an electronic sensor does. Most cameras used in digital cinematography employ a logarithmic encoding to efficiently capture and preserve the full dynamic range of the sensor for later color correction. The practice of log encoding in digital cinema cameras evolved out of Kodak's Cineon system, which scanned film into a log format that corresponded to the

density of the original film. The most significant advantage of log encoding is that it yields a huge increase in dynamic range captured for a nominal increase in file storage size. Rec 709 video gamma encoding 2.4 (as specified in ITU-R BT.1886), is designed to produce pleasing images on the limited dynamic range of video monitors, but there is a limit to how much scene dynamic range can be compressed into a video signal. The same image recorded in a log encoding holds considerably more usable color information over the entire exposure range.

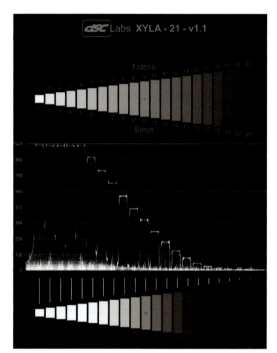

Figure 15.1 Log encoding maximizes dynamic range from sensors.

Figure 15.1 shows that when presented with a grayscale chart with 21 stops of latitude, this particular digital sensor can capture 14+ stops of latitude from the middle of the chart. The first four stops are clipped, the last four stops are indistinguishable in black, and middle gray is at about 38%. A real-world camera is constrained by the full well capacity saturation point of its photosites at the bright end of the scale, and by the noise floor of the sensor at the dark end of the tonal scale.

Each brand of camera uses a tailored custom log transfer function developed by its manufacturer to preserve the most dynamic range and latitude through a workflow and into color correction. Logarithmic curves from one camera to another are very different, tuned to the sensor design, and the function of a custom log curve is to preserve the full dynamic range of that camera. SONY uses S-Log, S-Log2, and S-Log 3, ARRI uses LogC, RED uses RED Log 3 G10, RED Gamma 3, RED Gamma 4, RED Log Film, and Panasonic uses V-Log. Each of these log curves has been designed to preserve as much information as possible from a specific sensor design, and make it easily usable during color correction.

Table 15.1 IRE and code values for black, middle gray and white for various log encodings

Log/Gamma Encoding Function	0.0088% Black (–13 stops) – IRE %	0% Black 10-Bit Code Value	18% Gray IRE %	18% Gray 10-Bit Code Value	90% White – IRE %	90% White 10-Bit Code Value
ARRI Log C (Sup 2.x)	8.00%	134	38.4%	400	58.00%	569
ARRI Log C (3.x & 4.x)	3.60%	95	38.4%	400	58.00%	572
Blackmagic 4.6K Film	1.00%	75	41.0%	420	68.00%	664
Blackmagic 4K Film	4.00%	95	38.0%	400	78.00%	743
Blackmagic Film	4.00%	95	38.0%	400	66.00%	642
Canon Log	7.30%	128	32.8%	351	62.80%	614
Canon Log 2	3.60%	95	39.2%	408	58.40%	575
Canon Log 3	7.00%	128	31.3%	351	59.00%	577
Cineon Film Log	3.54%	95	46.0%	481	70.90%	685
DJI D Log	0.00%	64	39.3%	498	86.00%	814
Gamma 2.2	0.00%	64	40.9%	444	100.00%	940
Gamma 2.6	0.00%	64	54.0%	536	100.00%	940
Linear	0.00%	64	18.0%	239	100.00%	940
Panasonic V Log	7.30%	128	42.1%	433	61.00%	602
Rec BT 709	0.00%	64	40.9%	444	101.10%	940
Rec 2100 HLG	0.00%	64	22.0%	260	50.00%	502
RED Log 3 G10	3.40%	94	31.6%	341	49.20%	495
RED Gamma 3	4.00%	95	45.0%	455	77.00%	736
RED Gamma 4	1.00%	72	45.0%	457	81.00%	778
RED Log Film	3.54%	95	46.1%	481	70.90%	685
SONY S Log	3.00%	90	37.6%	394	65.40%	637
SONY S Log 2	3.00%	90	32.3%	347	59.20%	582
SONY S Log 3	3.60%	95	40.6%	420	60.90%	598
sRGB	0.00%	64	48.0%	488	100.00%	940

Waveform Monitoring for Log Signals

Reading a Rec 709 signal from a monitor output, middle gray sits at 40.9%. As a cautionary note, standard dynamic range wave form monitors are not scaled to read log encoded signals. Using middle gray to set exposure from a log signal on an SDR wave form monitor is impractical unless one is familiar with the 18% gray numbers that one should expect to see when displaying each log function.

Figure 15.2 Log signal of a Chroma du Monde viewed on a monitor.

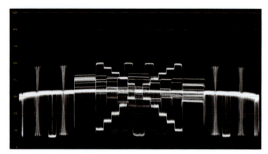

Figure 15.3 Log signal of Chroma du Monde viewed on a waveform monitor.

Gray cards and grayscales yield a wide variety of waveform graphs when viewed uncorrected and unlutted on a Rec 709 waveform monitor. It is valuable to closely examine the portion of the various log graphs where the values cross the 18% middle gray line. A closer graph of log encoding functions shows that for the various encodings, 18% reflectance varies widely in code value.

Log Functions in Detail

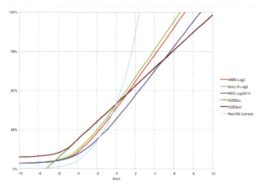

Figure 15.4 Sample of camera encoding log curve plots from –10 through +10 stops as a percentage of scene luminance vs. stops of light.

It is valuable to closely examine the portion of log plots where the values cross the 18% middle

gray line. The closer graph of log encoding functions shows that for the various encodings, 18% reflectance varies widely in luminance. Wave form monitors are not scaled to read log encoded signals. Using middle gray to set exposure is difficult when a log signal is presented on a wave form monitor unless one is familiar with these 18% gray numbers. It is very useful to view a Rec 709 signal through a monitor out from the camera using a gray card if one is armed with the knowledge that true middle gray for Rec 709 sits at 40.9%.

Also, exposing a green or blue screen for middle gray optimizes color saturation for the green record on a green screen, or the blue record on a blue screen. Darker than that increases the amount of noise in the mattes, and brighter than that increases the amount of red and blue contamination in a green screen, or green and red in a blue screen. The idea of color difference matting is to minimize noise and maximize color difference, and middle gray is that crossover point for either a blue screen or a green screen. For true Rec 709, that crossover point is 40.9%, and for log encodings it varies from camera to camera depending on the log encoding being used.

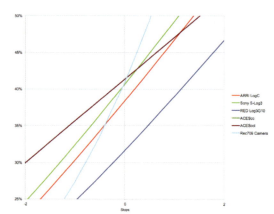

Figure 15.5 Closer on middle section of sample of log curve plots Figure 15.4 showing that 18% middle gray is different for every encoding!

Table 15.2 A guide to 18% middle gray values for a variety of log encodings when viewed on an SDR waveform monitor set to REC 709

Stop	Linear Light (% Reflectance)	ARRI LogC	Canon Log	Canon Log2	Canon Log3	DJI Dlog
0	0.1800	38.3540%	32.7954%	39.2026%	31.3435%	39.2621%
Panasonic Vlog	**Rec709**	**RED Log3G10**	**REDlogfilm**	**SonyS-Log**	**SonyS-Log2**	**SonyS-Log3**
42.1287%	40.9008%	31.6210%	46.0992%	37.6074%	32.3062%	40.6393%

Interfaces and Data Transport Streams

Serial digital interface (SDI) and high definition mechanical interface (HDMI) are digital video interfaces used for transmission of digital video signals including embedded audio and time code over hard wired electronic (and sometimes fiber optic) connections. A transport streams specifies a container format encapsulating packetized elementary streams with error correction and a synchronization pattern for maintaining transmission integrity when the channel carrying the stream is degraded. Program streams are designed for reasonably reliable media, such as DVDs while transport streams are designed for less reliable transmissions like terrestrial or satellite broadcasts. A transport stream may carry multiple programs.

HDSDI

Serial digital interface (SDI) is a family of digital video interfaces first standardized by the Society of Motion Picture and Television Engineers in 1989. ITU-R BT.656 and SMPTE 259M define digital video interfaces used for broadcast video.

A related standard, known as high-definition serial digital interface (HD-SDI), is standardized in SMPTE 292M to provide a data rate of 1.485 Gbit/s.

Additional SDI standards have been introduced to support increasing video resolutions (HD, UHD, and beyond), frame rates, stereoscopic (3D) video, and increased color depth. Dual link HD-SDI consists of a pair of SMPTE 292M links, standardized by SMPTE 372M in 1998 to provide a 2.970 Gbit/s interface for use in applications such as digital cinema or HDTV 1080P that require greater fidelity and resolution than standard HDTV can provide.

3G-SDI was standardized in SMPTE 424M and consists of a single 2.970 Gbit/s serial link that allows replacing dual link HD-SDI. 6G-SDI and 12G-SDI standards were published on March 19, 2015. These standards are used for passage and transmission of uncompressed digital video signals including embedded audio and time code.

SDI and HD-SDI are usually available only in professional video equipment because licensing agreements restrict the use of unencrypted digital interfaces in consumer equipment.

Table 15.3 HD SDI bit rates

Standard	Name	From	Bit Rates	Video Formats
SMPTE 259M	SD-SDI	1989	270 Mbits/s, 360 Mbits/s, 143 Mbits/s, & 177 Mbits/s	480i, 576i
SMPTE 344M	ED-SDI	2000	540 Mbits/s	480p, 576p
SMPTE 292M	HD-SDI	1998	1.485 Gbits/s and 1.485/1.001 Gbits/s	720p, 1080i
SMPTE 372M	Dual Link HD-SDI	2002	2.970 Gbits/s and 2.970/1.001 Gbits/s	1080p 60
SMPTE 424M	3G-SDI	2006	2.970 Gbits/s and 2.970/1.001 Gbits/s	1080p 60
SMPTE ST-2081	6G-SDI	2015	6 Gbits/s	1080p 120, 2160p 30
SMPTE ST-2082	12G-SDI	2015	12 Gbits/s	2160p 60
SMPTE ST-2083	24G-SDI	In Dev.	24 Gbits/s	2160p 120, 4320p 30

HDMI

HDMI (high-definition multimedia interface) is an audio/video interface for transmitting video and audio signals from an HDMI source device, such as a graphics card to a compatible computer monitor, video projector, television or digital audio device. HDMI is a digital replacement for analog video standards.

HDMI implements EIA/CEA-861 standards, which define video formats and waveforms, transport of compressed and uncompressed audio, auxiliary data, and implementations of the VESA EDID. CEA-861 signals carried by HDMI are electrically compatible with the CEA-861 signals also used by the digital video interface (DVI). No signal conversion is necessary, nor is there a loss of video quality when a

DVI-to-HDMI adapter is used. Several versions of HDMI have been developed and deployed since the initial release of the technology, but all use the same cable and connector.

Codecs, Containers, and Wrappers

Codec stands for *EnCode/Decode* and usually refers to a "file wrapper/container" system. A file wrapper/container is a multiplexing (or muxing as it is sometimes referred) scheme that enables video, audio, FX, titles, metadata, and a myriad of other digital resources to play out synchronously. Numerous wrapper/containers have been designed by a wide variety of hardware and software builders for everything from internet content to DVD, to Blu-ray, to digital cinema exhibition.

A container or wrapper defines the type of file it is, as identified by the file extension, like .mpeg, .mov, .mp4, .mxf, .m4v, etc. A container or wrapper format is a metafile format that defines how different elements of data and metadata function and interact in a computer file. Most container formats are specialized for use with multimedia file formats. Since audio, video, data, and text streams can be coded and decoded with many different algorithms, a wrapper or container format is used to present the multiple media files that go into that container as what appears to be a single file to the user.

MXF

Material exchange format (MXF) is a wrapper/container format for professional digital video and audio media defined by a set of SMPTE standards. MXF supports a number of different streams of media files encoded in any of a variety of video and audio compression formats, together with a metadata wrapper which describes the material contained within the MXF file, and timecode support. MXF was developed to carry a subset of the advanced authoring format (AAF) data, enabling MXF/AAF workflows between non-linear editing (NLE) systems using AAF and cameras, servers, and other devices. It is designed as a platform-agnostic stable standard for future professional video and audio applications.

MXF is in the process of evolving from standard to deployment, and the breadth of the standard can lead to interoperability problems as vendors implement different parts of the standard. There are an increasing number of professional non-linear editing systems that can work with MXF files natively, including Avid Media Composer, Adobe Premier 3.1 or higher, DaVinci Resolve, SONY Vegas Pro, Grass Valley Edius, and Final Cut Pro X.

Quicktime

QuickTime is an extensible multimedia wrapper/container framework that was developed by Apple Computer for handling a variety of digital video formats, pictures, and sound. The format specifies a multimedia container file that could contain multiple tracks to store data, audio, video, or text.

QuickTime has been available free of charge for both mac OS and Windows operating systems. There are some other free player applications that rely on the QuickTime framework, for example, iTunes can export audio in WAV, AIFF, MP3, AAC, and Apple Lossless file formats. Apple's professional applications Final Cut Studio and Logic Studio also included a QuickTime Pro license. Features enabled by the Pro license included editing clips through the cut, copy, and paste functions, merging separate audio and video tracks, and freely placing the video tracks on a virtual canvas with the options of cropping and rotation. Other features included, saving and encoding to any of the codecs supported by QuickTime. QuickTime 7 included presets for exporting video to a video-capable iPod, iPhone, or Apple TV, and saving as source. Another option allowed the user to save as QuickTime movie, to save the embedded video in a .mov file format no matter what the original container was.

QuickTime 7 is still available for download from Apple, but as of mid 2016, Apple ended support for the Windows version of QuickTime in 2016 and stopped selling registration keys for the Pro version. Apple ended support for QuickTime 7 and QuickTime Pro in 2018, and updated their download and support pages stating that QuickTime 7 "will not be compatible with future macOS releases."

Apple ProRes Codecs

Apple ProRes is a high quality, lossy video compression codec format developed by Apple Inc. for use in production and post production that supports up to 8K. The ProRes family of codecs use compression algorithms based on the discrete cosine transformation (DCT) techniques inside a Quicktime wrapper. ProRes is widely used as a final format delivery wrapper for HD broadcast files in commercials, features, Blu-ray, and streaming. ProRes is a line of intermediate codecs intended for use during acquisition, editing, but not for exhibition.

ProRes RAW provides a new standard compression for RAW Footage. The ProRes RAW algorithm creates smaller video file size, while retaining the high quality video data rates and editing capabilities, of the original uncompressed RAW video. This gives the user file sizes even smaller than the original ProRes formats, while still retaining the high quality level to be expected of working from RAW files.

Apple ProRes 4444 XQ is a very high quality version of ProRes for 4:4:4 image sources (including alpha channels), with a very high data rate to preserve the detail in high-dynamic-range imagery generated by today's highest-quality digital image sensors.

Apple ProRes 4444 XQ preserves dynamic ranges several times greater than the dynamic range of Rec 709 imagery – even against the rigors of extreme visual effects processing, in which the tone-scale of blacks or highlights may be stretched significantly. Like standard Apple ProRes 4444, this codec supports up to 12 bits per image channel and up to 16 bits for the alpha channel. Apple ProRes 4444 XQ features a target data rate of approximately 500 Mbps for 4:4:4 sources at 1920 × 1080 and 29.97 fps.

Apple ProRes 4444 is an extremely high-quality version of ProRes for 4:4:4 image sources (including alpha channels). This codec features full-resolution, mastering-quality 4:4:4 RGBA color and visual fidelity that is perceptually indistinguishable from the original material. Apple ProRes 4444 is a high-quality solution for storing and exchanging motion graphics and composites, with excellent multigeneration performance and a mathematically lossless alpha channel up to 16 bits. This codec features a remarkably low data rate compared to uncompressed 4:4:4 HD, with a target data rate of approximately 330 Mbps for 4:4:4 sources at 1920 × 1080 and 29.97 fps. It also offers direct encoding of, and decoding to, both RGB and Y'CBCR pixel formats.

A gamma correction setting is in the codec's advanced compression settings pane, which allows you to disable the 1.8 to 2.2 gamma adjustment that can occur if RGB material at 2.2 gamma is misinterpreted as 1.8. This setting is also available with the Apple ProRes 422 codec.

Apple ProRes 422 (HQ) codec offers the utmost possible quality for 4:2:2 or 4:2:0 sources (without an alpha channel) and also provides target data rate of approximately 220 Mbps (1920 × 1080 at 60i).

The Apple ProRes 422 codec provides a target data rate of approximately 145 Mbps (1920 × 1080 at 60i).

The Apple ProRes 422 (LT) codec provides roughly 70% of the data rate of Apple ProRes 422 (thus, smaller file sizes than Apple ProRes 422).

The Apple ProRes 422 (Proxy) codec is intended for use in offline workflows and provides roughly 30% of the data rate of Apple ProRes 422, high-quality offline editing at the original frame size, frame rate, and aspect ratio, and high-quality edit proxies for Final Cut Server.

REDCODE RAW

RED's proprietary wrapper/container and file format, REDCODE RAW encodes image data in a way that maximizes post production capabilities. REDCODE's efficiency helps increase image quality in smaller file sizes. REDCODE plays a critical role in managing the massive amounts of data contained in up to 8K images. RAW image capture maximizes image fidelity and preserves post production flexibility. REDCODE RAW provides tunable file sizes for superior image quality and lower storage requirements. REDCODE enables a RAW workflow with non-destructive editing, which is supported by all of the major post production software packages including Adobe, Apple, Avid, DaVinci Resolve, and others. Because the files are RAW, additional metadata is available. This gives content creators a window in to how the image was shot while preserving any relevant metadata for the post production process.

Cinema DNG

CinemaDNG is an Adobe-led open file format and wrapper container for digital cinema files. CinemaDNG is a wrapper for sequences of raw video images, accompanied by audio and metadata. CinemaDNG supports stereoscopic cameras and multiple audio channels. CinemaDNG specifies directory structures containing one or more video clips, and specifies requirements and constraints for the open format files (DNG, TIFF, XMP, and/or MXF), within those directories, that contain the content of those clips. CinemaDNG images are encoded with the Adobe DNG (digital negative) format used for still cameras. The image stream can then be stored in one of two formats: either as video essence using frame-based wrapping in an MXF file, or as a sequence of DNG image files in a specified file directory.

Avid DNx Codecs

There are a number of compression level and file size options available for cutting a project on

Avid editing systems, depending on budget, the eventual target screen of the project (TV, wide screen, etc.) and the editor's preference.

Avid DNxHD 444 provides the highest color fidelity and image quality in 1920 × 1080 progressive projects. Full resolution, 10-bit 4:4:4 RGB video sampling, and high bit-rate is excellent for multi-generational finishing and mastering. Absence of subsampling or averaging of chroma information preserves the original color information and ensures visually lossless compression.

Avid DNxHD 220x gives superior quality image in a YCbCr-color space for 10-bit sources. Data rate is dependent on frame rate. For example, 220 Mbps is the data rate for 1920 × 1080 30 fps interlace sources (60 fields) while progressive sources at 24 fps will be 175 Mbps

Avid DNxHD 220 works for high quality image when using 8-bit color sources. Data rates based on frame rates are the same as for Avid DNxHD 220x.

Avid DNxHD 145 is for high-quality mastering when using 8-bit lower data rate sources such as HDCAM and DVCPRO. 145 Mbps is the data rate for 1920 × 1080 30 fps interlaced sources (60 fields). Progressive sources at 24 fps will be 115 Mbps and at 25 fps will be 120Mbps.

Avid DNxHD 100 is for optimal visual impact where workflow speed and storage capacity are important factors. Suitable replacement for DV100 compression and offers lower processing overhead than AVC-Intra 50/100. DNxHD 100 subsamples the video raster from 1920 to 1440 or from 1280 to 960 to reduce compression artifacts, providing a balance of reduced compressed bandwidth and visual quality.

Avid DNxHD 36 is for high-quality offline editing of HD progressive sources only. Designed for projects using an offline/online workflow due to large quantities of source media and/or needing more real-time preview streams for craft editorial or multi camera editing.

Other Video Wrapper/Containers

AVI – the standard Microsoft Windows video wrapper/container.

CineForm RAW – an open source video codec and wrapper/container developed for CineForm Inc and acquired by GoPro for its 3D HERO System.

DVR – MS Microsoft Digital Video Recording, another video wrapper/container format developed by Microsoft.

Flash Video – (FLV, F4V) a wrapper/container for video and audio from Adobe.

IFF – a platform-independent video wrapper/container format.

Matroska – (MKV) an open source container format.

Motion JPEG 2000 – (MJ2) is a file format and wrapper/container, based on the ISO base media file format which is defined in MPEG-4 Part 12 and JPEG 2000 Part 12.

MPEG-1 and MPEG-2 wrapper/containers – MPEG-1 is used on DVD-Video discs. MPEG-2 is used on Blu-ray Discs.

MP4 – a standard audio and video wrapper/container for MPEG-4 media based on the ISO base media file format defined in MPEG-4 Part 12 and JPEG 2000 Part 12 (which was based on the QuickTime file format).

Real Media – (RM), a standard wrapper/container for RealVideo and RealAudio.

Image Compression

Digital motion image production generates an enormous amount of data. Camera builders have often seen the size of this data load as an impediment to the adoption of their cameras for general use, so many have invested a great amount of time, effort, and resource into creating compression schemes for recording cameras to lighten

Table 15.4 Editorial codecs compared in bandwidth

Editorial Codecs Bit Rate Comparison			
Format	Bit Depth	Sampling	Bandwidth
Apple ProRes 4444	10-bit	4:4:4:4 Sampling	330MB/sec
Apple ProRes 422 HQ	8-Bit	4:2:2 Sampling	220MB/sec
Apple ProRes 422	8-Bit	4:2:2 Sampling	145MB/sec
Apple ProRes 422 LT	8-Bit	4:2:2 Sampling	100 MB/sec
Apple ProRes Proxy	8-Bit	4:2:2 Sampling	44 MB/sec
Avid DNxHD 36	8-Bit	4:2:2 Sampling	36 MB/sec
Avid DNxHD 100	8-Bit	4:2:2 Sampling	100 MB/sec
Avid DNxHD 145	8-Bit	4:2:2 Sampling	145 MB/sec
Avid DNxHD 220	8- and 10-Bit	4:2:2 Sampling	220 MB/sec
Avid DNxHD 444	10Bit	4:4:4 Sampling	440 MB/sec

that data load. The debates over the advantages and drawbacks of these compression schemes have resulted in a wide variety of compression codecs, mechanisms, and ratios.

Image compression comes in two kinds, lossy and lossless. Uncompressed or at worst, lossless compression is preferred for archival. Lossy compression is more suitable for images where some minor loss of fidelity or resolution is acceptable in the name of substantially reducing bit rate and file size. Lossy compression that produces negligible differences may be called visually lossless. Here are a few examples:

Chroma Subsampling

Chroma subsampling is a lossy compression that takes advantage of the fact that the human eye perceives changes in brightness more acutely than changes of color. It works by averaging or dropping some of the chrominance information in the image. The green or Y luminance channel is sampled at full bandwidth, but the chroma channels Cb and Cr are sampled at lower bandwidth and applied to a larger image area. Chroma subsampling assumes that red and blue can be sampled at lower resolution (Cb as plus blue and minus blue values and Cr as plus red and minus red values) and then be given the appearance of greater apparent resolution by the detail in the luminance channel.

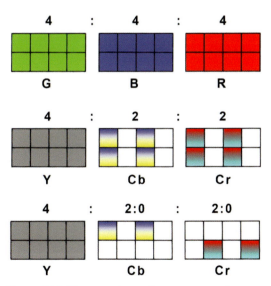

Figure 15.6 Chroma subsampling arrangements.

H.264 (MPEG-4 AVC)

H.264 (MPEG-4 AVC) is one of the most commonly used lossy discrete cosine transformation (DCT) compression formats for recording, compression, and distribution of video content. H.264 is a "family of standards" composed of a number of different profiles, used on Blu-ray discs and some satellite TV broadcasts, and supports resolutions up to 8K UHD.

High Efficiency Video Coding (HEVC, H.265, and MPEG-H Part 2)

High Efficiency Video Coding (HEVC, H.265) is a newer video compression standard designed as a successor to the widely used H.264 or MPEG-4 Part 10, AVC. In comparison to AVC, HEVC offers from 25% to 50% better data compression at the same level of video quality, or substantially improved video quality at the same bit rate. It also supports resolutions up to 8192 × 4320, and unlike the primarily 8-bit AVC, HEVC's higher fidelity Main10 profile has been incorporated into nearly all supporting hardware.

JPEG 2000 Wavelet Compression

JPEG 2000 (JP2) was created by the Joint Photographic Experts Group in 2000 with the intention of superseding their original DCT based JPEG standard with a newly designed, wavelet based method. JPEG 2000 code streams are regions of interest that offer several mechanisms to support spatial random access or region of interest access at varying degrees of granularity. It is possible to store different parts of the same picture using different quality. JPEG 2000 decomposes the image into a multiple resolution representation in the course of its compression process. The JPEG 2000 standard provides both lossless and lossy compression options in a single architecture.

The Panavision DXL2 and RED cameras use a form of JPEG 2000 wavelet compression. In addition, the Digital Cinema Initiatives standard for digital distribution, the Digital Cinema Package (DCP) utilizes JPEG 2000 wavelet compression for the digital delivery of movies to theaters.

The wavelet transform does not actually compress image data, but rather, it restructures the data so that it is easier to compress. Wavelets have a great deal in common with DCT compression, but with one important difference, wavelet images can be scaled in sample size from a single pixel to the entire image, depending on the content. If there is a lot of fine detail, smaller, more refined boxes will be used. If image detail is coarser than the designated quality setting requires, then the encoder will discard samples, revealing the lower resolution below. This results in more detail remaining in the areas that need it most and less detail where it would be unnecessary. JPEG 2000 can also achieve lossless compression at ratios of about 2.5:1.

Wavelets work well on images from digital cinema cameras, as they don't have high frequency grain like film does, enabling them to heavily compress low contrast areas without a reduction in the signal to noise ratio.

Wavelets offer some advantages over DCT. As compression is increased and file size is decreased, the image quality degrades more gracefully and organically. Instead of ending up with ugly image blocks, wavelet compression tends to let noisy, low contrast areas of the image go softer. In green screen work, this can actually be advantageous, as it intelligently reduces the noise in the large flat green areas while holding on to detail in the edges and hair.

A wavelet compressed image is made of progressively higher levels of detail, so stripping off a few top layers is relatively easy. The wavelet code stream can be partially decompressed for a low-resolution image, or the code stream can be fully decompressed to yield full resolution images. By specifying the highest resolution to be decoded, wavelet compressed footage can be displayed as a variable resolution proxy without re-encoding. This allows users to edit at proxy resolution and then render out a 4k conformed timeline; you get "free proxies" out of wavelets, which will reduce your bandwidth and processor requirements.

How JPEG 2000 Works

Figure 15.7 Stages of JPEG 2000 compression.

Pre-Processing

The Pre-Processing block deals with color conversion or decorrelation from RGB to YUV. This entails use of both ICT (Irreversible Color Transform) and RCT (Reversible Color Transform) steps.

Figure 15.8 A sample sRGB colorspace frame.

Figure 15.9 The frame (reversibly) transformed to XYZ color space and rendered in RGB color space.

Figure 15.10 The frame (irreversibly) transformed into Y'C'xC'z (decompressed inverse of YCbCr color space rendered in RGB color space).

The Discrete Wavelet Transform

JPEG 2000 partitions images into rectangular, non-overlapping blocks in a process called tiling; those tiles are compressed independently. Component mixing, wavelet transform, quantization, and coding are independently performed on each tile. During the wavelet transform, image components are passed recursively through low pass and high pass wavelet filters.

Figure 15.11 The frame after one DWT level to achieve two embedded resolutions.

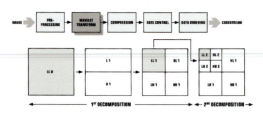

Figure 15.12 Decompositions of a frame for JPEG2000 compression.

The sub-band limits are highlighted. Clockwise, from top left, there is the LL sub-band, the LH sub-band, the HL sub-band, and the HH sub-band.

Figure 15.13 The frame after DWT into 5 resolutions.

The sub-band limits are highlighted. This enables the .n.

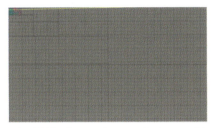

Figure 15-14 The frame after sample data partitioning.

Every different solid line width represents a different partitioning level (sub-band, precinct and code block).

Four sub-bands, with the upper left one containing all the low the frequencies, enable an intra-component decorrelation that concentrates the image information in a small and very localized area. Successive decompositions are applied on the low frequencies.

Compression of the Wavelet Coefficients

By itself the wavelet transform does not compress image data; it restructures the image information so that it is easier to compress.

Once the Discrete Wavelet Transform (DWT) has been applied, the output is quantified. The quantized data is then encoded in the Entropy Coding Unit (ECU).

The Entropy Coding Unit

The Entropy Coding Unit is composed of a coefficient bit modeler and the Arithmetic Coder itself. The Arithmetic Coder removes the redundancy in the encoding of the data. It assigns short code words to the more probable events and longer code words to the less probable ones. The Bit Modeler estimates the probability of each possible event at each point in the coding stream.

Figure 15.15 Code block weight after arithmetic coding.

Lighter colors denote that more bits are used to represent that code block. Code block weighting gives JPEG 2000 its Region of Interest (ROI) capability, which enables the user to select an area of an image to view at a high quality, while viewing the rest of the image at a lower quality.

Rate Control

Given a targeted bit-rate, the Rate-Control Module adjusts the coding precision of each pixel (actually small groups of pixels: the Code-Blocks).

Data Ordering

The Data Ordering Module embeds all groups of pixels in a succession of packets. These packets, along with additional headers, form the final JPEG 2000 Code-Stream. In the last "Data Ordering" block the Preferred Scalability (or Progression Order) is selected.

Compression

To understand compression, it's handy to first understand why we compress images – as compression would be a form of compromise over the image integrity, why on earth would we not always use uncompressed formats?

The simple answer is data rate. There is a significant amount of data that is generated from the recording of motion picture images, and a significant bottleneck of technology available – and viable in a real-world production setting – to record that stream of data.

Let's start with high definition – 1920 × 1080. As this would, with a few exceptions, be the minimum pixel count image for professional usage, we'll take a look at the data rates associated with this format and examine a 1920 × 1080 10-bit uncompressed signal.

We first calculate the number of pixels in the image, a simple product of the vertical and the horizontal pixel counts to give us 2,073,600 pixels. In a 10-bit system, that's 10 bits per pixel for a total of 20,736,000 bits of information. Of course, that's just gray information; to add color, we need to multiply those bits by 3 (red, green, blue) and we get 62,208,000 bits per frame of 1920 × 1080 10-bit uncompressed video.

That's a big number, which can be scary, so let's simplify it. We convert bits to Bytes by dividing by 8 (8 bits to a Byte) and get 7,776,000 Bytes per frame. We can convert that to kiloBytes by dividing by 1,024 (1,000 Bytes) to get 7593.75 kB, and then again to get 7.42 MegaBytes per frame.

Now that's a number most of us can wrap our heads around; 7.42 MegaBytes per frame is a pretty sizeable chunk of information. Since most data rates discuss Megabits, we can also convert that to 59.4 Megabits per frame.

Of course, in motion pictures, we don't just record one frame, we shoot 23.976 of them per second. So taking 7.42 MB per frame and multiplying that by 23.976 we get 177.9 MB per second or 1,423 Megabits per second.

That's an extraordinary amount of data.

At the time when HD was first becoming a viable tool for motion pictures, namely through the joint efforts between SONY, Panavision, and George Lucas to create the SONY HDW-F900 HDCAM camera, the highest quality digital tape available on the market was D5, which had a data rate of 32.25 MB/s or 258 Mb/s. A chasm away from 177.9 MB/s (1,423 Mb/s). Even if we ran D5 tape at four times its normal speed – which meant you only got 15 minutes of record time out of a 1-hour tape – that was 129 MB/s (1,032 Mb/s) still shy of full 10-bit uncompressed 1920 × 1080.

So what do we do? We compress the image.

Compression, by definition, is the methodology by which the overall data size can be reduced by eliminating information deemed unnecessary. Basically, we're dumping information considered "nonessential" in order to reduce the data rate. All compression schemes are based on limitations of human vision – presuming that we "won't know the difference" because we can't tell the difference visually. This is true of lossless compression schemes that compress the size of a data file, but completely restore all of the data information when the file is uncompressed; however, there are very few actual lossless video codecs (short for compressor/decompressor) in use today, mostly because they are inefficient at significantly reducing a file to a manageable file. Lossy compression algorithms reduce the data by eliminating information that is never recovered. They attempt to do this without degrading the image significantly,

but there is always an irretrievable loss of information in a lossy codec – most of which we deal with in motion picture imaging.

A true lossless compression means that when decompressed you have exactly the same information, all intact, as you did before you compressed it. A great example of this is a computer ZIP file or a RAR file, where the lossless compression algorithm serves to reduce the file size while maintaining the full integrity of the data so that, when decoded, everything is there. The drawback to lossless compression is that it doesn't significantly reduce file size as compared to lossy compression.

As was covered earlier, the bit is the basic unit of digital information. One bit is capable of defining two distinct states or levels of information, be that on/off, true/false, zero/one, yes/no or black/white. Each addition of a bit doubles the number of levels that can be defined. So if one bit can define two levels of information, two bits can define four levels, three bits can define eight levels, four bits can define 16 levels and so forth – like this:

1 bit = 2 levels
2 bits = 4 levels
3 bits = 8 levels
4 bits = 16 levels
5 bits = 32 levels
6 bits = 64 levels
7 bits = 128 levels
8 bits = 256 levels.

The more bits, the more levels of information can be described.

Translating this to image information, let's say we're trying to define levels or gradations between black and white. In a one-bit system, we have only two levels: black and white in which to describe the difference. In a two-bit system we have four levels so we can describe black, white, and two distinct variations of gray between them. As we increase our bits we can increase the subtlety with which we can describe the values between black and white.

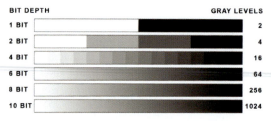

Figure 15.16 Bit depth increases the number of tones.

This translates to colors, as well. As we've already discussed, in an 8-bit RGB system we can define 16.7 million colors (256³). In a 10-bit system, we can define 1.07 billion colors (1024³). If we increase our acquisition format to 16 bits, we can capture 281.47 trillion colors.

This level of subtlety of gradation goes well beyond the visual ability of human eyes – we can't discern 281 trillion colors. It's even arguable that we can distinguish graduations between 16.7 million colors. However, the more bits we have to capture an image – the more dynamic range we have – levels of detail between black and white – in which to record our images.

Most of the display systems where we see our images are 8-bit systems (with the exception of theatrical presentation which the DCI – Digital Cinema Initiatives – sets at a 12-bit standard) so we have to "throw away" all those extra bits of information when we display our work on televisions, computers, phones, etc. Why do we need more bits to begin with? To give us flexibility of choice and manipulation of the image later in post production. 16-bit acquisition will allow us to maintain better detail in bright skies as well as deep shadows so that we can manipulate the image in post to get the proper representation.

Figure 15.17 Uncompressed image.

So all these bits are great! We want more bits! But, of course, more bits mean more data. If a 10-bit uncompressed HD signal is 177.9 MB/s or 1423 Mb/s, a 16-bit uncompressed HD signal is 284.4 MB/s or 2275.8 Mb/s! We already have trouble recording 10-bit – 16-bit becomes nearly impossible! Unless we compress that image.

Compression is often described as a ratio of the compressed image compared to the uncompressed image. The higher the ratio, the more compressed the image. 2:1 compression means that 1/2 of the image information from the original is present; 1/2 of that information has been discarded. 4:1 compression means that 25% of the image information from the original is present.

RED Epic has a minimum compression of 3:1. REDCode 36, which was popular for quite a while, had a compression of approximately 18:1. DVCProHD has a compression of 6.7:1, HDCAM has a compression of 4:1 and HDV or AVCHD (AVCCAM) has a compression of anywhere between 20:1 and 50:1.

Obviously, the higher the compression ratio, the more compromised the image. One of the reasons we can get away with super compression is because – on the surface – we can't really tell the difference.

Figure 15.18 The same image compressed.

These two images appear to be identical. They both have the same pixel count – 2,304 × 3,556. The first image has a file size of 6.54 MB and a compression of 3.58:1. The second image has a file size of 173 kB (.17MB) with a compression of 38:1. Looking at them compared we can't see a difference.

However, if we take a closer look:

Figure 15.19 The compressed image exhibits "blockiness."

Figure 15.20 The uncompressed image looks better close up.

We can easily see that the highly compressed image has significant image artifacts in it. Where there are subtle gradations (and a lot of noise) in the original image, that has become ugly blocks of color with no subtlety between them in the compressed image.

This loss of information becomes a significant issue in post production when we attempt to alter the color of the image through color correction. Any kind of even remotely aggressive changing

of the coloring will result in revealing these artifacts and the image will quickly "fall apart" and become an undesirable quality.

Keeping the theoretical data rates of uncompressed 10-bit HD in mind (177.9 MBs/1423 Mbs), these are some data rates for common compression formats:

DVCam/HDV = 21 Mb/s
XDCAM HD = 25, 35, or 50 Mb/s
CANON EOS H.264 = 40+ Mb/s VBR
DVCPro HD = 100 Mb/s
HDCAM = 140 Mb/s
HDCAM-SR = 440 Mb/s
PRO RES 4:2:2 = 145 Mbps (1920 × 1080 at 60i)
PRO RES 4:2:2 (HQ) = 220 Mbps (1920 × 1080 at 60i)
PRO RES 4:4:4:4 = 330 Mbps (1920 × 1080 at 60i)

Comparing 1423 Mb/s to 25 Mb/s, HDV is 57:1 compression ratio! This is a little misleading because there aren't any 10-bit HDV cameras, but 8-bit uncompressed HD would be 1137.9 Mb/s or 45.5:1 compression. This is how we can squeeze high definition images onto tiny MiniDV tape or onto tiny SD memory cards. Significant compression.

The data rate bottleneck has been widened substantially by moving away from videotape to recording images direct to hard drives. Faster drives and faster bus connection speeds allow for considerably higher data rates. This is good, because with increasing data rates, we're also increasing the digital pixel count of the images we're recording – up to 5K as in the case of the RED Epic (5120 × 2700) with frame rates far exceeding 24 fps – up to 120 fps! There's a bit of a moving target where data rates are concerned. Data transfer rates are increasing, yet so is the amount of data we need to record. It's a case we'll continue to see for many years.

Intraframe vs. Interframe Compression Schemes

There are two primary methods of compressing a sequence of images, Interframe and Intraframe – the terms are very close and often confused.

Interframe Compression

With interframe compression, the algorithms take a single frame as a reference frame (sometimes referred to as a "key frame") and then compare the changes in a set number of following frames. The algorithm looks for anything that has changed and discards anything that is the same between the frames. This works well for motion pictures as, normally, much of the image doesn't change from frame to frame – only a small portion of the image records movement. If you imagine a talking-head interview shot with a camera at a fixed position on a tripod, the only thing changing frame to frame is the person's head, mouth, eyes, etc. The background is the same from frame to frame. An interframe compression looks at that identical information and says "I don't need to keep this information for every frame, I only need it for a reference and I can discard it for all these other frames that have the same information."

Let's look at a more detailed example. If we imagining that we were shooting a shot of a simple red ball bouncing in front of a plain white wall, these might be the frames that make up that sequence:

Figure 15.21 Image sequence for group of pictures compression.

Now the algorithm will select the reference frame, frame one, and look at only the elements of the successive frames that are different from frame one:

Figure 15.22 How group of pictures (GOP) works.

All of the black represents the information that is identical in all six frames and, therefore, is considered redundant and can be discarded. By doing this, it can eliminate a large amount of data and significantly reduce the file size.

This process creates what is called a Group of Pictures or GOP as the successive frames are dependent on the initial, reference, frame, they're all collected into a group – typically of 7 to 15 frames before a new reference frame is selected and a new GOP is created.

The reference frame is called the intra frame or I frame and the subsequent frames are called P frames or predictive frames. The decoding system has to look at the P frame and fill in the missing information by referring back to the nearest I frame. In more advanced encoding there are also B frames, bi-directional frames, that require

the decoder to look at the previous I frame as well as the P frame before and after the B frame. This results in more accurate information filling, but also requires more hardware speed and video buffering to look back and forth and fill in the images on the fly. A typical advanced GOP frame structure looks like this: IBBPBBPBBPBB – and the sequence repeats with a new I frame.

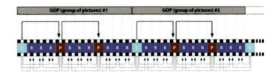

Figure 15.23 Group of Pictures compression sequence.

This technology was originally created for MPEG (Moving Picture Coding Experts Group) compression, the codec behind the eventual encoding of DVDs and digital video distribution (cable, satellite, Internet) in general. It was designed as an exhibition format where the file sizes of the media could be very small and the decoding of the GOPs was left to the hardware, IE your DVD player does the GOP decoding for the DVD, filling in the information missing in the compressed frames in real time. This ensures that the data on the physical DVD itself doesn't have to include the decoding algorithm or information and it can be significantly small compared to the final information decoded back from the player.

Variations of MPEG have been used for video CDs, DVDs, satellite and cable video distribution as well as Blu-ray discs, which now use the updated MPEG-4 encoding standard.

MPEG is also known by its International Telecommunication Union (ITU) standard code number, H.261 (MPEG-1), H.262 (MPEG-2), H.264 (MPEG-4)and H.265 (HEVC). H.262/MPEG-2 covered the standard definition 720 × 486 Rec. 601 format, MPEG-4/H.264 is an updated version that includes the 1920 × 1080 Rec. 709 format, and H.265 includes all the way up to 8K UHD.

These standards were created for exhibition – playback – allowing content producers to distribute very small data files that were decoded on the hardware/consumer side, allowing movie content to be placed onto CDs, and DVDs at very low bit rates with true broadcast standard quality.

It was observed, however, by the camera manufacturers, how successful MPEG and GOP encoding was for creating very small video files and MPEG started to make its way into acquisition formats. The first early popularity of

MPEG encoding in camera systems showed up in the HDV format adopted by Panasonic, SONY, Canon (and others) allowing users to record 1920 × 1080 images onto small Mini DV tape at 25 Mb/s (remember 8-bit uncompressed HD is 1137.9 Mb/s, HDV is highly compressed MPEG at 46:1). This created a boom of inexpensive HD cameras that recorded to standard DV tape and the impressive HD images were quickly adopted by consumers and professionals alike.

There is, however, a significant problem when attempting to edit a GOP encoded video. If the editor decides to cut on a P or B frame, it is not a full frame of video! That frame only has partial information and requires a reference back to the I frame to fill in the missing parts. This means the non-linear editing system either only cuts on I frames (making the precision of editing limited to every 7th or 15th frame) or it has to decode those P or B frames on-the-fly, which requires intensive computations. Many non-linear editing systems now have "native" editing in GOP formats, but most professional editors prefer to transcode their material to an intraframe codec before attempting to edit the footage.

When MPEG broadcast compression loses the I frame sequence reference, it can sometimes break in spectacular ways.

Figure 15.24 When Interframe compression breaks.

Intraframe Compression

The antithesis of interframe, intraframe encoding compresses the information in each individual frame discretely. There is no dependence on successive or previous frames – the cheese stands alone here.

A JPEG-like compression algorithm is used on each frame wherein the encoding process looks for redundancy in the frame and discards repetitive information. The image is mathematically divided up into sections – blocks of digital pixels called "macroblocks" – usually a minimum of 8 pixels by 8 pixels in size (although that varies depending on the algorithm). Using a mathemat-

ical process called discrete cosine transformation, the blocks are all analyzed and redundancy between them is discarded.

Looking back at the image of the bouncing red ball, the encoder can look at the red ball and say – this is one uniform color of red. So instead of encoding 200 digital pixels of red-red-red-red-red, it merely encodes one digital pixel of the actual color information and the rest refer back to that one color. The same would go for the white wall, the encoding algorithm looks at the wall and says – this is all one uniform color of white, I only need to remember one pixel of color and I can discard all the rest.

The image integrity of intraframe compression is vastly superior to interframe, but both are lossy compressions – which compress images by identifying marginally important information and discarding it.

Lossless compression does exist, which serves to remove statistically redundant information without any degradation to the actual image integrity, but there really isn't any lossless video compression algorithm in wide use today for acquisition of images, although there is a nearly lossless application from high-end H.264 encoding referred to as AVC (Advanced Video Coding) and JPEG2000 has a lossless encoding option.

REDCODE employs a wavelet encoding algorithm to reduce the size of their "raw" files ("raw" is in quotes here as the very fact that the file is compressed negates the true definition of raw). As opposed to using rectangular "macroblocks" to analyze and compress information, wavelet algorithms use circular patterns (like ripples on a pond) to compare and reduce information. It is still a lossy compression algorithm and some information captured from the Red sensor is discarded forever.

Interframe codecs:

HDV
AVCHD
AVCCAM
XDCAM EX
XDCAM HD
NXCAM
H.264
MPEG-2
MPEG-4.

Intraframe codecs:

DV
MJPEG
JPEG 2000

DVCPro HD
AVC-Intra
AVC-ULTRA
HDCAM
HDCAM-SR
Avid DNxHD
Apple ProRes 4:2:2
Apple ProRes 4:4:4:4.[1]

Post Production File Types

ALE Files

The Avid Log Exchange or ALE file format is a kind of spreadsheet file with a global header that has been universally adopted as an import/export means of exchanging metadata for editorial master clips and sub clips as well as to merge metadata into existing clips across production and post production applications. Avid Log Exchange is an application format that is used by external logging systems to bring metadata into the Avid Edit system. The .ALE format is in the form of an ASCII TAB formatted text file that can be imported and exported into and out of Avid editing systems.

XML Files

XML files are the method by which camera metadata is ingested into Final Cut Pro Editing systems. XML or Extensible Markup Language is an annotating markup language that defines a set of rules for encoding documents in a format that is both human readable and computer readable. XML is a description format that is easily parsed, and which can be opened in a text editor.

Avid can export XML from FilmScribe for specialized workflows, but XML export does not create an AAF file represented as XML. Film-Scribe fulfills much of the metadata management in Avid, such as pull lists, scan lists, and change lists and it can export (but not import) metadata as XML for use in downstream third party workflows.

AAF Files

For more complex sequence exchanges, the AAF or Advanced Authoring Format is a professional file interchange format designed for video post production and authoring environments, and it is used as a primary exchange format by Avid. It supports import and export of layers, effects, and much more metadata than an Edit Decision List.

EDL Files

An EDL or Edit Decision List is a simple format originally used for matching control of video tape decks to do a tape online edit. Edit Decision Lists are still in use today and can be imported and exported for simple cut to cut workflows.

AAF was created to address the problems of multi-vendor, cross-platform interoperability for computer-based non-linear digital video production. Video, audio, still image, graphics, text, animation, music, and other multimedia data can be exchanged using AAF. This type of data is called essence data, because it is the essential data within a multimedia program that can be seen or heard by the audience. Metadata that provides information on how to combine or modify essence data or which provides supplementary information about essence data is called metadata, defined as data about other data. The metadata in an AAF file can provide the information needed to combine and modify the sections of essence data in the AAF file to produce a complete multimedia program.

AIFF and WAV Audio Files

Audio Interchange File Format (AIFF) is an audio file format used for storing audio data for personal computers and other electronic audio devices. The format was developed by Apple in 1988 based on Electronic Arts Interchange File Format (IFF, widely used on Amiga systems) and is commonly used on Apple computer systems. The audio data in most AIFF files is uncompressed pulse code modulation (PCM). AIFF files use much more disk space than lossy compressed formats like MP3 – about 10MB for one minute of stereo audio at a sample rate of 44.1kHz at a bit depth of 16 bits. There is also a compressed variant of AIFF known as AIFF-C or AIFC, with various defined compression codecs. The file extension for the AIFF format is .aiff or .aif, and for compressed variants it is .aifc, but .aiff or .aif are also accepted by audio applications that support the format.

Waveform Audio File Format (.WAV) is an audio file format developed by Microsoft and IBM for storing an audio bitstream on a PC. It is the main format used on Microsoft Windows systems for raw and uncompressed audio. The bitstream encoding is linear pulse code modulation (LPCM) format.

Metadata

Metadata is data about the image. Metadata refers to all data besides image content. It is the writing on the back of the picture. Metadata in practical application holds the promise of automating many of the manual processes of filmmaking. We are on the verge of automating camera reports, lens data on a frame-by-frame basis, script reports, visual effects data collection, sound reports, and all of handwritten "metapaper" that has in the past so tediously consumed production time and which has been so prone to data entry errors.

As an example of the kinds of metadata about camera images supplied to editing systems via ALE or XML files, here is a list of the data columns that the ARRI ALEXA provides automatically: Camera Serial Number, Camera ID, Camera SUP Version, Sensor Fps, Shutter Angle, Manufacturer, Exposure Index, White Balance, White Balance CC, Gamma, Look, Image Size, Camera Model, Time Code, User Bits, UUID, Camera Tilt, Camera Roll, UMID, Lens Type, Zoom Distance, Focus Distance, Iris Value, Master/Slave Info, Channel Info, Reel Name, Take Name, Director name, Cinematographer Name, Location Name, Production Name, User Info 1, User Info 2, Sound Reel Name, SxS Serial Number, User Date, User Time, ND Filter Type, ND Filter Density.

Different types of metadata are also embedded into HD-SDI. This data is located in the HANC (horizontal ancillary data) and VANC (vertical ancillary data) space of the HD-SDI signal. Ancillary Time Code (ATC) is embedded in the HD-SDI stream according to SMPTE 12M. It represents the timecode of the camera. This timecode is also available in the Extended Metadata as "Master TC" with identical content. The camera can also deliver additional timecodes with different content. Timecode is inserted as "ATC_LTC" (Linear Time Code) and "ATC_VITC" (Vertical Interval Time Code) at the preferred locations in HANC space. Every sensor image has an ATC_LTC and ATC_VITC packet. For camera frame rates above 30 fps the implementation follows the "preferred implementation" in paragraph 12.1 of SMPTE 12M-1. This basically

says: the frame counter should increment every second image. ATC_LTC and ATC_VITC also carries the "Vari-Frame" flag.

Avid editing systems now have the ability to import and manage ASC CDLs when they are integrated with ALE files and provided as part of the transfer and grading process that precedes ingest. Two data column headers have been added to the ALE spec for storing and carrying ASC CDL data on a take-by-take basis. The ASC_SOP column carries ASC CDL Slope, Offset, and Power data, and the ASC_SAT column carries ASC CDL Saturation data. The values can be displayed in readable form by selecting Headings in the Bin menu, where they are kept on a per clip basis for all edits in a sequence. These values can be exported in an EDL by selecting the ASC template in the EDL Type menu. The same values can be included as comments by selecting Color Decision List in the Comments tab of the EDL settings. Once selected, the ASC CDL information can be used downstream in color correction and Digital Intermediate. Avid are also integrating the export of ASC CDL values from FilmScribe into XML output format.

The White Paper referred in the link below can provide insight into the mechanism by which ASC CDL's are ingested, stored, managed, and forwarded to the Digital Intermediate suite for use in final color correction:

https://resources.avid.com/SupportFiles/attach/HighRes_WorkflowsGuide.pdf

How Much Data?

Digital cinematography can produce volumes of data and then it can produce *enormous* volumes of data depending on the camera, recorder, media, and compression scheme one uses. Be absolutely certain that you, your producers, your post producers, and the studio know and understand what they have signed up for in terms of the data that will be generated as a result of the choice of camera and workflow.

Table 15.5 Digital cinematography camera single frame file sizes in MB

Camera Single Frame File Sizes	File Size – MB	GB at 24 fps
Camera & Codec at 24 fps	One Frame	One Hour
RED EPIC 4K (raw 3:1)	9 MB	759.4 GB
RED EPIC 4K (raw 5:1)	2.32 MB	195.75 GB
RED EPIC 5K (raw 5:1)	3.55 MB	299.53 GB
ALEXA ProRes (12-bit 1080p 4:4:4)	11 MB	928.12 GB

Camera Single Frame File Sizes	File Size – MB	GB at 24 fps
Camera & Codec at 24 fps	One Frame	One Hour
ALEXA ProRes (1080p HQ)	7.33 MB	618.48 GB
ALEXA ProRes (1080p 4:2:2)	4.9 MB	413.44 GB
ALEXA ProRes (1080p LT)	3.4 MB	286.87 GB
ALEXA ARRIraw (12-bit 16×9 1080p 4:4:4)	7 MB	590.62 GB
ALEXA DPX (12-bit 16×9 deBayered raw file)	18.7 MB	1577.82 GB
ALEXA ARRIraw (12-bit 4×3 1080p 4:4:4)	9.3 MB	784.69 GB
ALEXA DPX (12-bit 4×3 1080p 4:4:4)	24.9 MB	2100.93 GB
SONY F65 (raw 1–60 fps)	10.4 MB	877.5 GB
SONY F65 (raw 60–120 fps)	21.3 MB	1797.18 GB
SONY F65 (deBayered 4K 16-bit EXR)	53 MB	4471.86 GB
SONY F35 12-bit (1080p 4:4:4)	9.3 MB	784.68 GB
SONY F35 10-bit (1080p 4:4:4)	7.78 MB	656.44 GB

Bandwidth

When building custom solutions for near-set processing, bandwidth between components is the biggest concern. Whenever a custom solution is assembled, the speeds with which a production can move data from camera through to the various functions of the workflow become crucial. The problem is compounded when shooting on distant location, trying to move the massive amount of data across borders and from continent to continent requires significant effort, expense, and expertise.

10-Gig E/Fibre Channel

Facilities have long dealt with the problem of how to move media around from machine to machine and room to room. 10-GigE switches, fiber channel and the like are in fact much of what makes a facility. Now that digital production work is migrating to on-set and near-set environments, productions are having to find ways to implement such technologies in tight quarters on tight budgets often with little time for planning. Solid state technologies like Fusion IO may alleviate some of this problem in the future with compact super fast drives acting as transport devices from camera to post.

The Cloud

Cloud computing refers to the on-demand availability of computer system resources and data storage over the internet without direct active management by the user. Data movement, storage, and production and capabilities via the cloud and other remote services enable everything from reviewing footage to editing, to color grading and sound postproduction, and have been steadily accelerating as production has become more global.

Data Transport: Fiber Brokers and Data Synchronization across Sites

Once throughput has been addressed with respect to getting data from the camera to the near set environment and between the various components thereof, another challenge awaits. How to get the footage back via wide area network (WAN) to the studio archive, the VFX team in another city, and other creative participants is a major concern for productions on distant locations. In some business models a cloud data center not only provides storage and horsepower to store and manage files, but also the ability to move the files where they need to go as well.

Sohonet www.sohonet.com/ What began as a small consortium of post houses in London needing bandwidth to move files is now the market leader in providing bandwidth to the media and entertainment industry. Sohonet is currently working on its next generation plan to upgrade to provide more support for 10-gig and beyond connectivity.

Cogent www.cogentco.com/en/products-and-services/dedicated-internet-access Cogent provides On Network Internet access to more than 2,823 buildings directly connected to their IP backbone and Off Network Internet access to more than 206 markets.

Level (3) www.centurylink.com/business.html Level (3) has 450,000 route miles of fiber and a network of over 60 countries.

Comcast https://business.comcast.com/enterprise/products-services/data-networking Comcast networking services provide a secure, reliable, high-performance backbone that helps companies manage data, drive application performance, and safely access cloud and data center resources.

Aspera http://asperasoft.com/ Aspera has enjoyed a long reign as the leading provider of bandwidth acceleration tools. With fast file transfer and streaming solutions built on IBM FASP protocol, IBM Aspera software moves data of any size across any distance.

Signiant www.signiant.com/ Signiant provides solutions when there is a need to move large files with speed, reliability, and security.

Talon www.talonstorage.com/products The bandwidth as a service space is becoming more crowded with companies such as Talon Data offering solutions like FAST, which we tested at 450MB/sec transfer from LA to London. At that speed, an entire feature could be sent at digital cinema quality from one continent to another at just under 2 hours.

Ekinops www.ekinops.net/ Ekinops and others are offering wave division multiplexing, which makes better use of existing fiber to move data quickly. It seems likely that going forward, acceleration devices of some sort are likely to be seen more and more frequently on DIT carts and near-set environments as productions look to move files around more quickly and efficiently.

Zayo www.zayo.com/services/data-center-colocation/ Services diverse communication needs from fiber to colocation to the cloud.

Switch www.switch.com Vegas-based SwitchNAP, for example, is parked atop a nationwide hub of fiber connectivity acquired at fire sale prices from Enron.

Infrastructure as a Service: Raw Computing Resource Clouds

Large cloud data service providers are providing a multitude of cloud services. Raw data storage is a basic service available through multiple organizations, addressable and billable on an as used basis. Computing infrastructure is available in predefined or custom machine sizes to accelerate your task in the cloud. Compute Engine virtual machines live-migrate between host systems without rebooting, which keeps applications running even when host systems require maintenance.

> **Amazon Web Services (AWS)** https://aws.amazon.com/?nc2=h_lg
> **Google Cloud Service** https://cloud.google.com/
> **Microsoft Azure** https://azure.microsoft.com/en-us/
> **Oracle** www.oracle.com/index.html

Software as a Service

Software as service providers give developers cloud services that help to deploy and scale applications that run simultaneously on multiple computers. To the user these cloud services have a user interface that looks like one computer, but behind the scenes services are distributed as needed, allowing users to scale power to meet the time and computational needs of the job. When CGI companies require raw horsepower to process and render images for complicated sequences or on short deadlines, they turn to distributed rendering on the cloud. These services provide compute power billable on an as used basis.

> **Digital Ocean** www.digitalocean.com/
> **SDVI Rally** www.sdvi.com/
> **Cinnafilm** https://cinnafilm.com/products/
> **Conductor** www.conductor.com/

Cloud-Enabled Workflows

At the time of this writing, and hastened by the Covid-19 pandemic, cloud-enabled workflows are increasing in use, providing for new ways for film makers to work. The foundations of these changes are outlined in the whitepaper, *The Evolution of Media Creation – A 10-Year Vision for the Future of Media Production, Post and Creative Technologies*, https://movielabs.com/production-technology/, written by MovieLabs and its member studios.

Several recent movements have paved the way from working with artists on-premises with OCN or DI master media, to a remote model where media and applications are centralized, and artists work remotely with access granted as needed:

- Camera files are generally increasing in size due to capturing in higher resolutions with lower compression to elevate motion imaging quality.
- DI master media has increased dramatically due to mastering in 4k, 6k, or 8k resolutions in high dynamic range and in larger color gamuts (i.e., Rec 2020).
- Improvements in last-mile connectivity, in both bandwidth and latency, are enabling users to run high-quality virtualized desktop environments.
- Production and post workflows are dynamic, with many processes happening concurrently, rather than serially, as in the past.
- Film makers have the ability to use any available artist worldwide, rather than limiting to those in their geographic area.
- Everyone working on the project is verified, offering the potential of enhanced security and audit tracing.
- The digital dilemma is mitigated, as the data protection is the responsibility of the cloud provider(s). Popular providers are Amazon Web Services (AWS), Google Cloud Platform, Microsoft Azure, and Oracle Cloud.

In addition, remote workflows reduce capital expenditures, moving infrastructure costs to an operating expenditures model, drastically reducing business risk and exposure. Lastly, large facilities are burdened with expensive lease costs which may make up a large part of their operating budget.

Security

Security has always been a major concern in our industry, as intellectual property theft continues to threaten content owners. As we've shifted from physical content on-premises to digital content on-premises, then digital content moving between approved production and post facilities to, now, artists and related crew working from anywhere in the world, content security has never been more important. To help combat threat potential, the Trusted Partner Network (TPN) www.tpn. org provides a framework for third-party vendor assessments. The TPN is a joint venture between two major industry associations: the Motion Picture Association (MPA) www.motionpictures. org and the Content Delivery Security Association (CDSA) www.mesalliance.org/communities/ CDSA who provide industry guidelines and best practices for safeguarding content.

Note

1. This section was contributed by Jay Holben – Cinematographer, Author.

Chapter 16

Post Production and Digital Intermediate

Post production includes all the stages of production occurring after shooting or recording individual program segments. Post production consists of several processes that happen in parallel, culminating in final delivery of the project. There are specific points in the post production timeline when the cinematographer should be involved, most especially in color correction of dailies, and in the final color correction of the finished project in the Digital Intermediate.

Figure 16.1 Workflow from set to final delivery.

When delivering a high dynamic range (HDR) master in DolbyVision, HDR 10+ or Hybrid Log Gamma, the cinematographer should give thought to whether to finish the HDR version or the standard dynamic range (SDR) version first. If the choice is to do the SDR version first, there is a tendency to be very conservative when doing the subsequent HDR version, and if the choice is to do the HDR version first, the SDR grade can seem disappointing in comparison. It is sometimes helpful to consider the two deliverables almost as two separate projects.

The discussion of post production and finishing entails an examination of the path from set, to dailies, to editorial all the way through to digital intermediate and deliverables.

Handling of Original Media

The original files, shuttle disk drives, cards are archived and filed in a prescribed directory structure. In addition to the editorial proxy files, the lab usually provides storage path information on subclip bins and master dailies clip bins as part of the dailies package. The editorial department should be designated to give a final ok before drives or cards can be erased and recirculated into use on set. The camera package should have a sufficient supply of cards or media to allow for times when that media cannot be turned around and returned to set the next day.

Dailies Generation

At the end of each shoot day, digital files are archived and ingested by a lab, film footage is developed, images are color corrected under the supervision of the cinematographer (using LUTs and CDLs from the set). The color corrections performed are recorded and preserved as metadata as a starting point for digital intermediate. Well color corrected dailies and look managed images will embed a familiarity of the eventual desired look in the minds of the director, the producers, the studio, the editors and everyone involved in a project. This is an urgently important first step in arriving at a final look that reflects the cinematographer's intent! Once the creative team have wed themselves to the look of the dailies, making changes in that look frequently becomes an uphill battle! It frequently happens that a cinematographer may not be available for or invited to attend final color correction, so attention to look management during production is a very good step toward assuring the look of the final image.

Audio files are synced to picture, and editorial proxy files are generated for viewing by the director, the producers, the cinematographer, the editors, selected actors, and invited crew members. Dailies serve as a quality control step in evaluating the photography, for evaluating focus, for evaluating whether coverage is sufficient, and as an indication of how the shooting and the actors' performances are progressing.

Film Scanning

In the case of film acquisition or a hybrid film/digital mixed media project, a telecine or film scanner digitizes the selected film takes. When content is shot on 35mm film, after the film is developed the takes selected by the director and noted by the assistant camera person and the script supervisor are transferred to a high quality digital file format such as DPX or Open EXR from ADX (Academy Density Exchange) scans on a film scanner, color corrected under the supervision of the cinematographer, and rendered to an editorial proxy file format. The color corrections performed are recorded and preserved as metadata as a starting point for digital intermediate.

Figure 16.2 NorthLight film scanner.

Watching Dailies

Increasingly, the time pressures of production, budgets, long hours, and short schedules leaves little time for viewing of dailies. The cinematographer should make every effort to see dailies as often as possible, and on the largest screen available. Dailies can be viewed early in the morning before shooting starts, during a lunch break, or in the evening after shooting ends. An HD projector can be used if it is well calibrated; dailies provides a chance to evaluate focus, camera movement, performances, hair, makeup, and wardrobe, and dailies present an opportunity for team bonding. It is common for several members of the film crew including the director, cinematographer, editor, and others to view and discuss the dailies as a group, but today, many productions distribute the dailies for individual viewing via a dailies delivery service such as PIX or DAX.

Editing

Depending on the size and budget of a production, dailies proxies are almost always compressed, and the amount of compression is a budgetary tradeoff – the lower the budget the higher the compression. Remember when choosing a compression ratio for dailies proxies that the lower the compression, the better the picture looks when projected for screenings. Non-linear off-line picture editing creates a non-destructive Edit Decision List (EDL) to be forwarded to the lab for digital intermediate (DI) for conforming an on-line timeline from the original camera media. Non-linear editing usually manipulates compressed proxies of the original media such as AVID DNx or DNxHD files in order to optimize the performance of the computer edit station. These proxy files used in the final edit will eventually be used to generate an EDL to conform a timeline from the high-resolution camera original files. Each time the edited audio, video, or image is rendered, played back, or accessed from the non-linear editing system, it is reconstructed from the editorial source media and the accumulated editing procedures. The editorial process is computationally intensive, but preferable to directly modifying the original media, and it prevents generation loss as the proxy audio, video, or image is edited, and changing an edit is quick and efficient.

Visual Effects and Computer Generated Images

Work on VFX and CG Images is initiated by the VFX department and distributed to vendors through the editorial department. Plates for the

CG work and any accompanying clean plates or reference materials are supplied to the vendors, usually as Open EXR files or as DPX files along with applicable LUTs and CDLs. At the CG vendor, data is ingested as scan, linearized to gamma of 1 with the inverse of the camera encoding, and then is usually published as both scan.EXR and published as scan.JPG. The vendor's tracking department ingests distortion map footage (at this point the work of mapping lenses becomes very important! See Chapter 7 – Lenses – for instructions on how to shoot lens distortion maps), creates scan.JPG proxy files, and publishes distort nodes (nuke script) and flattened undistorted overscan plateBg.JPG sequences. The vendor GG department ingests the flattened undistorted overscan plateBg. JPG sequences and work on CG begins. The CG department then subscribes to scan.EXR sequences, subscribes to distort nodes from tracking department, and publishes flattened, undistorted overscan plate Bg.EXR sequences along with clean plates. When the GG work is complete, the EXR sequences are reverse distorted as the inverse of the flattening process, re-encoded from linear into the original encoding format, and output to editorial for director approval. The resulting versioned finished shots are returned to the editorial department, cataloged, cut into the project, and forwarded to the lab for inclusion in the conformed timeline.

Audio Finishing

Composing, scoring, recording, and editing of music are completed to fit and enhance the picture.

Foley

Foley is studio recorded sound effects created to fit the images, swishing of clothing, footsteps, squeaky doors, breaking glass, and any other sound effects suggested by the picture.

Sound Design

Sound design is the addition of sound effects, Automated Dialog Replacement (ADR), and looping (the process where actors re-record sync dialog).

Dubbing

Dubbing is the process of sound re-recording or mixing on an audio stage. After the sound editors have prepared all the additional sound tracks, dialogue, ADR, Foley, sound effects, and music, the dubbing mixers proceed to balance all of the elements and output the finished soundtrack.

Turnover

Turnover is the moment when a project is given to a lab or DI facility for the final finishing, online editorial, sound, and color correction. Creative editing and post production are considered the offline edit, using lower res proxy versions of the media. The online edit begins when the original media is ingested into a full bandwidth edit system and conformed to match the proxy edit timeline. Editorial prep is the process of consolidating and organizing the timeline for turnover.

Checklist for a Correct and Effective Turnover

- Editorial should deliver a collapsed, clean, and orderly timeline with each video track's media consistently organized.
- Editorial should also deliver a reference file with timecode burn in of the offline picture locked sequence.
- Media manage the cleaned, orderly timeline and include that media managed project file, so the online editor can refer back to it, if needed.
- Delivery should include a full-res textless Quicktime of the project with clean cuts; no dips to black, cross dissolves, or transitions.
- Deliver XML, AAF, and EDL files of the timeline to the online editor.
- Make sure all video and images are scaled properly.
- Meet with the online editor and confirm the workflow.

Ingest and Conform

When the editorial process completes the final approved cut of the project, Edit Decision List (EDL), Avid File Exchange (AFE), or Advanced Authoring Format (AAF) files, and XML (Extensible Markup Language) files are used in a full bandwidth edit system to recreate a full resolution timeline of the project with effects, fades, dissolves etc. The corresponding full resolution digital files are ingested onto a server, the conform edit system links the locked timeline to the subclip bins, master dailies clip bins and files in an automated process, replacing the proxy edit files with the full resolution media in a process referred to as conform.

Figure 16.3 Avid Symphony outputs conform AFE files.

Figure 16.4 Autodesk Smoke builds a conformed timeline from AFE files.

Next, the timeline is dustbusted by the VFX department. Dustbusting is the process of painting out silhouetted dust particles that remained after film was cleaned for scanning. The conformed full resolution timeline is then "pushed" into the color corrector, so that the color correction process can begin.

OpenColorIO

https://opencolorio.org/
Color management of the timeline as it is being ingested and set up in the color corrector is an important part of the process. The interface between visual effects, editorial and digital intermediate requires sophisticated color management, and Open Color IO is an open source tool set that helps to manage the process.

OpenColorIO (OCIO) is a complete color management solution geared towards motion picture production with an emphasis on visual effects and computer animation. OCIO provides a straightforward and consistent user experience across all supporting applications while allowing for sophisticated back-end configuration options suitable for high-end production usage. OCIO is compatible with the Academy Color Encoding Specification (ACES) and is LUT-format agnostic, supporting many popular formats.

OpenColorIO has two major goals: consistent color transforms, and consistent image display, across multi-application cinematic color pipelines. The design goal behind OCIO is to decouple the color pipeline API from the specific color transforms selected, allowing users to tightly manage (and experiment) with color pipelines from a single location. OpenColorIO is natively designed to handle both scene-referred and display-referred imagery. All color transforms are loaded at runtime, from a color configuration external to any individual application. OCIO does not make any assumptions about the imagery; all color transformations are "opt in." This is different from the color management often built-in to applications, where it is often difficult to track down the specific LUTs/gamma transforms automatically applied without the user awareness. OCIO color configuration files define all of the conversions that may be used. For example, if you are using a particular camera's color space, one would define the conversion from the camera's color encoding to scene linear. Users can also specify the display transforms (for multiple displays) in a similar manner. OCIO transforms can rely on a variety of built-in building-blocks, including all common math operations and the majority of common lookup table formats. OCIO also has full support for both CPU (Central Processing Unit) and GPU (Graphics Processing Unit) pathways, in addition to full support for CDLs and per-shot looks. OCIO ships with a configuration compatible with the Academy's ACES effort, allowing for experimentation with this next-generation color pipeline in existing applications. OpenColorIO is in use at many of the major visual effects and animation studios, and is also supported out of the box in a variety of commercial software.[1]

Digital Intermediate: Color Correction

The best quality, least compressed and highest resolution original image material should always be used in the DI session. The processes of color correction, visual effects, and resampling should be performed in a linear floating point mathematical environment. The original media is set to the eventual final resolution and new media renders are created out of the color correction platform. This process is also about assuring that the project meets quality control requirements for both sound and picture for final delivery, to broadcast, web streaming, theatrical exhibition, and any other markets.

Figure 16.5 Digital intermediate suite.

Color grading is the process of digitally painting, altering, and enhancing the color and contrast of the project, accomplished on any one of many possible color correctors. A skilled colorist operates a toolset in conjunction with the cinematographer and the director, which includes many powerful image manipulation functions. There are a wide variety of software and hardware platforms available for this work. The price tag for the hardware and software required varies widely according to the parameters of performance and functionality.

It is essential to the cinematographer to participate with the director and the colorist in this process, but participation frequently becomes an issue of budget. A good relationship with director, producer, and studio will help to assure the importance of the cinematographer's inclusion in this process.

Time spent in the digital intermediate suite is expensive and precious, so use it wisely. Color correction begins in the dailies process and applies the cinematographer's intent to the RAW or uncorrected footage, but dailies color correction is only meant to get the footage close to the final look for dailies screening and for the editorial process. DI is the final color correction process that will give the project a uniform, refined, and finished look.

In an all-digital acquisition project, once the low resolution and low bit depth editorial proxy materials in the timeline are replaced with full bandwidth original material, a skilled colorist grades the color and contrast of the entire motion picture timeline from scene to scene, under the willing and enthusiastic guidance of the cinematographer. At this point, final visual effects are inserted into the timeline, and rendering of digital opticals, fades, dissolves, titles, is performed. Clips can be shipped out of the DI suite to near line visual effects artists for small fixes and adjustments in the last moment.

The DI process uses powerful color correction tools to color grade every shot in the movie, allowing for precise control of color and contrast in specific areas of the image, and it also allows for fine adjustment of grain, and sharpness.

The Principal Tools of Color Correction

Primary color correction independently adjusts the lift, gain, and gamma of the RGB color channels from shot to shot, and from scene to scene. Secondary color correction isolates specific colors, modifying their hue, saturation and brightness.

Region-of-interest correction uses "power windows" or articulated mattes to isolate specific areas of the frame. These windows may follow or track moving subjects to make further primary and secondary corrections.

Stylized looks may be applied in order to emulate lab processes such as noise reduction (or enhancement), bleach bypass or ENR (a legacy film color-positive developing technique that utilized an additional black-and-white developing bath in a film print's processing in order to retain silver and increase contrast). Overall color-gamut manipulation may also be needed for output to various deliverables.

All of the operations of color correction, visual effects, resampling, and resizing should be performed in a linear mathematical environment on images that have been linearized for these purposes.

Primary Color Corrections

Primary color corrections are generally the broad, overall color corrections that affect the entire frame. They are the first step in setting the look for the scene and for individual clips in the scene. Primary corrections affect the overall color balance of the image, and generally refer to global adjustments of red, green, and blue, lift, gamma and gain, and hue and saturation. Film and digital cameras have different gamma characteristics for shadow, mid tone, and highlight detail, so the colorist first sets levels for each parameter on a shot-to-shot, scene-to-scene basis. A film or TV show might juxtapose a night scene after a day scene, or a violent scene next to a quiet scene. Color correction can serve both to harmonize the look of the images or to disrupt the flow. Primary color correction is the first layer correction of many layers that eventually add up to the final look of the project.

Lift, Gamma, Gain/Slope, Offset, Power/Hue/ Saturation

We are already familiar with lift, gamma, and gain, and their ASC Color Decision List "CDL" counterparts – slope, offset and power from Chapter 13 – Color Management.

In the digital intermediate suites, there are a few new wrinkles such as secondary color correction, curves, power windows, keys, and mattes.

Figure 16.6 DaVinci Resolve primary color correction screen.

These primary correction tools control highlights, mid tones, and shadows, either ganged to control overall levels, or independently to control individual RGB channels.

Numerous operations of the color corrector can affect the brightness and contrast of the image. Let's use a normal grayscale to illustrate the tools available for this purpose:

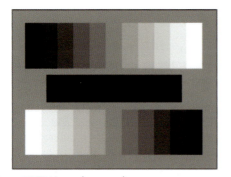

Figure 16.7 Normal grayscale.

Lift/Offset

Lift adjusts the images black or shadow levels. As black levels are pushed up or down, the mid tones are pushed up or down modestly and highlights are pushed up or down very slightly.

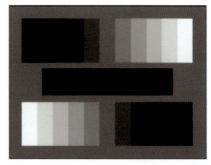

Figure 16.8 Grayscale demonstrating lift down – the entire tonal scale darkens and some steps at the dark end of the scale disappear.

Figure 16.9 Gray scale demonstrating lift up – the entire tonal scale lightens and some steps at the bright end of the scale disappear.

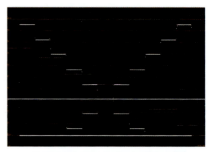

Figure 16.10 Waveform representation of grayscale demonstrating lift down.

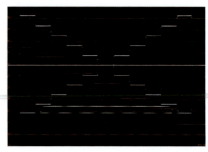

Figure 16.11 Waveform representation of grayscale demonstrating lift up.

Offset raises or lowers the value of a component, shifting the transfer function up or down while holding the slope constant. Offset is the approximate but not equivalent ASC CDL corollary for lift. For linear encodings, offset controls the overall "base fog" of the image. The values of the entire image are moved up or down together, affecting both brightness and contrast. This is not traditionally a common operation for linear data. The old telecine lift function – raising or lowering the darks while holding the highlights constant – can be achieved via a combination of offset and slope.

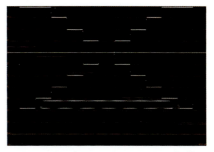

Figure 16.15 Waveform representation of offset up grayscale.

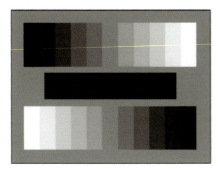

Figure 16.12 Normal grayscale.

Most color correction systems natively provide vendor-specific lift, gain, and gamma functions. The ASC CDL standard uses slope, offset, and power applied to each of the R, G, and B signals independently, and saturation which operates on R, G, and B in combination. Thus, ten parameters describe any ASC CDL color correction. Slope, offset, and power are similar to lift gamma and gain, but are mathematically purer functions. In most cases, vendor-specific lift, gain, and gamma can be translated into some combination of slope, offset, and power for interchange between systems.

Gamma/Power

Gamma stretches or squeezes the mid tone contrast levels between the shadows and the highlights. The middle steps of the chart become brighter or darker, the top end whites and bottom end blacks remain the same. The ASC CDL Equivalent of gamma is called power. For linear encodings, power controls the contrast of the image.

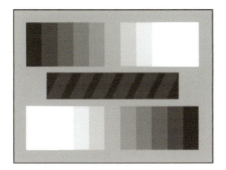

Figure 16.13 Grayscale demonstrating offset up – the entire tonal scale lightens and some steps at the bright end of the scale disappear.

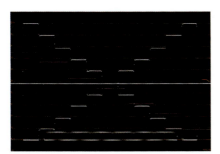

Figure 16.14 Waveform representation of normal grayscale.

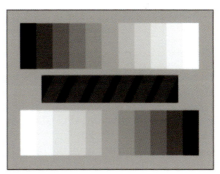

Figure 16.16 Grayscale demonstrating gamma up – black and white steps are unaffected but the rest of the tonal scale is redistributed brighter.

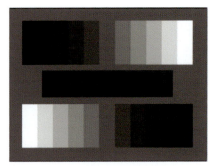

Figure 16.17 Grayscale demonstrating gamma down up – black and white steps are unaffected but the rest of the tonal scale is redistributed darker.

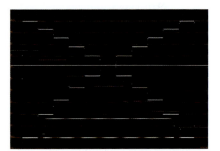

Figure 16.18 Waveform representation of gamma up on the grayscale – notice that the steps of the scale are slightly curved – this is a non linear function.

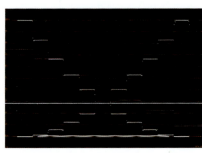

Figure 16.19 Waveform representation of gamma down on the grayscale – notice that the steps of the scale are slightly curved in the opposite direction.

Gain/Slope

Gain raises or lowers the overall level of the signal, and can either crush blacks as it lowers highlights, or lift black levels while clipping highlights. The approximate ASC CDL equivalent of gain is called slope. For linear encodings, slope controls the brightness of the image while maintaining contrast – like adjusting the *f*- or T-stop. The old telecine gain function can be achieved via a combination of ASC offset and slope controls.

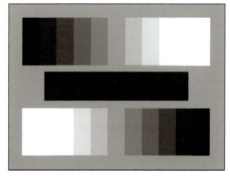

Figure 16.20 Grayscale demonstrating gain up.

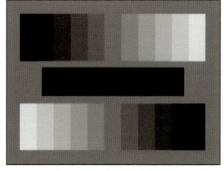

Figure 16.21 Grayscale demonstrating gain down.

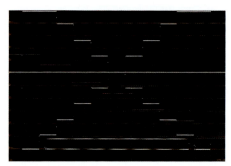

Figure 16.22 Waveform representation of gain up on the gray scale.

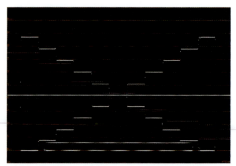

Figure 16.23 Waveform representation of gain down on the grayscale.

Hue

Hue refers to the overall color that is being selected and changes the range of colors available. An individual color selection can be rotated through 360 degrees of the color circle, moving it through every other hue, and giving the colorist tremendous selective control over both broad and narrow ranges of selected color.

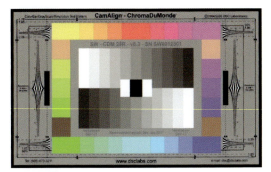

Figure 16.24 Normal hue setting.

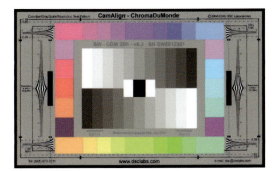

Figure 16.25 Hue rotated minus 90 degrees (note the 90 degree rotation in the color perimeter).

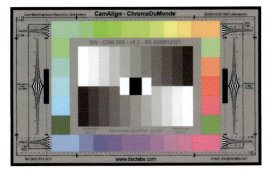

Figure 16.26 Hue rotated plus 90 degrees (note the opposite 90 degree rotation in the color perimeter).

Saturation

Saturation refers to the level of color or chrominance saturation or intensity in the image. Individual colors

or the entire picture can be made more or less vivid or intense in color with this tool, and accordingly, it can be a powerful aid in storytelling! Saturation is an amazing tool that we never had in film! ASC CDL also contains this tool, which functions identically.

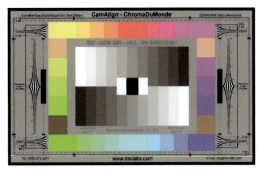

Figure 16.27 DSC Chroma Du Monde chart at normal saturation setting.

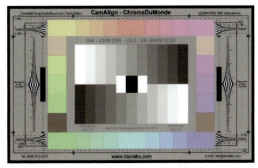

Figure 16.28 DSC Chroma Du Monde chart at reduced saturation setting.

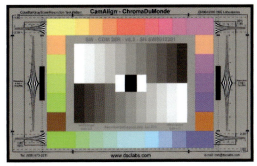

Figure 16.29 DSC Chroma Du Monde Chart at increased saturation setting.

ASC CDL is generally agnostic – when images in the color corrector are in a log format and a LUT transforms that log format into a displayable format, the ASC CDL can be applied either before or after the LUT. This is a powerful capability and can be a huge a source of confusion for those who don't understand the difference between applying standard operating procedure to log vs. displayable data.

Secondary Color Corrections

Secondary corrections are most often used to correct specific skin tones, or to isolate faces, and they are also frequently used to shape and "paint" specific areas of the frame.

Figure 16.30 Power windows can be used to isolate specific areas for secondary corrections.

Secondary color corrections also extend to yellow, cyan, and magenta colors, and further into isolated in-between colors. They are frequently used to control narrow ranges of color, and specific areas of the frame. Secondary corrections sometimes affect only a specific color or colors within an image, and secondary color isolation can be defined by hue, saturation, and luminance.

Power Windows and Shapes

Power windows and shapes can be used to isolate an area of the image for specific color adjustment. Colorists can use hand drawn shapes, such as squares, circles, or ovals, allowing for corrections to be made inside or outside those shapes, and softening can graduate the area affected to feather the edge.

Figure 16.31 An evening shot to be enhanced with secondary color correction.

Figure 16.32 A power window is set up to specify the area being corrected with a vignette.

Figure 16.33 The finished shot with vignette applied.

This technique is also commonly used to take down the exposure in distracting areas such as excessively bright windows with daylight outside.

Color Vectors

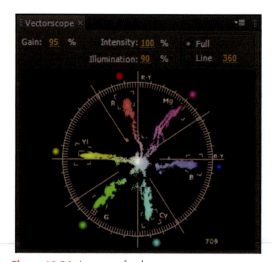

Figure 16.34 A range of color vectors.

Vectors can selectively isolate a single color within a scene for alteration without having to specifically pick a geographical area of the frame. This tool can be used to "grab" one (or more) small range(s) of color for manipulation without affecting any other colors.

Color Curves

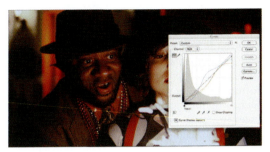

Figure 16.35 Color curves in action.

Curves can be used to bend a color range from a certain point while only slightly affecting the color or luminance below or above that point. Curves can be adjusted in the red, green, and blue channels independently, or as slaved RGB values.

Dynamics

Dynamics can be employed when a scene requires changing color correction and lighting conditions. The colorist can apply a gradual, key framed color change or animated color or contrast graduation to accentuate or repress the change. Instead of a constant grade throughout the scene, a key framed dynamic adjustment can be used to vary color, contrast, hue, saturation, or other adjustment parameters over part or all of a shot or scene over a selected duration.

Masks/Mattes/Keys

Masks/mattes/keys can be used to define a specific picture area that is being color corrected. They can be sued to specify correction areas with pixel and sub pixel precision, which is needed in many cases.

Figure 16.36 A shot requiring a matte for color correction.

Figure 16.37 Hold out matte for the subject

Figure 16.38 Counter matte for the background.

3D color correction requires pixel position accuracy. Color corrections that disagree from left eye to right eye in 3D assume their own position in 3D space, and that position almost never agrees with the scene data, resulting in left eye right eye discrepancies and rivalries, in other words, really bad 3D.

Color Correction and Decimation: Cautionary Notes

Decimation is defined as reducing the number of samples in a digital sampling scheme or system, and decimation can result from excessive re-sampling of color data in color correctors with low mathematical accuracy. This shows up most frequently as "crunchy" images, especially in mid tones and skin tones.

Decimation, Downsampling, or Subsampling

Decimation, downsampling, or subsampling refer to the processes of reducing the number of samples in a raster size or frame rate. When color, lift, gamma, and gain corrections are applied that result in fractional code changes in hue, contrast, or color, rounding errors can sometimes occur because there are no fractional code values available in a low accuracy integer color correction computation. A color code value that is altered upward or downward by a fraction of .49 of its original value as a result of a color correction will remain at the same code value. A color code value that is altered upward or downward by a fraction of .51 of its original value as a result of a color correction will jump to the next code value up or down. Enough accumulations of these rounding errors can result in color aliasing, or banding.

Figure 16.39 A gray graduation before resampling.

Figure 16.40 The same gray graduation after several re samplings.

The image on the left was subjected to three consecutive gamma corrections, resulting in the image on the right, which exhibits noticeable aliasing and banding, and a loss of overall smoothness to the graduation.

Noise Reduction (or Sometimes Amplification)

Noise in images is subjective. The cinematographer and his director may embrace noise and make it a part of their creative intent in storytelling. Adding noise is relatively easy. Other projects suffer from noisy images, and the creative team may ask the lab and the colorist to intervene to reduce noise. Noise reduction is more difficult.

Digital noise in motion images shows up as random fluctuations of color or luminance from pixel to pixel or from frame to frame on individual pixels. As seen in Chapter 2, noise is always present to some degree in digital images. Fixed pattern noise, readout noise, circuit noise, and photon noise all contribute to the overall noise character of the finished project. Removing noise from images is difficult because of the variety of noise sources and types. The type and contribution of noise sources can vary in different parts of the same image, from dark areas to light areas. Noise can be worsened in dark areas of the frame by lifting the exposure up in color correction. Basically, noise reduction tools analyze neighboring pixels across frames and frame ranges, and only allow certain types of variation in value.

A sophisticated set of tools is needed to manage noise from shot to shot, from scene to scene. Noise reduction (or amplification) may be applied to the footage to alter film grain or digital noise. Most color corrections systems include noise reduction tools, or can be supplemented with noise reduction plugins. When over-applied, noise reduction algorithms have the potential for reducing detail and contrast, and making images look very flat. Cinematographers need to be cautious not to over-soften the image when applying noise reduction. Studio quality control procedures will question excessive noise reduction and the resulting loss of picture detail as readily as they will question excessively noisy images. Noise reduction will blur any image details that it identifies as noise, so be careful not to sacrifice image detail. The finer the detail, the more likely it will be seen as noise by the noise reduction algorithm and blurred.

Reduction of chroma noise can create issues, and as chroma noise reduction is applied the risk of either color bleeding or desaturation of color increases. Contrast control can be used when attempting to restore some loss of picture detail experienced during noise reduction, but used excessively, contrast controls can sometimes result in areas patchy textures in images.

Film Grain and Film Look

Many cinematographers and directors still have a nostalgic fondness for the look of film, and one way to get that effect from digital acquisition is to add film grain to the finished image. Adding film grain also has the added benefit of helping to mask digital noise in the image. There are many libraries of digitally scanned film grain and numerous plugins for the purpose. Adding grain can be accomplished on many color correctors by adding a node to use a scanned grain plate as a matte. Using a layer mixer node to overlay the grain, the colorist can create a key to adjust the amount of grain using gain, and even adjust the size of the grain by using sizing to zoom in on the grain plate. The grain layer can be saturated more and less, increased or decreased in contrast, and even blurred. Using the layer mixer and matte functions in DaVinci Resolve to control the grain at the node level over the whole project, or per clip, is just one of several ways to add 35mm film grain to a project. For those creatives who have a strong nostalgia for the look of film, it is also possible to add film grain, gate weave, and even halation glow to images in the digital intermediate.

Sharpening

Spatial alterations of the image may include repositioning the frame, rotating the image, zooming, and panning. Resizing or resampling usually dictates applying a software resampling filter such as Bicubic, Lanxos, or a Mitchell sharpening kernel. Do not assume that the process of applying sharpening to images is easy or automated. Sharpening can become a source of great frustration if performed incorrectly.

Image sharpening is one of the most misunderstood areas of digital imaging. It is important for the cinematographer to have at least some basic familiarity with what image sharpening is and what it does. We are sometimes required to spatially resample or resize images in digital cinema. When scaling a raster image, a new image with a higher or lower number of pixels must be synthesized by software. Resampling is the mathematical technique used to create a new version of the image with a different width and/or height in pixels. Increasing the size of an image is called upsampling, and reducing its size is called downsampling. When we acquire (for example) in 6K and deliver in UHDTV, a fractional (or non-integer) downsample of the original image is required. When we acquire in 3.4K and deliver in 4K, a fractional (or non-integer) upsample is required.

When a digital sensor is presented with high contrast or high frequency edges that cross photosites at angles to the grid of the raster, they capture an average of what the individual pixels on the sensor see. In the greatly magnified example in Figure 16.41 and 16.42, we can examine the difference between the original real world image (left) and (greatly magnified) a digital sensor's attempt to capture that image (right).

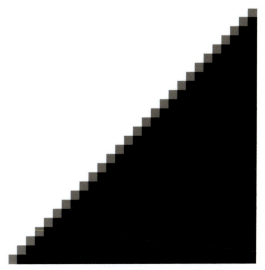

Figure 16.42 Greatly magnified – how a digital sensor sees that sharp edge.

When presented with very sharp real world high contrast edges, such as in Figure 16-41, a digital sensor sees something more like Figure 16-42 (greatly magnified).

When a high contrast high frequency image edge passes through any given photosite on the sensor, the photosite can only record a single value. In this case, the average value of the light hitting these individual photosites exactly along the edge is gray.

Isotropic capture of high contrast high frequency real world edges poses a challenge in digital imaging, which is exacerbated when we resize or resample those images larger or smaller, especially when we resize them by non-integer factors. For example, when we resize a 1920 pixel wide HD image up to 2048 pixels wide, we are upsampling that image by a factor of × 1.066666.

Frequently when questions of fractional scale upsampling and downsampling arise, it is useful to try using Nuke, a compositing package available from the Foundry, a British visual effects software package that is specifically designed for high end digital cinema use.

From the Foundry's *Nuke Online User Guide* on spatial transformations that involve remapping pixels from their original positions to new positions:

When question arises as to what values to assign remapped pixels, in the simplest case, they retain their original values. This can create problems with image quality, particularly in high contrast areas of the frame. For example, the figure below shows a close up of

Figure 16.41 Real world sharp edge in subject to be photographed.

a high-contrast feature that has been upsampled by a small percentage. The remapped pixels have retained their original values, but the result is a highly aliased, or jagged, edge.

The solution is to apply a more sophisticated filtering algorithm to determine the values of remapped pixels – one that takes into account, in some fashion, the values of neighboring pixels. When executing spatial transformations, Nuke lets you select from several filtering algorithms. Note that the effects of each filter shown represent the amount of sampling that occurs across a five pixel radius.

Figure 16.43 Magnified portion of original digital image from Figure 16.41 with different sharpening filters applied.

It must be stated that the choice of which filter to use is content dependent, test, test test! Several re sampling filter choices are shown:

- Impulse – Remapped pixels carry original values.
- Cubic (the Nuke default) – Remapped pixels receive some smoothing.

- Keys – Remapped pixels receive some smoothing, plus minor sharpening.
- Simon – Remapped pixels receive some smoothing, plus medium sharpening.
- Rifman – Remapped pixels receive some smoothing, plus significant sharpening.
- Mitchell – Remapped pixels receive some smoothing, plus blurring to hide pixelation.
- Parzen – Remapped pixels receive the greatest smoothing of all filters.
- Notch – Remapped pixels receive flat smoothing (which tends to hide Moiré patterns).
- Lanczos4 – Remapped pixels receive minor sharpening, good for scaling down. The filter number at the end of the filter name denotes the width of the filter (4 pixels).
- Lanczos6 – Remapped pixels receive some sharpening, good for scaling down. The filter number at the end of the filter name denotes the width of the filter (6 pixels).
- Sinc4 – Remapped pixels receive a lot of sharpening, good for scaling down. The filter number at the end of the filter name denotes the width of the filter (4 pixels).

When using filters that employ sharpening, such as Rifman, Lanczos, and Sinc, you may see a haloing effect as the filter becomes sharper.[2]

Using Sharpening Filters in Baselight

When using a Baselight color corrector, the basic scene settings (each timeline is a "scene"), the overall sharpening filter is selectable.

Figure 16.44 Sharpening scene settings menu in Baselight color corrector.

The default setting is "Adaptive." The info box for "Adaptive" states that "Adaptive interpolation uses an optional first pass average for large reductions followed by a 4-tap filter in X and Y where weights are fitted to the remaining resize ratio, and a blur is Sharpness less than 1.0 so the Sharpness slider can make the image softer even for large reductions." (This should not be necessary for correctly sampled images.)

The full pulldown list of other available filters (accessed by using a "Shift+click") shows these choices (Figure 16.45):

Adaptive

Adaptive (old)

Square Average

Circle Average

Composite

Fixed Cubic

Fixed Cubic Spline

Fixed Lanczos 4-tap

Fixed Lanczos 6-tap

Fixed Quintic 6-tap

Fixed Gaussian

Fixed Catmull-Rom

Fixed Simon

Fixed Linear

Fixed Nearest Pixel

Sharp Edge

Figure 16.45 Baselight menu of sharpening filter choices.

A new world of sharpening tools and textural enhancements is opening up, not just for resizing and resampling, but also for the creative manipulation of sharpness and texture in images. FilmLight Baselight is on the cutting edge of the innovation and evolution of this tool set.

FilmLight Texture Equalizer: A New Approach to Texture Management

The increase in the dynamic range of current HDR displays is also an increase of sharpness, as color contrast is a parameter of perceived sharpness. This might sound like an additional benefit of HDR technology, but we should not forget that sharpness and detail texture is also a strong visual attention cue. In the context of storytelling, an overall sharpness boost is not necessarily what a storyteller wants. Increased sharpness might draw the attention away from essential areas of the image that were once unimportant, distracting from the story.

Therefore, new spatial tools are needed to manage, control, and direct sharpness to where it is needed and control it where it might distract the audience. The simple, fixed-kernel based sharpening algorithms used for resampling images are not flexible enough to meet these new demands.

Texture Equalizer

Baselight's new Texture Equalizer tool allows tuning the contrast in different frequency bands by decomposing the image into temporally stable image pyramids.

Let's examine the test image in Figure 16.46.

Figure 16.46 Test image.

As we can see we have fine details and edges (for example the London underground map on the right) as well as smooth areas like the white shades.

Figure 16.47 Highest frequency decomposition of the image into image pyramids.

Figure 16.48 Second highest frequency decomposition of the image into image pyramids.

Figure 16.49 Third highest frequency decomposition of the image into image pyramids.

Figure 16.50 Fourth highest frequency decomposition of the image into image pyramids.

Figure 16.51 Fifth highest frequency decomposition of the image into image pyramids.

Figure 16.52 Lowest frequency decomposition of the image into image pyramids.

After the decomposition of the image into image pyramids in the frequency domain, we can see that the different features of the texture (edges vs. flat areas) are living in different image pyramids. We can now individually modulate the different spatial frequencies of the image with different weights.

One technical use-case of the tool is matching the appearance of different lenses. Here we have the same scene shot with two different lenses, a very sharp lens and a very soft one. In addition, the aperture is set differently, as we can see from the varying depth of field and bokeh.

Figure 16.53 Same scene captured with two different lenses at different stops.

We can mimic the softer MTF and apply this via Texture Equalizer onto the image captured with the sharp lens. As a result, we get a smoother picture of the image captured with the sharper lens.

Figure 16.54 Using Texture Equalizer to match the apparent sharpness of the softer lens.

We can also do the opposite, correcting the softer lens to match the sharpness of the sharper one. If carefully examined, we also get more noise in the modified image. This is because we are extensively boosting signals which had only a small amplitude in the original. Additional denoising would be required to further improve the match.

The tool can be applied to the image as a whole or to parts of the picture. In the case in Figure 16.55 the Texture Equalizer was only used on the subject in the foreground. This leaves the out of focus areas and bokeh untouched. With single-kernel sharpen filter the black–white top of the girl would have been amplified much more.

Figure 16.55 Matching the apparent sharpness of the sharper lens.

Other use-cases for Texture Equalizer are global changes of texture helping to create an abstraction of the real world and local application to surfaces such as skin.

This technology is not new and has been used in still photography for quite a while. The reason it was not used in motion pictures is that it is prone to temporal haloing and flicker artifacts. FilmLight modified and tuned the image pyramid construction to minimize those artifacts by using adaptive filters to generate the different pyramid levels.

Texture Highlight

It is almost impossible to capture all details of small practical lights while having enough exposure for the crucial parts of the image. This results in sensor-clipped highlights. This clipping produces artificial energy in the high spatial frequencies, which visually manifests in over sharp images.

Figure 16.56 shows an image and exposure parade of a horizontal frequency sweep captured by a theoretical lens with a typical MTF.

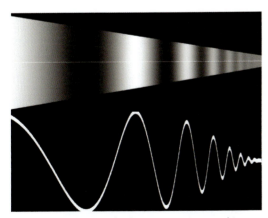

Figure 16.56 Image of a frequency sweep and its exposure parade.

In Figure 16.57, we see the same exposure parade and its Fourier transformation. We can see that any optical lens will decrease in contrast at higher frequencies.

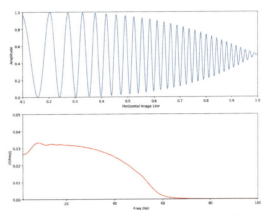

Figure 16.57 Exposure parade and Fourier transform of a horizontal frequency sweep.

But after the lens, the sensor of the camera can (and will) clip specular highlights due to the finite dynamic range a camera can capture. This artificial modification of the signal will introduce artificial energy in the higher frequencies. We cannot pre filter the signal really because the clipping is happening after the optical elements in the photon transfer process.

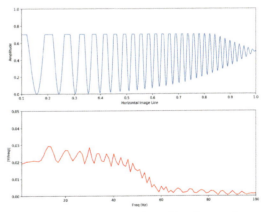

Figure 16.58 Exposure parade and Fourier transform of a horizontal frequency sweep – with clipped highlights.

Texture Highlight

Texture highlight applies a sophisticated frequency-based tuning of the image highlights, adding photographic qualities to overly sharp-looking content. It also helps to reintroduce variation in flat image parts, giving the picture more life in the highlights.

The issue is subtle in SDR but becomes significant when grading for an HDR release.[3]

Figure 16.59 Image with clipped highlights.

Figure 16.60 Image with clipped highlights – processed by texture highlights.

A Suggested Order of Operations in Grading on DaVinci

In this suggested order of operations for grading, it is important to first properly scale the images when conforming using the proper algorithms. It is advisable to scale and grade the entire timeline at the resolution desired for the final master. If the deliverable is to be a 4K master, all the files input for grading in the timeline should be scaled to match 4K. Scaling affects perceived sharpness and fine detail, so it is necessary to grade with scaled images, especially when adjusting sharpness as a last step in rendering. Before beginning the creative grade, it is necessary to properly color manage the project and set any specific input and output transforms (and/or LUTs).

Typically, for a feature it is helpful to prebuild a node tree to use as a starting point for every shot. There are numerous examples of prebuilt node trees on line, and the community of colorists is generous in their sharing.

A fixed node structure can be very useful to optimize a workflow and save time. A fixed template with pre-built tools can include power windows, keys for highlight recovery, vignettes, noise reduction, and film grain. The colorist might not use all of them in every shot, and will very likely always tweak settings for each shot. Having a pre-built node tree can save a lot of repetitive work in grading.

If you evolve a pre-built a node tree structure you intuitively know where everything is, which allows you to work much faster than building a

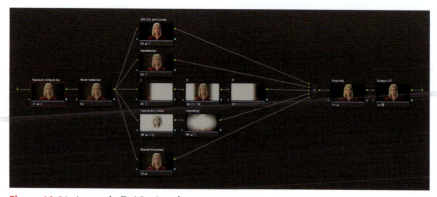

Figure 16.61 A sample DaVinci node tree structure.

node tree for each shot. It also makes managing changes and revisions much easier.

The first step in the grade is to balance the image and correct for things that happen on set like variations in exposure or white balance. We will call this first part of the process color correction. The aim of this step is to even out the "digital color negative" and optimize the footage from set. This first pass should remain "scene referred," and any adjustments made here should be made in the name of fixing mistakes and inconsistencies in the footage, so that any corrections, secondaries, keying, or processing will be "scene referred."

Figure 16.62 Node 1 – exposure, color temperature and tint pre trim.

Node 1 adjusts exposure to establish a consistent baseline so that subsequent grading will be based on a consistent exposure. This node also adjusts color temperature and tint to correct white balance or variance in color or tint due to inconsistency in lens color from shot to shot. Node 1 is also a "pre-trim" which will be the creative color correction following the "scene referred" color correction. This node will make fine adjustments to color on a shot to shot basis.

Now that the timeline is technically consistent, we can proceed to the next step in color grading to set the creative look. Any color corrections after this point can be applied to individual shots, groups of shots, or globally. This sample node tree is structured with parallel nodes that help colorists to blend numerous adjustments without those processes interfering with each other. Setting these

processes independently allows color grading to go faster and more efficiently. Most of the nodes we are adjusting from this point forward are based on the "scene referred" timeline values. This is why we do not do any secondary refinement or power windows in the "scene referred" nodes of the timeline. If (for example) we had keyed the sky and applied contrast before this point, we would have to re key the sky over again in the creative grade because it was based on a previous node.

Node 2 is a noise reduction, which is best adjusted after the exposure adjustment. Correcting exposure in an overexposed image will yield a cleaner image with less apparent noise, so noise should only be adjusted after the exposure has been corrected. Use caution when applying noise reduction – it can create motion artifacts and lose fine image detail.

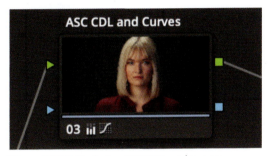

Figure 16.64 Node 3 – ASC CDL and curves.

Node 3 applies ASC-CDLs generated on set; this node can be readjusted to refine those looks using saturation and contrast. If both are applied in the same node, then contrast should be applied first in line as contrast amplifies saturation. If you want to adjust contrast and saturation using individual serial nodes, put the saturation node before the contrast node to avoid artifacts or decimation of chroma details. If you want to use a single node for these tasks, DaVinci automatically performs saturation adjustments before contrast adjustments.

More nodes can be added here to set the black and white point. These adjust small sections at the bottom and top part of the tone curve using the log control wheels.

Figure 16.63 Node 2 – noise reduction.

Figure 16.65 Node 4 – secondary color corrections.

Node 4 uses secondaries, refining the look with local selections such as a specific color to be shifted on different levels of luminance or hue vs. hue, soft clip, hue vs. saturation, etc.

Figure 16.66 Nodes 5-6-7 – dividing the image into three parts – left, center and right

Nodes 5-6-7, also applied on a parallel level, are preset to divide the image in three parts – left, middle, and right. These nodes, mostly using primary adjustments, are useful to grade scenes with dialog between two characters, or to direct attention to a character in the middle of the shot.

Figure 16.67 Faces node.

Node 8, also on a parallel level, is used to key and track faces. This node is for adjustments like tint, temperature, or any secondaries to affect the look of a character.

Figure 16.68 Node 9 – vignette node.

Node 9 adds some vignetting when needed. It is efficient to leave this node disabled with a preset adjustment, and then enable it when needed.

Figure 16.69 Node 10 – sharpness node.

Node 10 on another parallel level will adjust the sharpness/softness of the image. This first sharpness node may be used as a beauty tool. There are numerous tools available to adjust sharpness, which is mostly applied in the midtones. Softness can be applied almost anywhere, but some softness in the highlights can take some of the "digital" edge off the look.

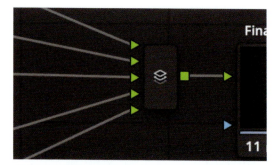

Figure 16.70 Parallel mixer.

A parallel mixer is used to merge all these adjustments all together.

Figure 16.71 Node 11 – final adjustments.

Node 11 is the final image adjustment, providing the last creative touches. There is no preset node for Open FX plugins or specific processes in this node tree since each should be at a specific place depending on the desired effect. There is no fixed node tree position for preset OFX; these nodes are task dependent.

Figure 16.72 Node 12 – output LUT node.

Node 12 is for the output Transform (or LUT) that is display referred, which will take the graded wide gamut log color space and apply a rendering to create a pleasing image and match different display devices. This node would replace the RRT-ODT in a non-ACES project. Always grade on the log image, never after any REC709 output LUT![4]

Output: The Digital Source Master (DSM)

Output is the final stage, where the color corrected images are rendered out to a master file sequence of the movie – a Digital Source Master, which is used to generate the myriad of deliverables required, or recorded out to film as a master negative(s) for lab use in making film deliverables.

Figure 16.73 Steps from digital intermediate to delivery.

From the color corrector, the digital source master (DSM) is used to generate the many deliverables of the project, including a Digital Cinema

Package (DCP), a DVD version, a Rec 709 HD master for broadcast TV and Blu-ray, an HDR version, an H-265 version for streaming, or a film output for traditional theatrical release.

The Digital Source Master created during the digital intermediate process can also be recorded to very stable archival yellow–cyan–magenta (YCM) separations on black-and-white film with an expected 100-year or longer life, and recorded to archival LTO tape for digital preservation to protect the value of the asset into the future.

Figure 16.74 ARRIlaser film recorder.

Figure 16.75 Lasers write the image to film.

The complexity of a deliverables list is massive, and the work involved in color correcting the project is not finished at the delivery of the DSM. Each transformation into another color space requires another "trim pass" of color correction to assure the closest possible correspondence to the artistic intent of the original look of the project.

What Possibilities Does ACES Hold for Color Grading?

Figure 16.76 shows a comparative color grading example of what grading in ACES color space can afford the cinematographer as opposed to grading in the de facto traditional 10-bit log color space. These are actual RAW images from an ARRIFLEX ALEXA, shot on location at Cape Canaveral Florida.

Figure 16.76 ARRI ALEXA image of the final space shuttle launch.

Source: Original images courtesy of: cinematographer Bill Bennett ASC; ARRI – Stephen Ukas Bradley; Gary Demos – NASA.

Figure 16.78 Waveform representation of the normal exposure.

The original shot, as captured and displayed in a conventional display workflow exhibits a tremendous overexposure in the exhaust of the rocket engines, an extreme challenge for any camera or color correction system.

In a traditional motion picture finishing 10-bit log Cineon color correction environment is employed, dialing down the overall exposure level in the shot to recover highlight detail which achieves a much different result; when the clipped highlights are brought down into a lower range, some small amount of additional detail is increased, but for the most part, the clipped highlight areas simply become gray highlights, and very little additional detail is introduced.

When the footage is linearized into an ACES 16-bit environment and the overall exposure is reduced in single stop increments the results are quite different. Each image in the color correction sequence is accompanied by a parade Waveform Monitor representation, so that the amount of image detail can be evaluated. Note the highlight clipping in the engines, and especially notice the graceful way in which detail and color are revealed in those highlight areas beginning at about five stops down!

Figure 16.79 Minus one stop corrected in a 10-bit log environment.

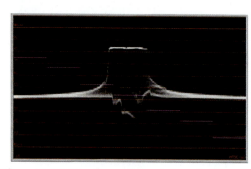

Figure 16.80 Waveform representation of minus one stop.

Images Corrected in a 10-bit Log Environment

Figure 16.77 Blowup and crop of the normal exposure.

Figure 16.81 Minus 2 stops corrected in a 10-bit log environment.

Figure 16.82 Waveform representation of minus 2 stops.

Figure 16.83 Minus 3 stops corrected in a 10-bit log environment.

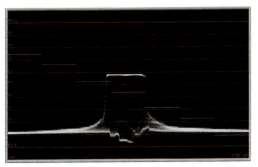

Figure 16.84 Waveform representation of minus 3 stops.

Figure 16.85 Minus 4 stops corrected in a 10-bit log environment.

Figure 16.86 Waveform representation of minus 4 stops.

Figure 16.87 Minus 5 stops corrected in a 10-bit log environment.

Figure 16.88 Waveform representation of minus 5 stops.

Figure 16.89 Minus 6 stops corrected in a 10-bit log environment.

Figure 16.90 Waveform representation of minus 6 stops.

Figure 16.93 Minus 1 stop corrected in a 16-bit ACES environment.

The images corrected in a 10-bit log environment for the most part maintain the clipped characteristics in the highlights and recover only a small amount of detail as they are corrected downward using the unity gain control. The overall highlight details retain the same waveform monitor profile, indicating that the highlight detail is not recovered, but rather, rendered as a gray tone of the original clipped highlights.

Images Corrected in a 16-bit ACES Environment

Figure 16.91 Normal blowup and crop of the normal exposure.

Figure 16.94 Waveform representation of minus 1 stop.

Figure 16.95 Minus 2 stops corrected in a 16-bit ACES environment.

Figure 16.92 Waveform representation of the normal exposure.

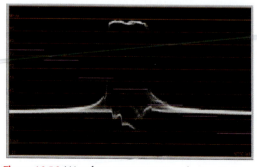

Figure 16.96 Waveform representation of minus 2 stops.

Figure 16.97 Minus 3 stops corrected in a 16-bit ACES environment.

Figure 16.101 Minus 5 stops corrected in a 16-bit ACES environment.

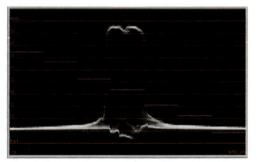

Figure 16.98 Waveform representation of minus 3 stops.

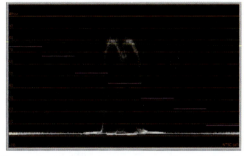

Figure 16.102 Waveform representation of minus 5 stops.

Figure 16.99 Minus 4 stops corrected in a 16-bit ACES environment.

Figure 16.103 Minus 6 stops corrected in a 16-bit ACES environment.

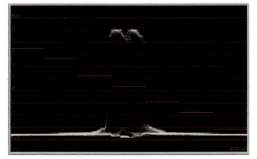

Figure 16.100 Waveform representation of minus 4 stops.

Figure 16.104 Waveform representation of minus 6 stops.

As we can see, the same 12-bit original images corrected in an ACES 16-bit environment actually reveal highlight detail in the overexposed areas that was heretofore unrecoverable when working in a 10-bit log environment. Working in an ACES environment has the potential to give cinematographers some amazing advantages in color correction!

Color Correction Systems

Some of the tools of digital intermediate are versions of the same tools used for on-set color correction, and have been discussed in prior chapters for use in look management. It is no surprise that many of those applications are smaller, more compact versions of much bigger horsepower feature quality color correction systems. Those tools were built to extend the capabilities of the DI suite to set, and conversely, to smooth the path from set to final color correction. Driving open source interoperability between all of these systems has been the focus of the American Society of Cinematographers Technical Committee for nearly a decade, and we are now reaching an era of maturity on that learning curve. Cinematographers everywhere will benefit in seeing their vision more efficiently and cost-effectively achieved by the use of these tool sets.

Assimilate Scratch

www.assimilateinc.com/products/

Figure 16.105 Assimilate Scratch screen.

Assimilate Scratch is a high end, real-time, nondestructive primary and secondary color grading system. Grading features include source-side adjustments for mixed color space workflows, match, and auto grading, 2D and shape tracking, keying based on Vector, Chroma, or Luminance, integrated Histogram, Waveform, Vectorscope, and Color Curve views, group shots, copy/paste color grades and reference libraries, key frames and animation curves, and import and save 1D and 3D LUTs based on primary color grades.

Scratch is ASC-CDL compliant, and integrates via XML with other tools such as Nuke, Shotgun, Avid and Final Cut Pro, and supports QuickTime, DPX, ACES, and over 50 additional formats, and blends color correction with 3D compositing and VFX tools in one unified, real-time system.

Scratch supports multiple camera formats including REDCODE raw R3D with support for multiple RED Rocket cards, ARRI raw, Sony F65, Phantom high speed cameras, SI2K, Panasonic P2/MXF and AVCHD, Canon C300, 5D, 7D, GoPro, and others.

Autodesk Lustre

www.autodesk.com/products/flame/overview

Figure 16.106 Autodesk Lustre color screen.

Autodesk Lustre is a software based high end configurable color-grading solution for film, television, and stereoscopic projects. Lustre uses parallel processing and graphical processing unit rendering technologies. It can share media and timelines with Autodesk Flame and Autodesk Smoke visual effects and finishing software. Functionality includes degrain, automatic region tracking, advanced keying tools for high-quality color isolation, a shape system with advanced controls like freehand shapes, hierarchical shape animations, and variable-edged softness.

Blackmagic DaVinci Resolve

www.blackmagicdesign.com/products/davinciresolve/

Figure 16.107 Blackmagic DaVinci Resolve color correction panels.

DaVinci Resolve is a high end (and yet at a modest budget) software-based color corrector that allows for image processing at 32-bit floating point YRGB, so that all correction math is at high bit depth in real time, with the ability to adjust luminance gain without rebalancing the color of whites, mids, or blacks. Functionality includes unlimited grades, primaries, secondaries, reframing, 3D object tracking, image stabilization, high dynamic range, RGB mixing, custom curves, custom HSL curve grading, power windows, grouped clip grading, dynamic timeline, color decision lists, gallery stills and grades, metadata management, export of 3D LUTs from grades, and copy and paste grades.

Resolve can grade directly from camera files, grade direct with ARRI ALEXA raw .ari files including v3 color science, RED One R3D files including RED color3 and REDgamma3 with premium deBayer and RED EPIC R3D files including 5K and HDRx with image blend. Also supports Phantom, GoPro, Canon C300 and 5D, Sony, and others natively.

Digital Vision Nucoda

https://digitalvision.world/products/nucoda/

Figure 16.108 Digital Vision Nucoda color correction screen.

Nucoda is a high end color correction system that supports EDLs and CUT lists, and can handle multiple format images, including 4K. Functionality includes timeline and shot bookmarks allow for better organization and retrieval of information and multiple versions of shots to the same time line. Isolation can be matte based, user-defined shape based or keyer based, and layers can be selectively cached to streamline operations and greatly enhance user interactivity.

Nucoda is interoperable with third-party systems supporting industry standard formats like Avid DNxHD, AAF, MXF and Apple ProRes. Nucoda reads and writes Avid DNxHD formats, MXF, and Quicktime formats natively. Raw Camera Support

includes Sony F65 raw, ARRI ALEXA raw, RED raw, EPIC HDRx blending support, Silicon Imaging SI-2k, and Phantom CINE.

FilmLight Baselight

www.filmlight.ltd.uk/

Figure 16.109 Baselight color correction control panels.

Baselight is a very powerful software-based, high end, resolution and format independent system that works with linear, video, log, and ACES image sequences. Baselight provides fully integrated editorial workflows with editorial systems including Avid and Apple Final Cut Pro. Integration includes AAF import and export, MXF reading, writing, and conform of multi-track timelines, and ALE export. Baselight systems incorporate Truelight, which provides color-accurate emulation on grading displays. The system also integrates directly with the Northlight, a high-resolution digital film scanner, and most other scanners and telecines. Baselight systems can share local storage, and allow third-party systems such as Autodesk Flame and Smoke, Pixel Farm PF Clean to read and write to common storage in the background.

Grass Valley Rio

www.grassvalley.com/products/rio/

Figure 16.110 Grass Valley Rio color correction panels.

Rio is Grass Valley's high end software-based color and finishing system. 8K 60p Rio can handle high frame rate file-based media and multi-layer Stereo3D projects. Rio will work from local, SAN, NAS in combination, configurable for video i/o or network-only connectivity, and Rio is scalable by adding GPUs, storage or i/o, and integrates into ACES pipelines, to deliver a standard, future-proof color space.

Rio includes 2D and S3D color and finishing toolsets for fixes, titles, compositing, re-editing or deliverables, working with media from high frame rate, Stereo3D, OpenEXR, RED HDRx. Rio supports ARRI, Canon, SONY, Phantom, Silicon Image, and GoPro. When color correction is complete, Rio holds an uncommitted master, from which all the deliverables can be created and played out in real time without rendering or using up any further workspace.

Mistika

www.sgo.es/mistika-ultima/

Figure 16.111 Mistika timeline screen.

Figure 16.112 Mistika color correction screen.

Mistika is a real-time, high-end time-line based DI, editing, compositing, effects, and color grading systems for both 2D and especially stereoscopic 3D productions, resolution and color space independent. It is a powerful, software-based, open architecture and hardware system, with open SAN connectivity useable across multiple systems, while third-party creative systems can read and write to the same storage in the background.

Pandora Revolution

https://pandoratek.global/products/revolution-product-page/

Figure 16.113 Pandora Revolution runs on off the shelf hardware.

Figure 16.114 Pandora Revolution color correction panels.

The Pandora Revolution Express color correction system supports the RED Rocket card giving real time play out of 4K R3D files in source or conform order, converting RED material to other file formats including ProRes, DNxHD, DPX, and TIFF. Revolution functionality includes scene change detector, FastTrack auto tracking, 1D and 3D LUTs, ASC CDL compatibility, Bezier Primaries, and multiple 6-vector corrections, unlimited secondary corrections, foreground and background keying and image defocus, clipping, blanking, and color space legalizing. Functionality includes XSan and ADIC compatibility, data management, play out of mixed format and resolution material, real time spatial processor to create files in other resolutions, import or creation of EDLs and scan lists, keycode, and timecode.

Red Giant Magic Bullet Colorista II

www.redgiant.com/products/magic-bullet-colorista

Figure 16.115 Red Giant Magic Bullet Colorista color correction screen.

At the cost-conscious end of the spectrum, Red Giant's Magic Bullet Colorista II software can color correct on a budget. Colorista II is a native plug-in for Final Cut Pro, After Effects, and Premiere Pro. A GPU accelerator and CPU render engine optimizes render speed on laptops, and CPU-only render farms can also run Colorista II.

Notes

1. These two paragraphs were contributed by Jeremy Selan – *Cinematic Color: From Your Monitor to the Big Screen*.
2. From the Foundry's *Nuke Online User Guide* on spatial transformations that involve remapping pixels from their original positions to new positions.
3. Contributed by Daniele Siragusano of FilmLight Ltd.
4. This section was contributed by Valentin Alt.

Chapter 17

Delivering and Archiving Digital Movies

Most of the motion pictures made over the last century have been photographed on film. In the last 20 years, evolutionary developments enabled cinematographers to capture images using digital technology. Digital workflows are dynamic and ever evolving, and to date, nearly every motion picture acquired digitally has used a different workflow in some aspect or another. The purpose of this chapter is to provide an understanding of how motion pictures that are photographed digitally are delivered and how they can be archived. The issues of long-term digital storage and the cost of the storage are part of this discussion.

Digital Cinema Initiatives, LLC (DCI): Architect of Digital Cinema

What digital cinema now does was defined by the major Hollywood motion picture studios in the Digital Cinema Specification, created by their collaborative group, Digital Cinema Initiatives, LLC, best known as DCI. The DCI Specification, first published in July, 2005 created a wide range of concepts supporting the studio's objectives for digital cinema. The standards and engineering specifics that define *how* it is done were later codified in SMPTE standards. (Digital Cinema by definition does not include HDTV or E-Cinema, a term largely used in theaters abroad.)

Between 1999 and 2002 it became apparent to the studios that Rec 709 color space high definition video was insufficient to differentiate the exhibition of theatrical motion pictures on big screens from home video viewing.

Furthermore, early efforts at putting digital onto theater screens were in chaos. Suppliers were scrambling to become "gatekeepers" of the new digital technologies, each hoping to develop an essential technology that everyone would have to buy, or at least license, from them. The main problem was these different manufacturers were all using different image resolution, compression, encryption, and file packaging.

This problem really became apparent when George Lucas, who had done a prototype digital presentation to a couple of theaters with paying customers for *Star Wars* Episode 1, photographed Episode II almost exclusively in digital. To show this movie in 85 theaters in the United States required post production to create a reported 11 unique digital masters to play on the various systems! At the time, a 35mm film print could be shown on 120,000 screens around the world.

DCI was formed and tasked with studying what new characteristics and practices would be needed to accommodate a level of quality that could elevate the theater viewing experience to better than both the home and existing theater viewing experience in order to continue to attract audiences.

Their initial goal was to create a system in theaters equivalent in quality to the first screening of a 35mm answer print – every time. Along with objectives of interoperability, extensibility, reliability, security, and quality control, it was decided it should also be free of IP. An additional objective of DCI was to develop a model for financing the change to digital. More on that later.

Engineers, compression, encryption, production, and post production experts were employed to construct a new digital system for finishing, distributing, and showing movies. They worked with SMPTE to assure interoperability and compatibility of content, moving from studios and distributors to exhibitors and with the American Society of Cinematographers to create open source content to rigorously stress test imaging systems. Continuing with SMPTE and studio support, they drove the codification, engineering, and publication of standards, including specifics for 2K and eventually 4K (and beyond) mastering resolution, audio mapping, multiplexing, and the JPEG 2000 layered scalable compression specifications that are the building blocks of the DCP.[1]

Delivering a Motion Picture

There are several possible output deliverables with which the cinematographer should be concerned.

1. Native 4K DCI P3 color space
2. Native 4K DCI Dolby Vision high dynamic range
3. UHD standard dynamic range
4. UHD high dynamic range HLG, HDR10+ or Dolby Vision
5. 2K DCI standard dynamic range
6. 2K DCI high dynamic range Dolby Vision
7. HD REC 709 standard dynamic range
8. HD high dynamic range HLG, HDR10+ or Dolby Vision
9. An original digital to film output negative from digital intermediate
10. An original cut picture negative (for projects originated on film – exceedingly rare!)

The cinematographer has the duty and responsibility to do a Rec 709 "trim pass" to create a video master for DVD and Blu-ray that resembles as closely as possible (within the smaller gamut of Rec 709 video) both the DCI P3 color space and high dynamic range finished digital intermediate renders.

The Digital Source Master and the Digital Cinema Distribution Master

The DSM (Digital Source Master) is the source data from the final color correction output render and the final audio master mix of a film. The DSM serves as the basis for the generation of DCDMs, which in turn combines all the elements that are needed to create a Digital Cinema Package (DCP). A Digital Cinema Distribution Master (DCDM) is a collection of all the images, sound, subtitles, metadata, and other language versions for generation of output referred display specific versions. A DCDM is normally encoded as 12-bit linear TIFF (Tagged Image File Format) files in x, y, z color space which is placed into the most significant bits of a 16-bit word, with the remaining 4 bits filled with zeros for color bit depth overhead and for flexibility in creation of the Digital Cinema Package. This 12-bit TIFF copy of the project is usually considered the main deliverable and the primary archival copy of the movie. If the

project was acquired at 23.976 frames per second then the picture is usually reparsed from 23.976 frames per second to 24 frames per second and audio is resampled to match for 24 frame per second playout of the DCP. The sound is stored as a 24-bit uncompressed Broadcast WAV file in 5.1 and sampled at 48 or 96kHz.

The DCDM serves as an uncompressed digital master for archival purposes and it can serve as a direct source for a demonstration of the material. From here, the studio or distributor will frequently aggregate the combined assets of the project into an Interoperable Mastering Format master structure. An archival picture negative may be made, and we have seen in Chapter 16 the mechanics of outputting digital pictures to film.

Interoperable Master Format (IMF)

Interoperable Master Format (IMF) is a SMPTE standard for providing a single, interchangeable master file format and structure for the distribution of content from a file-based final master. IMF is an evolution of the Digital Cinema Package (DCP) architecture, providing a complete file interchange unit to the distribution channel. While DCP is about theatrical content distribution, IMF is a master format for creating multiple tailored versions of the same piece of content for different audiences. It allows distribution of unique versions from content owners to service providers, distributors, and multiple final destinations such as Airlines, Broadcaster, OTT, streaming, DVD authoring, and more. IMF eliminates the need to create multiple master versions by separating each market requirement into Composition Play Lists (CPL) that reference the available MXF media files included in an IMF package. Individual CPLs are used to create versions based on the master essence components for each of the differing market audiences. An IMF package includes the following essence wrapped into MXF track files.

1. Video essence (J2K up to UHD)
2. Audio essence (24-bit uncompressed, any number of channels)
3. Data essence (subtitles and captioning using IMSC Timed Text)1
4. Dynamic metadata (metadata changes over time)
5. Composition Play List (CPL) – human readable XML, similar to an Edit Decision List
6. References track files referenced via UUID instead of directory paths
7. Packaging data XML (asset map, packing list, and volume index)

Archiving a Motion Picture in the Digital Age

The practice of archiving digital motion pictures is not close to achieving an ideal long-term solution. The current solutions for archiving movies currently include magnetic LTO tape (Linear Tape Opensource) developed by a consortium of magnetic media companies, and film, in the form of color negative(s) or separation masters filmed out from the finished RGB digital files.

The magnetic tape solution is prone to errors and must be media migrated on a regularly scheduled basis. Once every 3 to 5 years, the LTO tapes must be read out and cloned, error checked, and error corrected from multiple copies. The cost of migrating media regularly over the course of even 50 years will run into many tens of thousands of dollars, a cost which has never been factored into the life expectancy of a movie in the past. The process is prone to errors, and any data lost from all of the cloned digital copies is data lost permanently.

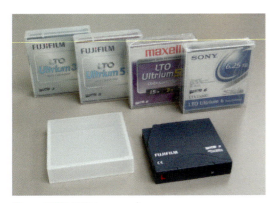

Figure 17.1 LTO tape media.

In addition, LTO stock is subject to the physical constraints of all magnetic media, such as cosmic rays, gamma rays, and sunspots such as the Carrington event, a series of solar coronal mass ejections that lasted from August 28 until September 2, 1859, which caused a geomagnetic storm.

The Carrington Event

According to NASA:

At 11:18 a.m. on the cloudless morning of Thursday, September 1, 1859, 33-year-old Richard Carrington – widely acknowledged to be one of England's foremost solar astronomers – was in his well-appointed private observatory. Just as usual on every sunny day, his telescope was projecting an 11-inch-wide image of the sun on a screen, and Carrington skillfully drew the sunspots he saw.

On that morning, he was capturing the likeness of an enormous group of sunspots. Suddenly, before his eyes, two brilliant beads of blinding white light appeared over the sunspots, intensified rapidly, and became kidney-shaped. Realizing that he was witnessing something unprecedented and "being somewhat flurried by the surprise," Carrington later wrote, "I hastily ran to call someone to witness the exhibition with me. On returning within 60 seconds, I was mortified to find that it was already much changed and enfeebled." He and his witness watched the white spots contract to mere pinpoints and disappear.

It was 11:23 a.m. Only five minutes had passed.

Just before dawn the next day, skies all over planet Earth erupted in red, green, and purple auroras so brilliant that newspapers could be read as easily as in daylight. Indeed, stunning auroras pulsated even at near tropical latitudes over Cuba, the Bahamas, Jamaica, El Salvador, and Hawaii.

Even more disconcerting, telegraph systems worldwide went haywire. Spark discharges shocked telegraph operators and set the telegraph paper on fire. Even when telegraphers disconnected the batteries powering the lines, aurora-induced electric currents in the wires still allowed messages to be transmitted.

"What Carrington saw was a white-light solar flare – a magnetic explosion on the sun," explains David Hathaway, solar physics team lead at NASA's Marshall Space Flight Center in Huntsville, Alabama.

Now we know that solar flares happen frequently, especially during solar sunspot maximum. Most betray their existence by releasing X-rays (recorded by X-ray telescopes in space) and radio noise (recorded by radio telescopes in space and on Earth). In Carrington's day, however, there were no X-ray satellites or radio telescopes. No one knew flares existed until that September morning when one super-flare produced enough light to rival the brightness of the sun itself.[2]

In view of such a history, the value of a magnetic media archive would seem to dictate that the archive should be kept very deep underground!

There are some promising non magnetic storage technologies being developed at the time of this printing such as DOTS: Digital Optical Technology System from Group 47.

This nonmagnetic, chemically inert technology promises to be archival for 100+ years, and immune from electromagnetic fields including electromagnetic pulse (EMP). DOTS will be a visual "eye-readable" method of storing digital files. With sufficient magnification, one can actually see the digital information. A "Rosetta Leader™" specification calls for microfiche-scale human readable text at the beginning of each tape with instructions on how the data is encoded and instructions on how to actually construct a reader. Because the information is visible, as long as cameras and imaging devices are available, the information can always be recoverable.

Taking Digital Out to Archival Film

The digital to analog solution for archiving a movie involves creating a yellow–cyan–magenta Color Separation Master set for a filmed out archival copy of the digital intermediate data on three separate negatives on Estar black and white film stock. This process is considered to be stable for hundreds of years after development (if properly stored) and is currently the only solution for long-term archival preservation and restoration, at least for as long as we still have film.

Figure 17.2 Archival YCM separations on black and white film.

The Digital Dilemma

The issues of archiving digital media prompted the Academy of Motion Picture Arts and Sciences to conduct studies that resulted in two very complete reports, which are freely available for download: *The Digital Dilemma*, and *The Digital Dilemma 2*. These reports go into great depth on the subject of archiving media, and are "must read" reports for cinematographers, directors, producers and studio executives.
www.oscars.org/science-technology/council/projects/digitaldilemma/
www.oscars.org/science-technology/sci-tech-projects/digital-dilemma-2
    It is important to maintain agreement between film makers and studios that will help protect both the creative intent of the film makers and

the investment of the studio both in the short and long term. The framework for creating a workflow starts on set with common "metadata" such as camera roll, sound roll, sc#, take#, script notes, etc., and then preserving that metadata through production and into the archive. In some cases, it may even be necessary to store some of the hardware and software used in the film making process with the footage and metadata for future reference. The task of an efficient metadata schema is to automate the collection and preservation of all of these important pieces of the media puzzle for each product that the studio creates, but also to make the data accessible on a day-to-day basis. The principal value of metadata in this case is to enable us to quickly and efficiently find the elements that we have invested so much time and money into creating.
    Due to constant changes in the technology of digital acquisition, it is vital to test any proposed workflow before starting principal photography. During camera testing, sample files or tapes should be run through the workflow in order to determine equipment compatibility. If at all possible, testing should extend all the way to film out and DCP and in the name of thoroughness, the film archival step should also be tested. Copies of setup files of the cameras being used should be preserved and turned over to production, and changes made to camera setups or firmware versioning during production should also be noted in writing and turned over to production. Generally, it is bad practice to change firmware on any camera during production, and it is generally agreed that a "version lock" should be declared at the commencement of principal photography, unless there is some deeply compelling reason to do otherwise.
    Following the creation of the editorial and production dailies, two LTO tape copies of the original material TAR (Tape Archive) per shot should be made at the end of each day of shooting. These tapes should include all footage shot that day and be written in a file format such as DPX or ACES Open EXR. One tape should be labeled as the Production Copy, the other should be labeled as the Archival Copy. In addition to the LTOs, copies of all the paperwork pertaining to that day's production should be turned over to the production department. These should include camera reports including "circled" takes, "star" takes, "burned" takes and all information relevant to that day's shooting. All of the metadata pertaining to a day's production coming from the disk recorder or tape deck should be captured in a file and turned over to production along with the LTOs on a daily

basis. XML is the preferred language but that is not exclusive.

VFX shots should be named by the editorial staff using an agreed naming convention, and should have a clear path noted to their location with relationship to the ODCN (Original Digital Cinema Negative) digital files. In addition, it is recommended that post production, director of photography, VFX supervisor, representatives from the digital intermediate post facility, and editorial agree on the workflow for VFX. Each VFX house should be supplied with a color space document specifying what the colors pace and color pipeline will be. The director of photography and the director should approve any LUTs used, and the methodology for use of log and linear workflows should be specified and followed throughout the production.

At the time when the "First Assembly" is loaded to a SAN, an LTO tape set of the entire assembly should be written TAR per scene. In addition, all metadata such as Avid AAF files or FCP EDLs and XML files pertaining to that version should be archived and delivered to production. As footage is subsequently added in the completion of the editing of the film, additional LTO protection copies should be made regularly.

The Digital Cinema Package or DCP

The DCP, or Digital Cinema Package, is a file wrapper and multiplexing system of digital files used for storing and playing digital cinema picture, sound, synchronization, and other data files on theatrical projection systems. It uses a material exchange format (MXF) file structure to multiplex PCM audio and heavily compressed JPEG 2000 picture files for delivery to theaters. A DCP has the ability to play at 4K or 2K resolution from the same media, a feature enabled by the flexible JPEG 2000 compression format's ability to decode more or fewer detail layers on demand.

DCP Delivery to Theaters

The DCP occasionally still arrives at a theater projection booth in a small Pelican Case which contains a hard disk drive mounted in a carrier rack unit (CRU) DataPort DX 115 Carrier that slides into a dock for ingest into either a cinema server or storage unit. Early servers used link encryption to securely get the data from the server to the projector, where its media block decrypted the content. In later units, the DCP content went from the storage unit to an integrated media

block (IMB) built into the projector. Today, new projectors may contain an integrated media server (IMS) with the storage on the same card as the IMB. All of these methods securely store the DCP's data files, picture, and sound, subtitle and encryption information, and decrypt and decode the DCP itself.

Figure 17.3 Digital Cinema Package on a disk drive.

A key delivery message (KDM) that is specific to the server/IMB/IMS, projector, and theater screen arrives separately to unlock the encrypted DCP for showing. These keys are digital security codes that activate access to the content for a specific amount of time on specific date(s) and are administered by the studio distribution department. The studio's physical distribution supplier (usually a facility-type company) generates the actual KDM. There are occasional problems in the projection booth when the KDM codes arrive corrupted, but distribution of movies on hard drives is less expensive than manufacturing release prints, and digital exhibition doesn't suffer from film dirt, scratches, or breaks, weaving, or bad splices. It is also much harder to pirate a digital movie than a film print. The KDM key system and advanced encryption technologies make it extremely difficult to pirate DCP files.

In the last decade, domestic (U.S.) delivery of physical hard drives yielded to more mass-distribution of DCPs by satellite directly to theaters, especially for wide releases. Hard drives continued to fill in for inaccessible sites (often in cities due to interference), site failures, smaller releases, or revisions.

In this decade, as domestic connectivity improves due to expanded Internet use and deployment, we are beginning to employ terrestrial electronic distribution of DCPs over IP on a variety of physical "last mile" connections such as fiber and high-performance cable to theaters. Each of these methods have their own set of economics, benefits, and shortcomings. Generally, these are progressive in terms of lower cost, immunity to weather and responsiveness to problems or changes.

The Migration from Film to Digital

Numerous factors have contributed to the transition from film projection to digital exhibition. The quality of the theatrical viewing experience has been significantly improved by digital projection, and will continue to do so. The economics of exhibition have been revolutionized in several ways by digital projection. The cost of distributing a movie digitally is now a smaller fraction of the cost of distributing on film prints. This cost will continue to decline.

One effective result has been a drastic reduction in the quantity of film used in Hollywood in the last few years. However, if you look back to 1990, it is clear that the total market for film has long been under intense technological attack. In the 1990s, digital still cameras began their capture of 93% of the total U.S. domestic market for film stock, which was formerly used primarily for snap-shots and to a lesser extent, professional still use. This left the 6% of 1990s' total film use that was motion picture and the 1% medical and special-use remaining largely unchanged.

One of the economic factors in the cost basis of film manufacturing has been the release print. A 100-minute film uses 9,000+ feet of film per print, which in quantity can cost around $1,000.00 dollars. If we multiply that by an order of 2500 prints for a studio movie, we get 225,000 feet of release print film, or a savings of about $2.5 million dollars on the release of a film. It's not hard to see what effect the loss of that kind of volume can do to disrupt the cost basis of manufacturing film (especially negative film) might be. With the subsequent dropoff of film negative sales to motion pictures, commercials, television, music videos, documentaries, plus the resulting loss in

interpositive, internegative, print stock and the aforementioned loss of the consumer film market, film manufacturers, and film developing laboratories have been forced to dramatically change what was left of their business models.

It is important to note that these cost savings did not immediately accrue to studios and distributors. The main *business* objective of DCI was to create a method to help finance the estimated $1–2 billion dollar investment required to change domestic exhibition to digital.

In DCI business meetings, studio's representatives were each paired with their lawyers to ensure the collaboration did not drift into antitrust behavior. The tone was "Collaborate on technology, compete on content."

The result of these discussions was a "Virtual Print Fee" (VPF) with the actual financing being done by early integrators, some equipment manufacturers, and others. Participating studios independently negotiated their own agreements with these third party lenders. This was essential to "jump start" a transition that would otherwise probably never have happened. In practice, using the hypothetical cost example above, and a similarly derived agreement example, the lions' share of the former release print cost would instead be paid to the financing entity by the studio. Another much smaller portion borne by the studio would cover the cost of DCDM mastering and hard drive replication, with small additional charges for shipping and recycling for reuse.

The initial term of the earliest VPFs were as long as 12 years. Later VPFs were for shorter periods and lesser amounts until the digital deployment exceeded its critical mass. The last new VPFs in the United State. were discontinued in the last five years, and the world is now converted to DCI digital cinema.

In the meantime, this global cinema standards-based system builds on its DCI foundation with improvements like immersive sound (Dolby Atmos, MCA), laser projection, HDR, and extended color/gamut presentation (Dolby Vision Cinema), additional frame rates, archival frame rates, and on into a bright future.[3]

A Simplified Source Material Digital Assets List for IMF Packaging Delivery

Interoperable Master Format (IMF) deliverables created according to SMPTE ST 2067-21.

IMF Application #2E.

Asset Map XML file
Packing List XML file

1 or more Composition Playlist (CPL) XML file(s), representing a single audio language each, containing;
1 image virtual track
1 surround audio virtual track (6 channels)
1 stereo audio virtual track (2 channels)
Volume Index and Output Profile List (OPL)

IMF Video
Native 4K DCI
UHD
Native 2K DCI
HD

IMF Audio
Surround audio
Stereo audio

ProRes 422 HQ
Primary mezzanine audio
Timed text timing
TTML 1
SCC
EBU STL
Lambda subtitles – Japanese language only

Subtitles as a separate file
Forced narrative subtitles

Accessibility files (SDH and CC)
SDH and closed captioning as separate file

Audio description
Acceptable audio description formats (non-QuickTime)
Acceptable audio description formats (QuickTime)

Alternate language audio as a separate file
Acceptable alternate language audio formats (non-QuickTime)
Acceptable alternate language audio formats (QuickTime)
5.1 Surround mix – mastering and archive
2.0 Stereo Mix – mastering and archive

Dolby Atmos TM deliverable requirements
Dub cards

Production materials
Production material filenames

Movie content metadata
Artwork
Display art – verticals, horizontals, title card and title treatment
Story art

A Simplified Motion Picture Studio Deliverables List for Film Projects

Here for cinematographers to consider is a list of the elements that a studio will require in the delivery of a finished motion picture on film. It is important to understand the depth of this list, if only to impact the seriousness of the job of the cinematographer, and the awesome responsibility that accompanies the creative process.

Media

One original cut picture negative or one original digital output negative, 2D and 3D

One each 2D and 3D 35mm camera original full aperture color cut negatives titled, assembled, and conformed to the final domestic release version, or one each 2D and 3D fully timed, digital 35mm archival negatives from the Digital Intermediate process.

Digital intermediate original data files 2D and 3D

One set of all the data files used to create the final version of the original digital output negative delivered on current version of LTO tape, delivered as a series of uncompressed frames in 10-bit log .dpx format, "DPX TAR format," uncompressed TAR per reel, labeled to identify its position in the sequence of tapes (e.g. 2 of 10 tapes). One single reel will be stored on each LTO tape.

D.I. delivered in both DCI P3 Color Space and Rec 709 Color Space

LTO tape backup details:
Each tape should have a label affixed to the tape reel and case that includes "DPX TAR format," and includes a Directory File for each tape logging the contents of the tape according in the following format:

Title
Picture language (e.g. English)
Reel number or content type: (e.g. Reel 3, textless backgrounds, etc.)
Color–Space (e.g. P3 or Rec 709)
If P3, state the film stock number the DI was calibrated to print to.
Texted/Textless (e.g. texted)
Stereo (e.g. 3D-left, 3D-right, 2D-mono)
Format (e.g. 10-bit log DPX)

Medium (e.g. LTO-4)
Image width (e.g. 2,048 pixels)
Image height (e.g. 1,156 pixels)
File size per frame (e.g. 12.2MB)
Frame count (e.g. 20,178 frames)
Frame in (e.g. 0001234.dpx)
Frame out (e.g. 0021413.dpx)
Reel size (in GB) (e.g. 239.69GB)
DI Lab (e.g. Tech)
Date rendered (create datestamp from first file; e.g. mm/dd/yyyy)
TAR archival software and version (e.g. GNU TAR version 1.23)
TAR segment (e.g. tar-per-reel)
TAR extract: (e.g. tar – xvf /dev/nst0 – b 256)
TAR restore path (e.g. immortals/im_r3/)

Documents should include instructions how to extract the data files, and specifying the blocking factor and the device and system used, so that byte order can be determined.

3D picture elements

The following elements must be delivered in addition to the 2D versions of these elements:

If made for the production, a set of three fully timed 35mm 3D separation masters YCM or RGB digital separation protection negatives for both left eye and right eye.

If made for the production, a 3D original digital output negative or digital archival negative for both left eye and right eye.

One set of the digital intermediate data files used to create the final version of the 3D original digital output negative. In addition, one full set of the 2D digital intermediate data files shall be delivered if they were created from a source other than the 3D left eye (or right eye) DI data files. If they were created using the 3D left eye or right eye DI data files, documentation of that should be provided.

One set of the 3D textless background masters.

Digital Cinema Package: two copies of the complete final talent approved color-timed 3D version of the feature in the DCI (P3) color space, delivered in JPEG 2000 files on Linear Tape-Open Format (LTO-4, LTO-5 or the most recent version available) the tape stock for the two sets should be made by different manufacturers. Picture and audio should follow the specifications in distribution elements.

35mm timed interpositives 2D and 3D

35mm final approved original or digital negative answer Print 2D and 3D

35mm internegative 2D and 3D
35mm internegative check print 2D and 3D
Textless backgrounds
ProRes 4.2.2 Mez File Quicktime proxy
Title elements

35mm YCM or RGB separation wet gate protective masters 2D and 3D

Distribution Elements

35mm 2D release prints
35mm 3D release prints
2D DCDM
2D DCP
3D DCDM
3D DCP

Digital Cinema Package details:
Two unencrypted copies of the complete final talent approved color timed version of the feature in the DCI (P3) color space, delivered in JPEG 2000 files on Linear Tape-Open Format (LTO-4, LTO-5 or the most recent version available. The tape stock from the two sets should be made by different manufacturers).

Picture specifications
File numbering scheme:

$01:00:00:00 = 86400$ = start of picture frame (8-second leader) Reel 1
$01:00:08:00 = 86592$ = program start Reel 1
$02:00:00:00 = 172800$ = start of picture frame (8-second leader) Reel 2
$02:00:08:00 = 172992$ = program start Reel 2
$03:00:00:00 = 259200$ = start of picture frame (8-second leader) Reel 3
$03:00:08:00 = 259392$ = program start Reel 3
And so on … (note – 60 mins × 60 secs × 24 frames = 86400)

Image must be provided with 8 second leader and tail pop.
3 channel, interleaved RGB, 16-bit tiff files no compression
the 12-bit gamma 2.6 XYZ values should occupy the high order 12 bits in the 16-bit data.
Image size: (1.85/FLAT) = 1998 × 1080, (1.85/SCOPE) = 1998× 836 (padded to 1998 × 1080)
(2.39/SCOPE) = 2048 × 858, (2.39/FLAT) = 1588 × 858 (padded to 2048 × 858)

Audio specifications:

Files must be provided in reels matching the image

Stereo interleaved WAV files – channel config: (1) left/right, (2) center/sub, (3) left surround/right surround

OR

single channel WAV files

48Khz @ 24 fps (2000 samples per frame)

24-bit

Ref level = –20 dbfs

Reels must be delivered with 8 seconds of preroll. 1st modulation of 2 pop must land at exactly 6 seconds (288,000 samples) and must be exactly 1 frame in duration (2000 samples) 1st modulation of 2 pop must be exactly 2 seconds (96,000 samples) from the start of the reel.

Handle audio of the reels before and after must be provided and should not be longer than 1 second.

Files must be delivered on CDs/DVDs, or on a Windows, Mac, EXT2, or EXT3 formatted HDD.

Editorial Items

All print film dailies

All "A" negative trims, outs, and lifts

All "B" negative

Two lined scripts

Two editor's code books

All camera and lab reports

Combined continuity/spotting script

All editorial materials + production screen tests

Sound Elements

One 35mm quad optical sound track negative

One 6+2 printmaster

One 2-track printmaster

One Dolby Magneto Optical Disc (MOD)

One Set of DTS audio master disc(s)

Two 6-track dialogue stem masters

Two 6-track music stem masters

Two 6-track effects stem masters

One 6 + 2 track music and effects (M&E) master

One 6-track DD/MM/EE master

Two (2) sets of all pre-dubs, LTO

All dubbing (re-recording) cue sheets

One set of all original production sound dailies

One complete set of all original sound dailies.

All original sound reports of dailies

International Elements

Subtitling disk and spotting list

Subtitling disk and spotting list for English subtitles.

Optical sound track negative

Dolby MO disc

Dolby SR-D/ 6+2-track dub discrete printmaster

6-track dub dialogue stem, MAG, LTO, DVD

One complete set of dub dialogue recordings only (raw stems)

Trailer Material

Pro-tools session

One MO disc Protools session of all mix elements

2K final output digital files on Firewire drive

35mm timed interpositive

35mm timed IP of the final version negative of the trailer

35mm color reference print

MO Disc ProTools session of all mix elements

Videotape Master Material

2D Home Video

HDCAMSR (2.40)

HDCAMSR (16 × 9)

HDCAMSR (4 × 3)

NTSC Digi-Beta (2.40)

NTSC Digi-Beta (16 × 9)

NTSC Digi-Beta (4 × 3)

PAL Digi-Beta (2.40)

PAL Digi-Beta (16 × 9)

PAL Digi-Beta (4 × 3)

Publicity Materials

Press kit materials

EPK materials

DVD Blu-Ray Bonus Materials

EPK

All available bonus material

Clearance Documents

Interviews/ featurettes / documentaries

Music cue sheets

Commentaries

QC delivery masters

Photo galleries

Legal Materials

- Short form assignments
- Chain-of-title documentation
- Final shooting script
- Laboratory access letters
- Laboratory list
- Residual documentation
- Credit documents
- Contracts
- Clearances
- Consultation and approval obligations
- IATSE seal
- MPAA
- Negative cost statement
- Dolby or Ultra Stereo License/D.T.S. License/ S.D.D.S. License
- Certificate of origin
- Insurance
- Security interest documentation
- Adam Walsh Child Protection and Safety Act Documentation

Broadcast Delivery Technical Specifications

Rec 709 Video Levels

Luminance must not exceed 714mv (100 IRE units).

Chrominance levels in the Y/Pr/Pb domain must not exceed 785mv (110 IRE).

Chrominance signals must remain within the legal 0–700mV range when measured in the RGB domain on a calibrated digital broadcast waveform monitor. A diamond waveform display or equivalent should be used to avoid gamut errors and prevent illegal colors during production.

Chrominance levels created in an RGB color space must result in a valid signal when transformed to Y'PrPb (709) color space in accordance with ITU-R Rec 709 for HDTV video.

Black level must be at zero IRE units as measured in the component digital domain.

HDR "Legal" Video Levels

Although specular highlights may sit above SDR nominal white with HDR, the video levels, for both HDR and SDR, must sit within the preferred minimum and maximum range as per EBU R 103. Narrow range parameters should be used as denoted in ITU-BT.2100. Overshoots exceeding the total video signal range will result in the content being rejected.

Notes

1. This section was contributed by Jay Spencer.
2. Source: NASA.
3. Contributed by Jay Spencer.

Index

Note: Numbers in **bold** indicate a table. Numbers in *italics* indicate a figure.